DATE DUE

			PRINTED IN U.S.A.

SOMETHING ABOUT THE AUTHOR

ISSN 0276-816X

SOMETHING ABOUT THE AUTHOR

**Facts and Pictures about Authors
and Illustrators of Books for Young People**

EDITED BY
DONNA OLENDORF

VOLUME 65

 **Gale Research Inc.** · *DETROIT* · *LONDON*

STAFF

Editor: Donna Olendorf

Associate Editor: James F. Kamp

Senior Editor: Hal May

Sketchwriters: Marilyn K. Basel, Barbara Carlisle Bigelow, Elizabeth A. Des Chenes, Janice E. Drane, Kevin S. Hile, Katherine Huebl, Thomas Kozikowski, Margaret Mazurkiewicz, Carol DeKane Nagel, Jani Prescott, Julia M. Rubiner, Edward G. Scheff, Neil R. Schlager, Kenneth R. Shepherd, Les Stone, Diane Telgen, Polly A. Vedder, and Thomas Wiloch

Research Manager: Victoria B. Cariappa

Research Supervisor: Mary Rose Bonk

Editorial Associates: Jane A. Cousins, Andrew Guy Malonis, and Norma Sawaya

Editorial Assistants: Mike Avolio, Reginald A. Carlton, Clare Collins, Theodore J. Dumbrigue, Shirley Gates, Sharon McGilvray, and Tracy Head Turbett

Production Manager: Mary Beth Trimper

External Production Assistant: Shanna P. Heilveil

Data Entry Supervisor: Benita L. Spight

Data Entry Associate: Merrie Ann Carpenter

Art Director: Arthur Chartow

Keyliner: C. J. Jonik

The paper used in this publication meets the minimum requirements of American National Standard for Information Sciences—Permanence Paper for Printed Library Materials, ANSI Z39.48-1984. ∞™

Copyright © 1991
Gale Research Inc.
835 Penobscot Bldg.
Detroit, MI 48226-4094

Library of Congress Catalog Card Number 72-27107

ISBN 0-8103-2275-7
ISSN 0276-816X

Printed in the United States

Published simultaneously in the United Kingdom
by Gale Research International Limited
(An affiliated company of Gale Research Inc.)

Contents

K

L

M

N

O

P

R

S

Introduction

Something about the Author (SATA) is an ongoing reference series that deals with the lives and works of authors and illustrators of children's books. *SATA* includes not only well-known authors and illustrators whose books are widely read, but also those less prominent people whose works are just coming to be recognized. This series is often the only readily available information source for emerging writers or artists. You'll find *SATA* informative and entertaining whether you are a student, a librarian, an English teacher, a parent, or simply an adult who enjoys children's literature for its own sake.

What's Inside SATA

SATA provides detailed information about authors and illustrators who span the full time range of children's literature, from early figures like John Newbery and L. Frank Baum to contemporary figures like Judy Blume and Richard Peck. Authors in the series represent primarily English-speaking countries, particularly the United States, Canada, and the United Kingdom. Also included, however, are authors from around the world whose works are available in English translation. The writings represented in *SATA* include those created intentionally for children and young adults as well as those written for a general audience and known to interest younger readers. These writings cover the entire spectrum of children's literature, including picture books, humor, folk and fairy tales, animal stories, mystery and adventure, science fiction and fantasy, historical fiction, poetry and nonsense verse, drama, biography, and nonfiction.

Obituaries are also included in *SATA* and are intended not only as death notices but as concise views of people's lives and work. Additionally, each edition features newly revised and updated entries for a selection of *SATA* listees who remain of interest to today's readers and who have been active enough to require extensive revision of their earlier biographies.

Two Convenient Indexes

In response to suggestions from librarians, *SATA* indexes no longer appear in each volume, but are included in alternate (odd-numbered) volumes of the series, beginning with Volume 57.

SATA continues to include two indexes that cumulate with each alternate volume: the Illustrations Index, arranged by the name of the illustrator, gives the number of the volume and page where the illustrator's work appears in the current volume as well as all preceding volumes in the series; the Author Index gives the number of the volume in which a person's Biographical Sketch or Obituary appears in the current volume as well as all preceding volumes in the series.

These indexes also include references to authors and illustrators who appear in Gale's *Yesterday's Authors of Books for Children, Children's Literature Review,* and the *Something about the Author Autobiography Series.*

Easy-to-Use Entry Format

Whether you're already familiar with the *SATA* series or just getting acquainted, you will want to be aware of the kind of information that an entry provides. In every *SATA* entry the editors attempt to give as complete a picture of the person's life and work as possible. A typical entry in *SATA* includes the following clearly labeled information sections:

● *PERSONAL:* date and place of birth and death, parents' names and occupations, name of spouse, date of marriage, and names of children, educational institutions attended, degrees received, religious and political affiliations.

● *ADDRESSES:* complete home, office, and agent's address.

● *CAREER:* name of employer, position, and dates for each career post; military service.

● *MEMBER:* memberships and offices held in professional and civic organizations.

● *AWARDS, HONORS:* literary and professional awards received.

● *WRITINGS:* title-by-title chronological bibliography of books written and/or illustrated, listed by genre when known; lists of other notable publications, such as plays, screenplays, and periodical contributions.

● *WORK IN PROGRESS:* description of projects in progress.

● *SIDELIGHTS:* a biographical portrait of the author's development, either directly from the person—and often written specifically for the *SATA* entry—or gathered from diaries, letters, interviews, or other published sources.

● *FOR MORE INFORMATION SEE:* references for further reading.

● *EXTENSIVE ILLUSTRATIONS:* photographs, movie stills, manuscript samples, book covers, and other interesting visual materials supplement the text.

How a SATA Entry Is Compiled

A *SATA* entry progresses through a series of steps. If the biographee is living, the *SATA* editors try to secure information directly from him or her through a questionnaire. From the information that the biographee supplies, the editors prepare an entry, filling in any essential missing details with research and/or telephone interviews. When necessary, the author or illustrator is sent a copy of the entry to check for accuracy and completeness.

If the biographee is deceased or cannot be reached by questionnaire, the *SATA* editors examine a wide variety of published sources to gather information for an entry. Biographical and bibliographic sources are consulted, as are book reviews, feature articles, published interviews, and material sometimes obtained from the biographee's family, publishers, agent, or other associates.

We Welcome Your Suggestions

We invite you to examine the entire *SATA* series, starting with this volume. Please write and tell us if we can make *SATA* even more helpful to you. Send comments and suggestions to: The Editor, *Something about the Author*, Gale Research Inc., 835 Penobscot Bldg., Detroit, Michigan 48226.

Acknowledgments

Grateful acknowledgment is made to the following publishers, authors, and artists whose works appear in this volume.

Patricia Baehr. Jacket of *Falling Scales,* by Patricia Baehr. Morrow, 1987. Jacket illustration (c) 1987 by Andrew Glass. Reprinted by permission of William Morrow & Company, Inc.

James W. Baker. Photograph by Elaine Baker. Courtesy of James W. Baker.

Sally Belfrage. Photograph by David Hobson.

Elizabeth P. Benson. Illustration from *An Olmec Figure at Dumbarton Oaks,* by Elizabeth P. Benson. Reproduced by permission of Dumbarton Oaks Studies.

Mildred Benson. Photograph courtesy of *The Blade,* Toledo, OH.

Alix Berenzy. Illustration by Alix Berenzy from her *A Frog Prince.* Henry Holt and Company, 1989. Copyright (c) 1989 by Alix Berenzy. Reprinted by permission of Henry Holt and Company, Inc./ Photograph courtesy of Alix Berenzy.

Lloyd Biggle, Jr. Caricature by Harlan Rector.

Barbara Birenbaum. Photograph courtesy of Barbara Birenbaum.

Robert H. Boyle. Photograph by Dr. Daniel Salzberg.

John W. Brainerd. Illustration from *The Nature Observer's Handbook: Learning to Appreciate Our Natural World,* by John W. Brainerd. The Globe Pequot Press, 1986. Copyright (c) 1986 by John W. Brainerd. Reprinted with permission of The Globe Pequot Press, Chester, CT 06412.

David Brin. Cover by Jim Burnes from *Startide Rising,* by David Brin. Copyright (c) 1983 by David Brin. Used by permission of Bantam Books, a division of Bantam Doubleday Dell Publishing Group, Inc./ Photograph (c) Jerry Bauer.

Kevin Brownlow. Cover of *The Parade's Gone By...,* by Kevin Brownlow. Copyright (c) 1968 by Kevin Brownlow. Cover photograph: Turner Entertainment Company.

Olive Ann Burns. Jacket of *Cold Sassy Tree,* by Olive Ann Burns. Ticknor & Fields, 1984. Jacket design by Wendell Minor (c) 1984. Reprinted by permission of Wendell Minor./ Photograph (c) 1984 John Sparks.

Dan Burr. Illustration courtesy of Dan Burr.

Leo Buscaglia. Illustration by Carol Newsom from *A Memory for Tino,* by Leo Buscaglia. Slack Incorporated, 1988. Illustrations copyright (c) 1988 by Slack Incorporated./ Photograph by C. Steven Short. Courtesy of Leo F. Buscaglia.

Eric Carle. Cover by Eric Carle from his *The Very Hungry Caterpillar.* Philomel Books, 1969. Copyright (c) 1969 by Eric Carle. Reprinted by permission of Philomel Books./ Illustration by Eric Carle from his *The Rooster's Off to See the World.* Picture Book Studio, 1972. Copyright (c) 1972, Eric Carle. Reprinted by permission of the publisher./ Illustration by Eric Carle from *Do Bears Have Mothers, Too?* by Aileen Fisher. Thomas Y. Crowell, 1973. Illustrations copyright (c) 1973 by Eric Carle. Reprinted by permission./ Cover of *The Very Busy Spider,* by Eric Carle. Philomel Books, 1984. Text and illustrations copyright (c) by Eric Carle Corp. Reprinted by permission of Philomel Books./ Photograph (c) Sigrid Estrada.

Hugh Maxwell Casson. Illustration by Sir Hugh Casson K.C.V.O. from *The Old Man of Lochnagar,* by H.R.H. The Prince of Wales. Hamish Hamilton Children's Books, 1980. Copyright (c) illustrations The Trustees of The Prince of Wales's Charities Trust 1980. Reprinted by permission of Sheil Land Associates Ltd./ Illustrations by Hugh Casson from *Pushkin the Polar Bear,* by Simon Gaul. Quartet/Visual Arts Book, 1983. Illustrations copyright (c) Hugh Casson 1983. Reprinted by permission of Quartet Books, Ltd./ Illustration from *Nanny Says,* by Sir Hugh Casson and Joyce Grenfell. Souvenir Press, 1987. Copyright (c) 1972 by Sir Hugh Casson and Joyce Grenfell. Reprinted by permission of Souvenir Press Ltd./

Photograph by Cathy Courtney. Courtesy of Hugh M. Casson./ Photograph of Casson with his sister, Rosemary, courtesy of Hugh M. Casson.

Yuan-tsung Chen. Cover of *The Dragon's Village,* by Yuan-tsung Chen. Penguin Books, 1980. Copyright (c) 1980 Yuan-tsung Chen. Cover illustration courtesy of Shanghai People's Publishing House. Used by permission of Viking Penguin, a division of Penguin Books USA Inc.

John Ciardi. Illustration by Robert Osborn from *I Met a Man,* by John Ciardi. Houghton Mifflin Company, 1961. Copyright (c) 1961 by John Ciardi. Reprinted by permission of Houghton Mifflin Company./ Illustration by Edward Gorey from *You Read to Me, I'll Read to You,* by John Ciardi. Harper & Row, Publishers, 1962. Copyright (c) 1962 by John Ciardi. Reprinted by permission of HarperCollins Publishers./ Illustration by Merle Nacht from Doddle Soup, by John Ciardi. Houghton Mifflin Company, 1985. Copyright (c) 1985 by Myra J. Ciardi. Reprinted by permission of Houghton Mifflin Company./ Photograph (c) Rollie McKenna.

Kinuko Y. Craft. Photograph courtesy of Kinuko Craft.

John Crowley. Photograph (c) Jerry Bauer.

Doug Cushman. Illustration by Doug Cushman from his *Nasty Kyle the Crocodile.* Grosset & Dunlap, 1983. Copyright (c) 1983 by Doug Cushman. Reprinted by permission of Grosset & Dunlap./ Photograph by John Massimino.

Amy Ehrlich. Jacket of *Where It Stops, Nobody Knows,* by Amy Ehrlich. Dial Books for Young Readers, 1988. Jacket painting (c) 1988 by Linda Benson. Reprinted by permission of Dial Books for Young Readers, a division of Penguin Books USA Inc./ Photograph courtesy of Amy Ehrlich.

Lillian Eige. Photograph courtesy of Lillian Eige.

Delia Ephron. Illustration by Edward Koren from *Teenage Romance: Or How to Die of Embarrassment,* by Delia Ephron. The Viking Press, 1981. Copyright (c) 1981 by Delia Ephron. Illustrations copyright (c) 1981 by Edward Koren. Used by permission of Viking Penguin, a division of Penguin Books USA Inc./ Illustration by Edward Koren from *Do I Have to Say Hello?* by Delia Ephron. Viking, 1989. Copyright (c) 1989 by Delia Ephron. Drawings copyright (c) 1989 by Edward Koren. Used by permission of Viking Penguin, a division of Penguin Books USA Inc./ Photograph (c) Bonnie Shiffman. Courtesy of Delia Ephron.

John Grant Fuller, Jr. Jacket of *Tornado Watch #21,* by John G. Fuller. Reprinted by permission of William Morrow & Company, Inc./ Photograph by Elizabeth Fuller.

Margaret Gaan. Jacket of *Little Sister,* by Margaret Gaan. Dodd, Mead, 1982. Jacket illustration and design (c) 1982 by Tim Gaydos. Reprinted by permission of Tim Gaydos./ Photograph by Henry Au.

Faye Gibbons. Jacket of *Mighty Close to Heaven,* by Faye Gibbons. Morrow, 1985. Jacket illustration (c) 1985 by Steve Marchesi. Reprinted by permission of William Morrow & Company, Inc.

Gene Gurney. Photograph courtesy of Gene Gurney.

Charles Hamilton. Illustration from *Cry of the Thunderbird,* by Charles Hamilton. New edition copyright (c) 1972 by University of Oklahoma Press. Reprinted by permission of University of Oklahoma Press./ Photograph courtesy of Charles Hamilton.

William Harmon. Photograph courtesy of William Harmon.

Torey Hayden. Photograph by Lee Chiu Hwan.

Mary Haynes. Jacket of *Catch the Sea,* by Mary Haynes. Bradbury Press, 1989. Jacket illustration copyright (c) 1989 by Catherine Stock. Reprinted by permission of Catherine Stock.

Marie H. Henry. Photograph courtesy of Marie H. Henry.

Barbara Ware Holmes. Jacket of *Charlotte the Starlet,* by Barbara Ware Holmes. Illustrated by John Himmelman. Harper & Row, Publishers, 1988. Jacket art (c) 1988 by John Himmelman. Reprinted by permission of HarperCollins Publishers.

SOMETHING ABOUT THE AUTHOR

ANTHONY, C. L.
See SMITH, Dorothy Gladys

      *   *   *

ANTHONY, John
See CIARDI, John (Anthony)

      *   *   *

ASHE, Arthur (R., Jr.) 1943-

PERSONAL: Born July 10, 1943, in Richmond, Va.; son of Arthur R. (a parks department guard) and M. C. Ashe; married Jeanne Moutoussamy (a photographer), 1976; children: Camera Elizabeth. *Education:* University of California, Los Angeles, B.S., 1966.

ADDRESSES: Office—c/o Pro Serv, 1101 Wilson Blvd. #1800, Arlington, VA 22209.

CAREER: Tennis player. President of Players Enterprises, Inc., 1969-85; member of U.S. Davis Cup Tennis Team, beginning 1963. Numerous tennis championships include National Indoor Junior Tennis Championship, 1960, 1961, U.S. Men's Hard Court Championship, 1963, U.S. intercollegiate championships, 1965, U.S. Men's Clay Court Championship, 1967, U.S. Amateur Title, 1968, U.S. Open Championship, 1968, Australian Open Championship, 1970, and Wimbledon Singles Championship, 1975. Lecturer and writer; correspondent, ABC Sports and HBO. Vice-president, Le Coq Sportif; tennis director, Doral Resort and Country Club, Miami, FL. National campaign chairman, American Heart Association, 1981-82; member of board of directors, Aetna Life and Casualty. Chairman of advisory staff, Head Sports. *Military service:* U.S. Army, 1967-69.

WRITINGS:

(With Clifford G. Gewecke, Jr.) *Advantage Ashe,* Coward, 1967.
(With Frank Deford) *Arthur Ashe: Portrait in Motion,* Houghton, 1975.
(With Louie Robinson, Jr.) *Getting Started in Tennis,* illustrated with photographs by Jeanne Moutoussamy, Atheneum, 1977.
(With Neil Amdur) *Off the Court,* New American Library, 1981.
A Hard Road to Glory: A History of the African-American Athlete, Volume 1: *1619 to 1918,* Volume 2: *1919 to 1945,* Volume 3: *1946 to the Present,* Dodd, 1987.

Contributor to newspapers and magazines, including the *New York Times, Tennis Magazine, Washington Post* and *People.*

SIDELIGHTS: "It's not merely because he is the only black male thus far to achieve superstardom in professional tennis that Arthur Ashe stands out from the crowd," says Jonathan Yardley in *Sports Illustrated.* "It's also because he is one of the few genuinely multidimensional individuals ever to achieve superstardom in any sport." Indeed, Ashe's life and career have provided material enough to fill a number of biographies and autobiographies. After working his way through the amateur and professional tennis circuits during the 1960s and 1970s, Ashe attained worldwide acclaim in his 1975 Wimbledon singles triumph over Jimmy Connors. He has also kept up careers as a writer and lecturer and visited South Africa as an anti-apartheid spokesman.

Arthur Ashe, American tennis champion.

Tennis was Ashe's top priority from an early age. As the son of a playground superintendent in then-segregated Richmond, Va., Ashe showed promise in tennis by age seven. A few years later, he studied the game under the tutelage of Dr. Robert Walter Johnson, a black physician who dedicated himself to developing young black tennis players in an era when the sport was the bastion of upper-class whites.

In his writings, Ashe often mentions the admiration he has for Johnson and discusses the racism black athletes encountered before the days of the civil rights movement. Although he was a top-ranked teenage player, for example, Ashe was barred from some tennis clubs when he toured. Later, as a member of the UCLA tennis team, Ashe alone was excluded from the team's invitation to compete at an exclusive country club tournament. But, far from openly retaliating, Ashe demonstrated a grace under pressure and a sense of self-control that he attributes to Johnson's training.

In 1979 Ashe was a member of the Davis Cup team and ranked as one of America's leading players when, after returning from a tournament, he began experiencing chest pains that culminated in a heart attack. He underwent quadruple bypass surgery and then endured a slow, but steady, recovery. While high blood pressure and heart disease run in Ashe's family, the athlete admits that he thought himself immune to their effects. "Why should I have worried?" Ashe remarked in an interview with Judy Kessler and Allan Ripp of *People* magazine. "My blood pressure and cholesterol are low, I don't smoke or take drugs, and with all the tennis I play I'm as physically fit as a 36-year-old man can be. People like me simply don't get heart attacks." As Ashe later explained to Richard K. Rein in *People,* "One thing I've learned is that it's not so much the heart attack that kills most people, though there are a few who die on the spot. Most people die because they deny it; they say it's indigestion or heartburn. A heart attack is not something that goes click,

boom. A heart attack can occur in a few minutes or over a period of days. If we could just get people not to go through the denial stage, then we would save even more lives."

The incident ended Ashe's professional tennis career, but he has remained active in the sport, serving as captain of the Davis Cup team. Ashe also became campaign chairman of the American Heart Association. "There's a hell of a lot I can do," he told Kessler and Ripp in *People.* "I am a determined person. I expect to live a long time."

WORKS CITED:

Kessler, Judy, and Allan Ripp, "For a Recovering Arthur Ashe, His Heart Attack May Not Be a Net Loss," *People,* September 17, 1979, pp. 86-89.
Rein, Richard K., "An Athlete Nearly Dying Young: A Tennis Champ Tells His History," *People,* September 21, 1981, pp. 113-14.
Yardley, Jonathan, "Booktalk: Arthur Ashe Steps off the Court to Reveal the Man Behind the Player," *Sports Illustrated,* September 7, 1981, pp. 14-16.

FOR MORE INFORMATION SEE:

BOOKS

Ashe, Arthur, and Clifford G. Gewecke, Jr., *Advantage Ashe,* Coward, 1967.
Ashe, Arthur, and Frank Deford, *Arthur Ashe: Portrait in Motion,* Houghton, 1975.
Ashe, Arthur, and Neil Amdur, *Off the Court,* New American Library, 1981.
MePhee, John, *Levels of the Game,* Farrar, Straus, 1969.
Robinson, Louie, Jr., *Arthur Ashe: Tennis Champion,* Doubleday, 1970.

PERIODICALS

Ebony, November, 1979.
Newsweek, September 7, 1964.
New Yorker, June 7, 1969; June 14, 1969; October 13, 1975.
New York Times Book Review, June 1, 1975; November 22, 1981.
People, March 12, 1979.
Time, August 13, 1965; July 14, 1975.
Times Literary Supplement, July 1, 1977.
Village Voice, January 6, 1982.
World Tennis, December, 1980.

*   *   *

AUGUSTINE, Mildred
   See BENSON, Mildred (Augustine Wirt)

*   *   *

BAEHR, Patricia (Goehner) 1952-

PERSONAL: Born May 14, 1952, in Long Island, NY; daughter of Herman and Doris (Powers) Goehner; married Edward W. Baehr (a police detective), October 14, 1972; children: Peter, Gemma. *Education:* Hofstra University, B.S., 1974, M.A., 1977.

ADDRESSES: Home—Bayville, NY. *Agent*—Jean V. Naggar Literary Agency, 216 East 75th St., New York, NY 10021.

CAREER: Archer Street and Leo F. Giblyn Schools, Freeport, NY, teacher of instrumental music, 1974-80; free-lance writer, 1980—. Clarinetist with the Long Island Original Music Ensemble, 1984-88.

MEMBER: Society of Children's Book Writers, Authors Guild.

AWARDS, HONORS: Jane Tinkham Broughton fellow, Bread Loaf Writers' Conference, 1980; Notable Children's Book in the Field of Social Studies citation, National Council for the Social Studies, 1989, for *School Isn't Fair!;* Pick of the Lists citation, *American Bookseller,* 1990, for *Summer of the Dodo.*

WRITINGS:

The Way to Windra, illustrated by Gail Owens, F. Warne, 1980.
The Dragon Prophecy, F. Warne, 1980.
Always Faithful, New American Library, 1983.
Indian Summer, New American Library, 1984.
Faithfully, Tru, Macmillan, 1984.
Falling Scales, Morrow, 1987.
Louisa Eclipsed, Morrow, 1988.
School Isn't Fair!, illustrated by R. W. Alley, Four Winds Press, 1989.
Summer of the Dodo, Four Winds Press, 1990.

WORK IN PROGRESS: The Pursuit of Happily Ever After.

SIDELIGHTS: "Because I did become a writer," Patricia Baehr writes, "I find it appropriate that I was baptized in a

Dustjacket for Patricia Baehr's 1987 novel about a teenage girl's coming of age. (Jacket illustration by Andrew Glass.)

library. When I was born, our church was a tiny wooden building, abandoned as soon as the parish raised the funds to build a new church. The old building came to house the library collection and was the place where I browsed for books when I was growing up. All I remember of it are creaking floors, dust, darkness, and the kind of deadly quiet that made me afraid to speak. Eventually the building was razed to make way for a parking lot, so I suppose I could say that I was baptized in a parking lot, but it doesn't have the same pertinence as saying I was baptized in a library.

"When I was growing up, I was fortunate to have an aunt who supplied me with wonderful books each birthday and Christmas, books that nurtured and influenced me tremendously. I came to identify strongly with Louisa May Alcott's Jo in *Little Women* since Jo was the second oldest of four girls in her family, and so was I. I identified with any family I read about that contained four children, assigning myself the role of the second eldest, whether that was male or female, but the Marches are the family I remember best. It helped that I saw Jo as the main charcter. I certainly considered myself the main character in my own family. Perhaps it's no wonder that since Jo put on plays and wanted to be a writer, so did I. The curious thing about it all is that I wound up marrying a man with the last name of Baehr, a name uncannily similar to that of Jo's gentle professor Bhaer.

"I don't think I've ever made a conscious decision to write for children and young adults. I always set out to tell a story that interests me, hopeful that it will interest others, as well."

HOBBIES AND OTHER INTERESTS: "Dogs are my favorite animals, and in my spare time I like to train and play with my flat coater retriever, Maggie. Reading is another activity I love, and I run a book discussion club for elementary school students at my local library."

*   *   *

BAKER, James W. 1926-

PERSONAL: Born December 20, 1926, in Emporia, VA; son of Otis Fletcher (a draftsman) and Hazel (a housewife; maiden name, Webb) Baker; married Elaine Campton (a librarian), December 15, 1951; children: James W., Glenn Campton. *Education:* College of William and Mary, A.B., 1951. *Religion:* Presbyterian.

ADDRESSES: Home—510 Spring Trace, Williamsburg, VA 23185.

CAREER: Richmond News Leader, Richmond, VA, reporter and education writer, 1951-63; U.S. Information Agency, Washington, DC, foreign service officer, 1963-83; *Virginia Gazette,* Williamsburg, VA, columnist and writer, 1983—. *Military service:* U.S. Marine Corps, 1945-46, served in Tientsin, China.

MEMBER: International Brotherhood of Magicians (vice president of Richmond branch), Society of American Magicians, Virginia Writers Club.

AWARDS, HONORS: Virginia Press Association, certificates of merit, 1956 and 1969; first place, American Trucking Association safety writing contest, 1958; U.S. Information

Magician-author James W. Baker.

Agency, director's award for creativity, 1972, meritorious honor awards, 1973 and 1982.

WRITINGS:

Illusions Illustrated: A Professional Magic Show for Young Performers, Lerner Publications, 1984.
Valentine Magic, Lerner Publications, 1988.
Halloween Magic, Lerner Publications, 1988.
Christmas Magic, Lerner Publications, 1988.
Birthday Magic, Lerner Publications, 1988.
New Year's Magic, Lerner Publications, 1989.
Presidents' Day Magic, Lerner Publications, 1989.
April Fools' Day Magic, Lerner Publications, 1989.
Thanksgiving Magic, Lerner Publications, 1989.
Columbus Day Magic, Lerner Publications, 1990.
St. Patrick's Day Magic, Lerner Publications, 1990.
Arbor Day Magic, Lerner Publications, 1990.
Independence Day Magic, Lerner Publications, 1990.

WORK IN PROGRESS: A book containing one hundred fifty columns from the *Virginia Gazette;* a syndicated newspaper column on simple magic tricks for children.

SIDELIGHTS: "I feel that I have been extremely fortunate in having three distinct careers, each of which was in its own way exciting, interesting, stimulating," the author told *Something about the Author.* "From 1951 to 1963 I was a reporter and education writer on the *Richmond News Leader,* covering at various times the county government, the police beat, the Virginia state legislature, courts, and general assignments. In early 1954 I was named education editor of the paper, and within months the U.S. Supreme Court ruled in the *Brown vs. Board of Education* decision, which outlawed racially segregated schools. Education became the hottest news subject in the South, and as a young reporter I was suddenly covering the paper's biggest stories. Because of legal battles, I ended up spending more time covering education from the courthouse than from the schoolhouse. Heady stuff for a reporter still in his twenties.

"During twelve years on the *News Leader* I covered just about every 'beat' the paper had. By the early 1960s I began to get itchy feet and a desire to see the world. Realizing I could never do this as a tourist on a reporter's salary, I began to look for a job that would take me overseas. I applied to the U.S. Information Agency (U.S.I.A.) and in 1963 was offered an appointment as a foreign service officer.

"In July, 1963, my family (my wife and our two sons, then seven and five years old) and I flew to Madras, India, for a three-year assignment. By the time the tour was over we had become committed nomads. I stayed with U.S.I.A. for twenty years, serving in Turkey, Pakistan, the Philippines, Tunisia, and Washington, DC. It was a wonderful, exciting two decades. We took advantage of opportunities most Americans never get. We traveled in more than sixty countries, once got hijacked to Cairo, Egypt, and saw most of the world's famous structures and places.

"Throughout my first two careers—on the newspaper and in the foreign service—I had avidly pursued a hobby I discovered at the age of nine: magic tricks and sleight of hand. I gave numerous shows in Richmond. In the foreign service I performed magic shows for schools, orphanages, hospitals, ambassadors and other diplomats, the mentally retarded, and the college educated in a couple of dozen foreign countries. I discovered that magic was an international ice-breaker that cut across language and cultural barriers like an invisible magic wand.

"Entering my third career—'retirement'—I began to combine my two loves, writing and magic, while writing a weekly column and numerous feature stories for the *Virginia Gazette.* This combination of writing and magic resulted in the publication of my first book, *Illusions Illustrated.* Some months afterward I got a phone call from Elizabeth Petersen, then the editorial director of Lerner Publications. Her words still ring clearly in my ear six years later. 'Children,' she said, 'love magic and they love holidays. Is there any way the two could be combined in a children's book?' It was as if she had turned on a one-hundred-fifty-watt light bulb inside my head. Of course; why hadn't I ever thought of that? The result is history."

FOR MORE INFORMATION SEE:

PERIODICALS

Richmond News Leader, April 30, 1984.
Richmond Times-Dispatch, October 31, 1988.

*   *   *

BEAR, Greg(ory Dale) 1951-

PERSONAL: Born August 20, 1951, in San Diego, CA; son of Dale Franklin (a naval officer) and Wilma (a secretary and homemaker; maiden name, Merriman) Bear; married Christina Nielsen, January 12, 1975 (divorced August, 1981); married Astrid Anderson, June 18, 1983; children: (second marriage) Erik William Anderson Bear, Alexandra Astrid Bear. *Education:* San Diego State College (now University), A.B., 1969.

ADDRESSES: Home—506 Lakeview Rd., Alderwood Manor, WA 98037. *Agent*— Richard Curtis, 171 East 74th St., New York, NY 10021.

CAREER: Writer. Worked in bookstores, a planetarium, and as free-lance teacher in San Diego, CA. Member of Citizen's Advisory Council on National Space Policy.

MEMBER: Science Fiction Writers of America (president, 1988-90).

AWARDS, HONORS: Nebula awards from Science Fiction Writers of America for best novelette (*Blood Music*) and for best novella (*Hardfought*), both 1984; Hugo Award for best novelette for *Blood Music;* Prix Apollo, 1986, for *Blood Music;* Nebula and Hugo Awards, 1987, for short story "Tangents."

WRITINGS:

SCIENCE FICTION

Hegira (novel), Dell, 1979.
Psychlone (novel), Ace, 1979.
Beyond Heaven's River (novel), Dell, 1980.
Strength of Stones (novel), Ace, 1981.
The Wind From a Burning Woman (short stories), Arkham, 1983.
Corona ("Star Trek" novel), Pocket Books, 1984.
The Infinity Concerto (novel), Berkeley, 1984.
Eon (novel), Bluejay Books, 1985.
Blood Music (novelette; first published in *Analog,* June, 1983), Arbor House, 1985.
The Serpent Mage (novel; sequel to *The Infinity Concerto*), Berkeley, 1986.
The Forge of God (novel), Tor Books, 1987.
Sleepside Story, Cheap St., 1987.
Eternity, Warner Books, 1988.
Hardfought (bound with *Cascade Point* by Timothy Zahn), Tor Books, 1988.
Early Harvest, New England SF Assoc., 1988.
Tangents, Warner Books, 1989.
Queen of Angels, Warner Books, 1990.
Heads, Legend, 1990.

Contributor to science fiction periodicals, including *Analog* and *Isaac Asimov's Science Fiction Magazine.* Editor with wife, Astrid Bear, of *SFWA Forum.* Book reviewer for *San Diego Union Book Review* supplement, 1979-82.

ADAPTATIONS: Greg Bear's story "Dead Run" was adapted for *The Twilight Zone* television series in 1986. *Blood Music* was broadcast as a radio play by the Canadian Broadcasting Corporation.

SIDELIGHTS: Greg Bear said, "I was born in San Diego, California, on August 20th, 1951, to Wilma M. and Dale F. Bear. My father was in the navy, and by the time I was twelve years old, I had traveled with my parents to Japan, the Philippines and Alaska, as well as touring various parts of the United States.

"It was in Alaska, at age nine, that I completed my first short story. I had been writing for a year or so already. At age thirteen or fourteen I began submitting stories to the magazines, and at fifteen I sold my first short short to Robert Lowndes' *Famous Science Fiction.* (It appeared when I was sixteen.) It took five years to sell my next story, and by the time I was twenty-three, I began selling regularly. My first novel, finished when I was nineteen, was recently rewritten and sold to Berkley; the first novel I sold . . . was written when I was twenty-three, and appeared in 1979. . . . In 1986, the paperback of *Eon* became a top science fiction bestseller.

"Occasional work as a freelance journalist has taken me to the Jet Propulsion Laboratory in Pasadena [CA], where I covered the Voyager Jupiter-Saturn fly-bys for the *San Diego Union.* I've written numerous articles on film for the *Los Angeles Times.* . . . I've also worked as a bookseller (my last formal job was at the late, lamented La Jolla bookstore, Mithras) and I frequently lectured for the San Diego City Schools, acting as a roving teacher and conducting short classes on ancient history, history of science and science fiction/fantasy.

"As an illustrator, my artwork has appeared on *Galaxy, Fantasy and Science Fiction,* and *Vertex,* and books both hardcover and paperback. I was a founding member of ASFA, the Association of Science Fiction Artists. I do very little artwork now, devoting myself almost exclusively to writing.

"My major interests (outside of writing and science fiction) are science—particularly astronomy and physics—and history. I frequently dabble in mythology and religions but belong to no organized religious group. Politically I am pragmatic and tend to vote for the candidate I judge most literate in science and technology, and the one most likely to further the causes of education, research and space exploration.

"In 1983, I married Astrid Anderson. We've collaborated in various writing projects, mostly journalism. Our son Erik was born in 1986 and daughter Alexandra in 1990. All in all, we're quite a team.

"All my life (or at least as long as I remember) I've enjoyed telling stories about marvelous people, events, and places. The pleasure I get from writing science fiction and fantasy is enormous. I do not limit myself as to what I will write or how I will write it, and I hope my readers enjoy the result as much as I do."

FOR MORE INFORMATION SEE:

Analog, April, 1980; August, 1982.
Science Fiction and Fantasy Book Review, April, 1982.
Village Voice Literary Supplement, October, 1984.
Washington Post Book World, February, 28, 1982.

*   *   *

BEE, Jay
See BRAINERD, John W(hiting)

*   *   *

BELFRAGE, Sally 1936-

PERSONAL: Born October 4, 1936, in Los Angeles, CA; daughter of Cedric (a writer) and Molly (a writer) Belfrage; married Sari Nashashibi, January 27, 1960 (died); married Bernard Pomerance (a playwright), November 21, 1965; children: Eve, Alexander. *Education:* Attended Hunter College, 1954-55, and London School of Economics, 1959-60.

ADDRESSES: Home—51 Randolph Ave., London W9, England. *Agent*— Anthony Sheil, 43 Doughty St., London WC1, England.

CAREER: John Calder (publisher), London, England, office worker, 1955-56; Cassells, London, in design and topography, 1956-57; Foreign Languages Publishing House, Moscow, U.S.S.R., translations editor, 1957-58; New American Library, New York, NY, reader, 1963-65; writer.

WRITINGS:

A Room in Moscow, Reynal, 1959.
Freedom Summer, Viking, 1965, reprinted, University Press of Virginia, 1990.
Flowers of Emptiness: Reflections on an Ashram, Dial, 1981.
Living with War: A Belfast Year, Viking, 1987, published as *The Crack: A Belfast Year,* Andre Deutsch, 1987.

WORK IN PROGRESS: A 1950s memoir.

SIDELIGHTS: Sally Belfrage's first book, *A Room in Moscow,* recounts her experiences living as a Muscovite during the winter of 1957-58, and as an employee of the Foreign Languages Publishing House. Belfrage commented that "the book was published in nine countries and supported its author at the London School of Economics and for a year of travel in the Middle East." *Freedom Summer* is Belfrage's autobiographical account of activities involving the Student Non-Violent Coordinating Committee (SNCC) in Mississippi during racial hostilities in 1964. *Flowers of Emptiness* details Belfrage's experiences in an Indian ashram. Accompanied by two friends, she traveled to Poona, India, to study under the tutelage of Guru Bhagwan Shree Rajneesh. Unlike her two friends, who had already accepted the guru's philosophy before journeying to India, Belfrage is largely skeptical of the guru and his methods. *Living with War* is a report on the war in Northern Ireland as seen by the fighting families on both sides, with whom Belfrage lived for a year in the mid-Eighties.

SALLY BELFRAGE

Belfrage explained, "When I began this work, it was generally agreed that the business of a writer was to write. Now it seems that publishers believe the business of a writer is to be a television personality. Faced with this challenge, I feel the same as Ferdinand the Bull did about the bullfights in Madrid, preferring 'to sit just quietly under the cork tree and smell the flowers' (which is rather like writing to me). So far the Banderilleros and Picadors and Matadors have failed to persuade me that they know what I want to do, or that the kind of writing I want to read or write can long survive this treatment. It's not that I can stop doing it, but how to communicate it? Designs for space capsules solicited."

FOR MORE INFORMATION SEE:

PERIODICALS

Atlantic, March, 1959.
Chicago Tribune, February 15, 1959.
Christian Science Monitor, February 12, 1959.
Manchester Guardian, October 24, 1958.
New Statesman, December 27, 1958.
New York Review of Books, July 1, 1965.
New York Times, April 19, 1959; April 17, 1981.
New York Times Book Review, May 3, 1981.
Newsweek, March 23, 1981.
Saturday Review, August 14, 1965.
Spectator, October 17, 1958.
Times Literary Supplement, October 31, 1958.
Washington Post, March 16, 1981.

* * *

**BELL, Frank
   See BENSON, Mildred (Augustine Wirt)**

* * *

BENSON, Elizabeth P(olk) 1924-

PERSONAL: Born May 13, 1924, in Washington, DC; daughter of Theodore B. (an attorney) and Rebecca (Albin) Benson. *Education:* Wellesley College, B.A., 1945; Catholic University of America, M.A., 1956. *Hobbies and other interests:* Poetry, fiction, music, painting, travel, Chinese food.

ADDRESSES: Home—Bethesda, MD. *Office*—8314 Seven Locks Rd., Bethesda, MD 20817.

CAREER: National Gallery of Art, Washington, DC, museum aide, 1946-51, curator, 1954-60; free-lance editor in New York, NY, 1960-62; Dumbarton Oaks (trustees for Harvard University), Washington, DC, director of Center for Pre-Columbian Studies and curator for Pre-Columbian collection, 1963-80. Institute of Andean Studies, research associate, 1980—. Lecturer at Catholic University of America, 1968, 1969; adjunct professor at Columbia University, 1973; lecturer to Smithsonian Institution Associates, 1978, 1982, 1984; senior lecturer, University of Texas at Austin, 1985; Andrew S. Keck Professor of Art History, American University, 1987.

MEMBER: Society of Women Geographers, Institute of Andean Studies, Literary Society.

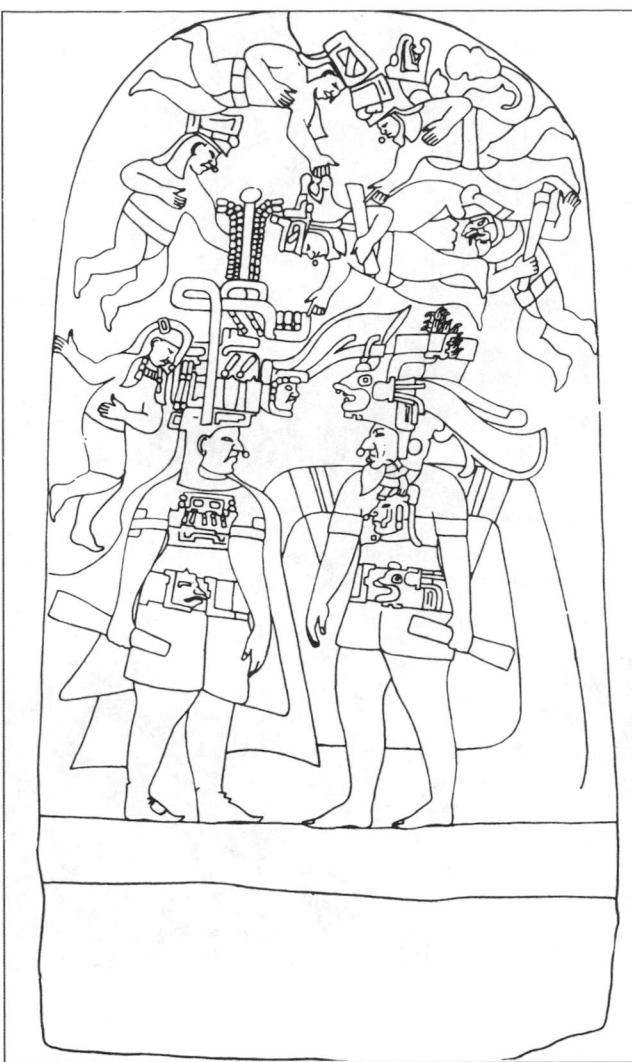

Reconstruction drawing of La Venta stone monument, representing the culture of a southeastern Mexican tribe that flourished c. 450-800 A.D. In her research, Elizabeth Benson uses the art of ancient peoples in an attempt to reconstruct their thought.

WRITINGS:

(With Michael D. Coe) *Three Maya Relief Panels at Dumbarton Oaks,* Dumbarton Oaks, 1966.

(Editor) *Dumbarton Oaks Conference on Chavin, October 26 and 27, 1968,* Dumbarton Oaks, 1971.

An Olmec Figure at Dumbarton Oaks, Dumbarton Oaks, 1971.

(Editor) *The Cult of the Feline: A Conference in Pre-Columbian Art and Archaeology, October 31 and November 1, 1970,* Dumbarton Oaks, 1972.

The Maya World, Crowell, 1972, revised edition, 1977.

The Mochica: A Culture of Peru, Praeger, 1972.

(Editor) *Mesoamerican Writing Systems: A Conference at Dumbarton Oaks, October 30 and 31, 1971,* Dumbarton Oaks, 1973.

Man and a Feline in Mochica Art (bound with *Thread of Life: Symbolism of Miniature Art from Ecuador* by Johannes Wilbert and *Further Explorations of the Rowe Chavin Seriation and Its Implications for North Central Coast Chronology* by Peter Roe), Dumbarton Oaks, 1974.

(Editor) *Death and the Afterlife in Pre-Columbian America: A Conference at Dumbarton Oaks, October 27, 1973,* Dumbarton Oaks, 1975.

(Editor) Dumbarton Oaks Collection Staff, *Pre-Columbian Art,* University of Chicago Press, 1976.

(Editor) *Pre-Columbian Metallurgy of South America, Proceedings: A Conference at Dumbarton Oaks, October 18 and 19, 1975,* Dumbarton Oaks, 1979.

(Editor) *Mesoamerican Sites and Worldviews: Conference at Dumbarton Oaks, October 16 and 17, 1976,* Dumbarton Oaks, 1981.

(Editor) *The Olmec and Their Neighbors: Essays in Memory of Matthew W. Stirling,* Dumbarton Oaks, 1981.

(With others) *Museums of the Andes,* Newsweek & Kodansha, 1982.

(Editor with Merle G. Robertson) *Fourth Palenque Round Table: 1980,* Pre-Columbian Art, 1985.

(With Michael Coe and Dean Snow) *Atlas of Ancient America,* Facts on File, 1987.

(Editor with Gillett G. Griffin) *Maya Iconography,* Princeton University Press, 1988.

Editor of *Studies in Pre-Columbian Art and Archaeology.* Contributor to professional journals and popular magazines, including *Americas* and *Smithsonian.*

WORK IN PROGRESS: A bestiary of the animals in Pre-Columbian art, to be published by Princeton University Press; research on the iconography of early north-coast Peruvian archaeological material.

SIDELIGHTS: Elizabeth Benson commented: "My research aim is to use the art of ancient peoples in an attempt to reconstruct their thought." She added, "I also write mystery stories."

*   *   *

BENSON, Mildred (Augustine Wirt) 1905-
(Mildred Augustine, Mildred Wirt Benson, Mildred A. Wirt; Frank Bell, Joan Clark, Don Palmer, Dorothy West, Ann Wirt, pseudonyms; Julia K. Duncan, Alice B. Emerson, Frances K. Judd, Carolyn Keene, Helen Louise Thorndyke, collective pseudonyms)

PERSONAL: Born July 10, 1905, in Ladora, IA; daughter of J. L. (a doctor) and Lillian (Mattison) Augustine; married Asa Alvin Wirt (affiliated with the Associated Press; died, 1947); married George A. Benson (editor of the Toledo, OH, *Times*), 1950 (died, 1959); children: (first marriage) Margaret. *Education:* University of Iowa, A.B., 1925, M.A., 1927. *Politics:* Republican. *Hobbies and other interests:* Golf, swimming, flying (holds commercial, private, seaplane and instrument pilot licenses), Pre-Columbian archaeology.

ADDRESSES: Office—Toledo *Blade,* 541 Superior St., Toledo, OH 43660.

CAREER: Author of books for children and young adults, 1927-59. Has held various jobs in journalism, including working for a newspaper in Clinton, IA, as a court reporter for the Toledo, OH, *Times,* and as aviation columnist for the Toledo *Blade.* Currently writes "On the Go" column for Toledo *Blade.* Taught swimming in Cleveland, OH.

Millie Benson shows the same spunk as her heroine sleuth Nancy Drew. (Photo courtesy of the Toledo *Blade.*)

AWARDS, HONORS: Boys' Life-Dodd, Mead prize, 1957, for *Dangerous Deadline;* Amos Ives Root Award, Ohio Aviation Trades Association, 1973, for articles on aviation; Ohioana Citation, Ohioana Library Association, 1989, for contributions to children's literature; Ohio Newspaper Women's Association citation for feature writing.

WRITINGS:

(Under name Mildred A. Wirt) *The Sky Racers,* Penn Publishing Co., 1935.
(Under name Mildred A. Wirt) *The Twin Ring Mystery,* Cupples & Leon, 1935.
(Under name Mildred A. Wirt) *Carolina Castle,* Penn Publishing Co., 1936.
(Under name Mildred A. Wirt) *Courageous Wings,* Penn Publishing Co., 1937.
(Under pseudonym Joan Clark) *Connie Carl at Rainbow Ranch,* Goldsmith, 1939.
(Under name Mildred A. Wirt) *The Mystery of the Laughing Mask,* Cupples & Leon, 1940.
(Under pseudonym Frank Bell) *Flash Evans and the Darkroom Mystery,* Cupples & Leon, 1940.
(Under pseudonym Frank Bell) *Flash Evans—Camera News Hawk,* Cupples & Leon, 1940.
(Under name Mildred A. Wirt) *Linda,* Cupples & Leon, 1940.
(Under name Mildred A. Wirt) *Pirate Brig,* Scribners, 1950.
Dangerous Deadline, Dodd, Mead, 1957.

Quarry Ghost, Dodd, Mead, 1959, published in England as *Kristie at College,* Children's Press, 1960.

Contributor to periodicals, including *St. Nicholas Magazine, Lutheran Young Folks,* and *Books at Iowa,* under names Mildred Augustine and Mildred Wirt Benson. Also contributor of a short story, "Mystery at the Lookout," to *Calling All Girls* magazine, under pseudonym Carolyn Keene.

"RUTH FIELDING" SERIES; UNDER COLLECTIVE PSEUDONYM ALICE B. EMERSON

Ruth Fielding and Her Great Scenario; or, Striving for the Motion Picture Prize, Cupples & Leon, 1927.
Ruth Fielding at Cameron Hall; or, A Mysterious Disappearance, Cupples & Leon, 1928.
Ruth Fielding Clearing Her Name; or, The Rivals of Hollywood, Cupples & Leon, 1929.
Ruth Fielding in Talking Pictures; or, The Prisoners of the Tower, Cupples & Leon, 1930.
Ruth Fielding and Baby June, Cupples & Leon, 1931.
Ruth Fielding and Her Double, Cupples & Leon, 1932.
Ruth Fielding and Her Greatest Triumph; or, Saving Her Company from Disaster, Cupples & Leon, 1933.
Ruth Fielding and Her Crowning Victory; or, Winning Honors Abroad, Cupples & Leon, 1934.

"RUTH DARROW FLYING STORIES"; UNDER NAME MILDRED A. WIRT

Ruth Darrow in the Air Derby; or, Recovering the Silver Trophy, Barse & Co., 1930.

Ruth Darrow in the Fire Patrol; or, Capturing the Redwood Thieves, Barse & Co., 1930.
Ruth Darrow in Yucatan, Barse & Co., 1931.
Ruth Darrow in the Coast Guard, Barse & Co., 1931.

"NANCY DREW MYSTERY STORIES"; UNDER COLLECTIVE PSEUDONYM CAROLYN KEENE

The Secret of the Old Clock, Grosset & Dunlap, 1930.
The Hidden Staircase, Grosset & Dunlap, 1930.
The Bungalow Mystery, Grosset & Dunlap, 1930.
The Mystery at Lilac Inn, Grosset & Dunlap, 1930.
The Secret at Shadow Ranch, Grosset & Dunlap, 1930.
The Secret of Red Gate Farm, Grosset & Dunlap, 1931.
The Clue in the Diary, Grosset & Dunlap, 1932.
The Clue of the Broken Locket, Grosset & Dunlap, 1934.
The Message in the Hollow Oak, Grosset & Dunlap, 1935.
The Mystery of the Ivory Charm, Grosset & Dunlap, 1936.
The Whispering Statue, Grosset & Dunlap, 1937.
The Haunted Bridge, Grosset & Dunlap, 1937.
The Clue of the Tapping Heels, Grosset & Dunlap, 1939.
The Mystery of the Brass Bound Trunk, Grosset & Dunlap, 1940.
The Mystery at the Moss-Covered Mansion, Grosset & Dunlap, 1941.
The Quest of the Missing Map, Grosset & Dunlap, 1942.
The Clue in the Jewel Box, Grosset & Dunlap, 1943.
The Secret in the Old Attic, Grosset & Dunlap, 1944.
The Clue in the Crumbling Wall, Grosset & Dunlap, 1945.
The Mystery of the Tolling Bell, Grosset & Dunlap, 1946.
The Clue in the Old Album, Grosset & Dunlap, 1947.
The Ghost of Blackwood Hall, Grosset & Dunlap, 1948.
The Clue of the Velvet Mask, Grosset & Dunlap, 1953.

"DORIS FORCE MYSTERY SERIES"; UNDER COLLECTIVE PSEUDONYM JULIA K. DUNCAN

Doris Force at Locked Gates; or, Saving a Mysterious Fortune, H. Altemus, 1931.
Doris Force at Cloudy Cove; or, The Old Miser's Signature, H. Altemus, 1931.

"MADGE STERLING" SERIES; UNDER PSEUDONYM ANN WIRT

The Missing Formula, Goldsmith, 1932.
The Deserted Yacht, Goldsmith, 1932.
The Secret of the Sundial, Goldsmith, 1932.

"KAY TRACEY MYSTERY STORIES"; UNDER COLLECTIVE PSEUDONYM FRANCES K. JUDD

The Mystery of the Swaying Curtains, Cupples & Leon, 1935.
The Shadow on the Door, Cupples & Leon, 1935.
The Six-Fingered Glove Mystery, Cupples & Leon, 1936.
The Green Cameo Mystery, Cupples & Leon, 1936.
The Secret at the Windmill, Cupples & Leon, 1937.
Beneath the Crimson Briar Bush, Cupples & Leon, 1937.
The Message in the Sand Dunes, Cupples & Leon, 1938.
The Murmuring Portrait, Cupples & Leon, 1938.
When the Key Turned, Cupples & Leon, 1939.
In the Sunken Garden, Cupples & Leon, 1939.
The Forbidden Tower, Cupples & Leon, 1940.
The Sacred Feather, Cupples & Leon, 1940.

"MILDRED A. WIRT MYSTERY STORIES"; UNDER NAME MILDRED A. WIRT

The Clue at Crooked Lane, Cupples & Leon, 1936.
The Hollow Wall Mystery, Cupples & Leon, 1936.
The Shadow Stone, Cupples & Leon, 1937.
The Wooden Shoe Mystery, Cupples & Leon, 1938.
Through the Moon-Gate Door, Cupples & Leon, 1938.
Ghost Gables, Cupples & Leon, 1939.

The Painted Shield, Cupples & Leon, 1939.

"PENNY NICHOLS MYSTERY STORIES"; UNDER PSEUDONYM JOAN CLARK

Penny Nichols Finds a Clue, Goldsmith, 1936.
Penny Nichols and the Mystery of the Lost Key, Goldsmith, 1936.
Penny Nichols and the Black Imp, Goldsmith, 1936.
Penny Nichols and the Knob Hill Mystery, Goldsmith, 1939.

"DANA GIRLS" MYSTERY SERIES; UNDER COLLECTIVE PSEUDONYM CAROLYN KEENE

The Secret at the Hermitage, Grosset & Dunlap, 1936.
The Circle of Footprints, Grosset & Dunlap, 1937.
The Mystery of the Locked Room, Grosset & Dunlap, 1938.
The Clue in the Cobweb, Grosset & Dunlap, 1939.
The Secret at the Gatehouse, Grosset & Dunlap, 1940.
The Mysterious Fireplace, Grosset & Dunlap, 1941.
The Clue of the Rusty Key, Grosset & Dunlap, 1942.
The Portrait in the Sand, Grosset & Dunlap, 1943.
The Secret in the Old Well, Grosset & Dunlap, 1944.
The Clue in the Ivy, Grosset & Dunlap, 1952.
The Secret of the Jade Ring, Grosset & Dunlap, 1953.
Mystery at the Crossroads, Grosset & Dunlap, 1954.

She stepped out into water which reached nearly to her knees. (Frontispiece for the 1930 edition of Nancy Drew's third adventure, *The Bungalow Mystery.* Illustration by Russell H. Tandy.)

"TRAILER STORIES FOR GIRLS"; UNDER NAME MILDRED A. WIRT

The Runaway Caravan, Cupples & Leon, 1937.
The Crimson Cruiser, Cupples & Leon, 1937.
Timbered Treasure, Cupples & Leon, 1937.
The Phantom Trailer, Cupples & Leon, 1938.

"HONEY BUNCH" SERIES; UNDER COLLECTIVE PSEUDONYM HELEN LOUISE THORNDYKE

Honey Bunch—Her First Little Treasure Hunt, Grosset & Dunlap, 1937.
Honey Bunch—Her First Little Club, Grosset & Dunlap, 1938.
Honey Bunch—Her First Trip in a Trailer, Grosset & Dunlap, 1939.
Honey Bunch—Her First Trip to a Big Fair, Grosset & Dunlap, 1940.
Honey Bunch—Her First Twin Playmates, Grosset & Dunlap, 1941.

"DOT AND DASH" SERIES; UNDER PSEUDONYM DOROTHY WEST

Dot and Dash at the Maple Sugar Camp, Cupples & Leon, 1938.
Dot and Dash at Happy Hollow, Cupples & Leon, 1938.
Dot and Dash in the North Woods, Cupples & Leon, 1938.
Dot and Dash in the Pumpkin Patch, Cupples & Leon, 1939.
Dot and Dash at the Seashore, Cupples & Leon, 1940.

"PENNY PARKER MYSTERY STORIES"; UNDER NAME MILDRED A. WIRT

Tale of the Witch Doll, Cupples & Leon, 1939.
The Vanishing Houseboat, Cupples & Leon, 1939.
Danger at the Drawbridge, Cupples & Leon, 1940.
Behind the Green Door, Cupples & Leon, 1940.
The Clue of the Silken Ladder, Cupples & Leon, 1941.
The Secret Pact, Cupples & Leon, 1941.
The Clock Strikes Thirteen, Cupples & Leon, 1942.
The Wishing Well, Cupples & Leon, 1942.
Ghost Beyond the Gate, Cupples & Leon, 1943.
Saboteurs on the River, Cupples & Leon, 1943.
Hoofbeats on the Turnpike, Cupples & Leon, 1944.
Voice from the Cave, Cupples & Leon, 1944.
The Guilt of the Brass Thieves, Cupples & Leon, 1945.
Signal in the Dark, Cupples & Leon, 1946.
Whispering Walls, Cupples & Leon, 1946.
Swamp Island, Cupples & Leon, 1947.
The Cry at Midnight, Cupples & Leon, 1947.

"BROWNIE SCOUT" SERIES; UNDER NAME MILDRED A. WIRT

The Brownie Scouts at Snow Valley, Cupples & Leon, 1949.
The Brownie Scouts in the Circus, Cupples & Leon, 1949.
The Brownie Scouts in the Cherry Festival, Cupples & Leon, 1950.
The Brownie Scouts and Their Tree House, Cupples & Leon, 1951.
The Brownie Scouts at Silver Beach, Cupples & Leon, 1952.
The Brownie Scouts at Windmill Farm, Cupples & Leon, 1953.

"DAN CARTER" SERIES; UNDER NAME MILDRED A. WIRT

Dan Carter, Cub Scout, Cupples & Leon, 1949.
Dan Carter, Cub Scout, and the River Camp, Cupples & Leon, 1949.
Dan Carter and the Money Box, Cupples & Leon, 1950.
Dan Carter and the Haunted Castle, Cupples & Leon, 1951.
Dan Carter and the Great Carved Face, Cupples & Leon, 1952.

Dan Carter and the Cub Honor, Cupples & Leon, 1953.

"GIRL SCOUT" SERIES; UNDER NAME MILDRED A. WIRT

The Girl Scouts at Penguin Pass; or, Trail of the Snowman, Cupples & Leon, 1953.
Girl Scouts at Singing Sands, Cupples & Leon, 1955.
The Girl Scouts at Mystery Mansion, Cupples & Leon, 1957.

"BOY SCOUT EXPLORERS" SERIES; UNDER PSEUDONYM DON PALMER

The Boy Scout Explorers at Emerald Valley, Cupples & Leon, 1955.
The Boy Scout Explorers at Treasure Mountain, Cupples & Leon, 1955.
The Boy Scout Explorers at Headless Hollow, Cupples & Leon, 1957.

SIDELIGHTS: Author, pilot, newswoman—Mildred Benson has played many roles in her long career. She was the first woman to receive a Master's degree from the University of Iowa's school of journalism. She holds a variety of pilot's licenses, she still flies regularly, and, since 1944, she has worked for the Toledo, Ohio, *Blade.* Moreover, between 1927 and 1959 she wrote well over a hundred juvenile series titles, some under her own name, but many others under pseudonyms. Under one of those pseudonyms— Carolyn Keene—Benson created Nancy Drew, the girl sleuth who in her more than sixty years of printed life has endeared herself to more than three generations of women.

"Carolyn Keene" still produces Nancy's adventures, but Mildred Benson no longer writes them. She was originally selected to begin Nancy's adventures by Edward Stratemeyer, head of the Stratemeyer Syndicate, a writing house that produced juvenile fiction, including the "Tom Swift," "Bobbsey Twins," and "Hardy Boys" series. Benson first met Stratemeyer in the late 1920s while on a trip to New York, looking for newspaper work and freelance writing assignments. He looked at her writing samples and contacted her after her return to Iowa, asking her to work on the Syndicate's established "Ruth Fielding" series, written under the collective pseudonym Alice B. Emerson. Pleased with Benson's work, Stratemeyer offered her the opportunity to write the first volume of the "Nancy Drew" mysteries, which he conceived as a counterpart to his newly successful "Hardy Boys Mystery Stories."

Stratemeyer's authors, including Benson, worked under strict rules when writing under Syndicate pseudonyms. With each Nancy Drew manuscript she submitted, Benson signed a contract giving up her right to royalty payments on the volume in exchange for a flat fee—usually about one hundred twenty-five dollars. She also agreed not to use the Syndicate pseudonym for any of her own books. In return, Stratemeyer provided her with an outline of the book's plot, indicating characters' names and other general information. "Pacing, characterization, and chapter delineation were left up to [Benson]," explains Geoffrey S. Lapin in the *Yellowback Library.* "Often . . . [Stratemeyer's] guidelines were either partially, or completely, ignored in favor of a well-written story."

"The plots provided me were brief," Benson records in a biographical article for *Books at Iowa,* "yet certain hackneyed names and situations could not be bypassed. Therefore I concentrated upon Nancy, trying to make her a departure from the stereotyped heroine commonly encountered in series books of the day." Benson turned

Stratemeyer's girl sleuth into a wish-fulfillment fantasy figure with a broad appeal to young girls. "When I asked my daughter why she had loved Nancy," reports Arthur Prager in his *Rascals at Large; or, The Clue in the Old Nostalgia*, "she thought for a moment, and then said simply, 'You can *identify* with her.' She meant that a little girl can plausibly pretend to be Nancy." Equipped with admiring friends and an indulgent, wealthy father who left her free to pursue her destiny in her own blue roadster, Nancy won a place in the hearts of millions of young girls. Today, more than sixty years after her debut, Nancy's adventures continue to attract readers. More than eighty million copies of her books have been sold.

After creating Nancy, Benson worked on several other Syndicate projects, including the "Doris Force," "Kay Tracey," "Dana Girls," and "Honey Bunch" series. In addition, she published several other volumes under her own pseudonyms. She also wrote many books under her own name, some of which introduced themes that Benson would later make a part of her own life. The "Ruth Darrow Flying Stories," for instance, sparked her interest in flying and Central American archaeology. The "Penny Parker Mystery Stories," started in 1939, featured a young reporter-sleuth whose father published a small-town newspaper. In 1944, Benson began reporting herself for local Toledo newspapers. She still works daily as a journalist for the Toledo *Blade* Co.

When approached by an editor to start a new series in the late 1960s, Benson relates in *Books at Iowa*, "For a moment I was tempted. Plots began to percolate. Then fog settled over my typewriter. The teenagers for whom I wrote lived in a world far removed from drugs, abortion, divorce, and racial clash. Regretfully, I turned down the offer. Any character I might create would never be attuned to today's social problems. In my style of writing there can be no time concept, no chains binding one to the present." "To be remembered for more than an hour, a tale must ride in a sealed capsule, isolated from everyday living," she explains. "A presentation should be as true to childhood aspiration in the year 2003 as in 1906. Such sentiments definitely identify an author with a swiftly receding past."

Nonetheless, Benson's work is fondly remembered by many readers. "All of her tales display a certain craftsmanship, a clear narrative line, and the suspense that Edward Stratemeyer said was essential in books for young readers," writes Anita Susan Grossman in the *San Francisco Chronicle*. "Many of her stories—long out of print—hold up surprisingly well, with an appeal that is not entirely due to their period charm. Adult collectors of children's books overwhelmingly prefer the old Nancy Drews to the updated, rewritten versions that have come along since 1959." In 1989, the Ohioana library honored Mildred Benson for her "special ability to entertain and motivate generations of children." "Mildred Wirt Benson's books," writes a contributor to the *Ohioana Quarterly*, "taught countless children to read and to enjoy reading."

WORKS CITED:

Benson, Mildred Wirt, "The Ghost of Ladora," *Books at Iowa*, November, 1973, pp. 24-29.
Grossman, Anita Susan, "The Ghost of Nancy Drew: The Story behind the Teenage Sleuth," *San Francisco Chronicle*, August 21, 1988, pp. 10-16.
Lapin, Geoffrey S., "Carolyn Keene, pseud.," *Yellowback Library*, July/August, 1983, pp. 3-5; September/Octo-

ber, 1983, pp. 16-17; November/December, 1983, pp. 13-17; September/October, 1985, p. 15.
Ohioana Quarterly, fall, 1989, p. S-4.
Prager, Arthur, "The Secret of Nancy Drew: Pushing Forty and Going Strong," *Rascals at Large; or, The Clue in the Old Nostalgia*, Doubleday, 1971, pp. 71-95.

FOR MORE INFORMATION SEE:

BOOKS

Girls Series Books: A Checklist of Hardback Books Published 1900-1975, Children's Literature Research Collections, University of Minnesota Libraries, 1978.
Hudson, Harry K., *A Bibliography of Hard-Cover Boys' Books*, revised edition, Data Print (Tampa, FL), 1977.
Mason, Bobbie Ann, *The Girl Sleuth: A Feminist Guide*, Feminist Press, 1975.
Nye, Russel B., *The Unembarrassed Muse: The Popular Arts in America*, Dial, 1970.
Paluka, Frank, *Iowa Authors: A Bio-Bibliography of Sixty Native Writers*, Friends of The University of Iowa Libraries, 1967.

PERIODICALS

Books at Iowa, April, 1989.
Detroit Free Press, June 8, 1969.
Hiram Magazine, summer, 1988.
Ohio Magazine, December, 1987.
People's Voice, December, 1974.
Publishers Weekly, September 26, 1986.
Toledo Blade, April 12, 1940.
Toledo Times, August 8, 1949; November 6, 1957.
Yellowback Library, September/October, 1986; March/April, 1987.

—Sketch by Kenneth R. Shepherd

*   *   *

BENSON, Mildred Wirt
See BENSON, Mildred (Augustine Wirt)

*   *   *

BERENZY, Alix 1957-

PERSONAL: Born August 3, 1957, in Queens, NY; daughter of George John (a roofing salesman) and Roberta (a free-lance illustrator; maiden name, Pommerer) Berenzy. *Education:* Attended Columbus College of Art and Design, 1974-76, and Philadelphia College of Art, 1979-81. *Hobbies and other interests:* Biking, skateboarding.

ADDRESSES: Home and office—849 South Seventh St., Apt. 3A, Philadelphia, PA 19147.

CAREER: Glassman Advertising Agency, Fairfield, NJ, assistant art director, 1977-78; free-lance sign painter, 1977-79; Mark Color Studios (advertising agency), Fairfield, art director, 1978-79; free-lance illustrator, 1982—; writer. Part-time art instructor at schools in Philadelphia, PA, including Hussian School of Art, 1989-90, and University of the Arts, 1990-91.

Works exhibited at Master Eagle Gallery, New York City, 1985 and 1986; Society of Illustrators show, 1990; group

ALIX BERENZY

exhibit "Worth a Thousand Words . . . ," Community Arts Center, Wallingford, PA, 1990; "Every Picture Tells a Story" exhibit in Los Angeles, CA, 1990; and at a one-woman show at the Children's Book Fair, Bologna, Italy, 1990.

MEMBER: National Organization of Women, People for the Ethical Treatment of Animals, Greenpeace, Sierra Club.

AWARDS, HONORS: Illustration honor, Philadelphia College of Art, 1982; *Touch the Moon, The Last Slice of Rainbow and Other Stories,* and *A Frog Prince* were named Book-of-the-Month by the Philadelphia Children's Reading Roundtable, Philadelphia Free Library, 1987, 1988, and 1990, respectively; *The Last Slice of Rainbow and Other Stories* was a Junior Literary Guild selection; *A Frog Prince* was a Junior Literary Guild selection and earned the Critici in Erba Prize at the Children's Book Fair, Bologna, Italy, 1990.

WRITINGS:

(Reteller) *A Frog Prince* (self-illustrated; loosely based on a fairy tale by Jacob and Wilhelm Grimm), Holt, 1989.
(Reteller) *Rapunzel* (self-illustrated), Holt, in press.

ILLUSTRATOR

Daniel Cohen, *America's Very Own Ghosts,* Dodd, 1985.
Marion Dane Bauer, *Touch the Moon,* Clarion, 1987.
Joan Aiken, *The Last Slice of Rainbow and Other Stories,* Harper, 1988.
Shirley Climo, *T. J.'s Ghost,* Harper, 1989.

Also illustrator of numerous book jackets.

SIDELIGHTS: Alix Berenzy told *SATA:* "My first interest was in horses—that's what started me drawing. I grew up in a

suburban community in New Jersey where keeping a horse in the backyard was out of the question. (Believe me, I worked very hard on my parents.) But on bus rides to school we would pass what few farms were left in the area, and I would always strain at the window to catch a glimpse of HORSES. Then, in school, when I should have been paying attention, I would draw what I'd seen out the bus window. I even drew horses on my test papers. Once I got back a test that the teacher had marked in red, 'Great horse, terrible math—D.' It was a good thing I loved to read. I was such an awful daydreamer in school, I never heard half of what was going on. So reading the great number of books that I did helped fill in my education.

"I went to Columbus College of Art and Design for two years. I liked doing all kinds of art but didn't know exactly what I could make a career of. Finally, because it seemed most practical, I chose 'advertising art' as my major. By the end of my second year I was still confused so I left college to work in an advertising agency back in New Jersey to see if I actually liked doing what I was majoring in. I did like it—the people were fun, if a bit frantic, and I enjoyed the high energy level. And it was really nice to get a steady paycheck. (I remember that fondly.)

"I also started a little sign painting business at home in the garage. I learned to do free-hand brush lettering and did big paper ('butcher') signs for stores, window lettering, and truck lettering. I even lettered a race car once. I worked on it all night and finished it at three in the morning. At seven o'clock they took it to the track and by ten o'clock it was in twenty different pieces. Race cars aside, I liked sign painting and found it to be quite creative.

"At the time my mother was doing free-lance commercial illustration— cartooning mostly. She is also a fine artist and does beautiful watercolors. I was not particularly interested in cartooning or in becoming a fine artist, but I knew by this time I wanted to be an illustrator of some sort. I went back to college, this time at the Philadelphia College of Art, firmly committed to majoring in illustration. In the two years I was there I saw a variety of art and types of illustration and I began to develop a distinct vision of the work I wanted to do.

"I'm very interested in light—how it creates a mood, moves over objects, and can conjure a magical feeling. Sometimes when I walk down the street, especially in the evening, I'll just stop and stare at the turn of a branch under a peach colored street light with an electric blue sky behind it, or a glass bottle crushed and glittering on the road, or a shadow on a stone wall. I have no memory for everyday practical things, but these images get stored away and come out when I am planning an illustration. Of course, they are adapted to another place and time, but it was in these ordinary scenes that I first saw something magical.

"Once, years ago, I happened upon an exhibit by James Turrell at the Whitney Museum in New York. His medium is light and space—rooms of it. You walk into his work. You can almost breath it, hear it. The intensity of his work made a deep impression on me. That, too, always seems to stay in the back of my mind.

"I work on black paper, so I can draw the light, as opposed to white paper, on which an illustrator renders shadows. I like the particular texture of the paper I use, and over the years I have developed a special technique. Mostly, though, I work

She was so lovely, the Frog hardly dared to approach. (From *A Frog Prince*, by Alix Berenzy. Illustrated by the author.)

on a black background because it is the most efficient way to record the images I have in my mind.

"I began my professional career doing adult book jackets—mysteries and science fiction—but soon moved to children's books. They offer a high degree of artistic freedom, picture books especially. There is also the challenge of writing. In 1990, I finished my first picture book, *A Frog Prince.* It's a fairy tale that I rewrote. The illustrations incorporate all the things I've learned from doing book jackets and also all the things I've always wanted to do. It was my first chance to immerse myself in the realm of the fairy tale, where I would really like to stay."

Berenzy reportedly became fascinated with fairy tales after her parents were involved in a serious automobile accident. Identifying with the sometimes horrifying aspects of fairy tales allowed her to cope with and overcome the grisly realities of life. In *A Frog Prince,* her retelling of the Grimm brothers' classic tale, Berenzy explores the inner feelings of an ugly frog searching for love and acceptance. The story reflects several notable themes, including the author's belief in the importance of treating all creatures with respect and the realization that inner beauty, kindness, and purity of heart matter more than outward appearances.

FOR MORE INFORMATION SEE:

PERIODICALS

Review-Chronicle West (Philadelphia), November 1, 1990.

*   *   *

BIALK, Elisa
See KRAUTTER, Elisa (Bialk)

*   *   *

BIGGLE, Lloyd, Jr. 1923-

PERSONAL: Born April 17, 1923, in Waterloo, IA; son of Lloyd B. (an electrician) and Ethel (Cruthers) Biggle; married Hedwig T. Janiszewski (a violin teacher), June 21, 1947; children: Donna Helene, Kenneth Lloyd. *Education:* Wayne University (now Wayne State University), A.B. (with high distinction), 1947; University of Michigan, M.M. (music literature), 1948, Ph.D. (musicology), 1953.

ADDRESSES: Home—569 Dubie St., Ypsilanti, MI 48198.

CAREER: Science fiction and mystery writer. University of Michigan, Ann Arbor, teacher of music literature and history, 1948-51; self-employed, 1951—. *Military service:* U.S. Army, 102nd Infantry Division, World War II; became sergeant; received Purple Heart with oak leaf cluster.

MEMBER: Science Fiction Oral History Association (founder; president, 1979-87; director, 1987—).

AWARDS, HONORS: Hugo Award nomination for short story, 1962; Nebula Award nomination, Science Fiction Writers of America, 1966, for *Watchers of the Dark;* New York Public Library Books for the Teenage list, 1980, for *Silence Is Deadly.*

WRITINGS:

SCIENCE FICTION NOVELS

The Angry Espers, Ace Books, 1961.
The Fury out of Time, Doubleday, 1965.
The Still, Small Voice of Trumpets, Doubleday, 1968.
The World Menders, Doubleday, 1971.
The Light That Never Was, Doubleday, 1972.
Monument, Doubleday, 1974.
(With T. L. Sherred) *Alien Main,* Doubleday, 1985.

"JAN DARZEK" SCIENCE FICTION SERIES

All the Colors of Darkness, Doubleday, 1963.
Watchers of the Dark, Doubleday, 1966.
This Darkening Universe, Doubleday, 1975.
Silence Is Deadly, Doubleday, 1977.
The Whirligig of Time, Doubleday, 1979.

OTHER

The Rule of the Door and Other Fanciful Regulations (short stories), Doubleday, 1967, published as *Out of the Silent Sky,* Belmont Books, 1977.
The Metallic Muse (short stories), Doubleday, 1972.
(Editor) *Nebula Award Stories Seven,* Harper, 1973.
A Galaxy of Strangers (short stories), Doubleday, 1976.
The Quallsford Inheritance: A Memoir of Sherlock Holmes (novel), St. Martin's, 1986.
Interface for Murder (mystery novel), Doubleday, 1987.
The Glendower Conspiracy: A Memoir of Sherlock Holmes (novel), Council Oak Books, 1990.
A Hazard of Losers (mystery novel), Council Oak Books, 1991.

LLOYD BIGGLE, JR.

Contributor to science fiction and mystery anthologies. Contributor of over seventy-five stories to magazines.

SIDELIGHTS: Lloyd Biggle, Jr., told *SATA:* "When I was nine years old, I decided to be a writer—a poet. I had poems published in the school paper at that age. One of them was my first science fiction story, written in the form of a poem. A few years ago I discovered a copy of it, so I am able to quote it:

"'A TALL MAN': 'A man once came to the earth. / He came to the Earth from Mars. / He stood in the traffic / And looked so giraffic / That people got out of their cars.'

"I have quoted that for audiences several times, and the reaction has been mixed. Many people seem to think that a professional writer should have been doing something more advanced than that at the age of nine— writing epics, perhaps. But if you are to write, the important thing is that you must start. I did start, and I did work to improve my writing—and I am still doing that. The longer I write, the more I learn from and about writing.

"I am a story teller. It is an ancient and honorable profession, though I don't know how many authors actually think of themselves in this light. To the story teller, the most important character in any story is the reader. Teachers will tell students to 'express themselves,' put themselves in what they write. That is the function of poetry. Most poems are long capital I's. I feel this, I see that. Prose, a story, is written *to* someone. When I autograph books, I often write, 'No book is complete without a reader.' This is the story teller's attitude.

"The question most frequently asked of science fiction authors is where they get those crazy ideas. Remember that the author lives in the same world you live in, resides in the same sort of community many of you reside in, walks his dog, mows his lawn, reads the same or similar newspapers, pays the same taxes, and has the same TV programs available (though he probably does not watch television nearly as much as you do!). The one major difference between authors and normal people is likely to be with their reading. Most authors read omnivorously (a good word for readers to know) and incessantly. Apart from that, writers see and experience many of the same things that you, the readers, see and experience. Their crazy ideas are no different from your crazy ideas—but they have trained themselves to turn ideas and events and experiences inside out, magnify them in different ways, color them differently, and make all sorts of whimsical changes in their search for story material. They must be able to recognize that material when they find it."

The author continued: "Look at everyday events, keep asking yourself the author's magic words *What would happen if* . . . and you quickly have more story material than you can make use of. What would happen if an alien from outer space enrolled in your school—or you enrolled in an alien school? What would happen if your school football team played a team from outer space? What would happen if the game were played on another world, one that has lower gravity than Earth? What would happen if there were no schools, and all students had to stay home and attend classes shown on television? (I have written that story; it is called, 'And Madly Teach.') See how it works?

"Your own background and interests will be strong factors in determining what you do with that material. . . . Musical 'themes' and art 'themes' run through my writing. If my background had been medicine, or athletics, or electronics, or mechanics, I still might have discovered the same ideas for stories in the same places, but the stories I wrote certainly would have been very different."

FOR MORE INFORMATION SEE:

BOOKS

Dictionary of Literary Biography, Volume 8: *Twentieth-Century American Science-Fiction Writers,* Gale, 1981.

*   *   *

BIRENBAUM, Barbara 1941-

PERSONAL: Surname is pronounced "beer-en-baum"; born Mary 24, 1941, in New York, N.Y.; daughter of Bernard (a physician) and Hazel (a nurse) Lapidus; married Mark Birenbaum (a corporate manager), November 25, 1965; children: two daughters. *Education:* University of South Carolina, B.A., 1961, M.Ed., 1963; Boston University, Ed.S., 1965; further graduate study at C. W. Post of New York and State University of New York at Stony Brook. *Hobbies and other interests:* Harp, piano, sewing, interior decorating, tending to flowers, loving a mini dachshund, and, above all, raising box turtles.

ADDRESSES: Home—Clearwater, Fla. *Office*—Peartree, P.O. Box 14533, Clearwater, Fla. 34629-4533.

CAREER: Richland County Schools, Columbia, S.C., elementary teacher, 1961-62, school psychologist, 1963-65; South Carolina Department of Vocational Rehabilitation, Columbia, rehabilitation psychologist, 1965; Clayton Schools, Clayton, Mo., school psychologist, 1966; University City Schools, University City, Mo., elementary teacher, 1966-67; Huntington Schools, Huntington, N.Y., teacher of creative writing workshops, 1976-78; Board of Cooperative Educational Services, Melville Center, Dix Hills, N.Y., school psychologist, 1978; Pinellas County, Fla., poet-in-schools, 1980-82; Peartree Publications, Clearwater, Fla., founder, 1985; free-lance author, illustrator, and composer, 1985—. Member of student advisory committees, ad hoc Clearwater Traffic Engineering Committee and Neighborhood Homeowners Association, 1979-87.

MEMBER: American Association of Composers, Authors and Publishers, Florida Reading Association, Florida Association for Instructional Materials, Southeast Bookseller Association, Pinellas County Arts Council, Psi Chi, Kappa Delta Epsilon.

AWARDS, HONORS: National Poetry and National Essay Anthology awards, 1958; first place sculpture awards, South Carolina Fine Arts Association, 1961 and 1962; Canadian Jewish Poet of the Year Award, 1963; grants for Poet-in-Schools program, 1981-83; *Light after Light* was nominated for Children's Literature Book Award by the Jewish Book Council of New York, 1985-86; *Lady Liberty's Light* was part of the Children's Festival to the Statue of Liberty Centennial celebration, 1986; honored centennial author, Punxsutawney Phil Groundhog Day centennial celebration, 1987, for *The Hidden Shadow;* honored Florida writer, Adler Literary Conference, 1987; *The Lost Side of the Dreydl* was nominated for Children's Literature and Illustrated Children's Book awards by the Jewish Book Council of New York, 1987-88.

BARBARA BIRENBAUM

WRITINGS:

Up Til Now, Yet . . . , Service Printing, 1964.
(With Guy Hoagland and Nancy Carter) *Breaking through to Poetry,* Pinellas Arts Council, 1982.
(With Hoagland and Carter) *A Dance of Words,* Pinellas Arts Council, 1982.
The Gooblins Night (self-illustrated children's book), Peartree, 1985.
Light after Light (self-illustrated children's book), Peartree, 1985.
Lady Liberty's Light (self-illustrated children's book), Peartree, 1986.
The Hidden Shadow (self-illustrated children's book), Peartree, 1986.
The Lost Side of the Dreydl (self-illustrated children's book), Peartree, 1987.
The Olympic Glow (illustrated by Pat Sapp), Peartree, 1988.

Author of poetry for children and adults. Composer of children's music titled "The Eight Lights of Hanukkah," "The Spinning Dreydl Song," "Lady Liberty's Light," and "Our Constitution."

WORK IN PROGRESS: The Lighthouse Christmas, The Birthday Wish, and *Candletalk.*

SIDELIGHTS: Barbara Birenbaum told *SATA:* "Most young people get encouragement from home and school. I had the 'mis'-happenstance of getting backward encouragement from my high school guidance counselor who discouraged college. I also found myself competing with an older brother. I'd study. He'd make good grades! I'd write. He'd get the awards!

"I believed in myself and felt confident that I knew the real me. So, as guidance recommended a 'no-go,' I just sent my counselor get well cards every time I received a degree. While guidance gave its advice based on the numbers, I was equally fortunate to have a wonderful creative writing teacher my senior year of high school.

"As I headed to English 4, Miss Patti Parker (Dreher High, Columbia, South Carolina) urged me into her class. As I looked for creative bones in my body, she was quietly motivating me: 'What you write will last. Other teens laugh at what you write because you look beneath the surface.' You must also realize that this came at a time when my brother, Richard, died suddenly at Georgia Tech, which motivated me into a self-competition to explore all my talents. But, never did I expect to win both the National Poetry and National Essay Anthology awards upon high school graduation!

"As I entered higher education, I made a promise to myself to always look at persons' strengths rather than weaknesses, to look for that ounce of creativity that was still untapped in students who felt 'unique' in the mainstream of education. I was the child whose middle name should have been 'Chatterbox' and who enjoyed recess as the major subject! As I progressed through school, I realized that what I thought was academic boredom was creative intelligence mowed down in the confines of academia and rote memorization. I found myself in college!

"I always kept a diary and wrote poetry ever since I could remember. I also played the piano for ten years and studied voice for five. I had a CBS show in 1959-1960 called *A Still Small Voice* every Friday at noon. Somehow, I also picked up the four string guitar and the harp. If I had a bent to compose music (four pieces now available) I never realized the talent. I just knew I got frustrated playing pieces as they were written for recitals.

"But 1956 and the Hungarian Revolution brought me to meet a sculptor, Hans Pawley, an emigre from Hungary. As he taught me the art of clay throwing—left-handed of course—I watched as he chiselled tree limbs into art that spoke its own language. Although he didn't teach me directly, he introduced me to raw house brick and supplied me with my first sculpting tools to go it alone. That I did, winning South Carolina Fine Arts Association awards in 1961 and 1962.

"But, it never really occurred to me that I was creative. My approach to music and art in my eyes was a way to cope, being raised in a small Southern community. Every time I felt bored, I worked at music, art, or writing out of frustration. I took every art class at high school just to fill up the schedule! I was actively involved with the Columbia Museum of Fine Arts by the time I was twenty. And by twenty-two I was the first woman school psychologist in South Carolina.

"It wasn't until the 1980s and through the encouragement of my husband, Mark, that I combined art, music, and my professional training into the Kindl series that fosters the 'Three E's to Reading: Education, Entertainment and Enjoyment.' How else could he get rid of the piles of manuscripts sitting on the floor in his computer room?

"Kindl, a walking, talking candle and symbol of light, is a recurring character in my books who crosses the boundaries of the superficial to give events a deeper meaning. He conquers the odds to learn more than those around him, seeking out the trivia of events as well as answering the often asked 'how comes?' He is no different than children today, groping in their knowledge, decisions, and feelings. Kindl also has the uncanny ability to go forward and backward in time."

FOR MORE INFORMATION SEE:

PERIODICALS

Belleair Bee (Belleair, Florida), April 3, 1986.
Carolina Alumni Quarterly, fall, 1982.
Clearwater Sun, March 29, 1986; February 2, 1987.
Clearwater Times, March 23, 1986; January 30, 1987; December 15, 1989.
Jewish Floridian (St. Petersburg), November 29, 1985.
Jewish Press of Pinellas County (Clearwater, Florida), December 12, 1986; August 26, 1988; November 18, 1988; November 23, 1990.
Pittsburgh Press, February 2, 1987.
St. Petersburg Times, July 6, 1986; December 7, 1986.
St. Petersburg Times Religious News, December 27, 1986; December 19, 1987; December 8, 1988.
State (Columbia, South Carolina), July 6, 1986.
Suncoast News (New Port Richey, Florida), October 3, 1985; September 7, 1988; October 27, 1988.
Tarpon Springs Leader, October 30, 1985.

*   *   *

BLAINE, John
See GOODWIN, Harold L(eland)

*   *   *

BOYLE, Robert H. 1928-

PERSONAL: Born August 21, 1928, in Brooklyn, NY; son of Robert H. (a ship's engineer) and Elizabeth (Condouris) Boyle; married Jane C. Sanger, January 7, 1956 (died, 1975); married Kathryn Belous, July 31, 1977; children: (first marriage) Stephanie, Peter, R. Alexander. *Education:* Trinity College, Hartford, CT, B.A., 1949; Yale University, M.A., 1950. *Politics:* Independent. *Religion:* Roman Catholic.

ADDRESSES: Home—Lane Gate Rd., Cold Springs, NY 10516. *Agent*—J.C.A. Literary Agency Inc., 27 West 20th St., New York, NY 10011.

CAREER: Employed by United Press, New York City, 1953-54; *Sports Illustrated,* New York City, staff writer, 1954-56, senior writer, 1960-1986, special contributor, 1986—; *Sports Illustrated* and *Time,* San Francisco, CA, and Chicago, IL, member of bureaus and staff correspondent, 1956-60; writer and editor. Visiting lecturer at Vassar College, 1988; director of Hudson River Foundation for Science and Environmental Research. *Military service:* U.S. Marine Corps, 1950-52.

MEMBER: Hudson River Fishermen's Association (president); Hudson Riverkeeper Fund (president).

AWARDS, HONORS: Salmo Award, Theodore Gordon Fishflyers, 1965, for conservation articles in *Sports Illustrated;* Trinity College alumni medal, 1971; *Outdoor Life*

Conservation Award, 1976, for work and writings on PCB contamination of the Hudson River; Conservation Communication Award, National Wildlife Federation, 1981, for articles on acid rain and the Florida environment.

WRITINGS:

Sport: Mirror of American Life, Little, Brown. 1963.
The Hudson River: A Natural and Unnatural History, Norton, 1969, expanded edition, 1979.
(With others) *The Water Hustlers,* Sierra Club, 1971.
(Editor with Dave Whitlock) *The Fly Tyer's Almanac,* Crown, 1975.
(Editor with Whitlock) *The Second Fly Tyer's Almanac,* Lippincott, 1978.
(With the Environmental Defense Fund) *Malignant Neglect,* Knopf, 1979.
Bass, Norton, 1980.
(With Eric Leiser) *Stoneflies for the Angler,* Knopf, 1982.
(With son R. Alexander Boyle) *Acid Rain,* Nick Lyons/Schocken, 1983.
At the Top of Their Game: Profiles from Sports Illustrated, Nick Lyons/Winchester, 1983.
(With Michael Oppenheimer) *Dead Heat: The Race against the Greenhouse Effect,* New Republic/Basic Books, 1990.

ADAPTATIONS: Dead Heat: The Race against the Greenhouse Effect is the basis for a fictional television movie on global warming to be produced by Robert Greenwald for ABC-TV.

SIDELIGHTS: Robert H. Boyle is concerned about the future of the earth's environment. Dangerous chemicals in the air, water, and land can be harmful to all living things. Boyle's book *Malignant Neglect* describes ways to avoid the cancer-causing agents that exist in our environment. *Dead Heat: The Race against the Greenhouse Effect,* which he wrote

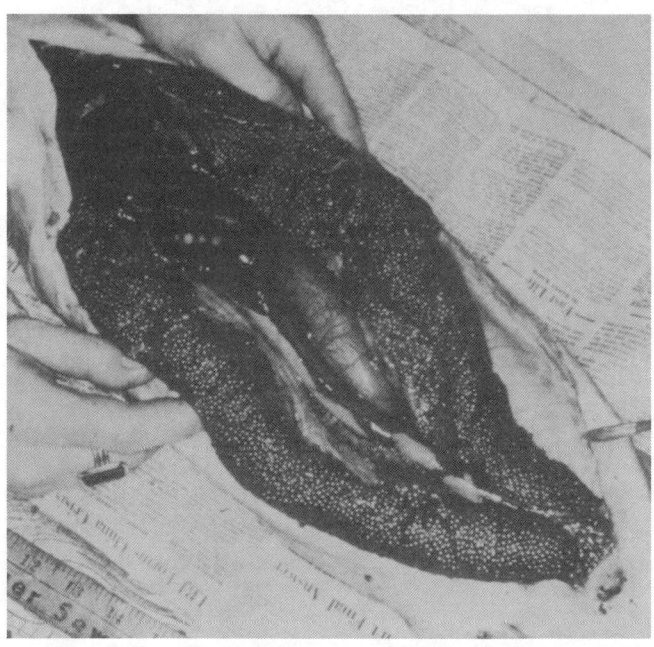

Future caviar, eggs inside a shortnosed sturgeon. (From *The Hudson River: A Natural and Unnatural History,* by Robert H. Boyle. Photo by Dr. Daniel Salzberg.)

with Michael Oppenheimer, deals with the subject of global warming. Global warming is believed to be caused by gases that are accumulating at an alarming rate in the air above the earth. These gases keep the heat of the sun's rays from escaping into space. Hot air collects in the earth's atmosphere, making temperatures rise throughout the world a little more every year. Boyle and Oppenheimer feel that global warming poses a serious threat to life on earth in the next century. According to their calculations, the process will cause certain disaster. Polar icecaps will melt, sea levels will rise, farm land will dry up, and the heat will become unbearable for humans. In *Dead Heat,* the authors urge that we reduce the effects of global warming by decreasing our use of fossil fuels. They further propose that we develop ways to harness the sun's energy, since solar energy is a safe and effective fuel form. Although some scientists do not agree that global warming is actually taking place, most recognize the need to follow the authors' recommendations.

In addition to his work as a writer, Boyle is active in the movement to conserve natural resources and decrease toxic waste. He is president of the Hudson River Fishermen's Association, and in 1980, he helped establish an agreement that forced utility companies using Hudson River water for cooling to endow an independent foundation for the river. The Hudson River Foundation for Science and Environmental Research now has an endowment of twenty-four million dollars and dispenses more than one million dollars a year in grants.

Boyle told *SATA:* "My big problem is that I'm five years ahead of the reading public and ten years ahead of the politicians."

FOR MORE INFORMATION SEE:

PERIODICALS

Chicago Tribune Book World, December 7, 1980.
Los Angeles Times, April 27, 1990.
New York Times, September 4, 1979; October 15, 1979; July 7, 1983; April 2, 1990.
New York Times Book Review, July 24, 1983; April 22, 1990.
Washington Post, June 7, 1979.

*   *   *

BRAINERD, John W(hiting) 1918-
(Jay Bee)

PERSONAL: Born February 14, 1918, in Dover, Mass.; son of Henry Boies (in business) and Eleanor (Shepard) Brainerd; married Barbara Hale (a librarian), June 25, 1941; children: Jill Brainerd Root, Roger W., Allen H. *Education:* Harvard University, A.B., 1940, M.A., 1941, Ph.D., 1949. *Religion:* Society of Friends.

ADDRESSES: Home—245 Varnum Rd., West Brooksville, ME 04617.

CAREER: Springfield College, Springfield, MA, professor of biology and conservation, 1949-1980; writer and illustrator. Volunteer art teacher in Maine elementary school; past chair of Springfield Conservation Commission. *Wartime service:* Civilian Public Service, 1942-46.

MEMBER: American Nature Study Society (past president), Association of Interpretive Naturalists (fellow), The Nature Conservancy (former state representative), National Audubon Society, Maine Audubon Society.

WRITINGS:

Nature Study for Conservation: A Handbook for Environmental Education (self-illustrated), Macmillan, 1971.
Working with Nature: A Practical Guide (self-illustrated), Oxford University Press, 1973.
The Nature Observer's Handbook: Learning to Appreciate Our Natural World (self-illustrated), Globe Pequot Press, 1986.

Also author of poems under pseudonym Jay Bee. Contributor of chapters to books, including *Short Essays: Models for Composition,* by Gerard Levin, Harcourt, 1977, and *Fifty Years of Resident Outdoor Education: Its Impact on American Education,* edited by William M. Hammerman, American Camping Association, 1980. Author of pamphlets and leaflets on natural areas, outdoor education, and environmental education. Contributor to education and conservation journals.

Creator of filmstrip series *Autumn Forests of the Northeast* and *Winter Forests of the Northeast,* Audio Instructional Devices; and *Shores: The Edge of Things,* Prentice-Hall Media, Inc.

ILLUSTRATOR

Herbert S. Zim and others, *Plants: A Guide to Plant Hobbies,* Harcourt, 1947.
Alexander C. Martin, Herbert S. Zim, and Arnold L. Nelson, *American Wildlife and Plants: A Guide to Wildlife Food Habits,* McGraw, 1951.

Also illustrator of *Travel*Vision Guides to Interstate 90,* by Robert Root and Jill Brainerd Root.

WORK IN PROGRESS: A book titled *Looking at the Landscape.*

SIDELIGHTS: John W. Brainerd was nurtured by artistic, nature-oriented parents in the countryside near Boston, Massachusetts. School teachers challenged him in languages, graphic arts, and natural history, and the Massachusetts Audubon Society urged him on in nature study. Harvard granted him three degrees in biology, supplemented by courses in geology, geography, and graphic art. In World War II he was drafted into civilian public service for timber management with the U.S. Forest Service and then for ecological research, illustrating, and cartography with the U.S. Fish and Wildlife Service.

For thirty-two years he taught biology and conservation at Springfield College in Massachusetts, developing courses in outdoor recreation, natural history, and environmental design for teachers and social workers. He has also been active in local, state, and national organizations in education and conservation of natural resources.

Now retired, he lives with his wife in West Brooksville, Maine, and is busy writing, illustrating, volunteer teaching, gardening, and traveling.

Brainerd told *SATA:* "Having been young once and having worked and played for many years with children, I know how

At least a bit of nature is close at hand wherever you are, even in the city. (From *The Nature Observer's Handbook,* written and illustrated by John W. Brainerd.)

important it is for children to learn joyfully about their environments and to share their joys with others by talking, writing, drawing, and—oh yes—singing and dancing."

*   *   *

BRENNAN, Tim
See CONROY, John Wesley

*   *   *

BRIGHTFIELD, Richard 1927-
(Rick Brightfield)

PERSONAL: Born September 28, 1927, in Baltimore, MD; son of Lloyd (a scientist) and Irene (a writer under name Irene Flesher; maiden name, Pool) Brightfield; married Glory Lesser (an artist and writer), April 22, 1972; children: Savitri (daughter). *Education:* Johns Hopkins University, B.A., 1949. *Politics:* Liberal Independent. *Religion:* Buddhist.

ADDRESSES: Home—366 Libertyville Rd., New Paltz, NY 12561.

CAREER: Columbia University, New York City, graphic designer of university publications, 1964-76; free-lance graphic designer and artist, 1976-82. Writer.

WRITINGS:

YOUNG ADULT ADVENTURE BOOKS

The Phantom Submarine, Bantam, 1983.

Secret of the Pyramids, Bantam, 1983.
The Dragon's Den, Bantam, 1984.
The Curse of Batterslea Hall, Bantam, 1984.
The Secret Treasure of Tibet, Bantam, 1984.
The Castle of Doom, Tor Books, 1984.
Island of Fear, Tor Books, 1984.
Terror under the Earth, Tor Books, 1984.
The Dragonmaster, Tor Books, 1984.
The Deadly Shadow, Bantam, 1985.
Revenge of the Dragonmaster, Tor Books, 1985.
Battle of the Dragons, Tor Books, 1986.
Trapped in the Sea Kingdom, Bantam, 1986.
Terror on Kabran, Bantam, 1986.
Star System Tenopia, Bantam, 1986.
The Forest of the King, Bantam, 1987.
The Caverns of Mornas, Bantam, 1987.
The Battle of Astar, Bantam, 1987.
Invaders of the Planet Earth, Bantam, 1987.
Hyperspace, Bantam, 1987.
Escape, Bantam, 1987.
Planet of the Dragons, Bantam, 1988.
Hurricane!, Bantam, 1988.
Master of Kung-Fu, Bantam, 1989.
Murder Comes to Life, Troll, 1989.
The Gruesome Guests, Troll, 1989.
China: Why Was an Army Made of Clay?, McGraw-Hill, 1989.
U.S.A.: What Is the Great American Invention?, McGraw-Hill, 1989.
Master of Tae Kwon Do, Bantam, 1990.
Hijacked, Bantam, 1990.
Master of Karate, Bantam, 1990.

UNDER NAME RICK BRIGHTFIELD

(With wife, Glory Brightfield) *Amazing Mazes,* Harper, 1973.
(With G. Brightfield) *Outer Space Mazes,* Harper, 1973.
Brightfield Mazes I, Barnes & Noble, 1974.
(With G. Brightfield) *More Amazing Mazes,* Harper, 1975.
Brightfield Mazes II, Barnes & Noble, 1975.
(With G. Brightfield and Mary Orser) *Instant Astrology,* Harper, 1976.
(With G. Brightfield) *Amazing Circle Mazes,* Harper, 1976.
(With G. Brightfield and Orser) *Predicting with Astrology,* Harper, 1977.
(With G. Brightfield and Orser) *What's My Sign?,* Harper, 1978.

Also author of *'Round the World Maze Trip Book* and *The Sea Kingdom;* co-author of *Astrorhythms* and *Star Games.*

SIDELIGHTS: Richard Brightfield has written over twenty-five "Choose Your Own Adventure" books for young adults. The reader becomes a character in these books, and can decide what action to take next in the story. As the reader picks a course of action, the book directs him to pick up the story on different pages. In *The Curse of Batterslea Hall,* for instance, the reader must figure out how to battle an evil woman living in an English castle. Depending on the reader's choice, the characters end up in situations that range from harmless to dangerous, with an ending that's either happy or sad. Because Brightfield's books have so many possibilities, young people can read them several times over and get a different story each time.

*　　*　　*

BRIGHTFIELD, Rick
See BRIGHTFIELD, Richard

*　　*　　*

BRIGHTON, Catherine 1943-

PERSONAL: Born May 20, 1943, in London, England; daughter of Stuart (an artist) and Vera (a writer; maiden name, White) Boyle; married Andrew Brighton (an art critic), July 16, 1966; children: Shane, Henry. *Education:* St. Martin's School of Art, Diploma in Art and Design, 1966; Royal College of Art, M.A., 1969.

ADDRESSES: Home—24 London Pl., St. Clements, Oxford, England. *Agent*—A. P. Watt Ltd., 20 John St., London WC1N 2DL, England.

CAREER: Writer.

AWARDS, HONORS: The Picture was exhibited at the Bologna International Children's Book Fair, 1985; *My Hands, My World* was chosen a Children's Book of the Year by the Child Study Association of America, 1986; Premio-Grafico Prize, 1987, for *The Fantastic Book of Board Games.*

WRITINGS:

FOR CHILDREN; SELF-ILLUSTRATED

Emily's Guzzleguts, Evans, 1979.
Cathy's Story, Evans, 1980.

My Hands, My World, Macmillan, 1984 (published in England as *Maria,* Faber, 1984).
The Picture, Faber, 1985.
(Editor) *The Voice,* Delacorte, 1986.
Five Secrets in a Box, Dutton, 1987.
Hope's Gift, Doubleday, 1988.
Nijinsky: Scenes from the Childhood of the Great Dancer, Doubleday, 1989.

OTHER

(Illustrator) Sian Victory, *Two Little Nurses,* Faber, 1983.
(Illustrator with Fulvio Testa, Ralph Steadman, Tony Ross and Quentin Blake) *The Fantastic Book of Board Games,* St. Martin's, 1988.

Also author of *Dearest Grandmama.* Contributor to *Modern Painters.*

WORK IN PROGRESS: Research for a picture book about Mozart's childhood.

FOR MORE INFORMATION SEE:

PERIODICALS

New York Times Book Review, February 20, 1990.
Times Literary Supplement, September 19, 1980.

*　　*　　*

BRIN, David 1950-

PERSONAL: Born October 6, 1950, in Glendale, CA; son of Herbert (an editor) and Selma (a teacher) Brin; married Cheryl Ann Brigham (a doctor of cosmochemistry), March, 1991. *Education:* California Institute of Technology, B.S., 1972; University of California, San Diego, M.S., 1979, Ph.D., 1981. *Hobbies and other interests:* Backpacking, music, science, and "general eclecticism."

ADDRESSES: Office—Heritage Press, 2130 South Vermont Ave., Los Angeles, CA 90007.

CAREER: Hughes Aircraft Research Laboratories, Newport Beach and Carlsbad, CA, electrical engineer in semiconductor device development, 1973-77; managing editor, *Journal of the Laboratory of Comparative Human Cognition,* 1979-80; Heritage Press, Los Angeles, CA, book reviewer and science editor, 1980—. Teacher of physics and writing, San Diego State University, 1982-85; post-doctoral research fellow, California Space Institute, 1983-86; visiting artist, Westfield College, University of London, 1986-87.

MEMBER: Science Fiction Writers of America (secretary, 1982-84), Planetary Society, British Interplanetary Society.

AWARDS, HONORS: John W. Campbell Award nomination for best new author of 1982; Locus Award, Locus Publications, Nebula Award, Science Fiction Writers of America, and Hugo Award, World Science Fiction Convention, all 1984, all for *Startide Rising;* Balrog Award, 1984, for *The Practice Effect;* Hugo Award, 1985, for short story "The Crystal Spheres"; Hugo Award nomination, Nebula Award nomination, Locus Award, John W. Campbell Memorial Award, and American Library Association Best Books for Young Adults citation, all 1986, all for *The Postman;* Hugo

DAVID BRIN

Award, Nebula award nomination, and Locus Award, all 1988, all for *The Uplift War.*

WRITINGS:

Sundiver, Bantam, 1980.
Startide Rising, Bantam, 1983, hardcover edition, Phantasia Press, 1985.
The Practice Effect, Bantam, 1984.
The Postman, Bantam, 1985.
(With Gregory Benford) *Heart of the Comet,* Bantam, 1986.
The River of Time (short stories), Dark Harvest, 1986.
The Uplift War, Phantasia Press, 1987.
Dr. Pak's Pre-School (novella), Cheap Street Press, 1988.
Earth, Bantam, 1990.

Contributor to *Far Frontiers,* 1985. Contributor of articles and stories to scientific journals, including *Astrophysical Journal,* and popular magazines, including *Analog* and *Isaac Asimov's Science Fiction Magazine.*

ADAPTATIONS: Warner Brothers has purchased the rights to make a film based on *The Postman;* the novella "The Loom of Thessaly" has been recorded on audio cassette by Off-Centaur Press.

WORK IN PROGRESS: More novels; a nonfiction academic book covering extraterrestrial intelligent life; continuing research on the nature and origins of the solar system.

SIDELIGHTS: David Brin told *SATA* that one of his heroes is "Mark Twain, because he was able to write innovative literature—breaking ground in style, characterization and social commentary—while nevertheless providing a bright thirteen-year-old with a terrific read. The two are not incom-

patible. One can both uplift and entertain. It may be arrogance, but I aspire to do as well."

Brin's novel *The Postman* is a step toward this goal, for while it deals with ideas like global ruin and survival, it has also been recognized by the American Library Association as a "Best Book for Young Adults." Other novels of nuclear disaster examine the total destruction of Earth, but *The Postman* describes "the real horror of such a war": the prospect of surviving in a holocaust-ravaged world, as Brin told Jean Ross in *Contemporary Authors New Revision Series* interview.

The main character of *The Postman* is Gordon Krantz, a loner who has lived through the destruction, but is attacked by bandits and stripped of his survival gear. Close to freezing, Gordon finds a mail carrier's body and borrows the dead postman's uniform. Gordon is accepted by people in the few small, suspicious settlements because of the uniform, and he begins to lie about his identity to gain their trust. He claims to be an agent of the government sent to set up mail service, and

Cover of the 1983 original paperback edition of David Brin's award-winning young adult novel that blends science fiction and social commentary. (Jacket art by Jim Burns.)

to support the lie he begins taking letters with him as he travels from town to town.

Gordon's story is suspicious, but the villagers accept him and see him "as a symbol of civilization," relates the *Washington Post Book World*'s Gregory Frost. But Gordon is forced to accept more responsibility along with his lies, until he is drawn into fighting against the organized war bands that trouble the villagers. The story develops "Brin's premise that people need something bigger than survival to believe in," notes *New York Times Book Review* writer Gerald Jonas. Even Gordon, a loner who thought he could live apart from others, discovers an urge to belong to something greater than himself, and begins a genuine service to the community.

Brin extends this concept to communities on a larger scale in *Earth,* his 1990 novel about ecological danger. As he related to *SATA,* the novel "extrapolates a tomorrow filled with both hope and tension weaving several major plot threads (computer networks and a black hole dropped into the Earth's core) through short vignettes showing details of life in the year 2038." Brin shows "a sense of community spreading partly via humanity's technology, and partly through a palpable and growing set of connections among all the planet's species." He also weaves the results of his research in geology, biology, and ecology with a rapid-paced plot.

Brin has also written *The Practice Effect,* which he described to Ross as "a light adventure-fantasy and romance which is accessible to bright children." Reviewers find *The Practice Effect* an enjoyable alternate-world tale in the tradition of Mark Twain's *A Connecticut Yankee in King Arthur's Court.* Like Twain's "Yankee," Brin's Dennis Nuel enters a strange world, rescues a princess, defeats a powerful enemy and contributes to progress by using skills that would be considered quite ordinary at home. This formula has been used often, but Brin gives it a new twist: Dennis finds himself in a world where repeated use improves objects instead of wearing them out. Through "practice" Dennis turns simple objects into complex tools: a zipper becomes a saw, while a combination of a hang glider and a cart becomes a plane. The result is a series of adventures "which can only be called rollicking," writes Baird Searles in *Isaac Asimov's Science Fiction Magazine.*

Brin's multi-award-winning novel *Startide Rising* contains exciting adventure as well, but it also deals with serious issues, such as genetic alteration and scientific responsibility. The novel is set in Brin's "Progenitors" universe, where the many races of the galaxy have "uplifted" intelligent creatures to self-awareness through genetic engineering. Humans themselves have uplifted dolphins and chimpanzees and work with them as comrades. In *Startide Rising* Earth's first dolphin-staffed starship, the *Streaker,* discovers an ancient spacecraft and is attacked by aliens who want the craft's secrets. The *Streaker* is forced to crash-land on a water planet, Kithrup, and the crew must overcome their own conflicts to repair the ship and escape detection by their galactic enemies.

The race to escape the galactics and return the *Streaker*'s valuable cargo to Earth creates a thrilling story. But *Startide Rising* contains something more than just excitement, according to Stephen B. Brown in the *Washington Post Book World.* In Brown's opinion, "the care and empathy with which Brin describes the relationships between his aquatic characters elevates this book into a substantial achievement." The book also features several young characters who mature during the struggle, including one of the crew's few

humans, a midshipman named Toshio. Brown praises Brin for consistently developing "the idea that a viable human-dolphin collaboration can be something greater than each race on its own."

The development of ideas is an essential part of Brin's work. His "Progenitors" universe, Brin told Ross in *Contemporary Authors New Revision Series,* "combines several ideas that I wanted to explore," as well as several "ethical questions." Science fiction has allowed him to investigate various questions, Brin added, for "one role of SF is to explore the limits of an idea. Fortunately, most people seem to find that this doesn't stand in the way of reading an entertaining story."

WORKS CITED:

Brown, Stephen B., review of *Startide Rising, Washington Post Book World,* April 22, 1984, p. 11.
Contemporary Authors New Revision Series, Volume 24, Gale, 1988, pp. 84-88.
Frost, Gregory, "Dreams and Nightmares of the Future," *Washington Post Book World,* December 22, 1985, p. 8.
Jonas, Gerald, "Science Fiction," *New York Times Book Review,* November 24, 1985, pp. 33-34.
Searles, Baird, "On Books," *Isaac Asimov's Science Fiction Magazine,* July, 1984, pp. 171-73.

FOR MORE INFORMATION SEE:

BOOKS

Contemporary Literary Criticism, Volume 34, Gale, 1985.

PERIODICALS

Amazing, January, 1984.
Analog: Science Fiction/Science Fact, November, 1983; July, 1984; March, 1986; November, 1987.
Chicago Tribune Book World, March 23, 1986.
Los Angeles Times, December 16, 1985; April 1, 1986.
Los Angeles Times Book Review, December 15, 1985; January 12, 1986.
Science Fiction Chronicle, December, 1985; March, 1987; June, 1987.
Science Fiction Review, August, 1984.
Voice Literary Supplement, December, 1983.

*   *   *

BROCK, Delia
See EPHRON, Delia

*   *   *

BROWNLOW, Kevin 1938-

PERSONAL: Born June 2, 1938, in Crowborough, Sussex, England; son of Robert Thomas and Nina (Fortnum) Brownlow; married Virginia Keane, August 1, 1969; children: Julia.

ADDRESSES: Office—Photoplay Productions, 21 Princess Rd., London NW1 8JR, England. *Agent*—Gloria Loomis, Watkins/Loomis Agency Inc., 150 East 35th St., New York, NY 10016.

CAREER: Film editor for World Wide Pictures, London, England, 1955-61, Samaritan Films, London, 1961-65, and

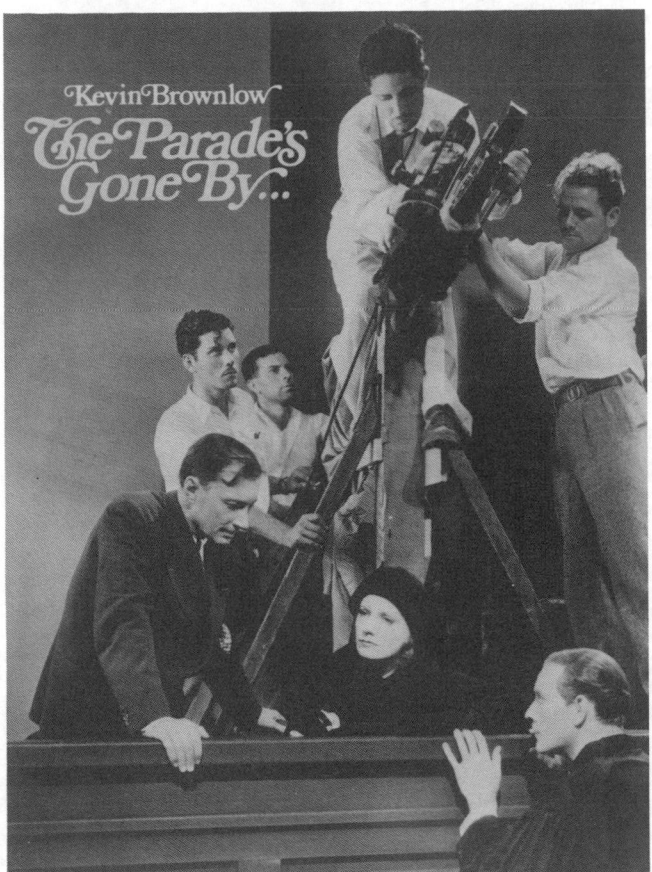

A 1929 photograph of Jacques Feyder directing Greta Garbo in *The Kiss* serves as the cover for Kevin Brownlow's paperback edition of *The Parade's Gone By*.

Woodfall Films, London, 1965-68; film director and producer; writer. Director of *Charm of Dynamite* (biographical television film of French movie innovator Abel Gance), 1967, with Andrew Mollo, of *Winstanley*, 1975, with David Gill, of *Unknown Chaplin* (three-part television series), 1983, of *Buster Keaton*, 1987, and of other documentaries.

MEMBER: British Film Institute (former member of board of governors).

AWARDS, HONORS: Award for best original screenplay, Writers Guild, 1966, for *It Happened Here;* special award, British Film Institute, c. 1975, for *Winstanley;* Emmy awards, National Academy of Television Arts and Sciences, c. 1983, for *Unknown Chaplin,* and c. 1987, for *Buster Keaton;* George Foster Peabody Broadcasting Award, University of Georgia's Henry W. Grady School of Journalism and Mass Communication, c. 1987, for *Hollywood* and other work.

WRITINGS:

(With Andrew Mollo; and director and producer, with Mollo) *It Happened Here* (screenplay), Lopert Pictures Corp., 1966.
How It Happened Here, Doubleday, 1968.
The Parade's Gone By (chronicle and analysis of silent films), Knopf, 1968.
(Editor) Karl Brown, *Adventures with D. W. Griffith,* Secker & Warburg, 1974.

The War, the West, and the Wilderness (film history and criticism), Knopf, 1979.
(And director, with David Gill) *Hollywood* (thirteen-part television series; also see below), Thames Television, 1980.
Hollywood: The Pioneers (based on *Hollywood* television series), pictures selected by John Kobal, Collins, 1980.
Napoleon: Abel Gance's Classic Film, Knopf, 1983.
(Author of introduction) Madge Bellamy, *A Darling of the Twenties,* Vestal, 1989.
Behind the Mask of Innocence: Sex, Violence, Prejudice, Crime—Films of Social Conscience, Random House, 1990.

Also author of *Harold Lloyd: The Third Genius,* 1989, and of screenplays. Contributor of articles on film history to film magazines. Supervising editor of *No Surrender,* 1986.

WORK IN PROGRESS: Three-part documentary on the career of American pioneer film director D. W. Griffith.

SIDELIGHTS: Kevin Brownlow told *SATA:* "I don't enjoy writing. I like searching for facts, but the only thing that makes me write books is guilt that the information may otherwise serve no useful purpose. I am supposed to be a film director, but I spend much more time behind a typewriter than behind a camera. Why is it that in order to make films you have to be able to write? Some of the greatest films ever made—such as those of Charlie Chaplin, Buster Keaton, and Harold Lloyd— were made without scripts. I should like filmmaking to be akin to the writing of novels—it doesn't matter how long you take or what method you use, so long as you get it right in the end. I should like to make films direct on to celluloid, as a novelist scribbles thousands of pages for the two hundred or so that eventually get printed. But film is a brutally industrial process; the miracle is that so much that is so good still gets made. One director said that making films these days is like running in front of a locomotive.

"Film history was always a relaxation for me in between making pictures. Now it's taken over my life completely, and while I still make films, they aren't features but documentaries. I miss that mad feature world of ecstasy and despair, but I now realize that the experience worked in a curious way: making films turned me into a better historian. I thought it would work the other way around—that knowing the history of films would force me to make better pictures. But having been a filmmaker, I can often guess the problems they had in making a silent film and can thus work out what happened and why.

"I now realize, with horror, that I have been studying the silent film era for as long as the silent era existed. Maybe I should do something else for a while. But my enthusiasm has never slackened. Relating the films to the history of their time, as I have done in *Behind the Mask of Innocence: Sex, Violence, Prejudice, Crime—Films of Social Conscience,* has given me a far wider interest. The only sad thing is that so many veterans of the silent era have died. Soon the period will be as remote as the American Civil War, and historians will have to work exclusively from documents. I am glad I was able to meet so many of the people who made the pictures; they were almost all extraordinary and impressive, as pioneers often are. One day, I hope to put all the memories I recorded into a book. But, as I think I told you, I hate writing."

FOR MORE INFORMATION SEE:

PERIODICALS

Film Comment, July-August, 1979.
Listener, May 8, 1980.
Los Angeles Times Book Review, March 9, 1980; November 20, 1983.
New Statesman, June 8, 1979.
Newsweek, February 26, 1979.
New York Times, December 11, 1968; July 5, 1979.
New York Times Book Review, March 25, 1979; November 13, 1983.
Time, April 2, 1979; May 5, 1980.
Times (London), June 9, 1983.
Times Literary Supplement, January 18, 1980; September 9, 1983.
Village Voice, July 9, 1979.
Washington Post Book World, April 13, 1980.

*　　*　　*

BURNHAM, Sophy 1936-

PERSONAL: Born December 12, 1936, in Baltimore, MD; daughter of George Cochran (an attorney) and Sophy Tayloe (Snyder) Doub; married David Bright Burnham (a journalist), March 12, 1960; children: Sarah Tayloe, Molly Bright. *Education:* University of Florence, certificate, 1957; Smith College, B.A. (cum laude), 1958. *Religion:* Episcopalian.

ADDRESSES: Home and office—1405 31st St. N.W., Washington, DC 20007.

CAREER: Smithsonian Institution, Washington, DC, assistant curator for Museum Service, 1962-64; free-lance writer, 1965—; David McKay Co., Inc., New York City, acquisitions editor, 1971-73; Department of Housing and Urban Development, Washington, DC, speechwriter for Secretary, 1977-79; affiliated with University of Alaska, Juneau, 1980; George Mason University, Fairfax, VA, adjunct lecturer, 1982-83; staff writer for *New Woman,* 1984—; staff writer and columnist for *Museum and Arts/Washington,* 1987-90. Studio Theatre, founding member, 1978—, chair of board, 1979-80; secretary, Women's International Theatre Alliance, 1979-81; D.C. Community Humanities Council, founding member, 1979-85, vice-chair, 1979-80; American Institute of Architects Foundation, member of Octagon committee, 1984-89, member of presidential search committee, 1984; affiliated with Heartworks, *New Art Examiner,* 1986 and 1987. Consultant to various organizations, including Mitre Corp., Veterans Administration, Public Citizen, Environmental Protection Agency, and Institute for Law and Social Research.

AWARDS, HONORS: Best magazine feature award, National Steeplechase and Hunt Association, 1970; named Daughter of Mark Twain, Mark Twain Society, 1974; grants from Advanced Drama Research of University of Minnesota, 1976, D.C. Arts and Humanities Council, 1980-81, Helen Wurlitzer Foundation of Taos, NM, 1981, 1983, and 1991; Episcopal Drama Award (third prize), National Episcopal Churches, 1979, and Women's Theatre Award (first prize), Seattle, WA, 1981, both for *Penelope; Witch's Tale* was named best children's radio play by the National Association of Community Broadcasters, 1980; award of excellence, *Realites,* 1980, for magazine article "Machu Picchu."

WRITINGS:

The Smithsonian's Whale (screenplay), Smithsonian Institution, 1963.
The Last Thieves (screenplay), Smithsonian Institution, 1964.
The Exhibits Speak, Smithsonian Institution, 1964.
The Art Crowd (Book-of-the-Month Club alternate selection; Saturday Review Book Club selection), McKay, 1973.
(Editor) *The Threat to Licensed Nuclear Facilities,* Mitre Corp., 1975.
Penelope (three-act play), staged reading at George Washington University, 1976, produced in Seattle, WA, 1981.
Buccaneer (young adult novel), Warne, 1977.
The Landed Gentry, Putnam, 1978.
The Dogwalker (young adult novel), Warne, 1979.
The Study (two-act play), staged reading at American Palace Theatre, 1980.
A Warrior (one-act play), staged reading in Alexandria, VA, 1988.
A Book of Angels: Reflections on Angels Past and Present and True Stories of How They Touch Our Lives, Ballantine, 1990.
Angel Letters: What They Gave to Us, Ballantine Books, 1991.
Revelations! (novel), Ballantine, in press.
For Writers Only, Ballantine, in press.

Author of television script *The Music of Shakespeare's England,* Smithsonian Institution, 1962. Author of children's radio plays, including *The Witch's Tale,* 1978, *Beauty and the Beast,* 1979, and *The Nightingale,* 1980.

Work represented in anthologies, including *Crime in the Cities,* edited by Dan Glaser, Harper, 1970; and *Cities in Trouble,* edited by Nathan Glazer, Quadrangle, 1970. Contributor of several essays and articles to periodicals, including *Esquire, New York Times Magazine, New York, Reader's Digest, Vogue, McCall's,* and *Saturday Review.* Contributing editor to *Town and Country,* 1975-80, *New Woman,* 1984—, *New Art Examiner,* 1985-86, and *Museum and Arts/Washington,* 1987-90.

Essays and articles reprinted in Great Britain, Japan, Australia, South Africa, and South America.

WORK IN PROGRESS: The President's Angel, a novel; *Love Stories: Men I Have Known,* short stories; film adaptation of *The Dogwalker.*

SIDELIGHTS: Sophy Burnham told *SATA:* "I think I didn't decide to be a writer: somehow, it decided me. I first learned I was a writer when I was ten and failed my fifth-grade English exam. The reason I failed this exam was that the first question was, 'Finish this paragraph,' and two bluebooks and forty-five minutes later I was still writing when, to my surprise, the bell rang and the exam was over. I hadn't finished and never got to the second question.

"I was startled at what happened. It was the first time that the writer's trance had fallen over me, and I went away disturbed by it and a little afraid of my teachers and parents nodding their heads and smiling knowingly at one another, 'Oh yes, *she's* going to be a writer.' I didn't know anything about being a writer or what you did, and anyway I was busy living life and had no intention of stopping to 'be a writer.'

"In college during my sophomore year I took a creative writing class (as it was called in those days) and wrote short stories, from which I learned that I was terrified of writing and, moreover, had nothing to say. The reason I was scared was because I was reading works by Leo Tolstoy, William Shakespeare, and other giants of literature, and it was easy to see that anything I had to say could not compare. It was years before I would dare to write.

"After college I found a job as a clerk-typist at the Smithsonian Institution in Washington, D.C., which was what you did in those days if you were a woman and had graduated with honors from a major university. But three years later I was making films and doing television work for the Smithsonian. My first film was sent by the United States Information Agency to the Venice Film Festival, and I had just decided that I wasn't going to be a writer after all but a film director, when my husband moved myself and our little baby up to New York City.

"I then discovered that young girls didn't write, produce, and direct films (at least in those days), and since I was not willing to give up control of the final product by being only a writer (but not director) or only a researcher (but not producer), I decided to teach myself to write. I thought the best way to do that was to get someone else to pay me to write. So I began free-lancing for magazines. Since then I have written I don't know how many articles for major national magazines, and from one article came the idea for my first book, *The Art Crowd.*

"But it is fiction that I like best. I had always thought of myself as a novelist. In 1973 we moved back to Washington, D.C., and fiction began to come over me. Suddenly I saw things as stories. In a fit of creativity, I began to write plays and novels, some for adults, some for children.

"For example, one day my little girl, Sarah, then ten, came up to me, saying, 'Mom, I want to write a horse story, will you help me?' 'Sure,' I said, and about thirty minutes later I was so engrossed I was waving her away: 'Leave me alone, I'm writing a book.' That became *Buccaneer.* When the book was published I opened it to the dedication page and read, 'To Sarah'—and suddenly realized I'd forgotten my *other* daughter, Molly. She'd been too young to be interested earlier, but I saw the confusion on her face. 'Don't worry,' I said. 'I'll write you a story of your own!' And that became *The Dogwalker.*

"For me, ideas seem to appear, asking to be written. An idea might begin with a sentence that pops into my mind, and if I follow the sentence, I will hear the next and the next, as if I'm moving along a rope, hand over hand, to the end. In some books I have no idea what's going to happen from one sentence to the next. That was so with *Buccaneer,* and very exciting to write! With other books (like *The Dogwalker*), I have a general idea of three or four scenes or actions, I know the beginning and the end, but nothing in between. And then I begin to write and the book unravels itself (with a lot of revisions and rewriting, of course, which is what writing is all about: it's hard, hard work). Sometimes I see the work in my mind's eye all at once, the way you see a painting, and then I put it down in the linear medium that is writing. But if this happens, then I can write any of it in any order, and it will all fit, because I have seen the whole and know who is talking and where and why. This happened with the play *Penelope.* You just watch the characters and write down what they say.

"After finishing *The Dogwalker* my children were both grown, and I had no one else to write a children's story for.

When I have grandchildren, perhaps, I will write more, and meanwhile I am writing other novels and nonfiction books and plays, stories, essays, and articles. The only thing I don't do any more is investigative journalism. But that is a wonderful way for a writer to begin, since it first teaches the craft of writing and secondly gives you a lot of experience, eating life alive—that is what the writer must do first, in order to be able to spin it out again in a new form (on paper, on film, on the stage) and make it for the second time come alive. All the time the writer must think of the reader, who is crying, 'Show me ME! I want to read about MYSELF!' For that the writer must live very alertly. For that reason I take no drugs and alcohol.

"But much of writing—and the business of publishing what you write—is luck. For that, I am truly humble: I have been so lucky.

"It's hard to know what's more fun about a writer's life. I adore writing. I feel happy writing. The bad times are when I have nothing to work on. (This happens less frequently now, because I keep two or three projects going simultaneously.) But the other nice thing is having your work received. To have an essay printed in Australia, or to be visiting in Alaska and have some stranger recognize your name—'Are YOU Sophy Burnham? I heard your play on the radio!'—then you sigh with utter satisfaction, glad that writing decided to be your work."

FOR MORE INFORMATION SEE:

PERIODICALS

Milwaukee Journal, May 20, 1973.
Newsday, March 22, 1973; July 9, 1978.
Newsweek, April 9, 1973.
New York Times, March 27, 1973.
New York Times Book Review, March 25, 1973; July 2, 1978.
Progressive, September, 1978.
Washington Post Book World, March 25, 1973.

*   *   *

BURNS, Olive Ann 1924-1990 (Amy Larkin)

PERSONAL: Born July 17, 1924, in Banks County, GA; died of heart failure while suffering from lymphoma, July 4, 1990; daughter of William Arnold (a farmers' cooperative executive) and Ruby (a homemaker; maiden name, Hight) Burns; married Andrew H. Sparks (an editor), August 11, 1956; children: Rebecca Marie, John Andrew. *Education:* Attended Mercer University, 1942-44; University of North Carolina at Chapel Hill, A.B., 1946. *Politics:* Democrat. *Religion:* Methodist. *Hobbies and other interests:* Reading, walking, camping, swimming, art, classical music, conversation, dancing to rock music, museums of all kinds, travel, public speaking ("not necessarily in this order").

ADDRESSES: Home—161 Bolling Rd. N.E., Atlanta, GA 30305. *Agent*—Mitch Douglas, International Creative Management, 40 West 57th St., New York, NY 10019.

CAREER: Staff writer for the *Coca-Cola Bottler* and the *Laundryman's Guide,* in Atlanta, GA, 1946-47; *Atlanta Journal and Constitution,* Atlanta, staff writer for the Sunday magazine, 1947-57; author of local newspaper advice column

"Ask Amy," under pseudonym Amy Larkin, 1960-67; writer and free-lance journalist.

MEMBER: Authors Guild, Atlanta Historical Society, University of North Carolina Alumni Association.

AWARDS, HONORS: Cold Sassy Tree was included in the annual lists of recommended selections for young adults by the New York Public Library, American Library Association, *School Library Journal,* and *Booklist,* all 1985.

WRITINGS:

Cold Sassy Tree (young adult novel; Book-of-the-Month Club alternate selection), Ticknor & Fields, 1984.

Contributor of articles to *Atlanta Weekly.*

Cold Sassy Tree has been published in Germany.

ADAPTATIONS: Cold Sassy Tree was adapted for audio cassette by Books on Tape and, in an abridged version, by Bantam Audio; Faye Dunaway starred in the television movie adaptation of the novel, which aired in 1989 on Turner Network Television.

SIDELIGHTS: Olive Ann Burns was a journalist who gained national attention in 1984 with her bestselling novel, *Cold Sassy Tree.* The book was praised by critics, and it appeared on several year-end lists of recommended books for young adults, including the 1985 American Library Association list. *Cold Sassy Tree* takes place in the early 1900s and is about an old man, Grandpa Blakeslee, who marries a young woman named Miss Love Simpson. The marriage, which takes place only a few weeks after Blakeslee's first wife dies, is

OLIVE ANN BURNS

nothing less than a scandal to the townspeople of Cold Sassy, Georgia. The story is told by Blakeslee's fourteen-year-old grandson, Will Tweedy, who defends the newlyweds. At first Tweedy believes his grandfather's description of the marriage as a practical exchange of housekeeping for a house (Miss Love Simpson will get the house after Blakeslee dies). As the story unfolds, however, Tweedy sees there is more to the relationship than a mere practical arrangement: the couple is actually in love. *Cold Sassy Tree* "is a novel about an old man growing young, a young man growing up, and the modern age coming to a small southern town," wrote Jeanne McManus in the *Washington Post Book World.*

Burns's novel contains much material that is from her own family history. Born in 1924 in Banks County, Georgia, Burns grew up in nearby Commerce, Georgia, which is the town she had in mind when she created the fictional town of Cold Sassy. She once commented, "From my father, who like Will Tweedy was fourteen in 1906, I got a vivid picture of Commerce at the turn of the century, and one of his favorite stories was about his Grandpa Power, a store owner, who married three weeks after his wife died and who (according to my father) said he loved Miss Annie but she was dead as she'd ever be and he had to git him another wife or hire a housekeeper one, and it would jest be cheaper to git married. I doubt Grandpa Power was anything like Grandpa Blakeslee and I know Miss Annie's successor was nothing like Miss Love, but I always thought the situation would make a good novel and that turn-of-the-century Commerce could be the model for a fictitious town."

Burns wrote *Cold Sassy Tree* after spending most of her career as a journalist in Atlanta, Georgia, writing news stories and an advice column under the name Amy Larkin. "Being a journalist," Burns said in 1984, "I never expected to get around to fiction. Then, nine years ago, an abnormal blood picture showed up in a routine physical, and the doctor said I would probably develop lymphoma or leukemia in a few months or a few years. As soon as he said the words, I decided I could handle the suspense if I had something new to do that was more exciting than whether I would not have cancer, and before I left the doctor's office it came to me to write a novel—which surprised me even more than his diagnosis had."

Burns carefully constructed *Cold Sassy Tree* over an eight-and-a-half-year period, an effort that was rewarded with good reviews and high sales. "I wasn't exactly trying to write a 'wholesome' book," she insisted. "Life is seldom wholesome. But I did try for 'refreshing.' I wanted to write a story, not a sociological treatise disguised as a novel. I wanted to express the lyric wonder and electric yearning between two people in love. I wanted to prove that a book about essentially decent people could be a page-turner without explicit sex and constant violence." *Cold Sassy Tree* was so successful that in 1989 it was adapted into a cable film starring Faye Dunaway.

After struggling with lymphoma for fifteen years, Burns died on July 4, 1990.

WORKS CITED:

Burns, Olive Ann, press release for *Cold Sassy Tree,* Ticknor & Fields, October 31, 1984.

McManus, Jeanne, "Southern Comfort," *Washington Post Book World,* November 25, 1984, pp. 3 and 11.

Dustjacket for 1984 edition of *Cold Sassy Tree.*
(Jacket design by Wendell Minor.)

FOR MORE INFORMATION SEE:

PERIODICALS

Atlanta Weekly, October 14, 1984.
New York Times Book Review, November 11, 1984.
Publishers Weekly, November 9, 1984.
Washington Post Book World, August 17, 1986.

OBITUARIES AND OTHER SOURCES:

PERIODICALS

Chicago Tribune, July 6, 1990.
Los Angeles Times, July 6, 1990.
New York Times, July 6, 1990.
Washington Post, July 8, 1990.

*   *   *

BURR, Dan 1951-

PERSONAL: Born November 14, 1951, in Red Oak, IA; son of Merrill and Dorothy (maiden name, Bills) Burr; married Debra Freiberg, June 11, 1988. *Education:* Attended University of Wisconsin—Milwaukee, 1975-80.

ADDRESSES: Home and office—2440 North Weil St., Milwaukee, WI 53212.

CAREER: Holoubek Studios, Butler, WI, screen printer, 1975-76, art production manager, 1976-77; *Skylarking in Milwaukee* (magazine), Milwaukee, WI, staff artist, 1980; Country Graphics, Greendale, WI, production artist, 1981-82; free-lance illustrator, 1982—.

AWARDS, HONORS: Will Eisner Awards for best new series for *Kings in Disguise* and for best single issue for *Kings in Disguise,* Number 1, both 1989; Harvey Award for best new series for *Kings in Disguise,* 1989.

ILLUSTRATOR:

James Vance, *Kings in Disguise* (comic magazine; also see below), Numbers 1-6, Kitchen Sink Press, 1988-89.
Isaac Asimov, *Projects in Astronomy,* Gareth Stevens, Inc., 1990.
James Vance, *Kings in Disguise* (graphic novel), Kitchen Sink Press, 1990.

WORK IN PROGRESS: Illustrating a *Classics Illustrated* comic book version Jules Verne's *Journey to the Center of the Earth,* published by Berkley/First.

SIDELIGHTS: Dan Burr told *SATA:* "Although I'm sure this is an old adage, I've been drawing as long as I can remember. My mother has claimed I was drawing recognizable objects as early as the age of eighteen months. My memory doesn't carry me back quite that far, but I do recall many afternoons in pre-school spent with coloring books or laying in front of the television trying to copy the images I saw on programs like *Crusader Rabbit* or *Robin Hood.* I was fascinated early on by the drawings and paintings I saw printed in books and believed, even then, I could draw as well as the artists in the books. Of course I couldn't, but I think that belief in an ability kept me motivated and helped me to improve.

"I remember being fascinated by different artists' varying styles and wondering why all art work didn't look the same. It didn't take me long to realize that certain styles appealed to me more than others, though I couldn't have explained why. Consequently, I spent many hours attempting to emulate the styles of artists I'd grown to admire. Most of these artists were American comic art masters. Hal Foster, Al Capp, V.T. Hamlin, Wallace Wood, and Jack Davis were among my favorites.

"By high school, my family had relocated to a suburb of Milwaukee. Following high school, my art briefly took a back seat to the rigors of independent living. After moving to Milwaukee, I went through a succession of non-art-related jobs while beginning to freelance as a cartoonist on the side. During a layoff I decided to enter the University of Wisconsin as a drawing and painting major. After a few years in college and a couple of art positions, I began to move into some of the areas of illustration I felt drawn to. This included the comic book field.

"In the fall of 1986 I was asked to try out for a proposed comic book series called *Kings in Disguise* about a twelve year old boy on a cross-country search for his father during the Depression in 1932. I read the script and was immediately impressed with the emotional depth the writing had. I began to feel a kinship to the boy, Freddie, at once. His fear, anger, and sense of duty to his friend were very accurately portrayed.

"Comic books have often been compared with movies—understandably, as they're both mediums which integrate words and pictures to tell a story. In fact, the comic format is very similar to storyboards for movies. When I'm reading a script, I seem to quite naturally 'become' the characters in the story . . . to feel what they feel, see what they

(From *Kings in Disguise* by Dan Burr. Illustration by Dan Burr and James Vance.)

see, and so on, as an actor might. My imagination will create images as I read. I then sketch these mental pictures out in loose form. After redrawing my rough sketches onto lettered art boards, I ink over the pencils with brush and pen.

"With *Kings in Disguise,* attention to historical accuracy was very important, so I would usually seek out the necessary reference photos or art. The library would supply me with whatever my personal files might not contain. I found it also helpful to watch old movies from the period. As someone who came into being in the 1950s, I can only make my best attempt to depict an era that predates my birth by twenty years. Recapturing history I have no direct contact with is a real challenge. One thing that helps is believing that there are common threads that run through the history of human experience. Things like poverty, loneliness, pride, anger, homelessness, and helplessness are universal and timeless.

"I think *Kings in Disguise* is the perfect example of a 'graphic novel.' It has all the depth, involvement, and continuity of a novel, and it is instructive and entertaining. I look forward to creating more work in this field and doing what I can to help prove that comic art books can be seen as an adult, mature, medium."

FOR MORE INFORMATION SEE:

PERIODICALS

Comics Journal, November, 1989.

*   *   *

BUSCAGLIA, (Felice) Leo(nardo) 1924-
(Leo F. Buscaglia)

PERSONAL: Professionally known as Leo F. Buscaglia; surname is pronounced "boo-*skal*-ya"; born March 31, 1924, in East Los Angeles, CA; son of Tulio Bartolomeo (a restaurant owner) and Rosa (Cagna) Buscaglia. *Education:* University of Southern California, A.B. (cum laude), 1950, general secondary school credential, 1950, special credentials in

speech correction and hearing, 1950, M.A., 1954, general administrative credential, 1960, Ph.D., 1963. *Hobbies and other interests:* Cooking, eating, good wines, traveling, meeting people, reading, movies, theater, and opera.

LEO F. BUSCAGLIA

ADDRESSES: Home—Los Angeles, CA. *Office*—Leo F. Buscaglia, Inc., P.O. Box 686, South Pasadena, CA 91030-0686.

CAREER: Pasadena City School System, Pasadena, CA, teacher and speech therapist, 1951-60, special education supervisor, 1960-65; lived in Asia, 1965-68; University of Southern California, Los Angeles, assistant professor, 1968-75, professor of education, 1975—. Has recorded more than a dozen speeches for Public Broadcasting System (PBS-TV); conducts lectures throughout the United States. President of Felice Foundation, 1984—. *Military service:* U.S. Navy, 1941-44; became medical corpsman second class.

AWARDS, HONORS: California Governor's Award, 1965; professor of the year award, 1970 and 1972, and award for teaching excellence, 1977-78, all from University of Southern California; recognition awards, American Academy of Dentistry for the Handicapped, 1972, and Royal Thai Navy, 1973; meritorious service award, International School, Bangkok, Thailand, 1973; excellence award, New Mexico State Federation of the Council for Exceptional Children, 1974; outstanding service award, U.S. Air Force, 1976; appreciation award, Public Broadcasting System (PBS), 1981; received keys to cities, including Charlotte, NC, 1981, Carbondale, PA, 1983, Scranton, PA, 1983, and Wilkes-Barre, PA, 1983; Dr. Leo F. Buscaglia Day proclaimed in Dunmore, PA, 1983.

WRITINGS:

PUBLISHED BY CHARLES B. SLACK, UNLESS OTHERWISE NOTED

Love, 1972.
Because I Am Human, photographs by Bruce Ferguson, 1972.
The Way of the Bull: A Voyage, 1974.
(Editor) *The Disabled and Their Parents: A Counseling Challenge,* 1975.
Personhood: The Art of Being Fully Human, 1978.
(Editor with Eddie H. Williams) *Human Advocacy and PL 94-142: The Educator's Roles,* 1979.
Living, Loving, and Learning, edited with photographs by Steven Short, introduction by Betty Lou Kratoville, 1982, 2nd edition published as *Living, Loving, and Learning II,* Nightingale-Conant, 1989.
The Fall of Freddie the Leaf: A Story of Life for All Ages, 1982.
Loving Each Other, 1984.
Bus Nine to Paradise: A Loving Voyage, 1986.
Seven Stories of Christmas Love, illustrated by Tom Newsom, 1987.
A Memory for Tino (for children), illustrated by Carol Newsom, 1988.
Papa, My Father: A Celebration of Dads, edited by Ann Bramson, 1989.
Celebrate Life!, Nightingale-Conant, 1989.
Sounds of Love, Nightingale-Conant, 1989.
Politics of Love, Nightingale-Conant, 1989.

ADAPTATIONS: Many of Buscaglia's books and lectures have been released on audio cassette.

WORK IN PROGRESS: A book on compromise; articles for magazines.

**"These photographs are full of memories for me,"
Mrs. Sunday told Tino.** (From *A Memory for Tino* by Leo F. Buscaglia. Illustrated by Carol Newsom.)

SIDELIGHTS: Leo Buscaglia is a populuar television lecturer and education professor who is sometimes called "Dr. Love" or "Dr. Hug." He first gained widespread attention during the 1970s through his speeches and bestselling books. Buscaglia's message is a positive one: he urges people to discover who they really are, to observe the wonder of life all around them, to accept both pleasure and pain as part of life, and to love one another. At the end of his lectures, people are often so inspired that they hug each other and Buscaglia as well. "My message is simple," Buscaglia said in a *Newsweek* article. "Let's get back a sense of personal dignity and individuality. We should all get in touch with our uniqueness and share it with other people."

Buscaglia was born on March 31, 1924, in Los Angeles, California. Shortly after, his family moved back to their hometown of Aosta, a village located in the mountains of Italy. During the first five years of his life Buscaglia enjoyed the company of his family and Italian neighbors—people who knew and cared for one another. In 1930, however, his family moved back to California, where people seemed cold and unfriendly compared to the Italians he knew as a child. When he went to elementary school in Los Angeles, for example, his classmates would tease him for wearing worn-out clothes and a garlic necklace, which his mother gave him to keep sickness away—a common Italian practice.

Life at home was better. Buscaglia was part of a large, extended family that kept together during both happy and sad times. Part of the good times occurred during dinner hour, when his father would ask the children to tell something new that they learned during the day. This practice helped Buscaglia develop his storytelling talents. He would retell these dinner-table stories to friends eager to learn new things. By the time Buscaglia was a teenager, he had decided to make teaching his career since he enjoyed talking and relating to other people so much.

Before he became a teacher, Buscaglia served in the U.S. Navy during World War II, after which he lived for a time in Paris, France. When he returned home he went to school at the University of Southern California (U.S.C.) and went on to become a teacher and speech therapist during the 1950s. In 1960 Buscaglia was placed in charge of special education for the Pasadena City School System. Although the job was an important career promotion, Buscaglia did not like being out of the classroom. In 1965 he quit and began teaching at U.S.C., but he was still dissatisfied. Buscaglia felt he needed to get away to learn more about himself. So he went on an extended leave-of-absence from the university, sold all of his material possessions, and traveled to Asia. There he lived in poverty among various people and studied Asian philosophy and religion, including Buddhism. His Eastern experiences made him realize that all religions "agree on the same principles for humanity," he explained in a *Time* article. "There is no religion that disagrees on the basic tenet being love. You can be a follower of Muhammad or Jesus or Buddha or whomever. Always they said that the most essential factor is to love your neighbor. And to love you."

Buscaglia decided to bring his message of love to the classroom when he returned to the United States. Specifically, the suicide of one of his students caused him to approach U.S.C. administrators to ask if he could teach a non-credit course on love. He was convinced students were missing out on basic life skills—skills that would help them deal with everyday problems like loneliness and depression without resorting to suicide. Buscaglia's request was granted, but some doubted whether there would be any interest. Buscaglia was not concerned. He said in *Time* magazine that he remembered thinking, "If nobody comes, I'll just sit . . . and meditate on love for the next three or four hours myself." People *did* come, and the class became so popular over the years that a waiting list developed with more than six hundred names on it. During the course students learned to have positive attitudes toward themselves and each other as well as toward life and death. The subject matter of this course led to his first book, simply titled *Love*.

Most of Buscaglia's later books are for adults interested in personal growth, but two of his works are for children. *The Fall of Freddie the Leaf* is a 1982 book that shows how death is part of life. Freddie the leaf talks to his other leaf friends about questions of life and death. They feel good when they realize that, even though they are similar, each of them is an individual. They also come to accept their fall from the tree as a natural part of their lives. *A Memory for Tino* is a 1988 book about how Tino, an eight-year-old boy, makes friends with an old woman named Mrs. Sunday. She lives in a run-down house, and Tino's friends think she is a vampire. Tino does too, until he gets to know her and discovers that she is just a lonely person. Tino decides to give her his family's television set to keep her company. At first his parents are upset, but they soon realize that Tino wanted to help Mrs. Sunday, so they let her keep the television. Although some critics found

the message of these stories too obvious, many reviewers thought children would enjoy the books.

Buscaglia continues to promote his message of love, harmony, and growth in his bestselling books and in lectures given throughout the country.

WORKS CITED:

Langway, Lynn and Janet Huck, "Dr. Hug Will Uplift You," *Newsweek,* May 9, 1983, p. 85.
Leo, John and Steven Holmes, "The Warm Success of Dr. Hug," *Time,* November 15, 1982, pp. 84-85.

FOR MORE INFORMATION SEE:

BOOKS

Buscaglia, Leo F., *The Way of the Bull: A Voyage,* Charles B. Slack, 1974.

PERIODICALS

Changes, January/February, 1988.
Current Health, December, 1981.
Los Angeles Times, May 5, 1982; February 16, 1983.
New York Times Book Review, May 16, 1982.
People, July 5, 1982.
Psychology Today, November, 1983.
Seventeen, February, 1983; November, 1983.

* * *

BUSCAGLIA, Leo F.
See BUSCAGLIA, Felice Leonardo

* * *

CARLE, Eric 1929-

PERSONAL: Born June 25, 1929, in Syracuse, NY; son of Erich W. (a civil servant) and Johanna (Oelschlaeger) Carle; married Dorothea Wohlenberg, June, 1954 (divorced, 1964); married Barbara Morrison, June, 1973; children: (first marriage) Cirsten, Rolf. *Education:* Graduated from Akademie der bildenden Kuenste, Stuttgart, Germany, 1950.

ADDRESSES: Home—231 Crescent St., Northampton, MA 01060.

CAREER: U.S. Information Center, Stuttgart, Germany, poster designer, 1950-52; *New York Times,* New York City, graphic designer, 1952-56; L. W. Frohlich & Co., New York City, art director, 1956-63; free-lance writer, illustrator, and designer, 1963—. Guest instructor, Pratt Institute, 1964. *Military service:* U.S. Army, 1952-54.

MEMBER: Authors League of America.

AWARDS, HONORS: New York Times Ten Best Picture Books of the Year citation, 1969, American Institute of Graphic Arts award, 1970, Best Children's Books of England citation, 1971, Selection du Grand Prix des Treize, France, 1972, Brooklyn Museum Art Books for Children citation, 1973, 1976, 1977, and Nakamori Reader's Prize, Japan, 1975, all for *The Very Hungry Caterpillar;* International Children's Book Fair first prize for picture books, 1970, and Deutscher

Jugendpreis citation, 1970, both for *1, 2, 3 to the Zoo;* American Institute of Graphic Arts award and Child Study Association book list citation, both 1970, for *Pancakes, Pancakes;* Children's Spring Book Festival honor book citation, 1971, International Children's Book Fair first prize for picture books, Deutscher Jugendpreis award, and American Library Association (ALA) notable book citation, all 1972, and Selection du Grand Prix des Treize, 1973, all for *Do You Want to Be My Friend?;* Selection du Grand Prix des Treize, 1973, for *Have You Seen My Cat?;* New York Times Outstanding Book of the Year, 1974, for "My Very First Library" series; *The Very Busy Spider* was named to *Horn Book*'s "Fanfare" list, 1986, and ALA's Best Books of the 80's list; Young Critics Award special mention, International Children's Book Fair, Parents Choice Award in illustration, 1986, and Kentucky Bluegrass Award, 1988, all for *Papa, Please Get the Moon for Me;* Silber Medal, City of Milano, 1989; *Redbook* Top Ten Picture Books of the Year award, 1989, for *Animals, Animals,* and 1990, for *The Very Quiet Cricket.* Also recipient of numerous other awards, including awards from New York Art Directors Show, New York Type Directors Show, Society of Illustrators Show, and Best Book Jacket of the Year Show.

WRITINGS:

SELF-ILLUSTRATED

The Say-with-Me ABC Book, Holt, 1967.
1, 2, 3 to the Zoo, World Publishing, 1968.
The Very Hungry Caterpillar, World Publishing, 1969.
Pancakes, Pancakes, Knopf, 1970.
The Tiny Seed, Crowell, 1970 (published in England as *The Tiny Seed and the Giant Flower,* Nelson, 1970).

ERIC CARLE

Do You Want to Be My Friend?, Crowell, 1971.
The Rooster Who Set Out to See the World, F. Watts, 1972, published as *Rooster's Off to See the World,* Picture Book Studio, 1987.
The Secret Birthday Message, Crowell, 1972.
The Very Long Tail (folding book), Crowell, 1972.
The Very Long Train (folding book), Crowell, 1972.
Walter the Baker: An Old Story Retold and Illustrated by Eric Carle, Knopf, 1972.
Have You Seen My Cat?, F. Watts, 1973.
I See a Song, Crowell, 1973.
All about Arthur (an Absolutely Absurd Ape), F. Watts, 1974.
The Mixed-Up Chameleon, Crowell, 1975.
Eric Carle's Storybook: Seven Tales by the Brothers Grimm, F. Watts, 1976.
The Grouchy Ladybug, Crowell, 1977 (published in England as *The Bad-Tempered Ladybird,* Hamish Hamilton, 1977).
(Reteller) *Seven Stories by Hans Christian Andersen,* F. Watts, 1978.
Watch Out! A Giant!, Philomel, 1978.
Twelve Tales from Aesop: Retold and Illustrated, Philomel, 1980.
The Honeybee and the Robber: A Moving Picture Book, Philomel, 1981.
Catch the Ball, Philomel, 1982.
Let's Paint a Rainbow, Philomel, 1982.
What's for Lunch?, Philomel, 1982.
The Very Busy Spider, Philomel, 1984.
All around Us, Picture Book Studio, 1986.
Papa, Please Get the Moon for Me, Picture Book Studio, 1986.
Eric Carle's Treasury of Classic Stories for Children, Orchard Books, 1988.
A House for Hermit Crab, Picture Book Studio, 1988.
The Very Quiet Cricket, Philomel, 1990.

"MY VERY FIRST LIBRARY" SERIES; SELF-ILLUSTRATED

My Very First Book of Colors, Crowell, 1974.
My Very First Book of Numbers, Crowell, 1974.
My Very First Book of Shapes, Crowell, 1974.
My Very First Book of Words, Crowell, 1974.
My Very First Book of Food, Crowell, 1986.
My Very First Book of Growth, Crowell, 1986.
My Very First Book of Heads and Tails, Crowell, 1986.
My Very First Book of Homes, Crowell, 1986.
My Very First Book of Motion, Crowell, 1986.
My Very First Book of Sounds, Crowell, 1986.
My Very First Book of Tools, Crowell, 1986.
My Very First Book of Touch, Crowell, 1986.

ILLUSTRATOR

Sune Engelbrektson, *Gravity at Work and Play,* Holt, 1963.
Engelbrektson, *The Sun Is a Star,* Holt, 1963.
Bill Martin, *If You Can Count to Ten,* Holt, 1964.
Aesop's Fables for Modern Readers, Pauper Press, 1965.
Louise Bachelder, editor, *Nature Thoughts,* Pauper Press, 1965.
Lila Perl, *Red-Flannel Hash and Shoo-Fly Pie: America's Regional Foods and Festivals,* World Publishers, 1965.
Samm S. Baker, *Indoor and Outdoor Grow-It Book,* Random House, 1966.
Bachelder, editor, *On Friendship,* Pauper Press, 1966.
Martin, *Brown Bear, Brown Bear, What Do You See?,* Holt, 1967.
Carl H. Voss, *In Search of Meaning: Living Religions of the World,* World Publishers, 1968.
Nora Roberts Wainer, *The Whale in a Jail,* Funk, 1968.
William Knowlton, *The Boastful Fisherman,* Knopf, 1970.

One fine morning, a rooster decided that he wanted to travel.
So, right then and there, he set out to see the world.
He hadn't walked very far when he began to feel lonely.

From *Rooster's Off to See the World*, Eric Carle's 1987 book featuring counting.

Martin, *A Ghost Story,* Holt, 1970.

Eleanor O. Heady, *Tales of the Nimipoo from the Land of the Nez Pierce Indians,* World Publishing 1970.

Aileen Fisher, *Feathered Ones and Furry,* Crowell, 1971.

George Mendoza, *The Scarecrow Clock,* Holt, 1971.

Vanishing Animals (posters), F. Watts, 1972.

Fisher, *Do Bears Have Mothers Too?,* Crowell, 1973 (published in England as *Animals and Their Babies,* Hamish Hamilton, 1974).

Isaac Bashevis Singer, *Why Noah Chose the Dove,* translated by Elizabeth Shub, Farrar, Straus, 1974.

Norma Green, reteller, *The Hole in the Dike,* Crowell, 1975.

Norton Juster, *Otter Nonsense,* Philomel, 1982.

Hans Baumann, *Chip Has Many Brothers,* Philomel, 1985.

Richard Buckley, *The Foolish Tortoise,* Picture Book Studio, 1985.

Buckley, *The Greedy Python,* Picture Book Studio, 1985.

Alice McLerran, *The Mountain That Loved a Bird,* Picture Book Studio, 1985.

Mitsumasa Anno, *All in a Day,* Dowaya (Tokyo), 1986.

Arnold Sundgaard, *The Lamb and the Butterfly,* Orchard Books, 1988.

Laura Whipple, editor, *Animals, Animals,* Philomel, 1989.

SIDELIGHTS: Even as a child, Eric Carle was fascinated by drawing. "Until I was six years old I lived in Syracuse, N.Y., where I went to kindergarten. I remember happy days with large sheets of paper, bright colors and wide brushes!" the author once told *Something about the Author (SATA).* Just after Carle started first grade, his family moved to Stuttgart, Germany. His father's mother had pleaded for the family to return to their native country. In a visit to America, Carle's grandmother "promised gifts and she told them about the rising leader, Adolf Hitler, and claimed that he had eliminated unemployment, inflation, and hunger," Carle recalled in *Something about the Author Autobiography Series.* "Her own children ignored her pleas, but in my mother the seed of homesickness had been planted."

"When I got to Germany I had to learn two languages and how to get along in a country that was far different from the one I was used to," Carle said in *Famous Children's Authors.* "Often I wished that a bridge could be built from Germany to America so I could get back home." Adjusting to school in his new country was very hard for Carle, even though he soon forgot his English and was speaking German fluently. When he was six, he began attending grammar school in Stuttgart. "School was strict," Carle told *SATA,* "corporal punishment not excluded. I also remember receiving a small piece of paper, a hard pencil and an eraser with the warning not to make mistakes." On his third day, Carle became the first in his class to get a whipping. For a small mistake, he received three whacks on each hand.

Carle's new life in Germany wasn't all troubles. Carle began making many friends at school, becoming popular because he was an American. He had a helpful art teacher who praised him for his drawings. He also had many relatives nearby, and

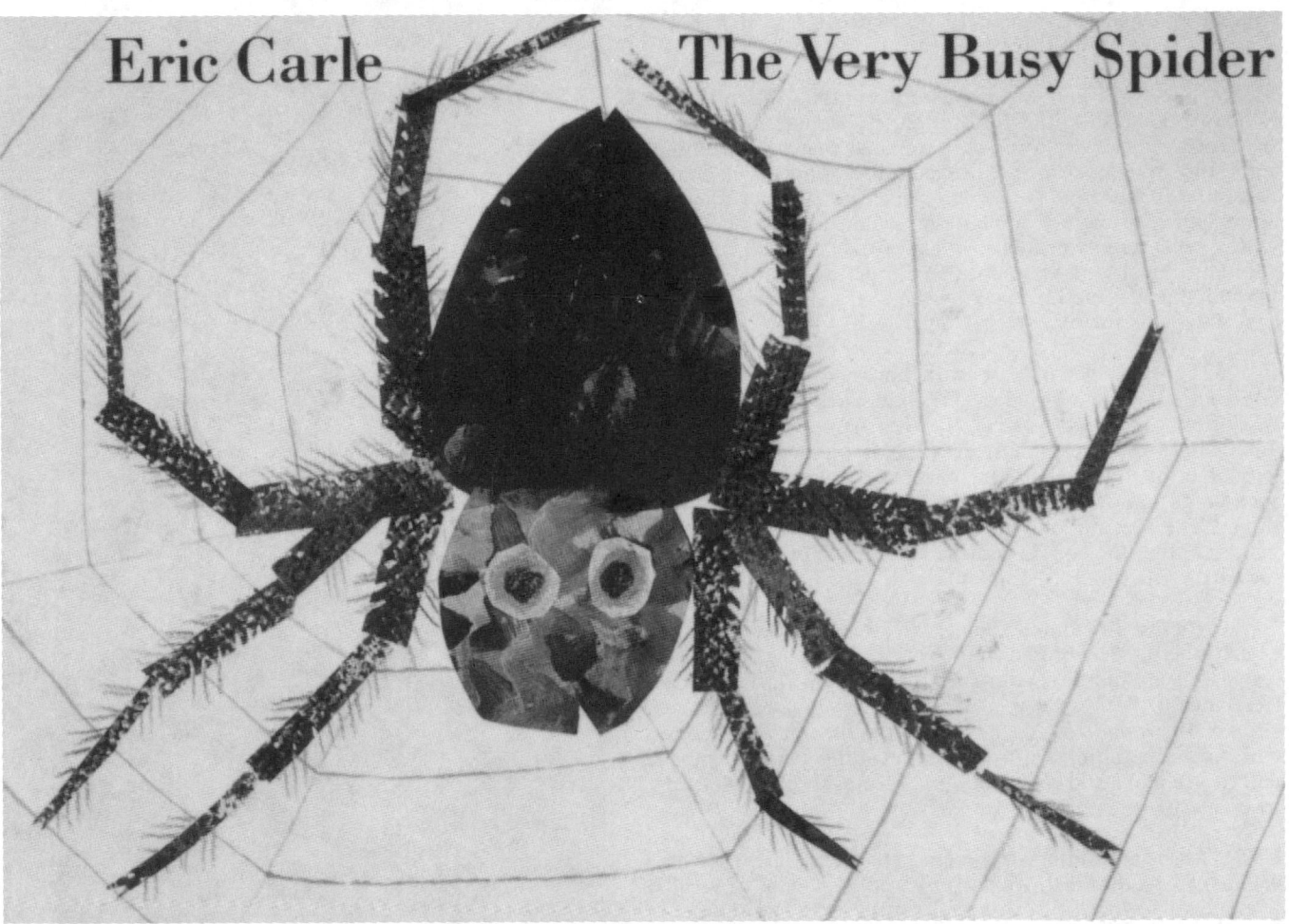

Eric Carle   The Very Busy Spider

Cover from Eric Carle's award-winning book that has been especially appealing to visually handicapped children, who can feel the spider on the pages.

often spent entire weekends with his aunt and uncle in their old house: "At the door my aunt would hug and kiss me, and push me into their kitchen to stuff me with goodies, fearing that I was near starvation," the author related in his *Something about the Author Autobiography Series* essay. Next "I would go into my uncle's studio, a small unused bedroom, sit down next to him, and listen to the stories he often had to tell."

But, along with these fond memories, Carle recalled an event that was to change history. "On my way to school I often passed a small department store on the Adolf Hitler Strasse," he wrote for the *Something about the Author Autobiography Series.* "Occasionally I had bought a toy there for myself, or some thread or canning jars for my mother. But one day as I passed, clothing, furniture, hardware, toys, and much more lay strewn and torn beyond the shattered windows. A large Star of David had been painted roughly across a broken door that was off its hinges. The damaged building was cordoned off, and a policeman ordered me to move on, to be on my way to school. This was the so-called Crystal Night, 1938, when open anti-Semitism erupted in Nazi Germany."

Soon afterward World War II broke out, and Carle's father was drafted into the German Army. "He was away for eight years and was a prisoner of war in Russia part of the time," Carle said in *Famous Children's Authors.* "I missed my father very much." During the early years of the war, Germany was

successful and the boy was impressed by the many German soldiers returning from victory. As he said in the *Something about the Author Autobiography Series,* he became "a loyal German patriot, along with all his German-born school-mates. Hitler's victories [were] intoxicating."

But Germany's fortunes changed and Allied forces started attacking Stuttgart, a major target. Even though Carle's family strengthened their basement with steel doors, it wasn't safe from the bombs falling on the city. The people began digging tunnels, which they called *Stollen,* around the area. Carle and his family were forced to take shelter there, some-times several times a night. For the last eighteen months of the war, Carle and his schoolmates were sent to a small town in the southwest of Germany to be safe from the bombing raids.

The war ended with Germany's surrender in 1945. Still Carle's family heard nothing about his father's whereabouts. Eventually rumors brought them word that he was in Russia, and in 1946 they finally received a note saying he was alive and would return soon. He arrived home in late 1947, sick and weighing just eighty pounds. Eight years away had changed his father so much, Carle stated in the *Something about the Author Autobiography Series* that he "would never really recover or 'belong' to our family again." The closeness he and his father had shared was gone, but Carle still "recalled the happiness he had offered to me in my early childhood, when he passed on to me his dreams which he had not been able to fulfill for himself.''

Meanwhile, Carle had begun art studies at the Akademie der bildenden Kuenste with Professor Ernst Schneidler. Because the professor's reputation was so great, as one of the professor's students Carle found a job easily after graduation. Even before he finished his studies he began working for a local American information center, designing posters. By 1952, the young artist had gained enough experience and had created enough artwork to feel confident about returning to the United States, something he knew he would do ever since his first day in Germany.

In 1952 Carle arrived in New York, and within two weeks he landed a job with the *New York Times.* Carle had only been working for five months when the U.S. Army recruited him, and he began two years in the service. He was soon stationed with an army unit back in Stuttgart, where he was allowed to spend nights and weekends at his parent's house. During this time, Carle met and married his first wife, Dorothea. After his discharge, the couple returned to New York, and there they had two children, Cirsten and Rolf.

Carle worked for almost ten years as a designer and art director before deciding to change his surroundings. In 1963, Carle quit his full-time company job to begin working as a free-lance artist. As he related in his *Something about the Author Autobiography Series* essay, ''I had come to the conclusion that I didn't want to sit in meetings, write memos, entertain clients, and catch commuter trains. I simply wanted to create pictures.''

Carle first became interested in children's literature when he was asked to do illustrations for a series of books by Bill Martin. ''I found Bill's approach to the world of the preschool and first grade child very stimulating; it reawakened in me struggles of my own childhood,'' Carle commented to Delores R. Klingberg in *Language Arts.* Remembering his difficult early schooldays in Germany, Carle added that the conflicts from that time ''remained hidden until the opportunity and insight presented themselves. Through my work with Bill Martin, an unfinished area of my own growing up had been touched.''

''I didn't realize it clearly then, but my life was beginning to move onto its true course,'' Carle said in the *Something about the Author Autobiography Series.* ''The long, dark time of growing up in wartime Germany, the cruelly enforced discipline of my school years there, the dutifully performed work at my jobs in advertising—all these were finally losing their rigid grip on me. The child inside me—who had been so suddenly and sharply uprooted and repressed—was beginning to come joyfully back to life.''

''It was then that I met Ann Beneduce (then editor with World), and with her kind help and understanding I created my first two books: *1, 2, 3 to the Zoo* and *The Very Hungry Caterpillar,*'' Carle told *SATA.* ''A mixture of negative and positive influences had led to a fruitful expression.''

Both of Carle's first books contain bold, collage pictures and feature many different animals. The author recalled in a *Books for Keeps* article that his early years with his father taught him about nature. ''We used to go for long walks in the countryside together, and he would peel back tree bark to show me what was underneath it, lift rocks to reveal the insects. As a result, I have an abiding love and affection for small, insignificant animals.''

Come little cub, don't look so blue. One little spank is nothing new. I love you both—you *know* I do. (From *Do Bears Have Mothers Too?* by Aileen Fisher and Eric Carle.)

1, 2, 3 to the Zoo was published in 1968 and follows several animals on their train trip to live in a zoo, with a tiny mouse observing each car. The book is full of ''superb paintings of animals, bold, lively, handsome, spreading over big double-spread pages,'' Adele McRae of the *Christian Science Monitor* wrote. ''His elephant is all magnificent power, his giraffes a precision of delicacy, his monkeys a tangle of liveliness. This is a book to grow with its owner. The tiny mouse lurking in every picture may remain invisible to the smallest reader and, as the title implies, the book is waiting to teach the art of counting.''

Carle's award-winning book *The Very Hungry Caterpillar* was published in 1969. ''I was just playfully punching holes in a stack of paper,'' the author told Molly McQuade of *Publishers Weekly,* ''and I thought to myself, 'This could've been done by a bookworm.' From that came a caterpillar.''

The Very Hungry Caterpillar ''tells the story of a caterpillar's life-cycle, from egg to butterfly,'' as John A. Cunliffe described it in *Children's Book Review.* ''He eats through a great many things on the way—one apple on Monday, two pears on Tuesday, and so on, to a list of ten exotic items on

Saturday—and the book's delight, and originality, lie in the way in which these cumulative items are shown." In addition, the critic noted, "the text is brief and simple, and has a satisfying cumulative effect that neatly matches the pictures, which are large and bold, in brilliant colours and crisp forms set against the white page, mainly achieved by the use of collage. This book has a direct appeal, true simplicity, and a strong play element that will endear it to the hearts of all children from about eight downwards. Their elder brothers and sisters, not to mention their parents, will find delight in it too, for such an outstanding book has a universal appeal."

Not only does *Caterpillar* contain brightly colored shapes designed to appeal to young children, it also has holes in the pages which match the path of the caterpillar. As Carle explained in *Books for Your Children,* the holes in *Caterpillar* "are a bridge from toy to book, from plaything, from the touching to understanding. . . . In the very young child the thought travels mightily fast from fingertips to brain. This book has many layers. There is fun, nonsense, colour, surprise. There is learning, but if the child ignores the learning part, let him, it's OK. Someday he'll hit upon it by himself. That is the way we learn." Carle's approach in *Caterpillar* has proved so popular that the book has sold over four million copies and been translated into fifteen languages.

Carle's book *Do You Want to Be My Friend?*, published in 1971, is his favorite, for he believes friendship is very important to the very young. In his *Something about the Author Autobiography Series* essay Carle recalled a childhood friend from Syracuse who wrote him letters after he moved to Germany. "Twenty years later, I went to his door unannounced and asked him, 'Do you know me?' Without a moment's hesitation, he answered, 'You're Eric!' Now, over fifty years later, I still have his precious letter[s]. In my heart, I have dedicated my book *Do You Want to Be My Friend?* to this first and deeply felt friendship."

Like *1, 2, 3 to the Zoo, Do You Want to Be My Friend?* is a picture book filled with bright and colorful animals. The only words in the story are the title question "Do you want to be my friend?" spoken by a lonely mouse, and a joyful "yes" from the new friend he finally discovers. Calling it "a perfect picture book for a small child," *Washington Post Book World* contributor Polly Goodwin added that *Do You Want to Be My Friend?* "offers a splendid opportunity for a pre-reader, with a little initial help, to create his own story based on the brilliantly colored, wonderfully expressive pictures."

The Rooster Who Set Out to See the World, later published as *Rooster's Off to See the World,* is another "brilliantly colored picture story that does double duty as a counting book," Lillian N. Gerhardt said in *Library Journal.* The story follows a rooster who decides to travel and see the world. As he travels, he adds friends in twos, threes, fours, and fives. "The sums are presented pictorially in the corners of the page," Marcus Crouch of *Junior Bookshelf* noted, but this doesn't distract from Carle's "exquisitely drawn coloured pictures. Mr. Carle is still the best of all artists for the very young," Crouch concluded.

Carle introduced another innovation in his 1978 book *The Grouchy Ladybug:* the pages grow in size as larger and larger animals appear on them. The story follows a bad-tempered ladybug as she challenges different creatures, starting with other insects and ending with the whale whose cut-out tail slaps her back to her home leaf. While Carle presents such instructive concepts as time and size, "this book is chiefly a pleasure to read and to look at," Caroline Moorhead wrote in the *Times Educational Supplement,* "with its cross and good-natured ladybirds . . . and its deep-toned illustrations of animals."

The Very Busy Spider follows a spider who spends her day spinning a web which grows larger with each page. Although she is interrupted by a number of farm animals, the spider continues her work until the web is finished and she catches the fly that has been bothering the other animals. Because the web and fly are raised above the page so that they can be felt, the book "is obviously of value to the visually handicapped," as Julia Eccleshare commented in the *Times Literary Supplement.* Denise M. Wilms agreed, writing in *Booklist* that "this good-looking picture book has just the ingredients" to become an "instant classic."

In addition to original stories, Carle has also written his own versions of familiar children's works, such as Grimm's fairy tales, Aesop's fables, and Hans Christian Andersen's stories. But whatever their topic, all of Carle's works are educational tools that interest children with their bold, imaginative drawings and whimsical presentations. "We underestimate children," Carle said in a 1982 *Early Years* interview. "They have tremendous capacities for learning."

This interest in education, fired by his own early experience, has been the driving force behind Carle's books, as he declared in *Books for Keeps.* "There are two major traumas in anyone's life, being born and going to school for the first time. . . . The transition for me from home to school was so horrible, and I want to make that transition better and easier for children by providing them with books which help to 'sweeten' the educational process." By including holes, cutouts, changing surfaces, and moving parts, Carle creates works that are both toys—things to be touched and played with—and books.

"But there is something else," the artist remarked in *Books for Keeps.* "So many 'learning' books for the young leave out the emotional side of life. I want to keep it in. There is a feeling, an emotional level quite consciously in each of my books. The emotion and feeling were all left out of my education in Germany, and that's why I think it's so important for me now. I also think of myself as an entertainer now. . . . Entertainment is an important part of books for the young." And, as Carle further explained in *Books for Your Children,* "I would like to make childhood something special and joyous, something that the child does not want to get over with fast, something that immunises him from such warnings as 'time to grow up,' 'be mature' and 'don't act like a child.'"

"I've had children come to me and say, 'I can do that!,' and I'm highly complimented," the author told McQuade in the *Publishers Weekly* interview. "Both the content and the art in my books reflect the child in me—with the help of the grownup." Indeed, as Donnarae MacCann and Olga Richard claimed in *Wilson Library Bulletin,* "Eric Carle is like a half dozen creative people rolled into one." Because of Carle's skill in writing for pre-schoolers, his "innovativeness and artistic discipline," and his ability to turn a book into a toy, the critics concluded, "a child reared on such books will blossom into a confirmed bibliophile." And, as Carle told *Early Years,* this would fulfill the one hope he has for all his books: "I would wish my books could have an effect on every child, every last one of them."

Dustjacket of Eric Carle's 1969 classic, *The Very Hungry Caterpillar*.

WORKS CITED:

Carle, Eric, "From Hungry Caterpillars to Bad Tempered Ladybirds," *Books for Your Children,* spring, 1978, p. 7.

Carle, Eric, "Authorgraph No. 2: Eric Carle," *Books for Keeps,* May, 1985, pp. 14-15.

Carle, Eric, *Something about the Author Autobiography Series,* Volume 6, Gale, 1988, pp. 33-51.

Crouch, Marcus, review of "Rooster Sets out to See the World," *Junior Bookshelf,* October, 1972, pp. 301-02.

Cunliffe, John A., review of *The Very Hungry Caterpillar, Children's Book Review,* February, 1971, p. 14.

Eccleshare, Julia, "Following the Thread," *Times Literary Supplement,* March 29, 1985, p. 351.

"Eric Carle's Children's Books Are to Touch, to Experience, and Most of All to Love," *Early Years,* April, 1982, p. 23.

Famous Children's Authors, edited by Shirley Norby and Gregory Ryan, Denison, 1988, p. 18.

Gerhardt, Lillian N., review of *The Rooster Who Set out to See the World, Library Journal,* June 15, 1973, pp. 1992-93.

Goodwin, Polly, review of *Do You Want to Be My Friend?, Washington Post Book World,* Part II, May 9, 1971, p. 4.

Klingberg, Delores R., "Eric Carle," *Language Arts,* April, 1977, p. 447.

MacCann, Donnarae and Olga Richard, "Picture Books for Children," *Wilson Library Bulletin,* January, 1989, pp. 90-91.

McQuade, Molly, "Ballyhooing Birthdays: Four Children's Classics and How They Grew," *Publishers Weekly,* September 29, 1989, pp. 28-29.

McRae, Adele, "Crayoned Morality Plays," *Christian Science Monitor,* May 1, 1969, p. B2.

Moorhead, Caroline, "Animal/Animal, Animal/Human," *Times Educational Supplement,* February 3, 1978, p. 45.

Something about the Author, Volume 4, Gale, 1973, pp. 42-43.

Wilms, Denise M., review of *The Very Busy Spider, Booklist,* June 1, 1985, p. 1398.

FOR MORE INFORMATION SEE:

BOOKS

Children's Literature Review, Volume 10, Gale, 1986.

PERIODICALS

Book Window, spring, 1979.
Children's Book Review Service, November, 1974.
Christian Science Monitor, November 11, 1971.
Graphis, Number 86.
Junior Bookshelf, August, 1972.
Lion and the Unicorn, Volumes 7 and 8, 1983-84.
New York Times Book Review, February 22, 1981.
Publishers Weekly, January 29, 1982.
Top of the News, June, 1971.
Wilson Library Bulletin, November, 1974.

CASSON, Hugh Maxwell 1910-

PERSONAL: Born May 23, 1910, in Hampstead, London, England; son of Randal (Indian Civil Servant and math professor) and Mary Caroline (Man) Casson; married Margaret Macdonald Troup (an architect), 1938; children: Carola Casson Zogolovich, Nicola Casson Hessenberg, Dinah Casson. *Education:* Attended Eastbourne College, Sussex, 1924-27; St. John's College, Cambridge, M.A., 1931; graduate study at Bartlett School of Architecture, University College, London, 1931-32, and British School at Athens, 1933. *Religion:* Church of England. *Hobbies and other interests:* Drawing, writing, travel, sailing.

ADDRESSES: Home—6 Hereford Mansions, Hereford Rd., London W2 5BA England. *Office*—Casson Conder Partnership, 35 Thurloe Place, London S.W.7 England.

CAREER: Private practice of architecture in London, England, 1933-39; Air Ministry, London, camouflage officer, 1940-44; Ministry of Town and Country Planning, London, technical officer, 1944-46; Casson Conder Partnership, London, senior partner, 1946-89. Royal Academy of Art, professor of environmental design, 1953-75, provost, 1976-84. Member of Royal Design for Industry Faculty, and Master of Faculty, 1969-71. Member of Royal Fine Art Commission, 1960-85, and Royal Mint Advisory Committee, 1972—. Director of Architecture for Festival of Britain, 1948-51. Council member and executive board member of National Trust, 1965—; member of British Rail Development Panel, 1977-85. Member of board of trustees of British Museum (Natural History) and National Portrait Gallery, 1976-85, and board of directors of British Council, 1977-80.

HUGH M. CASSON

MEMBER: Royal Institute of British Architects, Chartered Society of Designers (fellow), Society of Industrial Artists (fellow), Greater London Arts Association (1974-76); Royal Danish Academy (honorary member, 1954), American Institute of Architects (honorary associate, 1968), Royal Canadian Academy of Arts (honorary member, 1980).

AWARDS, HONORS: Named Royal Designer for Industry, Royal Society of Arts, 1951; Knight of the Order of the British Empire, 1952; Knight Commander of the Royal Victorian Order, 1978; Italian Order of Merit, Rome, 1980; Albert Medal, Royal Society of Arts, 1984; Companion of Honour, 1985. Honorary doctorates from Royal College of Art, 1975, and University of Southampton, 1977; LL.D.s from University of Birmingham, 1977, Loughborough University, 1979, and University of Glasgow, 1980; D.Litt., Sheffield University, 1986.

WRITINGS:

AUTHOR AND ILLUSTRATOR

New Sights of London, London Transport, 1937.
(Contributor) *Weekend Houses, Cottages and Bungalows,* Architectural Press, 1939.
Bombed Churches, Architectural Press, 1946.
(With Anthony Chitty) *Houses: Permanence and Prefabrication,* Pleiades Books, 1947.
Homes by the Million: An Account of the Housing Achievement in the U.S.A. 1940-1945, Penguin, 1947.
An Introduction to Victorian Architechture, Art and Technics Ltd., 1948.
Red Lacquer Days, Lion and Unicorn Press, 1956.
The Unseeing Eye, [London], 1958.
(With Joyce Grenfell) *Nanny Says,* edited by Diana, Lady Avebury, Dobson, 1972.
(Contributor) *Spirit of the Age,* British Broadcasting Corp., 1975.
Sketchbook, Lion and Unicorn Press, 1975.
(Contributor) Mary Banham and Bevis Hillier, editors, *A Tonic to the Nation: The Festival of Britain, 1951,* Thames & Hudson, 1976.
Indian Sketchbook, Workshop Gallery, 1979.
Diary, Macmillan (London), 1981.
(With others) *George Mackley: Wood Engraver,* Gresham Books, 1981.
(Author of introduction) *The Royal Academy of Arts Year Book, 1981,* Abner Schram, 1981.
Hugh Casson's London, Dent, 1983.
(Contributor) Andrew Morton, *The Royal Yacht Britannia,* Orbis, 1984.
(Contributor) *Night and Day* (anthology), Chatto & Windus, 1985.
(With others) *Hugh Casson: Architect, Etcetera,* Blueprint Press, 1985.
Hugh Casson's Oxford: A College Companion, Phaidon, 1988.
(Contributor) Michael Spender, *Visions of Venice,* David & Charles, 1990.
Hugh Casson's Cambridge, Phaidon, 1991.

ILLUSTRATOR

Ivan Morris, *The Pillow-Book Puzzles,* Bodley Head, 1969.
Morris, *The Lonely Monk,* Bodley Head, 1970.
George Bijur, *Wines with Long Noses,* Dobson, 1977.
Prince of Wales, *The Old Man of Lochnagar,* Farrar, Straus, 1980.
Simon Gaul, *Pushkin the Polar Bear,* Quartet Books, 1983.
Diana Avebury, *Zelda and the Corgis,* Picadilly Press, 1984.

Hugh M. Casson and his sister Rosemary.

Linda Yeatman, *Buttons,* Picadilly Press, 1985, Barron, 1988.
John Betjeman, *Summoned by Bells: The Verse Autobiography of the Century,* J. Murray, 1989.

EDITOR

E. M. Hatt, *Bridges,* Chatto & Windus, 1963.
Hatt, *Follies,* Chatto & Windus, 1963.
(And contributor) Hatt, *Monuments,* Chatto & Windus, 1963.
Hatt, *Museums,* Chatto & Windus, 1964.
(Hatt and others) *Sailing Tours: Solent,* Chatto & Windus, 1964.
(Hatt and others) *Sailing Tours: Thames and S.E.,* Chatto & Windus, 1964.

OTHER

Television and radio writer. Regular contributor to professional journals and popular magazines, including *Contact, Night and Day,* and *Decoration.* Architectural editor, *Arts and Technics,* 1947-50; member of editorial board, *Architectural Review,* 1948-65.

WORK IN PROGRESS: (With wife, Margaret Casson) travel books on Japan and Egypt.

ADAPTATIONS: The Old Man of Lochnagar, the book Casson illustrated for the Prince of Wales, was made into an animated film for release in 1991.

SIDELIGHTS: Hugh Maxwell Casson is a well-known British architect, writer and illustrator. His illustrations, like the sketches he prepares for building projects, are done in pen and ink and watercolor. Friends describe Casson as a gifted artist who is often seen drawing quick sketches in notebooks or on bits of paper. "I'm a compulsive drawer," Casson told an interviewer for *Something about the Author (SATA).* "I really am very unhappy anywhere without a surface and a weapon to draw with. If I've got a pen and torn off label waiting at Kemble Junction I'm all right because I can draw. I love it, I really love it."

Casson remembers the exact time when he focused on the interests that would later become a successful dual career. "I learned my early love of drawing from a great-uncle's bound volumes of *Punch* (1900-1925) and my love of buildings and ships from holidays spent walking and drawing the warehouses and wharves [and Atlantic liners] of Southampton where we lived," he wrote in *Hugh Casson: Architect Etcetera.*

Casson spent much of his childhood reading and exploring different forms of art because he had relatively poor health. When Hugh was born in Hampstead, England, his father was a civil servant in Burma. It was the custom for Britains abroad to send their pregnant wives home so that their children would be born in England. Casson needed special

A stitch in time saves nine. (From *Nanny Says* as recalled by Hugh Casson and Joyce Grenfell. Illustrated by Casson.)

care soon after he was born, and he was a delicate child. When strong enough to travel, he returned to Burma with his mother and his elder sister. While his father, a judge, traveled to small villages to try cases, Casson and his older sister Rosemary were looked after by a native woman. "We lived in an official house, two stories, in a place called Golden Valley, where all the Empire pith-helmeted characters lived, with a staff of about five servants and a dog and ponies and an Overland car, very high. The car was a sort of open tourer Ford, with a hood," Casson recalled in the *SATA* interview. He remembers little else about his life there "except there were a lot of starched dresses and white socks and panama hats," he said. They lived in Rangoon, Burma's capitol city, until war broke out in 1914 and all British children were sent home to England. Wives were given the choice of staying with their husbands or going home with their children. Hugh's mother chose to stay in Burma.

Back in England, Hugh lived mostly with his Aunt Jocelyn and Uncle Cecil, another Indian civil servant, now retired. He also lived for a time with his mother's parents in their seaside home at Folkstone, Kent. He loved living near the sea. "When it was rough," he said, "we had to close the shutters because pebbles were flung against the house. I loved it. We had the lighthouse from Cape Grisnez flash round the bedroom. The house was always full of cousins, I had about twenty cousins about my age. Their parents were always abroad, they were all in the Empire. So there were always six or seven of us."

In 1917, Casson lived with his grandparents at Hythe on the south coast, which "had a lot of German prison camps round it on the marshes and we used to sleep under the piano during air-raids, which was quite exciting," he said. When the war ended, eight-year-old Hugh celebrated by painting a watercolor in red, white and blue that included the word "PEACE" in large block letters.

That year, Casson was sent to boarding school near Canterbury. Still comparatively frail, he was not good at competitive sports. Instead, he became popular for his clever sense of humor. He kept score for the soccer and cricket teams, sang in the choir, learned to play the piano, and acted in plays. Eventually he became head boy of the school. He did well in school because of an exceptionally good memory which allowed him to remember full pages of material he had seen. He spent much time in the art room, where, in the British policy of the time, he was sent when not feeling well.

Casson was thirteen and had spent many holidays with his aunts and uncles by the time his father retired from the civil service. The family bought a house in Southampton, where Mr. Casson took a job teaching mathematics at the university. Hugh was interested in becoming an architect by this time, but his father warned him that he needed math skills to succeed in that field. At about this time he started to draw. Later, he was one of the few from his class at Eastbourne College to take an interest in art.

Casson was sent to Eastbourne College in Sussex because it was near the sea, where the climate was thought to be good for his health. While there, he studied Latin and Greek and read early Greek and Roman literature. After a year's study at Southampton University, he sat for Cambridge entrance exams. His test score on the classics was not as impressive as an essay he wrote about ancient Greek buildings, so he was advised to study architecture instead. He was enrolled at the Cambridge School of Architecture where he took his degree.

His days at Cambridge were filled with activity. He read a book a day from the local library—novels, biographies, and first-hand accounts of World War I combat. He also joined the college rowing club. "My father rowed for his college. He knew I couldn't row because I was too small but I liked boating and I liked steering so I was the cox of the college boat. A very successful one, in fact, and I became spare cox for the University," Casson told the interviewer. He said he enjoyed coxing for the Cambridge crew very much because the river is narrow, "and if you're in the Cambridge University boat, with light blue oars, you had a horn on the front and you could toot it on the corners and every boat had to scuttle into the banks and crouch until you'd gone sweeping by very grandly." In the evenings and on weekends, he worked backstage at the Festival Theatre, a small playhouse that presented a new play each week. Casson would help to strike the sets and paint the new scenery for the coming week's show. Robert Donat, Jessica Tandy, and other actors who later became famous were in the acting company there.

Casson learned the watercolor techniques he uses to illustrate children's books while studying to be an architect. He explained, "Everybody had to do what was called rendered drawings, which meant that you did your drawings in pencil and ink and then you put on very soft grey-brown washes, which had to be totally even." The artist cannot be interrupted when using this technique. He said, "If you stop for a minute or cough you'll never get the evenness. You actually paint with the water, not with the brush. You don't let the brush touch the paper."

The teacher at Cambridge who helped him most was the architect Harold Tomlinson. "He taught me to draw," Casson explained. "He wouldn't allow me to use a pencil or a rubber (eraser). I always had to draw with a fountain pen. If the line was wrong you put the right one along side it, you couldn't rub it out. He also insisted that everything was drawn in perspective." Eventually, Casson would have to make working drawings that would help others to put the actual buildings together. But Tomlinson made his students learn also to draw accurate pictures of what the finished buildings would look like. "So I got a fantastically good training for quick perspective drawing, for which I am eternally grateful," Casson said. Another most helpful teacher was Christopher Nicholson, who eventually was to become Casson's business partner.

After three years at Cambridge, Casson was given a travel grant from the school to go to Greece, where he wrote his thesis. "I decided to study Byzantine architecture and I went first to Ravenna and then I went to Athens, to the British School at Athens, which was my base for months, travelling all over Greece," he said. Unwilling to complete two more full years of study to earn his professional degree, he studied for his finals by correspondence course, and finished in fourteen months. At about this time, Casson's father inherited fifteen hundred pounds and gave him the legacy to spend as he liked. Casson used the money to design and build a house, then advertised and sold it by publishing the plans and photographs in *The Lady* magazine. The response was unexpectedly rewarding, and he gained another seven houses as a result.

In the early 1930s, he became the assistant to Christopher Nicholson, a former teacher who needed help in his latest job to build hangars and a clubhouse for the London Gliding Club. Nicholson's father William was an acclaimed painter, and his brother Ben was a leading figure in the modern movement. These contacts helped the small firm to land

The old man was by no means light, so the eagle had a very tough job getting his cargo airborne. (From *The Old Man of Lochnagar,* by H.R.H. The Prince of Wales. Illustrated by Hugh Casson.)

unusual jobs, such as recasting a small country house (oiginally designed by Sir Edwin Lutyens) using the designs of surrealist painter Salvador Dali. The house was to have features such as a two-story aquarium, swans exploding on the lake, and a sitting room designed to look like the insides of a sick dog. The client was Edward James, a lively young supporter of the surrealist movement in England.

Their work on that house was interrupted by the outbreak of World War II. Casson joined the London river firebrigade and, in 1938, married Margaret Macdonald Troup, an architect he had met at Bartlett School of Architecture. Her father, a doctor from Edinburgh, had gone to South Africa to serve in a war and had stayed there. Dr. Troup had sent his children home to England to boarding schools, so Casson and "Moggie," as he called her, had much in common. After their wedding in England, they voyaged to South Africa to visit the parents of the bride. The boat, which had been crowded with people fleeing wartime England on the trip south, was nearly empty for the return trip. "We had this most extraordinary voyage," Casson recalled, "it was totally blacked out, the ship, and when you went out on the deck you couldn't see." He added that "the ship's orchestra had nothing else to do so they played to us, a dozen passengers huddled in this five hundred seater dining room, it was creepy really. We could have gone into any cabin."

Back in England, Casson returned to the river firebrigade where the only emergency in the first six months of his service was when the firestation itself caught fire. He was called out from the firebrigade by the Air Ministry to camouflage aircraft, airfields, bomb dumps, and the like to hide them from the German bombers. For this job, Casson regularly had to fly in all kinds of aircraft from glider tugs to seaplanes. His most serious assignment was one of "dispersal" of new aircraft from the factories into places of natural and "assisted" concealment. The Germans would bomb the new planes as soon as they were built at the factories. To prevent this from continuing, Casson's camouflage force hid planes under trees along country roads. They painted strategic buildings to look like barns and farm houses, and they disguised the airfields, or aerodromes. Casson explained, "The interesting thing was that the aerodromes in those days were mostly grass and all the hedges had been taken up to clear the ground and then you'd paint the hedges back with black paint and from the air . . . you couldn't tell the hedges had gone."

Protecting Margaret and their first child during air raids was not easy. The couple had fortified their bed by making supports from stacked books and laid an old door across the top to make a canopy. Some time after a bomb destroyed buildings across the street, Casson noticed a glint of light reflected from the makeshift canopy and realized it was a painted-over plate glass door they had chosen for their protection.

When the danger of the air war had passed, Casson was assigned to the Ministry of Town and Country Planning, researching convenient and affordable new housing for the English. Casson studied the advantages of prefabricated homes (homes assembled from sections made in a factory) and published a book on the subject in 1947. *Houses: Permanence and Prefabrication* was not his first venture as an author. Before the war, London Transport had asked him to compile a guide to new buildings in London. They published it with the title *New Sights of London* in 1937.

In addition, Casson wrote so many articles for magazines and newspapers that some people thought of him more as a journalist than an architect. At the end of the war, he was assistant editor of a magazine founded by Robert Harling and edited by John Betjeman. "It was a quite interesting thing because in those days of paper rationing you weren't allowed to start a magazine but you could publish a magazine with hardback and call it a book. So he had a magazine called *Contact* and I was the architecture correspondent and everybody wrote in it," Casson said. He also told the *SATA* interviewer, "Then I worked for a magazine that was the English version of the *New Yorker* called *Night and Day,* which was founded by Graham Greene. This was after peace. Graham Greene was the editor and film critic. That was frightfully smart. Peter Fleming did the 'Londoner's Diary,' Anthony Powell was the literary editor and Elizabeth Bowen was the women's editor and Cyril Connolly wrote for it once a month."

After Nicholson returned from the Navy, he found that the small architectural firm he shared with Casson just barely survived. Building materials were being rationed, and there were very few jobs available. Casson's writing helped him to make it financially during those years. One of the newspapers he wrote for was the *News Chronicle,* edited by Gerald Barry. This contact turned out to be very important, because in 1948 when Barry was asked to oversee the Festival of Britain—an exhibition meant to revive the country's post-war spirits—he called Casson and Nicholson to work on it. "Round about the middle of the war," Casson explained, "somebody had suggested that when the war was over and we'd won it, which there was no doubt about, we ought to have a), a party, and b), an exhibition to prove that England was still on its feet." At first, it was to be an international "party" for all Europe, but other nations were as yet too damaged to participate. "So it was switched to being an English thing," Casson continued. "Then somebody wrote and said, 'Look, 1951 is the centenary of the 1851 exhibition, which was for exactly the same purpose, proving England was on its feet.'" Barry published this letter in the *News Chronicle* and Herbert Morrison—the Minister in charge of the project—authorized Barry to organize it. Casson was appointed to advise Barry on the architectural aspects of the Festival. He was paid one thousand pounds a year from the Festival budget, supplied by a government grant. Nicholson, a champion glider pilot, died tragically in a hangliding accident in the Olympics in Switzerland, so two assistants, Neville Conder and Patience Clifford, watched over the firm while Casson worked on the Festival.

The Festival was launched initially without popular support; everyone was tired and busy trying to rebuild their lives. The Prime Minister Winston Churchill thought the people working on it were trying to promote new political ideas. Others felt that the working class majority in Britain did not need upper-class people such as Barry to tell them how to celebrate the country's well-being. The only groups who seemed enthused about the Festival were people in media and the arts involved in designing, organizing, and building it. "It was really going to be a bonanza for them, with special commissioned operas, commissioned plays, commissioned poetry, commissioned ballet, commissioned buildings, commissioned music." Just as the creative community expected, the Festival brought attention to the work of many artists and a serious explosion of support for the arts in general. "It was genuinely nationwide fun," Casson recalls in *Hugh Casson: Architect Etcetera.* "All over the country the Festival was celebrated in locally organised events of every size and kind, bringing an unprecedented (for Britain) [enthusiasm] in national patronage of the arts—opera, films, painting, poetry, sculpture, and crafts. A lot of people enjoyed themselves and it was all a great success."

Immediately after the Festival was over, the men and women who had worked on it had to find other work. Casson and his wife helped establish Britain's first School of Interior Design at the Royal College of Art. In addition, they practiced professionally, traveled, gave lectures, and wrote for magazines. Finding work as builders was difficult because people thought an architect who had worked on so large and famous a project would not be happy to work on simpler or more modest jobs. Aware of this and grateful for Casson's work on the Festival, the British government offered to keep his firm busy. In 1952, the Casson Conder Partnership won a bid for work on the new faculty buildings at Cambridge University, where they have been employed ever since. They also worked on the street decorations for the Coronation of Elizabeth II and designed opera sets at Covent Garden and Glyndbourne. Most challenging in Casson's view was the work he did on the Royal apartments of Her Majesty's Yacht *Britannia* and the public rooms he furnished for the new P & O flagship *Canberra* being built in Belfast. Success with these projects led to another twenty years of design commissions from the Royal family.

Many of Casson's jobs involved issues of conservation and teamwork. He had discovered, while working on the Festival, a talent—later developed at the Royal Academy—for persuading creative people to work together on combined projects without bloodshed. The Festival had gained him a knighthood and, in 1970, election to the Royal Academy—an association of artists, run by artists, which had been founded in 1768 to display exhibitions and establish both an art school and a charity for the poor—the only academy of its kind in the world. In 1976 he became president of the Royal Academy and helped to make it a financial and professional success.

Meanwhile he continued writing, drawing, and painting, starting to illustrate children's books when the Prince of Wales asked him to illustrate *The Old Man of Lochnagar.* On a trip to Scotland with his younger brothers on the royal yacht, Prince Charles had written a book for them. All proceeds from the sale of *The Old Man of Lachnagar* were to be given to charities in Britain. The book tells the story of an unusual old man who has strange experiences, such as dining with birds who carry him through the air and conversing with a toad. Drawing the characters was a challenge for Casson, who had to invent them from descriptions in the story. "I just made them up as I went," Casson explained. "There was a funny lot of people called Gorms who looked rather like potatoes with legs. There were women Gorms as well, they were mostly sort of aproned housewives stirring saucepans, cheering the king when he was around, doing a general loyal

"Pushkin, is that you?" called his mother. (From *Pushkin the Polar Bear* by Simon Gaul. Illustrated by Hugh Casson.)

crowd effect in the distance. They were quite fun to draw." Since publication in 1980, *The Old Man of Lochnagar* has been translated into many languages. "It was curious that some of the languages that came first were unexpected, like Yiddish and Japanese, as it were, before German and French," the illustrator remarked. Steady sales of the book have raised much money for the Prince's charities.

Casson also illustrated *Buttons* by Linda Yeatman to raise money for Dogs for the Deaf. He explained, "Dogs, we know, are used for the blind, but they are also trained now for the deaf. They hear the telephone bells and tug your sleeve when the telephone goes and you can't hear it. So I did that one. Then I did a little one on the adventures of a little sort of Yorkshire Terrier fluffy thing, her adventures in the Kensington Gardens." That book is called *Zelda and the Corgis,* by Diana Avebury.

Casson also drew the pictures in *Nanny Says,* a book by Avebury and Joyce Grenfell. Casson knew Grenfell from her work on a display in the Festival of Britain in which she matched scenes from British life with witty captions. She wrote the book's introduction. Avebury collected the nanny sayings, proverbs and phrases familiar to many British children of Casson's generation, such as "Manners maketh man," and "You can't have the penny and the bun." This book, too, continues to sell steadily.

"About the same time I was doing these children's books I also did one called *Pushkin and the Polar Bear*," Casson said. "It was the adventure of a polar bear who ran away from home, decided to see what it was like at the other end. He walked across Europe so it was quite a test of my geography. He went to Egypt and he went to Leningrad and he went to Naples. I rather enjoyed doing this." Memories of trips to Russia helped him to recreate the horizontal fields, rows of thin trees, flat rivers, and pale moons of the Russian landscape for the book. Casson and his wife were in Greece when he worked on the drawings for *Pushkin the Polar Bear.* "Every morning at ten 'o clock I'd sit down. Each page has a biggish drawing on it, about ten inches by six in colour. I thought I'd never get it done unless I had some discipline. I think as a reasonably experienced illustrator in other fields I was fairly experienced in composition on the page and that sort of thing." Gaul has written a sequel to the Pushkin book which Casson plans to illustrate.

Casson was especially pleased to illustrate *Summoned by Bells,* a book by his friend John Betjeman the Poet Laureate. Casson was happy for the chance to add what he recalled of childhood to Betjeman's life story in verse, he said. "I wanted to do what I remembered of little boys ambushing you on the way home from school and throwing your cap over the wall and all those awful experiences and the humiliation of your father ordering a cup of tea and a poached egg in a rather grand restaurant when everybody else was having salmon flambe or something. All those experiences are so close to my

"Now, Pushkin, where have you been? Your mother and I have been very worried," said his father. (From *Pushkin the Polar Bear* by Simon Gaul. Illustrated by Hugh Casson.)

own—and haunting second hand bookshops and things." Casson had to visit some of the places Betjeman described in the book in order to draw them. He also needed to find out what kind of clothes the author had worn at home and at school. One of the houses Betjeman had lived in was no longer standing, so Casson had to guess what it looked like from the old houses near it.

The pictures in *Hugh Casson's London* also required him to do extensive research. Writing about a city as large as London seemed to be an unmanageable task, Casson said, "So, I thought the only solution was to talk about the buildings with which I'd had personal experience, either by working in them or living in them or having built them or done something with them. So I went through my life, my childhood when Selfridges was the top experience of my Christmas holidays—rather than the Victoria and Albert Museum, I may say. They were buildings in which I'd really had some personal contact. That made it handleable. It's largely a picture book with long captions, really." *London* was followed by *Hugh Casson's Oxford,* and *Hugh Casson's Cambridge.* Illustrated travel books on Japan and Egypt are planned under joint names of both the Cassons.

Since his retirement from the Royal Academy in 1984, Casson and his wife have spent more time traveling in the United States, and he is able to spend more time in the office. Looking back on his career as artist, architect, writer, and administrator in *Hugh Casson: Architect Etcetera,* he notes that everything he has learned has cost him something, and that various distractions have kept him from devoting himself to any single activity. Even so, he says he feels lucky to have been able for so long to enjoy being involved in more than one profession, and "the pleasures of parallel lives."

WORKS CITED:

Casson, Hugh, and others, *Nanny Says,* Dobson Books, 1972, pp. 22 and 26.
Casson, Hugh, interview with Catharine Courtney for *Something about the Author,* conducted in England in October, 1990.
Casson, Hugh, and others, *Hugh Casson: Architect Etcetera* (exhibition catalogue with author's memoirs), Blueprint Press, 1985.

FOR MORE INFORMATION SEE:

BOOKS

Banham, Mary and Bevis Hiller, editors, *A Tonic to the Nation: The Festival of Britain, 1951,* Thames & Hudson, 1976.
Dictionary of Design and Decoration, London and Glasgow, 1973.

PERIODICALS

Art Magazine, Number 3, 1983.
New York Times, May 3, 1983.
Spectator, May 23, 1981.
Times Literary Supplement, January 6, 1984.

—Sketch by Marilyn K. Basel

* * *

CAZEAU, Charles J(ay) 1931-

PERSONAL: Born June 25, 1931, in Rochester, NY; son of Floyd A. (a musician) and Nan M. (an artist; maiden name Barbehenn) Cazeau; married Janet G. Donovan (a therapist), August 11, 1960 (died, November, 1971); children: Sharon Lee, Suzanne Carroll. *Education:* University of Notre Dame, B.S., 1954; Florida State University, M.S., 1955; attended Virginia Ploytechnic Institute; University of North Carolina at Chapel Hill, Ph.D., 1962.

ADDRESSES: Home and office—8223 East Monte Vista Rd., Scottsdale, AZ 85257.

CAREER: Exxon Corp., Houston and Midland, TX, geologist, 1955-58; Clemson University, Clemson, SC, assistant professor of geology, 1960-63; State University of New York at Buffalo, associate professor of geology, 1963-86; consultant and science writer, 1986—. Member of Scientific Committee for the Investigation of Claims of the Paranormal; adviser and writer for skeptic societies.

WRITINGS:

(With Francis T. Siemankowski) *Physical Geology Laboratory Manual,* Kendall-Hunt, 1971, 3rd edition, 1982.
Earthquakes (juvenile), Follett, 1975.
Physical Geology, Harper, 1975.
Exploring the Unknown: Great Mysteries Reexamined, Plenum Press, 1979.
Science Trivia: From Anteaters to Zeppelins, Plenum Press, 1986.

Also author of column, "Let's Explore," Gannet News Service, 1978—.

SIDELIGHTS: "Writing is a powerful tool both in life and in death," writes Charles J. Cazeau. "In life, skillful writing is a key to worldly success whether you ever collect a royalty check or not. Top business executives have large vocabularies and they use them. Those better able to express themselves in writing are sought after, and they have greater personal satisfaction.

"In death, survival of your words is a legacy greater than a slab of polished granite. Those of us fortunate to have published books can stir the minds of those yet unborn. I came across an old letter for sale in an antique shop. It was dated 1864 and contained a handwritten letter from a woman in Wisconsin. She spoke of commonplace difficulties because the Civil War still raged. For the moments I read the letter and shared her experiences, this woman lived again and I was strangely affected by what she said.

"Note that I referred to this woman by saying, she spoke, she said. . . . Talking is writing put to paper. Everybody talks, so people ought to be able to write. Most people think 'creative'

CHARLES J. CAZEAU

writing is hard work. Sometimes it is. But you don't need to write a novel at one sitting. Get in the habit of writing something everyday, even a few sentences. I keep a deck of blank 5x8 file cards next to my typewriter. Whenever I have an opinion or comment rumbling in my mind, I peck it out on a file card. It might only take a couple minutes. Put a date on each. I am writing this right now on a file card. The tough thing about writing is getting started. If you say you will only set down a few sentences, you usually wind up writing much more. 25 words become 500. There is another thing. In looking back on what you have written, perhaps years ago, you find you are advising yourself, to wit, 'How could I have been so dumb as to really believe that?' In sum, writing aids your own intellectual growth."

* * *

CHEN, Yuan-tsung 1932-

PERSONAL: Born April 15, 1932, in Shanghai, China; came to the United States in 1972; daughter of Shi-cheng (an engineer) and Tung-yin (Chin) Chen; married Jack Chen (an artist and writer), April 26, 1958; children: Jay. *Education:* Empire State College of the State University of New York, B.A., 1975.

ADDRESSES: Office—East Asian Library, University of California, Berkeley, CA 94720.

CAREER: Film Publishing House, Peking, China, translator and editor, 1950-64; Cornell University, Ithaca, NY, instructor of Chinese, 1974-77; Chinese Culture Center of San Francisco, San Francisco, CA, researcher and writer, 1978-79; East Asian Library, University of California, Berkeley, library assistant, 1979—. Coordinator of Chinese Film Retrospective at San Francisco International Film Festival, 1981.

AWARDS, HONORS: New York Public Library Books for the Teen Age citation, 1982, for *The Dragon's Village.*

WRITINGS:

The Dragon's Village (novel), Pantheon, 1980, published in Chinese as *A City Girl Riding an Ox Cart,* Shanghai Literature and Art Publishing House, 1989.
A House of Her Own, Writers Publishing House (Beijing, China), 1989.

WORK IN PROGRESS: A novel about a young girl's pursuit of her literary career in revolutionary China between 1950 and 1957, a sequel to *The Dragon's Village.*

SIDELIGHTS: Yuan-tsung Chen writes, "I am a Chinese, born and raised in mainland China. After working in Peking for about fifteen years as translator and editor in the Film Publishing House, I came to the United States with my husband and son in 1972. Settled in the new country I adopted, I began writing my first novel, *The Dragon's Village,* dealing with the momentous land-reform movement in China. I am now working on my fourth novel (second in English), in which several important happenings which were the prelude to the Cultural Revolution are described. I prefer to write books which tell the individual stories of people caught up in crucial moments of the Chinese revolution, the

Dustjacket from 1980 edition of *The Dragon's Village: An Autobiographical Novel of Revolutionary China.*

land reform and Cultural Revolution, and other political movements which in different ways brought about fundamental transformations in China's economy and society.

"I follow the Chinese literary tradition of presenting the social background and events of the times through individual experiences. For this reason, my writing is different from many books written in the West about China and which have mostly been theoretical, academic studies or reportage. The emotional and spiritual realities of the Chinese people (especially after 1949) are little known in the West. My writing, I hope, helps to fill in this gap by revealing the inner world of its protagonists during those tumultuous, revolutionary times that I experienced."

"I had a lonely childhood. I was often confined to bed by a persistent, low fever that the doctors couldn't cure and that prevented me from attending elementary school. Fortunately, there was a window beside my bed and I could look out and watch the neighborhood children playing in the courtyard, but sometimes I felt so lonely that I started imagining that I was part of their games. The courtyard was small but in my imagination I transformed it into a large, beautiful garden with bushes, trees and flowers, and I invited all the youngsters on our block to enjoy this fairyland with me. This was the first fairytale I told to an audience of one—myself.

"Later on my health improved and my parents sent me to a very good junior high school. My favorite class was composition and I always got good marks for my writing. One day I wrote about my experience traveling by sea between Shanghai and Hong Kong during the Second World War. My teacher thought so highly of this that she asked me to read it to the entire class. It was a rare honor. I was thrilled. I thought to myself that writing was easy, pleasant and—and glamorous. So I wanted to become an author.

"Up to that time I had not given much thought to the form of government or the social system existing in China. Then came 1949. Since then my concept of what a writing career means to me and others has entirely changed. My years of growing up were a time of swift and radical change in every sphere of life. I was a pupil in a girl's high school founded by American Protestant missionaries in Shanghai and almost ready to graduate. The Kuomintang government headed by Chiang Kai-shek was defeated in its last big civil war against the insurgent Communist army and Chiang and his troops fled to the off-shore island of Taiwan. In mainland China, a new government was established by the Communist Party. Even then, many years before the great purge—"the Cultural Revolution"—their intellectual policies were rigid. They proclaimed that the function of art and literature was to propagate the policies of the ruling clique. This autocratic trend intensified and culminated in the so-called Cultural Revolution, when all dissent was ruthlessly crushed. That was not my idea of the role that a writer should play. I had been working as a translator and editor and writing in my spare time. But I had never got a single story published in China. I was frustrated, but the experience of those years was a revelation to me. Why were the diehard dogmatists so afraid of letting writers speak their minds? It was clearly because they well understood the power of writing, that writing can make a difference if a writer lives up to her or his social responsibilities. I believed literature should not only be a matter of self-fulfillment, should not only entertain readers, but should also be a social comment. It could help win a better world for humankind. And throughout the tragic and tumultuous years of the infamous 'Cultural Revolution' I never wavered from that belief.

"In 1971, my husband Jack, a journalist and writer, received invitations to lecture on more than 30 American university campuses, including Stanford, University of California at Berkeley, Illinois, Harvard, Yale, Princeton, Columbia and Cornell.

"When he left for America, I remained in Hong Kong with our small son Jay. I thought it would be easier for me to get published outside mainland China. I was wrong. At that time Chinese language publishers outside China could be basically classified as pro- or anti- the People's Republic and each group held very definite views on writing about China. Well, I am not a pro- or anti-writer. I write what I see and understand as truth, as reality. Reality, in my eyes, is not all rosy nor all dark. So neither group welcomed my writings.

"It was then that I decided to write in English. The switch was and still is difficult and painful. But at first it seemed an easy thing to do. I started learning English when I was about four, and in more than thirty years I had acquired quite a wide vocabulary. When I read, I kept my dictionary by me, but seldom had need of it. I was confident that I would not have much difficulty completing my new novel in English.

"Then gradually it dawned on me that I had been taught to use the English language merely as a tool. I used it to read and to socialize with English speaking people. But when it came to expressing my thoughts and feelings on a deeper level, I always switched to the Chinese language, which was as much a part of me as my limbs. When I was moved by a story or a poem written in English, I thought about it in Chinese terms. In my deepest being I thought in Chinese and I felt in Chinese. The English language, unlike the Chinese language, had never become a wholly integral part of me. It became clear to me that I had to study and to work doubly hard if I wanted to write in English. In writing my first novel in English, I was fortunate to have Jack's help. No matter how many times I re-wrote and revised my manuscript, he would re-edit it again and again for me. I would not have completed *The Dragon's Village* in English without his support.

"I would like to accomplish more, but I write very slowly when I don't write in my mother-tongue. However, I have the satisfaction of knowing that the story I have written is one of a kind, because my experience as a writer is one of a kind. I also have the satisfaction to say that along with my fellow writers in China, I have struggled in my way over the past thirty-some years, and now we have won a greater measure freedom of expression. I am happy to say that at long last in the last two years I have had two novels published in Chinese in China. One is the Chinese version of *The Dragon's Village,* and that was selected as one of the seven best novels in 1989 in the greater Shanghai area. Shanghai is China's equivalent of New York City here. The other one, titled *A House of Her Own,* deals with Chinese immigrants in the USA. It is reviewed as the first Chinese-style psychological novel."

FOR MORE INFORMATION SEE:

PERIODICALS

Los Angeles Times Book Review, June 22, 1980.
New York Times Book Review, May 4, 1980.
Times Literary Supplement, July 3, 1981.

JOHN CIARDI

CIARDI, John (Anthony) 1916-1986
(John Anthony)

PERSONAL: Surname pronounced *Char*-dee; born June 24, 1916, in Boston, MA; died of a heart attack, March 30, 1986, in Edison, NJ; son of Carminantonia (an insurance agent) and Concetta (De Benedictus) Ciardi; married Myra Judith Hostetter, July 28, 1946; children: Myra Judith, John Lyle Pritchett, Benn Anthony. *Education:* Attended Bates College, 1934-36; Tufts College (now University), A.B. (magna cum laude), 1938; University of Michigan, M.A., 1939. *Politics:* Democrat.

ADDRESSES: Home—359 Middlesex Ave., Metuchen, NJ 18840; and 725 Windsor Lane, Key West, FL 33040.

CAREER: Poet and critic. University of Kansas City, Kansas City, MO, instructor in English, 1940-42, 1946; Harvard University, Cambridge, MA, Briggs-Copeland Instructor in English, 1946-48, Briggs-Copeland Assistant Professor of English, 1948-53; Rutgers University, New Brunswick, NJ, lecturer, 1953-54, associate professor, 1954-56, professor of English, 1956-61; *Saturday Review,* New York City, poetry editor, 1956-72. Bread Loaf Writer's Conference, lecturer, beginning 1947, director, 1955-72; lecturer in American poetry, Slazburg Seminar in American Studies, 1951. Editor with Twayne Publishers, 1949; served as judge in Children's Literature Section of National Book Awards, 1969. Host of "Accent," a weekly educational program presented by Columbia Broadcasting System-Television, 1961-62. Has given public poetry readings. *Military service:* U.S. Army Air Forces, 1942-45; served as gunner on B-29 in air offensive against Japan; became technical sergeant; received Air Medal with Oak Leaf Cluster.

MEMBER: American Academy of Arts and Sciences (fellow), National Institute of Arts and Letters (fellow), National College English Association (director, 1955-57; president, 1958-59), Northeast College English Association (past president), Phi Beta Kappa.

AWARDS, HONORS: Avery Hopwood Award for poetry, University of Michigan, 1939; Oscar Blumenthal Prize, 1943; Eunice Tietjens Award, 1945; Levinson Prize, 1946; Golden Rose Trophy of New England Poetry Club, 1948; Fund for the Advancement of Education grant, 1952; Harriet Monroe Memorial Prize, 1955; Prix de Rome, American Academy of Arts and Letters, 1956-57; Litt.D., Tufts University, 1960; Junior Book Award, Boys' Clubs of America, 1962, for *The Man Who Sang the Sillies;* D.Hum., Wayne State University, 1963, and Keane College of New Jersey, 1976; LL.D., Ursinus College, 1964; L.H.D., Kalamazoo College, 1964, Bates College, 1970, Washington University, 1971, and Ohio Wesleyan University, 1971.

WRITINGS:

POETRY

Homeward to America, Holt, 1940.
Other Skies, Atlantic Monthly Press, 1947.
Live Another Day: Poems, Twayne, 1949.
As If: Poems New and Selected, Rutgers University Press, 1955.
I Marry You: A Sheaf of Love Poems, Rutgers University Press, 1958.
Thirty-Nine Poems, Rutgers University Press, 1959.
In the Stoneworks, Rutgers University Press, 1961.
In Fact, Rutgers University Press, 1962.
Person to Person, Rutgers University Press, 1964.
This Strangest Everything, Rutgers University Press, 1966.
An Alphabestiary, Lippincott, 1967.
A Genesis, Touchstone Publishers (New York), 1967.
The Achievement of John Ciardi: A Comprehensive Selection of his Poems with a Critical Introduction (poetry textbook), edited by Miller Williams, Scott, Foresman, 1969.
Lives of X (autobiographical poetry), Rutgers University Press, 1971.
The Little That is All, Rutgers University Press, 1974.
For Instance, Norton, 1979.
Selected Poems, University of Arkansas Press, 1984.
The Birds of Pompeii, University of Arkansas Press, 1985.
Echoes: Poems Left Behind, University of Arkansas Press, 1989.
Poems of Love and Marriage, University of Arkansas Press, 1989.

JUVENILES

The Reason for the Pelican (poetry), Lippincott, 1959.
Scrappy the Pup (poetry), Lippincott, 1960.
The Man Who Sang the Sillies (poetry), Lippincott, 1961.
I Met a Man (poetry), Houghton, 1961.
You Read to Me, I'll Read to You (poetry), Lippincott, 1962.
The Wish-Tree (fiction), Crowell-Collier, 1962.
John J. Plenty and Fiddler Dan: A New Fable of the Grasshopper and the Ant (poetry), Lippincott, 1963.
You Know Who (poetry), Lippincott, 1964.
The King Who Saved Himself from Being Saved (poetry), Lippincott, 1965.
The Monster Den; or, Look What Happened at My House—and to It (poetry), Lippincott, 1966.
Someone Could Win a Polar Bear (poetry), Lippincott, 1970.

Fast and Slow: Poems for Advanced Children and Beginning Parents, Houghton, 1975.
Doodle Soup, Houghton, 1986.

TRANSLATOR

Dante Alighieri, *The Inferno* (poetry), Rutgers University Press, 1954.
Dante, *The Purgatorio* (poetry), New American Library, 1961.
Dante, *The Paradisio* (poetry), New American Library, 1970.
Dante, *The Divine Comedy* (includes *The Inferno, The Purgatorio,* and *The Paradisio*), Norton, 1977.

RECORDINGS

"About Eskimos and Other Poems" (cassette phonotape), Spoken Arts, 1974.
"What Do You Know about Poetry?: An Introduction to Poetry for Children" (cassette phonotape), Spoken Arts, 1974.
"What is a Poem?: A Discussion of How Poems Are Made" (phonodisc), spoken Arts, 1974.
"Why Noah Praised the Whale and Other Poems" (cassette phonotape), Spoken Arts, 1974.

OTHER

(Editor) *Mid-Century American Poets,* Twayne, 1950.
(Author of introduction) Fritz Leiber and others, *Witches Three* (prose), Twayne, 1952.
(Contributor) William White, *John Ciardi: A Bibliography,* Wayne State University Press, 1959.
(Editor and contributor) *How Does a Poem Mean?* (prose), Houghton, 1960, 2nd edition (with Miller Williams), 1975.
Dialogue With an Audience (collection of *Saturday Review* essays), Lippincott, 1963.
(Editor with James M. Reid and Laurence Perrine) *Poetry: A Closer Look* (prose), Harcourt, 1963.
(Contributor) A. L. Bader, editor, *To the Young Writer* (prose), University of Michigan Press, 1965.
(Contributor) *Dante Alighieri: Three Lectures* (prose), Library of Congress, 1965.
(Author of introduction) John A. Holmes, *The Selected Poems,* Beacon Press, 1965.
(With Joseph B. Roberts) *On Poetry and the Poetic Process* (prose), Troy State University Press, 1971.
Manner of Speaking (selected *Saturday Review* columns), Rutgers University Press, 1972.
(With Isaac Asimov) *Limericks, Too Gross,* Norton, 1978.
A Browser's Dictionary and Native's Guide to the Unknown American Language, Harper, 1980.
(With Laurence Urdang and Frederick Dickerson) *Plain English in a Complex Society,* Poynter Center, Indiana University, 1980.
(With Asimov) *A Grossery of Limericks,* Norton, 1981.
A Second Browser's Dictionary and Native's Guide to the Unknown American Language, Harper, 1987.
The Complete Browser's Dictionary: The Best of John Ciardi's Two Browser's Dictionaries in a Single Compendium of Curious Expressions and Intriguing Facts, Harper, 1988.
Saipan: The War Diary of John Ciardi, University of Arkansas Press, 1988.
The Hopeful Trout and Other Limericks, Houghton, 1989.
Ciardi Himself, University of Michigan Press, 1989.

Also contributor of short story, under name John Anthony, to science fiction anthology *A Decade of Fantasy and Science Fiction: Out of This World Masterworks by Masterminds of the Near and Far Out.* Contributor of articles and essays to

HOW TO TELL A TIGER

People who know tigers
    Very very well
All agree that tigers
    Are not hard to tell.

The way to tell a tiger is
    With lots of room to spare.
Don't try telling them up close
    Or we may not find you there.

(From *You Read to Me, I'll Read to You,* by John Ciardi. Illustrations by Edward Gorey.)

periodicals. Contributing editor, *Saturday Review,* 1955-80, and *World Magazine,* 1970-72.

WORK IN PROGRESS: Additional volumes of *A Browser's Dictionary;* a book of juvenile poems; a book of "senile" poems.

SIDELIGHTS: From the time he was a small boy, the late poet John Ciardi loved words and books. "For some reason—I don't know why, because nobody in the family turned that way—I fell deeply into books and lived a lot of my life in books," the author told Linda Brandi Cateura in an interview for *Growing Up Italian.* Ciardi was a well-respected teacher and translator of classical poetry, including the works of Dante. A prolific poet in his own right, Ciardi was praised for his artful use of words and images. Perhaps his most enduring legacy, however, is the body of poetry he wrote for children. In collections such as *I Met a Man* and *The Reason for the Pelican,* Ciardi delighted generations of young readers with his funny rhymes and amusing characterizations.

Ciardi was born to Italian immigrants in Boston's North End, an area still referred to as "Little Italy." "I was born the fourth child and only male," Ciardi recalled in *Contemporary Authors Autobiography Series.* "I was born, that is to say, over-advertised, but these were the terms of the billing, as they were the terms of my ordination to stellar brathood."

When Ciardi was three years old, his life was abruptly changed by the death of his father in an automobile accident. "When my father died, my mother, who was a sort of hysterical woman, heroically so, decided I was his reincarnation and *I became my father,*" Ciardi noted in *Growing Up Italian.* "I was the man of the family; my [sisters] were just girls. I was the only son of an Italian family, and that meant I got what I wanted *at their expense.* No one questioned this. I was an insufferable brat, but I had been trained to be."

Ciardi's new responsibility in the family changed his relationship with his mother Concetta, a hard-working woman who spoke little English. In addition to being a favored Italian son, Ciardi became his mother's somewhat unwilling link to a language and culture she did not understand. In *Growing Up Italian,* Ciardi elaborated on their relationship: "My mother couldn't read. If I read something to her out of the paper, she had trouble recognizing it. I was terribly divided in this way because I loved my mother dearly. She would give me advice, for example, on how to behave outside the house, and it was loving advice, and I accepted it as such. But it was just dead wrong. She didn't know what she was telling me. So I learned to lie. I learned to be deceitful from the start and do what I had to do in order to get along. . . . From the start, I knew there was one culture at home and another in the world outside."

As he grew older, Ciardi discovered that there were some advantages to being part of two cultures. Ciardi noted in *Growing Up Italian* that "this separation is good. It sensitizes you to things outside, you see. When my friends did certain things my family did not do, I recognized that difference and noted it." Ciardi added that this sensitivity extended to his bilingual upbringing: "I have always felt that when you have a second language, you have three things: the first language, the second language, and the difference between them. That occupied some of my attention; I was fascinated by that."

Always a good student, Ciardi read voraciously. "Books were as important as what was going on around me," he related in his *Growing Up Italian* interview. "At first, I had no discretion at all about them—I read Frank Merriwell, Dick Merriwell, the Rover Boys, Horatio Alger, *Gulliver's Travels,* Hargrave's *Golden Treasury.*" Ciardi also found time to be an active boy scout and to hold numerous part-time jobs. He remained in high school an extra year because there was no money for college. After saving as much money as he could from odd jobs, Ciardi was directed by his high school teachers to attend Bates College. Ciardi immediately discovered that Bates College was not the right place for him. In his essay for *Contemporary Authors Autobiographical Series,* Ciardi wrote that "Bates is a good small school and more liberal now. It was then heavily Baptist and relentlessly concerned with my character. I had my own doubts about it, but I had dug ditches and saved my money in hope of acquiring useful information." After three semesters, Ciardi left Bates and moved back home to attend Tufts University.

Have You Met This Man?

Have you met this man? He has no head.
He has no house, but he stays in bed.
He is not too small, he is not too big.
He has no arms, but he knows how to dig.
He cannot swim, yet he goes to sea
Without a boat. Who can he be?

If he knew how, he would say, "I am
No other, sir, than MR. CLAM."

(From *I Met a Man* by John Ciardi. Illustration by Robert Osborn.)

It Makes No Difference to Me

I climbed a mountain three feet high
And banged my head against the sky.

"Watch out!" my sister's brother said.
"You climb that high, you'll lose your head!"

I didn't care. Mine is no use
To anyone. What's your excuse?

(From *Doodle Soup: Poems by John Ciardi,* by John Ciardi. Illustration by Merle Nacht.)

While at Tufts, Ciardi signed up for a writing class taught by John Holmes. Ciardi discovered Holmes to be patient, helpful, and inspiring. Ciardi recalled his first day in class for *Contemporary Authors Autobiographical Series:* "Almost at once, I knew what I was going to do with the rest of my life! I had no idea what I would do for food and shelter, but I was young, toughened to hard labor, and ready to go for broke. Somehow, I would earn enough to eat on and to give to my mother the little she needed, but what I would live for was poetry!" Ciardi came to look upon Holmes as both a mentor and father figure. Under Holmes's guidance, Ciardi refined his poetry skills by writing and re-writing countless poems. The effort paid off when Holmes arranged for Ciardi to attend graduate school at the University of Michigan.

A number of good things happened to Ciardi at Michigan. He got a scholarship to help with expenses, met his second mentor, Roy W. Cowden, and won the prestigious Avery Hopwood Award for poetry. Winning the award gave Ciardi both recognition and some much-needed financial freedom. "There I sat, a Master of Arts, holding a check for one thousand 1939 dollars!" Ciardi stated in *Contemporary Authors Autobiography Series.* "It was the largest piece of money I had ever held in my hand! Lucky John was rich! And more doors opened." Ciardi was able to pay off some debts, give his mother some money, and travel around the country. He also sold a poem to *Poetry* magazine, and a revised version of his Hopwood manuscript was accepted as a book by Henry Holt publishing. By 1940, Ciardi was offered a guest lectureship at the University of Kansas City at a salary of nine hundred dollars per semester.

Ciardi taught in Kansas City until 1942. As World War II escalated, Ciardi feared he would be drafted into the infantry, so he signed up for the aviation cadets. After much training, Ciardi became an aerial navigator and was offered a promotion to officer. Unfortunately, a routine security check was run on every service person before he or she was made an officer. Ciardi's security check revealed that he had signed some political petitions while he was a University of Michigan graduate student. These papers were found in the files of a special committee of the United States House of Representatives called the Dies Committee. Its purpose was to investigate actions of United States citizens who might threaten America's security. After reviewing Ciardi's file, the Army Air Forces demoted Ciardi to private and refused him permission to fly any combat missions.

Ciardi eventually became a B-29 gunner and flew many noncombat missions. Once his superiors learned of his writing skills, Ciardi was removed from his crew and given the job of handling military awards. He also wrote letters of condolence to next of kin whose loved ones died while in service. After the war, he returned to teaching in Kansas City and later accepted a position at Harvard.

In 1946, Ciardi married Judith Hostetter. Of his marriage, Ciardi told *Contemporary Authors New Revision Series* that he "did not marry until the age of thirty, which gave me some time to think about things. It has been a happy marriage. I chose with blessed fortune." About this same time, Ciardi began receiving a great deal of positive response to his poetry. The *New Yorker* began buying his poems almost as fast as he could write them, and in 1947 his collection entitled *Other Skies* was published by the Atlantic Monthly Press and Little, Brown.

Between writing, lecturing, and teaching, Ciardi also translated Dante, directed the Bread Loaf Writers' Conference, and acted as poetry editor for *Saturday Review.* Ciardi became interested in writing poetry for children while living with his sister and her family in the 1950s. He wrote a number of poems for his nieces and nephews, most of which eventually ended up in a neglected folder. An editor friend encouraged Ciardi to submit the folder of poems to a publisher. The immediate result was two volumes of poetry for children: *The Reason for the Pelican* (1959) and *Scrappy the Pup* (1960). Noted for their witty verse and catchy rhymes, both volumes were a success.

Ciardi claimed that a lot of his motivation for writing juvenile poetry came from his three children. "Their presence was all the motive there was for the poems," he once told *Something about the Author* (*SATA*). Ciardi's daughter Myra was the inspiration for one of his most popular books, *I Met a Man.* Houghton Mifflin had asked Ciardi to try a book based on a first grade reading vocabulary. Ciardi told *SATA* that he "knew nothing about school vocabularies but my daughter was then in kindergarten, and once I was supplied with the word list I found myself eager to write the first book she would read all the way through. . . . My reward was that my daughter not only had fun but learned to read in the course of playing with *I Met a Man.*"

Ciardi's goal was to write poetry that was natural and realistic to children. "I didn't see any way of getting my children sugar-coated," he wrote in *Ciardi Himself.* He explained: "It seems the language of childhood, the imagination of childhood, is naturally violent. . . . Children have a firm sense of the difference between real and pretend. When they lose this difference, they are sick. . . . Any healthy child knows the difference between real and pretend violence."

In his books such as *You Read to Me, I'll Read to You* (1962), and *The Hopeful Trout and Other Limericks* (1989), Ciardi explored both the light and dark aspects of childhood. When writing a book for children, he found it helpful to get input from his young readers. Ciardi noted in *Ciardi Himself* that he often visited grade schools, where he discovered "that one of the most joyous and natural and perfect audiences for poetry in this world is a class of bright third graders. Nothing matches it. Everything is immediate, real, alive, without inhibitions, all out-flowing identification and joy." On a more negative note, Ciardi disappointedly observed that somewhere between third grade and high school, many children lost their love for poetry. "I find myself wanting to ask some questions about it," he wrote in *Ciardi Himself.* "Why is it that every American child delivered to the school system starts as a natural audience for poetry and almost every child who leaves hates the stuff?"

Readers and critics have often wondered if Ciardi's books for young readers are based upon his own childhood experiences or memories. Ciardi maintained that he did not draw much on his own childhood as the basis for his poems. Writing in the "Manner of Speaking" column for *Saturday Review,* Ciardi summed up the impact of his juvenile poetry by writing that "whether the poems were good or bad, they were meant for fun. They were meant for the dance and joy of healthy children. Much of my own pleasure in writing children's poems has been in having my pleasure shared by children, individually, in groups, and many times in classrooms."

WORKS CITED:

Cateura, Linda Brandi, editor, *Growing Up Italian,* Morrow, 1987.
Ciardi, John, *Ciardi Himself,* University of Michigan Press, 1989.
Contemporary Authors Autobiography Series, Volume 2, Gale, 1985.
Contemporary Authors New Revisions Series, Volume 5, Gale, 1982.

FOR MORE INFORMATION SEE:

BOOKS

Ciardi, John, *Lives of X,* Rutgers University Press, 1971.
Contemporary Literary Criticism, Gale, Volume 10, 1979, Volume 40, 1986, Volume 44, 1987.
Dictionary of Literary Biography, Volume 5: *American Poets since World War II,* Gale, 1980.
Dictionary of Literary Biography Yearbook: 1986, Gale, 1987.
Hopkins, Lee Bennett, *Books Are by People,* Citation Press, 1969.
John Ciardi, Twayne, 1980.
Something about the Author, Gale, Volume 1, 1971, Volume 46, 1987.
White, William, *John Ciardi: A Bibliography,* Wayne State University Press, 1959.

PERIODICALS

America, July 27, 1957.
Book Week, September 29, 1963; November 1, 1964; November 8, 1970; September 24, 1972; September 28, 1980.
Booklist, December 1, 1972; February 1, 1975; October 15, 1979; July 15, 1980.
Chicago Review, autumn-winter, 1956; summer, 1957.
Chicago Tribune, December 16, 1979; September 8, 1980.
Christian Science Monitor, December 24, 1964; May 7, 1975; October 23, 1978; January 2, 1980.
Contemporary Literature, winter, 1968.
Detroit Free Press, February 28, 1964.
Nation, September 13, 1958.
New York Times Book Review, April 16, 1950; July 4, 1954; August 3, 1958; November 11, 1962; May 12, 1963; November 10, 1963; October 4, 1964; November 1, 1964; November 8, 1970; May 4, 1975; November 16, 1975; August 17, 1980.
Poetry, September, 1940; May, 1948; July, 1956; October, 1958; December, 1962; July, 1963; December, 1967; July, 1975.
Saturday Review, January 28, 1956; November 10, 1962; March 23, 1963; December 14, 1963; June 3, 1967; February 6, 1971; May 22, 1971; November 27, 1971; May 31, 1975.
Time, February 18, 1957; February 26, 1979.
Wall Street Journal, May 28, 1971.
Writer, March, 1964; August, 1976; June, 1980.
Yale Review, March, 1956.

OBITUARIES

Chicago Tribune, April 3, 1986.
Detroit News, April 2, 1986.
Milwaukee Sentinel, April 1, 1986.
Newsweek, April 14, 1986.
New York Times, April 2, 1986.
Time, April 14, 1986.
Washington Post, April 2, 1986.

* * *

CLARK, Joan
See BENSON, Mildred (Augustine Wirt)

* * *

CONROY, Jack
See CONROY, John Wesley

* * *

CONROY, John Wesley 1899-1990
(Jack Conroy; pseudonyms: Tim Brennan, Hoder Morine, John Norcross)

OBITUARY NOTICE—See index for *SATA* sketch: Born December 5, 1899, near Moberly, MO; died February 28, 1990, in Moberly, MO. Educator, editor, and author. Jack Conroy was a working-class writer who occasionally taught writing and folklore. During the Depression he published his semi-autobiographical novel *The Disinherited* and edited periodicals such as *Rebel Poet* and *Anvil.* Among his other books are *A World to Win, They Seek a City: A Study of Negro Migration,* and—with Arna Bontemps—the juvenile volumes *Fast Sooner Hound* and *Sam Patch, the High, Wide,* *and Handsome Jumper.* Conroy also wrote under the pseudonyms Tim Brennan, Hoder Morine, and John Norcross.

OBITUARIES AND OTHER SOURCES:

PERIODICALS

Chicago Tribune, March 2, 1990.
New York Times, March 2, 1990.

* * *

COOPER, Henry S. F., Jr.
See COOPER, Henry Spotswood Fenimore, Jr.

* * *

COOPER, Henry Spotswood Fenimore, Jr.
1933-
(Henry S. F. Cooper, Jr.)

PERSONAL: Born November 24, 1933, in New York, NY; son of Henry S. F. (a physician) and Katherine G. F. Cooper: married Mary Luke Langben, October 13, 1966: children: Elizabeth, Hannah, Mary. *Education:* Yale University, B.A., 1956.

ADDRESSES: Home—1165 Fifth Ave., New York, NY 10029. *Office*— *New Yorker,* 25 West 43rd St., New York, NY 10036. *Agent*— Robert Lescher, 155 East 71st St. New York, NY 10021.

CAREER: New Yorker, New York City, staff writer, 1958—. Wrexham Foundation, trustee, 1957—, chairman, 1965-68, 1974-77. New York Society Library, trustee, 1972—, chairman, 1984—. Trustee, Yale University Art Gallery, 1970—, Yale Library Associates, 1976—, and Glimmerglass Opera Company. Judge of National Book Awards, 1972. *Military service:* U.S. Army, 1956-58.

MEMBER: Authors Guild of Authors League of America, American Association for the Advancement of Science, Municipal Art Society (member of New York City board of directors, 1965-68), Century Association (member of board of trustees, 1973-76, 1984-87), Grolier Society, Coffee House.

AWARDS, HONORS: Guggenheim fellowship, 1975; science writing award from American Association for the Advancement of Science, 1977, for article "Life in a Space Station."

WRITINGS:

Apollo on the Moon, Dial, 1969.
Moon Rocks, Dial, 1970.
Thirteen: The Flight That Failed, Dial, 1973.
A House in Space, Holt, 1976.
The Search for Life on Mars: Evolution of an Idea, Holt, 1979.
Imaging Saturn: The Voyager Flights to Saturn, Holt, 1983.
Before Lift-Off: The Making of a Space Shuttle Crew, Johns Hopkins, 1987.

WORK IN PROGRESS: The Soviet Space Program.

SIDELIGHTS: Henry Spotswood Fenimore Cooper, Jr., once wrote *SATA:* "Having no academic background in the sciences myself, I proceed on the assumption that there is no basic division between the sciences and the humanities, and accordingly I try to treat science (in particular space science) as though it were simply another branch of human thought like poetry or art."

*   *   *

CRAFT, K. Y.
See CRAFT, Kinuko Y(amabe)

*   *   *

CRAFT, Kinuko
See CRAFT, Kinuko Y(amabe)

*   *   *

CRAFT, Kinuko Y(amabe) 1940-
(K. Y. Craft, Kinuko Craft)

PERSONAL: Born January 3 (one source says January 1), 1940, in Kanemaru, Ishikawa, Japan; daughter of Naoyoshi (in business) and Sugi Morita Yamabe; married Mahlon Frederick Craft (a book designer), March 21, 1965; children: Marie Charlotte. *Education:* Kanazawa Municipal College of Fine and Industrial Arts, B.F.A., 1962; attended the School of the Art Institute of Chicago, 1964-65.

ADDRESSES: Home—83 Litchfield Rd., Norfolk, CT 06058.

KINUKO Y. CRAFT

CAREER: Handelan Pederson, Inc. Chicago, IL, illustrator, 1966-67; Stephens, Biondi, DiCicco, Inc., Chicago, illustrator, 1967-69; free-lance illustrator, 1969—. *Exhibitions:* Columbia College, Chicago, IL, 1981; solo show at Society of Illustrators, New York, NY, 1983; Norfolk Public Library, 1985.

MEMBER: Society of Illustrators, American Portrait Society.

AWARDS, HONORS: Gold medal in advertising category and Hamilton King Award, both from Society of Illustrators 29 Annual Show, both 1987, for portrait of Queen Elizabeth of England commissioned by International Telephone and Telegraph; silver medal from Society of Illustrators, 1990, for portrait of Manon Lescault commissioned by an opera company in Washington, D.C.; merit awards from numerous organizations, including Illustration Chicago, *Communni Graphics, Communication Art,* Society of Publication Designers, Communicating with Children, Art Directors Club, and Art Annual.

ILLUSTRATOR:

Beverly Reingold, editor, *Classics—A Child's Introduction to Treasure Island, Black Beauty, Adventures of Tom Sawyer, and Robin Hood,* Putnam, 1977.
Margaret Hillert, *What Is It?,* Modern Curriculum, 1978.
Margaret Hillert, *Come Play with Me,* Modern Curriculum, 1978.
Paula Z. Hogan, *The Elephant,* Raintree, 1979.
Jacob Grimm and Wilhelm K. Grimm, *The Wolf and the Seven Kids,* Troll, 1979.
Corinne Denan, *Tales of the Ugly Ogres,* Troll, 1980.
(Under name Kinuko Craft) Robert Louis Stevenson, *Treasure Island,* adapted by Jane Edwards, Raintree, 1980.
(Under name Kinuko Craft) Anne Lindbergh, *Bailey's Window,* Harcourt, 1984.
(Under name Kinuko Craft) Joan Knight, *Journey to Japan,* Viking, 1986.
(Under name K. Y. Craft) Jacob Grimm and Wilhelm K. Grimm, *The Twelve Dancing Princesses,* retold by Marianna Mayer, Morrow, 1989.

WORK IN PROGRESS: Another book with Marianna Mayer, *Baba Yaga and Vasilisa the Brave,* publication by Morrow expected in 1992.

SIDELIGHTS: Kinuko Y. Craft is a well-known commercial artist and book illustrator. A native of Japan, Craft moved to the United States in 1964. Since then she has won many awards for illustrating magazine covers, magazine editorials, book jackets, and company advertisements. Recently, she has also earned praise for her work with children's books. She says she enjoys her art because she likes to escape into the world of fantasy. "I like dramatic things, not realistic stories," she noted in an interview with *Something about the Author (SATA).*

Craft's interest in stories and painting goes back to her early childhood in Kanemaru, a small village in Japan. Her grandfather owned a large collection of art books, and as a child Craft liked to look at the paintings in those books and make up stories about them. She also enjoyed creating her own pictures. She drew scenes based on her life and on the forests around her village. Sometimes, however, her family didn't approve of her artistic efforts. Once, when she was three years old, she drew a picture on the wall of her grandparents' house. The next day, her crayons disappeared. "My grandparents actually hid my crayons," she recalled with amusement.

Despite such incidents, Craft's family eventually supported her desire to become a professional artist. After graduating from an arts college in Japan, she thought about getting a job. But she didn't. "I wasn't ready to go into the real world. I still needed more time to waste or to look around." So she traveled to the United States in 1964 and enrolled in the School of the Art Institute of Chicago. For the next two years, she studied commercial design and explored the art institute's vast collection of famous paintings. Her time at the design school was an "incredible and interesting experience," she told *SATA*.

After leaving the school, Craft found work as a commercial artist. Since then, she has illustrated for magazines such as *Newsweek, Time,* and *National Geographic,* and for companies like Heinz and RCA. She has also designed jackets for books by many famous authors, including Stephen King, Isaac Asimov, and Isabel Allende, and she has illustrated children's books. She told *SATA* that she is becoming more interested in doing illustration for children's stories rather than commercial work because the stories offer her new challenges and opportunities. In addition, she stated that working on children's books lets her forget about the ugly, serious side of life, "like what's going on in the city, drug busts, and the cop and robber kind of thing. In pictures, I can escape from all of those troubles."

This desire to escape from reality is evident in Craft's illustrations. In Anne Lindbergh's *Bailey's Window,* for instance, Craft depicts a magic universe discovered by four children. One of the children, Bailey, draws a window on the wall in his aunt's house. He soon learns that the window is actually an opening to a new world. If Bailey paints a picture of a palm tree on the window, for instance, he finds himself on a tropical island. By changing the picture, Bailey can change his surroundings. He invites his friends into his new discovery, and together they explore an exciting land that includes "a blue elephant in a strawberry patch" and "a giant penguin who asks passersby for a dance," commented a *Publishers Weekly* critic. Craft highlights these events with a handful of detailed, realistic drawings. The *Publishers Weekly* reviewer called *Bailey's Window* a "spellbinding adventure" and added that "Craft's expert drawings are tuned in to the delightful doings."

For Marianna Mayer's *The Twelve Dancing Princesses,* Craft created a much different world. Instead of illustrating the book with drawings, Craft used full-color paintings. The story, based on an old fairy tale, is about twelve princesses who are under a strange spell. Each night they are locked in their bedchamber, but they don't sleep. Instead, they are drawn into a magic kingdom where they spend the night dancing. As a result of the dancing, they are exhausted the next morning. A common gardener, Peter, eventually solves the mystery and breaks the spell. He also falls in love with one of the princesses, Elise, and they have a beautiful wedding.

Craft's glowing illustrations for the book create a "luminous, romantic landscape," noted John Cech of the *Washington Post Book World.* There are forests of gold and diamonds, and gardens filled with flowers of red, orange, yellow, and blue. The flowing gowns of the princesses are lined with lace, ribbons, and jewels. Craft says that illustrating the book was

difficult and time-consuming. As she told *SATA,* it was a problem to squeeze in "twelve people all the time." The effort was worthwhile, though, since critics praised her work. "Craft's richly hued illustrations create a magical setting," wrote a *Publishers Weekly* reviewer. That same critic called *The Twelve Dancing Princesses* "a lavish feast for the eyes and the imagination."

The other books that Craft has illustrated include *Treasure Island,* adapted by Jane Edwards; *The Elephant,* by Paula Z. Hogan; *The Wolf and the Seven Kids,* by the famous German brothers Jacob and Wilhelm Grimm; and Corinne Denan's *Tales of the Ugly Ogres.* No matter what story she works on, Craft generally creates illustrations by mixing various painting techniques. She usually starts by using watercolor, which is a combination of paint and water. She uses watercolor because it dries so quickly. "I can even use the hair dryer to dry it," she told *SATA.* After that, she finishes the painting by using oil paint. This type of paint is not mixed with water and takes longer to dry, but it produces rich, full color. The combination of watercolor and oil paint gives Craft the quality she wants without taking too much time. "I like oil painting because of the sensitivity, but in most cases I just don't have the time to start in oil and finish in oil. If I have a wall painting and I have the luxury of working for six months or more, then I will start with oil color."

Whatever method she uses, Craft says she enjoys illustrating children's books and wants to do more of them. "I think my mind always stays in a juvenile state," she noted in the interview with *SATA.* "It's not something to do with trying to please young people. I think I try to please young minds of any age."

WORKS CITED:

A review of *Bailey's Window, Publishers Weekly,* April 27, 1984, p. 87.
Cech, John, "Pretty as a Picture," *Washington Post Book World,* May 14, 1989, pp. 15, 23.
Craft, Kinuko Y., interview with Marc Caplan for *Something about the Author,* May 5, 1990.
A review of *The Twelve Dancing Princesses, Publishers Weekly,* February 10, 1989, p. 68.

FOR MORE INFORMATION SEE:

BOOKS

Contemporary Graphic Artists, Volume 1, Gale, 1986.

*   *   *

CRAIG, M. F.
See CRAIG, Mary (Francis) Shura

*   *   *

CRAIG, M. S.
See CRAIG, Mary (Francis) Shura

*   *   *

CRAIG, Mary
See CRAIG, Mary (Francis) Shura

CRAIG, Mary S.
See CRAIG, Mary (Francis) Shura

* * *

CRAIG, Mary (Francis) Shura 1923-1991
(M. F. Craig, M. S. Craig, Mary Craig, Mary S. Craig, Mary Francis Shura; Alexis Hill, Meredith Hill, pseudonyms)

OBITUARY NOTICE—See index for *SATA* sketch: Born February 27, 1923, in Pratt, KS; died of injuries suffered in a fire, January 12, 1991, in Maywood, IL. Educator and author. Writing under a variety of pseudonyms, Craig published approximately seventy books for adults and children. Several of her children's novels were included on lists of best books, and one, *The Search for Grissi,* won the Carl Sandburg Award. Craig's first novel, *Simple Spigott,* appeared in 1960; another novel, *Gentle Annie: The True Story of a Civil War Nurse,* was scheduled to be published in 1991. Her other books include *The Third Blonde* and *Flash Point,* both for adults, and *Chester,* for children. Craig also worked as a lecturer and creative writing instructor and held administrative posts with the Mystery Writers of America.

OBITUARIES AND OTHER SOURCES:

PERIODICALS

Detroit Free Press, January 16, 1991.
Los Angeles Times, January 18, 1991.
New York Times, January 15, 1991.
School Library Journal, March, 1991.
Washington Post, January 16, 1991.

* * *

CROWLEY, John 1942-

PERSONAL: Born December 1, 1942, in Presque Isle, ME; son of Joseph B. (a doctor) and Patience (Lyon) Crowley. *Education:* Indiana University, B.A., 1964.

ADDRESSES: Home—Box 395, Conway, MA 01341.

CAREER: Photographer and commercial artist, 1964-66; free-lance writer, 1966—.

AWARDS, HONORS: American Book Award nomination, 1979, for *Engine Summer;* World Fantasy Award, 1982, for *Little, Big;* American Film Festival Award, 1982, for *America Lost and Found.*

WRITINGS:

SCIENCE FICTION

The Deep (novel), Doubleday, 1975.
Beasts (novel), Doubleday, 1976.
Engine Summer (novel), Doubleday, 1979.
Little, Big (novel), Bantam, 1981.
Aegypt (novel), Bantam, 1987.
Novelty (short stories), Bantam, 1989.

TELEVISION SCRIPTS

America Lost and Found, Public Broadcasting System, 1982.
No Place to Hide, Public Broadcasting System.

JOHN CROWLEY

OTHER

Contributor to the anthologies *Shadows,* Doubleday, 1977, and *Elsewhere,* Ace Books, 1981, and to *Omni.*

SIDELIGHTS: When he was a boy, John Crowley wanted to be a poet. His early efforts were quatrains written in grade school; by the time he was in college, Crowley seriously considered becoming a poet but abandoned the idea. "I had no calling," he is quoted as saying in the *Dictionary of Literary Biography.* "I really believe that you need a vocation to be a poet just as you do to be a priest. I was a fair versifier, but there's a big difference between poetry and verse. You can learn to be a versifier, you can't learn to be a poet."

After leaving college, Crowley worked as an assistant to a New York fashion photographer, wrote documentary films, and worked as a proofreader with the telephone company. His longtime desire to be a writer led him in the early 1970s to try his hand at a novel. Based on a manuscript he had first written in 1963, and which had never been accepted, the novel became *The Deep,* a science fiction story mixing the historical War of the Roses with an outer space setting. Crowley admits in the *Dictionary of Literary Biography* that he was led to writing science fiction because "I could write the sort of book I wanted and still get published. In science fiction, as long as everything takes place on another planet or in the future you can write what you like."

Crowley's second science fiction novel, *Beasts,* tells of a future in which mutated half-human/half-animal creatures work to rebuild America after the central government has collapsed. Inspired by traditional animal fables, Crowley's lion-men and fox-men resemble such medieval characters as Reynard the fox and Nobel the lion. A bitter struggle develops between rival factions; some want a rational, highly bureaucratized government which keeps firm control over society; others want a looser, more libertarian system. The struggle becomes one between those who live close to nature and those who wish to master it. In depicting this conflict, Crowley does not disguise the often violent side of nature, even as he depicts the wisdom of a harmonious relationship with nature. Sonya Dorman of *Analog Science Fiction/ Science Fact* declares that Crowley "is a strong, skillful writer who uses his wilderness lore and knowledge of birds . . . to point out healthy future possibilities for a ravaged planet."

With the publication of *Engine Summer* in 1979, Crowley won widespread attention for his work, garnering an American Book Award nomination. Again set in a future America, this time an America wrecked by war, the novel is structured as an interview with a young man, Rush That Speaks, who is obsessed with becoming a saint. As he narrates the story of his life, he provides a panoramic overview of his world. Rush That Speaks also reveals much about our own society, the scientific age his own world refers to as "the time of the angels." In this way, Crowley comments on what he sees as the destructive over-rational thinking of our time. John Clute of the *Magazine of Fantasy and Science Fiction* calls *Engine Summer* "one of the best novels yet to come out of the sf genre."

Crowley won the World Fantasy Award for *Little, Big,* a novel telling the story of five generations of the Drinkwater family, led by the outlandish John Drinkwater. The Drinkwaters have close friends among the fairyfolk who live in the woods near the ancestral home. In fact, the family's home is a crossover point between the world of Fairie and the world of men. The family even embodies this crossover as its children prove to be reincarnations of the Greek Fates and the legendary hero Barbarossa. Mixing together elements from fairy tales, fables, and science fiction, the novel is written in a complex and modernist style and spans a century of time. Speaking of the book's complexity, Crowley explained in the *Dictionary of Literary Biography* that *Little, Big* is "a tale within a tale, a series of paradoxes that, like Chinese boxes, are nested within one another." Critics praised the novel. Douglas Barbour in the *Science Fiction and Fantasy Book Review* calls *Little, Big* "a successful, richly populated novel." John Clute in the *Washington Post Book World* describes the novel as a "dense, marvelous, magic-realist family chronicle."

With *Aegypt,* published in 1987, Crowley began a story he plans to complete in a total of four novels. *Aegypt* has a circular structure in which the book being read is also the book the story's protagonist, Pierce Moffet, a Renaissance scholar, is writing. Moffet's book is to be about the meaning of the world, using ancient Egyptian mysticism as his inspiration. His research for the book leads him to Rosie Mucho, who helps him discover the last, unpublished book of famous historical novelist Fellowes Kraft. Kraft's book, concerned with ancient Egyptian mystical ideas, is also entitled *Aegypt.*

Some critics note that because the novel is self-referential, some readers will likely find it difficult. But they also note *Aegypt*'s many qualities. "Crowley writes most excellently, with extreme gifts of sensibility and description and characterization," Tom Easton notes in *Analog: Science Fiction/ Science Fact.* "But *Aegypt* may be the least finished book of the year. That is, people will buy it. They will recognize its quality and the interestingness of what Crowley has to say and the way he chooses to say it. But they will turn aside to other books and movies and parties of less intellectual interest and more excitement." "Beginning *Aegypt* is not half

the battle; it is very nearly the whole war," Clute claims in the *New York Times Book Review.* He goes on to call the book "a dizzying experience, achieved with unerring security of technique, in a prose of serene and smiling *gravitas.* . . . It will be of great interest to learn if he can reach a welcoming public with this daunting anomaly of a book, this gaping gateway that leaves us staring into a deeply strange world."

Called "a master of lyrical fantasy" by Michael Dirda of the *Washington Post Book World,* Crowley is a private person who seldom grants interviews. He explains: "Since I am a novelist, my opinions on other subjects are (or should be) without interest. My life (as that of most writers) is uneventful and sedentary. A distillation of its important occasions will be found (disguised or reinvented) in my . . . books."

FOR MORE INFORMATION SEE:

BOOKS

Contemporary Literary Criticism, Volume 57, Gale, 1990.
Dictionary of Literary Biography Yearbook 1982, Gale, 1983.

PERIODICALS

Analog: Science Fiction/Science Fact, June, 1977, August, 1987.
Berkshire Sampler, September 13, 1981.
Extrapolation, spring, 1990.
Magazine of Fantasy and Science Fiction, April, 1980.
New York Times Book Review, November 21, 1976, May 3, 1987.
Science Fiction and Fantasy Book Review, January-February, 1982.
Washington Post Book World, October 4, 1981, April 19, 1987.

*   *   *

CUMMING, Robert 1945-

PERSONAL: Born May 31, 1945, in Yorkshire, England; son of Alexander Ian (in business) and Beryl Mary (maiden name, Stevenson) Cumming; married Carolyn Alison Jenkins (a modern picture appraiser), June 7, 1975. *Education:* Trinity Hall, Cambridge, M.A., 1969.

ADDRESSES: Home—The Old Mill House, Maids Moreton, Buckingham MK18 7AR, England. *Office*—Christie's, 63 Old brompton Rd., London SW7, England.

CAREER: Tate Gallery, London, England, lecturer, 1974-77; Christie's Education, London, principal, 1978—, director, 1978-88, chairman, 1988—. Advisor, Arts Council, London, 1984—; director, Phaidon-Christie's Publishers, Oxford, 1987—; chairman, Contemporary Art Society, 1988—.

AWARDS, HONORS: Times Educational Supplement Information Book Award, senior division, 1983, for *Just Imagine: Ideas in Paintings.*

WRITINGS:

(Contributor) Trewin Copplestone and Bernard S. Myers, editors, *Encyclopaedia of Art,* Macmillan (London), 1979.
Just Look . . . A Book about Paintings, Scribner, 1980.

Just Imagine: Ideas in Paintings, Viking, 1982.
(Editor) *Christie's Guide to Collecting,* Prentice-Hall, 1984.
Looking into Paintings, Faber, 1985.

Contributor of articles and reviews to *Times Literary Supplement, Times Educational Supplement, Country Life, Burlington Magazine,* and other periodicals.

ADAPTATIONS: "Looking into Paintings" (four-part television series), London, 198?.

WORK IN PROGRESS: Discovering Turner, a guide book for the Tate Gallery, London; various television programs and books on modern and contemporary art.

SIDELIGHTS: Robert Cumming's *Just Look . . . A Book about Paintings* is designed to introduce young people to the vast world of art. A collection of more than fifty photographs of famous paintings, the book contains examples of the work of artists from seven hundred years past to the present time, and offers definitions of a number of art terms.

Just Look "is marvelous and could certainly stimulate an early interest in art," according to Barbara Karlin of the *Los Angeles Times Book Review.* Writing in the *Times Literary Supplement,* Lucy Miklethwait explains that Cumming "guides the reader around the paintings as if he were in an art gallery. . . . If the reader is left unsatisfied, and feeling that he ought to have been told more, both about the paintings and the artists, perhaps this is just the sort of curiosity that Mr. Cumming intended to stimulate."

Cumming once said: "I am excited by all areas of the fine and decorative arts although my main interest is modern and contemporary art. I believe we live in one of the great artistic centuries, and I am fascinated by our present-day view of our historical and cultural inheritance. My writings, teaching, and lecturing are aimed at making our art and our history accessible and exciting. I believe profoundly in the humanizing influence of great art."

FOR MORE INFORMATION SEE:

PERIODICALS

Los Angeles Times Book Review, August 24, 1980.
Times Literary Supplement, March 28, 1980.

*   *   *

CUSHMAN, Doug 1953-

PERSONAL: Born May 4, 1953, in Springfield, OH; son of Donald E. (a business manager) and Juney (a housewife; maiden name, Fasick) Cushman; married Kim F. Mulkey (an illustrator), June 16, 1979. *Education:* Attended Paier School of Art, 1971-75.

ADDRESSES: Home—31 West Prospect St., New Haven, CT 06515.

CAREER: Apprentice to book illustrator Mercer Mayer, 1975-77; writer and illustrator, 1977—. Instructor at Paier College of Art, 1980, and Southern Connecticut State University, 1981—.

MEMBER: Society of Children's Book Writers, National Cartoonists Society.

AWARDS, HONORS: Child Book of the Year Award, 1979, for *Haunted Houses on Halloween.*

WRITINGS:

JUVENILE; SELF-ILLUSTRATED

(And editor and contributor) *Giants* (stories and poems), Grosset, 1980.
(And editor) *Trolls* (stories), Groset, 1981.
Once Upon a Pig, Grosset, 1982.
Nasty Kyle the Crocodile, Grosset, 1983.
Aunt Eater Loves a Mystery, Harper, 1987.
Secret of the Nile: Missing Mystery, Macmillan, 1987.
Uncle Foster's Hat Tree, Dutton, 1988.
Possum Stew, Dutton, 1990.
Camp Big Paw, Harper, 1990.

ILLUSTRATOR

Lillie Patterson, *Haunted Houses on Halloween,* Garrard, 1979.
Elizabeth Norine Upham, *Little Brown Bear,* Platt & Munk, 1979.
F. Kaff, *Monster for a Day; or, The Monster in Gregory's Pajamas,* Gingerbread House, 1979.
Leonard Kessler, *The Silly Mother Hubbard,* Garrard, 1980.
Kessler, *Hickory Dickory Dock,* Garrard, 1980.
Michaela Muntean, *Bicycle Bear,* Parents Magazine Press, 1983.
The Pudgy Fingers Counting Book, Grosset, 1983.
Ida Lutrell, *Tillie and Mert,* Harper, 1985.
Suzanne Gruber, *Chatty Chipmunk's Nutty Day,* Troll Associates, 1985.

DOUG CUSHMAN

Once Doug Cushman captured the character of Nasty Kyle, the author-illustrator's story about an ill-tempered crocodile went very quickly. (From *Nasty Kyle the Crocodile,* by Doug Cushman.)

Michael J. Pellowski, *Benny's Bad Day,* Troll Associates, 1986.
Rose Greydanus, *Bedtime Story,* Troll Associates, 1987.
Sharon Gordon, *The Jolly Monsters,* Troll Associates, 1987.
Jack Long, *Sunken Treasure Mystery,* Macmillan, 1987.
Long, *The Vanishing Professor,* Macmillan, 1987.
Pellowski, *Mixed-Up Magic,* Troll Associates, 1988.
Terry Webb Harshman, *Porcupine's Pajama Party,* Harper, 1988.
Melanie Martin, *Itsy-Bitsy Giant,* Troll Associates, 1988.
Dorothy Corey, *A Shot for Baby Bear,* Albert Whitman, 1989.

SIDELIGHTS: Doug Cushman once said: "My earliest memories of books are of the bookmobile that arrived on our street every other week or so. I pored over every book my mother would let me check out, absorbing every detail, sometimes even copying the pictures on a pad of notebook paper. I've never stopped making my own books. Even today I like making stories and pictures out of everything I see. Character is the most important aspect of a book, I think. Once I got Nasty Kyle down as a solid character the stories went very quickly. A good character will almost write a book by himself with a little nudge or two from the author.

"My trip to Kenya provided a wealth of material that still has yet to be organized. I've done many paintings of the land and the Masai. But one of the most enjoyable moments was sitting one evening with our guide, a Kamba tribesman, and sharing folktales from our respective countries. His always began, 'Once upon a time when the lion lay down with the lamb . . . .' That's beautiful. I'd like to do something with that."

DAHL, Roald 1916-1990

OBITUARY NOTICE—See index for *SATA* sketch: Given name is pronounced "roo-aal"; born September 13, 1916, in Llandaff, Wales; died of an infection, November 23, 1990, in Oxford, England. Screenwriter and author. Dahl is remembered for his well-crafted macabre short fiction and children's books, sometimes criticized by adults for their violence, which include *Charlie and the Chocolate Factory*—later adapted by Dahl as the film *Willie Wonka and the Chocolate Factory.* He began his writing career with a *Saturday Evening Post* short story about the time his fighter plane was shot down over Egypt during World War II. It was later included in the volume *Over to You: Ten Stories of Flyers and Flying.* Dahl's first children's book was *The Gremlins,* in which mysterious malfunctions in planes are caused by tiny people inside them. Among Dahl's other well-known works are the children's books *James and the Giant Peach* and *Chitty Chitty Bang Bang,* which he later adapted as a film, and the screenplay for a James Bond movie, *You Only Live Twice.* Dahl's writings won Edgar Allan Poe awards from the Mystery Writers of America in 1954 and 1959.

OBITUARIES AND OTHER SOURCES:

BOOKS

Farrell, Barry, *Pat and Roald,* Random House, 1969.

PERIODICALS

Los Angeles Times, November 24, 1990.
New York Times, November 24, 1990.
School Library Journal, January, 1991.
Times (London), November 24, 1990; December 19, 1990.
Washington Post, November 24, 1990.

*   *   *

DHONDY, Farrukh 1944-

PERSONAL: Born in 1944 in Poona, Bombay, India; immigrated to England, 1964; son of an Indian Army officer. *Education:* Attended Bombay University for a year in the early 1960s; Cambridge University, B.A., 1967; received M.A. from University of Leicester.

ADDRESSES: c/o Jonathan Cape Ltd., 32 Bedford Sq., London WC1B 3SG, England.

CAREER: Henry Thornton Comprehensive School, Clapham, London, England, English teacher; Archbishop Temple School, Lambeth, London, 1974-1980, English teacher, beginning in 1974, became head of department; commissioning editor for multicultural television programs on Channel 4, London, 1984—. Writer of television scripts, plays, and fiction for adults and children.

AWARDS, HONORS: Children's Rights Workshop Other awards, 1977, for *East End at Your Feet,* and 1979, for *Come to Mecca, and Other Stories;* Collins/Fontana Award for books for multi-ethnic Britain, for *Come to Mecca, and Other Stories;* Dhondy's works were represented in "Children's Fiction in Britain, 1900-1990," an exhibition sponsored by the British Council's Literature Department, 1990.

WRITINGS:

FOR CHILDREN

East End at Your Feet (short stories), Macmillan (London), 1976.
Come to Mecca, and Other Stories, Collins, 1978.
The Seige of Babylon (novel), Macmillan, 1978.
Poona Company (short stories), Gollancz, 1980.
Trip Trap (short stories; contains "Herald," "The Bride" [also see below], "Homework," "The Mandarin Exam," "Batty and Winifred," "The Fifth Gospel," "Lost Soul," and "Under Gemini"), Gollancz, 1982.
Romance, Romance [and] *The Bride,* Faber, 1985.

OTHER

Mama Dragon (play), produced in London, England, for the Black Theatre Cooperative, 1980.
Trojans (adaptation of a play by Euripedes), produced in London, for the Black Theatre Cooperative, 1982.
(Coauthor) *The Black Explosion in British Schools,* Race Today Publications, 1982.
Kipling Sahib (play), produced in London, 1982.
Vigilantes (play; produced in 1985), Hobo Press, 1988.
King of the Ghetto (television series), broadcast by British Broadcasting Company (BBC1), 1986.
Bombay Duck (novel), J. Cape, 1990.

Also author of the stage plays *Shapesters; Film, Film, Film;* and, with John McGrath and others, *All the Fun of the Fair.* Author of additional television plays, including *Maids in the Mad Shadow,* 1981; *Good at Art,* 1983; *Dear Manju,* 1983; *Salt on a Snake's Tail,* 1983; *The Empress of the Munshi,* 1984; and *To Turn a Blind Eye,* 1986. Author of series of ethnic situation comedies for British television, including *No Problem,* with Mustapha Matura, 1983, and *Tandoori Nights,* 1985.

Contributor to Indian periodicals *Debonair* and *Economic and Political Weekly,* and to London periodicals, including *Race Today* and the *Listener.* Former editor of *Carcanet.*

SIDELIGHTS: Award-winning Indian writer Farrukh Dhondy is an important figure in modern children's literature. Although he was born in Bombay, India, Dhondy writes for an English-speaking audience about life among the many different cultures, races, and ethnic backgrounds in Great Britain. His juvenile fiction deals honestly with the confusion and anxieties young people experience as they mature. Dhondy is known for using humor, vivid descriptions, dialect, and slang expressions to bring his stories to life.

Before becoming a writer, Dhondy spent a year at the University of Bombay studying physics and engineering. But he found his courses dull and the thought of a life as an engineer unfulfilling. "I was completely bored with the great prospect that yawned before me," he told Anwer Bati in a *Times Literary Supplement* interview. So Dhondy left the university without really knowing what he wanted to do with his future. He explained to Bati, "I just sat in bed and I read. I read myself sick, a book a day," while trying to decide what to do next. He later received a scholarship to Cambridge University in England and pursued a career in the arts.

Dhondy's first short story collection, *East End at Your Feet,* focuses on children of different cultures who live on the East End of London, England. This book, along with the 1978 collection *Come to Mecca, and Other Stories,* led critics to characterize Dhondy as a writer who deals candidly with the racial problems facing Asian and West Indian teenagers living in England. But in the *Times Literary Supplement* interview with Bati, Dhondy claimed that he is not motivated by matters of race and discrimination. "All my work involves black persons, but I don't think any of it involves issues of race. I have to write from a locale: it has to start from somewhere."

Dhondy's first young adult novel, *Seige of Babylon,* was published in 1978. Critics noted that the book is written in a more serious tone than the author's earlier stories. *Seige of Babylon* is an account of the impact of poverty and frustration on the lives of young people. The story revolves around three black youths in Brixton, England, who bungle a robbery. Their inability to cope with the consequences of the crime leads them to commit a more reckless and serious offense.

The stories in Dhondy's 1980 collection *Poona Company* take place in India and portray the exciting, gossipy, spirited atmosphere of the Chowk tea-house, a crowded bazaar-like gathering place in Poona. The book captures the flavor of Indian culture and helps to promote among young people a greater understanding of the ways in which different ethnic groups are alike. In a review of *Poona Company* for the *Times Literary Supplement,* Dervla Murphy proclaimed that Dhondy's stories "are for anyone—aged nine to ninety—who enjoys good writing." The critic further stated that through his works, the author "is illuminating not merely a sliver of the Indian scene, but a chunk of universal human nature." Murphy also reviewed Dhondy's 1982 short story collection *Trip Trap* for the *Times Literary Supplement.* She noted that the volume portrays the problems of immigrant families with sympathy and intensity and concluded, "Mr. Dhondy has a lot to teach us all."

In addition to his works for young people, Dhondy has written several plays and a novel for adults titled *Bombay Duck.*

WORKS CITED:

Bati, Anwer, "Exposing the Fraud Squad," *Sunday Times* (London), May 13, 1990, p. H10.
Murphy, Dervla, "In the Chowk Tea-House," *Times Literary Supplement,* November 21, 1980, p. 1322.
Murphy, Dervla, review of *Trip Trap* in the *Times Literary Supplement,* November 26, 1982, p. 1303.

FOR MORE INFORMATION SEE:

PERIODICALS

New Statesman, November 28, 1980.
Sunday Times (London), May 13, 1990.
Times Educational Supplement, March 18, 1983; July 15, 1983.
Times Literary Supplement, July 15, 1977; April 7, 1978; June 1, 1990.

*   *   *

DONALDSON, Bryna
See STEVENS, Bryna

DUBROVIN, Vivian 1931-

PERSONAL: Born March 24, 1931, in Chicago, IL; daughter of Ross (a school superintendent) and Emilie (a teacher; maiden name, Robert) Herr; married Kenneth P. Dubrovin (a director of agricultural research), September 5, 1954; children: Kenneth R., Darryl, Diana, Laura, Barbara. *Education:* University of Illinois, B.S., 1953. *Religion:* Episcopalian.

ADDRESSES: Home—1901 Arapahoe Dr., Longmont, CO 80501.

CAREER: Cuneo Press, Chicago, IL, editor of "Cuneo Topics," 1953; U.S. Savings & Loan League, Chicago, staff writer for *News,* 1954; University of Wisconsin Press, Madison, editor, 1955-56; free-lance writer, 1971—. Director of numerous writing conferences. Consultant, lecturer, and participant in writing programs and workshops.

MEMBER: National League of American Penwomen (president, Central Colorado branch, 1978-80), American Association of University Women (member of executive board and chapter editor, 1978-79), Society of Children's Book Writers (Rocky Mountain chapter, vice-president, 1978-79, president, 1979-80), Western Women in the Arts (honorary life member).

WRITINGS:

Write Your Own Story, F. Watts, 1984.
Running a School Newspaper, F. Watts, 1985.
Creative Word Processing, F. Watts, 1987.
A Guide to Alternative Education and Training, F. Watts, 1988.
The ABC's of the New Print Shop, Sybex, 1990.

"SUMMER FUN/WINTER FUN" SERIES

Baseball Just for Fun, EMC Corp., 1974.
The Magic Bowling Ball, EMC Corp., 1974.
The Track Trophy, EMC Corp., 1974.
Rescue on Skis, EMC Corp., 1974.

"SADDLE UP" SERIES

A Better Bit and Bridle, EMC Corp., 1975.
A Chance to Win, EMC Corp., 1975.
Trailering Troubles, EMC Corp., 1975.
Open the Gate, EMC Corp., 1975.

OTHER

Contributor of stories and articles to *Highlights for Children, Jack and Jill, Humpty Dumpty, Curriculum Review, Focus, Instructor,* and other publications.

SIDELIGHTS: "I've been writing for as long as I can remember," Vivian Dubrovin states. "In elementary school, I wrote plays and pageants that my classmates performed on the school stage. In high school I worked on the school yearbook and newspaper.

"I can't remember ever deciding that I wanted to be a writer. My teachers, relatives, and friends all just assumed I would be. Perhaps that was because I was always writing.

"My father insisted that if I wanted to make writing my career, I'd need a degree in journalism. So, I graduated from the University of Illinois with a degree in journalism. I worked for several years as an editor and staff writer for trade publications and a publishing company while my husband earned his Ph.D. in Soil Chemistry at the University of Wisconsin.

"While raising our two boys and three girls, I became interested in children's literature. I began writing short stories for children's magazines. Our family was very active. I was a Camp Fire leader, a Cub Scout den mother, and a Sunday School teacher. The short stories and fiction books were based on our experiences.

"After the fiction books were published, I began to visit classrooms to tell boys and girls how I wrote the stories. One day, a young boy raised his hand and asked, 'Can you tell us how *we* can write stories, too?' I began working with teachers as a consultant. Since there was no book written for children on how to write short stories, I wrote *Write Your Own Story.* But boys and girls like to write many things and in some of the classrooms where I spoke, the children were trying to create classroom newspapers. So, I put my journalism training and experience into *Running a School Newspaper.* The newspaper book was created on a computer with word processing software. I enjoyed using word processing so much that I wanted boys and girls to enjoy it, too. *Creative Word Processing* tells boys and girls about projects they can do with word processing.

"In the summer of 1986, using the writing books as textbooks, I began teaching teachers in university workshops. Each year I stressed more strongly how easy it was for teachers to publish their students' writing. In 1989, I included desktop publishing in the workshops and began collecting and creating the material for a new book telling children how much fun it was to use desktop publishing."

FOR MORE INFORMATION SEE:

PERIODICALS

Boulder Town and Country, December 25, 1974.
Longmont Times-Call, October 31, 1974.
Loveland Reporter-Herald, April 19, 1975.

*   *   *

DUNCAN, Julia K.
See BENSON, Mildred (Augustine Wirt)

*   *   *

EATON, George L.
See VERRAL, Charles Spain

*   *   *

EGERMEIER, Elsie E(milie) 1890-1986

PERSONAL: Born July 28, 1890, near Sanborn, IA; died October 15, 1986, in Oklahoma City, OK; daughter of John Christopher (a farmer) and Sophia Emma (Weiss) Egermeier. *Education:* Educated in rural schools in Iowa, Tennessee, and Oklahoma; studied privately, Anderson, IN, 1910-14. *Religion:* "Vital Christianity."

CAREER: Gospel Trumpet Co. (now Warner Press, Inc.), Anderson, IN, copy writer, beginning 1908, editor and writer of juvenile literature, beginning 1911.

AWARDS, HONORS: Litt.D. from Anderson College, Anderson, IN, 1941.

WRITINGS:

Egermeier's Bible Story Book, Gospel Trumpet, 1922, new edition with story revisions by Arlene S. Hall, 1955, 5th revised edition, 1969.
John Wesley, the Christian Hero, Gospel Trumpet, 1923.
Bible Picture A-B-C Book, Gospel Trumpet, 1924, new edition with story revisions by Zelpha Henderson, 1957, new edition with story revisions by Arlene S. Hall, 1963.
Girls' Stories of Great Women, Gospel Trumpet, 1930.
Boys' Stories of Great Men, Gospel Trumpet, 1931.
Egermeier's Stories of Great Men and Women (contains *Girls' Stories of Great Women* and *Boys' Stories of Great Men*), Warner Press, 1962.
Picture Story Life of Christ (adapted from *Egermeier's Bible Story Book*), Gospel Trumpet, 1940.
Friends of Jesus, Reilly and Lee, 1940.
Egermeier's Favorite Bible Stories, Warner Press, 1964.
Egermeier's Picture Story Life of Jesus, Warner Press, 1966.

SIDELIGHTS: Elsie E. Egermeier's *Egermeier's Bible Story Book* has sold over two million copies; Kathleen Buehler of the *Church of God News* called the collection "perhaps the most widely used Bible story book of this century."

FOR MORE INFORMATION SEE:

PERIODICALS

Church of God News, December 7, 1986.

          *   *   *

EHRLICH, Amy 1942-

PERSONAL: Born July 24, 1942, in New York, NY; daughter of Max (a television writer and novelist) and Doris (Rubenstein) Ehrlich; children: Joss. *Education:* Attended Bennington College, 1960-62 and 1963-65.

CAREER: Early jobs for short periods include teacher in day-care center, fabric colorist, and hospital receptionist. Free-lance writer and editor for publishing companies; roving editor at *Family Circle* magazine; senior editor at Delacorte Press; senior editor at Dial Books for Young Readers, New York, NY, beginning 1982.

AWARDS, HONORS: New York Times Outstanding Book of the Year, 1972, *School Library Journal* Best Book of the Year, and *ALA Children's Books of Exceptional Interest* citations, all for *Zeek Silver Moon;* IRA-CBC Children's Choice citation, for *The Everyday Train; American Bookseller* Pick of the Lists, Kansas State Reading Circle, and *Booklist* Reviewer's Choice citations, all for *Leo, Zack, and Emmie; Booklist* Reviewer's Choice, IRA-CBC Children's Choice, Child Study Association Children's Book of the Year, and *American Bookseller* Pick of the Lists citations, all for *Thumbelina; Redbook* Children's Book of the Year citation, 1987, for *The Wild Swans; American Bookseller* Pick of the Lists and *Booklist* Reviewer's Choice citations, both for *The Snow Queen; American Bookseller* Pick of the Lists, Child Study Association Children's Book of the Year, and Kansas State Reading Circle citations, all for *Cinderella; Booklist* Young Adult Reviewer's Choice and Best of the

Decade citations, and Dorothy Canfield Fisher Award, 1990, all for *Where It Stops, Nobody Knows.*

WRITINGS:

Zeek Silver Moon, illustrated by Robert Andrew Parker, Dial, 1972.
(Adapter) Dee Brown, *Wounded Knee: An Indian History of the American West* (from Brown's *Bury My Heart at Wounded Knee*), Holt, 1974.
The Everyday Train, illustrated by Martha Alexander, Dial, 1977.
(Reteller) Hans Christian Andersen, *Thumbelina,* illustrated by Susan Jeffers, Dial, 1979.
(Reteller) Andersen, *The Wild Swans,* illustrated by Jeffers, Dial, 1981.
Leo, Zack, and Emmie, illustrated by Steven Kellogg, Dial, 1981.
(Reteller) Andersen, *The Snow Queen,* illustrated by Jeffers, Dial, 1982.
(Adapter) *Annie* (storybook from John Huston's movie of the same title), Random House, 1982.
Annie Finds a Home, illustrated by Leonard Shortall, Random House, 1982.
Annie and the Kidnappers, Random House, 1982.
(Editor and adapter) *The Random House Book of Fairy Tales,* illustrated by Diane Goode, Random House, 1985.
(Adapter) *The Ewoks and the Lost Children* (storybook from the George Lucas television film), Random House, 1985.
(Adapter) *Bunnies All Day Long,* illustrated by Marie H. Henry, Dial, 1985.
(Adapter) *Bunnies and Their Grandma,* illustrated by Henry, Dial, 1985.
(Adapter) *Bunnies on Their Own,* illustrated by Henry, Dial, 1986.
(Adapter) *Bunnies at Christmastime,* illustrated by Henry, Dial, 1986.

AMY EHRLICH

Leo, Zack, and Emmie Together Again, illustrated by Kellogg, Dial, 1987.

Buck Buck the Chicken, illustrated by R. W. Alley, Random House, 1987.

Emma's New Pony, photographs by Richard Brown, Random House, 1988.

Where It Stops, Nobody Knows (young adult novel), Dial, 1988.

(Adapter) *Pome and Peel,* illustrated by Laszlo Gal, Dial, 1989.

The Story of Hanukkah, illustrated by Ori Sherman, Dial, 1989.

(Adapter) Brothers Grimm, *Rapunzel,* illustrated by Kris Waldherr, Dial, 1989.

Lucy's Winter Tale, illustrated by Troy Howell, Dial, 1991.

The Dark Card (young adult novel), Viking, 1991.

WORK IN PROGRESS: Maggie, Silky, and Joe, a picture book to be published by Viking; *The Pigs Are in the Bathtub and Little Millie's All Wet* (working title), a picture book to be published by Dial; *The Blue Crib* (working title), an adult novel; *The Spell on Mr. Wren* (working title), a picture book.

SIDELIGHTS: "I always wanted to write, even from the time I was a young child," Amy Ehrlich said in an interview for *Something about the Author.* "I think it was because I liked to read so much and because my father was a writer. He wrote television scripts and novels, and the household sort of revolved around the fact that he worked at home. We always had to be quiet, and there was an enormous space around him so that he could do his writing. He was a distant man, because he was very involved with work. A lot of time you got the feeling that he didn't know who you were, like, 'Which daughter are you?' It was tough, but I guess I thought that was the way fathers were. I did read some of his books, and I think in a way that had a big influence on me as a writer. He always was very proud of my writing. He made a lot of money for his time by being a crack suspense writer. He said to me, 'There's got to be a handle on every page to make the person want to keep reading.' Although I don't feel I'm a suspense writer, I do really believe in the power of the story in books—not only in children's books, but also adult books.

"My mother was an enormously competent woman. She was a homemaker, and her house was a perfect place. Every detail was perfect. She could have run a corporation if she had come of age in another time. In fact, in her late middle age she and my father got divorced, and she wound up starting a travel agency. At the time of her death she had twenty people working for her. She was a very ambitious person who always upheld a standard of excellence—if it was to be the best housekeeper on the block or to have the best dressed children or to run the best business. I felt like I had to really fight not to get swallowed up by her and that I went in the other direction just to discover who I was.

"When I was five or six I'd lie in my bed, and I'd make up a story at night, pretending to be writing about a girl. Every night I'd resume the story in my mind as a way of putting myself to sleep. I was also a very serious reader, and I read a tremendous amount as a kid. I removed myself from circumstances by reading, and books were very important to me for that reason. I remember loving Laura Ingalls Wilder for her view of that simpler wonderful family and pure world and open spaces— the idea of boundlessness, of people striking out on their own. I remember waiting eagerly for every new Mary Poppins book that came out; I just loved that open-ended, fantasy world. It was like somewhere you could pre-

tend to actually go. I remember the *Babar* books were the same; if you opened a page of those books and saw a picture of the elephants' houses that were built in trees, it was like you could place yourself in one with no trouble at all. I think the first adult book that I really loved was *A Tree Grows In Brooklyn,* which I probably read when I was about thirteen. Again it romanticized a very completely drawn alternate reality.

"I was a pretty good student up until adolescence, when my attention went elsewhere. I grew up in New York and Connecticut, and I think that, like a lot of other people who become artists or writers later in life, I always felt like a misfit. Inside I always felt different—alienated and out of step. When I was in ninth grade I won a prize for writing a short story. It was a story about a firefly which I contributed to Nina [the heroine of] *Where It Stops, Nobody Knows.* That was the first time in my school career that I was ever set apart or praised for anything specific. It really made a strong impression on me.

"When I was a junior in high school I asked to be sent away to boarding school. I wasn't as popular as I wanted to be, and I was also fighting a lot with my mother. I wanted to get out of my house and have more freedom and to be left alone. I wound up going to a Quaker boarding school in Poughkeepsie, New York, for the last two years of high school. That was a very good experience because I was in an advanced English class in my senior year, and the teacher was very good. Since the values of the Quaker society were different from the values of southern Connecticut public schools, there was more of a premium placed on school work and academic work and intellectual activity, which prepared me for college pretty well those last two years.

"I went to Bennington College, but I never quite finished. I got in a lot of trouble because I was unable to write papers at school, and I experimented with drugs and alcohol, and lived in a lot of places and did a lot of hitchhiking. The 1960s were wild and I was a classic case.

"I was always able to get work. I lived in southern Vermont on a commune which was in an apple orchard on a mountain. I went up there off and on for probably three or four years, but mainly just in the summer when the weather was warm. At that time you didn't need very much money to live. I was able to live in Vermont in the summer and go to New York and get freelance or part-time work in publishing. I was a copywriter or an editorial assistant for children's books, and I'd go back and forth between living in Vermont and going to New York and living in other people's apartments and working on an hourly basis.

"I had wanted to write a children's book for a long time and my boss encouraged me to write one. I was writing a lot of copy, and she'd always say, 'Oh, your copy's so good— why don't you write a book?' I tried, but every time I started I'd get blocked and I couldn't do it. Then some friends of mine from California had a baby and named him Zeke Silvermoon. I wanted to send him a little story as a present, so I sat down and started writing this thing. After I got to the second page I realized I was writing a book. It was really exciting because I kind of tricked myself into it. It only took me a weekend to write it. I stayed up every night for about two and a half days and worked until I was finished. Not a word of the book was changed when it was published, and it's very representative of that family and how people were bringing up children then.

A·M·Y·E·H·R·L·I·C·H
Where It Stops, Nobody Knows

A real incident in her son's school life prompted Amy Ehrlich to write this 1988 novel about a troubled girl and her mother who move from place to place.

"After living in northern Vermont on another commune, my son's father and I lived in Jamaica in the Caribbean. He had a job building a campground, a small cottage resort on an abandoned part of the north coast, a part that had never been developed for tourism. It was a very intense, very difficult nine or ten months. I'm very glad I had the experience, but I don't know if it will ever come out in my writing in any clear way. It was frustrating at the time, but it taught me an enormous amount about the world. There were a lot of stresses on us because he had jobs for a lot of people, and people were really desperate for the money. There was a lot of fighting, and we had to figure out who was lying and who was telling the truth. I think he was about twenty-four, so we were really unequipped to deal with this.

"Jamaica kind of came as an intermission for the rest of my life. I dropped out of my life and dropped back in. I came back from Jamaica in 1973, and I got pregnant. . . . After my son was born my view of life changed dramatically. A friend of mine said recently that the mid-seventies were like the end of innocence. During the sixties and early sevenites you thought you could do what you wanted and have personal freedom and no structure, but once you started having kids you found out you couldn't do any of it.

"I broke up with my son's father about two years later, and when I came back to New York my situation had changed, the times had changed, and the economy had changed. All I wanted to do was work. Since I couldn't get right back into writing children's books, I did some proofreading for a medical magazine and then some free-lance work for a children's publisher. That led to a job offer from *Family Circle* magazine, where I worked for nine months, but it turned out to be a real mismatch. After that I was hired to be senior editor at Delacorte Press, and I continued working as

an editor in the publishing industry for eight years. When I look back at my life now, I can't believe I ever lived it. It was very hard because I was living in Brooklyn, I had an hour commute each way to work, and I was bringing up a child myself. But I still wanted to write, and, as the years went by and I became progressively more corporate and I went up the 'ladder,' I began to feel the same insecurities I had as a child. I felt I was impersonating an executive—that it wasn't really me, yet I'd have to go to these conventions and sales conferences and smile at all these people. I wasn't comfortable, and it was an enormous strain on me. Sometimes I'd have to work overtime, and I wouldn't get home until 7:30, even though I'd take a cab so I wouldn't be as late. I'd pick my son up at daycare and then have to cook dinner and put him to bed.

"After about five years of this I started really wanting to leave. Then my sister, who lived up in Vermont, became very sick with cancer and it became clear that she wasn't going to live. I decided I would sublet my house for ten months, and take a leave of absence from work, and move up to Vermont for ten months to be with her. During that time I started writing more and more, and I met a man whom I fell in love with who teaches business at one of the Vermont state colleges and raises cows. We married six years ago.

"I never really returned to work, though I continued to do editing through the mail and I'd go back for a week at a time here and there the first year after I'd left.

"I've just been discovering myself as a writer quite intensely over the past five years. Being an editor taught me to be scrupulous. Sometimes, though, I wish as a writer that I could get rid of the editorial part of my brain so I wouldn't censor myself so much. I'd write more pages a day. I know my writing looks smooth and seems to flow, but really it's very, very careful. I don't really write in drafts. I take a chunk, and I polish it; I can't go on until it's fixed.

"I got the idea for *Where It Stops, Nobody Knows* from a girl who was going to school with my son. We had just moved to Vermont from New York when my son was eleven, and the move was very hard on him. It was hard on me too, but I saw that he was really suffering. Eventually he did get used to it. Then sometime in the spring he came home and said, 'Hey, Mom, there's this new girl in our school, and you know she's so cool. She's had this really interesting life; she's lived in all these different places, and she and her mother travel around.' My son thought it was very cool, but for some reason I thought it was terrible. I'd seen him suffer when we had moved. I just thought it was very sad and that it was very selfish of the girl's mother to keep moving because her daughter would never be able to establish a community anywhere.

"It was during this time that my sister was ill and I was very sad. I think that something about this girl stuck in my head, not that I knew much about her—I had met her briefly, but something about her situation affected me. I remember once I was telling my husband about the girl when we were driving in the car, and I just started to cry. I'd been wanting to write a novel while I'd been working in New York as an editor full time, in addition to writing picture books, easy-to-reads, and retellings. Now that I had left New York I realized the novel was going to be about a girl, Nina, and her mother, Joyce, who moved all the time.

"The character of Sam Gordon in the book was based on my son. The girl—the real girl, not Nina—wrote him a couple of letters and called him collect on the phone from California, but then she eventually lost touch with him.

"I feel very strongly about the books that I'm writing and about the market in general; my books shouldn't preach or offer simple answers. I did get some criticism from librarians. They couldn't reconcile the fact that Joyce was basically a good mother even though she had kidnapped this child. They had a lot of trouble with that. I don't think kids have any trouble with any of it; I just think that some adults do.

"When I get up in the morning I start writing immediately. I write from about eight in the morning when my son and husband leave, until two or three, with just a short break to get the mail and another to have some lunch. Every now and then I'll work in the evening if I can get the energy. I can go over what I'd written the day before and really get myself ready to start again the next morning. I don't work absolutely every day, and I have a lot of internal conflicts between my social and family responsibilities and my responsibility to my own work. I'd like to opt in the direction of my own work, but I was raised a certain way so I find it hard to let the other stuff slide. If someone's coming to visit I find it hard not to clean the house, and cook a nice dinner, versus writing another page that day, or writing that day at all. I think it's something that a lot of middle-aged women writers probably are dealing with.

"My life has really changed. People call me up from New York and say, 'Oh have you heard that so-and-so left such-and-such place to do this,' and really I'm not interested because I'm not there. It doesn't have any bearing on my life. But if someone says to me, 'You know the corn is ripe down the road, why don't you check yours?', I'll go out to the garden. It's been very good for me not being in New York, because here I feel like I'm much more in touch with my own fantasies and my own ideas. I think any serious writer has to develop a kind of cavalier attitude about the market, because in the end you've got to be writing for yourself. The reader you're writing for is you."

WORKS CITED:

Ehrlich, Amy, from an interview by Mark Kaplin for *Something about the Author,* September 6, 1990.

FOR MORE INFORMATION SEE:

PERIODICALS

Bulletin of the Center of Children's Books, February, 1982; November, 1985.
Publishers Weekly, November 13, 1981.

*   *   *

EIGE, (Elizabeth) Lillian 1915-

PERSONAL: Surname is pronounced *eye*-g; born July 22, 1915, in Marshalltown, IA; daughter of Francis Joseph (a tailor) and Lillian (a homemaker; maiden name, McNary) Tuffree; married Gaylerd S. Eige (an engineer), October 17, 1937; children: Jonathan, Julia Eige Rula. *Education:* University of Iowa, correspondence courses, 1964-66; attended the Iowa Writers' Workshop, 1966-67. *Politics:* Independent. *Religion:* Methodist.

ADDRESSES: Home—401 Foote St. S.W., Cedar Rapids, IA 52404.

CAREER: Iowa Training School for Boys, Eldora, IA, secretary, 1933-34; Northwestern Bell, Marshalltown, IA, office worker, 1935-37; writer, 1970—. Chairperson for a unit of United Fund drive, 1969; co-chairperson for UNICEF home drive, 1973; board member, Campfire Girls, 1956-58, and United Nations board, 1960-80.

MEMBER: National League of American Pen Women.

AWARDS, HONORS: Cady was included on the New York Public Library's 1987 list of "100 Books for Giving and Sharing."

WRITINGS:

The Kidnapping of Mister Huey, Harper, 1983.
Cady (Junior Literary Guild selection), Harper, 1987.

Contributor to periodicals, including *Jack and Jill.*

ADAPTATIONS: Cady was recorded by the Library of Congress National Library Service for the Blind and Physically Handicapped in 1988.

WORK IN PROGRESS: If a Bird Sings, a novel about a child accepting the death of a parent; a novel about the friendship between a small town child and a girl from a show troupe; a picture book.

LILLIAN EIGE

SIDELIGHTS: Lillian Eige told *SATA:* "During my early years until I reached high school I lived in Belmond, a typical, small Iowa town. For most of that time our home was in a flat above my father's shop. It meant the family was closely confined in work, play and home. When you lived in a half block off Main Street, back of the hospital, across from the funeral home, and you could see the hotel from your front windows, you never lacked for excitement or entertainment.

"I learned, too, there were treasures to be found behind the stores in the alleys. I became a collector. I remember how rich I felt when I found a piece of foil and added it to the huge wad I already had. We lived near a Movie Palace (we didn't call it a theater) and I probably saw most of the movies that came to town. I haunted the library, too, that was only a half block down the street.

"But as in so many families there were good times and bad times. I was a depression child, and like many we went from a happy, secure time to struggling for survival. That is when I grew up and learned to understand people's actions. And it was the time when we ate home canned green beans and eggs until they came out our ears. I sometimes insist my characters eat green beans.

"I have been a dreamer, a pretender, and an actor all of my life. When I was a child I could entertain myself all afternoon by throwing myself about the room acting out everything from a sick child to being the most glamorous girl in the whole world.

"Most of us have to write from the child that we were, the child that we remember, and the child that we are. The part of us that refuses to grow up. We could not write for children otherwise. Some believe that children's books are for children only. That is not true. They are for everyone who hangs on to the magic and excitement of living.

"But sometimes writing for me has been like going to the grocery store for a dozen eggs and coming home with a sack of bananas. I usually start out with my characters and relationships, and I am not always sure what they are going to do. They surprise me.

"After years of raising children, dogs, orphan birds and rabbits, I decided to go back to school and to try to write. That is where I am today."

HOBBIES AND OTHER INTERESTS: "Theater, traveling, music, and of course, reading."

FOR MORE INFORMATION SEE:

PERIODICALS

Gazette (Cedar Rapids, IA), April 24, 1983.
Junior Literary Guild, April, 1987, September, 1987.
Marshalltown Times Republican, October 21, 1983.

* * *

EMERSON, Alice B.
See BENSON, Mildred (Augustine Wirt)

DELIA EPHRON

EPHRON, Delia 1944-
(Delia Brock)

PERSONAL: Born July 12, 1944, in Los Angeles, CA; daughter of Henry (a writer) and Phoebe (a writer; maiden name, Wolkind) Ephron; married Dan Brock (divorced, 1975); married Jerome Kass (a screenwriter), May 21, 1982; children: two stepchildren, Julie and Adam. *Education:* Barnard College, B.A., 1966.

ADDRESSES: Home—Los Angeles, CA. *Agent*—Amanda Urban, International Creative Management, 40 West Fifty-seventh St., New York, NY 10019.

CAREER: Writer. Worked for *New York* (magazine), New York City, 1975-1978. Free-lance writer, 1975—.

AWARDS, HONORS: New York Public Library Books for the Teen Age citation, 1982, for *Teenage Romance; or, How to Die of Embarrassment.*

WRITINGS:

(With Lorraine Bodger; under married name, Delia Brock) *The Adventurous Crocheter,* illustrated by Bodger, Simon & Schuster, 1972.
(With Bodger; under name Delia Brock) *Gladrags: Redesigning, Remaking, Refitting All Your Old Clothes,* illustrated by Bodger, Simon & Schuster, 1974.

How to Eat like a Child, and Other Lessons in Not Being a Grown-up (also see below), illustrated by Edward Koren, Viking, 1978.

(With Bodger) *Crafts for All Seasons,* Universe, 1980.

Teenage Romance; or, How to Die of Embarrassment, illustrated by Koren, Viking, 1981.

Santa and Alex, illustrated by Elise Primavera, Little, Brown, 1983.

(With John Forster and Judith Kahan) *How to Eat like a Child, and Other Lessons in Not Being a Grown-up* (musical revue based on Ephron's book of the same title), Samuel French, 1986.

Funny Sauce: Us, the Ex, the Ex's New Mate, the New Mate's Ex, and the Kids, Viking, 1986.

"Do I Have to Say Hello?" Aunt Delia's Manners Quiz for Kids and Their Grownups, illustrated by Koren, Viking, 1989.

(With sister, Nora Ephron) *This Is My Life* (screenplay; adapted from Meg Wolitzer's novel of the same title), Twentieth Century-Fox, 1990.

Contributor to magazines, including *Esquire, New York, New York Times Magazine, Vogue, Glamour, Cosmopolitan, Redbook, House and Garden, Savvy,* and *California.*

ADAPTATIONS: How to Eat like a Child was adapted as a musical special first broadcast by the National Broadcasting Corporation (NBC-TV), November, 1982.

WORK IN PROGRESS: A children's novel; several screenplays.

SIDELIGHTS: Delia Ephron is known for humorous books that appeal to both young people and adults. She first became an author with a "how-to" book about crocheting; since then, she has broadened her outlook and showed her readers how to laugh at life's minor misfortunes.

Who is riding the escalator properly?

(From *"Do I Have to Say Hello?"* by Delia Ephron. Illustrated by Edward Koren.)

Ephron grew up in Beverly Hills, California, where she led a very comfortable life. Her parents were Hollywood screenwriters known for their wit. Ephron has said that as a child she felt she also had to be clever. "There was a constant scurry for attention at the dinner table," she reported in a *New York Times* article by Judy Klemesrud. "If you said something funny, Father might write it down." Also competing for laughs were Ephron's three sisters, all of whom are also writers. "I think there was a lot of pressure from my parents for each of us to become writers and that psychically we weren't given as many choices as we ought to have been. Although it's taken us different lengths of time, we've all gone like robots into writing," Ephron told Alice Steinbach in the Baltimore *Morning Sun.* Ephron took up the family trade when she wrote a story about a local college basketball team while living in Providence, Rhode Island.

Although Ephron referred to herself in Klemesrud's *New York Times* article as "the kid in school who was a goody-goody . . . the teacher's pet," she has said that she didn't like school much and was usually bored. Journalism class, however, was different. "In the print shop, making up the page, correcting it, getting your hands full of ink, and then seeing the finished product was a great feeling," she said to Hank Winnicki in the *New York Daily News.* According to Ephron, she was not much of a rebel in school, though she did once cause a stir by announcing falsely in a high school debate that she had been married.

After high school Ephron went to college in New York City. She later married and moved to Providence, Rhode Island, where she began a crafts business. Ephron's first book, *The Adventurous Crocheter,* was published when she was only twenty-seven. She followed up that effort two years later with *Gladrags,* another "how-to" book, which showed readers new uses for old clothes. Though Ephron would write a third craft book in 1980, *Crafts for All Seasons,* her instruction books would soon take on a humorous tone.

In 1975 Ephron divorced and returned to New York City. With the help of older sister Nora, a well-known author and screenwriter, Ephron became a free-lance writer. One day while eating chocolate pudding with a friend, the author noticed that she and her friend had very different ways of eating pudding. "I was sitting here, eating it my way," she told Klemesrud, "which means that I make a little hole in the pudding and scoop out all the best parts and save the skin until last. I thought, Gee, I want to write a piece about it." So Ephron wrote an article titled "How to Eat like a Child" that was published in the *New York Times Magazine.* Soon she began receiving letters from adults with their own brands of childish eating. Editors at Viking Press saw a good idea for a book and in 1978 Viking published *How to Eat like a Child, and Other Lessons in Not Being a Grown-Up.*

How to Eat like a Child, aside from describing juvenile approaches to food, offers advice on how to deal with parents, behave at school, and treat siblings. In doing research for the book, Ephron found that children everywhere play the same pranks— some more serious than others—on their brothers and sisters. She spent much of her own childhood finding ways to bother her sisters. In a chapter called "How to Torture Your Sister," she recommends telling your sister that an invisible man lives under her bed, munching a prize tidbit saved from lunch in front of the hungry sister just before dinner, and pretending to eat shaving cream. Shaving cream seems to be a recurring theme in Ephron's life as sibling Nora once fed it to her, saying it was ice cream. Not always a victim, however, Ephron does recall once almost reducing her younger sister Amy to tears by insisting that the child's name was really Amila, which was, of course, untrue.

Well received by book reviewers, *How to Eat like a Child* paved the way for Ephron's next comical "how-to" book, *Teenage Romance; or, How to Die of Embarrassment.* Chapters include guidelines for teenage boys making passes at teenage girls, teenage girls attending slumber parties, and teenagers of both sexes hiding pimples. Although younger children may not always understand that Ephron is poking fun at the agonies of adolescence, teenagers and former teenagers are almost certain to get the joke and see themselves in the pages of *Teenage Romance.*

In researching the book, Ephron interviewed roughly seventy teenagers to refresh her memory and broaden her own understanding of what being a teenager is all about. She says that her own youthful fears and problems are the backbone of *Teenage Romance.* Ephron claims to have been an average teenager, sensitive and insecure, not "a zero in popularity," but not "the queen of the hop," she told Ray Richmond in the *New York Daily News.* She recalled a typical teenage tragedy in Steinbach's *Morning Sun* article: "I remember . . . being dropped abruptly, from one day to the next, by a boy. He broke my heart. I remember I just couldn't function." This incident is recalled in the *Teenage Romance* chapter titled "How to Go Steady" when a guitar-playing boy named Doug suddenly tells his girlfriend of two months that he thinks they should "just be friends."

Other flashbacks of Ephron's teenage life also appear in the book. She admits that she never actually attended a slumber party, but confessed to Peter Costa in the Wichita *Eagle-Beacon* that she did "worry about always being a friend and never a girlfriend, for example. I was pathetic in relation to boys—I used to wait by the telephone for them to call or I wouldn't go out if I expected them to call." Like the teen couples she presents, Ephron did occasionally find herself necking for hours in a car. And in a chapter called "How to Hang Out," the author suggests one of her own former methods of passing time. "One of my biggest activities then was driving past a particular guy's house to see if he was home," she reported to Jill Wolfson in the Jackson *News.*

"Adults think teen-agers have changed so much," Ephron told Wolfson. "They think kids are so different now. It's to the point where many grown-ups are scared of them. But the book points out that they have more in common than they realize. I wrote it so adults will remember those feelings that they've repressed."

Finished with her lighthearted effort to remind adults that teenagers are people too, Ephron penned her first children's book. Called *Santa and Alex,* the tale puts a twist on the traditional story of a child waiting up on Christmas Eve for Santa Claus to come down the chimney. Not content to sit patiently for Santa, Alex falls up the chimney, where he meets a boisterous team of reindeer led by Jeremy, a crotchety animal whose antlers constantly change color. Ephron's Santa is a yo-yo-spinning practical joker full of corny riddles and wacky rhymes who takes Alex along on his delivery route. Alex, Santa, and Jeremy share lots of adventures before Alex returns home by way of a magical star, promising to keep his fantastic night a secret. Whether or not Alex has dreamed the entire episode is left up to the reader.

In 1982 Ephron remarried and became the stepmother of two young children. Four years and many stepparenting stumbles later, Ephron focused her gently comic lens on the modern American extended family. As an ex-wife herself, and as second wife to a man with his own ex-wife and two kids, Ephron had gathered enough material to write *Funny Sauce: Us, the Ex, the Ex's New Mate, the New Mate's Ex, and the Kids.* With characteristic humor, Ephron takes on a subject that seems anything but funny. In *Funny Sauce* she sensitively discusses the trauma children and parents face when families split up and reform in new combinations. Although older children might gain some insight into the often complicated relationships holding these families together, *Funny Sauce* is really a book for adults.

Ephron's title came from an early incident involving her stepdaughter. When the author served dinner one night, the child informed her that she did not like chicken served in funny sauce, volunteering that her real mother did not make it that way. Ephron borrows from the "funny sauce" showdown in a chapter called "How to Talk to Your Stepmother." Ephron told Leslie Bennetts in the *New York Times:* "[My stepdaughter] used to torture me, by not eating anything I would cook. But I should add that now we have a very good relationship. Really, my inclination is to see things funny. I think you have to laugh about serious things."

In addition to being a stepmother of two, Ephron is also an aunt many times over. A visit from one of her nephews inspired the author to write a book that would teach good manners by providing hilarious examples of bad ones. *"Do I Have to Say Hello?" Aunt Delia's Manners Quiz for Kids and Their Grownups* was born when the author fetched her sister's seven-year-old from the Los Angeles airport. "His first words to me were 'Take me to the baseball-card store,'" Ephron told Valerie Helmbreck in the Nashville *Tennessean.* "Instead of reading him the riot act on how to greet your aunt, I said 'So your Aunt Delia picks you up at the airport. Do you say "Hi, Aunt Delia" and give her a kiss? Or do you say "No kisses. I hate kisses?" or do you say "Take me to the baseball-card store?"' Of course he picked 'Take me to the baseball-card store,' but he loved the game. He kept saying do another and that was the beginning of the quiz."

Very young children, who may not understand the book's good-natured sarcasm, might be confused by *"Do I Have to Say Hello?,"* but its silly responses to common manners clashes delighted older readers and critics. In keeping with the author's earlier investigation of eating habits, she has included chapters on table and restaurant manners and one called "The Eating Chart" that asks "Which of these food are you eating properly?" Other chapters offer quizzes on visiting manners, thank-you manners, and telephone manners. Ephron admits that her own manners as a child were not flawless. She particularly hated making the required appearance when her parents had guests.

"I was very nervous about being a writer because everyone in my family was a writer," Ephron told Hillel Italie in the *Trentonian.* "One day I wrote [*How to Eat like a Child*] and very quickly wrote it. I didn't think I was writing a book for children. I was writing an adult book. . . . I was absolutely shocked when kids thought it was funny. I suddenly knew that this was what I knew how to do." Warm critical response and Ephron's enthusiastic feedback from children and adults have helped make her books best-sellers and established her as a versatile writer who appeals to a wide variety of readers.

How to Pick Up a Girl.... "Uh, excuse me"-tap one of the girls on the shoulder. "My friend here's in love with you."
(From *Teenage Romance; or, How to Die of Embarrassment* by Delia Ephron. Illustrated by Edward Koren.)

WORKS CITED:

Bennetts, Leslie, "Becoming A Stepmother: A Writer's Story," *New York Times,* November 17, 1986, p. B10.
Costa, Peter, "Teen, 37, Shares Insights," *Eagle-Beacon* (Wichita, Kansas), October 8, 1981.
Helmbreck, Valerie, "And Never Say ... At the Table!," *Tennessean* (Nashville), December 25, 1989.
Italie, Hillel, "Book's Comical Quizzes Help Children Develop Etiquette for All Occasions," *Trentonian* (Trenton, New Jersey), January 16, 1990.
Klemesrud, Judy, "Childhood Fun," *New York Times,* November 17, 1978.
Richmond, Ray, "Teens: Awkward Love, Cool Times," *New York Daily News,* October 11, 1981, pp. 1, 4.
Steinbach, Alice, "Being a Teen Isn't Always Cool," *Morning Sun* (Baltimore), September 29, 1981, pp. B1-B2.
Winnicki, Hank, "Pimples and Privacy," *New York Daily News,* October 3, 1981.
Wolfson, Jill, "Author Exploits Those Awful, Embarrassing Teen-Age Years," *News* (Jackson, Mississippi), November 3, 1981.

FOR MORE INFORMATION SEE:

BOOKS

Ephron, Delia, *How to Eat like a Child, and Other Lessons in Not Being a Grown-up,* Viking, 1978.
Ephron, Delia, *Teenage Romance; or, How to Die of Embarrassment,* Viking, 1981.
Ephron, Delia, *Funny Sauce: Us, the Ex, the Ex's New Mate, the New Mate's Ex, and the Kids,* Viking, 1986.
Ephron, Delia, *"Do I Have to Say Hello?" Aunt Delia's Manners Quiz for Kids and Their Grownups,* Viking, 1989.

PERIODICALS

Jackson Sun (Jackson, Tennessee), December 6, 1981.
New York Times Book Review, September 5, 1982; October 12, 1986.
New York Times Magazine, September 14, 1986.
People, October 12, 1981.
Publishers Weekly, January 7, 1983.
Reader's Digest, March, 1979; August, 1979.
San Francisco Chronicle, October 15, 1986.

Saturday Evening Post, May, 1979.
Seattle Times, October 6, 1987.
Valley Journal (Sunnyvale, California), October 28, 1981.

* * *

EVANS, Nancy 1950-

PERSONAL: Born April 12, 1950, in Philadelphia, PA; daughter of Charles Restrick and Charlotte (maiden name, Burr) Evans. *Education:* Attended Wesleyan University, 1971-72; Skidmore College, B.A. (highest honors), 1972; Columbia University, 1973-74.

ADDRESSES: Home—321 West 77th St., New York, NY 10024

CAREER: College English, Middleton, CT, copy editor, 1972-73; Wesleyan University, Middleton, teacher of literature course, 1973; Harper's Magazine Co., New York City, associate editor of *Harper's Weekly,* 1974-76; co-founder of book marketing firm, 1979; vice-president and editor-in-chief, Book-of-the-Month Club, 1985-87; Doubleday & Co., Inc., New York City, president, beginning 1987—. Co-host, *First Edition,* television show on books and authors, 1984-87. Lecturer at various institutions, including Radcliffe Publishing Institute.

MEMBER: Authors Guild of Authors League of America, PEN, Players Club.

WRITINGS

(Contributor) Susan Cornillon, editor, *Images of Women in Fiction,* Popular Press, 1972.
(With Judith Applebaum) *How to Get Happily Published,* Harper, 1978.
(With Ann Banks) *Good-Bye House* (juvenile), Crown, 1980.

Editor of *Encyclopedia of the American Woman,* 1972-73. Contributing editor and book review columnist, *Glamour,* 1977-85. Contributor to numerous periodicals, including *MS, New York Times Book Review,* and *Esquire.*

* * *

FINNEY, Shan 1944-

PERSONAL: Born July 30, 1944, in Mexia, TX; daughter of Norris R. and Shirley (Caudle) Singer.

ADDRESSES: c/o Franklin Watts, Inc., 387 Park Avenue South, New York, NY 10016.

CAREER: Free-lance writer and author of juvenile books.

WRITINGS:

Basketball, F. Watts, 1981.
Cheerleading and Baton Twirling, F. Watts, 1982.
Dance, F. Watts, 1983.
(With Edward F. Dolan, Jr.) *The New Japan,* F. Watts, 1983.
(With Dolan) *Youth Gangs,* Simon & Shuster, 1984.
Noise Pollution, F. Watts, 1984.
Geared for Romance, Bantam, 1987.
Perfect Image (adult novel), Ballantine, 1987.
Trust in Love, Bantam, 1988.

SIDELIGHTS: Shan Finney commented: "I became a writer by chance and with help from my friends. My first big break came when I sold five hundred words on gold panning to my local newspaper. I write on assignment and view each project as a problem to be solved. My personal interests and skills are not so much reflected in the subject matter of my books as in the act of writing them. I like to look into a subject, examine it from many different angles, and move on to something new. The writing itself I find very difficult."

* * *

FITZHUGH, Percy Keese 1876-1950 (Hugh Lloyd)

PERSONAL: Born September 7, 1876, in Brooklyn, NY; died after a long illness July 5, 1950, in Oradell, NJ; son of William Wyvill and Mary (Keese) Fitzhugh; married Harriet Lloyd LePorte, July 13, 1900; children: Lawrence Stetson, Millicent Alden. *Education:* Attended Pratt Institute, Brooklyn.

CAREER: Journalist and author of books for children.

WRITINGS:

"BOY SCOUT" SERIES

Along the Mohawk Trail; or, Boy Scouts on Lake Champlain, Crowell, 1912.
For Uncle Sam, Boss; or, Boy Scouts at Panama, Crowell, 1913.
In the Path of La Salle; or, Boy Scouts on the Mississippi, Crowell, 1914.

"BUDDY BOOKS FOR BOYS" SERIES

Hervey Willetts, Grosset & Dunlap, 1927.
Skinny McCord, Grosset & Dunlap, 1928.
Spiffy Henshaw, Grosset & Dunlap, 1929.
Wigwag Weigand, Grosset & Dunlap, 1929.
Lefty Leighton, Grosset & Dunlap, 1930.
The Story of Terrible Terry, Grosset & Dunlap, 1930.

"PEE-WEE HARRIS" SERIES

Pee-Wee Harris, Grosset & Dunlap, 1922.
Pee-Wee Harris on the Trail, Grosset & Dunlap, 1922.
Pee-Wee Harris in Camp, Grosset & Dunlap, 1922.
Pee-Wee Harris in Luck, Grosset & Dunlap, 1922.
Pee-Wee Harris Adrift, Grosset & Dunlap, 1922.
Pee-Wee Harris, F.O.B. Bridgeboro, Grosset & Dunlap, 1923.
Pee-Wee Harris, Fixer, Grosset & Dunlap, 1924.
Pee-Wee Harris, As Good As His Word, Grosset & Dunlap, 1925.
Pee-Wee Harris Mayor for a Day, Grosset & Dunlap, 1926.
Pee-Wee Harris and the Sunken Treasure, Grosset & Dunlap, 1927.
Pee-Wee Harris on the Briny Deep, Grosset & Dunlap, 1928.
Pee-Wee Harris in Darkest Africa, Grosset & Dunlap, 1929.
Pee-Wee Harris Turns Detective, Grosset & Dunlap, 1930.

"ROY BLAKELEY" SERIES

Roy Blakeley, Grosset & Dunlap, 1920.
Roy Blakeley's Adventures in Camp, Grosset & Dunlap, 1920.
Roy Blakeley's Camp on Wheels, Grosset & Dunlap, 1920.
Roy Blakeley, Pathfinder, Grosset & Dunlap, 1920.
Roy Blakeley's Silver Fox Patrol, Grosset & Dunlap, 1920.
Roy Blakeley's Motor Caravan, Grosset & Dunlap, 1921.

Roy Blakeley—Lost, Strayed or Stolen, Grosset & Dunlap, 1921.
Roy Blakeley's Bee-Line Hike, Grosset & Dunlap, 1922.
Roy Blakeley at the Haunted Camp, Grosset & Dunlap, 1922.
Roy Blakeley's Funny Bone Hike, Grosset & Dunlap, 1923.
Roy Blakeley's Tangled Trail, Grosset & Dunlap, 1924.
Roy Blakeley on the Mohawk Trail, Grosset & Dunlap, 1925.
Roy Blakeley's Elastic Hike, Grosset & Dunlap, 1926.
Roy Blakeley's Roundabout Hike, Grosset & Dunlap, 1927.
Roy Blakeley's Happy-Go-Lucky Hike, Grosset & Dunlap, 1928.
Roy Blakeley's Go-As-You-Please Hike, Grosset & Dunlap, 1929.
Roy Blakeley's Wild Goose Chase, Grosset & Dunlap, 1930.
Roy Blakeley up in the Air, Grosset & Dunlap, 1931.

"TOM SLADE" SERIES

Tom Slade, Boy Scout, Grosset & Dunlap, 1915.
Tom Slade at Temple Camp, Grosset & Dunlap, 1917.
Tom Slade on the River, Grosset & Dunlap, 1917.
Tom Slade with the Colors, Grosset & Dunlap, 1918.
Tom Slade on a Transport, Grosset & Dunlap, 1918.
Tom Slade with the Boys over There, Grosset & Dunlap, 1918.
Tom Slade, Motorcycle Dispatch Bearer, Grosset & Dunlap, 1918.
Tom Slade with the Flying Corps, Grosset & Dunlap, 1919.
Tom Slade back Home, Grosset & Dunlap, 1920.
Tom Slade, Scout Master, Grosset & Dunlap, 1920.
Tom Slade at Black Lake, Grosset & Dunlap, 1921.
Tom Slade on Mystery Trail, Grosset & Dunlap, 1921.
Tom Slade's Double Dare, Grosset & Dunlap, 1922.
Tom Slade on Overlook Mountain, Grosset & Dunlap, 1923.
Tom Slade Picks a Winner, Grosset & Dunlap, 1924.
Tom Slade at Bear Mountain, Grosset & Dunlap, 1925.
Tom Slade, Forest Ranger, Grosset & Dunlap, 1926.
Tom Slade in the North Woods, Grosset & Dunlap, 1927.
Tom Slade at Shadow Isle, Grosset & Dunlap, 1928.
Tom Slade in the Haunted Cavern, Grosset & Dunlap, 1929.
The Parachute Jumper, Grosset & Dunlap, 1930.

Also author of *Tom Slade, Scout Hero*, Grosset & Dunlap.

"WESTY MARTIN" SERIES

Westy Martin, Grosset & Dunlap, 1924.
Westy Martin in the Yellowstone, Grosset & Dunlap, 1924.
Westy Martin in the Rockies, Grosset & Dunlap, 1925.
Westy Martin on the Santa Fe Trail, Grosset & Dunlap, 1926.
Westy Martin on the Old Indian Trail, Grosset & Dunlap, 1928.
Westy Martin in the Land of the Purple Sage, Grosset & Dunlap, 1929.
Westy Martin on the Mississippi, Grosset & Dunlap, 1930.
Westy Martin in the Sierras, Grosset & Dunlap, 1931.
Out West with Westy Martin, Grosset & Dunlap, 1933.

"YOUNG FOLKS COLONIAL LIBRARY" SERIES

The Story of Ethan Allen, the Green Mountain Boy, McLoughlin Brothers, 1906.
The Story of General Anthony Wayne (Mad Anthony), the Hero of Stony Point, McLoughlin Brothers, 1906.
The Story of General Johann De Kalb, McLoughlin Brothers, 1906.
The Story of General Richard Montgomery; Tale of the Invasion of Canada, McLoughlin Brothers, 1906.
The Story of John Paul Jones, McLoughlin Brothers, 1906.
The Story of General Francis Marion (The Bayard of the South), McLoughlin Brothers, 1907.

"HAL KEEN" MYSTERY SERIES; UNDER PSEUDONYM HUGH LLOYD

The Hermit of Gordon's Creek, Grosset & Dunlap, 1931.
Kidnapped in the Jungle, Grosset & Dunlap, 1931.
The Copperhead Trail Mystery, Grosset & Dunlap, 1931.
The Smugglers' Secret, Grosset & Dunlap, 1931.
The Mysterious Arab, Grosset & Dunlap, 1931.
The Clue at Skeleton Rocks, Grosset & Dunlap, 1931.
The Lonesome Swamp Mystery, Grosset & Dunlap, 1932.
The Doom of Stark House, Grosset & Dunlap, 1933.
The Lost Mine of the Amazon, Grosset & Dunlap, 1933.
The Mystery at Dark Star Ranch, Grosset & Dunlap, 1934.

"SKIPPY DARE" SERIES; UNDER PSEUDONYM HUGH LLOYD

Among the River Pirates, Grosset & Dunlap, 1934.
Held for Ransom, Grosset & Dunlap, 1934.
Prisoners in Devil's Bog, Grosset & Dunlap, 1934.

NOVELS

The Galleon Treasure, Crowell, 1908.
King Time; or, The Mystical Land of the Hours, Caldwell, 1908.
Uncle Sam's Outdoor Magic: Bobby Cullen with the Reclamation Workers, Harper, 1916.
Bobby Cullen on the Mississippi, 1920.
Mark Gilmore, Scout of the Air, Grosset & Dunlap, 1930.
Mark Gilmore, Speed Flyer, Grosset & Dunlap, 1931.
Mark Gilmore's Lucky Landing, Grosset & Dunlap, 1931.

OTHER

(Under pseudonym Hugh Lloyd) *The Story of a Fight from Concord Bridge to a Field at Yorktown*, McLoughlin Brothers, 1907.
(Editor) *Every Girl's Library*, ten volumes, Pearson, 1910.
The Boys' Book of Scouts (nonfiction), Crowell, 1917.
From Appomattox to Germany: Pictures of the Great Events in a Wonderful Half-Century, Harper, 1919.
(With wife, Harriet Lloyd Fitzhugh) *Concise Biographical Dictionary*, Grosset & Dunlap, 1935, revised and enlarged edition, 1949.

Also author of *The Golden Rod Story-Book*, 1906, *The Winning of the Golden Cross*, 1920, *Adventure of Holman Bareley*, 1934, and of adult novel, *The Wolves in the Barber Shop*, c. 1950.

ADAPTATIONS: Tom Slade: Boy Scout was released as a silent movie.

SIDELIGHTS: Percy Keese Fitzhugh's *Along the Mohawk Trail; or, Boy Scouts on Lake Champlain* was one of the first novels "officially approved" by the Boy Scouts of America. The book follows two boy scouts who are separated from their troop and must find their way out of the wilderness around Lake Champlain. Fitzhugh's scouts were realistic young men who were close to nature, unlike the rich city boys in other scouting series who fought spies and had other unbelievable adventures. The Boy Scouts of America were pleased with *Along the Mohawk Trail*, and asked Fitzhugh to start his own series. The "Tom Slade" books, begun in 1915, became so popular that Fitzhugh gave Tom's buddies Roy Blakeley, Pee-Wee Harris, and Westy Martin their own series.

Fitzhugh's Tom Slade was different from earlier scout heroes. "Tom was an antihero in the classic mold of Huckleberry Finn," Arthur Prager said in *Rascals at Large; or, The Clue in the Old Nostalgia.* Tom was poor, the son of the town drunk, and was a "hoodlum" until he discovered scouting. "Taken under the wing of a local businessman who sensed his innate goodness and . . . befriended by some of the boys in the town's one Scout troop, Tom soon 'fell for scouting with a vengeance,' " as M. Paul Holsinger related in the *Children's Literature Association Quarterly.* Tom faced many different problems as he helped the Allies in World War I, returned to America to lead his own troop, and even became a parachute jumper, but in each novel he succeeded, stated Holsinger, "thanks to his commitment to Scouting." Holsinger concluded: "By the end of the series in 1930, no other boy hero, with the possible exception of Tom Swift, was more famous or more read."

Fitzhugh's books had widespread influence, both with his readers and fellow writers. There was "a perceptible change in the tone of the many new volumes that began to appear with the advent of Tom Slade during the years of World War I," Holsinger wrote. Many of these "unofficial" Boy Scout volumes imitated Fitzhugh's style and realistic characters. In addition, thousands of boys read the Tom Slade books and were inspired to become Boy Scouts themselves. With almost seventy scouting books to his credit, Prager claimed, Percy Keese Fitzhugh "contributed greatly to the growth of the [Boy Scout] movement."

WORKS CITED:

Holsinger, M. Paul, "A Bully Bunch of Books: Boy Scout Series Books in American Youth Fiction," *Children's Literature Association Quarterly,* winter, 1989, pp. 178-181.
Prager, Arthur, *Rascals at Large; or, The Clue in the Old Nostalgia,* Doubleday, 1971, pp. 169-180.

OBITUARIES:

PERIODICALS

New York Times, July 7, 1950.
Publishers Weekly, August 5, 1950.

*   *   *

FULLER, John G(rant, Jr.) 1913-1990

PERSONAL: Born November 30, 1913, in Philadelphia, PA; died November 7, 1990; son of John G. (a dentist) and Alice (a housewife; maiden name, Jenkins) Fuller; married first wife (marriage ended); married Elizabeth Brancae (a writer), November 17, 1976; children: (first marriage) John G. III, Geoffrey Tousley, Judd Wheatley; (second marriage) Christopher Lewis. *Education:* Lafayette College, B.A., 1936. *Politics:* Democrat. *Religion:* Quaker.

ADDRESSES: Home and office—72 River Rd., Weston, CT 06883. *Agent*—Roberta Pryor, 24 West Fifty-fifth St., New York, NY 10016.

CAREER: Bakers Plays, Boston, MA, editor, 1938-41; Little, Brown & Co., Boston, advertising manager, 1941-43; American Optical Co., Southbridge, MA, member of public relations staff, 1943-48; National Broadcasting Co. (NBC-TV), New York City, promotion manager, 1949-53; staff writer for television programs, including *Home Show,* 1953-

JOHN G. FULLER

55, *Garry Moore Show,* 1956, and *Candid Camera,* 1957; writer and director of *Conquest,* 1957, *Twentieth Century,* 1958-59, and *Dupont Show of the Week,* 1962; producer of television series *Road to Reality,* 1960-61, *The Great American Dream Machine,* 1971, and *Countdown to 2001;* writer. Director and producer of films and television documentaries. Lecturer; guest on numerous television and radio talk shows.

MEMBER: Authors League of America, Writers Guild, Dramatists Guild, Delta Kappa Epsilon, Pi Delta Epsilon.

AWARDS, HONORS: Received award from the National Association for Improvement of Mental Health, 1961; National Association of Women's Clubs award, 1961, for *Road to Reality;* Sigma Delta Chi journalistic achievement award for best documentary, 1966, for *Light across the Shadow;* award from the National Association of Teachers, c. 1966, for *Incident at Exeter;* Emmy Award for outstanding achievement in magazine-type programming, National Academy of Television Arts and Sciences, 1971, for television documentary *The Great American Dream Machine;* distinguished alumni award, Lafayette College, 1972; Children's Science Book Awards honorable mention (older honor), New York Academy of Sciences, 1975, for *Fever: The Hunt for the New Killer Virus;* Belgrade Film Festival prize, 1977, and Golden Eagle Cine award, both for *Century III: The Oceans;* American Library Association Young Adult award, 1979, for *The Poison That Fell from the Sky.*

WRITINGS:

The Pink Elephant (play), produced on Broadway, 1953.
Love Me Little (play adapted from Amanda Vail's book of the same title), produced on Broadway, 1958.
The Gentlemen Conspirators, Grove, 1962.
The Money Changers, Dial, 1962.

Games for Insomniacs, Doubleday, 1966.

Incident at Exeter, Putnam, 1966.

The Interrupted Journey: Two Lost Hours, Dial, 1966.

The Day of St. Anthony's Fire (Literary Guild selection), Macmillan, 1968.

(Editor) *Aliens in the Sky*, Putnam, 1969.

The Great Soul Trial, Macmillan, 1969.

200,000,000 Million Guinea Pigs: New Dangers in Everyday Foods, Drugs, and Cosmetics, Putnam, 1972.

Fever: The Hunt for the New Killer Virus (for young adults; Literary Guild featured alternate), Reader's Digest Press, 1974.

Arigo: Surgeon of the Rusty Knife, Crowell, 1975.

We Almost Lost Detroit (Book-of-the-Month Club featured alternate), Reader's Digest Press, 1975.

The Ghost of Flight 401, Putnam, 1977.

The Poison That Fell from the Sky (for young adults), Random House, 1978.

The Airmen Who Would Not Die (for young adults), Putnam, 1979.

Are the Kids All Right? (for young adults), Times Books, 1983.

The Day We Bombed Utah: America's Most Lethal Secret, New American Library, 1984.

(With Lars-Eric Lindblad) *Passport to Anywhere*, Times Books, 1984.

Tornado Watch #211, Morrow, 1987.

The Pack (novel), St. Martin's, 1989.

Edgar Cayce Answers Life's Ten Most Important Questions, Warner Books, 1989.

(Dustjacket for 1987 edition of *Tornado Watch #211*.)

Writer of many documentary films, including *Earl Warren and the Supreme Court, American Welcome, The Handyman, Independence Day, U.S.A., Miracle in the Desert, Century III: The Oceans,* and *Labor of Love*, all for the U.S. Information Agency; and *Drug Abuse: A Call to Action, VD: A Call to Action,* and *Problem Drinking: A Call to Action*, all for Crowell-Collier-Macmillan Educational Film Division. Author of numerous television documentaries, including *Light across the Shadow*, NBC-TV, 1965.

Also author of column, "Trade Winds," *Saturday Review*, 1957-67. Fiction and film critic for *Playboy, Reader's Digest*, and various newspapers. Contributor of articles to periodicals, including *Look, Omni, Science Digest,* and *Reader's Digest*.

Grant's works have been translated into Spanish.

ADAPTATIONS: The Ghost of Flight 401 was made into a film by Paramount; *Arigo: Surgeon of the Rusty Knife* was made into a film starring Alan Arkin; *The Interrupted Journey* was made into a film for an NBC-TV, starring James Earl Jones and Estelle Parsons.

FOR MORE INFORMATION SEE:

PERIODICALS

Atlantic Monthly, August, 1966.

Book World, September 21, 1969.

Christian Science Monitor, June 30, 1966; December 31, 1975.

Commonweal, January 21, 1977.

Los Angeles Times, April 19, 1984.

New York Times Book Review, August 28, 1966; September 9, 1968; November 30, 1975; February 12, 1978; March 4, 1984; May 13, 1984; September 27, 1987.

Time, September 2, 1966; April 3, 1978.

Times Literary Supplement, May 13, 1983.

*   *   *

GAAN, Margaret 1914-

PERSONAL: Born August 18, 1914, in Shanghai, China; came to the United States in 1977; daughter of Antonio Martins (an accountant) and Marie (Lubeck) d'Oliveira; married E. Reginald Gaan, February 12, 1945 (died February 23, 1976). *Education:* Attended convent schools in Shanghai, China. *Politics:* None. *Religion:* Roman Catholic. *Hobbies and other interests:* Contract bridge—Gaan participated for Thailand in Far East bridge championships.

ADDRESSES: Home—3325 Northrop Ave., Sacramento, CA 95864. *Agent*—William Reiss, John Hawkins & Associates, 71 West Twenty-third St., New York, NY 10010.

CAREER: United Nations Children's Fund (UNICEF), Bangkok, Thailand, program officer for Asia region, 1950-65, chief of Asia desk in New York City, 1965-68, program officer in Bangkok, 1968-72, deputy regional director in Bangkok, 1972-74; writer, 1974—.

AWARDS, HONORS: Little Sister was listed as one of the American Library Association's Best Young Adult Books in 1982; *Blue Mountain* was selected as one of New York Library's Books for the Teenage in 1988.

MARGARET GAAN

WRITINGS:

Last Moments of a World, Norton, 1978.
Little Sister, Dodd, 1983.
Red Barbarian (first novel in trilogy), Dodd, 1984.
White Poppy (second novel in trilogy), Dodd, 1985.
Blue Mountain (third novel in trilogy), Dodd, 1987.

ADAPTATIONS: Last Moments of a World was recorded on audiocassette and released by Books for Listening.

WORK IN PROGRESS: His Name Is Today, a nonfiction account of UNICEF's work in Southeast Asia.

SIDELIGHTS: Margaret Gaan told *SATA:* "When I learned that Chinese author Han Suyin was writing a book entitled *The First Moment of the World* about the beginning of the Communist era in China, I called my own first book *Last Moments of a World* because the victory of the Communists in China ended the world into which I was born: the unique world of Shanghai, in which Britain (and other foreign powers who rode on Britain's coattails) dominated a Chinese city and imposed upon it their will and their laws in an early form of racial segregation similar to the apartheid system in modern South Africa.

"Imagine a Chinese city in which the Chinese people had no say: Chinese law had no application, the Chinese had to look for justice in foreign courts and foreign law, and could be punished, put in jail, even executed, by foreigners. Foreigners could put notices on park gates that read, 'No Dogs or Chinese Allowed.' Such a world is not possible, you say. But it was possible; it existed in the days before the Communist era. It was the Communists who finally ended that world, in violent upheavals.

"It was right that that world should end. Its end had been demanded, clamored for, by the Chinese people ever since it began a century earlier. Nevertheless, that world had its own strange and exciting life, a life that lingers now only in the memories of a diminishing number of people. We who lived it are growing old and disappearing. Soon there will be no one left to tell our children and their children and their children's children about the world in which they had their roots.

"There are so many stories to be told. There are stories about parents and grandparents, the houses, the old servants, the dogs, the hunting of boar and pheasant, the houseboats traveling up the creeks in the evenings, the pleasant, happy times. And later about the war, the bombing, the broken glass from the tall buildings that tinkled down to the road like music. There are stories about the refugees who fled the warlords in the countryside and poured into the cities, choking them. The beggars. The opium smokers. The many who died of exposure on the streets at night. Stories about being hungry. About laughing and crying. About the whole hustling, bustling life of that unique city, Shanghai. I wrote many of these stories into *Last Moments of a World* for my French and American and Australian nieces and nephews. If other people read the book and liked it, I am glad.

"Then I wrote another book, *Little Sister,* which told more about the strangeness of life in Shanghai. It describes the bravery and the heartbreak of it from the wider viewpoint of those Chinese who, on May 30, 1925, staged an enormous protest against the foreign domination of Shanghai, demand-

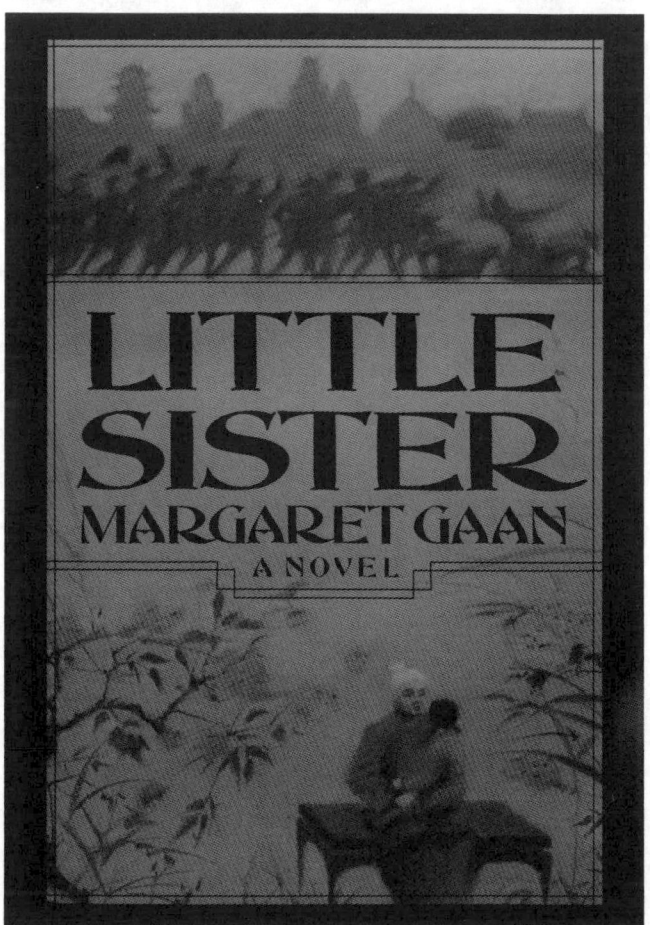

Dustjacket for Margaret Gaan's 1983 novel about Shanghai, China, the city of her birth.

ing the return of the city to the Chinese. On that day British police officers ordered gunfire against unarmed protestors. Many were killed. That "May Thirtieth Movement" sparked a tidal wave of protest that marked the high tide of the Chinese revolution which saw the Communists come to power. *Little Sister* is a book about people, people like me who lived in Shanghai, whose lives were engulfed and changed forever by violent politics.

"Then I wrote three books, *Red Barbarian, White Poppy,* and *Blue Mountain,* about opium. It was the opium trade in China that opened the door to British domination, to the creation of cities like Shanghai. In the seventeenth century, when the British took over India, they inherited from the Mogul emperor the monopoly on opium produced at Patna, the best opium in the world. The British started smuggling opium to China because they loved tea; they bought millions of pounds of tea from the Chinese every year, for which the Chinese demanded payment in silver. When the British began to run short of silver, they evened out the balance of payments by smuggling opium to China, for payment in silver.

"So started the opium trade, which was made legal in the mid−1800s by treaties that the British forced upon the Chinese to end the Opium Wars. These same treaties, called the "Unequal Treaties" by the Chinese, gave the British domination in China.

"I wrote the trilogy about opium because it is so astonishing and shocking to think that once it was legal to trade in opium—in fact, the opium trade was once the richest in the world—and because the legal opium trade was the beginning of today's worldwide drug problem. The three books span the lives and times of five generations of two families, one British, one Chinese, who were involved in building up the opium trade, in tearing it down, and, at last, after the Communists came to power, in its transfer to the Golden Triangle area of Burma, Laos, and Thailand, one of the richest sources of opium today.

"And now I am writing a book about being a UNICEF program officer in Southeast Asia, which was the most exciting, frustrating, happy, funny, sad, time of my life. When my Shanghai world ended in 1950, I went to Bangkok, Thailand, and got a job as a program officer in UNICEF, the United Nations Children's Fund, which helps governments around the world establish programs for the benefit of children. The problems of children are horrendous and nobody can hope to solve them all, but it is heart-stirring to work at it and sometimes to succeed.

"The people in this new book have different lifestyles from yours and mine, not better or worse, just different. Once the Inspector of Health of Central Java, a man with a ton of problems, little money, and few resources, said to his emissary, who was coming to confer with UNICEF, 'Tell Mrs. Gaan. She understands.' That's what the book is about: people and understanding and tolerance and compassion."

*   *   *

GIBBONS, Faye 1938-

PERSONAL: Born January 31, 1938, in Carter's Quarter, GA; daughter of George Manley (a welder and mechanic) and Alice Lenell (a mill worker; maiden name, Searcy) Junkins; married Benjamin Turner Gibbons III (a mathematician and computer analyst), August 29, 1964; children: Benjamin Turner IV, David. *Education:* Attended

(Dustjacket for 1985 edition of *Mighty Close to Heaven.*)

Oglethorpe University, 1960, and Emory University, 1961; Berry College, B.A., 1961; graduate study at Auburn University, 1965. *Religion:* Methodist.

ADDRESSES: Home and office—2536 Hwy. 143, Deatsville, AL 36022.

CAREER: Teacher at North Whitfield High School, Dalton, GA, 1961-63, at Waterman State Elementary School, Marietta, GA, 1963-64, at Beauregard High School, Lee County, AL, 1964-66, and at Lincoln Elementary School, Huntsville, AL, 1966-69; writer.

MEMBER: Society of Children's Book Writers, Alabama Library Association, Montgomery Creative Writers.

AWARDS, HONORS: Children's book of the year award from the Dixie Council of Authors and Journalists, 1983, and nominations for the Mark Twain Award, 1983, Alabama Children's Book Award, 1983, and Georgia Children's Book Award, 1984, all for *Some Glad Morning; Some Glad Morning* was selected two years in a row for the Alabama Emphasis on Reading Program; nominations for the Alabama Children's Book Award, 1986, and for the Georgia Children's Book Award, 1987, both for *Mighty Close to Heaven; Mighty Close to Heaven* was named an outstanding children's book by the American Library Association, 1986; *King Shoes and Clown Pockets* was named an outstanding children's book by *USA Today,* 1989.

WRITINGS:

Some Glad Morning (novel for young adults), Morrow, 1982.

Mighty Close to Heaven (novel for young adults), Morrow, 1985.
King Shoes and Clown Pockets (novel for young adults), Morrow, 1989.

Contributor of articles to newspapers and magazines, including *Old House Journal* and *Highlights*.

Gibbons's work has been recorded on audiocassette and *Some Glad Morning* is available in braille.

WORK IN PROGRESS: A book set in Alabama during the 1920s about a nine-year-old boy; several picture-book stories.

SIDELIGHTS: Faye Gibbons commented: "I grew up in mill towns and rural areas of north Georgia. When we lived in rural areas we experienced the kind of lifestyle that was more fitting to the 1800s than the 1900s: no electricity, no running water, no inside bathrooms, corn shuck mattresses, riding in wagons, and attending one-room school houses. All these things were extreme embarrassments to me when I was growing up and reading was my escape from what I saw as a harsh and ignorant world. Now that I am writing, of course, I see and appreciate the riches I gained back then. However, I wouldn't go so far as to say I'd want to live that way again!

"*Mighty Close to Heaven* had its beginnings in a hike my family and I made through a mountain wilderness area of Georgia when I was eight. Unemployed at the time and unable to afford either car or bus tickets for us, Daddy decided we would walk from my grandfather Junkins's farm to my mother's parents' farm. I wanted to capture my memory of those clean, wild mountains. The story of the boy lost in the mountains came later."

FOR MORE INFORMATION SEE:

PERIODICALS
New York Times Book Review, September 19, 1982.

*   *   *

GOLDMAN, Alex J. 1917-

PERSONAL: Born June 8, 1917, in Drohitin, Poland; immigrated to the United States, 1921; U.S. citizen; son of Julius David (a rabbi) and Sarah Esther (Rubinstein) Goldman; married Edith Borovay (an artist), March 1, 1942; children: Robert, Pamela. *Education:* DePaul University, J.D., 1939; Hebrew Theological College, Chicago, IL, Rabbi, 1944; University of Pennsylvania, certificate in marriage counseling, 1961.

ADDRESSES: Home—564 Hunting Ridge Rd., Stamford, CT 06903. *Office*—Temple Beth El, Roxbury Rd., Stamford, CT 06902. *Agent*— Bertha Klausner International Literary Agency, Inc., 71 Park Ave., New York, NY 10016

CAREER: Rabbi of temple in Tallahassee, FL, 1944-46; Temple University, Philadelphia, PA, teacher and director of Hillel Foundation, 1946-54; West Oak Lane Jewish Community Center, Philadelphia, rabbi, 1954-66; Temple Beth El, Stamford, CT, rabbi, 1966—. Director of Hillel Foundations, Florida State College for Women (now Florida State University), 1945-46, and Beaver College, Glenside, PA,

1953-54. Secretary of Philadelphia Zionist Youth Committee, 1951-52; vice president of the Stamford Clergy Association, 1974; president of the American Jewish Congress of lower Connecticut. Member of the National Conference of Christians and Jews, Philadelphia, 1946-54. Founder of the Covenant Lodge of B'nai B'rith.

MEMBER: Rabbinical Assembly, New York Board of Rabbis.

WRITINGS:

A Handbook for the Jewish Family: Understanding and Enjoying the Sabbath and Other Holidays, Bloch Publishing, 1958.
Blessed Art Thou: A Treasury of Prayers, Hebrew Publishing, 1961.
Giants of Faith: Great American Rabbis (young adults), Citadel, 1964, revised and expanded edition published as *The Greatest Rabbis Hall of Fame,* Shapolsky, 1987.
(Editor) John F. Kennedy, *The Quotable Kennedy,* Citadel, 1965.
A Child's Dictionary of Jewish Symbols, Feldheim, 1967.
John Fitzgerald Kennedy: The World Remembers (juvenile), Fleet Press, 1968.
(Editor) *The Truman Wit,* Citadel, 1968.
Power of the Bible (also see below), Fountainhead, 1972.
Power of the Bible [and] *The Eternal Books Retold* (also see below), introduction by Simon Greenberg, Fountainhead, 1974.
Judaism Confronts Contemporary Issues, Shengold, 1978.
The Eternal Books Retold, Pilgrim, 1982.
The Rabbi Is a Lady, Hippocrene, 1987.

Also author of *Experiencing China,* 1980, *A Passover Happening in the Ghetto,* 1980, and *Experiencing Jewish Communities in the Far East,* 1980.

WORK IN PROGRESS: Four novels: *My Blood Begins to Sing, Conceived in Liberty, I'm Lucky I Can Read in the Dark,* and *Peniel;* a novel-play, *My Path;* several other books on John F. Kennedy.

*   *   *

GOLDSZMIT, Henryk
See KORCZAK, Janusz

*   *   *

GOODWIN, Hal
See GOODWIN, Harold L(eland)

*   *   *

GOODWIN, Harold L(eland) 1914-1990
(Hal Goodwin; Hal Gordon, Blake Savage, pseudonyms; John Blaine, a joint pseudonym)

OBITUARY NOTICE—See index for *SATA* sketch: Born November 20, 1914, in Ellenburg, NY; died of cardiac arrest, February 18, 1990, in Bethesda, MD. Broadcaster, administrator, editor, journalist, and author. Goodwin is best remembered for his science adventure novels for young people featuring Rick Brant; the series, written under the pseudonym John Blaine and said to contain some of the most exciting and well-written juvenile fiction, includes *The Magic Talisman*. In addition to his writing, Goodwin held a variety of posts with radio stations, an advertising agency, a news service, the National Aeronautics and Space Administration, and the U.S. Department of Commerce. He wrote under different forms of his name as well as several pseudonyms, producing books such as *A Microphone for David, Rip Foster Rides the Gray Planet, All about Rockets and Space Flight,* and *Seafaring with Hal Goodwin.* Goodwin also edited *Americans and the World of Water.*

OBITUARIES AND OTHER SOURCES:

PERIODICALS

Chicago Tribune, March 4, 1990.
New York Times, February 23, 1990.

*   *   *

GORDON, Hal
See GOODWIN, Harold L(eland)

*   *   *

GREGG, Charles T(hornton) 1927-

PERSONAL: Born July 27, 1927, in Billings, MT; son of Charles Thornton (a broker) and Gertrude (Hurst) Gregg; married Elizabeth Whitaker (an operating room nurse), December 20, 1957; children: Paul, Diane, Brian, Elaine. *Education:* Attended Reed College, 1948-50; Oregon State University, B.S., 1952, M.S., 1955, Ph.D., 1959. *Politics:* Liberal. *Religion:* Unitarian Universalist. *Hobbies and other interests:* Reading, sailing, hiking, playing squash, bicycling.

ADDRESSES: Home—424 Kiva, Los Alamos, NM 87544. *Office*—Los Alamos Diagnostics, 2470 East Rd., Los Alamos, NM 87544.

CAREER: Oregon State University, Corvallis, instructor in agricultural chemistry, 1955-59; Johns Hopkins University, Baltimore, MD, research fellow in physiological chemistry, 1955-63; University of California, Los Alamos Scientific Laboratory, Los Alamos, NM, biochemist, 1963-85; Los Alamos Diagnostics, Los Alamos, vice president of research, 1986—. Visiting professor at Free University of Berlin, 1973-74. *Military service:* U.S. Navy, 1944-46; served in Pacific theater.

MEMBER: American Association for the Advancement of Science (fellow), American Society for Microbiology, Authors Guild, Authors League of America, American Society of Biological Chemistry and Molecular Biology.

AWARDS, HONORS: U.S. Public Health Service fellowship, 1959-63.

WRITINGS:

Plague! The Shocking Story of a Dread Disease in America Today (for young adults), Scribner, 1978, revised edition published as *Plague: An Ancient Disease in the Twentieth Century,* University of New Mexico Press, 1985.
A Virus of Love and Other Tales of Medical Detection, Scribner, 1983.
Tarawa, Stein & Day, 1984.

Contributor to scientific books, journals, and conference reports.

SIDELIGHTS: Charles T. Gregg wrote: "I considered myself a writer for a very long time before I had anything published. I wrote short stories, a two-act play, magazine articles, and half of a novel, and I accumulated a stack of rejection slips to attest to my status as a writer.

"I finally concluded that first I had to get a publisher's attention and could do that best by using my technical background to write on a subject that would be difficult for someone without my training (or the genius of French author Albert Camus) to handle. It worked—hence the book *Plague!*"

Of his second book, *A Virus of Love and Other Tales of Medical Detection,* Los Angeles Times book reviewer Carolyn See notes: "Several of the essays here—the ones based on both hard facts and accounts of detection—are interesting reading, particularly on Legionnaires' disease, a recent outbreak of botulism and the first part of a chapter on birth defects, dealing specifically with the marketing of Thalidomide in Europe."

In *Tarawa,* his third book of nonfiction, Gregg examines the U.S. Marines' attack on Tarawa Island, which was occupied by the Japanese during World War II.

WORKS CITED:

Los Angeles Times, March 16, 1983.

*   *   *

GURNEY, Gene 1924-

PERSONAL: Born July 4, 1924, in Fremont, Ohio; son of Jacob and Josephine (Mange) Gurney; married, 1951; wife's name, Clare (divorced, 1977); married Judith Scheirer, December 25, 1977. *Education:* Attended University of Florida, 1943; University of Maryland, B.S., 1954; George Washington University, M.A., 1966; Pacific Western College, Ph.D., 1980. *Hobbies and other interests:* "I collect replica scrimshaw and hope to do a definitive pictorial book about it. Writing books is also a hobby."

ADDRESSES: Home—4654 South 34th St., Arlington, VA 22206. *Office*—Federal Technology Transfer, 1200 Pennsylvania Ave., P.O. Box 7206, Washington, DC 20044.

CAREER: U.S. Air Force, 1943-73, retired as colonel; National Aeronautics and Space Administration (NASA), Washington, DC, program manager 1973-90.

MEMBER: Order of Daedalians.

AWARDS, HONORS: Aviation Space Writers Association awards, 1963, for *The War in the Air,* and 1965, for *Private Pilot's Handbook of Weather;* Silver Anvil Award from Public Relations Society of America, 1964, for his part in creating more than five hundred aviation books as director of the Air Force Book Program; Republic of Vietnam Gold Medal of Honor, 1971, for his public relations productions; named Public Affairs Officer of the Year, 1983, by Aviation Space Writers Association.

WRITINGS:

(With Mark P. Friedlander, Jr.) *Five Down and Glory: A History of the American Air Ace,* Putnam, 1959.

Journey of the Giants, Coward, 1961.

(With Carroll V. Glines) *Minutemen of the Air,* Random House, 1961.

Americans into Orbit: The Story of Project Mercury (for young adults), Random House, 1962.

(Editor with James Gilbert) *Test Pilots,* F. Watts, 1962.

The War in the Air, Crown, 1962.

The B-29: The Plane That Won the War, Fawcett, 1963.

Great Air Battles, F. Watts, 1963.

The Pentagon, Crown, 1964.

(With Joseph A. Skiera) *Private Pilot's Handbook of Weather,* Aero Publishers, 1964, 2nd edition, 1974.

Rocket and Missile Technology, F. Watts, 1964.

The Smithsonian Institution, Crown, 1964.

Flying Aces of World War I, Random House, 1965.

Arlington National Cemetery, Crown, 1965.

Chronology of World Aviation, F. Watts, 1965.

Library of Congress, Crown, 1966, revised edition, 1981.

A Pictorial History of the United States Army, Crown, 1966, revised edition, 1978.

Walk in Space: The Story of Project Gemini (for young adults), Random House, 1967.

(With James C. Elliott) *Private Pilot's Handbook of Navigation,* Aero Publishers, 1967.

P-38 Lightning, Arco, 1969.

Beautiful Washington, D.C.: A Picture Story of the Nation's Capital, Crown, 1969.

Americans to the Moon: The Story of Project Apollo (for young adults), Random House, 1970.

GENE GURNEY

The United States Coast Guard: A Pictorial History, Crown, 1973.

(With Friedlander) *Higher, Faster, and Farther,* Aero Publishers, 1973.

How to Save Your Life on the Nation's Highways and Byways, Crown, 1974.

(With Nick P. Apple) *The Air Force Museum,* Crown, 1975, revised edition, 1983.

America in Wax, Crown, 1977.

(With Harold Wise) *The Official Washington, D.C., Directory: A Pictorial Guide,* Crown, 1977.

(With Brian Sheehan) *Educational Guide to U.S. Service and Maritime Academies,* Van Nostrand, 1978.

Space Technology Spinoffs (for young adults), F. Watts, 1979.

(With Friedlander) *Handbook of Successful Franchising,* Van Nostrand, 1981, 3rd edition, 1989.

Kingdoms of Europe: An Illustrated Encyclopedia of Ruling Monarchs from Ancient Times to the Present, Crown, 1982.

(With Kurt Willinger) *The American Jeep in War and Peace,* Crown, 1983.

Vietnam, the War in the Air: A Pictorial History of the U.S. Air Forces in the Vietnam War; Air Force, Army, Navy, and Marines (for young adults), Crown, 1985.

Kingdoms of Asia, the Middle East, and Africa: An Illustrated Encyclopedia of Ruling Monarchs from Ancient Times to the Present, Crown, 1985.

Editor-in-chief, *Military Classics,* TAB Books, 1988-90.

WITH CLARE GURNEY

Mount Vernon (for children), F. Watts, 1965.

Monticello (for children), F. Watts, 1966.

F.D.R. and Hyde Park (for children), F. Watts, 1970.

Unidentified Flying Objects, Abelard, 1970.

The Colony of Maryland (for young adults), F. Watts, 1972.

Cosmonauts in Orbit: The Story of the Soviet Manned Space Program, F. Watts, 1972.

North and South Korea (for young adults), F. Watts, 1973.

The Launching of Sputnik, October 4, 1957: The Space Age Begins, F. Watts, 1975.

Women on the March (for young adults), Abelard, 1975.

The United States Treasury: A Pictorial History, Crown, 1978.

Agriculture Careers (for young adults), F. Watts, 1978.

WORK IN PROGRESS: Ethics in American Industry.

SIDELIGHTS: Gene Gurney commented: "I wrote some articles for the newspaper in high school and at the University of Florida. This was a very important base, I think. It set my style of writing quickly the facts of the story. Now I can easily 'do' a nonfiction book a year on almost any subject, some of considerable magnitude. Next point: Do your own basic research. I can read the Sunday *New York Times* and with little imagination come up with specific subjects for a dozen books. But even with nearly fifty books, I could never make a living writing. For the *publishers,* on the other hand, I could."

*   *   *

HACKETT, John Winthrop 1910-

PERSONAL: Born November 5, 1910, in Perth, Australia; son of Sir John Winthrop and Deborah Vernon (Drake-Brockman) Hackett; married Margaret Frena, 1942; children: Bridget, Elizabeth, Susan. *Education:* New College,

Oxford, B.A., 1933, B.Litt., 1936, M.A., 1945; postgraduate study at Graz University, 1948, and Imperial Defence College, 1951. *Hobbies and other interests:* Travel, fishing, books, wine, music, medieval history.

ADDRESSES: Home—Coberley Mill, Nr. Cheltenham, Gloucestershire GL53 9NH, England.

CAREER: British Army, career officer, 1931-68, commissioned to 8th King's Royal Irish Hussars, 1931-36, served in Palestine, 1936, with Transjordan Frontier Force, 1937-40, served in Syria, 1941, secretary of commission of control for Syria and Lebanon, 1941, served in tanks in Western Desert, general staff officer with 9th Army, 1942, and Raiding Forces Middle East Land Forces, 1942-43, commander of Fourth Parachute Brigade, 1943, served in Italy, 1943 and 1946, and Arnhem, 1944, wounded three times during World War II, head of British Intelligence Organization in Vienna, 1946, commander of Transjordan Frontier Force, 1947, deputy quartermaster-general of British Army of the Rhine, 1952, commander of Twentieth Armoured Brigade, 1954, general officer commanding Seventh Armoured Division, 1956-58, commandant of Royal Military College of Science, 1958-61, colonel-commandant of Royal Electrical and Mechanical Engineers, 1961-66, commander-in-chief of Northern Ireland Command, 1961-63, deputy chief of Imperial General Staff, 1963-64, deputy chief of general staff of Ministry of Defence, 1964-66, commander-in-chief of British Army of the Rhine and commander of Northern Army Group, 1966-68, retired as general; University of London, London, England, principal of King's College, 1968-75, fellow, 1968; writer, 1975—. Instructor at Royal Naval College, Greenwich, England, 1943-50; Lees Knowles Lecturer at Cambridge University, 1961; Kermit Roosevelt Lecturer in the United States, 1967; Alanbrooke Memorial Lecturer, 1968; Harmon Memorial Lecturer at U.S. Air Force Academy, 1970; Basil Henriques Memorial Lecturer for National Association of Boys' Clubs, 1970; lecturer at Woodrow Wilson Institute of International Studies, Princeton University, 1984, U.S. Army War College, U.S. Naval War College, National Defense University, Fort Leavenworth, and West Point; visiting professor in classics at King's College, 1976. ADC General to the Queen, 1967-68.

MEMBER: Classical Association (president, 1970-71), English Association (president, 1973-74), Cavalry Club, Carlton Club, United Oxford and Cambridge University Club, White's Club.

AWARDS, HONORS: Military—Distinguished Service Order and bar; Military Cross; honorary colonel of Tenth Battalion and Tenth Volunteer Battalion Parachute Regiment, Oxford University Officers Training Corps, and Queen's Royal Irish Hussars, 1969-75; mentioned four times in dispatches. *Other*—Member of Order of the British Empire, 1938, commander of order, 1953; companion of Order of Bath, 1962, knight commander, 1962, knight grand cross, 1967; deputy lieutenant of Gloucestershire, 1983; Chesney Gold Medal from Royal United Services Institution, 1985; LL.D. from Queen's University, Belfast, University of Western Australia, 1963, University of Exeter, 1977, and University of Buckingham, 1987; fellow of St. George's College, University of Western Australia, 1965, King's College, London, 1968; honorary fellow of New College, Oxford.

WRITINGS:

The Profession of Arms, Times Publishing Co., 1963, Macmillan, 1983.
I Was a Stranger, Chatto & Windus, 1977, Houghton, 1978.
(With others) *The Third World War: August, 1985* (novel), Macmillan, 1978, published in England as *The Third World War: A Future History,* Sidgwick & Jackson, 1978.
(With others) *The Third World War: The Untold Story* (novel), Macmillan, 1982.
Hitler's Generals, Weidenfeld & Nicolson, 1989.
Warfare in the Ancient World, Facts on File, 1990.

Also author of *Authority in a Changing Society,* 1969. Author of addresses, including *Reflections upon Epic Warfare,* Classical Association, 1971, and *Sweet Uses of Adversity: An Experience,* United Kingdom English Association, 1974. Contributor of articles and reviews to magazines. *I Was a Stranger* was read by John MacDonald on audio cassette and released by Books on Tape.

SIDELIGHTS: John Winthrop Hackett told *SATA:* "If my career as an undergraduate at Oxford at the turn of the 1930s had been of outstanding brilliance in either of the two quite separate degree courses (classics and history) that I completed, I should have become a don at once, for life as a university teacher, especially at Oxford, always greatly attracted me. Fortunately for me I was only very good and not brilliant, otherwise I should now be a retired professor in the later years of a rather humdrum life instead of having had the fascinating kaleidoscopic time that has been my lot.

"Another narrow escape was from a sackful of inherited wealth. My father, going out from Ireland to Australia (where I was born and lived until the age of seventeen) made a very great deal of money and never really knew how rich he was. When he died in 1916 he left a decent legacy to his widow and five children (I, the only son being the fourth) and the residue to the Church in Western Australia and the university he founded there. The university was better off by some twenty-seven million Australian dollars. As I have moved through a life of high variety and absorbing interest and seen the cares and responsibilities that go with the inheritance of great wealth, I have often been grateful to have been spared them. What is more important is that if I had been rich my life would have been different. I might not have been serving with Arab troops of a British colonial force in Jordan in the late 1930s, when I met my future wife. We were married in St. George's Cathedral in Jerusalem after war broke out.

"I hugely enjoyed my thirty-five years of military service, almost all spent overseas, and the chance it gave me to see so much of the world. I used periods of leave on historical research in Oxford and elsewhere and was awarded a research degree for my work on the Crusades. I learned modern languages (being now at home in four or five) to add to Latin and Greek, traveled widely, heard a great deal of music, drank a great deal of wine, played polo, skied, fished, and shot, and had a lovely time, always doing a bit of writing. What I was trying to do all the time, I now see, was to have my cake and eat it too, and on the whole I nearly succeeded. The outbreak of World War II found me as a horse cavalry soldier, moving through tanks in the Western Desert into parachuting and on to Arnhem, after which I lay in hiding in German-occupied Holland. For four and a half months I was nursed, protected, and cherished by a brave Dutch family in a house fifty yards away from German military police quarters, while I gathered strength for a final escape. In the year after the war I wrote down an account of this almost unbelievable experience while everything was still sharp in my mind and then put the manuscript away for thirty years. It was published in 1977 as *I Was a Stranger*. It is the best thing I have ever written—an undramatic, unheroic, low-key study of the unconquerable strength of the gentle.

"I became commander of Britain's largest land force, the British Army of the Rhine, and of NATO's Northern Army Group. Then, at long last, I went back to university life in 1968 as principal of King's College, London, and spent eventful years there before coming to live in an ancient mill house. The drawing room where I write, looking out over the mill pond to the meadows where my sheep are, is that part of the mill built about 1585, and all around is the beautiful Cotswold countryside. Here I read and go on writing, often in the early morning before the world wakes up, writing out of preference with a pen. I use modern aids too, but also like to push a pen because it is hard work—and that helps your writing to be terse and precise. The machines are too easy and a talkative person like me can easily become long-winded and verbose.

"I never forget the slogan 'use it or lose it' and try to let no week go by without reading something in Latin, Greek, French, German, Italian, and Arabic. I often find I have to run pretty fast just to stand still, but I like it like that."

FOR MORE INFORMATION SEE:

PERIODICALS

New York Times, March 21, 1980; September 22, 1982.
New York Times Book Review, March 25, 1979.
Times Literary Supplement, August 12, 1982.
Washington Post, June 18, 1979.

*   *   *

HAMILTON, Charles 1913-

PERSONAL: Born December 24, 1913, in Ludington, MI; son of Charles and Ethel Louise (Carr) Hamilton; married Diane Brooks, March 21, 1962; children: Carolyn, Charles, Cynthia, Brooks. *Education:* University of California, Los Angeles, B.A., 1937, M.A., 1939. *Hobbies and other interests:* Collecting old guns, swords, and books on snakes, insects, and witchcraft.

ADDRESSES: Home—166 East 63rd St., New York, NY 10021.

CAREER: Prentice-Hall, Inc. (publishers), New York City, sales correspondent, 1940-41; William H. Wise & Co., New York City, office manager, 1941-42 and 1946-47; Ben Sackheim, New York City, copywriter, 1948; Bibliotherapy, Inc., New York City, president, 1951-62; Charles Hamilton Autographs, Inc., New York City, president, 1953-85; founder and president of Charles Hamilton Galleries, Inc. (first auction house in America devoted exclusively to autographs), 1963-85. Consultant on manuscripts and documents and expert witness on forgeries for New York courts. *Military service:* U.S. Army Air Corps, 1942-45; became technical sergeant; awarded Bronze Star, Conspicuous Service Medal, five campaign medals, and six battle stars.

CHARLES HAMILTON

AWARDS, HONORS: Civil War Round Table of New York Prize for best book on Abraham Lincoln, 1963, for *Lincoln in Photographs: An Album of Every Known Pose;* Kentucky Colonel award, 1980.

WRITINGS:

(Editor) *Cry of the Thunderbird: The American Indian's Own Story,* Macmillan, 1950.
Men of the Underworld: The Professional Criminal's Own Story, Macmillan, 1952, published in England as *Crime U.S.A.,* 1956.
(Editor) *Braddock's Defeat,* University of Oklahoma Press, 1959.
Collecting Autographs and Manuscripts, University of Oklahoma Press, 1961.
(With Lloyd Ostendorf) *Lincoln in Photographs: An Album of Every Known Pose,* University of Oklahoma Press, 1963.
The Robot That Helped to Make a President: A Reconnaissance into the Mysteries of John F. Kennedy's Signatures, privately printed, 1965.
Scribblers and Scoundrels, Paul Eriksson, 1968.
(With wife, Diane Hamilton) *Big Name Hunting: A Beginner's Guide to Autograph Collecting,* Simon & Schuster, 1973.
The Book of Autographs, Simon & Schuster, 1978.
The Signature of America: A Fresh Look at Famous Handwriting, Harper, 1979.
(Contributor) *Book of Lists,* Morrow, Volume I: 1979, Volume II, 1980, Volume III, 1983.
Great Forgers and Famous Fakes: The Manuscript Forgers of America and How They Fooled the Experts, Crown, 1980.
Auction Madness, Everest, 1981.

American Autographs: Signers of the Declaration of Independence, Revolutionary War Leaders, Presidents, 2 volumes, University of Oklahoma Press, 1983.
Leaders and Personalities of the Third Reich, R. James Bender, 1984.
In Search of Shakespeare: A Reconnaissance into the Poet's Life and Handwriting, Harcourt, 1985.
The Illustrated Letter, Universe, 1987.
The Hitler Diaries: The World's Most Famous Fake, University Press of Kentucky, 1991.

Contributor of more than fifty articles on autographs to *Hobbies,* 1948-58; also contributor of numerous other articles on autographs and manuscripts to other periodicals. Also author of two privately printed pamphlets of poems.

WORK IN PROGRESS: Cardenio: Shakespeare's Lost Play; Sherlock: The Autobiography of Sherlock Holmes.

SIDELIGHTS: Charles Hamilton told *SATA:* "I am a handwriting expert, a jack-of-all-trades in everything that is written down with pencil or pen or even typewriter. I am also an author who has written some seventeen published books and quite a few that were not clever enough or marketable enough to get into print. I buy and sell letters and documents and signatures of famous people; I read character from looking at how a person writes; and I testify in court in cases of forged wills and other documents. I've been an expert handwriting witness in many exciting cases, some of them famous murder cases. I also deliver lectures about my adventures.

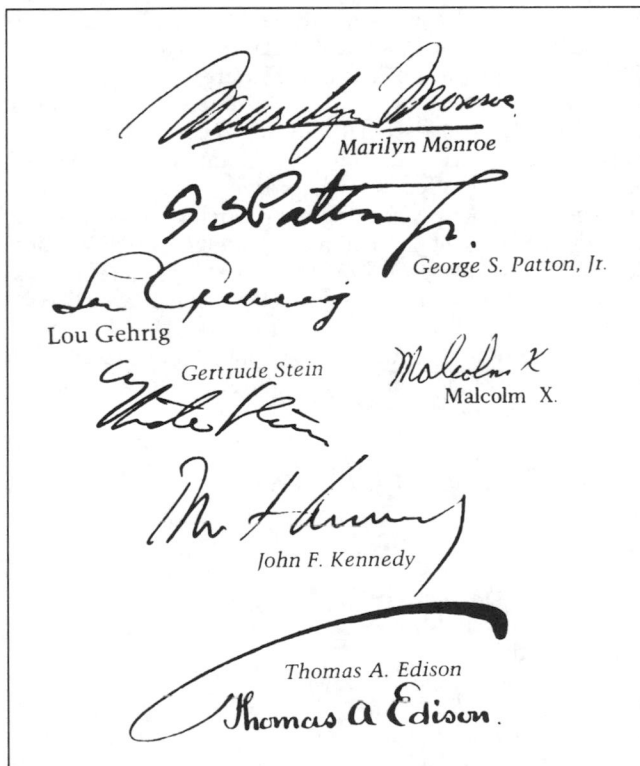

Signatures of famous twentieth-century Americans. (From *The Book of Autographs* by Charles Hamilton.)

"My career started in a trash can behind the house of old Judge Charles Wisner of my hometown, Flint, Michigan. Mrs. Wisner, the inventor's widow, had pitched out a lot of old documents signed by the judge and I stuffed my pockets with them. I was then ten years old and the year was 1924. I was fascinated by the quaint papers and immediately started a collection of old documents. I already had collections of butterflies, crayfish, polliwogs, rare rocks, Indian relics, pressed tree leaves, old clocks, Civil War souvenirs, stamps, old license plates, bird feathers, and other things. I even had a jar of bloodsuckers. I was also the member, and usually the leader, of our local knight's club, Indian club, Seven Sly Slickers, and pirate club.

"When I was in fifth grade I wrote my first book, a novel about World War I—long since thrown away. I wrote it while the other members of the class were studying geography. I also wrote poems in Scottish dialect in imitation of Robert Burns. Nevertheless, my teacher tried to persuade my parents to take me out of school so I could learn a useful trade and not be a burden on society when I grew up.

"My father's ambition for me was that I go to Harvard University and study law. However, he died when I was thirteen and our family moved to Los Angeles, where everything was, in those days, much cheaper. The Depression was on. Oranges were ten cents a bucket, bread was nine cents a loaf, and almost everything else was three for a nickel. The trouble was that a lot of people didn't have a nickel.

"By this time I had lost interest in all of my collections but autographs. Handwriting captivated me. I read everything I could find in the library about autographs and I wrote my first letter to a celebrity—my favorite British author, Rudyard Kipling. Kipling hated autograph hunters and Americans. His hostility was a real challenge for me. I told him in my letter: 'I am a boy twelve years old and I am enclosing ten cents for your signature. It's my week's salary for hauling out our furnace ashes. I hope it will be enough for your signature.' It was, and Kipling wrote his name for me on a slip of paper. Getting Kipling's autograph was one of the greatest thrills of my life. I set it various places in my room and walked around it and contemplated it for hours. Eventually I framed it with a portrait of Kipling. Within months I had increased the size of my collection with scores of other signatures and letters from people I enormously admired, such as Thomas A. Edison, Jane Addams, William Howard Taft, Katharine Lee Bates (author of 'America the Beautiful'), and John Philip Sousa, who told me how he happened to write, in only fifteen minutes, his famous march, 'The Stars and Stripes Forever.'

"The hobby of collecting autographs changed my whole life. I became intensely interested in the great men and women to whom I wrote and developed a keen interest in all knowledge. I was the valedictorian of my class at Beverly Hills High School and a distinguished scholar at the University of California, Los Angeles, where I took two degrees.

"After graduation, near the end of the Great Depression, I came to New York—as good a place to go hungry as anywhere else. I wrote a lot of stories and collected a lot of rejection slips, which I used as bookmarks. It didn't take me long to discover that I wasn't a very good writer. During World War II, I was a sergeant and served in the army for four years, two of them in combat zones, for which I was awarded two medals for conspicuous service, six battle stars, and five campaign medals.

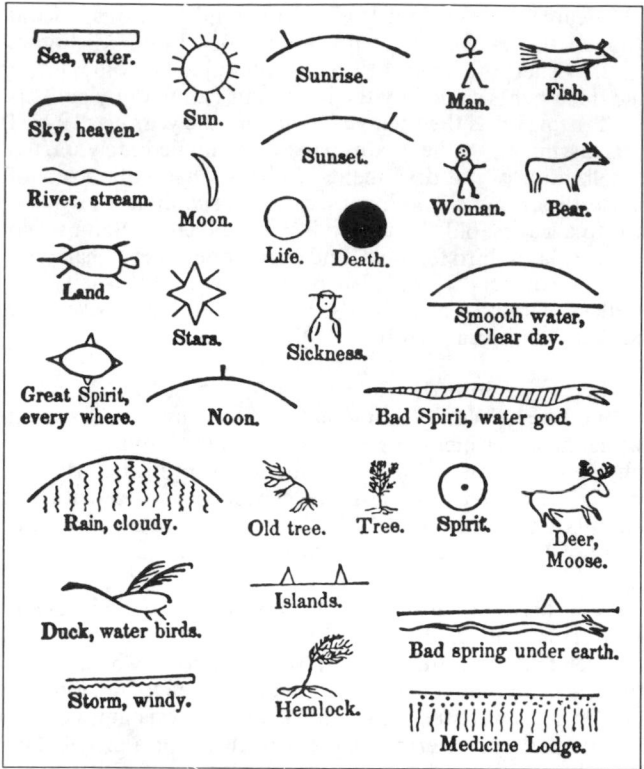

Characters used in Ojibway picture writing. (From *Cry of the Thunderbird* by Charles Hamilton.)

"At thirty-six I had my first book published, a semi-anthology called *Cry of the Thunderbird: The American Indian's Own Story.* It defended the Indians and described their way of life in their own words. I had always been fascinated by the Indians and as a boy I played with Ojibway kids in northern Michigan. I was so interested in Indians that I read almost every book on them in the Flint Public Library and even signed my name *Charles P. Hamilton,* borrowing the 'P' from Pitamakin, a Blackfoot Indian I much admired. I often wrote birchbark letters to my friends, sometimes drawing pictographs on them.

"Such was my interest in Indians as a boy that one fall my father cut for me a huge nine-foot-long sheet of birchbark from a young tree. My best friend, Bert Stull, and I worked for weeks stitching and caulking together a birchbark canoe. All winter it lay in the basement, but when the first spring thaw turned Gilkie Creek into a torrent of seething water we carried the canoe Indian-style on our heads to its snow-covered banks. Even though I couldn't swim I climbed into the canoe. Bert gave me a shove into the rapids. Almost at once the canoe started to crack and pop as the bark split open. Water poured in through the crevices. The canoe sank and so did I. Bert plunged into the icy water and pulled me out just in time. Afterwards we stood, drenched to the skin in the biting cold, laughing and embracing each other because we had cheated death. This perilous adventure just poisoned me for more excitement and interest in Indians.

"My second book, *Men of the Underworld,* was about professional crime in America. It explained exactly how professionals rob a bank. My descriptions were so detailed that for many years after the book was published I received propositions from criminals who needed an 'expert' to help them. My best offer came from Canada where a notorious bank robber,

who had already cased and was ready to rob a small bank, invited me to take part for an equal share. I declined.

"In 1961 I wrote the first of my books on autographs and handwriting, *Collecting Autographs and Manuscripts.* As I had been a collector since age ten and had written my first article about autographs at age fourteen, it was logical I should put my ideas on the subject into book form. In 1973 my wife Diane and I wrote a book on autographs especially for children titled *Big Name Hunting.* This little volume tells how to get valuable autographs for the price of a postage stamp. *The Book of Autographs* gives the values of famous autographs, some of which are worth many thousand dollars. The rarest modern autograph is that of actress Greta Garbo. Her signature is worth fifteen hundred dollars and a handwritten letter by her is worth about ten thousand dollars.

"More recently I revived a boyhood interest in William Shakespeare, my favorite writer. I was inspired to write *In Search of Shakespeare,* which is full of new information about the great dramatist and poet. Among other things, I discovered that Shakespeare might have been poisoned by his son-in-law. It is exciting to go back nearly four hundred years and find important evidence that thousands of other searchers have overlooked. I like nothing better than probing the secrets of the past.

"I often receive letters from young people and despite the fact that I am seventy-five years old and work a fourteen-hour day, I try to answer every letter. A few years ago I got a letter from a fourteen-year-old girl named Darla in the tiny town of Marshall, Kentucky. She explained that she had an assignment to write to her favorite celebrity. I couldn't resist the flattery and dispatched a speedy reply. Somehow a correspondence got started between Darla's class and myself. All the boys and girls wrote fascinating letters to me about life in a small town and sent me a portfolio of letters. On Valentine's Day they sent me a special and very beautiful valentine. Finally, they mailed their high school annual, in which all of them had written affectionate inscriptions to me. I, in turn, sent them long letters relating my escapades when I was a ninth-grade student at Thomas Starr King Junior High School in Los Angeles in 1929. As a final present to me, my young friends sent a round-robin letter to Governor Brown of Kentucky and asked him to appoint me a Kentucky Colonel. He did so in March, 1980, and I still treasure the certificate personally signed by the governor. It hangs on the wall in my summer home."

FOR MORE INFORMATION SEE:

PERIODICALS

Americana, May-June, 1978.
American Weekly, May 19, 1963.
Esquire, October, 1979.
Kirkus Reviews, August 1, 1985.
National Insider, September 12, 1965; November 14, 1965.
New York Herald Tribune, May 19, 1963.
People, July 31, 1978.
Saturday Evening Post, January, 1980.
Time, April 2, 1965; May 28, 1965.
Washington Post, June 15, 1983.
Washington Post Book World, November 24, 1985.

HANLEY, Boniface (Francis) 1924-

PERSONAL: Born September 27, 1924, in Brooklyn, NY; son of James Joseph and Mary (Riordan) Hanley. *Education:* St. Bonaventure College (now University), B.A., 1947; Holy Name College, M.S. (theology), 1951; received M.S. (in business) from Columbia University. *Politics:* Democrat.

ADDRESSES: Office—St. Joseph's Church, 454 Germantown Rd., Echo Lake, West Milford, NJ 07480.

CAREER: Entered Franciscan Order, 1945; ordained Roman Catholic priest, 1956; Bishop Timon High School, Buffalo, NY, teacher, 1951-53; Franciscan Provincial Headquarters, New York City, secretary, 1953-55; Franciscan Mission, La Paz, Bolivia, pastor, 1956-58; St. Francis College, Rye Beach, NH, master of students, 1958-67; Siena College, Loudonville, NY, superior of Franciscan Community, beginning 1967; St. Mary's parish, Pompton Lakes, NJ, pastor, 1973-76; Christ House (Franciscan retreat house), Lafayette, NJ, director, beginning 1976; became pastor of St. Catherine's parish, Ringwood, NJ; became rector of St. Francis Church, New York City; pastor of St. Joseph's Church, West Milford, NJ.

AWARDS, HONORS: Catholic Book Award from Catholic Press Association, 1985, for youth book *No Strangers to Violence, No Strangers to Love.*

WRITINGS:

(With Salvator Fink) *The Franciscans: Love at Work,* St. Anthony's Guild Press (Paterson, NJ), 1962.
Ten Christians: By Their Deeds You Shall Know Them, Ave Maria Press, 1979.
Maximilian Kolbe: No Greater Love (for young adults), Ave Maria Press, 1982.
No Strangers to Violence, No Strangers to Love (for young adults), Ave Maria Press, 1983.

Also author, with Fink, of biographical articles about saints and holy people.

WORK IN PROGRESS: A novel.

SIDELIGHTS: Boniface Hanley told *SATA:* "I was born on a farm in Springfield, New York, a place now covered with expressways. I grew up in Brooklyn, and consider it the greatest blessing of my life to have grown up on its streets. Our family embraced the whole block. We had fifty mothers watching us and one hundred and fifty sisters making sure we got home on time for supper. Our energies were absorbed by punchball, boxball, stickball, baseball, and football. We were Depression kids, but I never lived better. When I look at a basket of shrimp now and realize that we were eating it at a couple of cents a pound during those supposedly dark days, I chuckle.

"There were plenty of educational opportunities. Our teachers (Halifax Charity nuns) were top drawer. In the course of my life, I have attended some of the nation's most prestigious universities, but I never found teachers as competent and dedicated as those nuns. Along with my parents and a beloved aunt, they cultivated within me a love of poetry and reading and singing and dancing that has stayed with me all these years.

"I can not remember a time when I wasn't writing. It came to me as naturally as eating. But there came a time when I had to make a vocation choice and I chose to become a priest. This work absorbs most of my energies.

"My whole life has been a colorful one. I have traveled practically all throughout the world, lived in a number of places, and had many adventures. I have managed to turn out some books in the meanwhile. As you can see, my books have been mostly biographical. Men and women fascinate me. I believe each human being has a story. For the first time now, I am struggling to write a novel. It is based on the life of Father Franz Stock, a heroic German priest who served in the prisons of Paris during World War II. I hope I can meet the challenge."

*   *   *

HARMON, William (Ruth) 1938-

PERSONAL: Born June 10, 1938, in Concord, NC; son of William Richard (a textile executive) and Virginia (Pickerel) Harmon; married Lynn Chadwell, December 20, 1965 (divorced, 1984); married Anne Margretta Wilson, May 7, 1988; children: (first marriage) Sally Frances, William Richard Harmon II; (second marriage) Caroline Ruth. *Education:* University of Chicago, A.B., 1958, A.M., 1968; University of North Carolina, M.A., 1968; University of Cincinnati, Ph.D., 1970. *Politics:* Democrat. *Religion:* None.

ADDRESSES: Home—1919 Southwood Dr. Apt. 5, Durham, NC 27707. *Office*—Department of English, University of North Carolina, Chapel Hill, NC 27599-3520.

CAREER: University of North Carolina at Chapel Hill, instructor, 1970-71, assistant professor, 1971-72, associate

WILLIAM HARMON

professor, 1973-77, professor of English, 1977—, chairman of department, 1972-77. Texas A & M University, visiting distinguished professor, 1984-85. *Military service:* U.S. Navy, active duty as officer, 1960-67, reserve service, 1967—; currently a lieutenant commander; received Navy Commendation Medal with V and Vietnamese Staff Service Honor Medal, first class.

MEMBER: Modern Language Association of America, Academy of American Poets, American Anthropological Association, American Name Society, Poetry Society of America, Poe Studies Association, T. S. Eliot Society, Thomas Hardy Society, South Atlantic Modern Language Association.

AWARDS, HONORS: Rockefeller Foundation humanities fellowship; Ford Foundation fellowship; Elliston Poetry Fund scholarship; Kenan Fund research grants; Lamont Award for *Treasury Holiday: Thirty-four Fits for the Opening of the Fiscal Year;* William Carlos Williams Award for *Mutatis Mutandis: 27 Invoices.*

WRITINGS:

POETRY

Treasury Holiday: Thirty-four Fits for the Opening of the Fiscal Year, Wesleyan University Press, 1970.
Legion: Civic Choruses, Wesleyan University Press, 1973.
The Intussusception of Miss Mary America, Kayak Books, 1976.
One Long Poem, Louisiana State University Press, 1982.
Mutatis Mutandis: 27 Invoices, Wesleyan University Press, 1985.

OTHER

Time in Ezra Pound's Work (criticism), University of North Carolina Press, 1977.
(Editor) *The Oxford Book of American Light Verse,* Oxford University Press, 1979.
(With Louis Rubin) *Uneeda Review,* Nick Lyons, 1984.
(With C. Hugh Holman) *A Handbook to Literature,* 5th edition, Macmillan, 1986, 6th edition, 1991.
(Editor) *The Concise Columbia Book of Poetry,* Columbia University Press, 1990.

Work anthologized in *Quickly Aging Here: Some Poets of the 1970's,* edited by Geof Hewitt, Doubleday, 1969, and in a Pushcart selection. Contributor to journals, including *Antioch Review, Carolina Quarterly, Poetry, Kenyon Review, Sewanee Review, Ploughshares,* and *San Francisco Review.*

WORK IN PROGRESS: Poetry books entitled *Brass and Percussion: Prose Songs* and *Thingsomeness; A Scythian Suite,* a book of critical pieces; *What Rhymes,* a book about poetry.

SIDELIGHTS: "I've always loved laughter. School was pretty serious—the higher I went, the more serious—and the less room there was for comedy. But I kept up the interest as a hobby and sideline. When I began teaching in a university, I found that I was referring quite a bit to light verse, especially the lyrics of songs by Cole Porter, Johnny Mercer, Roger Miller, Paul Simon, and so forth. Eventually, in 1979, I made my hobby pay off when I got to edit *The Oxford Book of American Light Verse.* I know a lot of serious scholars who were made to feel ashamed and embarrassed in grade school because they preferred comic books and science fiction to the solemn books they used to call 'starred fiction.' Well, I think it was a mistake to make people ashamed; and now, we with our secret hobbies in childhood have now converted them into an academic discipline called 'popular culture.' I'm thinking of founding an Institute for the Study of Rock 'n Roll."

FOR MORE INFORMATION SEE:

BOOKS

Contemporary Literary Criticism, Volume 38, Gale, 1986.

PERIODICALS

Antioch Review, fall/winter, 1970-71.
Carolina Quarterly, winter, 1971.
Georgia Review, summer, 1983.
New York Times, August 9, 1979.
New York Times Book Review, February 13, 1972.
Poetry, March, 1972; December, 1973; January, 1974.
Sewanee Review, summer, 1978.
Washington Post Book World, August 19, 1979.

* * *

HAYDEN, Torey L(ynn) 1951-

PERSONAL: Born May 21, 1951, in Livingston, MT; daughter of Joyce Jansen (a secretary); married; children: one daughter. *Education:* Whitman College, B.A., 1972; Eastern Montana College, M.S., 1973; doctoral study at University of Minnesota, 1975-79.

ADDRESSES: Home—North Wales, U.K. *Agent*—P. Ginsberg, Curtis Brown Associates, Inc., 10 Astor Place, New York, NY 10003.

CAREER: Writer, 1979—. Has worked as a special education teacher for the emotionally disturbed, a university teacher, a psychiatric researcher, and a children's unit teacher in a state mental institution.

AWARDS, HONORS: Christopher Award, 1981, for *One Child; One Child* was chosen as a New York Public Library Books for the Teenager in 1981, and *Somebody Else's Kids* was chosen in 1982; *Murphy's Boy* named an American Library Association and *School Library Journal* Best Young Adult Book, 1983.

WRITINGS:

One Child (nonfiction), Putnam, 1980.
Somebody Else's Kids (nonfiction), Putnam, 1981.
Murphy's Boy (nonfiction), Putnam, 1983.
The Sunflower Forest (fiction), Putnam, 1984.
Just Another Kid (nonfiction), Putnam, 1988.
Ghost Girl (nonfiction), Little, Brown, 1991.

Contributor to professional journals.

ADAPTATIONS: Murphy's Boy was adapted as a television movie entitled "Trapped in Silence," starring Marsha Mason, 1986; *One Child, Somebody Else's Kids,* and *Murphy's Boy* are available on cassette tapes for the visually impaired.

WORK IN PROGRESS: A novel.

TOREY L. HAYDEN

SIDELIGHTS: "I don't remember when I first became interested in writing," Torey L. Hayden told *SATA.* "It seems like it has been something that has been with me, been a part of me, for as long as I have memories, but I have a very clear recollection of when the magic of writing took hold. I was eight, a none-too-enthusiastic third-grader in Miss Webb's class. At home I had a puppy, a dachshund my mother had given me for my seventh birthday. One day at school—it was October, I think—I spent my reading period writing a fairly lurid account of imagined kid and dog adventures. The class had been divided into reading groups and I was supposed to be at my desk doing my reading workbook, but I wrote instead on the back of an old math paper. Miss Webb came down the aisle unexpectedly, caught me and confiscated the story.

"That wasn't a particularly traumatic event. In fact, I forgot all about it until some days later when she was cleaning out her desk and found the story, which she returned to me. I don't recall now how much time had elapsed, a couple of weeks, I think. Anyway, I'd been ill earlier in the week and was now having to stay after school to make up work and she'd been cleaning her desk, I suspect, to occupy time. So, when I finished, she gave me back the story and I left the room with it.

"Among all the memories of my childhood, that particular moment is one of the clearest," Hayden remarked. She later added, "I remember the exhilaration of reading that story and finding it every bit as exciting to me as the day I wrote it. For the first time I discovered that, like a camera, words can capture the complexity, the beauty, the subtlety of life so precisely that one can return to them the next day, the next week, or years later and feel the experience they have created as powerfully as the moment it happened. That to me is magic of the first order.

"Writing remains an affair of the heart for me. I've been working as a full time writer for over ten years now and financial and family commitments force me to regard it as a profession, but I must admit, each time I sit down to the typewriter to start a new book, I write it for me. I *love* the process of writing, the nudge and jiggle of words until that ripe moment when *snap!* the emotional photograph is taken and all the complex beauty of being human is captured. I no longer have the leisure to write when in the mood. With a husband and a toddler to consider, I'm confined to writing weekday mornings, but I'm still fairly manic at the typewriter. I've never equalled the eight days it took to write *One Child,* but I still expect on average to finish a first draft of a book in six weeks.

"How did I come to write the books I did? In the case of the five nonfiction books, I think it was simply a desire to share my experiences, to open up to others a world that most people do not encounter firsthand and, if I'm honest, to open minds. All the stories told in these books are true; all the characters in them exist. They did the hard part by living. I did the easy part by writing about it.

"I'm frequently asked where the inspiration for the novel, *The Sunflower Forest,* came from, particularly as it is so diverse from my nonfiction books. The answer is rather mundane, I'm afraid. It was triggered by a newspaper article I read and my imagination took over from there. Gratefully, I've never had any personal experiences similar to those in the story and, yes, I *could* think all that up!

"I am still involved with my former work. I stopped teaching in 1980, when I moved permanently to North Wales, although I did continue on as a psychotherapist for two further years and continued to lecture on my research. Getting married and having my daughter in 1985 reoriented me for a few years and I devoted most of my time to my family. However, I have since returned to work in the areas of child abuse and family counseling on a volunteer basis."

FOR MORE INFORMATION SEE:

PERIODICALS

Library Journal, March 15, 1984.
Los Angeles Times, April 24, 1980.
New York Times Book Review, May 4, 1980; April 26, 1981; March 6, 1988.
Washington Post, May 8, 1981; July 6, 1984; April 19, 1988.
Washington Post Book World, August 15, 1982.
Wilson Library Bulletin, February, 1985.

*   *   *

HAYNES, Mary 1938-

PERSONAL: Born June 1, 1938, in Duluth, MN; daughter of Newton Edward (a minister) and Elizabeth (Tichenor) Moates; married David B. Haynes (an antiques dealer), June, 1963; children: Charlotte, Elizabeth. *Education:* Attended University of the Pacific, 1956-58, and University of Vienna, 1959-60; Drake University, B.A., 1961. *Politics:* Democrat.

ADDRESSES: Home—P.O. Box 226, Harpers Ferry, WV 25425.

CAREER: Teacher at public schools in Chicago, IL, 1963-64, and Jefferson County, WV, 1967-70; Bookend, Inc., Shepherdstown, WV, bookseller, 1968-73; Appalachian Trail Conference, Harpers Ferry, WV, editor, 1974; writer, 1974—. Bolivar-Harpers Ferry Public Library, president of board of trustees, 1977-87; Children's Book Guild of Washington, D.C., president, 1989-90.

WRITINGS:

Pot Belly Tales (juvenile), illustrated by Michael J. Deraney, Lothrop, 1982.
Wordchanger (juvenile), illustrated by Eric Nones, Lothrop, 1983.
Raider's Sky (juvenile), Lothrop, 1987.
Catch the Sea (juvenile), Bradbury, 1989.
The Great Pretenders (juvenile), Bradbury, 1990.

Also editor of *Appalachian Trail Conference,* 1974.

WORK IN PROGRESS: A novel.

SIDELIGHTS: Mary Haynes told *SATA:* "I spent my early years in Seattle, Washington. My sisters and brother were much older and seemed like the mountains that ringed the city: magical, powerful and far away.

"My love of books began in Seattle, where I learned to read. By the time I was in the fifth grade, I had read every book in the McGilvra School library. Suddenly (and not because I'd outgrown the library) we moved from Seattle to Des Moines, Iowa. Only my parents and I made this journey, my brother and sisters were grown now with lives of their own.

"I wasn't a 'good mover' and this change wasn't an easy adjustment. I didn't know how to make friends. I remember walking down a long, tree-lined street, thinking of Seattle's notorious weather and wishing, 'If only someone would ask me about *rain!*'

"Before long, I found the branch library some blocks from our house. On Saturdays, I went there and checked out as many books as I could carry. Then I went around the corner

Dustjacket for Mary Haynes's 1989 novel about an artistic family's summer on the seashore.

to the movie theater, where every Saturday they had a Kiddie Matinee. With my twenty cents (ten cents for the movie, ten for popcorn) I went in, delighted by the cartoons, the serial, the cowboy show, with my stack of books piled on the seat beside me like a promise.

"My parents (understanding my misery more than I thought) enrolled me in the after school classes of the Children's Theater, run as part of the Drake University drama department. The professor, Portia Boynton, was magnificent. She cared deeply about the theater, taught us acting by improvisation, following Stanislavsky, and showed by example what it meant to be 'professional.' I can still hear her voice from the back of a darkened room, saying, 'May-ry! Believe what you are doing. Just *believe!*'

"I remained an active student at the Children's Theater throughout junior high school and high school, soon being cast in the plays put on for the public four times a year. I played a nightshirt, a statue, the mother in countless plays, and only once, a princess.

"Ambition to become an actress grew, although I was still always reading. In college, to my surprise, the acting fell away and I tried other things: psychology, literature—still always reading—and became an English major.

"Writing came about more slowly. I started my first novel when I was twelve, handwritten on lined paper (the way I still start out today). I wrote what seemed like very many pages (fifteen or so), saw with dismay how many more it would take . . . and did something else instead.

"So it continued. I wrote little bits here and there, but it wasn't until I was married, with two daughters, and living in West Virginia, that I began in earnest. I had rediscovered children's literature through teaching homebound children to read and by buying books for a small bookstore. Soon I had my own characters in mind: children, on a journey, suddenly alone. The pile of books was still by my side. But there were other stories now, inside my mind.

"When my younger daughter went off to kindergarten, I told myself, 'This is it. Begin.' "

FOR MORE INFORMATION SEE:

PERIODICALS

Bulletin of the Center for Children's Books, May, 1982; October, 1983; June, 1987.
School Library Journal, September, 1983.

* * *

HENRY, Marie H. 1935-

PERSONAL: Born August 15, 1935, in Paris, France; daughter of Marc Fay and Anne Marie Stourme; married Hubert Henry (a barrister to the state council), September 12, 1962; children: Pascal, Benedicte. *Education:* Attended Conservatoire National de Musique, Versailles. *Religion:* Catholic.

ADDRESSES: Home—Avenue d'Eylau 4, Paris, France 75116.

MARIE H. HENRY

CAREER: Children's author and illustrator. Has had exhibitions of her art in Tokyo, Japan, 1986, 1987.

AWARDS, HONORS: Prix de la Famille, 1989, for *Praline s'ennuie;* Premier Prix d'Histoire de la Musique, Piano-Solfege.

WRITINGS:

ILLUSTRATOR

Amy Ehrlich, *Une Journee comme une autre,* Duculot, 1985, translation published as *Bunnies All Day Long,* Dial, 1985.

Ehrlich, *Une Journee chez Grandmere,* Duculot, 1985, translation published as *Bunnies and Their Grandma,* Dial, 1985.

Ehrlich, *Le Clairon de Praline,* Duculot, 1986, translation published as *Bunnies on Their Own,* Dial, 1986.

Ehrlich, *Et si on invitait le Pere Noel,* Duculot, 1986, translation published as *Bunnies at Christmastime,* Dial, 1986.

Ehrlich, *Praline s'ennuie,* Duculot, 1988.

Also illustrator of *The Wedding of Brown Bear and White Bear* and *The Rescue of Brown Bear and White Bear,* both for Little, Brown.

SIDELIGHTS: "When my daughter was eight, she went on holidays with her school," Marie H. Henry told *SATA.* "I wrote to her every day, illustrating each letter with drawings of bunnies. Afterwards, I collected all these drawings in a book. Many years after, the book was still in a drawer. But as my daughter wanted them, [so did the publishing company] Duculot from Belgium. That is why I started to draw again.

"I have to share my time between my family [and] music, which requires quite a lot of time. . . . I rarely have full-time days.

"In my opinion, drawings really complete musical pictures."

*   *   *

HENSON, James Maury 1936-1990
(Jim Henson)

OBITUARY NOTICE—See index for *SATA* sketch: Born September 24, 1936, in Greenville, MS; died of pneumonia, May 16, 1990, in Manhattan, NY. Puppeteer, filmmaker, and author. Creator and animator of the Muppets—foam-rubber creations part puppet, part marionette that included Kermit the Frog and Miss Piggy—Henson was one of the most ingenious, most successful, and best-loved puppeteers in history. Over the course of more than thirty years his furry, funny creatures—each a unique individual with its own virtues and faults—brought their master eighteen Emmy awards, seven Grammy awards, four Peabody awards, and numerous other honors. In addition to his television work with the popular educational show *Sesame Street,* network prime-time's *Muppet Show,* and cable's *Fraggle Rock,* Henson took his wizardry to feature films such as *The Muppet Movie, The Dark Crystal,* and *Labyrinth.* His success was attributed in part to his skill at adapting puppetry to television and film, but perhaps even more to the endearing humanity of the Muppets' personalities, with which their audiences, both child and adult, overwhelmingly identified. Henson served variously as puppeteer, writer, director, and producer for his projects; his screenplays include *Time Piece* and *The Cube;* he also wrote *The Muppet Show Book.*

OBITUARIES AND OTHER SOURCES:

BOOKS

Newsmakers 89, Issue 1, Gale, 1989.

PERIODICALS

Chicago Tribune, May 17, 1990.
Los Angeles Times, May 17, 1990.
New York Times, May 17, 1990; May 22, 1990.
Washington Post, May 17, 1990; May 18, 1990.

*   *   *

HENSON, Jim
See HENSON, James Maury

*   *   *

HILL, Alexis
See CRAIG, Mary (Francis) Shura

*   *   *

HILL, Meredith
See CRAIG, Mary (Francis) Shura

*   *   *

HILL, Ralph Nading 1917-1987

PERSONAL: Born September 19, 1917, in Burlington, VT; died of a stroke, December 10, 1987, in Burlington, VT; son of Ralph N. and Marion A. (Clarkston) Hill. *Education:* Dartmouth College, B.A., 1939.

CAREER: Shelburne Steamboat Co., Inc., Burlington, VT, president, 1950-53; *Vermont Life* magazine, Montpelier, VT, 1951-87, began as senior editor, became a member of the advisory board. Trustee, Shelburne Museum, Shelburne, VT, beginning 1950, Vermont Historical Society, 1950-62, and Dartmouth Alumni Council, 1958-60. *Military service:* U.S. Army, Counter-Intelligence Corps, 1943-46; served in Ninth Infantry Division in four European theater campaigns; became first lieutenant.

AWARDS, HONORS: Litt.D., Dartmouth College, 1964.

WRITINGS:

The Winooski: Heartway of Vermont, Rinehart, 1949.
Contrary Country: A Chronicle of Vermont, Rinehart, 1950, 2nd edition, Stephen Greene Press, 1960.
Sidewheeler Saga: A Chronicle of Steamboating, Rinehart, 1953, abridged edition published as *The Story of the Ticonderoga: A Chronicle of Steamboating,* Shelburne Museum, 1957.
(With Lilian Baker Carlisle) *The Story of the Shelburne Museum,* Shelburne Museum, 1955, 2nd edition, 1960.
(Co-editor) *A Treasury of Vermont Life,* A. S. Barnes, 1956.
Window in the Sea, Rinehart, 1956.
(Co-editor) *Green Mountain Treasury,* Harper, 1960.
(Editor) *The College on the Hill: A Dartmouth Chronicle,* Dartmouth Publications, 1964.
(Compiler with Walter R. Hard, Jr., and Murray Hoyt) *Vermont: A Special World,* Vermont Life Magazine, 1969, 7th edition, c. 1987.
Yankee Kingdom: Vermont and New Hampshire, Harper, 1960, revised edition, 1973.
(Author of text) *Vermont Album: A Collection of Early Vermont Photographs,* Stephen Greene Press, 1974.
Lake Champlain—Key to Liberty, Countryman Press, 1977.

FOR CHILDREN

Robert Fulton and the Steamboat, Random, 1954.
The Doctors Who Conquered Yellow Fever, Random, 1957.
The Voyages of Brian Seaworthy (mystery), Vermont Life Magazine, 1971.

OTHER

Contributor to periodicals, including *Atlantic Monthly* and *American Heritage.*

OBITUARIES:

PERIODICALS

New York Times, December 12, 1987.

[Sketch verified by Tom Slayton, editor of *Vermont Life*]

*   *   *

HIPPOPOTAMUS, Eugene H.
See KRAUS, (Herman) Robert

HOKE, Helen (L.) 1903-1990
(Helen L. Hoke Watts; Helen Sterling, a pseudonym)

OBITUARY NOTICE—See index for *SATA* sketch: Born in 1903 in California, PA; died of pneumonia, March 26, 1990, in Bethesda, MD. Educator, administrator, editor, journalist, and author. Hoke, who occasionally wrote under the pseudonym Helen Sterling, worked as a teacher and journalist before publishing her first book for children in 1940. She penned more than thirty volumes, including *Factory Kitty, Jokes and Fun,* and *Whales,* and edited many more, among them *Devils, Devils, Devils.* With her second husband's company, the publishing firm Franklin Watts, Inc., she worked as vice president and editor in chief beginning in 1948, and in 1956 Hoke formed her own consulting and publishing firm, Helen Hoke Associates.

OBITUARIES AND OTHER SOURCES:

PERIODICALS

Washington Post, March 31, 1990.

*   *   *

HOLMES, Barbara Ware 1945-

PERSONAL: Born September 2, 1945, in Roanoke, VA; daughter of Cecil O. (an air force pilot who died in Korea) and Dorris (a homemaker; maiden name, Vest) Savoy; stepdaughter of Robert H. Savoy; married David J. Holmes (a manuscript and autograph dealer), November 30, 1968; children: Sarah Anne. *Education:* In conjunction with studies at Springfield College, attended Institute of European Studies, Vienna, Austria, 1965-66, and Exeter College, Oxford, 1966; Springfield College, B.A., 1967; Northeastern University, M.A., 1968; graduate study at Connecticut College for Women (now Connecticut College), 1969.

ADDRESSES: Home—510 Park Ave., Collingswood, NJ 08108.

CAREER: Springfield City Library, Springfield, MA, reference librarian and clerk, 1968; Connecticut College, New London, secretary to the dean, 1969; elementary school librarian in Montville, CT, 1969-70, and Ketchikan, Alaska, 1970-72; National Association of Independent Schools, Boston, MA, advertising manager and assistant to editor of *Independent School Bulletin,* 1973-75; writer, 1975—.

MEMBER: Authors Guild, Authors League of America, Franklin Inn Club (Philadelphia).

WRITINGS:

Charlotte Cheetham, Master of Disaster (juvenile fiction), illustrated by John Himmelman, Harper, 1985.
Charlotte the Starlet (juvenile fiction), illustrated by Himmelman, Harper, 1988.
Charlotte Shakespeare and Annie the Great, illustrated by Himmelman, Harper, 1989.

Contributor of adult stories to magazines, including *Redbook, Samisdat, Moving Out,* and *Pig Iron.*

SIDELIGHTS: Barbara Ware Holmes told *SATA:* "I spent much of my childhood following relatives from room to room, entertaining them with readings from works in progress and, like the heroine of my books, telling a fair share of tall tales. It wasn't until the success of my riveting sixth-grade play on coffee beans in Brazil, however, that I began to consider the career of writing seriously. From there it was simply a matter of working for twenty-two more years to ready myself for publication.

"*Charlotte Cheetham: Master of Disaster* is the story of a fifth-grader who tells lies. How can she not, when the lies are there, waiting to be told, and seeming, to Charlotte, exactly like the truth? It is only later, when classmates demand she prove them true, that Charlotte is forced to distinguish between fantasy and truth. She decides to write, storing up her fictions for future books. The Charlotte Cheetham trilogy follows Charlotte's career as a writer of books and producer of a play which stars her unpredictable classmates.

"Surely the subject of lying is dear to any writer's heart, believing, as we must, that good fiction is truer than 'truth.' Children, I think, know this too, for they see that the world as it *is* is not the world as it should be, and only imagination can set it straight."

Dustjacket from the second book in the "Charlotte Cheetum" trilogy, which focuses on a fifth-grader who enjoys telling tall tales. (Illustration by John Himmelman.)

HOY, Linda 1946-

PERSONAL: Born March 27, 1946, in Sheffield, England; daughter of Len (a clerk) and Dorothy (a hospital handicraft teacher; maiden name, Mortimer) Potts; separated; children: Marcus, Mikita, Bevan. *Education:* Sheffield Polytechnic, Certificate of Education, 1973, B.Ed. (with honors), 1974. *Religion:* Society of Friends (Quakers).

ADDRESSES: Agent—Gina Pollinger, 222 Old Brompton Rd., London SW5 OB2, England.

CAREER: Worked as shop assistant, barmaid, and civil servant; English teacher at Gosforth Comprehensive School, near Sheffield, England, 1974-83; lecturer at Sheffield City Polytechnic, 1986—.

MEMBER: Sheffield Campaign for Nuclear Disarmament (chairperson, 1983-86).

WRITINGS:

FOR YOUNG PEOPLE

Your Friend Rebecca (novel), Bodley Head, 1981.
The Damned (novel), Bodley Head, 1983.
Emmeline Pankhurst (biography), Hamish Hamilton, 1985.
Kiss File JC 110 (novel), Walker, 1988.
Nightmare Park, Collins, Armada, 1989.
Ring of Death, Collins, Armada, 1990.

OTHER

The Alternative Assembly Book (for teachers), Longman, 1985.
"Emily" (television play), TV South, 1985.
(Editor) *Poems for Peace,* Pluto Press, 1986.

SIDELIGHTS: Linda Hoy told *SATA:* "The joy I experience in being alive has motivated me to work for the survival of our species, our planet, and our civilization. I am also a deeply religious person and, although not an orthodox Christian, my spiritual life is very important to me. I spend time in meditation and occasional weekends at monastic retreats. I have traveled widely, especially in the United States. I take pleasure in encouraging others who want to write, and I run regular workshops with writers groups and especially with teenagers in school."

FOR MORE INFORMATION SEE:

PERIODICALS

Times Literary Supplement, September 18, 1981; November 25, 1988.

*   *   *

HOYT, Erich 1950-

PERSONAL: Born September 28, 1950, in Akron, Ohio; son of Robert Emmett (a writer and television producer) and Betty Jane (an editor and public relations representative; maiden name, Shutrump) Hoyt; married Sarah Elizabeth Wedden (a developmental biologist and lecturer); children: Moses Erich. *Education:* Attended high school in Prairie du Chien, WI.

ERICH HOYT

ADDRESSES: Home and office—29 Dirleton Ave., No. 11, North Berwick, Scotland EH39 4BE, United Kingdom. *Agent*—Katinka Matson, John Brockman Associates, Inc., 2307 Broadway, New York, NY 10024.

CAREER: Studio, outdoor, and nature photographer in Toronto, Ontario, and Victoria, British Columbia, 1968-70; farmer near Nelson, British Columbia, 1970-73; documentary filmmaker in Vancouver, British Columbia, 1973-75; free-lance writer and photographer, 1975—. Owner and operator of a record store in Victoria, 1969-70; film score composer in Vancouver, 1973-78. Vannevar Bush Fellow at Massachusetts Institute of Technology, 1985-86. Visiting lecturer in writing at Massachusetts Institute of Technology, 1986-87. Consultant to International Board for Plant Genetic Resources, 1987-88; consultant, researcher, and writer for new exhibit halls "How Plants Become Food" for the New York Botanical Gardens and "In the Rain Forest" for the Missouri Botanical Gardens, both 1987-89. Project officer, World Wide Fund for Nature, 1987-88 and 1990-91.

WRITINGS:

The Whale Called Killer (nonfiction), Dutton, 1981, revised edition published as *Orca: The Whale Called Killer,* Firefly, 1984.
The Whale-Watcher's Handbook (nonfiction), Doubleday, 1984.
Whales of Canada (nonfiction), Firefly Books, 1988.
Seasons of the Whale (nonfiction), Chelsea Green, 1990.
A Reference Guide to Plant and Animal Extinction (nonfiction), Enslow, 1991.
Meeting the Whales (nonfiction), Firefly Books, 1991.

Co-author radio play "Cries and Whistles," broadcast by Canadian Broadcasting Corp., 1981. Field correspondent,

Defenders, 1985—. Contributing editor to *Equinox* (magazine), 1982—. Contributor to magazines, including *National Geographic, Owl, Dolphin Log, Reader's Digest, BBC Wildlife, International Wildlife, Oceans, Diver, Pacific Discovery,* and to numerous newspapers.

WORK IN PROGRESS: A book on the lives of insects; a series of children's books on the biomes of the world and the stories of the plants and animals that inhabit them.

SIDELIGHTS: Born in Akron, Ohio, on **September 28, 1950,** the eldest of a family of two boys and three girls. Hoyt was raised in northeastern Ohio, northern Virginia, Cambridge, Massachusetts, Michigan, and Toronto, Canada. His parents were journalists who encouraged their children to use the typewriter almost as soon as they could write. (One sister, Victoria Hoyt, is a poet; another sister, Gerard Elizabeth Hoyt, wrote a novel at age 11; his brother Douglass has written articles; but Hoyt is the only one who has pursued writing as a career.)

Hoyt told *SATA:* "Growing up, I was far more interested in playing baseball and making expeditions to 'the creek' to find turtles and toads than in reading books or writing stories. In third grade, I wrote a story about a visit to the creek to cut down a Christmas tree, aided by two of my younger sisters. It was something of a hit at home and school, but that was the exception.

"In eighth grade, a teacher introduced me to Charles Dickens' *David Copperfield,* at first reading it aloud in class. I took to Miss Peggotty and Mr. Micawber and all those other wonderful characters and read the book twice. Through high school at a Jesuit boarding school, I explored more books, though I rarely enjoyed those on the suggested reading lists. Some of my favorite authors—Camus, Rousseau, Joyce—were banned at the school because they were considered anti-Catholic."

Late 1960s. "In junior year of high school I began writing poetry and then wrote a one-act play. A school friend, David Haase, who has since become a fine investigative journalist in Washington, D.C., admired this early work and encouraged me. For two years, I wrote poems almost every day and, after I learned to play piano and guitar, I wrote songs. Some of these were performed in concerts, but none has been recorded. My music, however, was later used to score a number of documentary and dramatic films."

1968-1972. "Besides writing words and music after leaving home at age 17, I supported myself by starting a record store, making and selling jewelry and other crafts, farming for three years in the Rocky Mountains of western Canada, building musical instruments, taking and developing photographs, and producing, editing and recording sound for short films, especially documentaries. Once a year I would try to write something for publication. If not a poem, an article, short story, or a book idea."

1973. "When I was 22 I spent the summer working on a documentary film that proved the adventure of a lifetime—and hooked me on wanting to write for a living. It was a three-month sailing expedition along Canada's west coast in search of killer whales or orcas. At that time they had never been filmed in the natural habitat. We had no idea what to expect. After several weeks of searching through storms and other difficulties, we met a pod or family group of sixteen killer whales. In time, we found a remote bay where they spent most of their summer days and built a camp there. We came to know the whales as individuals; markings on their dorsal fins gave rise to names like Nicola, Stubbs, and Top Notch. Day after day, we loved to watch them play, eat, rest, and nurture their young."

1976-1980. "I began sketching notes for a book on killer whales, and after several more summers of visits, and a great deal of help from my father who served as my editor, I finally completed and published *The Whale Called Killer*. In the four years I worked on the book, I wrote my first magazine articles—mostly on whales, but I also wrote about kites, hot air balloons, and windsurfing. Later, I made an expedition in search of Canada's tallest trees. I rode an ice breaker with oceanographers in the Greenland Sea. I visited the tropical rain forests in Costa Rica, Paraguay, Brazil, and Mexico.

"From the start, my writing has been based on first-hand experiences and I have tried to give the reader the feeling of being 'right there.' To do this I try to write simply and to play on the senses, recreating, for example, the initial feeling of awe, surprise and a little fear when a whale three times the size of my small boat surfaced beside me, close enough to touch. The massive seven-ton mammal rocked the boat from side to side, then spouted and the spray drifted over me—oddly cooling on a hot day—and I was sweating!"

1981-1985. "My first book led to many articles on other conservation subjects for *National Geographic* and other magazines and to another book on all whales and dolphins, *The Whale-Watcher's Handbook*. The research—gathering facts and photos—for this book was fascinating. I wrote more than six hundred letters to scientists and conservationists in fifty to sixty different countries around the world. I worked closely with the superb natural science illustrator

Dustjacket for the book Erich Hoyt wrote about his seven summers spent observing the lives of killer whales.

Pieter A. Folkens who produced state-of-the-art illustrations of all the whales and dolphins for this book. We have since worked on other projects together.

"In 1986, I collaborated with a twenty-one year old Japanese woman on a story of her visit to the old whaling village of Taiji where the men carried out traditional whaling. She was torn between her deep love of whales and her respect for the traditions of her country. The story was published in the United States and in twelve other countries through *Reader's Digest.*"

1987 to the present. "In the last few years, I have helped design and write the text for a number of museum exhibit halls: The rainforest climatron of the Missouri Botanical Gardens; 'How Plants Become Food' at the New York Botanical Gardens; on electricity, electronics, and computers at the Museum of Art, Science, and Industry at Bridgeport, Connecticut; and two new museums on the invention of the telephone and the future of communications in Boston, Massachusetts.

"My future plans include writing a number of children's books. Among other things I am currently working on a series of children's science books, for age ten and up. The first book is about whales and future volumes will be on the geology of North America (how to read the rocks) and on other topics. I have also written one children's fiction book, as yet unpublished.

"I believe books on science and the natural world, if well presented, have the power to unlock our sense of wonder. The story is the key. And there are a million riveting stories in the stars, on the beaches, in the tropical rain forests, in the deep sea, in the rocks, in the magical flow of electrons. I hope through my writing that I can continue discovering the world—and recreating what I discover for others."

FOR MORE INFORMATION SEE:

PERIODICALS

Akron Beacon Journal, October 25, 1981.
Detroit Free Press, November 6, 1981.
Discover, September, 1981.
Globe and Mail (Toronto), January 16, 1982.
Montreal Gazette, October 17, 1981.
Publishers Weekly, June 26, 1981.
Seattle Times, March 7, 1982.
Westworld, September, 1981.

*   *   *

HUNTER, Jim 1939-

PERSONAL: Born June 24, 1939, in Stafford, England; son of David (a teacher) and Gwendolyn (Castell-Evans) Hunter. *Education:* Gonville and Caius College, Cambridge, M.A. (with first class honors), 1960; Indiana University, graduate study, 1960-61; University of Bristol, Certificate of Education (with distinction), 1962.

ADDRESSES: Office—White Cottage, The Street, Wickhambreaux, Canterbury CT3 1RP, England. *Agent*—Harold Matson Co., Inc., 22 East 40th St., New York, NY 10016.

CAREER: English master at Bradford Grammar School, Bradford, England, 1962-66, Bristol Grammar School, Bristol, England, 1966-75, and Broadoak School, Avon, England, 1975-78; headmaster of Weymouth Grammar School, Weymouth, England, 1978-81, and of Leighton Park School, Reading, England, 1981-86; Christ Church College, Canterbury, England, senior lecturer, 1986— .

AWARDS, HONORS: Authors Club Award for best first novel, 1961, for *The Sun in the Morning*.

WRITINGS:

The Sun in the Morning, Faber, 1961.
Sally Cray, Faber, 1963.
Earth and Stone, Faber, 1963, published as *A Place of Stone,* Pantheon, 1964.
(Editor and author of introduction) *Modern Short Stories* (high school anthology), Faber, 1964, Transatlantic, 1967.
The Metaphysical Poets, Evans Brothers, 1965.
The Flame, Pantheon, 1966.
Gerard Manley Hopkins, Evans Brothers, 1966.
(Editor) *The Modern Novel in English Studies in Extracts,* Faber, 1966.
(Editor) *Modern Poets,* Faber, Volumes 1-4, 1968, Volume 5, 1981, revised edition of Volume 4 published as *Modern Poets Four,* 1979.
(Editor) William Shakespeare, *Henry IV, Part 1,* Evans Brothers, 1969.
Walking in the Painted Sunshine, Faber, 1970.
(Editor) *The Human Animal* (stories), Faber, 1972.
Kinship, Faber, 1973.
Percival and the Presence of God, Faber, 1978.
Tom Stoppard's Plays, Grove, 1982.

Contributor to *Listener, Spectator, Guardian, Times Literary Supplement,* and *College English.*

SIDELIGHTS: In Jim Hunter's book, *Modern Short Stories,* fifteen short stories written by such talented authors as Dylan Thomas, Ernest Hemingway, and William Faulkner are presented with critical notes and study guides. Book critics have praised the wide and varied selection of short stories by a number of the most gifted authors of this century. A reviewer for *Horn Book* asks: "How often one looks for a good collection of modern short stories to serve as an introduction to some of our outstanding writers! Here is one."

WORKS CITED:

Horn Book, October, 1965.

FOR MORE INFORMATION SEE:

BOOKS

Dictionary of Literary Biography, Volume 14: *British Novelists since 1960,* Gale, 1983.

* * *

JACKSON, Jacqueline 1928-

PERSONAL: Born May 3, 1928, in Beloit, WI; daughter of Ronald Arthur (owner dairy and hybrid seed corn business) and Vera (musician; maiden name, Wardner) Dougan; mar-

ried Robert S. Jackson, June 17, 1950 (divorced, 1973); children: Damaris Lee, Megan Trever, Gillian Patricia, Jacqueline Elspeth. *Education:* Beloit College, B.A., 1950; University of Michigan, M.A., 1951. *Hobbies and other interests:* Biking (all over England, and Rock County, WI), hiking, swimming, rowing, doing activities with my kids and granddaughter, and playing cello in a chamber music group.

ADDRESSES: Home—816 North Fifth St., Springfield, IL 62702. *Office*—Department of English, Sangamon State University, Springfield, IL 62701. *Agent*—Marilyn Marlow, Curtis Brown Ltd., 60 East 56th St., New York, NY 10022.

CAREER: Kent State University, Kent, Ohio, lecturer in children's literature, 1964-68; Teacher Development Center, Rockford, IL, consultant in creative writing, 1968-70; Sangamon State University, Springfield, IL, associate professor of literature, 1970, professor of English, 1970—. Developed series of creative writing programs for children for University of Wisconsin, 1969-82; teacher in workshops on children's creativity. Producer of weekly radio program broadcast on public radio station WSSU, "Reading and Writing and Radio," 1975—.

MEMBER: National Council of Teachers of English, Modern Language Association of America, Popular Culture Association, Children's Reading Round Table.

AWARDS, HONORS: Notable book citation from American Library Association, 1966, and Dorothy Canfield Fisher children's book award, 1967, both for *The Taste of Spruce Gum;* D. Litt. from MacMurray College, 1976; D.H.L. from Beloit College, 1977.

WRITINGS:

FOR CHILDREN

Julie's Secret Sloth, Little, Brown, 1953.
(Self-illustrated) *The Paleface Redskins,* Little, Brown, 1958.
The Taste of Spruce Gum, Little, Brown, 1966.
Missing Melinda (Junior Literary Guild selection), Little, Brown, 1967.
Chicken Ten Thousand (Junior Literary Guild selection), Little, Brown, 1968.
(Self-illustrated) *The Ghost Boat* (Junior Literary Guild selection), Little, Brown, 1969.
Spring Song, Kent State University Press, 1969.
The Orchestra Mice, Reilly & Lee, 1970.
(With William Perlmutter) *The Endless Pavement* (Junior Literary Guild selection), Seabury, 1973.

OTHER

(Illustrator) Chad Walsh, *Knock and Enter,* Morehouse, 1952.
Turn Not Pale, Beloved Snail: A Book about Writing among Other Things (for all ages), Little, Brown, 1974.

Also author of dance-drama and operetta based on Jackson's book of same title, "The Endless Pavement." Contributor of about forty short stories and poems to periodicals, including *Children's Literature: An International Journal, Language Arts,* and *Illinois Library Journal.*

WORK IN PROGRESS: The Round Barn.

Jacqueline Jackson and her daughters Damaris, Megan, Jackie, and Gillian.

SIDELIGHTS: Jacqueline Jackson told *SATA:* "Books were the most enthralling things in the world to me, as a child. I was read to regularly by parents and sisters, and by the end of third grade had devoured all of George Macdonald, the Grimm tales and *East o' the Sun and West o' the Moon* (my own still treasured edition is illustrated by Kay Nielson), all the then-published *Oz* books, and standard classics such as *Tom Sawyer* and *Secret Garden.* I also produced my first book, an untitled collection of short stories. In fourth grade I wrote another book, and had a story published. In fifth grade, my Oz-esque novel, *Cloudlanders,* ran weekly for four months in a newspaper. All this was outside of school, writing (other than to master skills) was not a part of the curriculum. Now, as a university teacher working in writing classes with adult students, and with thousands of children through my radio program on writing, I've recently reread *Cloudlanders* and thought, 'Well, that little kid wasn't bad.'

"However, I wrote almost nothing from sixth grade to college, now being taught how, in school, with outlines, thesis sentences, and the necessity of knowing what it is you're going to say before you say it. This took all the creativity and joy out of writing. The joy returned with a surge when I entered Beloit College and found that creative writing was a legitimate subject. My major was Classics, but I worked with the writer Chad Walsh (a poet, and the first biographer of C. S. Lewis) for four years, and then with Roy Cowden, Hopwood Writing Director at the University of Michigan. At Michigan, I produced my first published book.

"When I had the opportunity to produce a weekly radio show for writing with children, over Wisconsin Public Radio in 1969, I tried to free kids from the kinds of inhibitions in composition and subject matter that I'd experienced, and that my own children were experiencing in their schools. This doesn't mean ignoring the 'skills' forever—one learns the skills by doing fascinating work, and rewriting and polishing have their own disciplined joy. But these are separate processes and need to be treated as such.

"The radio shows were the basis for *Turn Not Pale, Beloved Snail: A Book about Writing among Other Things.* This book is used in many grade schools, and a number of colleges as a 'non-text' on writing. If I were to pick a couple of main themes for inclusion here, I'd say to kids, 'Keep a journal: Keep your eyes and ears and all your senses alert. And put down everything and anything in your journal, especially the thoughts and feelings that go along with the events of your life. Include the ordinary and the she-sezes and he-sezes. Include dreams and plans and imaginings.' And a second would be, 'Collect your parents' stories, and your grandparents', and other relatives, or neighbors, and write them down, too.' A third would be, READ! And read all the great stuff. My older girls, when they found their little sister (by six years) refusing to read certain of their favorites because she wanted to be 'different' sat on top of her and read out loud Laura Ingalls Wilder and *Secret Garden* until Elspeth was hooked.

"I could tell a story on the writing of each of my books, all of which are different—no series—but for that I refer the reader to *Turn Not Pale, Beloved Snail: A Book about Writing among*

Other Things. Several such stories are given there, mainly as illustrations (you can start a book at the end, or middle, or beginning) but here's one that isn't. When I was at the lake, drawing the pictures for *Ghost Boat,* one of my children suggested that children's drawings ought to illustrate the stories the children tell, which punctuate the narrative rather like a Greek chorus. I agreed, and they and neighbor kids fell to. We ended up with five published children's drawings. Even my four-year-old had a share, in a composite of Liggle, Biggle, and In-Betwiggle, three germs who lived on a giant's foot. I needed derelict boats as models for the ghost boat itself, the word went out, and we ended up with so many wrecks on our beach that it became known as 'Jacksons' Graveyard.' We ultimately had the problem of disposing of them all, while *The Ghost Boat* characters had only to get rid of one!

"Though it robs writing time, I love teaching. Each semester I teach a literature class, a writing class, and produce the radio show for kids. My favorite literature class is fantasy: we read both adult and children's fantasies. Fantasy is my favorite genre, probably the hardest to write well, and my hero is Ursula LeGuin, author of the *Earthsea* books. I have a bathroom whose walls are completely covered with the maps of Earthsea. (My downstairs bathroom is an *Alice* one, papered with huge Tenniel drawings, and containing a large clock stuck at 6 p.m. The room holds so much *Wonderland* and *Looking Glass* memorabilia that guests vanish into it, staying so long that we begin to worry about their health.)

"I also teach Classics of Children's Literature; we read from Louisa May Alcott to Katherine Paterson. I have twice taken classes to England, for 'Sources of British Children's Literature.' For twenty days we slept and ate at youth hostels, visited Beatrix Potter's cottage, sailed on Arthur Ransome's Lake Windemere, walked Jane Eyre's moors, had tea with Rosemary Sutcliff, talked with C. S. Lewis's literary executor, picnicked with Richard Adams on top of Watership Down, picnicked also by the river at Godstow Nunnery where Lewis Carroll and his friend picnicked with Alice and her sisters, the afternoon Carroll began telling the girls of Alice's adventures underground. We listened to Tolkien's poetry atop an ancient burial barrow on the Ridgeway, one of the oldest footpaths in the world. We floated down Ratty and Moley's river.

"In my writing classes we do fun and foolish activities, such as sitting by a lake for an hour in complete silence, in the dark, or mimicking (at a discreet distance) people's body movement at the local mall, in order to 'feel into' their bodies. All my exercises are to stimulate creativity and to create a trusting community. This latter is extremely necessary if students are to write what they're really needing and wanting to write, and to be willing to share it. I teach the following classes: Perceptual Writing, Stories, Novel, and Personal Journal. I'm gearing up to teach Feminist Writing and Mother and Daughter Writing.

"The other major writing I do is to publish a newspaper, begun when Elspeth left for college in 1982: *The Empty Nest Newsletter.* It is six legal-size pages long, and I get out about seven issues a year. It started as a family newspaper but now has an international circulation of 150. It contains articles, cartoons, news notes on subscribers, editorials, and is not just written by me: my daughter Megan's account of the Loma Prieta earthquake, which she experienced in Santa Cruz, is an example of at-the-scene reporting. No news is too old to print, no item too insignificant, and our contributors, while mostly people, are sometimes dogs, cats, cows, or plants.

"I've done some work on a book for kids on the childhood writings of well known adult authors such as the Brontes, Jane Austen, and C. S. Lewis. Eric Eddison's adult fantasy, *The Worm Ouroborus,* was conceived and much of it written—and illustrated between the ages of five and fourteen. But that's a sabbatical down the pike."

FOR MORE INFORMATION SEE:

PERIODICALS

Language Arts, March, 1981.
Library Journal, May 15, 1970.
Washington Post Book World, October 6, 1968; May 4, 1969.
Young Reader's Review, December, 1967; November, 1968; April, 1969.

*   *   *

JOHNSON, Lissa H(alls) 1955-

PERSONAL: Born May 1, 1955, in Pasadena, CA; daughter of James Langdon (a camp administrator) and Patricia (Froats) Halls; married Tom S. Johnson, June 1, 1974 (divorced July, 1988) married Jeff Oliver, February 24, 1990; children: (first marriage) Trevor Michael, Stacie Michelle, Misty Amber. *Education:* Attended Santa Ana College, 1973, and Biola University, 1973.

ADDRESSES: Office—P.O. Box 2813, Antioch, CA 94531. *Agent*—S. Rickly Christian, P.O. Box 4285, Diamond Bar, CA 91765.

LISSA H. JOHNSON

CAREER: Writer. Lecturer and speaker at schools, organizations, and writing conferences.

MEMBER: California Writer's Club.

AWARDS, HONORS: Campus Life Book of the Year Award for Excellence in fiction, 1987, for *No Other Choice.*

WRITINGS:

NOVELS FOR YOUNG READERS

Just Like Ice Cream, Bantam, 1981.
Runaway Dreams, Regal, 1985.
No Other Choice, Revell, 1986.
Something to Live For, Revell, 1987.
Lambs of the Lie, Revell, 1987.

OTHER

(Editor) Nancy Michels, *Helping Women Recover from Abortions,* Bethany House.
(Editor) Charles Ludwig, *Defender of the Faith,* Bethany House.
(Editor) Rokelle Lerner, *Affirmations for the Inner Child,* Health Communications, Inc.

Also author of *The Secret of Lucidia* (a fantasy for children), and of radio scripts for "Teen Scene" program. Contributor of short stories and articles to periodicals, including *Young Ambassador, Clubhouse, Christian Herald, Brio, Reader's TQ,* and *Teen Power.*

SIDELIGHTS: Lissa H. Johnson told *SATA:* "I fell in love with books when I was very young. My mother said that when I was two, I would sit for hours on the couch 'reading' books without pictures. I learned to read early, and instantly, books became my life, my world. Not only did I read them, I lived them.

"It wasn't long before I decided I wanted to write a book. I could feel and smell the joy of creating a story others could get lost in. Almost immediately I realized my dream was foolish and unobtainable. You had to be a 'somebody' to write a book. I was a nobody. Little Lissa. The kid who got bloody noses on hot days. The one who feared life. The wisest thing I could do was give up this impossible dream and confine my writing to journals and school reports.

"The years passed. I got married and had a child. All around me, high school kids were getting pregnant, having abortions and babies. These girls were wounded and bleeding on the inside. They didn't feel they had anyone to help, or at least didn't know where to find that help. They stumbled along, trying to make adult decisions with only a child's background.

"Somebody had to help these kids. I wanted to help. I put my thoughts into a notebook. Thoughts of what the kids needed to know, and where they could find help. Those thoughts triggered more creative thoughts. I flipped to a clean section of the notebook, and began to write a story about two kids, Kyle and Julie. Then I put the notebook away in the back of my desk. 'How foolish I've been,' I thought. 'I'm still a nobody. Who do I think I'm kidding?'

"In the fall of 1979, I decided I had to write or I would die. I had to write stories. I had to write something, anything. I confided in my cousin Joni that I wanted to write a book. She

didn't laugh or even smirk. She looked me straight in the eye. 'Well, if that's what God wants you to do, you'll do it.' I whispered the dream to my friend Karen. 'Don't let go of your dream, Lissa. I know you can do it.'

"Circumstances led me to a small, beginning writer's conference in Southern California. There, the instructor, who never complimented anyone unless she really felt they deserved it, put her arm around me and said, 'You have a lot of inborn talent. You'll be a writer someday.'

"From there, I graduated to a larger writer's conference. I went, terrified of the 300 writers present. I had brought with me all I had written in that notebook about Kyle and Julie—two typed chapters. I slipped in and out of classes, wanting desperately to be a writer, but knowing it was clearly out of my reach. The conference had hired many people to tell me just that. 'No one wants to read a story about teen pregnancy. That problem is passe'; 'Your dialogue is stilted, unnatural, the story contrived'; 'Go home and write for newspapers. Fiction writers are born, not taught.'

"My crushed spirit limped to my crotchety old fiction teacher, Lee Roddy. 'Lee,' I said quietly, 'I want you to tell me the truth. Tell me how bad my story is.'

"Lee was silent, rubbing his stubbled chin while he glanced at the manuscript in front of him. 'Little one,' he said in his gruff voice, 'this is *good.* The dialogue is very real. I can *see* your characters. You have a great story. Don't give up.' I protested, telling him what the other teachers had said. 'Don't listen to them. Not one of them has published thirty novels as I have,' he said.

"I went home, sent out a proposal, and within four days had a phone call from a publisher offering me a contract. That little book, *Just Like Ice Cream,* has now sold over 100,000 copies. It is being used in schools as curriculum, in juvenile detention centers, high school and junior high camps, churches, and homes, to discuss teen sexuality and pregnancy. High school libraries can't keep the book (or any of my others) on the shelves. There is always a waiting list.

"You would have thought my writing career would have soared after that. But my confidence still remained low. I believed *Just Like Ice Cream* could only be acknowledged as a freak accident. But others had confidence in me. I received phone calls from five publishers asking me to write for them. The result of negotiations, led to the book, *Runaway Dreams.*

"My third book, *No Other Choice,* was written at the request of a friend, who opened my eyes to the severe emotional pain of many women who have abortions. In 1987, this book received the Campus Life Book of the Year Award for Excellence in fiction.

"*Something to Live For* was a very difficult book to write. Perhaps it is because suicide is an irreversible solution to pain. My other stories dealt with problems that at least carried hope that life could use the pain for growth. Perhaps it was a more difficult book to write because I had been suicidal a short time before. But *Something to Live For* is a story that ends in hope and healing, in spite of the tragic circumstances.

"*Lambs of the Lie* is a real deviation from my usual style and purpose of writing. I had been given the story as an assignment, rather than a story of my own choosing. To keep my own interest, I wrote it as a novel of intrigue, in the manner Ray Bradbury suggests. I followed the characters down the hall and simply wrote what happened. As a result, I did not know what would happen to the characters two chapters before the end.

"Each of my books is written as a novel—a couple of kids facing a crisis. The story is stuffed with facts, so the kids who would never pick up a non-fiction book can learn. Each book is written with the underlying theme of compassion. My hope, my purpose, my prayer, is that my readers, upon completion of my books, will walk away with a better understanding of their fellow man . . . and perhaps reach out to hold them, to listen, to understand and even to help. And if the reader is a kid facing the same sort of crisis in his or her life, perhaps they can come away knowing they are not alone, knowing people care, knowing there is help available and where to begin to find it.

"After writing my books, I began to branch out, writing radio scripts and short stories. In September of 1988, I completed a ghostwriting project; an autobiography for a psychologist. Following that, I wrote a fantasy for children (tentative title, *The Secret of Lucidia*). I discovered I love the world of fantasy where everything is not always what it seems, and good always triumphs over evil.

"When I first began to write, if told I would have to also become a speaker, I would have ended my writing career right then. Today, I thoroughly enjoy my speaking engagements. I love to meet new people, and encourage them in their writing just as I was encouraged as a new writer. I also enjoy speaking to kids in school. I enjoy encouraging them to dream and to become. They are all persons of value and their dreams are too.

"Since writing *Runaway Dreams,* I realized I am a writer. I never was a nobody, I have always been a somebody. The world does not contain nobodies. Only somebodies. And those who reach for their dreams, and never give up, will one day see their dream come true."

*   *   *

JUDD, Frances K.
See BENSON, Mildred (Augustine Wirt)

*   *   *

KEENE, Carolyn
(Collective pseudonym)

WRITINGS:

"DANA GIRLS" MYSTERY SERIES

By the Light of the Study Lamp, Grosset & Dunlap, 1934.
The Secret at Lone Tree Cottage, Grosset & Dunlap, 1934.
In the Shadow of the Tower, Grosset & Dunlap, 1934.
A Three-Cornered Mystery, Grosset & Dunlap, 1935.
The Secret at the Hermitage, Grosset & Dunlap, 1936.
The Circle of Footprints, Grosset & Dunlap, 1937.
The Mystery of the Locked Room, Grosset & Dunlap, 1938.
The Clue in the Cobweb, Grosset & Dunlap, 1939.
The Secret at the Gatehouse, Grosset & Dunlap, 1940.
The Mysterious Fireplace, Grosset & Dunlap, 1941.
The Clue of the Rusty Key, Grosset & Dunlap, 1942.
The Portrait in the Sand, Grosset & Dunlap, 1943.
The Secret in the Old Well, Grosset & Dunlap, 1944.
The Clue in the Ivy, Grosset & Dunlap, 1952.
The Secret of the Jade Ring, Grosset & Dunlap, 1953.

The Mystery at the Crossroads, Grosset & Dunlap, 1954.
The Ghost in the Gallery, Grosset & Dunlap, 1955, reprinted as Volume 13 of series, 1975.
The Clue of the Black Flower, Grosset & Dunlap, 1956.
The Winking Ruby Mystery, Grosset & Dunlap, 1957, reprinted as Volume 12 of series, 1974.
The Secret of the Swiss Chalet, Grosset & Dunlap, 1958, reprinted as Volume 7 of series, 1973.
The Haunted Lagoon, Grosset & Dunlap, 1959, reprinted as Volume 8 of series, 1973.
Mystery of the Bamboo Bird, Grosset & Dunlap, 1960, reprinted as Volume 9 of series, 1973.
The Sierra Gold Mystery, Grosset & Dunlap, 1961, reprinted as Volume 10 of series, 1973.
The Secret of Lost Lake, Grosset & Dunlap, 1963, reprinted as Volume 11 of series, 1974.
Mystery of the Stone Tiger, Grosset & Dunlap, 1963, reprinted as Volume 1 of series, 1972.
The Riddle of the Frozen Fountain, Grosset & Dunlap, 1964, reprinted as Volume 2 of series, 1972.
The Secret of the Silver Dolphin, Grosset & Dunlap, 1965, reprinted as Volume 3 of series, 1972.
Mystery of the Wax Queen, Grosset & Dunlap, 1966, reprinted as Volume 4 of series, 1972.
The Secret of the Minstrel's Guitar, Grosset & Dunlap, 1967, reprinted as Volume 5 of series, 1972.
The Phantom Surfer, Grosset & Dunlap, 1968, reprinted as Volume 6 of series, 1972.
The Curious Coronation, Grosset & Dunlap, 1976.
The Hundred-Year Mystery, Grosset & Dunlap, 1977.
The Mountain-Peak Mystery, Grosset & Dunlap, 1978.
The Witch's Omen, Grosset & Dunlap, 1979.

"NANCY DREW MYSTERY STORIES"

The Secret of the Old Clock (also see below), Grosset & Dunlap, 1930, revised edition, 1959.
The Hidden Staircase (also see below), Grosset & Dunlap, 1930, revised edition, 1959.
The Bungalow Mystery, Grosset & Dunlap, 1930, revised edition, 1960.
The Mystery at Lilac Inn, Grosset & Dunlap, 1930, revised edition, 1961.
The Secret at Shadow Ranch, Grosset & Dunlap, 1930, revised edition, 1965.
The Secret of Red Gate Farm, Grosset & Dunlap, 1931, revised edition, 1961.
The Clue in the Diary, Grosset & Dunlap, 1932, revised edition, 1962.
Nancy's Mysterious Letter, Grosset & Dunlap, 1932, revised edition, 1968.
The Sign of the Twisted Candles, Grosset & Dunlap, 1933, revised edition, 1968.
The Password to Larkspur Lane, Grosset & Dunlap, 1933, revised edition, 1966.
The Clue of the Broken Locket, Grosset & Dunlap, 1934, revised edition, 1965.
The Message in the Hollow Oak, Grosset & Dunlap, 1935, revised edition, 1972.
The Mystery of the Ivory Charm, Grosset & Dunlap, 1936, revised edition, 1974.
The Whispering Statue, Grosset & Dunlap, 1937, revised edition, 1970.
The Haunted Bridge, Grosset & Dunlap, 1937, revised edition, 1972.
The Clue of the Tapping Heels, Grosset & Dunlap, 1939, revised edition, 1969.
The Mystery of the Brass Bound Trunk, Grosset & Dunlap, 1940, revised edition, 1976.

"Thought you'd be smart, didn't you!" she sneered.
(Frontispiece from the 1930 Nancy Drew adventure,
The Mystery at Lilac Inn.)

**"It is I, Nancy Drew," she whispered, removing the
bonnet and veil.** (Frontispiece from the 1933 edition
of *The Password to Larkspur Lane*.)

The Mystery at the Moss-Covered Mansion, Grosset &
Dunlap, 1941, revised edition, 1971.
The Quest of the Missing Map, Grosset & Dunlap, 1942,
revised edition, 1969.
The Clue in the Jewel Box, Grosset & Dunlap, 1943, revised
edition, 1972.
The Secret in the Old Attic, Grosset & Dunlap, 1944, revised
edition, 1970.
The Clue in the Crumbling Wall, Grosset & Dunlap, 1945,
revised edition, 1973.
The Mystery of the Tolling Bell, Grosset & Dunlap, 1946,
revised edition, 1973.
The Clue in the Old Album, Grosset & Dunlap, 1947, revised
edition, 1977.
The Ghost of Blackwood Hall, Grosset & Dunlap, 1948,
revised edition, 1967.
The Clue of the Leaning Chimney, Grosset & Dunlap, 1949,
revised edition, 1967.
The Secret of the Wooden Lady, Grosset & Dunlap, 1950,
revised edition, 1967.
The Clue of the Black Keys, Grosset & Dunlap, 1951, revised
edition, 1968.
The Mystery at the Ski Jump, Grosset & Dunlap, 1952,
revised edition, 1968.
The Clue of the Velvet Mask, Grosset & Dunlap, 1953, revised
edition, 1969.

The Ringmaster's Secret, Grosset & Dunlap, 1953, revised
edition, 1974.
The Scarlet Slipper Mystery, Grosset & Dunlap, 1954, re-
vised edition, 1974.
The Witch Tree Symbol, Grosset & Dunlap, 1955, revised
edition, 1975.
The Hidden Window Mystery, Grosset & Dunlap, 1957,
revised edition, 1975.
The Haunted Showboat, Grosset & Dunlap, 1958.
The Secret of the Golden Pavilion, Grosset & Dunlap, 1959.
The Clue in the Old Stagecoach, Grosset & Dunlap, 1960.
The Mystery of the Fire Dragon, Grosset & Dunlap, 1961.
The Clue of the Dancing Puppet, Grosset & Dunlap, 1962.
The Moonstone Castle Mystery, Grosset & Dunlap, 1963.
The Clue of the Whistling Bagpipes, Grosset & Dunlap, 1964.
The Phantom of Pine Hill, Grosset & Dunlap, 1965.
The Mystery of the 99 Steps, Grosset & Dunlap, 1966.
The Clue in the Crossword Cipher, Grosset & Dunlap, 1967.
The Spider Sapphire Mystery, Grosset & Dunlap, 1968.
The Invisible Intruder, Grosset & Dunlap, 1969.
The Mysterious Mannequin, Grosset & Dunlap, 1970.
The Crooked Bannister, Grosset & Dunlap, 1971.
The Secret of Mirror Bay, Grosset & Dunlap, 1972.
The Double Jinx Mystery, Grosset & Dunlap, 1973.
The Mystery of the Glowing Eye, Grosset & Dunlap, 1974.
The Secret of the Forgotten City, Grosset & Dunlap, 1975.
The Sky Phantom, Grosset & Dunlap, 1976.

The Strange Message in the Parchment, Grosset & Dunlap, 1977.
The Mystery of Crocodile Island, Grosset & Dunlap, 1978.
The Thirteenth Pearl, Grosset & Dunlap, 1979.
The Triple Hoax, Wanderer, 1979.
The Flying Saucer Mystery, Wanderer, 1980.
The Secret in the Old Lace, Wanderer, 1980.
The Greek Symbol Mystery, Wanderer, 1981.
The Swami's Ring, Wanderer, 1981.
The Kachina Doll Mystery, Wanderer, 1981.
The Twin Dilemma, Wanderer, 1981.
Captive Witness, Wanderer, 1981.
Mystery of the Winged Lion, Wanderer, 1982.
Race against Time, Wanderer, 1982.
The Sinister Omen, Wanderer, 1982.
The Elusive Heiress, Wanderer, 1982.
Clue in the Ancient Disguise, Wanderer, 1982.
The Broken Anchor, Wanderer, 1983.
The Silver Cobweb, Wanderer, 1983.
The Haunted Carousel, Wanderer, 1983.
Enemy Match, Wanderer, 1983.
The Mysterious Image, Wanderer, 1984.
The Emerald-Eyed Cat Mystery, Wanderer, 1984.
The Eskimo's Secret, Wanderer, 1985.
The Bluebeard Room, Wanderer, 1985.
Phantom of Venice, Wanderer, 1985.
The Double Horror of Fenley Place, Minstrel, 1987.
The Case of the Disappearing Diamonds, Minstrel, 1987.
The Mardi Gras Mystery, Minstrel, 1988.
The Clue in the Camera, Minstrel, 1988.
The Case of the Vanishing Veil, Minstrel, 1988.
The Joker's Revenge, Minstrel, 1988.
The Secret of Shady Glen, Minstrel, 1988.
The Mystery of Misty Canyon, Minstrel, 1988.
The Case of the Rising Stars, Minstrel, 1989.
The Search for Cindy Austin, Minstrel, 1989.
The Case of the Disappearing Deejay, Minstrel, 1989.
The Puzzle at Pineview School, Minstrel, 1989.
The Girl Who Couldn't Remember, Minstrel, 1989.
The Ghost of Craven Cove, Minstrel, 1989.
The Case of the Safecracker's Secret, Minstrel, 1990.
The Picture Perfect Mystery, Minstrel, 1990.
The Silent Suspect, Minstrel, 1990.
The Case of the Photo Finish, Minstrel, 1990.
The Mystery at Magnolia Mansion, Minstrel, 1990.
The Haunting of Horse Island, Minstrel, 1990.
The Secret at Seven Rocks, Minstrel, 1991.
A Secret in Time, Minstrel, 1991.
The Mystery of the Missing Millionairess, Minstrel, 1991.
The Secret in the Dark, Minstrel, 1991.
The Stranger in the Shadows, Minstrel, 1991.
The Mystery of the Jade Tiger, Minstrel, 1991.

"NANCY DREW FILES" MYSTERY SERIES

Secrets Can Kill, Archway, 1986.
Deadly Intent, Archway, 1986.
Murder on Ice, Archway, 1986.
Smile and Say Murder, Archway, 1986.
Hit and Run Holiday, Archway, 1986.
White Water Terror, Archway, 1987.
Deadly Doubles, Archway, 1987.
Two Points for Murder, Archway, 1987.
False Moves, Archway, 1987.
Buried Secrets, Archway, 1987.
Heart of Danger, Archway, 1987.
Fatal Ransom, Archway, 1987.
Wings of Fear, Archway, 1987.
This Side of Evil, Archway, 1987.
Trial by Fire, Archway, 1987.

Never Say Die, Archway, 1987.
Stay Tuned for Danger, Archway, 1987.
Circle of Evil, Archway, 1987.
Sisters in Crime, Archway, 1988.
Very Deadly Yours, Archway, 1988.
Recipe for Murder, Archway, 1988.
Fatal Attraction, Archway, 1988.
Sinister Paradise, Archway, 1988.
Til Death Do Us Part, Archway, 1988.
Rich and Dangerous, Archway, 1988.
Playing with Fire, Archway, 1988.
Most Likely to Die, Archway, 1988.
The Black Widow, Archway, 1988.
Pure Poison, Archway, 1988.
Death by Design, Archway, 1988.
Trouble in Tahiti, Archway, 1989.
High Marks for Malice, Archway, 1989.
Danger in Disguise, Archway, 1989.
Vanishing Act, Archway, 1989.
Bad Medicine, Archway, 1989.
Over the Edge, Archway, 1989.
Last Dance, Archway, 1989.
The Final Scene, Archway, 1989.
The Suspect Next Door, Archway, 1989.
Shadow of a Doubt, Archway, 1989.
Something to Hide, Archway, 1989.
Wrong Chemistry, Archway, 1989.
False Impressions, Archway, 1990.
Scent of Danger, Archway, 1990.
Out of Bounds, Archway, 1990.
Win, Place, or Die, Archway, 1990.
Flirting with Danger, Archway, 1990.
Date with Deception, Archway, 1990.
Portrait in Crime, Archway, 1990.
Deep Secrets, Archway, 1990.
A Model Crime, Archway, 1990.
Danger for Hire, Archway, 1990.
Trail of Lies, Archway, 1990.
Cold as Ice, Archway, 1990.
Don't Look Twice, Archway, 1991.
Make No Mistake, Archway, 1991.
Into Thin Air, Archway, 1991.
Hot Pursuit, Archway, 1991.
High Risk, Archway, 1991.
Poison Pen, Archway, 1991.
Sweet Revenge, Archway, 1991.
Easy Marks, Archway, 1991.
Mixed Signals, Archway, 1991.
The Wrong Track, Archway, 1991.
Final Notes, Archway, 1991.
Tall, Dark, and Deadly, Archway, 1991.

"RIVER HEIGHTS" SERIES

Love Times Three, Archway, 1989.
Guilty Secrets, Archway, 1989.
Going Too Far, Archway, 1990.
Stolen Kisses, Archway, 1990.
Between the Lines, Archway, 1990.
Lessons in Love, Archway, 1990.
Cheating Hearts, Archway, 1990.
The Trouble with Love, Archway, 1990.
Lies and Whispers, Archway, 1991.
Mixed Emotions, Archway, 1991.
Broken Hearts, Archway, 1991.
Junior Class Trip ("Super Sizzler"), Archway, 1991.
Hard to Handle, Archway, 1991.
A Mind of Her Own, Archway, 1991.

Nancy made a wild scramble to save herself. (Frontispiece from the 1941 Nancy Drew story, *The Mystery at the Moss-Covered Mansion.*)

WITH FRANKLIN W. DIXON

Nancy Drew and the Hardy Boys: Super Sleuths! (short stories), Wanderer, Volume 1, 1981, Volume 2, 1984.
Nancy Drew and the Hardy Boys Camp Fire Stories, Wanderer, 1984.
Nancy Drew & the Hardy Boys Be a Detective Mystery Stories: The Secret of the Knight's Sword, edited by Betty Schwartz, Wanderer, 1984.
Nancy Drew & the Hardy Boys Be a Detective Mystery Stories: Danger on Ice, edited by Schwartz, Wanderer, 1984.
Nancy Drew & the Hardy Boys Be a Detective Mystery Stories: The Feathered Serpent, edited by Schwartz, Wanderer, 1984.
Nancy Drew & the Hardy Boys Be a Detective Mystery Stories: Secret Cargo, edited by Schwartz, Wanderer, 1984.
Nancy Drew & the Hardy Boys Be a Detective Mystery Stories: The Alaskan Mystery, edited by Diane Arico, Wanderer, 1985.
Nancy Drew & the Hardy Boys Be a Detective Mystery Stories: The Missing Money Mystery, edited by Arico, Wanderer, 1985.
Nancy Drew & the Hardy Boys Be a Detective Mystery Stories: Jungle of Evil, edited by Arico, Wanderer, 1985.

Nancy Drew & the Hardy Boys Be a Detective Mystery Stories: Ticket to Intrigue, edited by Arico, Wanderer, 1985.

OTHER

(Contributor) Stephen Dunning and Henry B. Maloney, editors, *A Superboy, Supergirl Anthology: Selected Chapters from the Earlier Works of Victor Appleton, Franklin W. Dixon, and Carolyn Keene,* Scholastic Book Services, 1971.
The Nancy Drew Cookbook: Clues to Good Cooking, Grosset & Dunlap, 1973.
Mystery of the Lost Dogs (Nancy Drew picture book), Grosset & Dunlap, 1977.
The Secret of the Twin Puppets (Nancy Drew picture book), Grosset & Dunlap, 1977.
The Hardy Boys and Nancy Drew Meet Dracula (based on episodes of "The Hardy Boys/Nancy Drew Mysteries"), Grosset & Dunlap, 1978.
The Haunted House and Flight to Nowhere (based on episodes of "The Hardy Boys/Nancy Drew Mysteries"), Grosset & Dunlap, 1978.
The Nancy Drew Sleuth Book: Clues to Good Sleuthing (short stories and police procedures), Grosset & Dunlap, 1979.
Nancy Drew Book of Hidden Clues, Wanderer, 1980.
Nancy Drew Ghost Stories (short stories), edited by Meg Schneider, Wanderer, Volume 1, 1983, Volume 2, 1985.

A modern-day Nancy Drew graces the cover of this 1987 episode from the Nancy Drew files. (Cover artwork by Enric.)

Nancy Drew Mystery Stories: Back-to-Back Edition, Putnam, 1987.

Double Crossing: A Nancy Drew & Hardy Boys Supermystery, Archway, 1988.

A Crime for Christmas: A Nancy Drew & Hardy Boys Supermystery, Archway, 1988.

Shock Waves: A Nancy Drew & Hardy Boys Supermystery, Archway, 1989.

Dangerous Game: A Nancy Drew & Hardy Boys Supermystery, Archway, 1989.

Last Resort: A Nancy Drew & Hardy Boys Supermystery, Archway, 1989.

Buried in Time: A Nancy Drew & Hardy Boys Supermystery, Archway, 1990.

Mystery Train: A Nancy Drew & Hardy Boys Supermystery, Archway, 1990.

Paris Connection: A Nancy Drew & Hardy Boys Supermystery, Archway, 1990.

Best of Enemies: A Nancy Drew & Hardy Boys Supermystery, Archway, 1991.

High Survival: A Nancy Drew & Hardy Boys Supermystery, Archway, 1991.

New Year's Evil: A Nancy Drew & Hardy Boys Supermystery, Archway, 1991.

Also author of *The Secret of the Old Clock* [and] *The Hidden Staircase*, revised editions, published in the early 1970s.

SIDELIGHTS: Of all the Stratemeyer Syndicate series stars, perhaps none has shone as brightly as Nancy Drew. "Since the '30s," declares Deborah Kaplan in the *Detroit Free Press*, "she has steered the Silent Generation, Woodstock Generation and Me Generation of women through their tender years as the model of a Junior Leaguer." Supported by her lawyer father, Carson Drew, aided by chums George Fayne and Bess Marvin as well as boyfriend Ned Nickerson, driving her blue roadster around River Heights, Nancy has sleuthed her way into the hearts of millions of young readers for more than fifty years. Nancy is "the most popular girl detective in the world," says Bobbie Ann Mason in her book *The Girl Sleuth: A Feminist Guide.* "There had been nothing in children's books like the success of Nancy Drew." She began her detecting career in 1929, Mason declares, "serenely ignoring the world crashing all around." By 1933, she adds, Nancy was outselling the most popular boys' series by nearly two to one. Today, more than fifty years after her debut, Nancy's adventures continue to attract readers; more than eighty million copies of her books have been sold.

Part of Nancy's success, critics believe, derives from the way her adventures mix elements of three different genres: detective, series, and Gothic fiction. Russel B. Nye reports in *The Unembarrassed Muse: The Popular Arts in America* that all of Nancy's exploits "are based on the mystery-adventure-Gothic pattern developed by Mary Roberts Rinehart, geared to the level of the early teen." Nancy is locked in Heath Castle's dusty tower in *The Clue in the Crumbling Wall. The Witch Tree Symbol* interweaves Pennsylvania Dutch hex signs and a thief who pursues Nancy with deadly intent, while in *The Invisible Intruder,* the young detective and her friends search for a ghost. "This seesaw pattern of pursuit, confinement, and release, in turn," Carol Billman asserts in *The Secret of the Stratemeyer Syndicate: Nancy Drew, the Hardy Boys, and the Million Dollar Fiction Factory,* "wrings out readers' emotions by exciting alternating feelings of tension and exhilaration."

Often these elements are used repeatedly in different volumes of the series, sometimes—in the opinion of certain critics—to the detriment of the reader's imagination. "A common complaint" of reviewers, notes *New York Times Book Review* contributor Karla Kuskin, "is that 'Nancy Drew books are the same books written over and over again.'" Proponents of series fiction recognize this; Mason observes, "The plots of Nancy Drew mysteries are like sonnets—endless variations on an inflexible form." But some of Nancy's supporters see this repetitiousness as a positive factor in the series' success. "Perhaps," Kuskin continues, "that is also part of the charm they hold for their readers. A series combines the excitement of the unknown cushioned by the known." "In a world of gaudy exhibitionism," declares Arthur Prager in *Rascals at Large; or, The Clue in the Old Nostalgia,* "sub-teens find refuge in Nancy's enviable, secure, conservative world."

Another part of the series' attraction lies in the figure of the girl sleuth herself. Anita Susan Grossman, writing in *Ohio Magazine,* states, "Nancy represents an ideal: Well-to-do, attractive, intelligent, she is eternally poised on the edge of adulthood, without ever having to take on grown-up worries and responsibilities." "At the same time," she adds, "Nancy is endowed with any number of skills . . . and is mature beyond her years." Nancy has her own car and is largely free of parental supervision; she can do anything, and does it superbly well. The young investigator, says Mason, "is as immaculate and self-possessed as a Miss America on tour. She is as cool as Mata Hari and as sweet as Betty Crocker." In *The Password to Larkspur Lane* she makes a championship dive while at a swank resort, then rescues a small child who has fallen in the lake. She shoots a lynx with a revolver in *The Secret at Shadow Ranch,* and even repairs her car in *The Sign of the Twisted Candles.* "As a symbolic figure," declares Billman, "the young female private eye is everything girl readers could ask for."

Yet Nancy also has a certain accessibility and appeal that other, more exotic, heroines lack. Prager reports, "When I asked my daughter why she had loved Nancy, she thought for a moment, and then said simply, 'You can *identify* with her.' She meant that a little girl can plausibly pretend to be Nancy. She is an example of the fantasy world in which pre-pubescent girls live in day-dreams." Carol King, a regional director of the National Organization for Women, told Kaplan, "You could relate to a young woman who wasn't just timidly sitting back playing dolls, watching life go by, waiting for her knight in armor to come and sweep her off her feet." "She gave girls the idea you could be something other than Pollyanna or the Bobbsey Twins. Nancy Drew *did* stuff," women's studies librarian Pat Padala informed Kaplan. She is a paragon of young women's aspirations. Young readers, says Nye, "find in her what they hope soon to be—a poised, capable, self-sufficient girl in control of her life; one who can take care of herself and who needs neither guidance nor exhortation."

Although Nancy has her proponents as a symbol of female liberation, some critics note that she fails as a role model. Nora Faires, a woman's historian, told Kaplan that Nancy "never seemed to have a future." "Totally protected from want, gainful employment, boredom and despair," says Kuskin, "Nancy would seem to be more of a suburban princess than a symbol of liberation from anything except real life." "Living in the nearly fantastic land of River Heights, she is hermetically sealed off from change, growth, failure," asserts Billman. "Yet," she continues, "it is precisely because [Nancy] is so far removed from the little qualms and the big frustrations and decisions facing real girls and women that she cannot be considered a helpful fictional model of successful womanhood." "Cool Nancy Drew figures it is better to be locked in the timeless role of girl sleuth—forever young, forever tops, above sex, above marriage—an inspiring symbol of freedom," states Mason. "But was she? . . . She always has it both ways—protected and free. She is an eternal girl, a stage which is a false ideal for women in our time." "Maybe in the end that's why I didn't like her," Faires concludes. "Her world never gets more complicated. Like Peter Pan, she never had to grow up."

If Nancy has never had to grow up, still she has evolved over the years. Juvenile lifestyles changed after the Second World War, and volumes written in the 1930s seemed dated to later readers. In 1959 Harriet Adams, head of the Stratemeyer Syndicate, began rewriting the earlier series books in order to bring Nancy up-to-date and to eliminate racial stereotypes. Villains lost their ethnic qualities and dialect-speaking characters switched to standard English, but the young sleuth herself stayed basically the same. In 1986, however, Simon & Schuster launched the "Nancy Drew Files" series, which featured an entirely revamped Nancy. "In keeping with Eighties feminism," says Grossman, "Nancy has become more the professional detective who is hired for 'cases' and has a 'career.'" Nancy Wartik writes in *Ms.,* "The blue roadster is now a Mustang GT convertible, Ned Nickerson's demure pecks on the cheek have turned into lingering kisses and romantic liaisons in a Jacuzzi." "To some readers," relates Grossman, "it has all been too much." One reviewer, she continues, "blasted the new Nancy Drew as a '*Dynasty* bimbo,' finding her 'a hot little number looking for "hunks" who acts like something out of a Jackie Collins novel.'"

Revised, revamped, and renewed, Nancy seems destined to continue forever. Although many critics agree that her adventures lack literary quality, they continue to enthrall readers—and, Kuskin emphasizes, "they have helped lead many children past River Heights or Bayport further into the bewitched byways of reading for pleasure. It's a destination well worth the trip." Librarians, executives, and authors such as Frances Fitzgerald, Ellen Goodman, and Eileen Goudge Zuckerman all have acknowledged Nancy's influence in their early years. "Whatever literary or life experiences readers graduate to," Billman declares, "Nancy does seem to be in American girls' bloodstream; and as part of their larger reading and developmental pattern, she not only has won—but *has*—her place."

The Stratemeyer Syndicate also used the Carolyn Keene pseudonym for the "Dana Girls" series, combining elements of Nancy Drew and the Hardy Boys in the adventures of two sister sleuths, Louise and Jean Dana. Mildred Benson originated the "Nancy Drew" series for Edward Stratemeyer, and also contributed volumes to the "Dana Girls." Walter Karig, Leslie McFarlane, Harriet S. Adams, James Duncan Lawrence, and Nancy Axelrad were among the other writers who contributed to these series. For more information, see the entry on Mildred Benson in this volume, or the *Something about the Author* or *Contemporary Authors* indexes for entries on Harriet S. Adams, James Duncan Lawrence, and Edward L. Stratemeyer.

ADAPTATIONS: Four black and white films featuring Nancy Drew were made in 1938-39. They all starred Bonita Granville as Nancy, John Litel as Carson Drew, and Frankie Thomas as "Ted" Nickerson: "Nancy Drew—Detective" (loosely based on *The Password to Larkspur Lane*), Warner Bros., 1938; "Nancy Drew—Reporter," Warner Bros., 1939;

"Nancy Drew, Trouble Shooter," Warner Bros., 1939; and "Nancy Drew and the Hidden Staircase," Warner Bros., 1939. More recently, Pamela Sue Martin and Janet Louise Jackson have portrayed the girl sleuth in "The Nancy Drew Mysteries," which later became "The Hardy Boys/Nancy Drew Mysteries," and ran on ABC-TV from 1977 to 1979, and then went into syndication. Four Nancy Drew filmstrips, each an adaptation of a Nancy Drew book, appeared in 1979 from the Society for Visual Education: "The Secret of the Old Clock," "Nancy's Mysterious Letter," "The Mysterious Mannequin," and "The Sky Phantom." The girl sleuth has also appeared in other media. Parker Brothers released a *Nancy Drew Mystery Game* in 1958. "The Clue in the Old Stagecoach," a recording of the novel of the same title, was issued in 1972, and recently actress Eve Plumb has narrated Nancy's adventures for the Cassette Book Company. In 1979, Grosset & Dunlap published two coloring books and Wanderer issued a Nancy Drew diary and date book. Simon & Schuster has recently announced plans for the girl detective that include Nancy Drew stationery, clothes, and jewelry.

FOR MORE INFORMATION SEE:

BOOKS

Authors in the News, Volume 2, Gale, 1976.
Bargainnier, Earl F., editor, *Ten Women of Mystery,* Bowling Green State University Popular Press, 1981.
Billman, Carol, *The Secret of the Stratemeyer Syndicate: Nancy Drew, the Hardy Boys, and the Million Dollar Fiction Factory,* Ungar, 1986.
Johnson, Deidre, editor and compiler, *Stratemeyer Pseudonyms and Series Books: An Annotated Checklist of Stratemeyer and Stratemeyer Syndicate Publications,* Greenwood Press, 1982.
Mason, Bobbie Ann, *The Girl Sleuth: A Feminist Guide,* Feminist Press, 1975.
Nye, Russel B., *The Unembarrassed Muse: The Popular Arts in America,* Dial, 1970.
Penzler, Otto, editor, *The Great Detectives,* Little, Brown, 1978.
Prager, Arthur, *Rascals at Large; or, The Clue in the Old Nostalgia,* Doubleday, 1971.

PERIODICALS

Americana, September-October, 1986.
Ann Arbor News, February 19, 1980.
Chicago Tribune, July 10, 1986.
Children's Literature, Volume 7, 1978.
Detroit Free Press, October 10, 1975; June 17, 1986; September 7, 1986.
Detroit News, February 17, 1980; August 13, 1986.
Family Weekly, August 10, 1980.
Hobbies, March, 1981.
Journal of Popular Culture, spring, 1973.
Language Arts, November-December, 1975.
Ms., January, 1974; September, 1986.
New Yorker, August 18, 1986.
New York Times, April 4, 1968; March 27, 1977.
New York Times Book Review, May 4, 1975.
Ohio Magazine, December, 1987.
People, April 28, 1980.
Publishers Weekly, March 5, 1979; May 30, 1986.
Redbook, April, 1980.
Saturday Review, January 25, 1969.
Seventeen, December, 1979.
TV Guide, June 25, 1977.
Vogue, May, 1980.

ANDREI KELEINIKOV

KELEINIKOV, Andrei 1924-

PERSONAL: Born April 23, 1924, in Ouglich, United Soviet Socialist Republics (U.S.S.R); son of Alexander Mihkailovich (professor of engineering) and Eugene (teacher of foreign languages) Keleinikov; married Svetlana I. Eremeeva, March 4, 1947; children: Tatiana, Olga. *Education:* Moscow State University, diploma and university degree, 1950, diploma and magister in biology, 1954. *Politics:* "Non-party." *Religion:* Orthodoxy.

ADDRESSES: Home—Avenue 60th, Block 2, Flat 24, Moscow 117036, U.S.S.R.

CAREER: Pencil artist and illustrator. Member of biological faculty and chairman of department of zoology, Moscow State University. Research worker for Institute of Virology. *Military service:* Russian artillery, 1942-44; became junior lieutenant; received numerous awards, including two orders of Patriotic War of the First Degree and Victory over Germany Awards.

MEMBER: Moscow Artist's Union, Moscow Society of Naturalists.

ILLUSTRATOR:

V. Bianki, *How a Little Ant Was in a Hurry,* Detgis, 1952.

(With L. Godin) A. Shahkov, *A Terrible Canyon,* Detgis, 1954.

Charles Roberts, *A Little House Under Water,* Detgis, 1955.

S. Vasiliev, *The Feathered's Council,* Detgis, 1956.

G. Skrebitsky, *Our Natural Reserves,* Detgis, 1957.

L. Golosnitsky, *Travelling into the Past,* Detgis, 1957.

G. Skrebitsky, *On the Shore of a New Sea,* Detgis, 1957.

(With G. Nickolsky) N. Rakovskaya, *Devoted Friends,* Detgis, 1958.

Vera Horol, *Belianka,* Detgis, 1958.

(With N. V. Vitka) *Squirrel's Sorrow—Stork's Summer,* Detgis, 1958.

J. Shamshourin, *Why do Birds Fly to the South?,* Detgis, 1959.

G. Skrebitsky, *Born in the Fall,* Detgis, 1960.

(With L. Godin) A. Shahkov, *With the Spring to the North,* Detgis, 1960.

G. Skrebitsky, *Welcoming the Spring,* Detgis, 1960.

A. Gazoukina, *A Hairy Laundress,* Detgis, 1960.

G. Skrebitsky, *New Acquaintances: Stories,* Detgis, 1960.

M. Zverev, *How Does Everybody Play?,* Detsky Mir, 1960.

M. Zverev, *Mergen Is Following in the Tracks Of. . . Juzushi,* Alma-Ata, 1960.

G. Skrebitsky, *What Happens and When?,* Detgis, 1961.

G. Skrebitsky, *Domesticated and Wild Things,* Detgis, 1961.

G. Skrebitsky, *About Our Birds, Starling, and Tits,* Detsky Mir, 1962.

G. Skrebitsky, *A Little Badger,* Detgis, 1962.

G. Skrebitsky, *A Devoted Friend,* Detsky Mir, 1962.

G. Skrebitsky, *A Little House on the Birch,* [U.S.S.R.], 1962.

Y. Dmitriev, *Ordinary Miracles,* Detsky Mir, 1962.

G. P. Dementiev, *Birds of Our Country,* Moscow State University, 1962.

G. Skrebitsky, *Winged Neighbours,* Detgis, 1962.

G. Skrebitsky, *In the Forest and in the Fields,* Detgis, 1963.

G. Skrebitsky, *Animals: Big and Little Ones,* Detgis, 1963.

(With L. Godin) G. Skrebitsky, *Behind the Forest Curtain,* Detgis, 1963.

M. Zverev, *Mysterious Feathers,* Detgis, 1963.

I. Abroskin, *The Boy Omkaj and His Oumkies,* Detsky Mir, 1963.

V. Chaplina, *Intolerable Pupil,* Detgis, 1963.

G. Skrebitsky, *The Little Forest Voice,* Children's Literature, 1964.

V. Balashov, *The Marked,* Malysh, 1964.

L. Markov, *Starlings: Twins and the Brave Kiki,* Malysh, 1964.

Anton Chehkov, *Near the Very Border,* Moscow Worker, 1965.

V. Astafiev, *The Little Swift Scrip,* Children's Literature, 1965.

A. Shahkov, *Traveller's Stories,* Children's Literature, 1966.

M. Zverev, *The Golden Saiga,* Children's Literature, 1966.

A. Vladimirov, *When Do the Bluebells Wake Up?,* Malysh, 1966.

E. Dokoukina, *An Elusive Carabid,* Malysh, 1966.

O. Serdiukova, *An Enigmatic Feather,* Malysh, 1966.

N. Sladkov, *Songs under the Ice,* Children's Literature, 1967.

Y. Dmitriev, *Forest Riddles,* Children's Literature, 1967.

P. Doudochkin, *Singularity in the Ordinarily,* Education Press, 1967.

K. Medjidov, *Kind Neighbours,* Children's Literature, 1968.

(With G. Nickolsky) G. Skrebitsky, *The Friends of My Childhood,* Children's Literature, 1968.

(With G. Nickolsky) *How the Cats Fish: Stories by Russian Writers,* Children's Literature, 1968.

M. Zverev, *Unbetrayed Mysteries,* Education Press, 1968.

Y. Dmitriev, *Stories By My Little Meadow,* Children's Literature, 1969.

V. Bocharnikov, *Silk Ears,* Children's Literature, 1969.

Keleinikov aims to capture the grace of living creatures by exactness and expression of lines of drawing. (From *Silk Ears* by V. Bocharnikov.)

G. Skrebitsky, *Cheerful by Streams*, Children's Literature, 1969.

E. Skim, *Who's Lost a Hoof?*, Children's Literature, 1969.

B. Dijour, *Why Have You Abandoned Your Friend?*, Children's Literature, 1969.

Y. Dmitriev, *Hello, Squirrel! How Are You, Crocodile?*, Children's Literature, 1970.

N. Nickonov, *Forest Days*, Children's Literature, 1970.

V. Fetissov, *The Morning in a Winter Woodland*, Malysh, 1970.

D. Tardjemanov, *Shouktougan*, Children's Literature, 1970, translation by Natalie Wood, Progress Publishers, 1975.

K. Oushinsky, *Bishka*, Children's Literature, 1970.

A. Barkov, *Winter Birds*, Malysh, 1970.

A. Smirnov, *Red-Haired*, Children's Literature, 1971.

B. Pavlov, *Forest Pictures*, Children's Literature, 1971.

A. Lelievre, *Why Does the Monkey Need a Tail?*, Children's Literature, 1971.

E. Skim, *Fairy Tales Found in the Grass*, Children's Literature, 1972.

E. Nijt, *The Little Hare "Black Eyes,"* Children's Literature, 1972.

An ABC Book of Birds and Beasts, Malysh, 1972.

M. Zverev, *The Owner of Celestial Mountains*, Children's Literature, 1972.

A. Green, *The Story of a Hawk*, Children's Literature, 1973.

M. Konstantinovsky, *Adventures of a Sea Puppy*, Malysh, 1973.

I. Bodrov, *In the Place Where the Lotus Blooms*, Malysh, 1973.

B. Dijour, *Complaints Book of Nature*, Children's Literature, 1973.

L. Tolstoj, *The Ant and the She-Dove*, Children's Literature, 1973.

V. Simonov, *The Sun in the Hollow*, Malysh, 1974.

N. Sladkov, *What's Being Done By Whom?*, Malysh, 1974.

N. N. Plavilshikov, *To Young Nature Lovers*, Children's Literature, 1975.

V. Bocharnikov, *Koriajonok*, Children's Literature, 1975.

E. Moshkovskaja, *A Greedy Thing*, Malysh, 1975.

S. Fineshtein, *Domesticated Beasts and Birds*, Malysh, 1975.

A. Ivanov, *Homa's Adventures*, Malysh, 1975.

V. Horol, *A Little Goat*, Children's Literature, 1975.

A. Babenyshev, *The Most, the Most . . . .* , Malysh, 1976.

Igor Akimushkin, *These Are All Dogs*, Malysh, 1976.

S. Younatov, *How Long Does the Turtle Live?*, Malysh, 1976.

M. Kravchuk, *In the Morning*, Malysh, 1976.

I. Polouianov, *Peas on a Thousand Roads*, Children's Literature, 1977.

M. Zverev, *A White Maral*, Children's Literature, 1977.

I. Akimushkin, *These Are All Antelopes*, Malysh, 1977.

K. Tile, *The Single Magpie's Island*, Children's Literature, 1977.

K. Oushinsky, *A Hen and Little Ducks*, Malysh, 1977.

M. Myshlina, *A Little Sparrow "Chick-Chirick,"* Malysh, 1977.

V. Maximov, *Who Makes the Water Clean?*, Malysh, 1978.

(With O. Basrykina) B. Pavlov, *Who Sings in a Winter Forest?*, Malysh, 1979.

A. Mihkailov, *How Do Animals Hide?*, Malysh, 1979.

V. Bocharnikov, *One More Friend of Ours*, Children's Literature, 1979.

E. Smolin, *Wonderful Tails*, Malysh, 1979.

M. Zverev, *The Young Wolf from Betpuck-Dala*, Malysh, 1980.

V. Bocharnikov, *The Red Sun*, Children's Literature, 1980.

V. Astafiev, *Uncle Kouzia: Hen's Chief,* Children's Literature, 1981.

G. Snegirev, *At the Zoo in the Spring,* Malysh, 1982.

I. Akimushkin, *Builders in the Wild,* Malysh, 1982.

G. Skrebitsky, *The Woodland Grand-grand-father,* Children's Literature, 1982.

S. Younatov, *Giants of Ocean,* Malysh, 1982.

(With daughter, Olga Keleinikov) A. Tambiev, *The Spring Has Come,* Malysh, 1983.

I. Akimushkin, *There Lived a Hedgehog,* Malysh, 1984.

G. Skrebitsky, *A Cunning Bird,* Malysh, 1984.

G. Snegirev, *At Money's Place,* Malysh, 1985.

G. Snegirev, *In Winter,* Malysh, 1985.

V. Tanasiitchouk, *How Many Eyes Has a Dragonfly?,* Malysh, 1986.

G. Snegirev, *At the Natural Reserve,* Malysh, 1986.

V. Flint, *About the Animals from the Red Book,* Malysh, 1986.

S. Younatov, *The Most Beautiful Fishes,* Malysh, 1987.

G. Mushkin, *The Parent's Day,* Children's Literature, 1988.

SIDELIGHTS: Andrei Keleinikov told *SATA:* "I don't know whether I was simply lucky enough or lead by my passion for nature, for animals, for all the living creatures but I didn't hesitate in choosing my profession. I was admitted to the biological faculty of Moscow State University, chair of zoology where the job is connected with permanent expeditions and trips. This decision made my father very sorry, he hoped that I'd choose the profession of an artist. I began to draw very early and in the opinion of those who surrounded me I did it very successfully. I think now if not for the university I would probably not have become an artist. There I was helped in realizing my destiny and in choosing the proper road. On entering the university I did not give up

Keleinikov spent years observing animals in the wild as part of his development as an illustrator. (Cover reproduction from the Russian edition of *Forest Riddles* written by Y. Dmitriev.)

drawing. Here I was taught by V. Vatagin—an excellent animalist, painter, and sculptor. I drew a lot during my expeditions and trips. My scientific leader, Professor G. P. Dementiev was very enthusiastic about my being fond of animalistics. He was a highly educated person, of a great cultural level. At his request I illustrated his book *Birds of Our Country* and I did it with really great pleasure. The author left it to me to decide upon the type and character of illustrations.

"My passion for art increased with time. I began to realize that to elicit secrets from nature was foreign to my nature. The cheerful contemplation of this world and wish to make other people more familiar with this joy were in more conformity with the state of my soul.

"Nevertheless, after defending my thesis I didn't have the nerve to give up science and I started working as a research worker at the Institute of Virology. I drew all my spare time and grew fond of landscape painting. I realized at last that it was no longer possible to 'sit on two chairs'; it was high time to choose between science and art. By this time I was already married and we had two children. It was not a very responsible decision to give up the prestige and well-paying job and to become a free-lance artist with occasional wages. My relatives considered it unjustified tomfoolery. The more so that I was not skilled as a painter. They predicted a failure, crash, hunger, cold, prayed to think of the family. I was lucky to have a wife who supported me completely; she realized that I couldn't be happy unless I was involved in creative work. The very thought that a wife and children could play a role of irons to a man was insulting to her. In 1956 I said good-bye to science and left for the 'liberated bread.' My wife started working and those small wages and her parent's help aided us to survive the most difficult time of my formation as a professional artist. My teacher and friend, a wonderful animalist also graduated from Moscow State University—G. E. Nickolsky—played not the last role in my decision. On obtaining freedom I began to work as if I were possessed. Almost everyday I made sketches at the zoo together with Nickolsky. We rode all over the middle part of Russia reaching Askania Nova and Karelia in the North penetrating into the most wild places in our desire to see animals under natural conditions in untouched nature.

"I visited by myself and also with expeditions practically all the regions of the country except the far east and the extreme North. Domesticated and wild animals—interchangeable pets of all the family inhabited our home. Dogs, hares, rock squirrels, guinea pigs, snakes, frogs, turtles, beetles, crickets, and other beasts and insects in turn or in common were inhabitants of our flat. Beasts felt at home at our place and often, to guests' mind, behaved 'impudently.' Our pet hare 'Trouska' didn't allow strangers to sit down on the couch which he considered to be its (or rather his) own area. If somebody forgot it or simply not knowing about it sat down on the sofa, the hare attacked this person from behind and beat him on the back with his front legs uttering some sounds very much like growling. He was very fond of company and if he was driven out of the room when guests had come he tried to force the door, pulled the door with his teeth and, if not managing it, he began to gnaw it.

"Since my childhood I was fond of fishing and hunting. With the age passion for hunting was forced out with the profound feeling of the unity with the surrounding world, nature, and animals, and with the desire to express this attitude to the world in my creative work. My creed of an artist-animalist is my wish to express my state of admiration and love for animals. Every animal is beautiful, harmonious, always natural and peaceful under natural conditions. Children feel it very keenly and their attitude towards animals is as a rule kind and trustful. Probably that's the reason why I'm engaged in illustrating children's books.

"I believe that it's possible to show grace and perfection of living things by exactness and expression of lines of drawings—that's what I always aimed at in my work."

* * *

KELLY, Jeff
See KELLY, Jeffrey

* * *

KELLY, Jeffrey 1946-
(Jeff Kelly)

PERSONAL: Born May 22, 1946, in Yonkers, NY; son of Thomas P. (in business) and Carol Lee (Sierk) Kelly; married wife, Carolyn (a teacher); children: Sarah, Rebecca. *Education:* Pace University, B.A., 1969; Lesley College, M.Ed., 1976.

ADDRESSES: Home and office—170 Elm St., Andover, MA 01810.

CAREER: English teacher, 1970-81; free-lance journalist, 1978—; Cole Surveys, Inc., Boston, MA, publicity director, 1982-84; Bentley College, Waltham, MA, news director and adjunct professor of English, 1984-87; children's book writer, 1984—; free-lance writing teacher.

MEMBER: PEN, Society of Children's Book Writers.

WRITINGS:

(Under name Jeff Kelly) *Tramp Steamer and the Silver Bullet* (children's book), Houghton, 1984.
The Basement Baseball Club (children's book), Houghton, 1987.

Also author of the children's book *An Old-Fashioned Ghost Story,* 1989. Contributor to newspapers and magazines, including the *Boston Globe.*

WORK IN PROGRESS: How to Handle a Bully, for fourth- to seventh-graders.

SIDELIGHTS: Jeffrey Kelly told *SATA:* "As a children's book writer, I am hired by many New England schools to act as 'writer-in-residence.' During these two-day to three-week stays I teach writing primarily to third to sixth graders, the ages for whom I write. In addition to supplementing my income, my work with children (which includes a healthy dose of storytelling) continues to act as an inspiration for my own writing for children. I use much of what I learn from children to supplement my talks and lectures to adult audiences on children's literature and writing for children. I teach writing for children at the Cambridge Center for Adult Education, all of which is lots of fun—and work, as is the writing."

KESLER, Jay (L.) 1935-

PERSONAL: Born September 15, 1935, in Barnes, WI; son of Herbert E. and Elsie (Campbell) Kesler; married Jane Smith, June 7, 1957; children: Laura, Bruce, Terri. *Education:* Attended Ball State University, 1953-54; Taylor University, B.A., 1958.

ADDRESSES: Home—711 Reade Ave., Upland, IN 46989. *Office*— President's Office, Taylor University, Upland, IN 46989.

CAREER: Youth for Christ/USA, Wheaton, IL, director of Marion, IN, branch, 1955-58, crusade staff evangelist, 1959-60, director of Illinois-Indiana region, 1960-62, director of college recruitment, 1962-63, vice-president for personnel, 1963-68, vice-president for field coordination, 1968-73, president, 1973-85, current member of board of directors; Taylor University, Upland, IN, president, 1985—. Chief executive officer, Youth for Christ/USA's interdenominational ministry to high school students. Publisher of *Campus Life* (magazine), 1973-83. Faculty member, Billy Graham Schools of Evangelism. Lecturer, Staley Distinguished Christian Scholar lecture program. Co-pastor, First Baptist Church of Geneva, Geneva, IL, 1972-85. Speaker on daily radio broadcast *Family Forum.*

Chairman of board of directors, Christian College Coalition; member of board of directors, Youth for Christ International, Prison Fellowship International, National Association of Evangelicals, Christianity Today, Evangelical Council for Financial Accountability, Christian College Consortium, Institute for Nonprofit Organizations, Independent Colleges and Universities of Indiana, Associated Colleges of Indiana, Brotherhood Mutual Insurance Co., and Marion, IN, Easter pageant; member of advisory board, International Council on Biblical Inerrancy, Venture Middle East, Christian Bible Society, Discovery Network, Inc., Evangelicals for Social Action; adviser to various groups and societies.

MEMBER: Christian Educators Association International, National Educators Fellowship, Christian Camps, Inc., Project Partner.

AWARDS, HONORS: D.D., Barrington College, 1977, Asbury Theological Seminary, 1984; L.H.D., Taylor University, 1982, John Brown University, 1987; H.H.D., Huntington College, 1983; Angel Award, Religion in Media, 1985; Gold Medallion Award, *Parents and Teenagers;* Outstanding Youth Leadership Award, Religious Heritage of America, 1989.

WRITINGS:

Let's Succeed with Our Teenagers, David Cook, 1973.
I Never Promised You a Disneyland, Word, Inc., 1975.
The Strong Weak People, Victor Books, 1976.
Outside Disneyland, Word, Inc., 1977.
I Want a Home with No Problems, Word, Inc., 1977.
Growing Places, Revell, 1978.
Too Big to Spank, Regal Books, 1978.
Breakthrough, Zondervan, 1981.
Family Forum, Victor Books, 1984.
(Editor) *Parents and Teenagers,* Victor Books, 1984.
(With Tim Stafford) *Making Life Make Sense,* Tyndale, 1986.

JAY KESLER

(Editor with others) *Parents and Children*, Victor Books, 1986.
Being Holy, Being Human, Word, Inc., 1988.
Ten Mistakes Parents Make with Teenagers (And How to Avoid Them), Wolgemuth & Hyatt, 1988.
Is Your Marriage Really Worth Fighting For?, Cook, 1989.
(With Paul Woods) *Energizing Your Teenagers's Faith*, Group Books, 1990.

Contributor to numerous evangelical publications, including *Christianity Today, Christian Herald, Partnership, Focus on the Family,* and *Today's Christian Woman.* Also author of column "I Never Promised You a Disneyland," *Campus Life* magazine, 1974-75. Member of editorial review committee for *New King James Bible.*

*   *   *

KLEEBERG, Irene (Flitner) Cumming 1932-

PERSONAL: Born April 21, 1932, in Chicago, IL; daughter of James Coale (an advertising executive) and Elsie (a professional volunteer; maiden name, Battin) Cumming; married Fred Martin Kleeberg (a printing consultant), October 20, 1957; children: John Martin, Margaret Anne. *Education:* Wellesley College, B.A., 1954. *Politics:* "Registered Democrat, socialist at heart." *Religion:* Humanist.

ADDRESSES: Home—350 East 30th St., New York, NY 10016.

CAREER: Thames Advertising Service Ltd., London, England, copywriter, 1954-55; L. Bamburger and Co., Newark, NJ, buyer, 1955-56; *Women's Wear Daily,* New York City, editor, 1956-58; American correspondent for several British trade publications, beginning in 1958; *Homesewing Trade News,* New York City, fashion and education editor, beginning in 1971; writer. Volunteer, New York City Commission for the United Nations and Consular Corps, 1966—; chair, Seventeenth Precinct Community Council (police department), 1966-68; member of board of directors, International Community Center, 1973—; member of acquaintanceship committee, New York Wellesley Club, 1973—.

MEMBER: Authors Guild, Authors League of America, Women's Fashion Fabrics Association (vice-president), Embroiderer's Guild of Great Britain, Danish Handicraft Guild.

AWARDS, HONORS: Certificate of merit from the police department, City of New York; certificate of appreciation from the City of New York.

WRITINGS:

Make Your Own Pants and Skirts, Bantam, 1971, revised edition, 1972.
Making School Clothes for Boys and Girls, Bantam, 1971.
The Blue Jeans Book, Bantam, 1972.
(Translator) Rob Herwig, *128 House Plants You Can Grow,* Macmillan, 1972.
Fashion Tops, Drake, 1973.
Bicycle Repair, F. Watts, 1973.
Sewing for Bazaars, Bantam, 1974.
(Editor) *The Butterick Fabric Handbook: A Consumer's Guide to Fabrics for Clothing and Home Furnishings,* Butterick Publishing, 1975.
Bicycle Touring, illustrated by Michael Horen, F. Watts, 1975.
The Butterick Home Decorating Handbook: A Consumer's Guide to Selecting, Purchasing, and Caring for Home Furnishings, Butterick Publishing, 1976.
Christianity, F. Watts, 1976.
(Editor with R. Patrick Cash) *The Management of Fashion Merchandising: A Symposium,* National Retail Merchants Association, 1977.
The Home Energy Saver: All the Facts You Need to Save Energy Dollars, illustrated by Barbara Knight, Butterick Publishing, 1977.
(Editor) Nora Hana, *Embroidery,* Two Continents Publishing, 1977.
(Editor) Rite van der Klip, *Crochet,* Two Continents Publishing, 1977.
Going to Camp, illustrated by Tom Huffman, F. Watts, 1978.
The Moving Book: How Not to Panic at the Thought, Butterick Publishing, 1978.
Latchkey Kid, illustrated by Anne C. Green, F. Watts, 1985.
Ethiopia, F. Watts, 1986.
Separation of Church and State, F. Watts, 1986.
Fund Raising, edited by Jennie Rakos, F. Watts, 1988.

Ghostwriter of a weekly fashion and retailing newsletter. Contributor of fiction to children's magazines and of articles to *Women's Wear Daily, Baby Talk, Stores Magazine,* and other trade publications.

SIDELIGHTS: Irene Cumming Kleeberg told *SATA:* "When I ask myself 'Who am I?' I always answer 'a writer'—and this is true whether I am teaching, working in an office, helping people new to New York, or free-lancing, when I work at home, writing, and try to sell my work.

"I like to write. I like it so much that when, for one reason or another, I don't have time to write, I find myself making stories up in my head, just like I used to do on the way to school.

"I like to learn things, too. Oh, not a lot of the things that other people think you should learn but things that help me with my writing. I love going to the library and going through books until I can find something to use in my writing that makes it just a little more colorful. When I can't find the answer to one of my questions in the library I get on the telephone and try to persuade an expert to answer my question.

"Perhaps because my books and my writings for magazines and newspapers have been mainly nonfiction, most of it has been done on assignment from a publisher, following that publisher's ideas. This usually means that I have written to the publisher saying, 'I want to write a book for you about this and that,' and the publisher replies, 'We're not interested in that but would you like to try something else?'

"This is why I have written for adults, young adults, and children, and also why I have a dream—to write and publish a novel.

"As one may have guessed, I am more interested in writing than in what I write. I'm almost as pleased when I finish an article on how leather jackets are selling as I am when I finish a book that I hope will help young people understand Ethiopia. I am, you see, a writer—first, foremost, and always."

*   *   *

KLEMIN, Diana

PERSONAL: Born in New York, NY; daughter of Alexander (a professor of aeronautical engineering and writer) and Ethel (a poet; maiden name, Murton) Klemin. *Education:* Vassar College, A.B., 1944; studied with Robert Josephy, 1946, with Reginald Marsh, Art Students League, 1947-48, with Alexei Brodovitch, New School for Social Research, 1948-49, with William Baziotes, Museum of Modern Art, 1951-52. *Hobbies and other interests:* Reading, gardening, swimming, and "the rearing of one exceptional cat, Christopher Chester."

ADDRESSES: Home—26 Anderson Rd., Greenwich, CT 06830. *Office*— Doubleday Book and Music Clubs, Inc., 245 Park Ave., New York, NY 10167.

CAREER: G. P. Putnam's Sons, New York City, book designer and production assistant, 1944-45; Doubleday and Co., Inc., New York City, book designer, 1945-52, art director, 1953-87, art director of Doubleday Book and Music Clubs, Inc., 1988—. Chairman, American Institute of Graphic Arts Young Book Designers Show, 1948, and Swiss Book Show, 1953; lecturer, Parsons School of Design, 1974. *Exhibitions:* Work represented at a three-man show, "Exhibit of Book Design," at the American Institute of Graphic Arts, 1952; an exhibition of the original art from *The Art of Art for Children's Books* was held at Gallery 303, New York City, 1966, and traveled to Little Rock, AR, Salt Lake City, UT, and Hattiesburg, MS.

AWARDS, HONORS: Young Book Designer award, 1947; awards from Fifty Books of the Year, *Children's Books,* Society of Illustrators, and Art Director's Club of New York; Trade Book Clinic and other awards from the American Institute of Graphic Arts.

WRITINGS:

Young Faces (monograph), Composing Room, 1963.
The Art of Art for Children's Books, C. N. Potter, 1966.
The Illustrated Book: Its Art and Craft, C. N. Potter, 1970.
(Compiler) *A Christmas Sampler of Feasts: Menus and Recipes for the Twelve Days of Christmas,* Doubleday, 1981.

Contributor to *American Artist, Publishers Weekly,* and *Book Production.*

WORK IN PROGRESS: Compiling *A Treasury of Book Illustrations;* a children's story to be published in 1991 or 1992.

SIDELIGHTS: Diana Klemin told *SATA:* "Book illustration has been one of my lifelong delights. As a child I always looked at the pictures in storybooks before reading the text. The look of the entire book was as important to me as the story. I would ask why the frontispiece was repeated on the book cover or jacket. How could the same painting be used twice? I adored the Christmas annuals sent from England by one aunt and the books illustrated by Rex Whistler from another. Before I could really read I would search my parents' books for illustrations. I examined the entire 'Har-

Cover from the 1981 paperback edition of Diana Klemin's holiday cookbook. Originally prepared as a momento for Doubleday authors and agents, the 64-page volume proved popular enough to market for public sale. (Illustrated by Mona Mark.)

vard Classics Five Foot Bookshelf' and found its one illustration, a frontispiece, in *The Arabian Nights.* My mother's *Pepys Diary* had line drawings by E. H. Shepherd. I loved the *Saturday Evening Post* illustrations and traced the cover lettering on *Harper's* and the *Atlantic Monthly,* only to discover years later that these beautiful letterforms were designed by D. W. Dwiggins, the famous calligrapher, book designer, and puppeteer. Rose Fyleman's *Tea-Time Tales* had different decorative pastel borders at the top and bottom of each page. Hans Christian Andersen's *Fairy Tales* had exquisite paintings by Edmund Dulac. *The Old Testament Bible Stories* illustrations were far more interesting than those in *The New Testament Bible Stories.* I would invariably ask to be shown Moses looking angry.

"*Millions of Cats* by Wanda Gag was read and reread. The gift of this book by publisher Tom Coward started my career in publishing. As my father was writing the children's book *If You Want to Fly* for Coward-McCann publishers, he took Mother and me to meet Coward, who sat me on his long, dark brown table covered with books and manuscripts and gave me *Millions of Cats.* From that moment I knew I wanted to work in a world of books, in a room full of books, and to help make beautiful books filled with pictures.

"When I began reading the classics, I noticed an occasional frontispiece by Phiz (Hablot Knight Browne) in works by Charles Dickens, or a few poorly reproduced black and white paintings by uninspired artists in other novels. Even my bible had just two nondescript sepia reproductions. So I turned to museums for pictures—the Metropolitan Museum of Art, the Whitney Museum, the British Museum, the Louvre, the Luxembourg, and the Philadelphia Museum of Art. I would be allowed to buy a colored postcard or two. Thus I began a self-taught study of art history which I have never stopped to this day. In my senior year of high school I discovered science and at Vassar College I started as a chemistry major. Wisely I realized I needed to know more about the entire world. As an English major I took other courses—economics, French, psychology—a splendid foundation for my career in book publishing. One summer I had an editorial job at G. P. Putnam's, Coward-McCann, and John Day. The dark brown table where Coward presented me with *Millions of Cats* was still there, as cluttered as ever.

"After graduation I was a design/production assistant at Putnam's and the next year I started at Doubleday as a book designer and, in time, became an art director. I read everything about the making of beautiful books. I went to galleries and book shows; I designed catalogs and hung a show of Swiss books for the American Institute of Graphic Arts. I studied drawing with Reginald Marsh, book design with Robert Josephy, and graphic journalism with Alexei Brodovitch.

"In the early 1960s I began to buy art for all kinds of books and book jackets as well as illustrations for a forty-eight-volume children's classics series with N. C. Wyeth and Howard Pyle as my touchstones. For the 'Best-in-Children's Books' book club, an anthology of stories and art, I asked Maurice Sendak, Andy Warhol, Edy LeGrand, Susanne Suba, Leonard Joseph Weisgard, Irene Hass, Feodor Stepanovich Rojankovsky, and Lawrence Beall Smith, among others, to do drawings and paintings. I helped to make forty-two volumes of literature a treasury of book illustration for thousands of young readers.

"Because of my work on these anthologies, Robert Leslie, a medical doctor and a co-owner of the New York City type house Composing Room, asked me to prepare a monograph, *Young Faces,* as a keepsake for the publishing world. Leslie was so pleased with the results that he said I should write a book about art for children's books, and when it was published he would put on a show of the entire book at the Composing Room gallery.

"In 1966 C. N. Potter published *The Art of Art for Children's Books* and Leslie gave the party. For a month the sixty-seven pieces of original art by the sixty-three fabulous artists in the book were displayed. I chose examples of works by contemporary artists for this project, and explained why these artists' books appealed especially to children or why they were personal expressions of an artist that were for artists or adults only. It was a statement of my eternal love for and devoted interest in children's book illustration.

"In 1970 Potter published *The Illustrated Book: Its Art and Craft.* Many publishers and many readers thought illustration was only for children. With this work I set out to collect contemporary adult books that had illustrations and to write about the way an artist contributed to the book; the enjoyment, the setting, the enhancement of the author's word.

"During this time I was also buying art for Doubleday's Anchor Books, including *The Anchor Bible,* and for children's books. I worked with Ben Shahn, Eugene Berman, George Guisti, Kiyoshi Kanai, Rolf Bruderer, Norman Ives, Alvin Eisenman, and Milton Glaszer, just to mention a few of the artists who made beguiling and appropriate book jackets, covers, and illustrations.

"For more than ten years I prepared the memento that Doubleday sent at Christmas to its authors, artists, literary agents, and other friends in the book world. These small, sixty-four-page volumes became keepsakes for readers. Doubleday even printed some to sell in subsequent years, including *A Christmas Sampler of Feasts,* which I compiled, creating menus for use from Christmas Eve through Twelfth Night from the fabulous array of cookbooks Doubleday had published.

"I still spend two days a week as art director for the Doubleday Book and Music Clubs, where I am working with Robert Byrd, Ann Schweninger, Lauren Jarrett, Warren Chappell, Chris Demarest, and Barry Moser on beautiful books. I still adore looking at pictures for books, whether I am selecting artists to work on a particular project, being inspired by a book exhibition, or just browsing in a bookstore."

*   *   *

KOCH, Kenneth 1925-

PERSONAL: Surname is pronounced "coke"; born February 27, 1925, in Cincinnati, OH; son of Stuart J. and Lillian Amy (Loth) Koch; married Mary Janice Elwood, June 12, 1954 (died, 1981); children: Katherine. *Education:* Harvard University, A.B., 1948; Columbia University, M.A., 1953, Ph.D., 1959.

ADDRESSES: Home—25 Claremont Ave., New York, NY 10027. *Office*— 414 Hamilton Hall, Columbia University, New York, NY 10027.

KENNETH KOCH

CAREER: Rutgers University, Newark, NJ, lecturer, 1953-58; Brooklyn College (now of the City University of New York), Brooklyn, NY, lecturer, 1957-59; Columbia University, New York City, assistant professor, 1959-66, associate professor, 1966-71, professor of English and comparative literature, 1971—. Director of Poetry Workshop, New School for Social Research, 1958-66. Taught poetry-writing to elementary schoolchildren. *Military service:* U.S. Army, 1943-46, served in the Pacific theatre.

AWARDS, HONORS: Fulbright fellow, 1950-51, 1978, and 1982; Guggenheim fellow, 1960-61; National Endowment for the Arts grant, 1966; Ingram Merrill Foundation fellowship, 1969; Harbison Award, 1970, for teaching; Frank O'Hara Prize, *Poetry,* 1973; Christopher Book Award and Ohioana Book Award, both 1974, both for *Rose, Where Did You Get That Red?;* National Institute of Arts and Letters award, 1976; *Sleeping on the Wing* was named a New York Public Library Book for the TeenAge, 1982; Children's Book of the Year, 1986, for *Talking to the Sun;* Award of Merit for Poetry, American Academy and Institute of Arts and Letters, 1986; *One Thousand Avant-Garde Plays* was shortlisted for the National Book Critics Circle award for poetry, 1988.

WRITINGS:

POETRY, EXCEPT AS INDICATED

Poems, Tibor de Nagy Gallery, 1953.
Ko; or, A Season on Earth, Grove, 1959.
Permanently, Tiber Press, 1960.
Thank You and Other Poems, Grove, 1962.
Poems from 1952 and 1953 (limited edition), Black Sparrow Press, 1968.
The Pleasures of Peace and Other Poems, Grove, 1969.
When the Sun Tries to Go On, Black Sparrow Press, 1969.

Sleeping with Women (limited edition), Black Sparrow Press, 1969.
(With the students of P.S. 61 in New York City) *Wishes, Lies, and Dreams: Teaching Children to Write Poetry* (nonfiction), Chelsea House, 1970.
(With Alex Katz) *Interlocking Lives* (fiction), Kulchur Foundation, 1970.
Rose, Where Did You Get That Red? Teaching Great Poetry to Children (nonfiction), Random House, 1973.
(Contributor) *Penguin Modern Poets 24,* Penguin, 1974.
The Art of Love, Random House, 1975.
The Red Robins (novel; also see below), Random House, 1975.
The Duplications, Random House, 1977.
I Never Told Anybody: Teaching Poetry Writing in a Nursing Home (nonfiction), Random House, 1977.
Les Couleurs des voyelles (nonfiction), Casterman, 1978.
The Burning Mystery of Anna in 1951, Random House, 1979.
Desideri, Sogni, Bugie (nonfiction), Emme, 1980.
(With Kate Farrell) *Sleeping on the Wing: An Anthology of Modern Poetry, with Essays on Reading and Writing* (nonfiction), Random House, 1981.
Days and Nights, Random House, 1982.
Selected Poems, 1950-1982, Random House, 1985.
(Selector with Farrell) *Talking to the Sun: An Illustrated Anthology of Poems for Young People,* Metropolitan Museum of Art/Holt, 1985.
On the Edge, Viking, 1986.
Seasons on Earth, Viking, 1987.
One Thousand Avant-Garde Plays, Knopf, 1988.
Selected Poems, Carcanet, 1991.

Contributor of fiction, poetry, and plays to magazines, including *Art and Literature, New York Review of Books, Poetry, Grand Street,* and *Raritan.* Member of editorial board, *Locus Solus,* 1960-62.

PLAYS

Little Red Riding Hood, produced Off-Broadway at Theatre De Lys, 1953.
Bertha and Other Plays (also see below; contains "Bertha" [opera; music by Ned Rorem], produced in New York at Living Theatre, 1959; "Pericles," produced Off-Broadway at Cherry Lane Theatre, 1960; "George Washington Crossing the Delaware," produced Off-Broadway at Maidman Playhouse, 1962; "The Construction of Boston," produced Off-Broadway at Maidman Playhouse, 1962, produced as an opera with music by Scott Wheeler in Boston, MA, at the Old South Church, 1988; "Guinevere; or, The Death of the Kangaroo," produced in New York at New York Theatre for Poets, 1964; "The Gold Standard," produced in New York, 1975; "The Return of Yellowmay"; "The Revolt of the Giant Animals"; "The Building of Florence"; "Angelica"; "The Merry Stones"; "The Academic Murders"; "Easter"; "The Lost Feed"; "Mexico"; "Coil Supreme"), Grove, 1966.
The Artist (opera based on poem of the same title; music by Paul Reif), produced in New York at the Whitney Museum, 1972.
A Little Light, produced in Amagansett, NY, 1972.
A Change of Hearts: Plays, Films, and Other Dramatic Works, 1951-1971 (contains the contents of *Bertha and Other Plays* and "E. Kology"; "The Election," produced in New York at Living Theatre, 1960; "The Tinguely Machine Mystery; or, The Love Suicides of Kaluka," produced in New York at the Jewish Museum, 1965; "The Moon Balloon," produced in New York in Central Park, 1969; "Without Kinship"; ten filmscripts:

"Because," "The Color Game," "Mountains and Electricity," "Sheep Harbor," "Oval Gold," "Moby Dick," "L'Ecole Normale," "The Cemetery," "The Scotty Dog," "The Apple"; "Youth"; "The Enchantment"), Random House, 1973.

Rooster Redivivus, produced in Garnerville, NY, 1975.

The Red Robins: A Play (based on novel of the same title; produced in New York at Theatre at St. Clement's, 1978), Theatre Arts, 1979.

The New Diana, produced in New York at New York Art Theatre Institute, 1984.

A Change of Hearts, produced in New York by Medicine Show Theatre Ensemble, 1985.

Popeye among the Polar Bears, produced in New York by Medicine Show Theatre Ensemble, 1986.

Koch's work, including *Wishes, Lies, and Dreams,* is available on audiocassette, distributed by Spoken Arts.

WORK IN PROGRESS: A book of short stories and a volume of poetry.

SIDELIGHTS: Kenneth Koch told *SATA:* "I've always hoped children would read my work, but the only two books of mine really written for children are *Sleeping on the Wing,*

SPIDER

> With what voice,
> And what song would you sing, spider,
> In this autumn breeze?
>
>   Bashō, 1644–1694

A verse from Kenneth Koch's *Talking to the Sun,* a children's anthology that pairs poetry with works of art from the Metropolitan Museum. (Woodblock print by Kitagawa Utamaro from *Picture Book of Selected Insects,* 1788.)

an anthology of modern poetry with essays on the poets, that I wrote with Kate Farrell (this book is specifically addressed to high-school students), and *Talking to the Sun,* also an anthology, this time not with essays but with works of art from the Metropolitan Museum. This book, also written in collaboration with Farrell, is for children of all ages, and I suppose some adults as well.

"The principle behind the choice of poems in these two books is the same: to give children the best poems that have been written. Though Farrell and I took care to avoid unduly difficult and/or distressing subject matter as well as poems with vocabularies and concepts that would require so many notes as to overburden the poetry, we didn't include any poems that we didn't genuinely admire—I mean, of course, as adults, not imagining we were children.

"I discovered while I was teaching schoolchildren to write poetry that my students could understand and be excited and inspired by poems by such writers as John Donne, Wallace Stevens, and Federico Garcia Lorca. Sometimes the intellectual understanding wasn't complete, but there was some strong imaginative communication going on, as one can see in the poems my students wrote in response to these and other great poets (these students' poems are in *Rose, Where Did You Get That Red?*).

"I know that there are poems specifically written for children that children like. It seems obvious, though, that the greatest poetry has been written by adults for adults. Since, with a little help from a teacher or a book, and sometimes even without that, children are capable of liking and responding to this poetry, I've been happy to work on a few books that could help them to do so. *Rose, Where Did You Get That Red?* and the earlier *Wishes, Lies, and Dreams* weren't specifically written for children, rather for their parents and others who teach them, but the poetry by other children in the books is something they like to read."

FOR MORE INFORMATION SEE:

BOOKS

Contemporary Literary Criticism, Gale, Volume 5, 1976, Volume 8, 1978, Volume 44, 1987.

Dictionary of Literary Biography, Volume 5: *American Poets since World War II,* Gale, 1980.

O'Hara, Frank, *Standing Still and Walking in New York,* edited by Donald Allen, Grey Fox Press, 1975.

PERIODICALS

Los Angeles Times Book Review, March 6, 1983; April 14, 1985.

New Leader, January 25, 1971.

New Republic, August 2, 1969; July 11, 1970.

Newsweek, September 16, 1985.

New York Review of Books, May, 1963; August 14, 1980.

New York Times, November 21, 1970; January 19, 1978; January 12, 1979.

New York Times Book Review, February 11, 1968; December 23, 1973; September 28, 1975; April 10, 1977; April 20, 1986.

Poetry, May, 1967; September, 1969; November, 1972.

Saturday Review, March 20, 1971.

Shenandoah, Spring, 1978.

Time, April 4, 1977.

Washington Post Book World, August 3, 1975; January 12, 1986; April 13, 1986.

KORCZAK, Janusz 1878-1942
(Henryk Goldszmit)

PERSONAL: Born Henryk Goldszmit, 1878, in Warsaw, Poland; died in 1942 in Treblinka (concentration camp) in Malkinia Gorna, Poland; son of Jozef Goldszmit (a lawyer). *Education:* Earned a medical degree in Warsaw. *Religion:* Jewish.

CAREER: Doctor, writer, teacher, radio personality. Doctor in Jewish children's hospital in Warsaw, Poland, 1904-05 and 1907-10; counselor in summer camps for boys, 1907-10; co-founder with Stefania Wilczynska and director of The Orphan Home for Jewish Children on Krochmalna St. in Warsaw, 1911-42; co-founder with Maryna Falska, of public orphanage for Christian children in Warsaw, 1918-36; hosted popular radio broadcasts as "The Old Doctor" during the 1930s; visited Palestine (now Israel) several times between 1934 and 1938; arrested with Jewish orphans and taken to Treblinka, where he was executed by the Nazis in 1942. *Military service:* Russian Army, doctor, served on the Eastern Front during World War I; served on hospital train in China during Russo-Japanese War, 1905-06. Also fought in the Polish-Soviet War of 1920.

AWARDS, HONORS: Literary awards in Europe; Golden Laurel Award, Polish Academy of Literature, 1937; UNESCO declared 1978-79 the Year of Korczak to coincide with the celebration of the Year of the Child.

WRITINGS:

Krol Macius Pierwszy (juvenile), [Poland], 1923, published with illustrations by Jerzy Srokowski, Nasza Ksiegarnia, 1955, adaptation in English by Edith and Sydney Sulkin published as *Matthew the Young King,* illustrations by Irena Lorentowicz, Roy Publishers (New York), 1945, translation by Richard Lourie published as *King Matt the First,* introduction by Bruno Bettelheim, Farrar, Straus, 1986.

Krol Macius na wyspie bezludnej (juvenile; title means "King Matt on the Desert Island"), [Poland], 1928, reprinted with illustrations by J. Srokowski, Nasza Ksiegarnia, 1957, published with illustrations by Waldemar Andrzejewski, 1978.

Big Business Billy, translation from the Polish by Cyrus Brooks, Minerva (London), 1939.

Jak kochac dzieci (title means "How to Love a Child"), Ksiaznica Polska, 1944.

Tajemniczy przyjaciel (short stories; title means "Mysterious Friend"), Iskry, 1957.

Wybor pism pedagogicznych (title means "Selected Writings on Education"), two volumes, Panstwowe Zaklady Wydawnictwo Szkolnych, 1957.

Wybor pism (title means "Selected Writings") four volumes, Nasza Ksiegarnia, 1957-58.

Prawo dziecka do szacunku (a manifesto for children's rights), Panstwowe Zaklady Wydawnictwo Szkolnych, 1958.

Bankructwo malego Dzeka (title means "Children of the Street"), Nasza Ksiegarnia, 1960.

Kiedy znow bede maly, Nasza Ksiegarnia, 1961, reprinted, 1983.

Maly czlowiek (title means "Little Man"), Arkady, 1965.

Selected Works of Janusz Korczak, compiled by Martin Wolins, translation from the Polish by Jerzy Bachrach, Scientific Publications Foreign Cooperation Center of Central Institute for Scientific, Technical and Economic Information (Warsaw), 1967.

Kajtus czarodziej (novel; title means "Confessions of a Butterfly"), illustrations by Gabriel Rechowicz, Nasza Ksiegarnia, 1973, published with illustrations by Tomasz Borowski, 1978.

Ghetto Diary, translation from the original Polish manuscript, *Pamietnik z getta,* Holocaust Library (New York), 1978, translation with introduction and notes by E. P. Kulawiec published as *The Warsaw Ghetto Memoirs of Janusz Korczak,* University Press of America, 1979, translation published as *The Ghetto Years, 1939-1942,* Hakibbutz Hameuchad (Tel Aviv), 1980.

Fragmenty utworow, compiled by Danuta Stepniewska, Nasza Ksiegarnia, 1978.

Pisma wybrane (title means "Selected Writings"), Nasza Ksiegarnia, 1978, Volume 1: *Wielka synteza dziecka, oto co mi sie snilo,* Volume 2: *Praktyka to moje zycie,* Volume 3: *Otworzmy wrota szkoly szeroko,* Volume 4: *Jestem czlowiekiem samotnej drogi.*

Dat ha-yeled (in Hebrew), Hakibbutz Hameuchad, 1978.

Mysl pedagogiczna Janusza Korczaka: Nowe zrodla, Nasza Ksiegarnia, 1983.

Also author of many other books, including a semiautobiographical first novel in 1906. Contributor of articles and essays to professional journals.

SIDELIGHTS: The writer known to readers around the world as Janusz Korczak was born Henryk Goldszmit in Warsaw, Poland. His grandfather was a Jewish surgeon who wrote about medicine in Hebrew, and his father was a lawyer who wrote about the Talmudic law in Polish. When Henryk became a writer, he adopted the pen name Janusz Korczak, naming himself after a character from a Polish novel written in the 1800s. The founder of an orphanage for Jewish children, Korczak became an expert on child psychology and an advocate of human rights who taught moral values to disadvantaged children. He is remembered for remaining with his orphans when they were deported by the Nazis to the Treblinka death camp after turning down many opportunities to escape. People in Poland and in Israel think of Korczak as a national and spiritual hero. During the 1970s, Korczak clubs were organized in many European countries to share his ideas and to translate his writings. His ideas about children's rights and education have brought about changes throughout the world.

The story of Korczak's life's work with children became known to American readers largely through Betty Jean Lifton's book *The King of Children: A Biography of Janusz Korczak,* published in 1978. She wrote, "Korczak felt that within each child there burned a moral spark that could vanquish the darkness at the core of human nature." Another factor also accounted for his dedication to children. His father had spells of madness and died when Korczak was eighteen. Because of his father's illness, the young doctor felt that he should never marry and have children of his own. The only family he would have would be the children he taught.

Korczak's early writings expressed his belief that the welfare of children was the key to a better future for all mankind. He also complained that modern parents seemed to regard children as worthless and senseless creatures who distracted adults from productive work. His first article, published when he was eighteen, lamented the way parents were putting their own pleasures ahead of the needs of their children.

Korczak formed his view of children as an oppressed group in need of liberation very early in life. A middle-class child with many advantages, he was not allowed to play with the poorer children in his neighborhood. They felt rejected and resented Korczak. Those same boys prevented him from burying his canary under a cross in his backyard, claiming that a Jewish canary should not be buried that way. From that time forward, Korczak fought against social systems that denied basic rights to some groups while giving special rights to others.

In medical school in Warsaw Korczak met a group of social activists who shared his views. They believed they could build a system of government that would not treat people differently because of wealth or racial background. This group also secretly worked against the Russian leaders to win back Polish independence. After he graduated, Korczak was drafted to serve in the Russo-Japanese War. He was a doctor on a medical train that traveled between the cities of Harbin and Mukden in northeastern China. While he was there, a four-year-old child befriended him and began to teach him Chinese. This experience helped to confirm his views about the intelligence of children and their importance as ambassadors of peace.

Korczak was to participate in three other wars—two world wars and the Polish-Soviet War of 1920—and his views about war were complicated. He strongly felt that Poland's independence as a nation and other goals were clearly worth fighting for. He was proud of his years as a soldier against the Russians and often wore his Polish uniform in later years to express that pride. But he also hated what war did to the lives of children.

Korczak published his first children's book in 1923. In *King Matt the First,* the adults go to school while the children, under King Matt's leadership, run the country. *King Matt the First* expresses what Korczak had learned from letting children have a larger voice in their own "government" at the orphanage. The book teaches children that having strong faith in their own ideals is not enough to build a better world. In their attempts to change their world, the children in King Matt's domain discover that all change is not necessarily for the better. The process of making rules about living together as a people can take a long time, if everyone is to have a voice in making those rules. And they learn that some people may have to give up some of their goals in order to achieve the most important ones.

In the book, King Matt the reformer learns these lessons the hard way, and many of his ideals fail. The children turn out to be no wiser and no less selfish than adults. Furthermore, Matt is rejected for trying to make a meaningful change in his society. He loses his throne and is carried off to exile on a desert island. However, the spirit of reform is not destroyed by these disappointments. Korczak "wanted to provide a vivid and realistic picture of those forces that undermine progressive change so that children and adult reformers would know what obstacles to expect and would not abandon their struggle," Jack Zipes commented in the *New York Times Book Review.*

Korczak's second book for children, *King Matt on the Desert Island,* was also a best-seller. King Matt looks back on his disappointments and sees that even though he can't change the entire world, he can improve himself and inspire others to do the same. Together, the King Matt books influenced the thinking of an entire generation. A number of great works of Polish literature show this influence, repeating the plot device of letting children and adults trade places. Witold Gombrowicz's novel *Ferdydurke* and Ryszard Kapuscinski's

The Emperor both have passages similar to passages in the King Matt books.

Some critics warn that black characters in *King Matt the First* behave in ways that reveal the racist attitudes common in Europe at that time. In the book, a black child from Africa, for example, was an uncivilized cannibal. The same child was also bright, reasonable, and open-minded. Critics say that it is unlikely the author agreed with the racist stereotypes of his day. Korczak probably intended to show that even people from cultures that others considered primitive were qualified to have a voice in the making of a new and better world.

In many ways, King Matt represented Korczak, who learned the same lessons in his work to improve the world by investing in the lives of children. Under Korczak's direction, the Orphan Home for Jewish Children was a "children's republic." Adults and children alike were subject to the same rules, and at times Korczak himself was tried before the "children's court." Outsiders saw that he insured fairness by keeping final authority. The children contributed much to their own "government," but the system remained secure because Korczak watched over it to keep it from getting out of hand. It was often in danger of this, since the children were not always fair or accurate in their judgements. Successful in many ways, this system of self-government was least effective when individual children tried to dominate others in the group.

When Korczak became the director of the orphanage, he disciplined the children by encouraging them to discipline themselves. Older children were given responsibility to look after the younger ones. Thus he built "family" relationships among the orphans. He weighed the children every week, at which time he would also see if any one was ill or unhappy. With his encouragement, they wrote articles for their own newspaper. He motivated them to correct their bad habits in an unusual way. Every week, he made bets with them that they could quit those habits by the end of the week; if they succeeded, they won candy. The children adored him. "He was loved by children—many of them tough street kids unused to exchanging love—not for his theories about child-rearing but for his tenderness, his instinct for the fabulous, his fierce attention to the individual," wrote Geoffrey Wolff in the *New York Times Book Review.*

The system of self-government at the orphanage was part of Korczak's lifetime work as a champion of changes in education. Threatening children with harsh punishments in the traditional way was not the best way to keep order, he believed. He demonstrated that when all members of a group—especially the most powerful ones—were equally accountable to keep the same rules of conduct, individuals and groups more easily reached their goals. He found that leading by example was the most effective way to teach values. For instance, he cleared the tables for the children after dinner in order to show that all kinds of work are honorable. Korczak measured teaching methods the way he measured everything, by looking closely at each method's final impact on the well-being of children.

Korczak left the orphanage briefly to serve as a doctor in the Russian army during World War I. During this time he wrote *Jak kochac dzieci* ("How to Love a Child"). It explained his belief that all children have a right to be respected and protected by adults, who should treat them as equals as much as possible. Children were not possessions to be ordered about and used by their parents. Rather, each child belonged to his extended family and to the larger family of mankind.

He wrote that rules for child care and schedules for achievement should be determined by the child's needs, not imposed from above by adults.

While on the Eastern front during the war Korczak became ill with typhus and returned to Poland. His mother nursed him back to health, but she caught the disease and died from it. The loss was devastating for Korczak, who tried to take his own life while mourning at her grave. While struggling to cope with this and other losses, he wrote a book of prayers in which he argues with God. The book's title means "Tete a Tete with God: Prayers for the Unbelieving." He dedicated the book to his parents.

In the following years, the political movements that divided Poland into communists and anti-communists, Jews and anti-Semites, Zionists and Poles, were extremes that hurt children. When teachers went on strike for political reasons, the children fell behind in their education. Political strife also produced destructive stress. Speaking as "The Old Doctor" in popular radio broadcasts, Korczak expressed these views to a large audience.

Korczak did not strongly identify with any single one of the opposing political parties. The different social groups that coexisted in the old Poland could coexist in the new Poland. He believed the new Poland should be like it was in the days when Catholics and Jews respected each other as native citizens of the same homeland.

Even though Korczak spoke up for Polish unity, he was victimized because of his Jewish heritage. He was not completely trusted among Jews, either. The Jewish community did not understand why he chose to write in Polish instead of Hebrew or Yiddish. Literary critics felt his works taught too much and entertained too little; educators thought the books didn't teach well enough. While his new ideas made him seem dangerous to many Poles who respected old traditions, his views on liberty for all were too radical for the communists and the socialists. In 1936 he was forced to leave the board of the public orphanage and to terminate his radio broadcasts. He was also fired from his job as an adviser to the juvenile court. At the same time, many prominent Poles defended Korczak. For example, in 1937 Poland's Academy of Literature gave Korczak its Golden Laurel Award.

During these years Korczak visited Palestine (now Israel) a number of times and thought about settling there with other Jews who were reclaiming their ancestral homeland. Compared to the strife in Poland, a life in Palestine near his friend and former colleague Stefa Wiloczynska seemed more comfortable. "He dreamed, in moments of enthusiasm, of what Jews, once independent, would do to help the oppressed in China, South Africa, and India. Perhaps Palestine would become a League of Nations, whose center, Jerusalem, would proclaim the rights of all to a spiritual life," Marie Syrkin related in the *New Republic*. But he felt that to leave his orphans in Poland during troubled times would be heartless and disloyal, like "leaving a sick child in the night." Soon after he returned to Poland the Germans invaded.

The Nazis forced Korczak to relocate the Orphan Home for Jewish Children to a building within the walls of the Warsaw Ghetto. Korczak resisted the Nazis whenever he could. He refused to wear the Star of David patch that identified Jews, and he confronted Gestapo officers who had stolen a wagon of coal and potatoes. The officers threw him in jail, but Korczak's friends bailed him out. His diary shows that through all of this, Korczak felt no bitterness against his enemies, continually thinking to himself that they might be better people than they appeared to be. He wrote that Hitler could not remain in power long because most Germans would not excuse his war crimes. Several times, concerned friends offered to hide or export Korczak and some of the children, but the dedicated teacher refused to escape if even one child had to be left behind. The intensity of their efforts to prevent his deportation alerted many to the fact that Jews who were being deported by the Nazis were actually being killed.

Korczak's resistance included the production of a play in which the Jewish children made an emotional appeal to the audience to work toward liberation from the Nazis. The play, Rabindranath Tagore's *Post Office*, presented a dying boy who longs to be freed from confinement in his darkened room. The boy waits for a doctor who is older and wiser to rescue him from illness. Korczak said that he chose the play in order to teach his orphans not to be afraid to die. The play, produced on July 18, 1942, made a powerful impression on those who saw it. Later, when the head of the *Judenrat* (the Jewish leadership) heard that Korczak's orphans would be deported with the other Jews as "nonproductive elements" of society, he killed himself.

Korczak's friends took great risks to provide his way of escape, but when the Nazis came to haul the children away to Treblinka in 1942, their teachers went with them. One of the orphans carried a green flag, the standard of King Matt. It is said the group of two hundred children was singing as they marched away. Other stories spread that the whole group escaped at the last minute to live in the woods. It is generally assumed that Korczak and the Jewish orphans were killed by the Nazis soon after their arrest in 1942. "However," wrote Zipes in the *New York Times Book Review*, "the Nazis were never able to annihilate the record of Korczak's deed and his remarkable contributions to the fields of child psychology and children's literature."

WORKS CITED:

Ascherson, Neal, "A Polish Hero," *New York Review of Books,* September 29, 1988, pp. 7-8, 10.

Korczak, Janusz, *Ghetto Diary,* Holocaust Library, 1978.

Lifton, Betty Jean, "Janusz Korczak: Shepherd of the Ghetto Orphans," *New York Times Biographical Service,* April 20, 1980, pp. 545-547.

Lifton, Betty Jean, *The King of Children: A Biography of Janusz Korczak,* Farrar, Straus, 1978.

Syrkin, Marie, "The Saint in the Ghetto," *New Republic,* June 6, 1988, pp. 44-48.

Sziazakowa, Alicja, *Janusz Korczak,* Wydawniczy Szkoline i Pedagogiczne, 1978.

Tryforos, Laurel Anderson, "Reign of the Boy King," *Fantasy Review,* June, 1987, pp. 42-43.

Wolff, Geoffrey, "A Saint's Life in Warsaw," *New York Times Book Review,* July 31, 1988, pp. 16-17.

Woloszyn, Stefan, *Korczak,* Wiedza Powszechna, 1978.

Zipes, Jack, review of *King Matt the First, New York Times Book Review,* July 20, 1986, p. 24.

FOR MORE INFORMATION SEE:

BOOKS

Gutman, Israel editor, *Encyclopedia of the Holocaust,* Yad Vashem, Sifriat Poalim/Macmillan, 1990.

Korczak, Janusz, *Ghetto Diary,* Holocaust Library, 1978.

Mortkowicz-Olczakowa, Hanna, *Janusz Korczak*, Czytelnik (Warsaw), 1978.

Newerly, Igor, *Rozmowa w sadzie piatego srerpnia*, Czytelnik, 1978.

Newerly, Igor, *Zywe wiazanie*, Czytelnik, 1978.

PERIODICALS

Bookbird, Number 16, 1978.
Child Education, Fall, 1989.
Education Leadership, May, 1986.
New York Times Book Review, July 20, 1986.
Prospects, Volume 17, number 1, 1987.
Publishers Weekly, April 25, 1986.
Time, March 2, 1981.

—Sketch by Marilyn K. Basel

* * *

KRAUS, (Herman) Robert 1925-
(Eugene H. Hippopotamus, E. S. Silly, I. M. Tubby)

PERSONAL: Born June 21, 1925, in Milwaukee, WI; son of Jack (in real estate business) and Esther (Rosen) Kraus; married Pamela Wong, December 11, 1946; children: Bruce, William. *Education:* Attended Layton Art School, Milwaukee, 1942, and Art Students' League of New York, 1945.

ADDRESSES: Home—Ridgefield, CT.

CAREER: Cartoonist for national magazines, and author and illustrator of children's books; president of Windmill Books, Inc., New York, NY, beginning 1965; president of Springfellow Books, Inc., beginning 1972.

AWARDS, HONORS: Whose Mouse Are You? was named a notable children's book of 1970 by the American Library Association; *Herman the Helper* appeared on the *Horn Book* honor list and received the Children's Trade Book Award; *Milton the Early Riser* and *Owliver* were named notable children's books by the American Library Association; *Leo the Late Bloomer* was read on national television by First Lady Barbara Bush as part of her literacy campaign.

WRITINGS:

Harriet and the Promised Land, Windmill Books, 1968.
Unidentified Flying Elephant, Windmill Books, 1968.
The Children Who Got Married, Windmill Books, 1969.
Animal Etiquette, Windmill Books, 1969.
Don't Talk to Strange Bears, Windmill Books, 1969.
Rumple-Nose Dimple and the Three Horrible Snaps, Windmill Books, 1969.
The Christmas Cookie Sprinkle Snitcher, Windmill Books, 1969.
The Rabbit Brothers, Anti-Defamation League of B'nai B'rith, 1969.
I'm Glad I'm a Boy, I'm Glad I'm a Girl, Windmill Books, 1970.
Whose Mouse Are You?, Macmillan, 1970.
Vip's Mistake Book, Windmill Books, 1970.
Bunya the Witch, Windmill Books, 1971.
Shaggy Fur Face, Windmill Books, 1971.
Ludwig, the Dog Who Snored Symphonies, Windmill Books, 1971.
Pipsqueak, Mouse in Shining Armor, Windmill Books, 1971.

Lillian Morgan and Teddy Morgan, Windmill Books, 1971.
The Tree That Stayed Up Until Next Christmas, Windmill Books, 1971.
Leo the Late Bloomer, Windmill Books, 1971.
Milton the Early Riser (Junior Literary Guild selection), Windmill Books, 1972.
How Spider Saved Halloween, Parents' Magazine Press, 1973.
Big Brother, Parents' Magazine Press, 1973.
Pip Squeaks Through, Springfellow Press, 1973.
Poor Mister Splinterfitz!, Dutton, 1973.
Rebecca Hatpin, Windmill Books, 1974.
Pinchpenny Mouse (Junior Literary Guild selection), Windmill Books, 1974.
Owliver (Junior Literary Guild selection), Windmill Books, 1974.
Herman the Helper (Junior Literary Guild selection), Windmill Books, 1974.
Three Friends (Junior Literary Guild selection), Windmill Books, 1975.
I'm a Monkey, Windmill Books, 1975.
The Night-Light Story Book, Windmill Books, 1975.
The Gondolier of Venice (Junior Literary Guild selection), Windmill Books, 1976.
Boris Bad Enough, Windmill Books, 1976.
Dinosaur Do's and Don'ts, Windmill Books, 1976.
Kittens for Nothing, Windmill Books, 1976.
The Good Mousekeeper, Windmill Books, 1977.
(With son, Bruce Kraus) *The Detective of London* (Junior Literary Guild selection), Windmill Books, 1977.
Noel the Coward, Windmill Books, 1977.
Another Mouse to Feed, Windmill Books, 1980.
Mouse Work, Windmill Books, 1980.
Mert the Blurt, Windmill Books, 1980.
Puppet Pal Books (contains *Herman the Helper Lends a Hand*, *Leo the Late Bloomer Bakes a Cake*, *Milton the Early Riser Takes a Trip*, and *Owliver the Actor Takes a Bow*), four volumes, Windmill Books, 1981.
The King's Trousers, Windmill Books, 1981.
Leo the Late Bloomer Takes a Bath, Windmill Books, 1981.
Herman the Helper Cleans Up, Windmill Books, 1981.
See the Christmas Lights, Windmill Books, 1981.
(With wife, Pam Kraus) *Box of Brownies*, four volumes, Windmill Books, 1981.
Where Are You Going, Little Mouse?, Greenwillow Books, 1986.
Screamy Mimi, Simon & Schuster, 1987.

AUTHOR AND ILLUSTRATOR

Junior, the Spoiled Cat, Oxford University Press, 1955.
All the Mice Came, Harper, 1955.
Ladybug, Ladybug, Harper, 1956.
The Littlest Rabbit, Harper, 1957.
I, Mouse, Harper, 1958.
The Trouble with Spider, Harper, 1962.
Miranda's Beautiful Dream, Harper, 1964.
Penguin's Pal, Harper, 1964.
Mouse at Sea, Harper, 1964.
Amanda Remembers, Harper, 1965.
My Son, the Mouse, Harper, 1967.
Little Giant, Harper, 1967.
(Under pseudoynm Eugene H. Hippopotamus) *Hello, Hippopotamus*, Windmill Books, 1969.
Daddy Long Ears, Windmill Books, 1970.
How Spider Saved Christmas, Windmill Books, 1970.
The Tale Who Wagged the Dog, Windmill Books, 1971.
Animal Families, Windmill Books, 1980.
See the Moon, Windmill Books, 1980.
How Spider Saved Turkey, Windmill Books, 1981.

A former cartoonist for *New Yorker* **magazine, Robert Kraus has delighted young readers in more than fifty children's books he has written and illustrated.** (From *Ludwig, the Dog Who Snored Symphonies.*)

The *Detective of London* is one of many titles published by Windmill Books, the children's publishing house founded by Robert Kraus in 1965.

The Old-Fashioned Raggedy Ann and Andy ABC Book, edited by Pam Kraus, Windmill Books, 1981.
Squeaky, Simon & Schuster, 1982.
Bumpy the Car, Putnam, 1985.
Ferddy the Fire Engine, Putnam, 1985.
How Spider Saved Valentine's Day, Scholastic Inc., 1986.
Spider's First Day at School, Scholastic Inc., 1987.
Happy City, Simon & Schuster, 1987.
Happy Farm, Simon & Schuster, 1987.
Spider's Home Town: A Story to Color, Scholastic Inc., 1988.
Here Comes Tardy Toad, Silver Press, 1989.
Ella the Bad Speller, Silver Press, 1989.
Good Morning, Miss Gator, Silver Press, 1989.
Miss Gator's School House, Messner, 1989.
Buggy Bear Cleans Up, Silver Press, 1989.
How Spider Saved the Baseball Game, Scholastic Inc., 1989.
Phil, the Ventriliquist, Greenwillow, 1989.
Daddy Long Ears Christmas Surprise, Simon & Schuster, 1989.
Daddy Long Ears Halloween, Simon & Schuster, 1990.
Private Eyes Don't Blink, Warner Books, 1990.
Spider's Baby-Sitting Job, Scholastic Inc., 1990.
Spider's Draw-a-Long Book, Scholastic Inc., 1990.
Creepy Hollow Ghostly Glowing Haunted House, Warner Books, 1990.
Boogie Woogie Bears Go Back to Nature, Warner Books, 1990.
Boogie Woogie Bears' Picnic, Warner Books, 1990.
Jack Galaxy, Space Cop, Bantam, 1990.
Klunky Monkey, New Kid in Class, Bantam, 1990.
Mixed-Up Mice Clean House, Warner Books, 1990.
Mixed-Up Mice in the Big Birthday Mix-Up, Warner Books, 1990.
Mummy Knows Best, Warner Books, 1990.
Mummy Vanishes, Warner Books, 1990.

Musical Max, Simon & Schuster, 1990.
The Phantom of Creepy Hollow, Warner Books, 1990.
(With Bonnie Brook) *Squirmy's Big Secret,* Silver Press, 1990.

"THE BUNNY'S NUTSHELL LIBRARY" SERIES

The Silver Dandelion, Harper, 1965.
Juniper, Harper, 1965.
The First Robin, Harper, 1965.
Springfellow's Parade, Harper, 1965.

"THE NIGHT LIGHT LIBRARY" SERIES

Good Night, Little One, Springfellow Books, 1972.
Good Night, Little ABC, Springfellow Books, 1972.
Good Night, Little Richard Rabbit, Springfellow Books, 1972.

UNDER PSEUDONYM E. S. SILLY

Squeaky, Windmill Books, 1982.
Squeaky's One Man Band, Windmill Books, 1982.

UNDER PSEUDONYM I. M. TUBBY

I'm a Little Airplane, Tubby Books, 1982.
I'm a Little Fish, Tubby Books, 1982.
I'm a Little House, Tubby Books, 1982.
I'm a Little Tugboat, Tubby Books, 1982.

EDITOR

Robert J. Flaherty, *Nanook of the North,* Windmill Books, 1971.
Reggie Jackson's Scrapbook, Windmill Books, 1978.

ILLUSTRATOR

Paul Anderson, *Red Fox and the Hungry Tiger,* Addison-Wesley, 1962.
Carla Stevens, *Rabbit and Skunk and the Spooks,* Scholastic Book Services, 1968.
Stevens, *Rabbit and Skunk and the Scary Rock,* Scholastic Book Services, 1970.
Cleveland Amory, *Cleveland Amory's Animail,* Dutton, 1976.
Stevens, *Rabbit and Skunk and the Big Fight,* Scholastic Book Services, 1976.

SIDELIGHTS: A noted children's writer and illustrator, former president of Windmill Books, and a magazine cartoonist, Robert Kraus has enjoyed a long and varied career.

Kraus began as a cartoonist, selling his first cartoon at the age of 10 to a local newspaper in his native Milwaukee. By the age of 16, he was selling cartoons to such magazines as the *Saturday Evening Post* and *Esquire.* His big break came with a sale to the *New Yorker,* the premiere cartoon market in the country. Soon Kraus was a regular cartoonist for the magazine, contracted to draw 50 cartoons a year.

After 15 years with the *New Yorker,* Kraus decided to try something new, turning his talents to writing and drawing children's books full time. This led him in 1965 to begin a new publishing company, Windmill Books, which specialized in children's picture books. At first, Kraus wrote the stories and his artist friends from the *New Yorker,* like Charles Addams and William Steig, drew the pictures. Soon Windmill Books was publishing a wide variety of children's books by many authors; some of the books were award winners. Jean F. Mercier, writing in *Publishers Weekly,* says that Windmill Books has "an enviable reputation." Among Kraus's publishing innovations was Tubby Books, small waterproof books for children to read in the bathtub. (The slogan: "They

Float! The Unsinkable Book!") Unfortunately, in the early 1980s Windmill Books experienced financial difficulties as well as problems with its distributor. Because of these troubles, Kraus was obliged to sign over the company and all its books to Simon and Schuster.

Since that time, he has focused his attention on writing and illustrating books for a number of different publishers. Kraus often writes of animal characters. Among the most popular are Owliver, an owl who likes to act, Herman, a well-meaning octopus, and Spider, a problem-solving insect.

A collection of Kraus's manuscripts is at Syracuse University.

FOR MORE INFORMATION SEE:

Growing Point, April, 1977.
New Yorker, December 7, 1981.
Publishers Weekly, February 27, 1978.

*   *   *

KRAUTTER, Elisa (Bialk) 1912(?)-1990
(Elisa Bialk)

OBITUARY NOTICE—See index for *SATA* sketch: Born October 4, 1912 (one source says c. 1909), in Chicago, IL; died of cancer, February 28, 1990, on Hilton Head Island, SC. Publicist, educator, and writer. Under her maiden name of Elisa Bialk, Krautter had a long and varied writing career. Beginning as a journalist for such Chicago-area papers as the *Daily News* and the *Lincoln-Belmont Booster,* she became a free-lance writer of short stories and magazine articles after her marriage in 1934. She adapted one of her stories, "The Sainted Sisters," into a play that later became a feature film. As Krautter's children grew she became interested in juvenile literature; beginning in 1948 with *The Horse Called Pete* she wrote dozens of children's books, including her "Tizz" series and *Orville Mouse at the Opera House.* Krautter also taught writing workshops and served as publicity chairperson of the Lawrence Hall Home for Boys from 1948 to 1952.

OBITUARIES AND OTHER SOURCES:

BOOKS

Current Biography, H. W. Wilson, 1954, May, 1990.

PERIODICALS

New York Times, March 7, 1990.

*   *   *

KURIAN, George 1928-

PERSONAL: Born October 24, 1928, in Kottayam, India; son of K. K. (a plantation owner) and Accamma (Mani) Kurian; married wife, Susannah (a doctor), February 6, 1964. *Education:* University of Madras, B.A., 1950; Institute of Social Studies [Netherlands], M.A., 1955, M.S.Sc., 1956; State University of Utrecht, D.Lit. and D.Phil., both 1961.

ADDRESSES: Office—Department of Sociology, University of Calgary, 2920 24th Ave. N.W., Calgary, Alberta, Canada T2N 1N4.

CAREER: Osmania University, Hyderabad, India, reader in sociology, 1962-63; Victoria University of Wellington, Wel-

lington, New Zealand, lecturer in Asian studies, 1963-66; University of Calgary, Calgary, Alberta, assistant professor, 1966-69, associate professor, 1969-75, professor of sociology, 1976—.

MEMBER: Canadian Association for South Asian Studies (vice-president, 1977), National Council on Family Relations, Royal Asiatic Society of Great Britain and Ireland (fellow), Indian Sociological Society, Association of Asian Studies.

WRITINGS:

The Indian Family in Transition, Mouton, 1961.
The Family in India: A Regional View, Mouton, 1974.
(Editor) *Cross-Cultural Perspectives of Mate-Selection and Marriage,* Greenwood Press, 1979.
(Editor with Ratna Ghosh) *Women in the Family and the Economy: An International Comparative Survey,* Greenwood Press, 1981.
Encyclopedia of the Third World, three volumes, revised edition, Facts On File, 1981, 4th edition, 1990.
(Editor with Ram P. Srivastava) *Overseas Indians: A Study in Adaptation,* Vikas Publishers, 1982.
New Book of World Rankings, Facts On File, 1983, 3rd edition, 1989.
(Editor) *Geo-Data: The World Almanac Gazetteer,* Gale, 1983.
What's What in American Business: Facts and Figures about the Biggest and the Best, Probus, 1985.
Dictionary of Biography, Laurel, 1985.
(Editor) *Parent-Child Interaction in Transition,* Greenwood Press, 1986.
Sourcebook of Global Statistics, Facts On File, 1986.
Handbook of Business Quotations, Prentice-Hall, 1987.
New American Gazetteer, Signet, 1987.
Yearbook of American Universities and Colleges, Garland, 1988.
World Education Encyclopedia, three volumes, Facts On File, 1988.
Global Guide to Medical Information, Elsevier, 1988.
World Police Forces, Facts On File, 1988.
(Editor) *Encyclopedia of World Police Forces and Penal Systems,* Facts On File, 1989.
World Gazetteer of Boundaries, ABC-Clio, 1989.
Glossary of the Third World, Facts On File, 1989.
(Editor) *Teachers as Writers,* G. Kurian, 1989.
Encyclopedia of the First World, Facts On File, 1989.
Atlas of the Third World, 2nd edition, Facts On File, 1989.
World Legal Encyclopedia, three volumes, Facts On File, 1990.
Encyclopedia of the Second World, Facts On File, 1990.

"FACTS ON FILE NATIONAL PROFILES" SERIES

Facts On File National Profiles: Mexico and Central America, Facts On File, 1989.
. . . *Benelux Countries,* Facts On File, 1989.
. . . *East Africa,* Facts On File, 1989.
. . . *Scandinavia,* Facts On File, 1989.
. . . *British Isles,* Facts On File, 1989.
. . . *North America,* Facts On File, 1990.
. . . *Japan,* Facts On File, 1990.
. . . *Middle East,* Facts On File, 1990.
. . . *Australia and New Zealand,* Facts On File, 1990.

OTHER

Author of *Historical and Cultural Dictionary of India,* Books On Demand, University of Michigan. Contributor of more than thirty-five articles to professional journals. Founder and editor of *Journal of Comparative Family Studies,* 1970—.

* * *

LANE, Margaret 1907-

PERSONAL: Born June 23, 1907, in Cheshire, England; daughter of Harry George (a newspaper editor) and Edith (Webb) Lane; married Bryan Edgar Wallace, June 23, 1934 (divorced, 1939); married Francis John Clarence Westenra Plantagenet Hastings, fifteenth earl of Huntingdon (an artist), becoming countess of Huntingdon, February, 1944; children: (second marriage) Selina, Harriet. *Education:* St. Hugh's College, Oxford, M.A., 1928.

ADDRESSES: Blackbridge House, Beaulieu, Hampshire, England SO4 7YE.

CAREER: Novelist, biographer, and book reviewer for *Daily Telegraph. Daily Express,* London, England, reporter, 1928-31; special correspondent in New York and for International News Service in the United States, 1931-32; *Daily Mail,* London, special correspondent, 1932-38.

MEMBER: Women's Press Club (president, 1958-60), Society of Authors, Bronte Society (president, 1976), Dickens Fellowship (president, 1959-61, and 1970), Johnson Society (president, 1971), Jane Austen Society (president, 1983).

AWARDS, HONORS: Prix Femina-Vie Heurese, 1935, for *Faith, Hope, No Charity.*

WRITINGS:

JUVENILE

(Illustrated by Kenneth Lilley) *The Squirrel,* Dial, 1981.
(Illustrated by Patricia Casey) *Operation Hedgehog,* Methuen, 1981.
(Illustrated by David Nockels) *The Beaver,* Dial, 1981.
(Illustrated by John Butler) *The Stickleback,* Methuen, 1981, published in United States as *The Fish: The Story of a Stickleback,* Dial, 1981.
(Illustrated by Lilley) *The Fox,* Dial, 1982.
(Illustrated by Grahame Corbett) *The Frog,* Dial, 1982.
(Illustrated by Barbara Firth) *The Spider,* Dial, 1982.
(Illustrated by Denise Finney) *The Chimpanzee,* Random House, 1985.
(Illustrated by David Wright) *The Elephant,* Random House, 1985.
(Illustrated by Wright) *The Giraffe,* Random House, 1985.
(Illustrated by Nockels) *The Lion,* Random House, 1985.

OTHER

Faith, Hope, No Charity (novel), Harper, 1935.
At Last the Island (novel), Harper, 1937.
Edgar Wallace: The Biography of a Phenomenon (nonfiction), Harper, 1938, revised edition with introduction by Graham Greene, Hamilton, 1965, reprinted, Arden Library, 1980.
Walk into My Parlor (nonfiction), Harper, 1941.
Where Helen Lies (novel), Duell, Sloan & Pearce, 1944.
The Tales of Beatrix Potter (nonfiction), Warne, 1946, published as *The Tale of Beatrix Potter: A Biography,* 1959, revised and enlarged edition, 1968.

The Bronte Story: A Reconsideration of Mrs. Gatskill's Life of Emily Bronte (nonfiction), Duell, Sloan & Pearce, 1953, reprinted Greenwood Press, 1971.
A Crown of Convolvulus, Heinemann, 1954.
A Calabash of Diamonds (nonfiction), Duell, Sloan & Pearce, 1961, published in England as *A Calabash of Diamonds: An African Treasure Hunt,* Heinemann, 1961.
Life with Ionides (nonfiction), Viking, 1963.
A Night at Sea (novel), Knopf, 1965.
A Smell of Burning: A Novel, Hamilton, 1965, published as *A Smell of Burning,* Knopf, 1966.
Purely for Pleasure (literary-biographical essays), Hamilton, 1966, Knopf, 1967.
The Day of the Feast, Knopf, 1968, published in England as *The Day of the Feast: A Novel,* Hamish Hamilton, 1968.
Frances Wright and the Great Experiment (nonfiction), Rowman & Littlefield, 1972.
Samuel Johnson and His World, Harper, 1975.
Flora Thompson, Murray, 1976.
The Magic Years of Beatrix Potter, Warne, 1978.
(Editor) Flora Thompson, *A Country Calender and Other Writings,* Oxford University Press, 1980.
The Drug-Like Bronte Dream, Humanities, 1981.
The Beatrix Potter Country Cookery Book, Warne, 1982.

Contributor to periodicals, including *Punch, Cornhill,* and *Times Literary Supplement.*

FOR MORE INFORMATION SEE:

BOOKS

Wakeman, John, editor, *World Authors,* H.W. Wilson, 1975.

PERIODICALS

America, February 28, 1976.
Christian Science Monitor, January 4, 1939; March 15, 1967.
Hornbook, November, 1946.
Ladies Home Journal, May, 1936.
New Statesman, January 23, 1976.
New York Times, March 19, 1939.
New York Times Book Review, December 12, 1965; October 13, 1968.
Saturday Review, February 7, 1942; June 30, 1953.
Spectator, December 9, 1938; October 1, 1954.
Time, November 11, 1946.
Times Literary Supplement, December 3, 1938; July 2, 1964; November 25, 1965; January 5, 1967; March 28, 1968; March 17, 1972; March 27, 1981.

* * *

LARKIN, Amy
See BURNS, Olive Ann

* * *

LASENBY, Jack 1931-

PERSONAL: Born March 9, 1931, in Waharon, New Zealand; son of Owen Liberty (a secretary) and Linda (a housewife; maiden name, Bryce) Lasenby; married wife, Elizabeth, 1963 (deceased, 1969); children: Rebecca, Kimberly; stepchildren: Anne, Jeremy. *Education:* Attended Auckland University, 1950-51.

*ADDRESSES: Home—*14 A Trevor Terrace, Paremata, Plimmerton, New Zealand.

CAREER: Worked variously as a deer culler, possum trapper, and teacher, c. 1950-68; New Zealand Department of Education, Wellington, editor of *School Journal,* 1969-75; Wellington Teachers' College, Wellington, New Zealand, senior lecturer in English, 1975-87; full-time writer, 1987—.

AWARDS, HONORS: Esther Glen Award, New Zealand Library Association, 1989, for *The Mangrove Summer.*

WRITINGS:

Charlie the Cheeky Kea (picture book), Golden Books, 1976.
Rewi the Red Deer (picture book), Golden Books, 1976.
The Lake (children's novel), Oxford University Press, 1989.
The Mangrove Summer (children's novel), Oxford University Press, 1989.
Uncle Trev Stories, Cape Catley Press, 1991.

Also author of school bulletins *Lost and Found,* 1970, and *The Chatham Islands,* 1973, both published by the New Zealand Department of Education. Contributor of poems, stories, plays, and articles to numerous magazines and journals.

WORK IN PROGRESS: A novel set in New Zealand of the future.

SIDELIGHTS: Jack Lasenby wrote, "I only regret that circumstances prevented me from becoming a full-time writer earlier. I enjoyed much of the work I did in my various jobs, but writing was always my aim. Much of my material to date has been drawn from direct experience. I choose to write for

JACK LASENBY

children because much of the best prose is being written for them; for example, by Cynthia Voight, Philippa Pearce, and Margaret Mahy. I hope it's not too wild an ambition to be of their company. It seems to me that there are few authors for adults who share their competence."

FOR MORE INFORMATION SEE:

PERIODICALS

Publishers Weekly, May 12, 1989.
School Library Journal, August, 1989.
Times Literary Supplement, July 29, 1988.

*　　*　　*

LAWRENCE, Jerome 1915-

PERSONAL: Born July 14, 1915, in Cleveland, OH; son of Samuel (a printer) and Sarah (a poet; maiden name, Rogen) Schwartz. *Education:* Ohio State University, B.A., 1937; graduate study at University of California, Los Angeles, 1939. *Politics:* Democrat.

ADDRESSES: Home and office—21056 Las Flores Mesa Dr., Malibu, CA 90265. *Agent*—(literature) Mitch Douglas, International Creative Management, New York, NY; and Ben Benjam, International Creative Management, Los Angeles, CA.

CAREER: Wilmington News Journal, Wilmington, OH, reporter and telegraph editor, 1937; *New Lexington Daily News,* New Lexington, OH, editor, 1937; Radio Station KMPC, Beverly Hills, CA, continuity editor, 1937-39; Columbia Broadcasting System, New York City and Los Angeles, CA, senior staff writer, 1939-41; scenario writer for Paramount Studios, 1941, and for Samuel Goldwyn, 1946, both Hollywood, CA; Lawrence & Lee, New York City and Los Angeles, playwright and director in partnership with Robert E. Lee, 1942—, president, 1955—.

Has directed numerous productions, including the premiere productions of *The Incomparable Max, The Crocodile Smile,* and *Jabberwock: Improbabilities Lived and Imagined by James Thurber in the Fictional City of Columbus, Ohio;* also staged the first arena production of *Mame* and the Dublin Theatre Festival production of *The Night Thoreau Spent in Jail.* Master playwright, New York University, 1967-69; visiting professor and playwright-in-residence, Ohio State University, 1968-69; professor, Salzburg Seminar in American Studies, 1972; professor of graduate study, Professional Writers Program, University of Southern California, 1984—. Member of California State Universities Distinguished Artists Forum and adviser to Chancellor W. Ann Reynolds in "The State of the Arts." Lecturer at University of Alberta, University of California, Los Angeles, American University, Yale University, Tufts University, Villanova University, University of Southern California, California State University, Boston University, Midwestern State University, Pepperdine University, and Pasadena Playhouse. American Playwrights Theatre, Columbus, OH, president, 1968-69, co-founder and trustee. Member of board of directors, National Repertory Theatre, American Conservatory Theatre, and East-West Players; member of board of standards, Living Theatre; member of advisory board, Eugene O'Neill Memorial Foundation, California Education Theatre Association, 1981—, Ohio State University School of

JEROME LAWRENCE

Journalism, and U.S.D.A.N. Center for Creative and Performing Arts. Co-founder of William Inge Festival. Has also lectured in Japan, Thailand, Egypt, Greece, France, India, Romania, Spain, Poland, the Philippines, Turkey, and England. Co-founder and judge, Margo Jones Award; expert consultant to Secretary of War, 1942-45; member of drama panel, Cultural Exchange Committee, U.S. State Department, 1964-69. Member of board of governors, Law and Humanities Institute, 1979-88. *Military service:* U.S. Army, 1943-44; correspondent in North Africa and Italy; cofounder of Armed Forces Radio Service; became staff sergeant; received Battle Star and special citation from Secretary of War.

MEMBER: American National Theatre and Academy (vice-president and director), American Society of Composers, Authors and Publishers (ASCAP), Academy of Motion Picture Arts and Sciences, National Academy of Television Arts and Sciences, Dramatists Guild (council member, 1968—), Authors League of America (council member, 1972—), Writers Guild of America (West; co-founder and board member), Radio Writers' Guild (founder; president, 1954-55), Ohio State University Association (member of board of directors), Phi Beta Kappa, Sigma Delta Chi.

AWARDS, HONORS: New York Press Club Award, 1942; Peabody Awards, 1948, for United National Radio series, and 1950; *Radio-TV Life* awards, 1948, 1952; *Radio-TV Mirror* awards, 1952, 1953; *Variety*'s Showmanship Award, 1954; Donaldson Award, Outer Circle Award, and *Variety* New York Drama Critics Poll, all 1955, and London Critics Award for best foreign play, 1960, all for *Inherit the Wind;* "Tony" Awards, 1955 and 1966; D.H.L., Ohio State University, 1963; Moss Hart Memorial Award, 1967; selected "Man of the Year," Zeta Beta Tau, 1967; D. Litt., Fairleigh Dickinson University, 1968; U.S. State Department Medal, 1968;

D.F.A., Villanova University, 1969; Pegasus Award, 1970; American Theatre Association Lifetime Award, 1979, for "distinguished service to the theatre"; National Thespian Association Directors Award, 1980; honorary Doctor of Letters, College of Wooster, 1983; Writers Guild of America's Valentine Davies Award, 1984, for "contributions to the entertainment community which have brought dignity and honor to writers everywhere"; named to Theatre Hall of Fame, 1990; elected College of Fellows of American Theatre at Kennedy Center, 1990; has also received numerous other awards and honors.

WRITINGS:

Oscar the Ostrich (juvenile), Random House, 1940.
Off Mike: Radio Writing by the Nation's Top Radio Writers, Essential Books, 1944.
Live Spelled Backwards: A Moral Immorality Play (produced in Beverly Hills, CA, 1966), Dramatists Play Service, 1970.
Actor: The Life and Times of Paul Muni, Putnam, 1974.
Laugh, God!, published in *Six Anti-Nazi One-Act Plays,* Contemporary Play Publications, 1939.

PLAYS WITH ROBERT E. LEE

Inside a Kid's Head, first published in *Radio Drama in Action,* edited by Erik Barnouw, Farrar & Rinehart, 1945.
Look Ma, I'm Dancin'!, produced on Broadway, 1948.
Inherit the Wind (three-act; produced on Broadway, 1955), Random House, 1955, acting edition, Dramatists Play Service, 1958, revised acting edition, 1963.
(Also with James Hilton) *Shangri-La* (musical; based on the book *Lost Horizon* by James Hilton; produced on Broadway, 1956), Morris Music, 1956.
Auntie Mame (two-act; based on the novel by Patrick Dennis; produced on Broadway, 1956), Vanguard, 1957, acting edition, Dramatists Play Service, 1960 (also see below).
The Gang's All Here (three-act; produced on Broadway, 1959), World Publishing, 1960, acting edition, Samuel French, 1961.
Only in America (three-act; based on book by Harry Golden; produced on Broadway, 1959), Samuel French, 1960.
A Call on Kuprin (three-act; based on the novel by Maurice Edelman; produced on Broadway, 1961), Samuel French, 1962.
Sparks Fly Upward (produced on Broadway as *Diamond Orchid,* 1965; rewritten and produced as *Sparks Fly Upward* in Dallas, 1967), Dramatists Play Service, 1967.
Mame (two-act musical comedy; based on the book *Auntie Mame* by Patrick Dennis and the play by Lawrence and Lee; music and lyrics by Jerry Herman; produced on Broadway, 1966), Random House, 1967.
Dear World (two-act musical comedy; based on Maurice Valency's adaptation of *The Madwoman of Chaillot* by Jean Giraudoux), produced on Broadway, 1969.
The Night Thoreau Spent in Jail (produced through American Playwrights Theatre in Columbus, OH, 1970), Hill & Wang, 1971.
The Incomparable Max! (based on Max Beerbohm's *Trips beyond Reality;* produced in Abingdon, VA, 1969), Hill & Wang, 1972.
The Crocodile Smile (produced as *The Laugh Maker* in Los Angeles at Players Ring Theatre, 1952; rewritten and produced as *Turn on the Night* in Philadelphia, 1961; rewritten and produced as *The Crocodile Smile,* in Flat Rock, NC, 1970), Dramatists Play Service, 1972.
Jabberwock: Improbabilities Lived and Imagined by James Thurber in the Fictional City of Columbus, Ohio (inspired

by *My Life and Hard Times* by James Thurber; produced in Columbus, OH, 1972), Samuel French, 1974.
First Monday in October, (produced in Cleveland, 1975), Samuel French, 1979.

Also co-author with Lee of unpublished and unproduced plays, *Top of the Mark, Paris, France, Eclipse, Dilly, Some Say Ice, Houseboat in Kashmir, Short and Sweet,* and *The Angels Weep.*

ONE-ACT OPERAS; WITH ROBERT E. LEE

Annie Laurie, Harms, Inc., 1954.
Roaring Camp, Harms, Inc., 1955.
Familiar Stranger, Harms, Inc., 1956.

SCREENPLAYS; WITH ROBERT E. LEE

My Love Affair with the Human Race, 1962.
The New Yorkers, 1963.
The Joyous Season, 1964.
The Night Thoreau Spent in Jail (based on play of same title), 1976.
First Monday in October (based on play of same title), produced by Paramount, 1982.

Also co-author with Lee of *Billion Dollar Baby, Whitewater,* and *The Clock Struck One.*

OTHER

Writer, director, and producer of television and radio programs, including "Hollywood Showcase," 1940-41, "I Was There," 1940-42, and "They Live Forever," 1942. Also

Daily Variety advertisement for the 1988 television adaptation of Jerome Lawrence and Robert E. Lee's award-winning play.

writer, director, and producer with Lee of many television and radio programs, including "Columbia Workshop," 1942-43, "Request Performance," 1945-46, "Orson Welles Theatre," 1945-46, "Favorite Story," 1945-48, "Frank Sinatra Show," 1947, "The Railroad Hour," 1948-54, "Hallmark Hall of Fame," 1949-51, "Halls of Ivy," 1950-51, "Date with Judy," "The Unexpected," "Times Square Playhouse," "Song of Norway," "West Point," and "Lincoln: The Unwilling Warrior," as well as "Hallmark Playhouse" productions of their plays "Shangri-La" and "Inherit the Wind." Writer and director with Lee of the official Army-Navy programs for D-Day, V-E Day, and V-J Day. Also writer of original lyrics and music with Lee for radio program, "Railroad Hour." Also writer and director with Lee of record album "One God," and Decca dramatic albums, "Musi-Plays." Adapter and director of record albums with Lee, "Rip Van Winkle," "Cask of Amontillago," "A Tale of Two Cities," and "One God." Contributor of numerous articles and short stories to *Saturday Evening Post* and other periodicals. Contributing editor, *Dramatics* magazine, 1980—.

ADAPTATIONS: Auntie Mame, starring Rosalind Russell, Forrest Tucker, and Roger Smith, was adapted for film by Warner Brothers, 1958; *Inherit the Wind,* starring Fredric March, Spencer Tracy, and Gene Kelly, was adapted for film by United Artists, 1960, and was adapted as a television movie starring Kirk Douglas and Jason Robards by NBC-TV, 1988; *Mame,* starr-ing Lucille Ball, Robert Preston, and Beatrice Arthur, was adapted by Warner Brothers-Seven Arts, 1974.

WORK IN PROGRESS: Whisper in the Mind, a stage play in collaboration with Norman Cousins and R. Lee.

SIDELIGHTS: Playwrights Jerome Lawrence and Robert E. Lee accidentally met at the ground-floor restaurant of the Columbia Broadcasting System (CBS) Building in New York City in 1942. They started what they thought would be a simple conversation. The men told each other of their love of writing, their desire to create quality entertainment for radio, and their interest in the theatre. One week later the pair became collaborators and formed the writing partnership of Lawrence & Lee.

This association would prove to be successful, well-respected, and long-lasting. Together Lawrence and Lee have written over nineteen produced plays and four screenplays. They are also responsible for numerous radio plays and scripts, operas, and many unproduced or unpublished plays. "Our collaboration started with six radio plays," Lee described the partnership's beginning to Sidney Fields in the *Daily News.* "By some fluke they all were aired the same week."

As they began writing together, Lawrence and Lee felt it was important to lay a good foundation in order for their partnership to work. This involved discussing their goals and dreams. In order to achieve their goals, the men had to take steps to make sure their working environment promoted individuality and creativity. At the same time, they wanted to create as little friction as possible.

A good solid partnership would take work and compromise. "In the beginning, we each had to make some adjustments," Lawrence recalled to Ernest Schier in the *Evening Bulletin.* "Bob had the habit of snapping pencils in half. I would shout

'No!' when I didn't like a line or an idea. He doesn't break pencils any more and I say 'Maybe.'" Lawrence and Lee shared the same ideas on what they thought a good writing partnership was. "Most collaborations fail because their base is emotional," Lawrence pointed out in *Theatre Arts.* "Writing is lonely, and it is nice to have a kindred spirit to tell you everything is great. But the spirits of collaborators should not be too kindred; they should differ as widely as working habits will permit."

There is one major reason the playwrights' partnership flourished and survived nearly fifty years. While they are different in certain ways, Lawrence and Lee are also alike in important ways. They both have similar backgrounds. Both men were born and raised in Ohio in the heart of the Midwest. They also had solid hardworking parents who provided a strong, stable family life. And finally, Lawrence and Lee are true professionals who take their writing seriously.

Jerome Lawrence was born on July 14, 1915, in Cleveland, Ohio. His parents were Samuel, a printer, and Sarah Schwartz, a poet. His sister, Naomi, was an actress at the Cleveland Playhouse. Both children showed interest in drama at a early age. Although he started acting in grade school, Lawrence switched to writing in college. He recalled his early encounters with drama in a commencement address at Fairleigh Dickinson University. "I *began* in the theatre as an actor—and I want you to know why I quit," Lawrence told the audience. "Our first grade Sunday-school class, headed up by Miss Barth, was presenting for an assembly a great 'epic drama' entitled: *Adam and Eve in the Garden of Eden.* Hilda, age six, was Eve. Marvin, age six, was Adam. And I, not a very mature five-and-a-half, had a hell of a part. I was the off-stage Voice of God. Well, I was a sensation. Because when the Voice of God was supposed to thunder: 'Where art thou, Adam? Where art thou, Eve?'— God spake in the highest-pipsqueak boy-soprano you every heard—and brought the house down. And that's why I quit as an actor. After you've played God, where can you go? But the point of the story is that during rehearsals, I was sulking off-stage, digging my fists into my short-pants pockets, and not liking the play very much. So I paraded on stage and told Miss Barth that she was doing it all wrong. If Marvin was really Adam and Hilda was really Eve . . . what were they doing with their clothes on? And Miss Barth said: 'Jerome, you get off stage, and be a good little Voice of God, and shut up!' Well, then I really sulked, because I thought if I were God I ought to have something to say about it. And I swore that someday I'd bring back a production of *Adam and Eve,* starring Marvin and Hilda, and, by God, they'd do it *stark naked!*"

"In high-school, Eugene C. Davis [my acting teacher] dared to present (and let me act in) the mature plays of O'Neill, Chekhov, even a pre-*Nicholas Nickleby* epic drama based on *A Tale of Two Cities,*" Lawrence told the California Educational Theater Association. "At Ohio State, Herman Miller [my professor] inspired me with a love of theatre, and numerous campus playwriting contests helped flame my desire to write for the living stage. My first published one-act play, *Laugh, God!,* was the result of such a contest, published in a volume of *Six Anti-Nazi One-Act Plays.*"

After he received his degree from Ohio State University in 1937, Lawrence stayed in Ohio as a reporter and telegraph editor for the *Wilmington News Journal,* and then as editor of the *New Lexington Daily News.* In 1939, Lawrence moved to California and worked briefly as continuity editor for KMPC Radio in Beverly Hills. Between 1939 and 1940 he did

graduate work at University of California, Los Angeles while he worked as a senior staff writer for Columbia Broadcasting System (CBS) in Hollywood and then in New York City. He also wrote scripts for Paramount Pictures.

Also an Ohioan, Robert E. Lee was born in Elyria on October 15, 1918, to Claire Melvin, an engineer, and Elvira Taft, a teacher. He attended Northwestern University, Ohio Wesleyan University, Western Reserve University, and Drake University. While still in college, Lee worked first as astronomical observer and technician at the Perkins Observatory in Delaware, Ohio and then as announcer at WHK-WCLE Radio in Cleveland. Between 1938 and 1942 he was a director for the advertising agency, Young and Rubicam, in Hollywood and New York City.

Lawrence and Lee's chance meeting at the New York City restaurant led to a formal and legal writing partnership established in 1942. The pair wrote radio plays until World War II called them into service. As Expert Consultants to the Secretary of War, Lawrence and Lee were two of the founding fathers of the Armed Forces Radio Service. They also wrote and directed the official Army/Navy broadcasts for such important World War II events as the Allied invasion of France (D-Day), the Allied victory in Europe (V-E Day), and the Japanese surrender to the United States (V-J Day). During their time in the service Lawrence was also correspondent in North Africa and Italy, while Lee was an Air Force pilot.

In 1943, the two men returned to civilian life and continued their partnership writing and directing radio plays. During this time in history, radio was a very important means of mass communication and entertainment. "Technically, we can span the world," Lawrence declared in his book about the power of radio, *Off Mike: Radio Writing by the Nation's Top Radio Writers.* "At a flip of a switch, we can pick up New Guinea, Cairo, a ship at sea, or a plane in the stratosphere. The greatest voices of the entertainment world and the world's greatest music are now on the air. Production has reached a fine hair of perfection. Frequency modulation will make every harmonic, every overtone of a violin string crystal clear. Television is closer than tomorrow. How much farther can we go in those directions? The wide road of progress that lies ahead will depend upon the writer, and upon the awareness of the radio industry that it is the written word that makes a radio program great or makes a radio program trash."

While writing for radio Lawrence and Lee began collaborating on plays for the theatre. In 1948 their first show, *Look Ma, I'm Dancin'!,* was produced on Broadway. This musical told of the life of ballet dancers and their difficult climb to success. It was considered a bit ahead of its time because of its plot and its underlying theme of selflessness vs. selfishness. However, *Look Ma, I'm Dancin'!* was generally well-received by audiences. "We were very lucky on that show because we had George Abbott as director," explained Lawrence to Georgia High in the *Independence Reporter,* "Jerome Robbins as choreographer and the star was Nancy Walker. And (the show) was way ahead of its time because it was about the then not widely-popular world of ballet." "My partner, Jerry Lawrence, and I wrote *Look Ma, I'm Dancin'!* because we felt a need to show that selfishness dampens the artistic spirit," added Lee in the *Writers' Digest.*

The duo's next play *Inherit the Wind* premiered in 1955. This play was inspired by the famous Scopes "Monkey Trail," in which a young schoolteacher, John Scopes, was put on trial in the summer of 1925. Scopes was accused of defying a Tennessee Statute that prohibited the teaching of any theory of creationism other than the idea that a supreme being created the world. Scopes was arrested for teaching Darwin's theory of evolution which suggested that man evolved from apes. Drawing their ideas from the actual persons in involved in the trial, including William Jennings Bryan, the prosecutor, and Clarence Darrow, who represented the defendant, Lawrence and Lee brought to the stage "one of the best serious dramas to hit Broadway and one of the best rounded," believed a reviewer for *Newsweek*. "Its dialogue moves easily, sometimes brilliantly." Describing the play as "splashed together in bold colors like a circus poster," a writer for *Life* declared *Inherit the Wind* "a vivid provocative piece of U.S. history."

Not only was the plot considered daring, controversial, and too serious for Broadway to tackle, *Inherit the Wind* was written during a politically shaky time in American history. A powerful movement, referred to as "McCarthyism," was grabbing America's attention. The movement questioned the loyalty of many people, including politicians, entertainers, and writers to the United States. People in the public eye were more vulnerable to attack from this group because their actions were so visible. Leaders of this movement, such as Wisconsin Senator Joseph McCarthy, were unduly suspicious of almost everyone. They demanded proof of an individual's denouncement of communism and liberalism or the group would publicly accuse the person of being a traitor against the United States. Many people were afraid to tackle controversial issues for fear of drawing undue attention to themselves.

Lawrence and Lee were unhappy about this movement and felt a pressing need to express their thoughts on the political climate of the day. "When we were writing *Inherit the Wind,* we were concerned about thought control or McCarthyism, where people were told what they should think," Lawrence commented to Allen Smith in the *Independence Daily Reporter*. "Instead of attacking the subject head on, we went back to a parallel incident in the 1920s, where freedom of thought was being attacked in the Scopes trial."

Lawrence and Lee saw beyond the straight details of the Scopes trial. They used the facts of this event as a stepping stone to discuss the broader issues and important freedoms that the United States Constitution provides its citizens. "*Inherit the Wind* is not history," Lawrence and Lee explained in the introduction to their play. "The events which took place in Dayton, Tennessee during the scorching July of 1925 are clearly the genesis of this play. It has, however, an exodus entirely its own. . . . Only a handful of phrases have been taken from the actual transcript of the famous Scopes Trial. Some of the characters of the play are related to the colorful figures in that battle of giants; but they have life and language of their own—and, therefore, names of their own. So *Inherit the Wind* does not pretend to be journalism. It is theatre. It is not 1925. The stage directions set the time as 'Not too long ago.' It might have been yesterday. It could be tomorrow."

The actual writing of *Inherit the Wind* took place after the pair spent a great deal of time researching the facts of the original trial. They wanted to know everything possible about the trial, people, and political issues involved in this project before they started writing. "For more than a year we haunted libraries and secondhand bookstores," Lawrence and Lee remarked in the *New York Herald Tribune*. "We read the complete files of the *New York Times* and the *Chattanooga Times,* the day-to-day and hour-to-hour accounts of Dayton's sweltering carnival." The men continued to explain that their "notes would have made six plays. Having allowed the juices to flow through us, we put aside the facts and let the fiction take over."

"The writing of the play was a joy," the men remembered in the *New York Herald Tribune*. "We met at six each morning, alternating houses. We acted out all the parts, noisily if not expertly. We cried and we laughed. And the characters . . . sat down beside us and started to speak their lines."

Originally, Lawrence and Lee found it impossible to bring *Inherit the Wind* to the Broadway stage. After being rejected by every New York producer, the play finally premiered at the Margo Jones Theatre in Dallas before a very enthusiastic audience. After the Dallas production opened, producer Herman Shumlin agreed to produce and direct the play in New York. "We were delighted by his daring approach to the production," remarked Lawrence in *Theatre Arts*. "He was determined to get all the fever and fervor of that inflamed community onto the stage, regardless of cost."

Inherit the Wind turned out to be one of the most popular plays in the history of American theatre. The play was considered a Broadway blockbuster, played to packed houses, and had a three year run. *Inherit the Wind* has been translated into thirty-five languages and performed in theatres around the world. In 1990-91, in honor of the two hundredth anniversary of the U.S. Bill of Rights, *Inherit the Wind* was staged and performed in actual courtrooms all over America.

In 1960, United Artists adapted *Inherit the Wind* into a motion picture starring Frederic March, Spencer Tracy, and Gene Kelly. The movie was widely praised and very successful. Twenty-eight years later, in 1988, NBC-TV produced and broadcast an updated version of *Inherit the Wind* starring Kirk Douglas and Jason Robards in the key roles.

After *Inherit the Wind*, Lawrence and Lee began writing their next play, *Auntie Mame,* which opened on Broadway in 1956. After reading a book of sketches written by Patrick Dennis about an eccentric and adventurous woman, the men asked for the opportunity to dramatize the book for the stage. The end result was *Auntie Mame,* a play revolving around a woman who is lively and curious and lives life to the fullest. Mame gives numerous parties in her fashionable apartment on New York's Beekman Place, shuttles between making a living, touring the world with her new husband, a southern gentleman, and living an exciting, colorful life. Some of the play takes place during Prohibition, a time when alcoholic was outlawed in the United States. Mame disregards the law, and served alcoholic beverages at her home when it was daring and illegal to do so. During the course of the story, Mame takes in her orphaned nephew and provides him with a lively homelife and liberal education. Eighteen years later she does the same for his young son.

When *Auntie Mame* opened in New York, Wolcott Gibbs described the play in the *New Yorker* as "rich in situations whose comic effect I have no reason to suppose has been diminished by age; and the chances are that it will run forever."

"Dramatizing *Auntie Mame* was an interesting challenge, because everybody agreed on one thing: it was impossible," stated Lawrence and Lee in the introduction to the book version of the play. "It is not easy to pinpoint the lady's hypnotic fascination, but there is a fiercely familiar quality

Rosalind Russell starred in the 1956 Broadway production of *Auntie Mame*, which was adapted for the stage by Jerome Lawrence and Robert E. Lee.

about her. Something of her determination to do, be, and see everything in human experience bubbles in everyone's blood stream.

"Perhaps Mame is a symbol of this century," continued Lawrence and Lee. "From all the recent miracles of communication and mobility, a new kind of human being has emerged: the *multi-person*. And because Mame is the multi-person personified, we could no more squeeze her into a single set than a single snapshot could portray the limitless panorama of her life and adventures."

"Mame has a serious undertone," maintained Lawrence in the *Independence Reporter*. *Auntie Mame* "seems like chocolate-covered candy, but underneath it is a blast against bigotry, against living the one-track life, against prejudice. . . . It's about the dignity of the individual and not limiting yourself, a challenge to live a full and total life." Lawrence and Lee agreed that they wrote *Auntie Mame* because they "felt a need to affirm the surging force of feminism and to reinforce the precious spirit of nonconformity," Lee stated in *Writer's Digest*.

The play, starring Rosalind Russell as Mame, was considered the biggest Broadway hit since *My Fair Lady*. Its performances sold out regularly and mail orders for advance tickets often reached thirty-five thousand a day. Ten years later, Lawrence and Lee reworked the play as a musical entitled

Mame. This production, starring Angela Lansbury, was received with similar enthusiastic response as Lawrence and Lee's earlier *Auntie Mame*.

Mame was a perfect example of Lawrence and Lee's philosophy on writing plays. Even after their plays opened and their job as writers appeared to be finished, the two men never cease to look at ways to improve the productions. "We never are finished with a show until the curtain comes down on the last night of its run," Lawrence observed to Whitney Bolton in the *Morning Telegraph*. "We agreed that there was a moment in *Mame* that could be improved with a small rewrite. We sat down and wrote the new lines, took them over to the theater, told Miss Lansbury and Gene Saks, the director, about them, rehearsed them in the afternoon and the new point of view went in that night. As it turned out, it did improve the scene and the fact that *Mame* is a hit didn't deter us from making the change." Lawrence believed that "no show ever should be left alone and most particularly a hit should not. It always can stand improvement and refreshment."

It is perhaps this dedication to turning out the best product humanly possible that has made the writing partnership of Jerome Lawrence and Robert E. Lee respected and admired. Besides their enormously popular plays *Inherit the Wind*, *Auntie Mame*, and *Mame*, the duo have been responsible for other hits such as *The Gang's All Here*, *The Night Thoreau*

Spent in Jail, Jabberwock, and *First Monday in Ooctober.* Lawrence and Lee have also written entertaining screenplays, and numerous popular and enjoyable television and radio programs.

Over the years, Lawrence and Lee have unselfishly shared their ideas and philosophy on writing with others. Both men have lectured extensively and have held prestigious teaching positions, including professorships at numerous universities in America and abroad.

Lee has taught playwriting at the University of California, Los Angeles and has lectured at colleges and universities through the world. He discussed in an interview with Russell Lee Lawrence the following thoughts he stresses to all his students. "Look beyond yourself, too," Lee suggested in *Writer's Digest.* "We live in a multidimensional world." Lee feels that a writer should look carefully at every aspect and side of a story or idea. In the beginning the story starts out simply. After much thought, the writer should explore and consider all the elements and factor and bring this knowledge into the writing material. "We start to dig," Lee continued. "We go below the surface. We probe for the why of what we see. We venture into other dimensions of space and time. This process of delving is what we hope gives substance to our work."

In his capacity as visiting professor at various universities, including New York University, the Salzburg Seminar in American Studies, and University of Southern California, Lawrence has also emphasized the importance of looking within oneself to search for truth as an essential element in creative writing. "Dig out the lies, the deceptions, sandpaper through the false fronts, the fake gilt, the flashy window dressing," Lawrence recounted in *Writer's Digest.* "Use your own senses and sensitivity as a sensor (never as a censor) in this digging. But be careful not to be entirely negative. Ask yourself: What makes me laugh? What gives me goose bumps? What makes me vomit? What makes me want to hug somebody? What makes me want to slug him? What makes my hair stand on end? What gives me hope that the world will still be around at the turn to the 21st century and even the 22nd? Vital plays are startling REVELATIONS, the uncovering of layers of self-deception, angers never spilled out, relationships never really defined, hopes never fully hoped."

In a later edition of *Writer's Digest,* Lawrence gave Christopher Meeks even more insight into the objectives he hopes to accomplish in his teaching. "In teaching, I ask students to begin by writing brief biographies of themselves," Lawrence explained. "With that, and with questioning on my part, I hope to dig out something that I (and all the rest of us in the workshop) can uncover. I try to find the gold inside that each student doesn't know is there. There are an infinite number of plays in everybody, if he or she only knows how to get to them."

Lawrence also stressed several other important rules of writing that both men work hard pass on to students. "We want to hear *your* voice," Lawrence insisted in *Writer's Digest.* "Never try to ape Arthur Miller, or copy Sam Shepard, or imitate Tennessee Williams or Samuel Beckett or Lanford Wilson or David Mamet or even us. *Be as much like yourself as possible.*

"Finding that special voice isn't always easy. Turning inward may begin as centripetal, but it must whirl out onto a page or a stage as a centrifugal force. You're not a very good playwright, and certainly not a very good human being, if your plays are entirely concerned with the lint-count of your own navel. The personal must expand until it connects with the universal."

In addition to helping students develop and tune their creative writing skills, Lawrence and Lee have also sought to assist their fellow playwrights in achieving their dream of seeing their plays produced. In 1963, the two men co-founded the American Playwrights Theater, an organization of leading dramatists intent on providing more opportunities for playwrights to showcase their material in regional and university theaters all over the United States. "There should be a platform other than Broadway," Lawrence declared in *Variety.* "This way the plays will have a chance to prove themselves before the people and not just before a few New York critics who virtually hold the key to a play's success or failure— the hardened, blase first-nighters. We thought if we had fifty subscribing communities it would work. But we have already counted 154 subscribers who will stage local productions. This gives the playwright a bigger guaranteed platform than a play opening in New York, without sacrificing any earning potential."

"We have done all we can to encourage truly national and international theatre, not confined to a few blocks of real estate in Manhattan or London's West End," reflected Lawrence in *Contemporary Dramatists.* "Thus, we have sought to promote the growth of regional and university theatres through the formation of American Playwrights Theatre, to bring new and vital and pertinent works to all of America and all of the world."

While the bulk of their writing projects have been done as a team, Lawrence and Lee have occasionally worked independently of each other. For example, some of Lawrence's solo literary creations included *Oscar the Ostrich,* a book for children, the play *Live Spelled Backwards: A Moral Immorality Play,* and a critically acclaimed book entitled *Actor: The Life and Times of Paul Muni.* Several of Lee's successful independent ventures include the book *Television: The Revolution,* as well as *Ten Days That Shook the World,* a play produced in Los Angeles, and *Sounding Brass,* a drama. "We write prose separately, we write books separately and occasionally plays, but Bob and I do most of our plays together," Lawrence explained in the *Independence Reporter.*

As witnessed by their great success, Lawrence and Lee have formed a professional and personal bond built on mutual respect and admiration for each other's ability. Over the years they spent as a writing team, Lawrence and Lee have described their partnership numerous times. In an in-depth article published in *Theatre Arts,* they wrote about their feelings concerning their collaboration. "The theatre is our most gregarious art form. Creating for the theatre, as well as attending it, is a basically *social* adventure. And it is enriched by collaboration.

"We belong to the peripatetic school of playwriting. Good plays are basically good conversation. We *converse* a play. We talk about it for months, even years, before beginning the actual writing. During this time we play Boswell [a Scottish lawyer and biographer famous taking detailed notes] to each other, taking copious and usually disorganized notes. Often we discover that an attractive idea does not have the substance for an evening in the theatre. Most of the failures of responsible dramatists are plays that should not have been written. Vast sums of energy and money, major portions of creative lifetimes, have been squandered because an author followed his unbridled fancy. Counsel with a conscientious

Cover from the paperback edition of Lawrence and Lee's popular play examining individual freedom.

partner might have eliminated this waste, or turned the energy into effective channels.

"Years of working together have diluted the contentious acid of proprietorship. After hours of polishing a scene, neither of us can say who wrote a particular line. Only when the partners can lose themselves in mutual craftsmanship is a collaboration worth while.

"A bonafide partnership provides a permanent two-way street for the exchange of opinion; it elevates counsel to the dignity and responsibility of coauthorship. All of our own conversations are private; we rarely discuss our ideas with outsiders before the actual writing, for they would be, in a sense, *performed*. We would find ourselves responding to the reactions of an irresponsible and often prejudiced audience."

Commenting on their contribution of American theatre as playwrights in *Contemporary Dramatists*, Lawrence and Lee remarked: "In our plays we have hoped to mirror and illuminate the problems of the moment—but we have attempted to grapple with universal themes, even in our comedies. We have tried for a blend between the dramatic and the entertaining: our most serious works are always leavened with laughter (*Inherit the Wind* is an example) and our seemingly frivolous comedies (*Auntie Mame, Mame, Jabberwock*) have sub-texts which we hope say something important for the contemporary world."

WORKS CITED:

Bolton, Whitney, "Lawrence and Lee—Long Lasting Team," *Morning Telegraph,* October 25, 1966.

"Dramatist-Professors Spark Much New U.S. Writing; Ohio State's Broadway Seminars," *Variety,* March 26, 1969, pp. 1, 95.

Fields, Sidney, "Has Pen, Will Travel," *Daily News,* November 11, 1966.

Gibbs, Wolcott, *New Yorker,* November 10, 1956.

High, Georgia, "Lawrence Talks About His 'Good Friend,'" *Independence Reporter,* April 19, 1983, p. 2.

Jampel, Dave, "U.S. Theatre Must Be International In Jet Age," *Variety,* May 13, 1964, pp. 63-64.

Kirkpatrick, D. L., editor, *Contemporary Dramatists,* St. James Press, 1988, pp. 314-318.

Lawrence, Jerome, editor, *Off Mike: Radio Writing by the Nation's Top Radio Writers,* Essential Books, 1944, p. 6.

Lawrence, Jerome, Commencement Address on receiving the Degree of Doctor of Literature from Fairleigh University," Teaneck, New Jersey, June 8, 1968.

Lawrence, Jerome, "Discovering Your Playwriting Voice," *Writer's Digest,* November, 1989, pp. 31-33.

Lawrence, Jerome, Response to questionnaire of the California Educational Theatre Association.

Lawrence, Jerome, and Robert E. Lee, *Inherit the Wind,* Random House, 1955, introduction.

Lawrence, Jerome, and Robert E. Lee, "The Genesis and Exodus of the Play," *Theatre Arts,* August, 1957, pp. 33, 94.

Lawrence, Jerome, and Robert E. Lee, *Auntie Mame,* Vanguard, 1957, introduction.

Lawrence, Jerome, and Robert E. Lee, "Which One Can't Spell?," *Theatre Arts,* June, 1958, pp. 63-65.

Lawrence, Russell Lee, "An Exclusive Interview with Playwrights Jerome Lawrence, Robert E. Lee," *Writer's Digest,* January, 1967, pp. 21-23.

Lee, Robert E., "The Only Playwriting Tools You'll Ever Need," *Writer's Digest,* May, 1989, pp. 34-36.

Life, May 9, 1955.

Meeks, Christopher, "The Greatest Sport in the World," *Writer's Digest,* May, 1986, pp. 31-36.

Newsweek, May 2, 1955.

Schier, Ernest, "It Takes Two to Write One Like 'Mame'," *Evening Bulletin,* July 18, 1968.

Smith, Allen, "Jerome Lawrence Explains How to Dramatize a Historical Event," *Independence Daily Reporter,* April 19, 1983, p. 1.

FOR MORE INFORMATION SEE:

PERIODICALS

Cue, February 15, 1969.

Chicago Sunday Times, February 14, 1971.

Dallas Morning News, July 18, 1966.

Morning Telegraph, July 27, 1970; July 7, 1971.

Newsweek, October 22, 1945.

New York, February 24, 1969; October 16, 1978; March 21, 1988.

New Yorker, June 10, 1961.

New York Times, April 22, 1955; October 18, 1970; December 23, 1970; October 13, 1985; February 1, 1987.

Time, January 11, 1960; November 3, 1975.

Theatre Arts, July, 1955; July, 1957; October, 1959.

TV Showpeople, May, 1975.

Variety, October 28, 1959; March 15, 1967; January 1, 1969; February 12, 1969; May 11, 1988.

Washington Post, October 30, 1970.
Women's Wear Daily, November 26, 1974.
Writer's Digest, January, 1967.

*   *   *

LEE, Robert E(dwin) 1918-

PERSONAL: Born October 15, 1918, in Elyria, OH; son of Claire Melvin (an engineer) and Elvira (a teacher; maiden name, Taft) Lee; married Janet Waldo (an actress), March 29, 1948; children: Jonathan Barlow, Lucy Virginia. *Education:* Attended Northwestern University, 1934, Ohio Wesleyan University, 1935-37, Western Reserve University (now Case Western Reserve University), 1938, and Drake University, 1943-44. *Politics:* Democrat. *Religion:* Congregationalist.

ADDRESSES: Home—15725 Royal Oak Rd., Encino, CA.

CAREER: Perkins Observatory, Delaware, OH, observer and technician, 1936-37; WHK-WCLE, Cleveland, OH, director, 1937-42, became director of Hollywood, CA office; Lawrence & Lee, New York, NY and Los Angeles, CA, playwright and director in partnership with Jerome Lawrence, 1942—; vice-president, 1955—. Producer of radio and television program, "Favorite Story," 1946-54; Pasadena Playhouse College of Theatre Arts, Pasadena, CA, professor of playwrighting, 1962-63; University of California, Los Angeles, lecturer in theatre arts, 1967—; playwright. Lecturer at colleges and universities throughout the world. Member of board of trustees and co-founder, Margo Jones Award, Inc., 1960—; co-founder and member of board of governors of American Playwrights Theatre, 1963—. *Military service:* U.S. Army Air Forces, 1942-45; co-founder of Armed Forces Radio Service.

MEMBER: Dramatists Guild, Writers Guild of America (West), Academy of Motion Picture Arts and Sciences, National Academy of Television Arts and Sciences, Broadcasting and Film Commission, National Council of Churches (member of broadcasting and film commission, 1962-72), The Players, Alumni Association of Ohio Wesleyan University (president, 1963-64), Theta Alpha Phi.

AWARDS, HONORS: New York Press Club Award, 1942; Peabody Award, 1948, for United National radio series; *Radio-TV Life* awards, 1948, 1952; *Radio-TV Mirror* awards, 1952, 1953; Donaldson Award, Outer Circle Award, and *Variety's* New York Drama Critics Poll, all 1955, and London Critics Award for best foreign play, 1960, all for *Inherit the Wind;* "Tony" Awards, 1955 and 1966; D. Litt., Ohio Wesleyan University, 1962; honorary M.A. in theatre, Pasadena College of Theatre Arts, 1963; Moss Hart Memorial Award, 1967; has also received numerous other awards and honors.

WRITINGS:

Television: The Revolution, Essential Books, 1944.

PLAYS

Ten Days That Shook the World (based on reports from Russia by John Reed), first produced in Los Angeles, 1973.

Sounding Brass (produced in New York City, 1975), Samuel French, 1976.
(With John Sinn) *Quintus* (screenplay), 1971.

PLAYS WITH JEROME LAWRENCE

Inside a Kid's Head, first published in *Radio Drama in Action,* edited by Erik Barnouw, Farrar & Rinehart, 1945.
Look Ma, I'm Dancin'!, produced on Broadway, 1948.
Inherit the Wind (three-act; produced on Broadway, 1955), Random House, 1955, acting edition, Dramatists Play Service, 1958, revised acting edition, 1963.
(Also with James Hilton) *Shangri-La* (musical; based on the book *Lost Horizon* by James Hilton; produced on Broadway, 1956), Morris Music, 1956.
Auntie Mame (two-act; based on the novel by Patrick Dennis; produced on Broadway, 1956), Vanguard, 1957, acting edition, Dramatists Play Service, 1960 (also see below).
The Gang's All Here (three-act; produced on Broadway, 1959), World Publishing, 1960, acting edition, Samuel French, 1961.
Only in America (three-act; based on book by Harry Golden; produced on Broadway, 1959), Samuel French, 1960.
A Call on Kuprin (three-act; based on the novel by Maurice Edelman; produced on Broadway, 1961), Samuel French, 1962.
Sparks Fly Upward (produced on Broadway as *Diamond Orchid,* 1965; rewritten and produced as *Sparks Fly Upward* in Dallas, 1967), Dramatists Play Service, 1967.
Mame (two-act musical comedy; based on the book *Auntie Mame* by Patrick Dennis and the play by Lawrence and Lee; music and lyrics by Jerry Herman; produced on Broadway, 1966), Random House, 1967.
Dear World (two-act musical comedy; based on Maurice Valency's adaptation of *The Madwoman of Chaillot* by Jean Giraudoux), produced on Broadway, 1969.
The Night Thoreau Spent in Jail (produced through American Playwrights Theatre in Columbus, OH, 1970), Hill & Wang, 1971.
The Imcomparable Max! (based on Max Beerbohm's *Trips beyond Reality;* produced in Abingdon, VA, 1969), Hill & Wang, 1972.
The Crocodile Smile (produced as *The Laugh Maker* in Los Angeles at Players Ring Theatre, 1952; rewritten and produced as *Turn on the Night* in Philadelphia, 1961; rewritten and produced as *The Crocodile Smile,* in Flat Rock, NC, 1970), Dramatists Play Service, 1972.
Jabberwock: Improbabilities Lived and Imagined by James Thurber in the Fictional City of Columbus, Ohio (inspired by *My Life and Hard Times* by James Thurber; produced in Columbus, OH, 1972), Samuel French, 1974.
First Monday in October (produced in Cleveland, 1975), Samuel French, 1979.

Also co-author with Lawrence of unpublished and unproduced plays, *Top of the Mark, Paris, France, Eclipse, Dilly, Some Say Ice, Houseboat in Kashmir, Short and Sweet,* and *The Angels Weep.*

ONE-ACT OPERAS; WITH JEROME LAWRENCE

Annie Laurie, Harms, Inc., 1954.
Roaring Camp, Harms, Inc., 1955.
Familiar Stranger, Harms, Inc., 1956.

SCREENPLAYS; WITH JEROME LAWRENCE

My Love Affair with the Human Race, 1962.
The New Yorkers, 1963.
Joyous Season, 1964.
The Night Thoreau Spent in Jail (based on play of same title), 1976.

First Monday in October (based on play of same title), produced by Paramount, 1982.

Also co-author with Lee of *Billion Dollar Baby, Whitewater,* and *The Clock Struck One.*

OTHER

Also writer, director, and producer with Lawrence of many television and radio programs, including "Columbia Workshop," 1942-43, "Request Performance," 1945-46, "Orson Welles Theatre," 1945-46, "Favorite Story," 1945-48, "Frank Sinatra Show," 1947, "The Railroad Hour," 1948-54, "Hallmark Hall of Fame," 1949-51, "Halls of Ivy," 1950-51, "Date with Judy," "The Unexpected," "Times Square Playhouse," "Song of Norway," "West Point," and "Lincoln: The Unwilling Warrior," as well as "Hallmark Playhouse" productions of their plays *Shangri-La* and *Inherit the Wind.* Writer and director with Lawrence of the official Army-Navy programs for D-Day, V-E Day, and V-J Day. Also writer of original lyrics and music with Lawrence for radio program, "Railroad Hour." Also writer and director with Lawrence of record album "One God," and Decca dramatic albums, "Musi-Plays." Adapter and director of record albums with Lawrence, "Rip Van Winkle," "Cask of Amontillago," "A Tale of Two Cities," and "One God." Contributor of numerous articles and short stories to *Saturday Evening Post,* and other periodicals.

ADAPTATIONS: Auntie Mame, starring Rosalind Russell, Forrest Tucker, and Roger Smith, was adapted for film by Warner Brothers, 1958; *Inherit the Wind,* starring Fredric March, Spencer Tracy, and Gene Kelly, was adapted for film by United Artists, 1960 and was adapted as a television movie starring Kirk Douglas and Jason Robards by NBC-TV, 1988; *Mame,* starring Lucille Ball, Robert Preston, and Beatrice Arthur, was adapted by Warner Brothers-Seven Arts, 1974.

WORK IN PROGRESS: A stage play, "Whisper in the Mind," in collaboration with Norman Cousins and J. Lawrence.

SIDELIGHTS: Robert E. Lee and Jerome Lawrence have collaborated on all significant dramatic works, so a joint Sidelights has been written. The essay on their lives and works appears in this volume under Lawrence's entry.

*   *   *

LEFFLAND, Ella 1931-

PERSONAL: Born November 25, 1931, in Martinez, CA; daughter of Sven William (an auto painter) and Emma (Jensen) Leffland. *Education:* San Jose State College (now University), B.A., 1953. *Hobbies and other interests:* Music, painting, swimming, travel in Europe.

ADDRESSES: Home—San Francisco, CA. *Agent*—Wallace & Sheil, 177 East 70th St., New York, NY 10021.

CAREER: Writer and painter. Lived two years in Europe. Has worked as a journalist, a salesgirl, a researcher for *Encyclopedia Britannica,* and mess girl on a Norwegian freighter. City of San Francisco, San Francisco, CA, city hall reporter for legal newspaper, 1960-63, *Sun Reporter* (black newspaper), San Francisco, copy editor, 1963-66; part-time typist in San Francisco, 1967-70.

AWARDS, HONORS: Excellence in Literature awards, Commonwealth Club of California, 1970 for *Mrs. Munck,* and 1975, for *Love Out of Season;* O'Henry award, 1977, for the short story "Last Courtesies."

WRITINGS:

Mrs. Munck, Houghton, 1970, reprinted, Graywolf, 1985.
Love Out of Season, Atheneum, 1974.
Rumors of Peace, Harper, 1979.
Last Courtesies and Other Stories (includes "The Linden Tree," "Vienna, City of My Dreams," "Last Courtesies," "Eino," "Conclusion," "The Forest," "Monsieur Scream," "The House of Angels," "Glad Offerings," "The Famous Toboggan of Laughter," "Water Music," "Inside," "The Queen of the Ivisira," and "Gorm"), Harper, 1980.
The Knight, Death and the Devil (novel based on the life of Hermann Goering), Morrow, 1990.

Contributor to *Best Short Stories of 1976;* short stories represented in *Atlantic, Harper's, New Yorker, Cosmopolitan, Epoch,* and *Quarterly Review of Literature.*

ADAPTATIONS: The film rights to *Mrs. Munck* have been sold to Diane Ladd.

WORK IN PROGRESS: Another novel.

SIDELIGHTS: Ella Leffland commented, "I started writing at about ten, and all I can say is that it's gotten harder ever since." She sent a story to the *New Yorker* when she was fourteen. After mailing submissions to them for the next fourteen years, they finally published "Eino," a story she sent in after her second trip to Europe. Now the author of five

ELLA LEFFLAND

novels and an acclaimed collection of short stories, she is known for her ability to draw insightful portraits of her characters. In some of her works, characters who seek approval from others learn to be more independent; in other stories, Leffland looks at lonely characters whose independence separates them from other people.

Leffland's interest in relationships stems from her heritage as an American raised in a Danish household. The author explained to *Contemporary Authors, New Revision Series* interviewer Jean W. Ross, "Of course, as a child I wasn't really aware of this. But now, looking back, I am. Another language was spoken at home and they always talked about home as Denmark. I thought we were on a vacation here for years! I do think that probably everyone who turns to writing or painting or anything like that has an ingredient of the outsider. . . . I think coming from a family that was different and had a different attitude toward things had a bearing on the people I wrote about, certainly."

Leffland's novel *Rumors of Peace* shows what is was like for a northern California girl to grow up during World War II. The book, says Wayne Warga of the *Los Angeles Times,* is "packed with the aches and pains of adolescence and emotionally armed by the impact of the war." Suse, a girl from a happy family, nurses her fear and rage by following daily news reports of the war and calms herself to sleep by picturing dead and wounded Japanese soldiers. This obsession is interrupted by her crush on a Jewish refugee. Her friendship with two sisters, Peggy and Helen Maria, also helps Suse to see that there is more to her life than her concern about the war.

"Suse . . . brings to life Leffland's concern with the nature of moral growth," Linda B. Osborne observes in the *Washington Post Book World.* Throughout the novel, Suse grapples with questions about war that lead her into the mysterious heart of human nature: "Why do diplomats argue with detached elegance while soldiers die? Why do some people persecute others? Why does mankind repeat the mistakes of war? Finding no answers from adults, she attacks these questions with her own curiosity, stubbornness, and anger," Osborne relates. And when the bombing of Hiroshima ends the war, Suse understands that the event "brings no resolution to the puzzle of war itself," the reviewer adds.

Like the young heroine of *Rumors of Peace,* Leffland was deeply affected by the human cost of World War II. Though the war came no nearer to her childhood home than Pearl Harbor, Leffland was terrified of dying in a bombing raid. She also felt intense loathing for the German invaders who were trampling her ancestral homeland.

Leffland was still a girl when she became fascinated with the figure of Nazi Reichsmarschall Hermann Goering, who loomed larger-than-life in stories her European relatives told about him. Her fascination with him has claimed a great deal of her attention.

"I became interested in him as a child during the second world war," Leffland explained to Ross. "The war was very real to me. Living on the West Coast, we thought we were going to be bombed. Whereas that came to seem very unlikely for most thinking people, for me it never did. The idea of being bombed, being attacked, was a very plausible thing in my mind, and the sense of threat didn't stay just with the Japanese, it spread out to the Nazis too. I saw Goering in newsreels and magazines, and I always thought of him as the archvillain. As I grew up, I continued to be interested in the

second world war and to read a good deal about it. The more I read about Goering, the more he fascinated me, because he was such a paradox.

"When I wrote *Rumors of Peace,* I went back to that period and read even more for background material. It was at that time that I knew I must write about Goering. He embodied some of the questions of evil, although I never used the word in the book. . . . He represented to me the old Germany and the new, all the traditions of the officer corps, all the strong moral values of the German middle class, which *were* very strong. And yet when he underwent the disillusionment that everybody underwent after the first world war, he was able to incorporate into himself qualities and values that didn't fit into his earlier belief—through, I think, personal weaknesses. It was a very slow process. He went step by step just as national socialism did. People didn't really believe anything was going to happen. A strong sense of ordinariness prevailed practically until the second world war. During that time Goering signed his whole soul away bit by bit to Hitler and to the movement in order to keep power. He identified so closely with Germany that he and Germany were one; he was keeping power for himself and also for Germany.

"I've never been able actually to paraphrase what it was that motivated me to write about him. That's about as close as I can come to it. I don't think I'd have written a book about Goebbels or Hitler. They didn't represent the human situation, and I felt that Goering did. . . . The more I learned about his personality, the more complex and deep it became. That would be true of anyone whose life you studied. But there was something I wasn't really aware of when I began. He had not been involved directly with the extermination camps, though a great deal is always made of his having signed the order, and I'm afraid that really means nothing. But he was very much involved in the horrendous happenings in Eastern Europe as far as starvation of the populace went. This I hadn't been aware of to that extent. I saw some of his dreadful choices in a clearer light than I had before."

On a trip to Yugoslavia in 1977, the author took a sidetrip to Germany where she visited the places where Goering had lived as a child, had risen to power, and had been condemned for war crimes. After finishing *Rumors of Peace,* she studied German and began to gather information on Goering's life and to collect the names of people who could answer her questions.

In 1979, Leffland went to Germany looking for information on Goering and was aided by his nephew, who had collected a room full of Goering materials. She was also fortunate to find a man who had once served as Goering's bodyguard; he put her in touch with others who had known the Reichsmarschall. Leffland's book makes use of many of the facts she discovered on that trip, she told *Publishers Weekly* interviewer Sonja Bolle: "The book is as truthful as I could make it. . . . But I was free to invent where there were no facts, and of course to omit or to change unimportant minor facts, because of the necessity of making a novel as balanced and believable as possible. In the course of my research, I am sure there must be things I misinterpreted or misunderstood. But I came across inaccuracies in history books, too." She also told Bolle, "I hope that my presentation of Goering shows the sides of him that are overlooked in the various biographies."

Leffland told Ross that it was very difficult to write the book. "I worked on it for eight years, plus one year of revision. . . . It was depressing, especially after I got into the second part of the book. When Goering began to deteriorate so much and

Cover of Ella Leffland's 1979 novel about a young girl's fear and confusion during World War II.

involve himself in the persecution of the Jews and all that, it was very hard to live with every page as it was being written."

Critics agree that Leffland's portrait of the creator of the Gestapo and the concentration camps is as insightful as her treatment of fictional characters. She shows that he was weak as well as powerful, and eventually lost his position as Hitler's advisor. Don G. Campbell notes in the *Los Angeles Times Book Review* that Leffland's Goering "emerges as probably the most . . . popular, and perhaps the brightest mind in that twisted inner circle of perverted talents surrounding Hitler. . . . We are left to wonder: What turns would those massive talents have taken against a different historic background?"

Leffland studied painting in college and still paints, even though writing has become her major activity. When she was still in school, "I did both with the same intensity and interest," she told Ross. "Perhaps it was simply that painting requires money: you have to buy canvasses and paints, and you have to show your painting somewhere. In those days I didn't have much money. It was certainly cheaper to use the backs of papers from my Kelly Girl jobs, and a pencil. But I don't know if that was the reason. I had some very early successes in writing. A story that was taken by the *New Yorker* when I was in my twenties really spurred me on. With painting, I didn't have that same kind of early response. As far as my interest goes, though, they remain the same."

Leffland plans to write more about people and their relationship to society. She also told Ross that writing continues to be a challenge: "When you begin, you've had no experience with

having been accepted. As you go on, you think, Oh, is this going to live up to what I've published? I think you become more of a perfectionist. I've talked to other writers about this, and they all seem to feel the same way, that it doesn't become easier even technically. It's got to be that you compare what you did in the past with what you're doing now."

WORKS CITED:

Bolle, Sonja, "Publisher's Weekly Interviews: Ella Leffland," *Publisher's Weekly,* February 2, 1990, pp. 68-69.
Campbell, Don G., "Storytellers: New in February," *Los Angeles Times Book Review,* January 21, 1990, p. 12.
Leffland, Ella, interview with Jean W. Ross in *Contemporary Authors, New Revision Series,* Volume 33, Gale, 1991.
Osborne, Linda B., "Growing Up under Fire," *Washington Post Book World,* July 29, 1979, pp. C1-C4.
Warga, Wayne, "Writer Who Practices the Right Rites," *Los Angeles Times,* October 31, 1980, p. 6.

FOR MORE INFORMATION SEE:

BOOKS

Contemporary Literary Criticism, Volume 19, Gale, 1981.
Dictionary of Literary Biography Yearbook 1984, Gale, 1985.

PERIODICALS

Chicago Tribune Book World, September 16, 1979; November 16, 1980.
Los Angeles Times Book Review, November 30, 1980; December 15, 1985.
Newsweek, November 3, 1980.
New York Times, August 10, 1970; September 5, 1974; March 14, 1990.
New York Times Book Review, October 11, 1970; July 22, 1979; August 10, 1980; October 5, 1980; January 5, 1986; February 11, 1990.
Publishers Weekly, December 1, 1989.
Tribune Books (Chicago), February 11, 1990.
Variety, December 16, 1970.
Washington Post Book World, October 19, 1980; February 25, 1990.

*   *   *

LERNER, Gerda 1920-

PERSONAL: Born April 30, 1920, in Vienna, Austria; came to U.S., 1939, naturalized citizen, 1943; daughter of Robert and Ilona (Neumann) Kronstein; married Carl Lerner (a film maker), October 6, 1941 (deceased); children: Stephanie, Daniel. *Education:* New School for Social Research, B.A., 1963; Columbia University, M.A., 1965, Ph.D., 1966. *Hobbies and other interests:* Music, gardening, backpacking.

ADDRESSES: *Office*—University of Wisconsin—Madison, Department of History, 5123 Humanities Bldg., 455 North Park St., Madison, WI 53706.

CAREER: Professional writer and translator, 1941—; New School for Social Research, New York City, lecturer and historian, 1963-65; Long Island University, Brooklyn, NY, assistant professor, 1965-67, associate professor of American history, 1967-68; Sarah Lawrence College, Bronxville, NY, member of history faculty, 1968-80, director of masters program in Women's History, 1972-76 and 78-79; University of

Wisconsin—Madison, Madison, Robinson-Edwards professor of history, 1980—, Wisconsin Alumni Research Foundation Senior Distinguished Research Professor, 1984—, and director and co-director, graduate program in Women's History, 1981-90.

Scholar in residence, Rockefeller Foundation Conference Center, Bellagio, Italy, 1975. Educational director, Summer Institute Program in Women's History, 1976 and 1979. Co-director, FIPSE grant for Promoting Black Women's History, 1980-83. Member of the Columbia University seminar in American civilization, and Seminar on Women and Society.

MEMBER: PEN, Organisation of American Historians (president, 1981-82), American Historical Association, American Association of University Women, American Studies Association, Author's League of America.

AWARDS, HONORS: National Endowment for the Humanities grants, 1976 and 1987; Ford Foundation grant, 1978-79; Guggenheim fellow, 1980-81; Educational Foundation Achievement Award, American Association of University Women, 1986; Lucretia Mott award, 1988; eight honorary degrees.

WRITINGS:

No Farewell (novel), Associated Authors (New York), 1955.

GERDA LERNER

Black Like Me (screenplay), Walter Reade Distributors, 1964.

The Grimke Sisters from South Carolina: Rebels Against Slavery, Houghton, 1967, new edition published as *The Grimke Sisters from South Carolina: Pioneers for Women's Rights and Abolition,* Schocken Books, 1967.

The Woman in American History (textbook), Addison-Wesley, 1971.

Black Women in White America: A Documentary History, Pantheon, 1972.

The Female Experience: Documents in U.S. Social History, Bobbs-Merrill, 1976, published as *The Female Experience: An American Documentary,* Macmillan, 1979.

The Majority Finds Its Past: Placing Women in History, Oxford University Press, 1979.

Teaching Women's History, American Historical Association, 1981.

A Death of One's Own, University of Wisconsin Press, 1985.

Women and History, Volume 1: *The Creation of Patriarchy,* Oxford University Press, 1986.

Author of *Women Are History: A Bibliography in the History of American Women,* 1986. Also author, with Eve Merriam, of musical, "Singing of Women," 1956. Contributor of short stories to literary magazines, and of articles and reviews to professional journals; has written numerous professional translations.

WORK IN PROGRESS: The Rise of Feminist Consciousness, Volume 2 of *Women In History.*

SIDELIGHTS: Gerda Lerner is a professor of history at the University of Wisconsin—Madison, who has written a number of important books on women and women's history. She had written short stories, novels, a screenplay, and a musical before devoting her attention to the subject of women's history. In 1972, she became one of the first American educators to found a Women's Studies program. Because she believes that every woman has a right to know the history of women, she has set out to provide information on women's lives most frequently left out of other histories.

The first history book Lerner wrote, *The Grimke Sisters of South Carolina: Rebels against Slavery,* describes the lives of two women who worked for abolition and women's rights during the 1800s. When she began to write *The Grimke Sisters,* it was a novel based on historical fact. But after she enrolled in graduate school at Columbia University, she decided to make it a historical biography.

Critics recommend Lerner's books to beginning students of women's history. Reading Lerner's *The Female Experience: An American Documentary* is the best "way . . . to begin the study of woman's past in America," Willie Lee Rose writes in the *New York Review of Books.* One can learn from the book how to place people from the past into their historical settings. Lerner's arrangements of sources and comments also teach readers how to sort out important facts from other historical details.

In her study of history at the New School for Social Research, Lerner discovered that the history of Western civilization had left the accomplishments of women largely untold. She entered the graduate program at Columbia University "to make women's history respectable," she told Catharine R. Stimpson in a *Ms.* interview. Lerner also called women's history "an absolute lifeline to self-recognition and to giving our life meaning."

Lerner's desire to make women's history available to young women has taken her far back in time. "In order to answer the questions I was interested in, I had to find out when men and women began to think that men and women are essentially different," she told Ashkor Chandrasekhar for a *New York Times Book Review* feature. The search led Lerner back to cultures in the ancient Near East. The attitude that men have a right to dominate women must have had a beginning somewhere, she points out. Therefore, it is important to find that beginning so that people can correct those ideas in their new thinking.

Looking back over women's roles in various Mesopotamian cultures in the second and third millenium B.C., Lerner traced the development of male dominance in ideas and institutions such as marriage and in places such as schools, temples, and courts of law. The first volume of her book *Women and History, The Creation of Patriarchy,* explains how women yielded some of their rights to men in exchange for protection and security. Women's own choices still determine their roles, she shows in *The Female Experience.* The book contains personal documents in which women describe the opportunites and the choices that have determined the direction of their lives.

Lerner's own life has taken many directions. The daughter of a successful businessman in Vienna, Austria, Lerner was headed for a college education. These plans were interrupted when she was put in jail six weeks before her college entrance exam. Her father had fled the country to escape Nazi executioners, and Lerner feared that her life, too, was in danger because of her participation in underground activities against the fascists. She was given reduced food rations for weeks and feared she would be taken to a concentration camp. The day after she was freed from prison, she took the exam and graduated from high school *magna cum laude.*

"My first academic career ended that day," Lerner told Stimpson. "For the next twenty years, I was an unskilled, and later a skilled worker; a housewife; and an organizer. I always was a writer as well. My first job before I left Europe was as a governess for a Swiss family. Then, in America, I did typical women's jobs: office work, waitress, salesgirl. It was a great triumph when I worked my way up to being an X-ray technician."

Lerner has never forgotten those weeks in jail, or the experience of preparing herself for death. She feels these experiences gave her a strength that some American social activists seem to lack. She told Stimpson, "I think most younger people don't really . . . know what it's like to keep something going when there's no hope, and to keep hope going when there's no hope, and to know that you can be defeated and yet prevail."

"That's something black people know," Lerner continued. "I guess that's what attracted me to trying to understand black women and their enormous strength. Like many immigrants, I felt like an outsider to America for a long time. In a way, I could relate more closely to the black experience than to the mainstream." Lerner's 1972 book *Black Women in White America: A Documentary History* was one of the first books to provide first-hand information about the experiences of black women in the United States. Lerner's selection of black women's letters, manuscripts, speeches, and other documents presents in detail the experiences of black women since 1830.

The documents collected here prove that many racial stereotypes are not accurate. More importantly, according to some critics, they show black women fighting not only for their civil rights, but also for their rights as women. For example, *Library Journal* contributor Janet G. Polacheck feels that *Black Women in White America* should be read by everyone who is interested in black culture and the women's rights movement. "However much this may be a book for blacks it is even more a book for whites," Alden Whitman notes in a *Book World* review. He feels that whites need to become familiar with the experience of black Americans if they are to work with them to build a just and racially diverse society. Much about the nature of black experience is in *Black Women in White America,* he observes.

Breaking into print in America was not easy for Lerner. Her first book, a novel set in Austria, was written in English, a language new to Lerner. Writing the novel took so long, she told Stimpson, "that the subject—the coming of fascism—was unpopular by the time I finished it." Only after it was printed in German in Austria did an American publisher agree to print it in English. Her second novel was about racial strife in New York City. Appearing several years before the civil rights movement became a national issue, the novel was never published.

Lerner believes that women writing today should leave a record of their experiences—especially those experiences not likely to be included in the newspapers or the formal histories of our times. To this category of writing, Lerner has herself contributed *A Death of One's Own,* the story of her husband's fight against cancer and his death in 1973.

In a *Ms.* magazine review, Joan Kron compares the book to a tapestry made from memories of her husband Carl's illness, diary entries, and memories from her life in Austria. "In the weaving," says Kron, "it is revealed that helping Carl to die well was not an isolated act but an inherited code of conduct. . . . It was something Gerda's aunt did for her grandmother; her father did for her mother; her uncle did for another aunt; an unbroken chain of people who do not abandon people." Kron values the book as an important source for people who feel that dying loved ones should not be hidden away in hospitals or nursing homes. "Gerda Lerner's book was not written as a how-to-book, but because of its maturity, because of its total honesty about her positive and, yes, her *negative* feelings, it can be a how-to book for those who share the Lerners' belief about one's right to die 'appropriately.'"

Lerner sees herself as part of another unbroken chain that connects women of the past to women of the future through their written history. Her inspiration, she told Stimpson, came from work by women of the 1920s who determined to preserve their history. "I hooked into this feminist inheritance," Lerner said. "I trust that we will leave something equally important to the generation that comes after us."

WORKS CITED:

Chandrasekhar, Ashok, "The Roots of Hierarchy," *New York Times Book Review,* April 20, 1986, p. 12.
Kron, Joan, "Death as a Pact of Life," *Ms.,* October, 1978, p. 28.
Polacheck, Janet G., review of *Black Women in White America, Library Journal,* May 1, 1972, p. 1696.

Rose, Willie Lee, "The Emergence of American Women," *New York Review of Books,* September 15, 1977, pp. 31-32.

Stimpson, Catharine R., "Gerda Lerner on the Future of Our Past," *Ms.,* September, 1981, pp. 51-52, 93-95.

Whitman, Alden, review of *Black Women in White America, Book World,* April 16, 1972, p. 12.

FOR MORE INFORMATION SEE:

BOOKS

American Women Writers, Volume 2, Ungar, 1980.

PERIODICALS

America, December 13, 1986.
Choice, October, 1986.
Chronicle of Higher Education, June 8, 1981.
Los Angeles Times Book Review, November 17, 1985.
Ms., September, 1980.
New York Review of Books, September 15, 1977.
New York Times Book Review, March 20, 1977; April 20, 1986.
Washington Post Book World, August 13, 1978; January 27, 1980; February 15, 1981.
Women's Review of Books, January, 1987.
Yale Review, spring, 1982.

—Sketch by Marilyn K. Basel

*   *   *

LEROUX, Gaston 1868-1927

PERSONAL: Born May 6, 1868, in Paris, France; died of uraemia (due to malfunctioning kidneys) after a long illness, April 16 (some sources say April 15), 1927, in Nice, France; son of shop owners. *Education:* Schooled in Normandy, France; studied law in Paris.

CAREER: French lawyer, journalist, drama critic, and author. Worked as a clerk for a law firm. Theater critic and court reporter for *L'Echo de Paris,* beginning c. 1890; roving reporter and interviewer for *L'Echo de Paris* and *Le Matin,* 1892-1907; author, 1907-27.

AWARDS, HONORS: Mysteries of a Great City was a Queen's Quorum selection.

WRITINGS:

La maison des juges: Piece en trois actes (drama), Imprimerie de l'Illustration, 1906.

Le mystere de la chambre jaune (novel), P. Lafitte, 1908, published as *The Mystery of the Yellow Room,* Brentano's, 1908, Remploy (London), 1978.

The Perfume of the Lady in Black (originally published as *Le parfum de la dame en noir,* 1908), Brentano's, 1909, Buccaneer, 1975.

The Double Life, J. E. Kearney, 1909.

Le fantome de l'Opera, P. Lafitte, 1910, published as *The Phantom of the Opera,* Bobbs-Merrill, 1911, abridged edition, with foreword by Peter Haining, Dorset Press, 1985.

Le fauteuil hante (novel), P. Lafitte, 1911, published as *The Haunted Chair,* Dutton, 1931.

L'homme qui a vu le diable: Piece en deux actes (drama), published in *L'Illustration theatrale,* August 24, 1912.

M. GASTON LEROUX

The Man with the Black Feather, translation by Edgar Jepson, Small, Maynard & Co., 1912.

Aventures extraordinaires de Joseph Rouletabille, reporter, Chatenet, 1912.

L'epouse de soleil (novel), P. Lafitte, 1913, published as *The Bride of the Sun,* McBride, Nast & Co., 1915, edited by R. Reginald and Douglas Melville, Ayer, 1978.

Rouletabille chez le tsar, P. Lafitte, 1913.

The Secret of the Night: Further Adventures of Rouletabille, Macaulay, 1914, Buccaneer, 1975.

(With Pierre Wolff) *Le lys,* A. Fayard, 1915.

Cheri-Bibi and Cecily (originally published as *Cheri-Bibi et Cecily,* 1916), translation by Hannaford Bennett, T. W. Laurie, 1923, published as *Missing Men: The Return of Cheri-Bibi,* Macaulay, 1923.

(With Lucien Camille) *Alsace: Piece en trois actes* (drama), P. Lafitte, 1916.

Le chateau noir (novel), P. Lafitte, 1916.

Les etranges noces de Rouletabille, P. Lafitte, 1916.

L'homme qui revient de loin, P. Lafitte, 1917.

Confitou, P. Lafitte, 1917.

Jalousie: Conte americain, Imprimerie Nouvelle, 1919.

Le capitaine Hyx, P. Lafitte, 1920.

Premieres aventures de Cheri-Bibi, P. Lafitte, 1921.

Nouvelles aventures de Cheri-Bibi, P. Lafitte, 1921.

Le coeur cambriole: Un histoire epouvantable, La hache d'or (novel), P. Lafitte, 1922, published as *The Burgled Heart,* translation by Hannaford Bennett, J. Long, 1925, published as *The New Terror,* Macaulay, 1926.

Le crime de Rouletabille (novel), P. Lafitte, 1922.

Rouletabille chez les Bohemiens, P. Lafitte, 1923.

Wolves of the Sea, Macaulay, 1923.

Tue-la-mort, P. Lafitte, 1923.

Le sept de trefle, P. Lafitte, 1923.

The Dark Road: Further Adventures of Cheri-Bibi, Macaulay, 1924.

La poupee sanglante: Roman d'aventures et de mystere (novel), J. Tallandier, 1924, translation published as *The Kiss That Killed,* Macaulay, 1934.

La machine a asassiner: Roman d'aventures et de mystere (novel), J. Tallandier, 1924, published as *The Machine to Kill,* Macaulay, 1935.

The Dancing Girl, J. Long, 1925.

La farouche aventure; ou, La cocquette punie (novel; English translation published as *The Adventures of a Coquette,* 1926), Gallimard, 1925.

The Slave Bangle, translation by Hannaford Bennett, J. Long, 1926, published as *The Phantom Clue,* Macaulay, 1926.

The Sleuth Hound, translation by Hannaford Bennett, J. Long, 1926, published as *The Octopus of Paris,* Macaulay, 1927.

Mister Flow (novel), Baudiniere, 1927, published as *The Man of a Hundred Faces,* Macaulay, 1930.

The Son of Three Fathers, translation by Hannaford Bennett, J. Long, 1927, Macaulay, 1928.

L'Agonie de la Russie blanche, edited by Mme. G. Leroux, Hachette, 1928.

The New Idol, translation by Hannaford Bennett, J. Long, 1928.

The Masked Man, translation by Hannaford Bennett, Macaulay, 1929.

Lady Helena; or, The Mysterious Lady, E. P. Dutton, 1931.

(With Stanislas Andre Steeman) *Les fils de Balaoo,* Librairie des Champs-Elysees, 1937.

Les Mohicans de Babel, Humanoides Associes (Paris), 1977.

Le roi mystere, Baudiniere, 1977.

Un homme dans la nuit, Presses de la Renaissance, 1977.

La reine du Sabbat, Livre de Poche, 1979.

La double vie de Theophraste Longuet, Presses de la Renaissance, 1980.

Pouloulou: Roman inedit, Michel Lafon, 1990.

Also author of *Balaoo,* 1909, *Cheri-Bibi,* 1914, *The Man Who Came Back from the Dead,* 1916, *Cheri-Bibi, Mystery Man,* 1916, *Les tenebreuses,* and *La mansarde en or.*

COLLECTIONS

Cheri-Bibi (includes *Les cages flottantes, Cheri-Bibi et Cecily, Palas et Cheri-Bibi: Fatalitas!, Le coup d'etat de Cheri-Bibi*), four volumes, R. Laffont, 1961.

Romans fantastiques, Volume 1: *Le fantome de l'Opera,* R. Laffont, 1961, Volume 2: *L'homme qui revient de loin* and *Le fauteuil hante,* Cercle du Bibliophile, 1970, Volume 3: *L'homme qui a vu le diable, Le coeur cambriole* and *La double vie de Theophraste Longuet,* Cercle du Bibliophile, 1970.

Rouletabille (includes *Le mystere de la chambre jaune, Le parfum de la dame en noir, Rouletabille chez le tsar, Le chateau noir, Les etranges noces de Rouletabille, Rouletabille chez les Bohemiens, Rouletabille chez Krupp: Le crime de Rouletabille*), seven volumes, Cercle du Bibliophile, 1969.

Romans d'aventures, Volume 1: *Mister Flow* and *Une histoire epouvantable,* Volume 2: *Les Mohicans de Babel,* Volume 3: *La reine du Sabbat,* Volume 4: *Le roi mystere,* Volume 5: *Balaoo,* Cercle du Bibliophile, 1970.

The Gaston Leroux Bedside Companion: Weird Stories by the Author of "The Phantom of the Opera" (includes "A Terrible Tale," "The Mystery of the Four Husbands," "The Inn of Terror," "The Woman with the Velvet Collar," "The Crime on Christmas Night," "The Letters of Fire," "The Gold Axe," "The Waxwork Museum," and "The Real Opera Ghost"), edited by Peter Haining, Gollancz, 1980.

Oeuvres (includes *Le fantome de l'Opera, La reine du sabbat, Les tenebreuses,* and *La mansarde en or*), Laffont (Paris), 1984.

Also author of story collections *The Count's Chauffeur,* 1907, *The Lady in the Car,* 1909, *"Cinders" of Harry Street,* 1916, *The Secret Telephone,* 1920, *Mysteries of a Great City,* 1920, and *The Crimes Club,* 1927. Author of stories including "The Inn of Terror," "The Woman With the Velvet Collar," and "In Letters of Fire," most having been written in the early 1900s and appeared in translation in *Weird Tales* magazine.

ADAPTATIONS:

MOTION PICTURES

The Mystery of the Yellow Room, starring Lorin Baker, Realart, 1919.

The Phantom of the Opera, starring Lon Chaney, Mary Philbin and Norman Kerry, directed by Rupert Julian, Universal, 1925.

Phantom in Paradise (based on character Cheri-Bibi), starring John Gilbert, Leila Hyams, Lewis Stone, Jean Hersholt, and C. Aubrey Smith, directed by John Robinson, M.G.M., 1931.

The Phantom of the Opera, starring Claude Rains and Nelson Eddy, and Suzanna Foster, directed by Arthur Lubin, Universal, 1943.

The Phantom of the Opera, starring Herbert Lom, Heather Sears, Edward de Souza and Michael Gough, directed by Terence Fisher, Hammer (British), 1962.

Phantom of the Paradise, starring William Finley, directed by Brian de Palma, Twentieth Century-Fox, 1974.

The Phantom of the Opera, starring Robert Englund, directed by Dwight H. Little, 21st Century Productions, 1989.

PLAYS

The Mystery of the Yellow Room, produced in 1912.

The Phantom of the Opera (adapted by Andrew Lloyd Webber and Richard Stilgoe, lyrics by Charles Hart and Stilgoe, starring Michael Crawford and Sarah Brightman), produced at Her Majesty's Theatre, London, October 6, 1986, produced at Majestic Theater, N.Y., January 26, 1988.

The Mystery of the Yellow Room and *The Phantom of the Opera* have both been recorded on audiocassettes. *The Phantom of the Opera* has also appeared as a television movie and in comic book form.

SIDELIGHTS: Gaston Leroux was born on **May 6, 1868,** the only child of well-to-do shop owners. He acquired a taste for literature at an early age. Although sent to Paris to study law, he preferred to spend his time writing stories and verse; his first published work consisted of a sequence of sonnets about Parisian actresses. At the age of twenty-one, he inherited nearly one million francs from his father, but Parisian night life— drinking and gambling—quickly reduced his inheritance. Within six months he was penniless, and turned to his writing as a means of support. He became a court reporter on the staff of *L'Echo de Paris,* combining his legal training with his writing skills.

1892. Tired of simply reporting court cases, Leroux launched his own career as an investigative reporter by trying to solve a case before the verdict came in. "He was convinced the accused man was innocent, and the reason he was being kept under such tight security before his court appearance in the town of Bourges was to protect some incompetent officials," explains Peter Haining in his introduction to the Dorset Press edition of *The Phantom of the Opera.* Passing himself off as a prison inspector, Leroux obtained access to the prisoner and interviewed him. Haining quotes from a 1925 interview with Leroux: "'I got my paper to publish a full report which completely exonerated the prisoner—and as a result the Prefect of Police was disgraced and the Prison Director was sent packing! Curiously, it was my newspaper colleagues who were the most annoyed. I had interviewed an accused man in prison before his trial—it was something that had never been heard of before in law reporting!'"

This case established Leroux's reputation as a reporter, and led to many other interviews with influential figures, including the Duc d'Orleans, pretender to the throne of France, and the Swedish antarctic explorer Nils Nordenskjold. It also led to a job with *Le Matin,* an important daily newspaper, and assignment as a roving reporter. Over the next fifteen years, Leroux became famous for his adventurous reporting from crisis spots throughout Europe and in Africa and Asia. A master of disguise, he covered the Russian Revolution of 1905 and posed as an Arab while reporting on European imperialism in Morocco—an assignment that could have cost him his life.

These escapades gained Leroux a reputation as a reporter "who could get a story out of even the most unlikely situation," says Haining. For example, in an attempt to interview British Colonial Secretary Joseph Chamberlain during the Boer War, Leroux slipped into the minister's private study without permission. When he was discovered by a secretary and ejected, Leroux composed an article on "How I Failed to See Chamberlain," which, according to Haining, "delighted French readers and was widely hailed as 'a masterpiece of good humour and wit.'" Eventually, however, Leroux tired of the travelling and hazards that his journalism demanded, and turned to writing fiction and plays. Much of his work drew on his experiences as a reporter, and "right from the start," declares Haining, "he proved himself an ingenious storyteller with a flair for pace and excitement."

1908. Leroux's first success as a novelist came with the publication of *The Mystery of the Yellow Room,* which introduced his amateur detective hero, Joseph Rouletabille. Like Leroux himself, Rouletabille is a reporter whose reasoning ability far outpaces that of the dull, regular police. With his assistant Sainclair, Rouletabille solves one of the first "locked-room" mysteries, in which a crime is committed in a place no one could have entered or left. Leroux is also credited with introducing to the genre the plot device of the "least-likely person" as the criminal.

The Mystery of the Yellow Room was successfully translated into English and established Leroux as a major figure in the field of mystery writing. "*The Mystery of the Yellow Room,*" wrote Howard Haycraft in 1941 in his *Murder for Pleasure,* "is generally recognized, on the strength of its central puzzle, as one of the classic examples of the genre. For sheer plot manipulation and ratiocination—no simpler word will describe the quality of its Gallic logic—it has seldom been surpassed. It remains, after a generation of imitation, the most brilliant of all 'locked room' novels."

1909. The sequel to the *Mystery of the Yellow Room*—*The Perfume of the Lady in Black*—featured the second appearance of Rouletabille and confirmed his reputation as an amateur sleuth who out-thought professional detectives. Although popular, *The Perfume of the Lady in Black* did not meet with the acclaim that had greeted *The Mystery of the Yellow Room.* Rupert Ranney, a contemporary reviewer, wrote in *The Bookman:* "*The Perfume of the Lady in Black* is no better than its predecessor, and it is no worse, which implies neither high praise nor serious disparagement. The faults and merits of one book are the faults and merits of the other." Other adventures of Rouletabille failed to duplicate the success of the first volume.

1910. Leroux's most famous work, *Le fantome de l'Opera,* or *The Phantom of the Opera,* was serialized in France and Britain, then published as a novel in 1911. It was based in part on actual events. Leroux had visited the Paris Opera House several times while working as a drama critic and was familiar with its architecture and history. Begun in 1861, the Opera was finished in 1879, and enclosed seventeen stories with mazes of corridors and stairways, private suites for then-Emperor Napoleon III, and stables for horses, as well as an underground lake on the lowest level. There were dressing rooms for five hundred performers and storage cellars for costumes. There were also rumors of some sort of ghost or mysterious being who haunted the depths of the building and who had been responsible for several mysterious deaths.

Universal Studios advertisement for the first film production of Leroux's enduring tale, starring Lon Chaney.

Most frightening of all, the main chandelier had fallen upon the audience in 1896, a detail Leroux worked into his novel.

Influenced by Victor Hugo's *Hunchback of Notre Dame,* Leroux created for his book a horribly disfigured central character, named Erik. Erik is a wonderful musician with a beautiful voice, but he is so ugly that from birth his mother required him to wear a mask. He builds a home for himself on the underground lake beneath the Opera and prowls its corridors unseen, leaving notes signed "O.G." (for Opera Ghost) instructing the management on how the theater is to be run.

To his underground residence the Phantom brings young Christine Daae, a lovely understudy he has fallen in love with, and whose career he is advancing. But Christine is in love with Raoul, a young nobleman she has known since she was a child, and is terrified of the Ghost. Eventually, however, she begins to understand Erik's longing, and comes to pity him. In Leroux's final scenes, writes Drake Douglas in *Horror!,* "when Erik speaks of the wonder of being looked upon without fear by a beautiful woman, of actually feeling the warmth of a woman's kiss on his horrible face, surely then we cannot feel too much fear and hatred for this monster who had the misfortune to be born with a great heart and a terrible ugliness."

1912. A dramatized version of *The Mystery of the Yellow Room* was made into films in France and America. The American version starred Lorin Baker.

1916-1925. Leroux wrote a series of detective novels about his new hero, a magician named Cheri-Bibi. He also wrote a number of gruesome short stories which were published after his death in *Weird Tales.* Among his novels of this period were *The Man Who Came Back from the Dead, The Bride of the Sun* and *The Man of a Hundred Faces.*

1925. The first of several movie versions of *The Phantom of the Opera* was produced in a silent film version. Comedian Lon Chaney Sr.— "The Man of a Thousand Faces," best known today for his performances in films such as *The Hunchback of Notre Dame* and *The Unholy Three*—was selected for the title role, and his performance was noted by *New York Times* film critic Mordaunt Hall as one of the highlights of the piece. "It is a role suited to [Chaney's] liking," Hall wrote, "and one which he handles with a certain skill, a little exaggerated at times, but none the less compelling. One has to remember that this is a fantastic tale and therefore strange things can happen; and they do."

Now regarded as a silent classic, Chaney's *Phantom* is probably the best-known version of Leroux's story. It has terrified audiences for over fifty years with its grotesque effects, especially Chaney's horrifically made-up face. In the climactic scene where Christine steals the mask from the Phantom's face and faints at the sight of him, wrote Hall, "a woman behind us stifled a scream. . . . [The Phantom] is hollow-eyed, with a turned-up nose which has long nostrils. His teeth are long and separated and his forehead is high. There is no doubt that he is a repellant sight."

Chaney achieved his character's "Death's Head" effect without a mask, using only makeup. "It was the use of paints in the right shades and the right places—not the obvious parts of the face—which gave the complete illusion of horror," Haining quotes the actor. "My experiments as a stage manager, which were wide and varied before I jumped into films, taught me much about lighting effects on the actor's face and

the minor tricks of deception. These I have been able to use in achieving weird results on the screen. I've never worn a mask in my life, save at Halloween parties. It's all a matter of combining paints and lights to form the right illusion."

April 16, 1927. Leroux died in Nice, France, after a two year lingering illness. It is unclear whether he was able to see the film that immortalized his novel.

1931. M.G.M. released a film titled "Phantom in Paradise" about the magician Cheri-Bibi, another of Leroux's heroes, who is wrongly accused of murder and must assume the murderer's identity to prove his own innocence. The film starred John Gilbert.

1943. A second *Phantom* film, starring Claude Rains and Nelson Eddy, was released. In this version, the Phantom is actually the father of the understudy and manipulates her career from afar. But, when a concerto he has written is stolen, he kills the thief, who had thrown acid at him in a dispute over the concerto. Disfigured and disillusioned, he goes to extreme lengths to assure his daughter's success, including dropping the chandelier on the audience. Claude Rains played the Opera Ghost, and Nelson Eddy was the girl's lover and co-star.

1962. Another film version of the Phantom story was located in England and starred Herbert Lom as the Phantom. His most poignant scene was a closeup of him watching his stolen concerto being performed while a tear rolled down his masked face.

1974. Brian de Palma directed a fourth movie version, this one set in a rock-and-roll theater in New York. The film starred William Finley.

October 6, 1986. Andrew Lloyd Webber's musical, *The Phantom of the Opera,* opened at Her Majesty's Theatre in London. Directed by Harold Prince and choreographed by Gillian Lynne, the production starred Michael Crawford—a comedian, as Chaney was—and Sarah Brightman, then Lloyd Webber's wife. Lloyd Webber said of his work: "You can't categorize music, and anyone who tries is playing with fire. I don't think any audience of mine really knows what they're expecting to see. A lot of people came to 'Phantom' in London in the first two or three previews there, thinking the combination of Andrew Lloyd Webber, 'Phantom of the Opera' and comedy actor Michael Crawford was going to mean an evening of Crawford swinging around on ropes, like an up-market version of 'The Prisoner of Zenda.' Or they thought it would be very campy and very funny. Instead they got my most mainstream romantic score."

"Funnily enough," Lloyd Webber continued, "the audience was right-footed by it pretty quickly; they took to it at once. The critics, however, were a little bit unprepared and not quite certain what it was. One or two of the reviews made inane comments about how I didn't go into the murky depths of 'Sweeney Todd.' Well, I wasn't writing 'Sweeney Todd,' I was writing a mainstream romantic musical based on what I found in the book."

January 26, 1988. When Lloyd Webber brought his show to the Majestic Theater in New York it quickly sold out. Eighteen million tickets were sold in advance of the opening, the highest in the history of the American musical theater. *Phantom* opened amid controversy: Sarah Brightman was not a member of Actor's Equity, the actor's union. The union wanted to replace Brightman with an American actress.

Chaney menaces a trembling Mary Philbin in the 1925 silent classic.

Lloyd Webber, on the other hand, insisted that she be allowed to perform the part of Christine Daae; he had written it for her, and would not permit the play to open in New York unless she was performing. Actor's Equity backed down; Brightman was reinstated and allowed to perform in New York.

Lloyd Webber's romantic version of *The Phantom of the Opera* has brought Leroux's story before thousands of theater-goers in the years since its opening, and its popularity shows no sign of abating. Recently a new film starring Robert Englund—Freddy Krueger of the *Nightmare on Elm Street* series of horror films—was released in the United States. The figure of the Phantom himself has become a staple of popular culture. Whether through Lloyd Webber's theatrical extravaganza or Lon Chaney's menacing performance, Leroux's Phantom seems destined for immortality.

WORKS CITED:

Authors and Artists for Young Adults, Volume 1, Gale, 1989, pp. 142-44.
Douglas, Drake, *Horror!,* Collier Books, 1969, pp. 196-220.
Haining, Peter, "Foreword" to *The Phantom of the Opera,* Dorset Press, 1985, pp. 7-24.
Hall, Mordaunt, "A Fantastic Melodrama," *New York Times,* September 7, 1925, p. 274.
Haycraft, Howard, "The Continental Detective Story," *Murder for Pleasure: The Life and Times of the Detective Story,* Appleton-Century, 1941, pp. 103-11.
Ranney, Rupert, *The Bookman,* April, 1909, pp. 199-200.

FOR MORE INFORMATION SEE:

BOOKS

Ashley, Mike, *Who's Who in Horror and Fantasy Fiction,* Taplinger, 1977.
Contemporary Authors, Volume 108, Gale, 1983.
Keating, H. R. F., *Whodunit?,* Van Nostrand Reinhold, 1982.
Kunitz, Stanley J., and Howard Haycraft, *Twentieth Century Authors,* H. W. Wilson, 1942.
Laffont-Bompiani, *Dictionnaire biographique des auteurs,* Societe d'Edition de Dictionnaires et Encyclopedies, 1956.
Steinbrunner, Christ, and Otto Penzler, editors, *Encyclopedia of Mystery and Detection,* McGraw, 1976.
Sullivan, Jack, editor, *The Penguin Encyclopedia of Horror and the Supernatural,* Viking, 1986.
Twentieth Century Literary Criticism, Volume 25, Gale, 1988.

PERIODICALS

Comics Journal, June, 1988.
New York Times Film Reviews, September 7, 1925; October 15, 1943; August 24, 1962.
People Weekly, December 26, 1988/January 2, 1989.
Publishers Weekly, November 25, 1988.
Time, February 8, 1988.

*   *   *

LEVINE-FREIDUS, Gail
  See PROVOST, Gail Levine

JACK PEARL LEWIS

LEWIS, Jack P(earl) 1919-

PERSONAL: Born March 13, 1919, in Midlothian, TX; son of Pearl Gaunce (a farmer) and Anna Elizabeth (Holland) Lewis; married Lynell Carpenter, August 3, 1943 (died, June 19, 1975); married Annie May Alston, November 23, 1978; children: John Robert, Jerry Wayne. *Education:* Abilene Christian College (now University), B.A., 1941; Sam Houston State Teacher's College (now Sam Houston State University), M.A., 1944; Harvard University, S.T.B., 1947, Ph.D., 1953; Hebrew Union College, Ph.D., 1962. *Politics:* Democrat. *Religion:* Church of Christ. *Hobbies and other interests:* Woodworking, flying, photography.

ADDRESSES: Home—1132 South Perkins Rd., Memphis, TN 38117.

CAREER: Minister, serving in churches in Texas, Rhode Island and Kentucky, 1941-54; Harding Graduate School of Religion, Memphis, TN, associate professor, 1954-57, professor of Bible, 1957-89. Member of board of directors, University Christian Center, Oxford, MS, 1966—. Honorary Dean, Japanese School of Evangelism, Tokyo, Japan, 1989—.

MEMBER: Society of Biblical Literature, American Academy of Religion, National Association of Professors of Hebrew (membership secretary, 1986—), Evangelical Theological Society (chairman, southern section, 1969-70).

AWARDS, HONORS: American Schools of Oriental Research (Jerusalem), Thayer fellow, 1967-68; Christian Education Award, *Twentieth-Century Christian*, 1968; distinguished service award, Harding University, 1979; senior fellow, W. F. Albright Institute of Archaeological Research, 1983-84; a festschrift published in Lewis's honor, *Biblical Interpretation Principles and Practices*, was published by Baker Book in 1986; Distinguisehd Christian Service Award, Harding University, 1988.

WRITINGS:

The Minor Prophets, Baker Book, 1966.
The Interpretation of Noah and the Flood in Jewish and Christian Literature, E. J. Brill (Leiden), 1968.
Historical Backgrounds of Bible History, Baker Book, 1971.
Archaeology and the Bible, Abilene Christian University, 1975.
(Editor) *The Last Things*, R. B. Sweet, 1976.
The Gospel According to Matthew, R. B. Sweet, 1976, reprinted in two volumes, Abilene Christian University, 1984.
Archaeological Background to Bible People, Baker Book, 1977.
The English Bible from the KJV to the NIV, Baker Book, 1981, 2nd edition, 1991.
Leadership Questions Confronting the Church, Christian Communications, 1985.
Understanding Genesis, Gospel Advocate, 1987.
Exegesis of Difficult Passages, Research Publications AR, 1988.
(Editor) *Interpreting Second Corinthians 5:14-21: An Exercise in Hermeneutics*, E. Mellen, 1989.
Questions You've Asked about Bible Translations, Resource Publications, 1990.

Contributor to numerous books on theology and Christian education. Contributor of articles to *Journal of Bible and Religion, Gospel Broadcast, World Vision, Twentieth Century Christian, Gospel Advocate*, and *Teenage Christian*. Member of editorial board, *Restoration Quarterly*, 1957—, and *Journal of Hebraic Studies*, 1969—.

WORK IN PROGRESS: A commentary on the twelve minor prophets.

SIDELIGHTS: Jack P. Lewis has a reading knowledge of German, French, Hebrew, Aramaic, Greek, and Latin. He has led twenty-eight tours to the Holy Land. He told *SATA* that he "sees the scholar as primarily the servant of the church." While most of his writing is directed at "the person in the pew," he says some of his writing is for scholars. Since his retirement from Harding Graduate School of Religion in 1989, he gives lectures, writes, and serves an an elder in his church. He is also the Honorary Dean of the Japanese School of Evangelism in Tokyo, Japan.

*   *   *

LLOYD, Hugh
See FITZHUGH, Percy Keese

*   *   *

LOTZ, Wolfgang 1912-1981

PERSONAL: Born April 19, 1912, in Heilbronn, Germany; died of a heart attack, October 24, 1981; son of Hermann and Clara (Meyer) Lotz; married Hilde Bauer, August 5, 1941; children: Christoph, Irene, Corinna. *Education:* Attended University of Freiburg, 1932-33, and University of Munich, 1934-35; University of Hamburg, Ph.D., 1937.

CAREER: German Institute for Art History, Florence, Italy, research fellow, 1937-39; Central Institute for Art History, Munich, Germany, curator of photographs, 1939-42, deputy director, 1946-52; Vassar College, Poughkeepsie, NY, professor of fine arts, 1952-58; New York University, New York City, professor of fine arts, 1959-62; Max Planck Institut, Rome, Italy, director of Bibliotheca Hertziana, 1963-80. Member of Institute for Advanced Study, Princeton, NJ, 1966; Kress Professor at National Gallery of Art, Washington, DC, 1976-77. *Military service:* German Army, 1939-45.

MEMBER: College Art Association of America, Renaissance Society of America, Society of Architectural Historians.

WRITINGS:

(With L. H. Heydenreich) *Architecture in Italy, 1400-1600*, Pelican, 1974.
(With J. Cooldige, C. Thoenes, and others) *Jacopo Barozzi da Vignola*, Vignola, 1974.
Studies in Italian Renaissance Architecture, M.I.T. Press, 1977.

Contributor to scholarly journals in the United States, Italy, and Germany.

SIDELIGHTS: Wolfgang Lotz's parents wanted him to study law, but Erwin Panofsky, the famous art historian, inspired him to study art history at Hamburg University. During World War II Lotz was trained as an English interpreter, a skill which was very useful when he was interned in an American prisoner-of-war camp at Remagen when the war ended. After his release he worked at the "Collecting Point" in Munich, Germany, where works of art that had been stolen by the Nazis were brought together. Here he met American art historians. In 1952 he took his family to Vassar College in New York state where he taught as professor of fine arts for six years.

While teaching at Vassar he did his creative work at night, working through until the early hours of the morning. He sought to write in a sober, straightforward style, rather than the complicated romantic language that had been prevalent among German art historians. He wanted to write, not only for professional historians, but for ordinary lay readers, while always striving for the highest quality of original research and scientific standards.

While at Vassar, as throughout his life, he engaged in endless discussions with colleagues and students. He often made original investigations and passed his notes to others freely for use in their own work. He was interested in twentieth-century art, although he specialized in Renaissance architecture. One of his closest friends in the United States was the painter and sculptor Alton Pickens, with whom he played scrabble and table tennis. During his later years in Rome, Italy, he visited the flea market at Porta Portese every Sunday morning, collecting curiosities such as ostrich eggs as well as paintings and maps.

Lotz had few hobbies. He hardly went to the movies or theater or engaged in sport, although he enjoyed growing tomatoes and other vegetables. Most of his waking hours were engaged in his work, either teaching, reading, or discussing. Writing was difficult for him because he wrote very slowly.

In the 1960s, especially in his work on the Spanish Steps in Rome and on town planning in Italy, Lotz studied works of art from the social and political background from which they sprang. He had already begun to work with this method long before it became fashionable during the late 1960s.

After returning to Europe in 1963, Lotz traveled and lectured extensively in many countries. He made hundreds of trips within Italy to study architecture. He traveled throughout Germany, Portugal, France, Greece, Spain, and Great Britain and made a visit to Istanbul, Turkey, as well as to the East and West coasts of the United States.

During the period of his directorship at the Max Planck Institute's Bibliotheca Hertziana in Rome, Lotz carried a heavy administrative burden. He supervised a major extension of the institute's building. The strain of this tore him away from his teaching and research, which were his true vocation. When he died suddenly from a heart attack in October 1981, he was already preparing a number of lecture tours in the United States.

[Date of death provided by daughter, Corinna Lotz]

* * *

MAGID, Ken(neth Marshall)

PERSONAL: Education: University of South Florida, M.A. (sociology), 1969, M.A. (counseling), 1972; University of Denver, Ph.D., 1975.

ADDRESSES: Office—K. M. Productions, Inc., P.O. Box 280334, Lakewood, CO 80228; and Golden Medical Clinic, 1823 Ford St., Golden, CO 80401.

CAREER: Tampa Times, Tampa, FL, news and feature reporter, 1969-71; free-lance journalist (stringer for *Newsweek,* United Press International, and Associated Press); director of psychological services at Golden Medical Clinic, Golden, CO; co-chairman of behavioral science department for family practice physicians at St. Joseph Hospital of Denver, Denver, CO. Instructor in psychology at Metropolitan State College and at Denver's federal prison. Host of psychology talk show on KIMN-Radio, health program on KMGH-TV, 1981-83, and talk show on KNUS-Radio, 1985-86; guest on national television programs, including *The Today Show, Hour Magazine,* and *The Oprah Winfrey Show;* public speaker. Affiliated with K. M. Productions, Inc., Lakewood, CO.

MEMBER: American Psychology Association, Colorado Psychology Association.

WRITINGS:

(With Walt Schreibman) *Divorce Is: A Kid's Coloring Book,* Evergreen Consultants Press, 1980.
(With Carole A. McKelvey) *High Risk: Children Without a Conscience,* M & M Publishing, 1985, Bantam, 1988.

Columnist for News America Syndicate and *Rocky Mountain News.* Contributor to magazines, including *Woman's Day.*

WORK IN PROGRESS: A television documentary inspired by *High Risk;* a sequel to *High Risk.*

FOR MORE INFORMATION SEE:

PERIODICALS
Los Angeles Times Book Review, February 21, 1988.

* * *

MALMGREN, Dallin 1949-

PERSONAL: Born April 5, 1949, in Albany, NY; son of Carl E. (a mining engineer) and Ascia (a homemaker; maiden name, Salich) Malmgren; married Karen Kleppinger (a homemaker), August 27, 1977; children: Bethany, Nathan, Zachary. *Education:* University of Missouri, B.S., 1981. *Politics:* "Every four years." *Religion:* "Floating Christian."

ADDRESSES: Home and office—218 Avenue E, Converse, TX 78109.

CAREER: High school teacher; writer. Worked in hospitals as a psychiatric aide and storeroom clerk, during 1970s; Ste. Genevieve High School, Ste. Genevieve, MO, English teacher, 1981-84; Judson High School, Converse, TX, journalism teacher, 1984-86; Samuel Clemens High School, Schertz, TX, English teacher and tennis coach, 1986—.

DALLIN MALMGREN

MEMBER: National Council of Teachers of English, National Education Association.

AWARDS, HONORS: The Whole Nine Yards received an Honorable Mention, Delacorte Press Prize, 1984, was named among Recommended Books for Reluctant Young Adult Readers, Young Adult Services Division of the American Library Association, 1987, and selected as one of the Top Twenty-five Titles of 1987, Books for Young Adults Program, University of Iowa; *The Ninth Issue* was listed among the Notable Children's Trade Books in the Field of Social Studies, National Council for Social Studies.

WRITINGS:

The Whole Nine Yards, Delacorte, 1986.
The Ninth Issue, Delacorte, 1989.

WORK IN PROGRESS: Split Ends, about an illicit romance between a student and a teacher; a collection of essays about teaching in high school.

SIDELIGHTS: Dallin Malmgren told *SATA:* "I first sensed that I could become a writer in the seventh grade, when I wrote a short story for my English class. I used the word 'hell' in the last sentence. My teacher put a huge circle around it in red ink, accused me of thinking I was Ernest Hemingway, and gave me a D-. I knew I was on my way.

"Actually, I think my desire to write came out of my love for reading. I owe that to my father. At the end of fifth grade I brought home a report card that said, 'Dallin is a very slow reader.' That concerned my dad, so he decided I would read a book a week all summer, and write a book report! That was like a death sentence to a ten-year-old boy. But my father had the wisdom to assign great books. I can remember staying up at night with a flashlight, just so I could keep reading *The Earth is the Lord's* by Taylor Caldwell or *Beau Geste* by P. C. Wren, or *The Count of Monte Cristo* by Alexander Dumas. By the end of the summer, I was addicted.

"I think the best training I got for being a writer came from working in a mental hospital for six years. I was just a psychiatric aide, the lowliest position in the power structure, but we were the ones who spent the most time with the patients. In the hospital we were trained to watch people and to record our observations. The population within a mental hospital (both patients and staff) provides a microcosm for all the diversity within the bounds of human nature. It was a fascinating job, and it gave me a motivation to write and a wealth of material to work with.

"In 1979 I faced a career crisis. I was working in a medical hospital as a storeroom clerk, and my wife was pregnant with our first child. Although I was twenty-nine years old, that was the first time it really hit me that I would be working for the rest of my life. I knew I was capable of more than delivering hospital supplies. I decided I would like to either write or teach. Becoming an English/education major seemed like a good way of pursuing both.

"I've been teaching for several years now. I still can't tell much difference between the mental patients and the high-school kids. I suppose it was being a teacher that led me to focus on writing young adult books. As a matter of fact, I wrote *The Whole Nine Yards* because I was disturbed that so few boys in high school seem to want to read for enjoyment. I wanted to write a book they would like.

"I share most of what I write with my students. They're tough critics. They are also great sources of material. I think a lot of teenagers are looking for adults who will listen to them. I'm not as good of a listener as I'd like to be, but I know I'm getting better. I do know that they're worth listening to.

"I don't know how successful I'll be, but I know I'll keep writing. I'm not sure if it's a compulsion or an urge or just a wish fulfillment, but I know it feels good to finish putting something down on paper. It's a way for me to put my own world in perspective, and it gives me something to think about. And somewhere deep inside, I suppose there's a desire to leave my mark on the world, too."

*   *   *

MANCHESTER, William (Raymond) 1922-

PERSONAL: Born April 1, 1922, in Attleboro, MA; son of William Raymond and Sallie (Thompson) Manchester; married Julia Brown Marshall, March 27, 1948; children: John Kennerly, Julie Thompson, Laurie. *Education:* Massachusetts State College (now University of Massachusetts), A.B., 1946; University of Missouri, A.M., 1947.

ADDRESSES: Office—Wesleyan University, 329 Wesleyan Station, Middletown, CT 06457. *Agent*—Don Congdon Associates, Inc., 156 Fifth Ave., Suite 625, New York, NY 10010.

CAREER: Daily Oklahoman, Oklahoma City, OK, reporter, 1945-46; *Sun,* Baltimore, MD, reporter, Washington correspondent, and foreign correspondent in the Middle East, India, and Southeast Asia, 1947-54; Wesleyan University, Middletown, CT, managing editor of Wesleyan University Publications, 1955-64, member of university faculty, 1968-69, member of faculty of East College, 1968—, writer in residence, 1975—, adjunct professor of history, 1979—. Associate fellow of Pierson College, Yale University, 1991—. Friends of the University of Massachusetts Library, president of board of trustees, 1970-72, trustee, 1970-74. *Military service:* U.S. Marine Corps, 1942-45; became sergeant; awarded Purple Heart.

MEMBER: American Historical Association, Society of American Historians, PEN, Authors Guild, Authors League of America, Williams Club, Century Club.

AWARDS, HONORS: Guggenheim fellow, 1959-60; Wesleyan Center for Advanced Studies fellow, 1959-60; honorary doctorates from University of Massachusetts, 1965, University of Richmond, 1967, University of New Haven, 1979, Skidmore College, 1986, and Russell Sage College, 1990; Prix Dag Hammarskjoeld au Merite Litteraire, 1967; Overseas Press Club citation for best book on foreign affairs, 1968; University of Missouri Honor Award for distinguished service in journalism, 1969; Connecticut Book Award, 1975; National Book Award nomination, 1980, for *American Caesar: Douglas MacArthur, 1880-1964;* American Library Association Notable Book citation, 1980, for *Goodbye, Darkness: A Memoir of the Pacific War;* President's Cabinet Award, University of Detroit, 1981; Frederick S. Troy Award, University of Massachusetts, 1981; McConnaughty Award, Wesleyan University, 1981; *Los Angeles Times* Biog-

WILLIAM MANCHESTER

raphy Prize nomination, 1983, and Union League/Abraham Lincoln Literary Award, 1984, both for *The Last Lion: Winston Spencer Churchill,* Volume 1: *Visions of Glory: 1874-1932;* Connecticut Bar Association Distinguished Public Service Award, 1985.

WRITINGS:

Disturber of the Peace: The Life of H. L. Mencken (originally serialized in *Harper's,* July-August, 1950), Harper, 1951, 2nd edition edited by Stephen B. Oates and Paul Mariani, University of Massachusetts Press, 1986.

The City of Anger (novel), Ballantine, 1953, reprinted, Little, Brown, 1987.

Shadow of the Monsoon (novel), Doubleday, 1956.

Beard the Lion (novel), Morrow, 1958.

A Rockefeller Family Portrait: From John D. to Nelson, Little, Brown, 1959.

(Contributor) Bredemier and Toby, editors, *Social Problems in America,* Wiley, 1960.

The Long Gainer: A Novel, Little, Brown, 1961.

Portrait of a President: John F. Kennedy in Profile, Little, Brown, 1962, 2nd edition, 1967.

(Contributor) Don Congdon, editor, *Combat World War I,* Dial, 1964.

(Contributor) Poyntz Tyler, *Securities Exchanges and the SEC,* Wilson, 1965.

The Death of a President: November 20-November 25, 1963 (originally serialized in *Look,* January 24-March 7, 1967; Book-of-the-Month Club selection), Harper, 1967, published with revised introduction, Arbor House, 1985,

published with new addition by the author, Harper, 1988.

The Arms of Krupp, 1587-1968 (originally serialized in *Holiday,* November, 1964-February, 1965; Literary Guild selection), Little, Brown, 1968.

The Glory and the Dream: A Narrative History of America, 1932-1972 (Literary Guild selection), Little, Brown, 1974, reprinted, Bantam, 1989.

Controversy and Other Essays in Journalism, Little, Brown, 1976.

American Caesar: Douglas MacArthur, 1880-1964 (Book-of-the-Month Club selection), Little, Brown, 1978.

Goodbye, Darkness: A Memoir of the Pacific War (Book-of-the-Month Club selection), Little, Brown, 1980.

One Brief Shining Moment: Remembering Kennedy (Book-of-the-Month Club selection), Little, Brown, 1983.

The Last Lion: Winston Spencer Churchill, Volume 1: *Visions of Glory: 1874-1932* (Book-of-the-Month Club selection), Little, Brown, 1983, Volume 2: *Alone: 1932-1940* (Book-of-the-Month Club selection), Little, Brown, 1987.

(Contributor) *A Sense of History: The Best Writing from the Pages of American Heritage,* American Heritage/Houghton, 1985.

(Contributor) Annie Dillard and Robert Atwan, editors, *Best American Essays 1988,* Ticknor & Fields, 1988.

(Author of text) *In Our Time: The World as Seen by Magnum Photographers,* Norton, 1989.

Also author of introduction for *Thimblerigger: The Law v. Governor Marvin Mandel.* Contributor to *Encyclopaedia Britannica.* Contributor to *Atlantic, Harper's, Reporter, Saturday Review, Holiday, Nation, Esquire,* and *Saturday Evening Post.*

WORK IN PROGRESS: The Last Lion: Winston Spencer Churchill, Volume 3: *Defender of the Realm: 1940-1965;* and *A World Lit Only by Fire: The Age of Magellan.*

ADAPTATIONS: The City of Anger, adapted from Manchester's novel of the same title, aired on NBC-TV in 1955. *American Caesar,* a television miniseries based on Manchester's biography of Douglas MacArthur, was narrated by John Huston, produced by John McGreevey, aired on the Ted Turner cable network in 1985, and is available on videocassette.

SIDELIGHTS: "Power," said writer William Manchester in *People,* "[is] the one thing that has fascinated me ever since I was a kid in Springfield, Mass. What exactly is power? Where are its roots? How do some people get it and others miss it entirely? How do they hold it or lose it?" The study of power, Manchester suggested, is the thread that connects all his books.

Manchester began his study of power when he became a journalist as a young man. After working briefly at the *Daily Oklahoman* he joined the staff of the Baltimore *Sun* in 1947 and served for the next seven years as a reporter, a Washington correspondent, and foreign correspondent throughout Asia. His first book, *Disturber of the Peace,* was about *Sun* legend H. L. Mencken, whose strongly worded commentary on public affairs and human failings made him one of the most renowned journalists of his time. Manchester went on to write a string of novels, often describing the use and abuse of power, that seem inspired in part by what he learned about the world while he was covering stories for the *Sun.*

By the 1960s Manchester had left newspaper work and begun to write the kind of book that would become his trademark: historical biography. His *Portrait of a President: John F. Kennedy in Profile* was an affectionate study of the newly elected American president that appeared in 1962. When President Kennedy was tragically assassinated in 1963, members of the Kennedy family remembered Manchester's work and authorized him to write the inside story of the president's last days. The resulting book, *The Death of a President: November 20-November 25, 1963*, appeared in 1967. In a new edition issued in 1985, Manchester wrote: "Here . . . I have attempted to lead the reader back through historical events by recreating the sense of immediacy people felt at the time, so that he sees, feels, and hears what was seen, felt, and heard—mourns, rejoices, weeps, or loves with mourners, rejoicers, weepers, or lovers long since vanished: figures whose present has become our past." Such use of detail and emotion to make the past come alive is considered a basic part of how Manchester writes: over the years, this style would please many thousands of readers and make Manchester a bestselling author.

Before *Death of a President* was released to the public, however, Manchester was drawn into one of the best-known court cases in American publishing history. Both Manchester and his publisher had received telegrams from the Kennedy family that seemed to give permission to publish the completed manuscript of *Death of a President,* but on the eve of publication the president's widow Jacqueline developed misgivings. Soon she filed a lawsuit to ban the book, claiming that Manchester's work would cause her harm and sensationalize the president's death. The suit was settled quietly after Manchester's publisher persuaded Mrs. Kennedy to read the manuscript. In his 1985 preface, Manchester observed: "*The Death of a President* was not written for Jackie or any of the others. I wrote it for the one Kennedy I had known well and deeply loved, the splendid man who had been cruelly slain at 12:30 p.m. Texas time on Friday, November 22, 1963." The author's profits from the book—approximately $1.5 million—were donated to the Kennedy Library in Boston.

In the years since *Death of a President* made him famous, Manchester has written several more highly popular historical biographies. *The Arms of Krupp* tells the story of a family that grew wealthy by supplying weapons to German governments, including the Nazis, the most brutal fascist regime of World War II. *American Caesar* and *The Last Lion* portray two of the most vivid personalities who led the fight against fascism during that war: American general Douglas MacArthur and British prime minister Winston Churchill.

Manchester also turned the biographical spotlight on himself in *Goodbye, Darkness: A Memoir of the Pacific War.* He wrote the book in the late 1970s after having nightmares about his younger days as a U.S. Marine during World War II, when he fought against fascist Japanese forces in the Pacific. To come to terms with the memories of his youth, Manchester visited old Pacific battlegrounds such as the island of Okinawa, where in 1945 he was severely injured by the explosion of a Japanese artillery shell and went temporarily blind. In the long run, *Goodbye, Darkness* is a book about two kinds of power: the monstrous brutality of war, and the love of America and its people that enabled young men such as Manchester to endure war's horrors.

WORKS CITED:

Kanfer, Stefan, "Author William Manchester Unmasks the Man behind the Corncob Pipe: MacArthur," *People,* November 27, 1978, pp. 55-62.
Manchester, William, *The Death of a President: November 20-November 25, 1963,* revised edition, Arbor House, 1985.

FOR MORE INFORMATION SEE:

BOOKS

Authors in the News, Volume 1, Gale, 1976.
Bestsellers 89, Issue 2, Gale, 1989.
Corry, John, *The Manchester Affair,* Putnam, 1967.
Manchester, William, *The City of Anger* (novel), Ballantine, 1953, reprinted, Little, Brown, 1985.
Manchester, *Goodbye, Darkness: A Memoir of the Pacific War,* Little, Brown, 1980.

PERIODICALS

Newsweek, November 25, 1974; September 11, 1978; December 12, 1988.
New York Times, January 14, 1951; July 13, 1953; April 8, 1956; August 9, 1959; April 3, 1967; December 6, 1968; November 15, 1974; September 20, 1978; September 17, 1980; May 25, 1983.
New York Times Book Review, September 10, 1961; September 30, 1962; April 9, 1967; November 24, 1968; November 17, 1974; August 31, 1980; June 5, 1983; November 27, 1988.
Time, January 8, 1951; December 20, 1968; November 18, 1974; September 11, 1978; October 31, 1988.

—Sketch by Thomas Kozikowski

*   *   *

MARTIN, Eva M. 1939-

PERSONAL: Born April 24, 1939, in Woodstock, Ontario, Canada; daughter of Harvey Attlin (a tool and die maker) and Daisybelle (Blake) Martin. *Education:* University of Toronto, B.A., 1960, B.L.S., 1961, M.L.S., 1972. *Hobbies and other interests:* Music (singing in a choir which specializes in liturgical music), cooking, gardening.

ADDRESSES: Home—401 Sackville St., Toronto, Ontario, Canada M4X 1S6. *Office*—Anglican Book Centre, 600 Jarvis St., Toronto, Ontario.

CAREER: Librarian. Toronto Public Library, Toronto, Ontario, children's librarian, 1961-63, head of children's department, 1963-71, head of Community Branch, 1971-77; Scarborough Public Library, Scarborough, Ontario, coordinator of services for children and young adults, 1977-89; affiliated with Anglican Book Centre, Toronto. Lecturer at University of Toronto, 1975-76, 1988—.

MEMBER: International Board on Books for Young People (chairperson of Canadian section, 1985-87), Canadian Library Association, Canadian Association of Children's Librarians, Canadian Association of Toy Libraries (chairperson, 1984-86), Book Publishers Professional Association, American Library Association, Ontario Library Association (chair of children's services guild, 1979-80, and vice-president, 1981-83; chair of teen services guild, 1986-87), Ontario Puppetry Association, Ontario Association for Children With Learning Disabilities, Storytellers School of Toronto.

WRITINGS:

Canadian Fairy Tales, Groundwood Books (Toronto), 1984, published as *Tales of the Far North,* Dial, 1986.

Contributor to *Meeting the Challenge* and to periodicals.

WORK IN PROGRESS: Another collection of fairy tales; picture books and a novel for children.

SIDELIGHTS: Eva M. Martin told *SATA:* "I have loved fairy tales since childhood, and as I am a children's librarian the opportunity to tell stories to children has delighted me. When my publisher invited me to put together and retell a collection of Canadian fairy tales, I was only too pleased to do so. I hope to pursue writing for children in more depth and eventually to create a novel.

"I live in downtown Toronto in a house that was built in 1870, and there I indulge my passions for gardening and cooking and share my thoughts with two mischievous cats. When I chaired the Canadian section of the International Board on Books for Young People (IBBY), I traveled to the IBBY congress in Japan and was thrilled to be plunged into oriental society, where everyone has a garden, however small."

Dustjacket from Eva Martin's first collection of fairy tales, illustrated by László Gál.

MATHER, Kirtley F(letcher) 1888-1978

PERSONAL: Surname rhymes with "rather"; born February 13, 1888, in Chicago, IL; died May 7, 1978, in Albuquerque, NM; buried in Maple Grove Cemetery, Granville, OH; son of William Green (a railroad ticket agent) and Julia S. (King) Mather; married Marie Porter, June 12, 1912 (died September 17, 1971); married Muriel Speare Williams, May 31, 1977; children: Florence Margaret (Mrs. Sherman A. Wengerd), Julia Carolyn (Mrs. Leroy G. Seils), Jean Marie (Mrs. Dean W. Seibel). *Education:* Denison University, B.Sc., 1909; University of Chicago, Ph.D., 1915. *Politics:* Independent. *Religion:* Baptist.

CAREER: University of Arkansas, Fayetteville, instructor, 1911-12, assistant professor of geology, 1912-14; Queen's University at Kingston, Kingston, Ontario, associate professor of geology, 1915-17, professor of paleontology, 1917-18; Denison University, Granville, OH, professor of geology, 1918-24; Harvard University, Cambridge, MA, associate professor of physiography, 1924-27, professor of geology, 1927-54, professor emeritus, beginning in 1954, director of summer school, 1934-42. University of Chicago, fellow, 1914-15; visiting professor at Carleton College, 1954, and University of New Mexico, 1971-78; Phi Beta Kappa visiting scholar, 1960-61 and 1965-66; Danforth lecturer, 1961-62. U.S. Geological Survey, geologist, 1910-45; Richmond Levering and Co., field geologist in Bolivia, 1919-20; attended International Geological Congresses in England, Algeria, Mexico, Denmark, and India, 1948-64. Educational Research Corp., president, 1946-53; Foundation for Integrative Education, president, 1946-69. Gave *Science by the Fireside* radio talks in Boston, MA, beginning in 1920s; consultant for educational science films to Pathe Films, during 1920s and 1930s. Curry College, trustee, beginning in 1913; Newton (MA) School Committee, member, 1927-34; Boston Center for Adult Education, president, 1930-36; Newton Community Forum, chairman, 1936-41. *Military service:* U.S. Army, Engineer Officers Reserve Corps, 1919-27; became captain.

MEMBER: American Association for the Advancement of Science (fellow; president, 1951), American Academy of Arts and Sciences (fellow; president, 1957-61), Geological Society of America (fellow), Royal Geographical Society (fellow), American Association of Petroleum Geologists, American Geophysical Union, Young Men's Christian Association (president of Massachusetts-Rhode Island committee, 1942, president of national council, 1947-48, member of world council, 1955-61, representative to United Nations, 1957-60), Oliver Wendell Holmes Association (president, 1962-70), Ohio Academy of Science (president, 1923-24), Civil Liberties Union of Massachusetts (chairman, 1946-49), Phi Beta Kappa (senator, 1952-64), Sigma Xi, Masonic Order, Twentieth-Century Club (president, 1930-35), Boston Authors Club, Century Club of New York, Harvard Travelers Club, Harvard Mountaineering Club, Harvard-Yale-Princeton Club of New Mexico.

AWARDS, HONORS: Honorary doctorates from Denison University, 1929, Colby College, 1936, Union College, 1942, Bates College, 1943, Beloit College, 1949, and Curry College, 1966; Distinguished Service Medal, University of Chicago, 1941; Abraham T. Alper Award, Civil Liberties Union of Massachusetts, 1961; Bradford Washburn Medal, Boston Museum of Science, 1964; Cullum Medal, American Geographical Society, 1965; Thomas Alva Edison Foundation award for best book on science for young people, 1965, and Publication Award from American Geographical Society, both for *The Earth Beneath Us.*

WRITINGS:

Old Mother Earth, Harvard University Press, 1928.
Science in Search of God, Holt, 1928.
Sons of the Earth, Norton, 1931.
(With W. W. Atwood) *Physiography and Quaternary Geology of the San Juan Mountains, Colorado* (monograph), U.S. Geological Survey, 1932.
(With C. J. Roy) *Laboratory Manual of Physical and Historical Geology,* Appleton-Century, 1934.
(With Dorothy Hewitt) *Adult Education: A Dynamic for Democracy,* Appleton, 1937.
(With Shirley L. Mason) *A Source Book in Geology,* McGraw, 1939, reprinted, Hafner, 1964, published as *A Source Book in Geology: 1400-1900,* Harvard University Press, 1970.
Enough and to Spare, Harper, 1944.
Crusade for Life, University of North Carolina Press, 1949.
A Laboratory Manual For Geology, Appleton-Century-Crofts, Volume 1: (with C. J. Roy and L. R. Thiesmeyer) *Physical Geology,* 1950, Volume 2: (with C. J. Roy) *Historical Geology,* 1952.
(Contributor) Harlow Shapley, editor, *Science Ponders Religion,* Appleton, 1960.
The World in Which We Live, Pilgrim Press, 1961.
The Earth Beneath Us, Random House, 1964, revised edition, 1975.
(Contributor) Jerry R. Tompkins, editor, *D-Days in Dayton: Reflections on the Scopes Trial,* Louisiana State University Press, 1965.
Source Book in Geology: 1900-1950, Harvard University Press, 1967.
The Permissive Universe, edited by daughter, Florence Mather Wengerd, and son-in-law, Sherman A. Wengerd, University of New Mexico Press, 1986.

Also author of *Geologist at Large,* a privately printed autobiography. Chairman of editorial board of Scientific Book Club, Inc., 1930-46; editor of Appleton's "Earth Science" series, 1934-65; judge for Nonfiction Book Club, 1946-48; consulting editor for Mcgraw-Hill, 1950-66. Contributor to *Atlantic Monthly, Forum,* and other popular and scientific periodicals. Editor, "Scientist's Bookshelf," *American Scientist,* 1942-54; member of book committee, Phi Beta Kappa's *Key Reporter,* 1950-75.

SIDELIGHTS: Kirtley F. Mather was a pioneering field geologist who searched successfully for oil deposits in places as varied as the American West and mountains of Bolivia. The report on his Bolivian expedition, which he gave to the Geological Society of America in 1921, led to his thirty-year appointment as a teacher at Harvard University.

In addition to his scientific work, Mather was widely respected for showing how science, religion, and freedom of speech could work together productively in everyday life. To Mather, only science, including the principle of evolution, could explain the rock formations that he found as a geologist; religion, however, remained needful as a guide to moral conduct. Only in an atmosphere of free thought could science and human progress flourish.

Mather defended such principles publicly throughout his life. In 1925, when Tennessee schoolteacher John T. Scopes was put on trial for discussing evolution with his students, defense lawyer Clarence Darrow brought Mather to the stand in order to show the jury that a religious man could also be a modern scientist. When Mather was in his eighties he summed up his ideas about the relationship between religion and science in the book *The Permissive Universe.* Left among his papers at the time of his death, the manuscript was edited by his daughter Florence and her husband and was published in 1986.

[Date of death provided by son-in-law, Sherman A. Wengerd]

*   *   *

MAXWELL, Gavin 1914-1969

PERSONAL: Born July 15, 1914, in Mochrum (some sources say Wigtown), Scotland; died September 6, 1969, in Inverness, Scotland; son of Aymer Edward (an army officer) and Lady Mary (Percy) Maxwell; married Lavinia Joan Lascelles, February 1, 1962 (divorced, 1964). *Education:* Hertford College, Oxford, M.A., c. 1937.

ADDRESSES: Home—Isle Ornsay Lighthouse, Isle of Skye, Inner Hebrides, Scotland; Kyleakin Lighthouse, by Kyle, Ross-shire, Scotland; Sandaig, by Kyle of Lochalsh, Ross-shire, Scotland.

CAREER: Free-lance journalist, c. 1937-39; Soay Shark Fisheries, Hebrides, Scotland, owner, 1944-49; portrait painter, 1949-52; writer, 1952-69. President, British Junior Exploration Society; member of advisory committee, Wildlife Youth Service of the World Wildlife Fund; trustee, Danilo Dolci Trust. *Military service:* Scots Guards, 1939-41, small arms instructor with Special Operations Executive, 1941-44; disabled, 1944; became major.

MEMBER: International Institute of Arts and Letters (fellow), Royal Society for Literature (fellow), Royal Geographic Society, Zoological Society (scientific fellow), American Geographical Society (fellow), P.E.N., Fauna Preservation Society, Wildfowl Trust (honorary life member), Special Forces Club, Guards Club, Puffin Club, Third Guards Club, Household Brigade Yacht Club.

AWARDS, HONORS: Heinemann Award, Royal Society of Literature, 1957, for *A Reed Shaken by the Wind.*

WRITINGS:

Harpoon Venture, Viking, 1952, published in England as *Harpoon at a Venture,* Hart-Davis, 1952.
Bandit, Harper, 1956, published in England as *God Protect Me from My Friends,* Longmans, Green, 1956.
People of the Reeds, Harper, 1957, published in England as *A Reed Shaken by the Wind,* Longmans, Green, 1957.
The Ten Pains of Death (Book Society selection), Longmans, Green, 1959, Dutton, 1960.
Ring of Bright Water (first book in "Camusfearna" trilogy; Book Society and Book-of-the-Month Club selections), Dutton, 1960, adaptation for children published as *The Otter's Tale,* Dutton, 1962, adaptation for children by Dorothy Welchman published as *Ring of Bright Water,* Hutchinson, 1981.
The Rocks Remain (second book in "Camusfearna" trilogy), Dutton, 1962.

Young Gavin Maxwell with a family of rooks.

The House of Elrig (childhood and adolescent autobiography), Dutton, 1965.

Lords of the Atlas: The Rise and Fall of the House of Glaoua, 1893-1956, Dutton, 1966.

(With John Stidworthy and David Williams) *Seals of the World,* Houghton, 1967.

Raven Seek Thy Brother (third book in "Camusfearna" trilogy), illustrations by Robin McEwen, Longmans, Green, 1968, Dutton, 1969.

Contributor to *The Pan Book of Animal Stories,* edited by J. Montgomery, Pan Books, 1964. Contributor of poetry and travel stories to periodicals, including *New Statesman, Saturday Review, Twentieth Century, National Geographic, American Magazine of Natural History,* and *Observer.* Member of advisory panel, *Animals.*

Lords of the Atlas has been translated into Spanish.

ADAPTATIONS: Ring of Bright Water was adapted into a film of the same title, starring Bill Travers and Virginia McKenna, Palomar Pictures, 1969; an abridged edition of *Ring of Bright Water* was narrated by Christopher Timothy on two audio cassettes, Durkin Hayes, 1982.

SIDELIGHTS: Reclusive Scottish author Gavin Maxwell gained international attention with the 1960 publication of *Ring of Bright Water,* a bestselling book in Britain and America. The story, which was made into a 1969 movie, is about Maxwell and his life with his pet otters at Camusfearna, a cottage located in the West Highlands of Scotland. *Ring of Bright Water* was so successful that Maxwell adapted it into a book for children entitled *The Otter's Tale,* and he continued to write about his otters in two later books: *The Rocks Remain* and *Raven Seek Thy Brother.*

In addition to his "Camusfearna" trilogy, Maxwell wrote other books that both young adults and adults have enjoyed. His first book, entitled *Harpoon Venture,* is about hunting basking sharks, which are among the largest creatures in the sea. *People of the Reeds* concerns Maxwell's trip to Iraq and his visit with the Ma'dans, the primitive people who live around the marshes of southern Iraq. *Lords of the Atlas* is about the history of a famous Moroccan family, the Berbers, who sought complete power of their country in the 1950s. And *The Ten Pains of Death* describes the social and economic problems of the Italian island of Sicily. Known for carefully researching his works, Maxwell traveled to several countries to gather information for his books, many of which are written in the first person point of view in Maxwell's voice.

Maxwell was born on July 15, 1914, in southwest Scotland, where his family's aristocratic roots date back to the late seventeenth century. Just three months after his birth, Maxwell's father died from combat wounds suffered during World War I. This left young Maxwell to grow up with his mother, sister, and two brothers in an isolated Scottish home called Elrig. His mother designed the home, and her artistic tastes—he later recalled in his childhood autobiography, *The House of Elrig*—had an early influence on him: "She preferred the bare windswept moors of Kielder to the gentle parklands and gracious gardens of her southern homes. . . . In all her appreciation of beauty there was that which I either inherited or acquired from her, an inherent approach of melancholy or nostalgia, so that splendour could not be splendid were it not desolate too."

Being part of an upper-class family separated Maxwell at an early age from other children. Raised by governesses, he and his sister and brothers spent much of their time together. They often amused themselves by drawing and writing short stories, and they occasionally staged very short original plays, using servants as their audience. But even while playing as a child, Maxwell felt a strong sense of isolation: "Our games and our theatricals we played alone; we lived in a closed circle and met no other children," he explained in *The House of Elrig.* "Except among ourselves we were as shy as wild animals, and the sound of unseen wheels upon the steep drive sent us scuttling for cover like rabbits. To us this segregation seemed natural enough; we did not question it because we were self-sufficient."

Self-sufficiency, which played a key role in Maxwell's adult life, was evident throughout his childhood, though it was often accompanied by—if not caused by—painful shyness. Maxwell attended a number of private schools for boys and always felt like the "odd-man-out" at each of them, much like his father and grandfather before him. During those early years he derived his greatest happiness from spending long afternoons outdoors alone in the English countryside or the Scottish Highlands. There he acquired his love of nature and his general preference of the company of animals to humans.

When Maxwell was sixteen he was diagnosed as having a rare blood disease that forced him to leave school for a few months. In *The House of Elrig* he recounted how the disease affected his thoughts: "As my condition worsened and I sank towards the crisis, my moments of consciousness and clarity became fewer; and in them, besides the pain, I suffered agonies of thirst which I was not allowed to quench. I knew where I wanted to drink from, a small stream at Elrig, where the water ran shallow over small pebbles, and in my mind I would lie prone at its bank and part the overhanging heather to bury my face in the sweet chill of its flow." Maxwell gradually recovered and, thanks to help from family members, was able to continue his studies during his convalescence. Christian, his sister, would read to him to help pass the many hours he lay in bed, and soon Maxwell began writing stories of his own, adapting the styles of the authors he heard.

Maxwell went on to study at Hertford College of Oxford University, and after graduation he began a career as a freelance journalist. He accompanied a bird-watching expedition to East Finnmark, Norway, but returned home to join the Scots Guard at the outbreak of World War II in 1939. Witnessing the daily death and destruction of war had a significant impact on Maxwell. He grew weary of the human world and longed to retire to an island of his own. Maxwell spoke of his idea of buying an island to a fellow officer, and together they examined a map of Scotland, looking for prospects in the islands in the Hebrides. "After an hour there were rings drawn round several islands," wrote Maxwell in *Harpoon Venture.* "I had drawn an extra ring round the island of Soay, an island unknown to either of us, below the Cuillin of Skye. We were still playing at make-believe; Soay was my Island Valley of Avalon, and Avalon was all the world away."

The dream of purchasing Soay gained momentum in 1943 after Maxwell visited the island with another officer from the Scots Guard. Although Maxwell was there for only two hours, he quickly fell in love with the quiet beauty of the island. Nearly a decade later Maxwell recalled in *Harpoon Venture:* "I decided to buy Soay if I could do so at a figure that would show me, from rentals and feu-duties, the small rate of interest that I received from my invested capital. I entered almost immediately into prolonged negotiations with the owner, Flora Macleod of Macleod, and the island became my property about a year later."

While still with the Scots Guard, Maxwell devoted much of his attention to figuring out how to make his island investment profitable. At first, prospects seemed dim because someone else owned the salmon fishing rights in the area. One day, though, Maxwell and a friend were in a boat near Soay when they spotted a basking shark. They decided to harpoon it, but after several hits and a long struggle, the shark got away. "I was intrigued by this first adventure," Maxwell remembered in *Harpoon Venture*, "and it made me curious to know more about basking sharks. It was only then that I began to understand that here was an unexplored field; an amazing blank upon the neatly, if superficially, filled-in map of the world's natural history. Here was the largest fish of European waters, a creature as large as any land animal in the world, and yet virtually nothing was known of it."

Encouraged by his basking shark encounter, Maxwell decided to start a shark fishery after he left the Scots Guard in November of 1944. The project was riddled with problems, but the main difficulty was in determining how to work with a fish that weighed several tons. His advisers told him that since almost every part of the basking shark had commercial value, the best thing to do was to process the entire fish. This proved unmanageable. There was simply too much fish to handle, and in *Harpoon Venture* Maxwell regretted that he did not concentrate on the most valuable part of the shark: "I know now that the shark's liver is the elephant's ivory." Frustrated with a number of unsuccessful fishing seasons and complicated governmental procedures, Maxwell sold the company in 1949. He went on to work as a portrait painter and started writing about his shark fishing adventures.

Publishing his shark business story in 1952 as *Harpoon Venture*, Maxwell spent the rest of his career as a writer. Shortly after its publication, *Harpoon Venture* was praised by a *Times Literary Supplement* reviewer, who remarked that the book "contrives so skillfully to be three things at once—the record of a practical enterprise, the fulfilment of one man's private dream and an evocation of one of the most beautiful places in the world." The same critic also observed that *Harpoon Venture* was written "in taut, exact prose, which now and then rises to descriptive brilliance."

Maxwell's later literary efforts were based on his international travels. A 1956 journey to Sicily, an island off the coast of Italy, yielded both *Bandit,* about a famous Sicilian pirate named Salvatore Giuliano, and *The Ten Pains of Death,* a collection of interviews with Sicilians describing the appalling social conditions of the island. During the 1950s Maxwell also traveled to Iraq and wrote *People of the Reeds,* which, when published in England as *A Reed Shaken by the Wind,* won the Royal Society of Literature's Heinemann Award.

But Maxwell's greatest publishing success came in 1960 with *Ring of Bright Water,* the first book in the "Camusfearna" trilogy about his pet otters at his home in the Scottish Highlands. The series—which also includes *The Rocks Remain* and *Raven Seek Thy Brother*— describes Maxwell's relationship with three otters named Mijbil, Teko, and Edal. These otters shared a bond with Maxwell that he considered as important as any of his human relationships. Otters are temperamental creatures, and Maxwell went to great lengths to please them, just as many people do for their dogs or cats. When Teko first moved into his new home, for example, Maxwell stayed with him to get acquainted. "I put my camp-

bed in his house and for the first few nights I slept there myself," recalled Maxwell in *The Rocks Remain,* "for sharing sleeping quarters with an animal is the most certain way of establishing mutual confidence. It was not, in this case, an entirely comfortable procedure, for no sooner had I manoeuvred myself into the sleeping-bag than he would begin to explore my face with his fingers, pushing mobile digits between my lips and into my nostrils and ears, uttering the while a curious snuffle that led me to believe he had contracted a cold; only after the first few days did I discover that this was a sound of pleasure and contentment, like the purring of a cat."

Ring of Bright Water sold extremely well in English-speaking countries and was warmly received by critics. Gerald Durrell, writing in the *New York Times Book Review,* thoroughly enjoyed the work: "Maxwell's book has made me laugh, and as it is the first one that has done this in goodness knows how many arid years of reading animal books, I must perforce commend it with all my might." Durrell concluded that the author "makes otters seem so delightful . . . that one feels one must get one at once. This is an enchanting, beautifully written, and, above all, a very funny book." Encouraged by its success, Maxwell adapted *Ring of Bright Water* into a children's book entitled *The Otter's Tale.*

Although the frivolity of many of his travel and animal tales might suggest Maxwell was simply an enthusiastic naturalist, close examination of his personal life reveals another side to this complex man. He was a chain-smoker, for instance, who kept several cigarette boxes throughout his house and smoked up to eighty cigarettes a day. He was not only an animal-lover but an avid hunter as well. (Maxwell was said to be an expert shot with the rifle.) Rather than consider this a contradiction, Maxwell felt that since hunting was an integral part of his early life, he naturally had grown accustomed to viewing death as a part of life. Thus he felt no conflict between hunting sharks and loving otters. In addition, Maxwell's living arrangements set him apart from the average person. While he was married between 1962 and 1964 he carried on affairs with other women. Maxwell also lived with two young men at Camusfearna. Perhaps the best characterization of Maxwell is the one John Lister-Kaye includes in *The White Island,* in which he quotes Maxwell's description of himself as "a half-poet with a hyper-sensitive temperament."

Maxwell's personal difficulties began to multiply in the 1960s. Due to his popularity, unannounced visitors came to Camusfearna at all hours of the day and night, causing Maxwell to lose much of the privacy he had cherished all his life. In 1967 a fire destroyed Camusfearna, killing one of Maxwell's otters. Around the same time, the author's health began to decline. He was diagnosed as having lung cancer, and during the late 1960s he was in and out of hospitals. Maxwell died on September 6, 1969, at the age of fifty-five.

WORKS CITED:

Durrell, Gerald, "An Otter Is Generous," *New York Times Book Review,* February 26, 1961, p. 22.
Lister-Kaye, John, "Hospital," *The White Island,* Longman, 1972, pp. 69-81.
"Loss and Profit," *Times Literary Supplement,* June 13, 1952, p. 394.
Maxwell, Gavin, *Harpoon Venture,* Viking, 1952.
Maxwell, Gavin, *The Rocks Remain,* Dutton, 1962.
Maxwell, Gavin, *The House of Elrig,* Dutton, 1965.

Elrig, where Maxwell was born and grew up, provided the locale for his autobiography, *The House of Elrig.*

FOR MORE INFORMATION SEE:

BOOKS

Frere, Richard, *Maxwell's Ghost: An Epilogue to Gavin Maxwell's Camusfearna,* Verry, 1976.
Oxbury, Harold, *Great Britons: Twentieth-Century Lives,* Oxford University Press, 1985.
Wakeman, John, editor, *World Authors, 1950-1970: A Companion Volume to Twentieth Century Authors,* H.W. Wilson Co., 1975.

PERIODICALS

Home, February, 1963.
New Statesman, October 8, 1965.
New Statesman and Nation, June 7, 1952.
New York Times, June 29, 1952; February 27, 1961.
Time, February 28, 1969.

OBITUARIES

Antiquarian Bookman, September 29, 1969.
Newsweek, September 22, 1969.
New York Post, September 8, 1969.
New York Times, September 9, 1969.
Publishers Weekly, October 13, 1969.
Time, September 19, 1969.
Times (London), September 8, 1969.

McCUE, Lisa (Emiline) 1959-

PERSONAL: Born February 16, 1959, in Brooklyn, NY; daughter of Richard (a television director and producer) and Emiline (an artist; maiden name, Dyer) McCue; married Kenneth Stephen Karsten, Jr. (an electrical engineer), 1986. *Education:* Attended University of Hartford, 1978-79; University of Southeastern Massachusetts, B.A., 1981.

ADDRESSES: Home—Bethlehem, PA. *Agent*—c/o Publisher's Graphics, 251 Greenwood Ave., Bethel, CT 06801.

WRITINGS:

WRITER AND ILLUSTRATOR

Fun and Games in Fraggle Rock, Holt, 1984.
Corduroy's Day, Penguin, 1985.
Corduroy's Party, Penguin, 1985.
Corduroy's Toys, Penguin, 1985.
The Little Chick, Random House, 1986.
Ten Little Puppy Dogs, Random House, 1987.
Corduroy Goes to the Doctor, Viking, 1987.
Corduroy on the Go, Viking, 1987.
Corduroy's Busy Street, Penguin, 1987.
Puppy Peek-a-Boo (*Publishers Weekly* children's bestseller), Random House, 1989.
Kittens Love, Random House, 1990.
Puppies Love, Random House, 1990.
Whose Little Baby Says . . . ?, Random House, 1990.
Bunnies Love, Random House, 1991.

"Cheep! Cheep!" said Little Chick.
"Neigh!" said the startled colt.
"I thought you were a dandelion!"

Most of Lisa McCue's books feature fuzzy, friendly animals. (From *The Little Chick*, written and illustrated by the author.)

Ducklings Love, Random House, 1991.

ILLUSTRATOR; WRITTEN WITH DICK McCUE

Ducky's Seasons, Simon & Schuster, 1983.
Froggie's Treasure, Simon & Schuster, 1983.
Teddy Dresses, Simon & Schuster, 1983.
Kitty's Colors, Simon & Schuster, 1983.
Puppy's Day School, Simon & Schuster, 1984.
Bunny's Numbers, Simon & Schuster, 1984.
Kitten's Christmas, Simon & Schuster, 1985.
Baby Elephant's Bedtime, Simon & Schuster, 1985.
Panda's Playtime, Simon & Schuster, 1985.
Raccoon's Hide and Seek, Simon & Schuster, 1985.

ILLUSTRATOR

Marguerite Muntean Corsello, *Who Said That,* Western
    Publications, 1982.
Anonymous (retold by Carol North), *The Three Bears,* West-
    ern Publications, 1983.
Michaela Muntean, *They Call Me Boober Fraggle,* Holt,
    1983.
M. Muntean, *The Tale of the Traveling Matt,* Holt, 1984.
Louise Gikow, *Sprocket's Christmas Tale,* Holt, 1984.
M. C. Delaney, *Henry's Special Delivery,* Dutton, 1984.
Marilyn Elson, *Duffy on the Farm,* Western Publications,
    1984.
L. Gikow, *Wembley and the Soggy Map,* Holt, 1986.
Katharine Ross, *The Baby's Animal Party,* Random House,
    1986.
Hans Christian Andersen (retold by Ben Cruise), *The Ugly
    Duckling,* Western Publications, 1987, released in audio
    and video formats, Western Publications, 1987.
K. Ross, *Bear Island,* Random House, 1987.

Cover for one of several books in the "Corduroy" series illustrated by McCue.

K. Ross, *My Little Library of Fuzzy Tales: A Fuzzy Fussy
    Tale, A Fuzzy Sleepy Tale, A Fuzzy Wake Up Tale, A
    Fuzzy Friendly Tale,* Random House, 1987.
K. Ross, *Farm Fun,* Random House, 1987.
Stephanie Calmenson, *Spaghetti Manners,* Western Publica-
    tions, 1987.

S. Calmenson, *One Red Shoe,* Western Publications, 1987.
Jane Thayer, *The Puppy Who Wanted a Boy* (Reading Rainbow selection), Morrow, 1988.
K. Ross, *Nighty-Night, Little One,* Random House, 1988.
Jan Wahl, *Timothy Tiger's Terrible Toothache,* Western Publications, 1988.
K. Ross, *Animal Babies Book and Puzzle Set,* Random House, 1988.
K. Ross, *Sweetie and Petie,* Random House, 1988.
Judy Delton, *Hired Help for Rabbit,* Macmillan, 1988.
K. Ross, *The Fuzzytail Friends' Great Egg Hunt,* Random House, 1988.
Bill Wallace, *Snot Stew,* Holiday House, 1989.
Diane Namm, *Little Bear,* Grolier, 1989.
Ann Turner, *Hedgehog for Breakfast,* Macmillan, 1989.
J. Thayer, *The Popcorn Dragon,* Morrow, 1989.
J. Delton, *My Mom Made Me Go to Camp,* Dell, 1990.
Ted Bailey, *Skunks! Go to Bed!,* Western Publications, 1990.
J. Delton, *My Mom Made Me Go to School,* Dell, 1991.
Jim Latimer, *Fox under First Base,* Macmillan, 1991.

ILLUSTRATOR; "SEBASTIAN (SUPER SLEUTH)" SERIES; ALL WRITTEN BY MARY BLOUNT CHRISTIAN

Sebastian (Super Sleuth) and the Hair of the Dog Mystery, Macmillan, 1982.
. . . *Crummy Yummies Caper,* Macmillan, 1983.
. . . *Bone to Pick Mystery,* Macmillan, 1983.
. . . *Santa Claus Caper,* Macmillan, 1984.
. . . *Secret of the Skewered Skier,* Macmillan, 1984.
. . . *Clumsy Cowboy,* Macmillan, 1985.
. . . *Purloined Sirloin,* Macmillan, 1986.
. . . *Stars-in-His-Eyes Mystery,* Macmillan, 1987.
. . . *Egyptian Connection,* Macmillan, 1988.
. . . *Time Capsule Caper,* Macmillan, 1989.
. . . *Baffling Bigfoot,* Macmillan, 1990.
. . . *Mystery Patient,* Macmillan, 1991.

McCue has often been told that she draws people like animals and animals like people. (Illustration from *Hired Help for Rabbit,* written by Judy Delton. Illustrated by McCue.)

OTHER

Illustrator of book covers, *Wretched Robert,* written by Lois I. Fisher, Dodd, 1983; *The Trouble with Soap,* written by Margery Cuyler, Dutton, 1983; and *Ape Ears and Beaky,* written by Nancy J. Hopper, Dutton, 1984.

SIDELIGHTS: Lisa McCue is an illustrator of more than seventy children's books, including the canine detective series "Sebastian (Super Sleuth)," several "Fraggle Rock" books, and her self-authored books for infants. Born in Brooklyn, New York and raised twenty minutes north of New York City in the town of Tappan, McCue explained to *Something about the Author* how her interest in drawing developed: "My mother was a big influence on me. She is an artist. Ever since I can remember, she was painting and drawing and doing every kind of craft. I was always involved in crafts. In elementary school, every time there was a classroom party or art involved, everybody would turn and say, 'Oh, Lisa could do it.' So I was always zeroed in on as the artist of the class. The more you're told you're good at something, the more you head towards that area."

McCue spent a happy childhood growing up in the New York City area. "My parents liked to go to museums, so I ended up going with them. I would always go to the Metropolitan Museum and go to their costume exhibit, that was my favorite place. I loved all the costumes and stepping back in history and seeing how the people dressed, just trying to imagine lifestyles. I had so many interests, and art was just one of them. Music and dance were big interests of mine. I played a lot of sports. In school, I ran track and I played soccer, but my main sport is skiing."

Eventually, drawing began to play a more important role in McCue's schooling. In 1980, while studying art at Southeastern Massachusetts University, McCue met Dutch author Loek Kessels. At Kessels' suggestion, McCue sent a portfolio of her artwork to the editors of a children's book Kessel had been working on. The editors liked her work, and even before she graduated from college McCue had illustrated her first book. "It was the best thing I ever did. I said, 'Wow! This is what I want to do!' So the rest of my junior and senior years I really pushed in that direction. I got right into children's books the summer after I graduated. I haven't had much time for anything else."

From the beginning, most of McCue's books have featured animal characters. "When I started I was much more comfortable doing animals, and my portfolio had a lot of animal drawings, so as my agent showed my portfolio around, clients tended to give me a lot of animal books, and it snowballed from there." Some have compared her style to that of Garth Williams, illustrator of E. B. White's *Charlotte's Web* and Laura Ingalls Wilder's "Little House" books. McCue admits the influence of Williams but said she never consciously tried to imitate him. "Growing up, I never even knew who he was. When I was younger, my favorite books were *Stuart Little* and *Charlotte's Web* and even small 'Golden' books that he did. I never even knew who the illustrator was, and I didn't pay any attention to it until I was at school and was interested in illustration. I went back thinking, 'What were my favorite books?' Every single one of them was the same illustrator. It was Garth Williams."

When asked to describe her drawing style, McCue said she concentrates on accuracy and finds that her everyday experiences are as helpful as animal picture books. "I have an extensive library of animal encyclopedias, but if you go through my books, you'll see all the neighborhood animals and children. My own cat and dog have since starred in many books, and bits and pieces of my home and places around my neighborhood and places I travel to show up in all the books. I try and make everything very happy. I try to give as much life and personality as I can. And since I have so much fun when I'm drawing, I think that comes through in the art work.

"I start with a sketch just like any other illustrator. You get your story, you do sketches, and you send it to the publisher for an 'okay.' As I'm reading a story for the first time, I visualize. I see things in my mind, and I don't really go too far from what my initial reaction to the story is—everything down to what I think characters should be wearing, what type of setting they should be in, if it's a rabbit, what kind of rabbit.

"I'll start with a very, very rough, scribbly sketch, put a piece of tracing paper over it, and start neatening it up—maybe changing action and motion a little bit to get more of the feeling that I want, or enlarge or make things smaller to fit in better. I think when I'm figuring out a book and I'm working at a very steady pace, I can average a page a day. But this average varies with the size of the book and the amount of background and characters on each page.

"I use acrylics a lot in a background because they won't bleed later. When I'm doing my animals, I like colored inks because I can get a nice fine line with them, and they're waterproof to an extent. If I'm doing a background with watercolors, a lot of times I get brighter colors. Luma dyes also get nice bright colors, and I'll use those for clothing or things that need to be brighter, more colorful than I might be able to get with some of the acrylics or colored inks."

McCue has distinguished herself among illustrators with her unique, wooly-haired animal renditions. Though she prefers drawing animals, McCue has depicted people in some of her books. She explained how she adapts her distinctive style to the drawing of people. "If I'm drawing animals and people together in a book, I'll lean towards relying on a photograph. All of a sudden, the clothing folds become a little more realistic, or I start to overwork them. They start looking too much like the photograph more than a personality. If I keep away from that and just deal with trying to give them a personality, I think I end up with a better result. If the character's personality is very strong, I'll usually visualize somebody I know that has a personality like that. If I'm making the character angry, all of a sudden I'll find out that my face is in a tense, angry position."

When choosing an illustrating project, McCue tries to avoid the tedious aspects of drawing. "I think in terms of what type of pictures I would enjoy doing. Sometimes I've gotten stories where I thought the story was just wonderful but it took place in the same room. The characters were doing something different but it all took place in the same background. I like books where there's a lot going on. The characters will be outdoors one time, indoors one time. On every page there's something new going on so that it doesn't all start to look alike. You just get tired of drawing if you're drawing an animal in a kitchen and the kitchen is the background for every page. You get tired of drawing that stove and all the little doo dahs on top of that stove over 100 times. So I look for books that I think I can make interesting pictures from. I like upbeat stories, funny, silly stories."

With her first child on the way, McCue has relied in the past on other children for reaction to her books. "I have good friends and relatives that all have little babies now, and they'll always call and say, 'Oh, so and so loves this page and every time we open the book up she only wants to skip right to that because she loves the kitty popping his head out of the bag.' And they tell me what pictures and what books tend to go over big with their children and why. I keep that in mind for the next stories. It's funny. My favorite pictures are the ones that compositionally work perfectly, but that's not necessarily the one's the kids go for. They tend to like the ones where there's a character that's being a little naughty or hiding or searching for something where the child could get involved."

McCue now lives in Bethlehem, Pennsylvania with her husband and seems content with the steady work she has found illustrating children's books.

WORKS CITED:

McCue, Lisa, interview conducted by Marc Caplan for *Something about the Author.*

* * *

McELRATH, William N. 1932-

PERSONAL: Surname is accented on first syllable; born March 1, 1932, in Murray, KY; son of Hugh M. (a dentist) and Gladys (Thomas) McElrath; married Elizabeth F. Hendricks (a musician and missionary), August 28, 1958; children: Timothy Paul, James Conrad. *Education:* Murray State University, B.A., 1953; Southern Baptist Theological Seminary, M.Div., 1956, Th.M., 1959. *Religion:* Baptist.

ADDRESSES: Home—Jalan Jamuju 17, Bandung 40114, Indonesia. *Office*—Southern Baptist Foreign Mission Board, 3806 Monument Ave., Box 6767, Richmond, VA 23230; and Box 70161, Pasadena, CA 91117-7161.

CAREER: Free-lance writer and editor, 1951—; pastor of Baptist church, Carrollton, KY, 1957-59; Baptist Sunday School Board, Nashville, TN, editor, 1959-64; Southern Baptist Foreign Mission Board, Richmond, VA, missionary, 1964—.

MEMBER: Indonesian Baptist Mission (member of executive committee, 1970-73, 1975-77), Indonesian Baptist Literature Society (editorial coordinator, 1966—).

AWARDS, HONORS: Prizes received from Broadman Press for hymns.

WRITINGS:

CHILDREN'S AND JUVENILE BOOKS

Butch Discovers America, with teacher's manual, Home Mission Board, 1962.
Great Passages of the Bible, with teacher's manual, Broadman, 1962.
A Bible Dictionary for Young Readers, Broadman, 1965.
Music in Bible Times, with teacher's manual, Convention Press, 1966.
Me, Myself, and Others, with teacher's manual, Convention Press, 1968.
Bible Guidebook, Broadman, 1972.

Cover of the 1984 children's book that helped author William N. McElrath discover his Kentucky roots.

Winding Road, Convention Press, 1973, 2nd edition, Broadman, 1976.
Four Fishers of Men: An Anytime Play (or Easter Play) for Teens, Broadman, 1978.
Sing His Song around the Earth, with teacher's manual, Convention Press, 1979.
I Sailed with Saul of Tarsus, Broadman, 1980.
Church in the Big Top, Convention Press, 1982.
Indian Treasure on Rockhouse Creek, Broadman, 1984.

BIOGRAPHIES FOR CHILDREN

Jamie Ireland, Freedom's Champion, Broadman, 1964.
To Be the First: Adventures of Adoniram Judson, America's First Foreign Missionary, Broadman, 1976.
Judges and Kings: God's Chosen Leaders, Broadman, 1979.
Oz and Mary Quick: Taiwan Teammates, Broadman, 1984.
Bold Bearers of His Name: Forty World Mission Stories, Broadman, 1987.

LIBRETTOS

Samuel!, Broadman, 1970.
God's Word in Their Hearts, Broadman, 1975.
William N. McElrath Anthem Series, Van Ness, 1986.

OTHER

Contributor of over 600 articles and stories to periodicals, including *Midwest Folklore, Living with Teenagers, Youth Alive!,* and *Accent.* Contributor to books, *Southern Baptist Encyclopedia,* Volumes 1, 2, 4, Broadman, 1958, 1982; *Survival Kit for New Christians: A Practical Guide to Spiritual Growth,* Convention Press, 1979; and *Unreached Peoples '80: The Challenge of the Church's Unfinished Business,* David

Cook, 1980. Hymns represented in numerous anthologies, including *Junior Hymnal,* Broadman, 1964; *Baptist Hymnal,* Convention Press, 1975, new edition, 1991; and *New Broadman Hymnal,* Broadman, 1979. Contributing editor to *International Christian Digest.*

McElrath is also the author of 35 books in the Indonesian language and has had his English-language work translated into numerous foreign languages, including Spanish and Indonesian.

WORK IN PROGRESS: Two juvenile novels, *New Worlds at the World's Fair,* and *The Crazy Cougars of Camp Crabmont;* two young adult novels, *Son of David, Son of Jezebel,* and *A Bridge of Days;* and a nonfiction juvenile book, *Rival Kings in Bible Times.*

SIDELIGHTS: William N. McElrath told *SATA:* "For twenty centuries, followers of the Lord Jesus Christ have used the word 'calling' in a special sense. It means the way God gets us into the kind of work He wants us to do and then equips us to do it.

"That's why I like to say that I have been called as a writer. At different times I've been a camp counselor, a part-time cafeteria employee, a part-time music and youth director of a church in the suburbs, a schoolteacher in the inner city, and a pastor in the backwoods; for many years I've been both a foreign missionary and an editor of books, magazines, and Sunday School quarterlies; but all this time I've also kept on being a writer.

"I started writing stories, nonfiction, poems, and plays when I was in the third grade. Some of my writings began to be published in school papers and annuals by the time I was in the sixth grade, and in newspapers and magazines of much wider circulation while I was still in my teens. I have written more than sixty books in all, about half of them in the Indonesian language. The books listed above are only those in English that have gotten published so far. I still have hopes for several more to make it into print!

"One of the most interesting things about my calling as a writer is the people I get to meet. Some of my best friends in Indonesia are a troupe of young circus stars—highwire walkers, trapeze artists, bareback riders, clowns, tumblers, jugglers, animal trainers, and all the rest. I've already done one book about them for a rather specialized audience (*Church in the Big Top*), and hope someday to write another book about them for young readers in general.

"The last time I got to attend the worship service they always hold in the main tent every Sunday morning, one of the speakers was Iwan. He's the tallest boy in the pyramid on the tightrope, and also the one who once rescued a dwarf clown from the fangs of a runaway tiger. I've known Iwan and his three younger brothers since they were small enough for me to carry them on my shoulders.

"Five of my books are biographies, and those have helped me meet some interesting people, too. For *Oz and Mary Quick: Taiwan Teammates,* I had fun eating Chinese food as I hear the Quicks themselves tell me about all those hair-raising adventures they had as missionaries in China, Japan, the Philippines, and Taiwan during and after World War II.

"I didn't get to meet *Jamie Ireland, Freedom's Champion,* because he died in 1806. But as I sat in the rare books vault of a library and leafed through the musty pages of Ireland's autobiography, I realized what a lively freedom fighter he must have been during colonial days in Virginia. And I knew I'd have to try to bring Jamie Ireland back to life again for readers of today.

"*To Be the First: Adventures of Adoniram Judson, America's First Foreign Missionary* was another book that took me back into the past. Yet I felt a special closeness with Adoniram Judson: He, like me, ventured out from the United States of America to become a missionary in a troubled country of Southeast Asia, and some things about such an experience don't change very much across two centuries.

"In writing *Bold Bearers of His Name: Forty World Mission Stories,* I also got to meet—in person and through their writings— several fascinating men and women from East and West whose biographical sketches are included.

"All the biographical subjects in *Judges and Kings: God's Chosen Leaders* have been dead for two thousand years and more. Yet their stories still blaze up like bonfires from the pages of the Old Testament. I suspect I'll have to write at least one more book from Bible times before I'm done.

"*I Sailed with Saul of Tarsus,* a novel for young adults, brought me a different kind of acquaintance. Of course I had known and read about the Apostle Paul (also known as Saul) ever since I was tiny. But as I mapped out the most complete record of a sea voyage still preserved for us from ancient times (you can read it yourself in the Acts of the Apostles, chapters 27 and 28), I got to know that first great missionary in a special way. What would it really have felt like to be a teenage slave boy on the same ship with Saul of Tarsus? That's what my book is all about.

"A favorite among my books is *Indian Treasure on Rockhouse Creek,* because it helped me dig down into my own family's roots in western Kentucky. That novel for boys and girls took me 25 years to write, off and on, and it was turned down by 18 different publishers before Broadman Press finally brought it out in 1984. Maybe this experience of mine will give encouragement to other boys and girls who have a way with words, and who feel that the Lord is also calling them to be writers.

"You can't write much unless you live a lot. God has been good to me: He's given me a faithful wife, two strong sons, two daughters-in-love, and one grandchild so far. Plus, I've lost count how many nephews and nieces, both blood kin and borrowed. God has let us hike up Vesuvius and the Great Wall of China, splash in the surf of the Malacca Strait, weather a hailstorm in Bryce Canyon, cruise through a fjord in Norway, and hydrofoil down the Danube. For a quarter of a century He's let us live in a gorgeous tropical country where you can sleep out on the slopes of a live volcano and see lava flows glowing red in the night, where you can swim outdoors 365 days a year and climb temple towers built six centuries before Columbus sailed. And all this time God has let us meet all kinds of people—as many different shades of skin among them as you'd find candy colors in a Whitman's Sampler. My job is to tell all the people I meet the Good News about Jesus Christ, the Saviour of the world. And I especially like to do it in writing. After all, that's my calling."

McWILLIAMS, Karen 1943-

PERSONAL: Born October 12, 1943, in Alexandria, LA; daughter of Paul F. (retired Air Force officer) and Bee McWilliams; married Julio Espinosa, July 26, 1980 (divorced, 1988). *Education:* Attended University of Madrid, Spain, 1963; University of Northern Colorado, B.A., 1966; University of San Diego, M.A., 1976.

ADDRESSES: Home—1763 Wellesley Circle #1, Naples, FL 33999. *Agent*—Meredith Bernstein, 2112 Broadway, Suite 503A, New York, NY 10023.

CAREER: Grade-school teacher in Placerville and Redlands, CA, 1966-69, in Germany, Japan, and Philippines, 1969-77; school librarian in St. Croix, U. S. Virgin Islands, 1977-83; writer, 1983—.

MEMBER: Authors Guild, Society of Children's Book Writers.

AWARDS, HONORS: Work-In-Progress Grant, Society of Children's Book Writers, 1985.

WRITINGS:

Pirates, Watts, 1989.

KAREN McWILLIAMS

Contributor of articles to *Lincoln Homework Encyclopedia.*

WORK IN PROGRESS: A series of pirate stories; a series of nonfiction pirate picture books for Kindergarten through 3rd graders, titled "Pirates throughout the Ages"; a collective biography of America's pre-Revolutionary War pirates, titled *Pirates of the Colonial Coast;* and a picture book with overseas settings.

SIDELIGHTS: Karen McWilliams told *SATA:* "I think I was an appreciator of books almost from the day I was born. Before I began school, I loved to hear my mother read fairy tales, the poems of Robert Louis Stevenson, Rudyard Kipling's *Just So Stories,* and Helen Bannerman's *Little Black Sambo.*

"When I was in second grade, she gave me a brown spiral notebook, and in big block letters I laboriously printed *The Witch That Said 'Boo!'* It was at that moment that I decided when I grew up I would write children's stories."

FOR MORE INFORMATION SEE:

PERIODICALS

Gulfcoast, June, 1989.

* * *

MILLER, Marvin

ADDRESSES: Home—New Jersey.

CAREER: Works in advertising. Writer; magician and inventor of magic tricks.

AWARDS, HONORS: Best Books for the Teenager, humor category award, New York Public Library, 1982, for *Wordoodles;* Reader's Choice Award, Silver Burdett & Ginn Reading Series, 1989, for short story "The Pirates of Sandy Harbor," in *T*A*C*K Secret Service.*

WRITINGS:

Wordoodles, Bantam, 1980.
Your Own Super Magic Show, Scholastic Inc., 1984.
You Be the Jury (illustrated by Bob Roper), Scholastic Inc., 1987.
You Be the Jury: Courtroom II, Scholastic Inc., 1989.
You Be the Jury: Courtroom III, Scholastic Inc., 1990.
You Be the Jury: Courtroom IV, Scholastic Inc., 1991.
You Be the Detective, Scholastic Inc., 1991.

"T*A*C*K" SERIES; WITH NANCY K. ROBINSON; ILLUSTRATED BY ALAN TIEGREEN

T*A*C*K to the Rescue, Scholastic Inc., 1982.
T*A*C*K Secret Service, Scholastic Inc., 1982.
T*A*C*K against Time, Scholastic, Inc., 1983.
T*A*C*K into Danger, Scholastic Inc., 1983.

OTHER

Contributor of short stories to several reading series; contributor of puzzles to numerous magazines and puzzle books. Creator of mystery plots for television, produced by Universal Studios and Twentieth Century Fox. Contributing Editor, *Games* magazine, 1977—.

Did Billy Hoffman's parrot ransack the living room? Or is his story a cover-up? (From *You Be the Jury* by Marvin Miller. Illustrated by Bob Roper.)

SIDELIGHTS: Marvin Miller told *SATA:* "I always had a special curiosity about things and became interested in magic at an early age. By the time I entered college, I was regularly performing on the east coast and worked my way through college as a stage magician. This curiosity expanded to puzzles and who-done-it mysteries. I find this curiosity very useful in advertising, which is my profession. I have tried to introduce concepts of curiosity and ingenuity into the books I have written."

* * *

MORINE, Hoder
See CONROY, John Wesley

* * *

MORRISON, Joan 1922-

PERSONAL: Born December 20, 1922, in Hinsdale, IL; daughter of Werner Lars (a contractor) and Neva (Lewis) Wehlen; married Robert Thornton Morrison (a writer), June 19, 1943; children: Robert Kirby, James Vaughan, Susan Signe. *Education:* University of Chicago, B.A., 1944. *Politics:* Democrat. *Religion:* Protestant.

ADDRESSES: Home—64 Spring Brook Rd., Morristown, NJ 07960. *Agent*—John Ware, 392 Central Park West, New York, NY 10025.

CAREER: Free-lance writer, 1948—. Adjunct professor at County College of Morris, 1976—, and New School for Social Research, 1987—.

MEMBER: National Society of Arts and Letters, American Association of University Women, American Studies Association, Oral History Association.

AWARDS, HONORS: Books Across the Sea Ambassador Book Award, English-speaking Union of the United States, and Notable Book of the Year award, *New York Times,* both 1980, both for *American Mosaic.*

WRITINGS:

(With Charlotte F. Zabusky) *American Mosaic: The Immigrant Experience in the Words of Those Who Lived It,* Dutton, 1980.
(With Robert K. Morrison) *From Camelot to Kent State: The Sixties Experience in the Words of Those Who Lived It,* Times Books, 1987.

Contributor of articles to numerous periodicals, including *New York Times, Mademoiselle, McCalls,* and *Better Homes and Gardens.*

WORK IN PROGRESS: A television adaptation of *American Mosaic.*

SIDELIGHTS: Joan Morrison told *SATA:* "I have always been interested in history, particularly in finding out what

happens to people living through periods of great change, and that probably explains why I concentrated on oral history. So far the two areas I worked on have been the American immigrant experience and the 1960s—both periods involving great change in both our national and our personal lives. By editing the transcripts of my interviews in a way that preserves the integrity of the narrator and reveals the 'short story' that I believe exists in every one's life, I hope to make those periods real and interesting both to present and future readers. To me reality is fascinating and absorbing and I want to share that feeling with others.

"My own career is an example of my belief that chance plays a role in all our lives. I had worked on my college newspaper and vaguely wanted to be 'a writer' but my first opportunity came on a canoe trip (with my husband) in the remote wilds of Canada when I was 22 years old. We were camped on a secluded campsite, far removed we thought from civilization, when a *Mademoiselle* photographer paddled up and asked if he could take our photo for a 'Young People in Canada' issue. That led to an offer to write an article to go with the photos and to a 20—year career as a free-lance writer."

FOR MORE INFORMATION SEE:

PERIODICALS

Morris County Record, November 15, 1987.
Newark Star Ledger, January 3, 1988.
New York Times (New Jersey Section), October 12, 1980.

*   *   *

MUIR, Helen 1937-

PERSONAL: Born March 4, 1937, in West Kirby, Wirral, England; daughter of John Gordon (a roofing consultant) and Mary Hazle (a speech therapist; maiden name, Syminton) Muir. *Education:* Attended school near Shrewsbury, England. *Politics:* "Middle and Green." *Religion:* Anglican.

ADDRESSES: Home—Primrose Hill, London, England. *Agent*— Jennifer Kavanagh, 39 Camden Park Rd., London NW1, England.

CAREER: Worked variously as a salesperson in an antique shop and a sports shop; reporter for the *Birkenhead News,* 1955-57, Hampstead *Highgate Express,* 1959, and London *Sunday Times,* 1973-1980; writer.

WRITINGS:

NOVELS

Don't Call It Love, Duckworth, 1975.
Noughts and Crosses, Duckworth, 1976.
The Belles Lettres of Alexander Bonaparte, Hutchinson, 1980.
Many Men and Talking Wives, Duckworth, 1981.
Nothing for You, Love, Gollancz, 1988, David & Charles, 1990.
Leo Dancing, Gollancz, in press.

CHILDREN'S BOOKS

Jack Russell Jackson, Gollancz, 1983.
Dan's Secret Pony, Blackie, 1985.
Lila the Edible Frog, Collins, 1986.

JOAN MORRISON

HELEN MUIR

Montagu Mountain Goat, Blackie, 1987.
Wonderwitch, Macdonald & Co., 1988, Simon & Schuster, 1989.
The Racing Witch, Methuen, 1988.
Modge and Podge, Methuen, 1988, Dial, 1989.
Tiger Trouble, Blackie, 1989.
Magic Mark, Simon & Schuster, 1990.
Wonderwitch and the Rooftop Cats, Simon & Schuster, 1991.

OTHER

Contributor of short stories to women's magazines, and of articles to periodicals, including *Punch, Observer* and *Times Literary Supplement.*

SIDELIGHTS: Helen Muir commented: "On the whole I am mostly interested in writing that amuses me. I like character studies rather than a lot of plot. I like a short, delicate study rather than a saga. I want extraordinary characters in an ordinary setting, and not ordinary people having extraordinary adventures. I hope I have enough humor and perception. If I can make a reader laugh, or if I can make a reader exclaim: 'Of course, that's just how it is. I'd never thought of it!,' then I feel reassured. I have admired Evelyn Waugh and Flann O'Brien.

"My children's books are mostly about animals. The writing is therapeutic, I find, whereas the inner churning necessitated by the adult novel strains my relationships. My father could go to a cocktail party and talk about dogs from the time we arrived to the time we left. I feel much the same. I belong to a cat rescue network—we take in unwanted cats until they find homes—and many of my children's stories come from ideas based on my own experiences with cats, horses, dogs, and other animals.

"I also work for the Compassion in World Farming movement every month. It is a fight against factory farming. If we are to use animals as we do, they must surely have a decent life and a decent death. I cannot understand how we make ourselves so superior and cause such suffering and abuse to the animals we eat."

FOR MORE INFORMATION SEE:

BOOKS

Dictionary of Literary Biography, Volume 14: *British Novelists Since 1960,* Gale, 1983.

PERIODICALS

Literary Review, June, 1988.
Sunday Times (London), July 3, 1988.
Times Literary Supplement, November 11, 1988.

*   *   *

MURPHY, Joseph E., Jr. 1930-

PERSONAL: Born March 13, 1930, in Minneapolis, MN; son of Joseph E. (a newspaperman) and Ann (Hynes) Murphy; married Diana Esther Kuske, July 24, 1958; children: Michael J., John E. *Education:* Princeton University, B.A., 1952; graduate study at University of Minnesota, 1956-60. *Politics:* Democrat.

JOSEPH E. MURPHY, JR.

ADDRESSES: Home—2116 West Lake Isles Blvd., Minneapolis, MN 55405. *Office*—Midwest Communications Inc., 90 South 11th St., Minneapolis, MN 55403. *Agent*—Vicki Lansky, 18326 Minnetonka Blvd., Deephaven, MN 55391.

CAREER: Writer. Woodard Elwood & Co. (brokerage firm), Minneapolis, MN, director of investment research and financial analysis, corporate secretary, 1961-67; Northwestern National Bank, Minneapolis, vice-president, 1967-83; writer, 1983—. Midwest Communications, Inc., Minneapolis, director, 1956-87, vice-chairman, 1986-89, chairman, 1990—. Member and co-leader of American expedition to Istor-o-Nal, Pakistan, 1955; member of American expedition to Peak Nun, India, 1980; leader of American expeditions to Minya Konka, China, 1982, Shisma Pangma, China, 1984, and Mount Everest, China, 1986; member of international South Pole Overland Expedition, 1988-89. Member of board of directors for various civic and political organizations, including Minnesota Council on Quality Education, 1971-77, Minnesota Opera Company, 1971-80, Macalester College, 1973-85, Minnesota Arthritis Foundation, 1982-86, Voyager Outward Bound School, 1986—, and Midwest China Center, 1987-88. *Military service:* U.S. Army, 1952-55; became second lieutenant.

MEMBER: Authors Guild, American Alpine Club (board of directors and vice-president, 1975-81), Explorers Club, Himalayan Club, Institute of Chartered Financial Analysts.

AWARDS, HONORS: Second prize, juvenile division, Friends of American Writers, 1986, for *Adventure Beyond the Clouds: How We Climbed China's Highest Mountain and Survived.*

WRITINGS:

Adventure Beyond the Clouds: How We Climbed China's Highest Mountain and Survived! (juvenile), Dillon, 1986.
With Interest: How to Profit from Interest Rate Fluctuations, Dow Jones-Irwin, 1986.
Stock Market Probability: How to Improve the Odds of Making Better Investment Decisions, Probus, 1988.
The Random Character of Interest Rates, Probus, 1990.
South to the Pole by Ski, Marlor Press, 1990.

Contributor of articles to *Financial Analysts Journal, Journal of Portfolio Management, Trusts and Estates, Princeton Alumni Weekly, Financial Management,* and *Journal of Financial and Quantitative Analysis.* Associate editor, *C.F.A. Digest,* 1971-88.

SIDELIGHTS: Joseph E. Murphy, Jr., commented: "I'd always been interested in mountain climbing, from grade school, I think, but where I lived—Minnesota—there were no mountains and not much chance to climb. At that time, back in the late 1940s, not many people climbed mountains anyway, at least in the United States, though climbing was quite common in Europe. In grade school and high school I read books by the early English explorers and climbers who not only explored and climbed, but who wrote fascinating accounts of their travels. It gradually became my ambition to do the same, though I wasn't very confident that I could."

Murphy began climbing during the summers between college, when he traveled to the western United States. "Those trips led to my first expedition to the Himalayas to the northwest frontier of Pakistan on the Pakistan-Afghanistan

Dustjacket for Joseph E. Murphy, Jr.'s 1986 book for young people about mountain climbing, a hobby that has led the author to expeditions in Asia and Antarctica.

border where no Americans had ever been and only some early British explorers had climbed," Murphy said.

"The expedition started out as a two person trip, much like the early British expeditions, but by the time we left for the mountains we had fifty porters, a liaison officer and an interpreter/cook. That expedition, seeing the strange country, drinking tea with the local people and talking with them through three translations—English, Urdu, and Chitrali—and climbing high in the mountains whetted my appetite for more." Murphy did not climb again until 1980, however, when his former climbing partner suggested a trip to India. "The trip with him to India led to the China expedition which is what *Adventure Beyond the Clouds* is about."

The author continued, "Writing the book was much harder and took a lot longer than I'd expected. I started by working through my diary and telling what happened. But the result lacked a good story line and I had to rework it considerably, ultimately going through five revisions. In the process I learned how to write a book which was much different than the kinds of things I'd written most of my life. Although I'd planned to finish the book in a summer, it took a full two years.

"Two unexpected things happened in writing the book. One was the joy of reliving the expedition—it was as though I experienced going to China all over again. The second was the clarity of recall that I developed in the course of writing.

Once I'd completed the first draft, the subsequent drafts were done largely from memory.

"*Adventure Beyond the Clouds* is a shortened version of a longer book which has not been published. Although I still hope to get the longer book published, I haven't given up writing and am now working on my fourth book. I must admit that writing that, and writing the other two, is a lot more fun than being the banker that I was for twenty-five years, even though it doesn't pay as well—to put it mildly. But being your own boss, working on your own schedule and doing what you want to do is hard to beat."

*   *   *

NELSON, Richard K(ing) 1941-

PERSONAL: Born December 1, 1941, in Madison, WI; son of Robert King (a state employee) and Florence (an independent business person; maiden name, Olson) Nelson; married Nita Couchman; children: Ethan Esterline. *Education:* University of Wisconsin, B.S., 1964, M.S., 1968; University of California, Santa Barbara, Ph.D., 1971.

Richard K. Nelson's 1980 book, *Shadow of the Hunter*, is a descriptive account of Eskimo culture that he wrote after living among Alaska's North Slope people for fourteen months. (Illustrated by Simon Koonook.)

ADDRESSES: Agent—Susan Bergholz, 340 West 72nd St., New York, NY 10023.

CAREER: University of California, Santa Barbara, teaching associate, 1968-69, research fellow in anthropology, 1969-71; University of Hawaii, Honolulu, assistant professor of anthropology, 1971-72; Memorial University of Newfoundland, St. Johns, assistant professor of anthropology, 1972-73; University of Alaska, Fairbanks, research associate, 1973-77; University of California, Santa Barbara, visiting lecturer, 1978; University of California, Santa Cruz, visiting lecturer, 1979; University of Alaska, visiting professor, 1980, affiliate associate professor, 1982—. Member of field expeditions to Kodiak Island, Alaska, 1961, Anangula Island in the Aleutians, 1963, and four extended ethnographic field studies among Alaskan Eskimos and Athapaskan Indians.

AWARDS, HONORS: New York Film Festival, silver medal, 1987, and Alaskan Press Club public service award, 1987, both for *Make Prayers to the Raven* television series; Pacific Northwest Booksellers Association book award, 1990, for *The Island Within.*

WRITINGS:

Alaskan Eskimo Exploitation of the Sea Ice Environment, Arctic Aeromedical Laboratory, U.S. Air Force, 1966.
Hunters of the Northern Ice, University of Chicago Press, 1969.
Hunters of the Northern Forest: Designs for Survival among the Alaskan Kutchin, University of Chicago Press, 1973, 2nd edition, 1986.
(With Douglas Anderson and others) *Kuuvangmiit: Contemporary Subsistence Living in the Latter Twentieth Century,* National Park Service, 1977.
(With Kathleen Mautner and Ray Bane) *Tracks in the Wildland: A Portrayal of Koyukon and Nunamiut Subsistence,* National Park Service, 1978.
Shadow of the Hunter: Stories of Eskimo Life, University of Chicago Press, 1980.
Harvest of the Sea: Coastal Subsistence in Modern Wainwright, North Slope Borough (Barrow, Alaska), 1982.
Make Prayers to the Raven: A Koyukon View of the Northern Forest, University of Chicago Press, 1983.
The Athapaskans: People of the Boreal Forest, with teacher's guide, University of Alaska Museum (Fairbanks), 1983.
(Editor) *Interior Alaska: A Journey Through Time,* Alaska Northwest Publishing, 1985.
The Island Within, North Point Press, 1989.

ADAPTATIONS: (And associate producer) *Make Prayers to the Raven* (five-part television series), Public Broadcasting System, 1987.

SIDELIGHTS: "I have always been fascinated by nature and deeply moved by the beauty of wild things," Richard K. Nelson states. "My earliest memories are of chasing butterflies behind our house in Madison, Wisconsin, putting them in jars and admiring the colors in their wings. By the time I started high school, my interests had turned to turtles, lizards, and snakes. I kept dozens of them, large and small, harmless and poisonous, in cages I made myself, filling my bedroom and spilling over into the garage. I read every nature book I could get my hands on, but never dreamed of writing a book myself. Incidentally, I later realized it was cruel and unfair to make captives of the animals I loved, and that I could learn more by watching them free in the outdoors.

"Of course, when it came time for college, I chose to study biology. But modern biology had much to do with anatomy, physiology, and chemistry, and little to do with ways of animals and other wild things. Through courses in cultural anthropology, I discovered that traditional people like the American Indians and Eskimos have a vast knowledge of nature and live intimately with their surrounding environment. So I decided to become an anthropologist, because I could then live with native American people and learn what I most wanted to know about nature. I still never considered the possibility of being a writer, and I did rather poorly in English classes.

"As an undergraduate student, I had an opportunity to join two summer research projects in Alaska. Then, in 1964, after my first semester of graduate school, I was given a chance to live for a year with the Eskimos on Alaska's arctic coast, studying their ways of hunting and travelling on the sea ice, recording their knowledge of the animals and the surrounding environment. I was twenty-two years old, and had never been away from home for more than a few months, when I went to spend a year in the Eskimo village of Wainwright. It was the most important experience of my life, and I came back a very different person. Through the year that followed, I sequestered myself in a basement office at the University of Wisconsin and wrote voluminous ethnographic reports on what I had learned. Still, I never considered the idea of a book, though by now I'd begun to imagine writing one someday. Then came an unexpected meeting with an editor from the University of Chicago Press, followed by an offer to publish my reports as a book. *Hunters of the Northern Ice* appeared a year later. It was also accepted in lieu of a masters thesis at the University of Wisconsin.

"My second book, *Hunters of the Northern Forest,* is based on research I did for my doctoral dissertation at the University of California. It is like a non-identical twin to *Hunters of the Northern Ice,* except it's about Kutchin Athabaskan Indians who live in interior Alaska just south of the Eskimo people.

"In *Shadow of the Hunter,* I tried to get beyond the limitations of scientific description, to give a better sense of the Eskimo people and the environment they live in. This book also reflects my interest in putting more life into scientific description, giving myself more chance for creative expression, and making the results of my studies interesting to people other than anthropologists. After writing the manuscript, it took me years to gather enough courage to show it to a publisher. What has gratified me most about this book is the favorable comments about it by Eskimo people and the fact that it is used in Alaskan schools to teach Eskimo children about their own tradition.

"*Make Prayers to the Raven* explores Koyukon Athabaskan Indian traditions regarding the natural world. I thoroughly enjoyed living and working with the Koyukon people, and their teachings about respectful behavior toward nature have profoundly influenced the way I conduct my life. In this book, I tried to express my own feelings about Koyukon people and their traditions, while also staying within the bounds of scientific description. *Make Prayers* is about living in right relationship with our environment, and I believe the lessons it contains are of universal importance, not just as

ethnography but as vital perspectives on preserving our earthly habitat.

"My latest book, *The Island Within,* is a personal exploration of the natural community surrounding my home on the northwest Pacific coast. It draws on the teachings of Koyukon tradition and western natural science, as the foundations of my own relationship to nature. *The Island Within* contains stories of my encounters with brown bears, black-tailed deer, humpback whales, harbor seals, salmon, halibut, and other animals; with storns and mountains and wilderness seacoast . . . experiences shared with family, friends, and a retired sled dog named Shungnak. It is my first step into the creative nonfiction usually called 'native writing,' and into work that focuses on my own life rather than the lives of others. This is the most difficult writing I've ever done, but by far the most enjoyable and rewarding.

"Although I never thought of being an author until I was an adult, I've come to love writing and now center my life around it. Writing is the most solitary work imaginable, and spending long days alone is sometimes very difficult. But as I move toward more creative ways of expression, I find the enjoyment far outweighs the hardship. The greatest rewards for me are in the daily work of writing, the fulfillment of dealing with words and expressing my feelings about the world outside myself, and the sense of doing something to educate others about the places where I've lived and the people who have taught me. This means much more than holding a book in my hands and thinking, 'I wrote this.'

"I have gone from a person who never intended to write to one who never intends to stop writing. I've found the most important things about writing are: to believe that I can do it, to accept huge sacrifices and little pay, to spend some time writing every day, to write about what means the most to me and what I know best, and to remember that I am writing to serve my subject rather than to serve myself."

HOBBIES AND OTHER INTERESTS: Surfing, bicycling, water polo, natural history, environmental activism.

* * *

NOEL HUME, Ivor 1927-

PERSONAL: Born 1927 in London, England; son of Cecil and Gladys Mary (Bagshaw Mann) Noel Hume; married Audrey Baines. *Education:* Attended Framingham College, Suffolk, England, 1936-39, and St. Lawrence College, Kent, England, 1942-44.

ADDRESSES: Home—P. O. Box 1711, Williamsburg, VA 23185. *Office*—Department of Archaelogy, Colonial Williamsburg, VA 23185.

CAREER: Guildhall Museum, London, England, archaeologist responsible for recovery of antiquities in postwar London, 1949-57; Colonial Williamsburg, VA, chief archaeologist, 1957-64, director of department of archaeology, 1964-72, resident archaeologist, 1972—. Honorary research associate, Smithsonian Institution, 1959—. Vice-chairman, Governor's advisory committee, Virginia Research Center for Historical Archaeology, 1969-70, member, 1971-76; member of review panel, National Endowment for the Humanities, 1973-77, and of Institute for Early American History and Culture, 1974-77. Consultant to government of

Jamaica, 1967-69. *Military service:* Indian Army, 1944-45; invalided out.

MEMBER: American Association of Museums, Zoological Society of London (fellow), Society of Antiquaries of London (fellow), Society for Historical Archaelogy, Society for Post-Medieval Archaeology (vice-president, 1967-76), Kent Archaeological Society, Virginia Archaeological Society, English Ceramic Circle, Glass Circle.

AWARDS, HONORS: Society of Colonial Wars in the State of New York best book award and American Association for State and Local History award of merit, both 1964, both for *Here Lies Virginia;* special award for historical archaeology, University of South Carolina, 1975; L.H.D., University of Pennsylvania, 1976; Professional of the Year Award, 1980, from Virginia Archaeological Society.

WRITINGS:

Archaeology in Britain, Foyle, 1953.
(With A. Noel Hume) *Handbook of Tortoises, Terrapins, and Turtles,* Foyle, 1954.
Treasure in the Thames, Muller, 1956.
Great Moments in Archaeology, Phoenix House, 1957.
Here Lies Virginia (American Heritage selection), Knopf, 1963.
1775: Another Part of the Field, Knopf, 1966.
Historical Archaeology, Knopf, 1968.
(And director) *Doorway to the Past* (film), 1968.
A Guide to Artifacts of Colonial America, Knopf, 1969, reprinted, 1991.
Archaeology and Wetherburn's Tavern, Colonial Williamsburg, 1969.
Glass in Colonial Williamsburg's Archaeological Collections, Colonial Williamsburg, 1969.
Pottery and Porcelain in Colonial Williamsburg's Archaeological Collections, Colonial Williamsburg, 1969.
Wells of Williamsburg: Colonial Time Capsules, Colonial Williamsburg, 1969.
James Geddy and Sons: Colonial Craftsmen, Colonial Williamsburg, 1970.
All the Best Rubbish, Harper, 1974.
Digging for Carter's Grove, Colonial Williamsburg, 1974.
(And narrator) *The Williamsburg File* (television film), 1976.
Early English Delftware from London and Virginia, University Press of Virginia, 1977.
(And narrator) *Search for a Century* (television film), 1980.
Martin's Hundred, Knopf, 1982, published as *Martin's Hundred: The Discovery of a Lost Colonial Virginia Settlement,* Dell, 1983.
Discoveries in Martin's Hundred, Colonial Williamsburg, 1984.

Also author of two novels published under undisclosed pseudonyms in England, 1971 and 1972. Also author of pamphlets and more than forty archaeological reports, and contributor of articles to *Archaeologia Cantiana, Illustrated London News, Antiques, Journal of Glass Studies, Connoisseur,* and *Country Life.*

SIDELIGHTS: In 1976 archaeologist Ivor Noel Hume, while examining the site of Carter's Grove, an eighteenth-century Virginia mansion, made a startling discovery—the remains of an early seventeenth-century settlement called Martin's Hundred. The 220 English settlers who built the small community had arrived in the New World some time before the *Mayflower* sailed. They had faced a tenuous

existence; those pioneers who survived disease and starvation were massacred during an Indian uprising in 1622.

As Noel Hume shows in his *Martin's Hundred,* the excavation and identification of the site yielded many valuable facts about the living conditions and sociology of America's earliest known settlers. In her review of *Martin's Hundred* for *Nation,* Frederika Randall points out that Noel Hume "tells us how pottery used by the landholding class can be distinguished from that used by servants and gives us the mathematical formula for dating a site by the size of the stem end of a clay tobacco pipe. He traces a few rusty chain links to a coat of mail and a fragment of blue and white tile to an example of delftware depicted in a seventeenth-century Dutch painting. He ponders the gash in the skull of one of the soggy skeletons and decides, finally, that a blow from a garden spade was the probable cause of death."

But "if the importance of the Martin's Hundred site is historical, the emphasis of Noel Hume's book is on the archeological," writes *Newsweek* critic Peter S. Prescott. The reviewer notes that the author "is especially candid regarding the difficulties and disappointments attending his profession." Speaking in the book of an archaeologist's motivation, Noel Hume writes: "It is the thrill of a chase that excites an archaeological historian, pursuing the proof with all the intensity of a hunter, the adrenalin flowing until the moment of the kill; then an instant of elation—and it's done. The excitement drains away."

FOR MORE INFORMATION SEE:

BOOKS

Noel Hume, Ivor, *Martin's Hundred,* Knopf, 1982.

PERIODICALS

Nation, August 7-14, 1982.
Newsweek, July 5, 1982.
Times Literary Supplement, January 7, 1983.
Washington Post Book World, July 4, 1982.

* * *

NORCROSS, John
See CONROY, John Wesley

* * *

O'MEARA, Walter A(ndrew) 1897-1989

PERSONAL: Born January 29,1987, in Minneapolis, MN; died after second heart attack, September 29, 1989; son of Michael (a logger) and Mary (Wolfe) O'Meara; married Esther Molly Arnold, August 18, 1922; children: Donn, Ellen O'Meara Woolf, Deidre O'Meara Humphrey, Wolfe. *Education:* Attended University of Minnesota, 1914-15; University of Wisconsin, B.A., 1920. *Politics:* Democrat.

ADDRESSES: Home—164 North Main St., Cohasset, MA 02025.

CAREER: Reporter in Duluth, MN, 1918; J. Walter Thompson Co. (advertising), Chicago, IL, copywriter, 1920-31; Benton & Bowles, Inc., New York City, creative director, 1932-40; J. Walter Thompson Co., creative director, 1940-50; Sullivan, Stauffer, Colwell & Bayles, Inc. (advertising), New

WALTER O'MEARA

York City, creative consultant, 1951-69; writer. U.S. government, chief of planning staff, Office of Strategic Services, 1942-43, deputy price administrator for information, Office of Price Administration, 1943-44. Director, National Conference of Christians and Jews. *Military service:* U.S. Army, 1918; became sergeant.

MEMBER: Deadline Club, The Players, Phi Beta Kappa, Sigma Delta Chi.

AWARDS, HONORS: Award from the American Association for State and Local History, 1951, for *The Grand Portage;* citation for distinguished services to journalism, University of Wisconsin, 1957.

WRITINGS:

The Trees Went Forth (novel), Crown, 1947.
The Grand Portage (novel), Bobbs-Merrill, 1951.
Tales of the Two Borders (collection of short stories), Bobbs-Merrill, 1952.
The Spanish Bride (novel), Putnam, 1954, reprinted, Friends of the Palace Press, 1990.
Minnesota Gothic (novel), Henry Holt, 1956, reissued as *Castle Danger,* Manor Books, 1966.
Just Looking (columns from *Advertising Age*), SSC&B, 1956.
The Devil's Cross (novel), Knopf, 1957.
The Savage Country (nonfiction), Houghton, 1960.
The First Northwest Passage (juvenile), Houghton, 1960.
The Last Portage (nonfiction), Houghton, 1962, reissued as *In the Country of the Walking Dead,* Universal Publishing, 1972.
(Contributor) *The Golden Book on Writing,* Viking, 1964.
Guns at the Forks (nonfiction), Prentice-Hall, 1965.
The Duke of War (novel), Harcourt, 1966.

The Daughter of the Country: The Women of the Fur Traders and Mountain Men (nonfiction), Harcourt, 1968.
The Sioux Are Coming (juvenile), Houghton, 1971.
We Made It through the Winter (memoir), Minnesota Historical Society, 1974.

Author of column, "Just Looking," in *Advertising Age.* Short stories have appeared in numerous periodicals, including the *Saturday Evening Post.* Also contributor of articles and critical reviews to periodicals.

SIDELIGHTS: The late Walter O'Meara began his writing career at an early age. In an interview with *Something about the Author (SATA),* O'Meara recalled: "The first literary production I remember was a poem I wrote at the age of twelve immortalizing the trailing arbutus. It was printed in our local paper under a pseudonym (I was a cagey lad)." O'Meara continued writing in high school and college with the ambition of becoming an author. After college, however, he began a successful career in advertising. Around age forty, O'Meara remembered his youthful desire to be a full-time writer. He decided the time was right to give his aspiration another chance. After agreeing to act as creative director at his office for six months every year, O'Meara was given the other six months off to write.

O'Meara's novels and historical works are noted for their attention to detail. *We Made It through the Winter,* O'Meara's memoir of his boyhood in northern Minnesota, is a good example. *We Made It through the Winter* offers a vivid

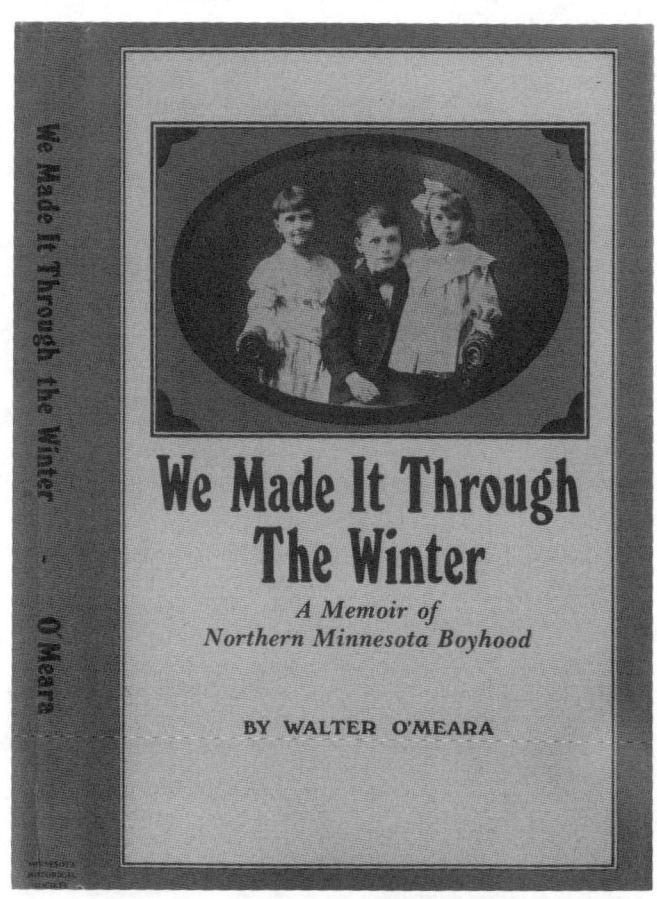

Walter O'Meara's 1974 autobiography offers a vivid description of his boyhood hometown and the colorful people who lived there.

physical description of O'Meara's hometown of Cloquet, as well as a detailed examination of the colorful people who lived there. O'Meara made a habit out of visiting all the places he wrote about. He told *SATA:* "I may have made a fetish of research, spending as much time on it as on writing. . . . I have enjoyed my field research, perhaps more than my writing. But I have tried never to let it show through—to leave a 'smell of lamp' in my prose."

O'Meara lived in many areas of the United States, including Chicago, New York, and Arizona. He also travelled extensively with his wife to Europe, Canada, and South America. In his *SATA* interview, O'Meara described his travels, both for work and pleasure, by saying: "I have always felt at home wherever I lived and in whatever I was writing."

FOR MORE INFORMATION SEE:

BOOKS

Contemporary Authors, Volumes 13-14R, First Revision Series, Gale, 1975.

PERIODICALS

The Patriot Ledger, September 30, 1989.
New York Times, September 29, 1989.

*   *   *

O'NEILL, Gerard K(itchen) 1927-

PERSONAL: Born February 6, 1927, in Brooklyn, NY; son of Edward G. (a lawyer) and Dorothy (Kitchen) O'Neill; married Sylvia Turlington, 1950 (divorced, 1966); married Renate Steffen, April, 1973; children: Janet, Roger, Eleanor, Edward. *Education:* Swarthmore College, B.A., 1950; Cornell University, Ph.D., 1954. *Politics:* Independent. *Hobbies and other interests:* Flying, mountain hiking.

ADDRESSES: Home—Princeton, NJ. *Office*—c/o Space Studies Institute, P.O. Box 82, Princeton, NJ 08542. *Agent*—John Brockman Associates, Inc., 2307 Broadway, New York, NY 10024.

CAREER: Princeton University, Princeton, NJ, instructor, 1954-56, assistant professor, 1956-59, associate professor, 1959-65, professor of physics, 1965-85, professor emeritus, 1985—; O'Neill Communications, Inc., Princeton, founder, 1986-89. Massachusetts Institute of Technology, Hunsaker Professor of Aeronautics and Astronautics, 1976-77. Space Studies Institute, president, 1977—; Geostar Corporation, founder and director, 1983-86. *Military service:* U.S. Navy, radar technician, 1944-46.

MEMBER: American Institute of Aeronautics and Astronautics, American Physical Society, American Association for the Advancement of Science, Experimental Aircraft Association, Phi Beta Kappa, Sigma Xi.

AWARDS, HONORS: Glover Medal, 1977, for *The High Frontier: Human Colonies in Space;* D.Sc., Swarthmore College, 1977; Phi Beta Kappa Science Book Award, 1978, for *The High Frontier: Human Colonies in Space;* Government Industry Service Award, Institute of Electrical and Electronic Engineers, 1986, for the invention and founding of Geostar.

GERARD K. O'NEILL

WRITINGS:

The High Frontier: Human Colonies in Space, Morrow, 1977.
(Editor with Brian O'Leary) *Space-based Manufacturing from Non-Terrestrial Materials,* American Institute of Aeronautics and Astronautics, 1977.
(With David Cheng) *Elementary Particle Physics: An Introduction* (graduate textbook), Addison-Wesley, 1979.
2081: A Hopeful View of the Human Future, Simon & Schuster, 1981.
The Technology Edge: Opportunities for America in World Competition, Simon & Schuster, 1984.

Contributor of over one hundred articles to scientific journals, including *Physical Review, Science,* and *Nature.*

SIDELIGHTS: Gerard K. O'Neill told *SATA:* "One of my books [*Elementary Particle Physics: An Introduction*] is a textbook, intended for college graduates who specialize in physics in graduate school. The other three are very different. Of those, [*The Technology Edge: Opportunities for America in World Competition*] came about as a result of my sense of urgency that America compete effectively with the rest of the world in developing and making high-technology products. When I wrote that book I had no intention of going into business. But within a year after publication I started the Geostar Corporation. I did that to bring to reality a system I had patented, designed originally for aircraft collision avoidance. The system has other applications, to land vehicles, boats, aircraft, and individual people. Geostar is based on satellites, computers, and miniaturized electronic terminals, some of them hand-held. Geostar had two satellites in operation by 1988, and began service in the middle of that year for surface vehicles and some aircraft. It is being implemented under license as LOGSTAR in Europe on a much faster time schedule and with much higher funding.

"The two books that concentrate on my hopes and dreams about the future are [*The High Frontier: Human Colonies in Space*], which presents the concept of space colonies, and [*2081: A Hopeful View of the Human Future*], which gives my view of the next hundred years. I developed the idea of space colonies because of my strong belief that human beings find the greatest satisfaction when they are free both in thought and in action. I also believe that the human race is at its best and most creative when it is expanding into new areas, whether they be geographic, intellectual or artistic. There was a powerful movement a few years ago to limit all human freedoms, even in democratic nations. The reasoning behind that movement was that the energy and material resources of the Earth were finite (which was, by itself, a true statement), and that therefore human beings had to be rationed in every respect, and limited even in their freedom of thought. That was, to me, a terrible prospect for humanity, bad enough for the present generation, and totally unacceptable as a legacy for our children.

"I reacted sharply against the conclusion, and challenged the unspoken basic assumption—which was that there will never be any resources other than those of our planet, and that the environmental range of humanity will be confined forever to the Earth.

"When I looked at the physical and social needs of human beings, and calculated the energy and material resources available in space, I was drawn to designing space colonies. They would run entirely on solar energy, and could be as Earth-like as the most attractive areas of our planet. Logically, I find that space colonies are the only way that humanity can expand both intellectually and in territory, while preserving and protecting the fragile environment of the Earth.

"In *2081* I view the Earth of the late 21st Century as it would be seen by a young space colonist who has never before set foot on a planet. I am fascinated by the opportunities that lie just ahead, all of them within the range of science that we already know. Those opportunities include personal aircraft totally guided from takeoff to landing by a computer system that assures safe flight; and 'floater' transportation at speeds of thousands of miles per hour, within vehicles supported by magnetic fields, flying in vacuum tunnels underground.

"My own life has been shaped by some unique people and by the challenges of the historical era that I've lived in. My parents were great readers, with wide interests, and I recall their frequent quotations aloud to each other, each from the book that was the current interest. Reading, interrupted by conversation, quotations and laughter, was their regular fare after dinner most nights.

"In high school I was fortunate in a number of my teachers, particularly for English, Latin and physics. World War II was the central fact of my high school years, and I joined the Navy on my 17th birthday. My two years in the Navy, much of it working on radar and high-frequency radio on a small ship, led me to major in physics when I returned to go to college. Physics opened up a world of understanding and insight that has enriched my whole life.

"During the 1960's the most exciting fact of American life was, to me, the Apollo Project. I went through the selection process to be an astronaut, only to be disappointed by the cancellation of the post-Apollo space program. My work on space colonies began in 1969, and was stimulated, I believe, by three things that were all happening at once: the first landings on the Moon, the attempts by many scholars to argue for a limitation on human freedoms, and my meeting the girl who later became my wife.

"In the 1970's, while teaching as a professor at Princeton, and doing research in elementary particle physics, I was also pursuing the calculations and library research needed for the practical design of space colonies. The space colony concept was so foreign to current thinking at that time that it took me five years of persistent effort to get the work published in a reviewed scientific journal. Once that happened, the idea spread very rapidly. As one of my friends said not long afterward, 'I don't think the genie will ever be pushed back inside the bottle.'

"During the five years when I was trying to get the new ideas published, I also took up a lifelong dream: flying. I learned to fly sailplanes in 1972. I will always be grateful to my wife, who was my crew chief in 1973-74 as I worked my way to the flight goals that earned the International Diamond Badge in sailplanes. Experiences like motorless climbs to 27,000 feet, and a sailplane flight of more than 300 miles over the deserts of California and Nevada, are not things that one forgets. In 1975 I made the transition to flying with an engine, and have flown small airplanes for business, family travel, and sheer fun ever since.

"The idea of going into business never occurred to me until I was 55 years old. Indeed, the notion of 'engaging in trade' was something that I and my scholarly colleagues had rather looked down on. By the early 1980's my work was an enjoyable mix of teaching, research, writing books and lecturing. I left all that in 1983 and took the risk of starting a new company, Geostar, simply because I could find no other way to bring my concept of a satellite navigation and communication system from the drawing board to reality. Once I was in the business world of a high-technology startup, I found that I liked it. When my first company got past the startup stage and I retired from it, I chose to start another, OCI. And there are other projects that I hope to do. If I had to put a single label on the work I've done in the past twenty years that means the most to me, it would probably be 'taking dreams of a better future for humanity and turning them into practical reality.' Many people, in their own ways, follow that same career, and I'm glad to be in their company."

FOR MORE INFORMATION SEE:

PERIODICALS

Los Angeles Times Book Review, February 12, 1984.
New York Times, July 7, 1981.
New York Times Book Review, May 3, 1981; May 9, 1982; April 29, 1984.
Saturday Review, May, 1981.
Washington Post, March 14, 1978.

*   *   *

OLDHAM, Mary 1944-

PERSONAL: Born June 7, 1944, in Nottinghamshire, England; daughter of Alec (a milkman) and Marjorie (Pickford)

Oldham. *Education:* Attended College of Librarianship, Wales, 1965-66; London School of Economics and Political Science, B.Sc., 1977. *Politics:* "Left of center." *Religion:* Anglican.

ADDRESSES: Home—5 Milford Cottages, Newtown, Powys, Wales. *Agent*—Herta Ryder, Toby Eady Associates, Ltd., 7 Gledhow Gardens, London SW5 0BL, England.

CAREER: Schools librarian at Montgomeryshire, County Library, 1969-72; Clwyd Library Service, Clwyd, Wales, organizer of school libraries, 1972-74; information officer for British Steel Corp., 1978-81; Gwasg Gregynog (The Gregynog Press), Newtown, Powys, Wales, administrative assistant, 1987—.

WRITINGS:

A Horse for Her, Hastings House, 1969 (published in England as *A Dream of Horses,* Harrap, 1969.
The White Pony, Hastings House, 1981.

WORK IN PROGRESS: Secret Feasts, a sequeal to *The White Pony; Lamb to the Slaughter: A Welsh Romance.*

*   *   *

OSTENDORF, (Arthur) Lloyd (Jr.) 1921-

PERSONAL: Born June 23, 1921, in Dayton, OH; son of Arthur Lloyd (an architect) and Edith C. (a homemaker; maiden name, Stomps) Ostendorf; married Rita Mary Hoefler (a dance teacher), December 30, 1941; children: Daniel Lee, Thomas Lloyd, Roxanne Louise. *Education:* Attended School of the Dayton Art Institute, 1939-42.

LLOYD OSTENDORF

ADDRESSES: Home—225 Lookout Dr., Dayton, OH 45419.

CAREER: Dayton Journal-Herald, Dayton, OH, newspaper artist, 1936-39; free-lance artist for periodical and book publishers, 1939—; Milton Caniff & Associates, New York City, cartoonist assistant, 1940; U.S. Government, Wright Field, artist and illustrator, 1941; Ostendorf Art Academy, Kettering, OH, instructor in commercial art and painting and director, beginning in 1969. *Lincoln Herald,* art editor, 1957—. St. Joseph's Orphanage Society, member, beginning in 1950. *Military service:* U.S. Army Air Forces, 1941-45; became technical sergeant.

MEMBER: Royal Society of Arts (London; fellow), Illinois State Historical Society, Montgomery County Historical Society (vice-president, Dayton, 1957-59), Dayton Society of Painters and Sculptors, Civil War Round Table of Dayton (president, 1955-56, 1958-59, and 1965), Manuscript Society, Nature Conservancy.

AWARDS, HONORS: First prize for design for "Chicago Lincoln" statue, 1958; honorary member, Lincoln National Sesquicentennial Commission, 1959; Benjamin Barondess Award from Civil War Round Table of New York, 1964, for *Lincoln in Photographs;* New Jersey Institute of Technology Award, religious category, 1964, for *The Quiet Flame: Mother Marianne of Molokai;* Lincoln Memorial University, Lincoln Diploma of Honor, 1966, doctor of arts, 1974; Litt.D. from Lincoln College, 1968; George Washington Honor Medal from Freedoms Foundation.

WRITINGS:

Mr. Lincoln Came to Dayton, Otterbein Press, 1959.
A Picture Story of Abraham Lincoln, Lothrop, 1962, published as *Abraham Lincoln: The Boy and the Man,* Lamplight Publishing, 1977.
(With Charles Hamilton) *Lincoln in Photographs: An Album of Every Known Pose,* University of Oklahoma Press, 1963.
The Magnetism of Lincoln, The Faces of Lincoln, Lincoln College, 1968.
The Photographs of Mary Todd Lincoln, Illinois State Historical Society, 1969.
(With Adin Baber) *Sarah and Abe in Indiana,* Moore Publishing, 1970.

ILLUSTRATOR

Illustrated Catechism, Bruce Publishing, 1941.
Sister Margaret Patrice, *Keeper of the Gate,* Bruce Publishing, 1941.
Gerald T. Brennan, *The Man Who Dared a King,* Bruce Publishing, 1941.
Albert Paul Schimberg, *The Larks of Umbria,* Bruce Publishing, 1942.
Arthur R. McGratty, *I'd Gladly Go Back,* Newman Press, 1951.
Philip J. Furlong, Sister Margaret, and Don Sharkey, *A Nation United* (textbook), W. H. Sadlier, 1952.
Floyd Anderson, *The Bishop's Boy,* Bruce Publishing, 1957.
Howard E. Crouch, *Brother Dutton of Molokai,* Bruce Publishing, 1958.
Frank Dell'Isola, *The God-Man Jesus,* Bruce Publishing, 1959.
Our Faith, God's Great Gift, Bruce Publishing, 1959.
Charles J. Carmody, *Learning to Serve: A Book for New Altar Boys,* Bruce Publishing, 1961.

Anamae Martin, *Columbus: The Buckeye Capital,* C. E. Merrill, 1962.
Eva Betz, *The Quiet Flame: Mother Marianne of Molokai,* Bruce Publishing, 1963.
V. H. Cassidy, *Long Ago in the Old World,* C. E. Merrill, 1964.
Gladys E. Deck, *Meet the Holy Family,* Prow Books, 1978.
Helen B. Walters, *No Luck for Lincoln . . . ,* Abingdon, 1981.

SIDELIGHTS: Since his early teens Lloyd Ostendorf has been fascinated by Abraham Lincoln; he has said, "A quarter of a century of collecting his pictures and drawing his likeness for fun and for publication was bound to result some day in a book." He told *SATA* that he is making "ongoing progress in finding unknown and unpublished photographs of Lincoln and his family, associates, and contemporaries."

* * *

PALMER, Don
See BENSON, Mildred (Augustine Wirt)

* * *

PANATI, Charles 1943-

PERSONAL: Born March 13, 1943, in Baltimore, MD; son of Charles and Mary Panati. *Education:* Villanova University, B.S., 1965; Columbia University, M.S., 1966. *Religion:* Roman Catholic.

ADDRESSES: Home—West Sayville, NY. *Agent*—Ellen Levine Literary Agency, Inc., 15 East 26th St. S., Suite 1801, New York, NY 10010.

CAREER: Columbia University, New York City, associate physicist at medical center, 1966-68; RCA Corporation, Clark, NJ, head physicist, 1968-71; *Newsweek,* New York City, science editor, 1971-77, television broadcaster for Newsweek Broadcasting Service, 1972-75; writer, 1977—. Consulting physicist. Guest on television programs, including *Today, Good Morning America, The David Letterman Show,* and *Merv Griffin.*

MEMBER: American Institute of Physics, American Association for the Advancement of Science, New York Academy of Sciences.

WRITINGS:

Supersenses: Our Potential for Parasensory Experience (nonfiction), Quadrangle, 1974.
(Editor) *The Geller Papers: Scientific Observations on the Paranormal Powers of Uri Geller* (nonfiction), Houghton, 1976.
Links (novel), Houghton, 1978.
Death Encounters (nonfiction), Bantam, 1979.
Breakthroughs: Astonishing Advances in Your Lifetime in Medicine, Science and Technology (nonfiction), Houghton, 1979.
(With Michael Hudson) *The Silent Intruder: Surviving the Radiation Age* (nonfiction), Houghton, 1981.
The Pleasuring of Rory Malone (fiction), St. Martin's, 1982.
The Browser's Book of Beginnings: Origins of Everything under (and Including) the Sun (nonfiction), Houghton, 1984.

CHARLES PANATI

Extraordinary Origins of Ordinary Things (nonfiction), Harper, 1987.
Panati's Extraordinary Endings of Practically Everything and Everybody (nonfiction), Harper, 1989.

Contributor of articles to magazines.

ADAPTATIONS: The Browser's Book of Beginnings was the basis for the television series *The Start of Something Big,* broadcast from January to April, 1985, for which Panati was series writer and associate producer.

SIDELIGHTS: Charles Panati earned bachelor's and master's degrees in physics and began his career in the field, but more recently he has become known for his writings. His books of unusual facts include *Breakthroughs, The Browser's Book of Beginnings,* and *Extraordinary Origins of Everyday Things.*

Breakthroughs is "a survey of the present state of the art in medicine, science, and technology," wrote Christopher Lehmann-Haupt in the *New York Times.* Among other things, the book describes new ways to diagnose schizophrenia, advances in transportation and telephone services, and new uses for computers and miniature memory banks. The critic felt that Panati overlooked negative aspects of some of the advances, but he still recognized the book's merits. "For anyone who enjoys thinking about the human body or the future of energy or the subparticles of quarks or the possibilities of living in space, 'Breakthroughs' provides a 10-course banquet for the imagination," said Lehmann-Haupt.

In *The Browser's Book of Beginnings* Panati offers essays on the origins of such items as croissants, chocolate, baseball, pens, bathrooms, and the wheel. Lehmann-Haupt, in another *New York Times* review, said he "came away from this book bubbling with new information.... You'll find utterly calming its graceful little essays on every subject from the origin of the universe to the invention of the rubber eraser." A *New Yorker* critic wrote that the book is full of "generally sparkling essays."

Books like Panati's require a lot of research. "In a short time one has to unearth and assimilate information a specialist might take a lifetime to sift," observed Ed Zotti in the *New York Times Book Review.* While a book is in progress Panati works about ten hours a day, every day, until it is done. "Panati says he enjoys the hours of research required by his books," related Jeanne Jackson in *Newsday.* Admitting that he is fairly solitary to begin with, he is able to cut down on social time and concentrate on his work. Jackson reported that the author also "enjoys the freedom writing offers him." Explained Panati, "You have no boss, there's no one looking over your shoulder. You set your own deadlines."

WORKS CITED:

Jackson, Jeanne, "A Book of Beginnings," *Newsday,* July 12, 1984.
Lehmann-Haupt, Christopher, "Books of The Times," *New York Times,* March 28, 1980, p. C32.
Lehmann-Haupt, "Books of the Times," *New York Times,* July 13, 1984.
New Yorker, September 3, 1984, p. 96.
Zotti, Ed, "That's All, Folks," *New York Times Book Review,* September 24, 1989, p. 22.

FOR MORE INFORMATION SEE:

PERIODICALS

Los Angeles Times, September 8, 1987.

* * *

PERCY, Charles Henry
See SMITH, Dorothy Gladys

* * *

POORTVLIET, Marien
See POORTVLIET, Rien

* * *

POORTVLIET, Rien 1932-
(Marien Poortvliet)

PERSONAL: Born August 7, 1932, in Schiedam, Netherlands.

ADDRESSES: Home—Soestdunen, Utrecht, Netherlands.

CAREER: Artist, author, and illustrator. Worked as an advertising executive for fifteen years.

AWARDS, HONORS: Golden plaque from the Committee for General Promotion of the Dutch Book, 1974, for *Het*

wereldje van Beer Ligthart; honors listing from the International Board on Books for Young People, 1980, for *The Sea Lord.*

WRITINGS:

SELF-ILLUSTRATED

Jachtekeningen, Van Holkema & Warendorf, 1972.
De vossen hebben holen, Van Holkema & Warendorf, 1973, translation by Marlies Comjean published as *The Living Forest: A World of Animals,* preface by the author, introduction by Robert Elman, Abrams, 1979.
Te hooi en te gras, Van Holkema & Warendorf, 1975, translation published as *The Farm Book,* introduction by Elman, Abrams, 1980.
Het brieschend paard, Van Holkema & Warendorf, 1978.
Van de hak op de tak, translation by Maria Milne published as *Dutch Treat: The Artist's Life, Written and Painted by Himself,* Abrams, 1981.
Braaf, translation published as *Dogs,* Abrams, 1983.
Langs het tuinpad van mijn vaderen, Kok, 1987, translation published as *In My Grandfather's House,* Abrams, 1988.

Also author of self-illustrated books translated as *Noah's Ark,* Abrams, 1986, and *The Book of the Sandman: And the Alphabet of Sleep,* Abrams, 1989.

ILLUSTRATOR

P. Fentener van Vlissingen, *Roodwild op de korrel,* Roelofs van Goor, 1966.
Wil Huygen, *Alleen woor jagers,* De Bilt, De Fontein, 1967, published as *Niet alleen voor jagers,* Luitingh, 1975.

Self-portrait of *Gnomes* illustrator Rien Poortvliet. (From *Gnomes,* text by Wil Huygen.)

WOODLAND GNOME

275 years old

in the prime of life

actual height (without cap)

15 cm.

his frowning is due to posing in harsh daylight...

Tool kit attached to belt

Rien Poortvliet's double-page illustration for his internationally bestselling book on gnomes. (From *Gnomes*, text by Wil Huygen.)

Just imagine if some animal species of giant proportions occurred.

(From *Dutch Treat: The Artist's Life, Written and Painted by Himself*, by Rien Poortvliet.)

Wilfried Reimann, *Der Lady. Heiteres aus cinem Jagerleben,* F. C. Mayer, 1967.

Huygen, *Met een kluitje in het riet,* De Bilt, De Fontein, 1968.

Ingrid Dobloug and Lise Forfang, *Dyr i kalde land,* Fabritius, 1969.

Dobloug and Forfang, *Dyr i varme land,* Fabritius, 1969.

Jaap ter Haar, *Het Sinterklass book,* Van Holkema & Warendorf, 1969.

ter Haar, *Het Kerstboek,* Van Holkema & Warendorf, 1970.

Huygen, *Leven en werken van de kabouter,* Van Holkema & Warendorf, 1976, translation published as *Gnomes,* Abrams, 1977, pop-up book published as *The Pop-up Book of Gnomes,* paper engineering by Tor Lokvig, handwriting by Diana Kosowski, Abrams, 1979.

Huygen, *Gnomes Games,* games designed by Larry Evans, Troubador Press, 1980.

Huygen, *Teeny Tiny Gnomes Tomes,* three volumes, adapted by Bill Nygren, Abrams, 1981.

Huygen, *De opreop der kabouters,* Van Holkema & Warendorf, 1981, translation published as *Secrets of the Gnomes* (Book-of-the-Month-Club alternate selection), Abrams, 1982.

Also illustrator of books translated as *Boris,* Delacorte, 1969, and *King Arthur,* Crane-Russak, 1977, both by Jaap ter Haar; *Gnomes and Princes,* Paideia, 1979, *The Uninhabited Island,* Paideia, 1979, *Captains, Pirates, and Runaways,* Paideia, and *The Runaway Balloon,* Paideia, both 1980, all by Godfried Bomans; *Gnomes and Their Families,* Abrams, and pop-up book *Gnomes with Animals,* Abrams, both 1983, both by Wil Huygen; and *The Sea Lord,* by Alet Schouten.

Also illustrator of *The Small Dutch Farm, Hunting,* and *Horses, Horses; Het wereldje van Beer Lighthart,* by Jaap ter Haar, translation published as *Beer Lighthart's Little World;* and *Hij was een van ons,* 1976, by Hans Bouma, translation by Brian McDermott published as *He Was One of Us: The Life of Jesus of Nazareth,* Doubleday, 1978.

Poortvliet's works have been translated into Danish, Swedish, German, and French.

SIDELIGHTS: Rien Poortvliet, one of Holland's most popular living artists, was born in Schiedam, the Netherlands on August 7, 1932. Although he showed artistic talent while still in school, Poortvliet's parents wanted him to follow a more traditional career, so he started working in advertising. For fifteen years the artist worked in that field, drawing "happy families eating TV dinners," as he described it to John Sparrow in *US* magazine. Eventually, he became very important in his advertising company. Poortvliet's professional success, however, failed to satisfy his creative needs and he began to devote more of his time to book illustration.

Poortvliet became known internationally in 1978 when he teamed up with doctor and author Wil Huygen to create *Leven en werken van de kabouter,* which was translated into English as *Gnomes.* The book is a detailed study of the life and work of the legendary six-inch-high forest dwellers. In *Us* magazine, Poortvliet claimed to have received the inspiration for the book while hunting near his home in Soestdunen with Holland's Prince Bernhard. "I was wandering in the woods when I saw something red, white, and blue," the artist continued. "A flag, perhaps, or a candy wrapper, I thought. A closer look astonished me, for it was a full-grown gnome, standing all of fifteen centimeters high." Poortvliet sat quietly in the cold woods at night to watch the gnomes, who spotted him right away despite his efforts to blend in with the trees. The little creatures responded by laughing at him, the artist reported. Poortvliet also described how he got down on the ground to imagine what it would be like to be just over a foot tall.

Gnomes was a huge success in Holland, Great Britain, and the United States, where it sold over a quarter of a million copies in prepublication orders alone. Huygen and Poortvliet followed this best-seller with a sequel, the English title of which is *Secrets of the Gnomes.* This book led to gnome dolls, calendars, Christmas decorations, jigsaw puzzles, stationery, and a gnome home designed by the artist. The gnome craze reached its height in 1980 when an animated show about the tiny characters appeared on American television.

Though Poortvliet earned fame for his gnomes, the bulk of his work is made up of realistic paintings of animals; because of this, he has been compared to the great wildlife illustrators John James Audubon and Louis Agassiz Fuertes. In his introduction to Poortvliet's book *The Living Forest: A World of Animals,* Robert Elman, the wildlife editor of *Outdoor Life* magazine, wrote, "As in *Gnomes,* Poortvliet's work . . . is a glorious celebration of nature. Again he reveals his enduring fascination for the natural world around him in his own unique style of scientific exactitude, wit and imagination."

Poortvliet has also illustrated two biblical works: *He Was One of Us: The Life of Jesus of Nazareth,* and *Noah's Ark.* When commenting on his animal paintings in his preface to *The Living Forest,* Poortvliet used biblical quotations to provide a greater understanding of his work, writing "Foxes have holes, and birds of the air have nests (Luke 9:58). . . . And God made the beasts of the earth according to their kind (Genesis) . . ." Elman noted the artist's strengths both as an observer and interpreter of nature, pointing out his "sharpness of observation, insatiable curiosity, limitless patience in studying each subject, an absolute greed for detail, and a mind both creative and pragmatic."

WORKS CITED:

Poortvliet, Rien, *The Living Forest: A World of Animals,* preface by the author, introduction by Robert Elman, Abrams, 1979.
Sparrow, John, "You've Met Gnomes? Now Meet the Man Who Invented Them," *Us,* March 21, 1978, pp. 72-73.
"Those Golden Gnomes," *Time,* April 3, 1978, p. 55.

FOR MORE INFORMATION SEE:

BOOKS

Poortvliet, Rien, *Dutch Treat: The Artist's Life, Written and Painted by Himself,* translated by Maria Milne, Abrams, 1981.

PERIODICALS

International Wildlife, May-June, 1980.

Library Journal, November 15, 1982.
New Yorker, December 6, 1982.
New York Times, December 11, 1983.
New York Times Book Review, December 11, 1983.
Publishers Weekly, June 4, 1982.
School Library Journal, April, 1985.
Times Literary Supplement, March 26, 1982.
TV Guide, August 28, 1982.

*   *   *

PROVOST, Gail Levine 1944-
(Gail Levine-Freidus)

PERSONAL: Surname is pronounced "Provo"; born November 12, 1944, in Augusta, GA; daughter of Arnold J. (a dentist) and Marjorie (a homemaker; maiden name, Rubinstein) Levine; married Frederic Freidus, August 7, 1966 (divorced, October, 1982); married Gary Provost (a writer, teacher, and lecturer), December 29, 1984; children: (first marriage) Scott, Randy. *Education:* University of Bridgeport, B.S., 1966. *Politics:* Liberal Democrat. *Religion:* "Jewish upbringing."

ADDRESSES: Home and office—74 Bolton Rd., South Lancaster, MA 01561. *Agent*—Sterling Lord Agency, Inc., 660 Madison Ave., New York, NY 10021.

CAREER: Art teacher in Devon and Wayne, PA, 1966-68; private art teacher, 1972-74; public speaker and teller of fairy tales, 1982-84; writer, 1984—. Manager of Write It/Sell It Seminars, 1986—, and Writers Retreat Workshop in Connecticut, 1987—. Free-lance artist; cofounder and president of Backstage Theatre Group, Bolton; former member of arts councils of Bolton and Lancaster, MA.

MEMBER: National Writers Union, Association of Writers' Conferences and Retreats.

AWARDS, HONORS: National Jewish Book Award for children's literature, 1985, for *Good If It Goes.*

WRITINGS:

(Composer and lyricist) *Mixed Upon a Time* (play), produced in Bolton, MA, May, 1977.
(With husband, Gary Provost; under name Gail Levine-Freidus) *Good If It Goes* (juvenile), Bradbury, 1984.
(With Gary Provost) *Popcorn* (juvenile), Bradbury, 1985.
(With Gary Provost) *David and Max* (juvenile), Jewish Publication Society, 1988.

WORK IN PROGRESS: William and the Wrestlers of Bamboor, a children's picture book, with David Addison Small; *Dreamality,* a contemporary fantasy novel.

SIDELIGHTS: Gail Levine Provost commented: "My two sons have throughout their lives been unusually open and honest with me about their thoughts and feelings, and in the end, they are the two responsible for my wanting to tell a story or two. Scott, my oldest (sports fanatic, sweet, and funny), was the source of inspiration for the main character of *Good If It Goes* and *David and Max.* Randy, four years younger (creative, expressive, and a risk-taker), was the model for Markie, of *Popcorn.*

Book cover of *David and Max*, a story inspired by Levine-Provost's oldest son, Scott.

"My art and theater background has, I suppose, influenced my visualization technique of working out first drafts of scenes. I, as set-designer, arrange the scene; as director, explain the situation to my characters; as actor, come to terms with each character's motivation by understanding what each character *wants;* and then, as audience, watch what happens next. Then I write.

"The creative part of the writing process—the making something out of nothing—is what actually makes my heart pound madly, and yet it is the other part of the process—the polishing, the editing—that seems to give me the greatest sense of fulfillment. It's a strange business.

"When I was seventeen I began a list—of heroes. By now it looks like this: Vincent Van Gogh, Claude Debussy, Woody Allen, William Goldman, Neil Simon, James Kirkwood, George Shearing, Michael Franks, Ruth ('Maude') Gordon, Ann Tyler, and my husband, Gary Provost. How lucky can a gal get, to be married to one of her heroes? How lucky can a couple be, a couple of writers, to spend their lives together doing what they both love? Being married to a writer, for a writer, might be the greatest gift of all. As Gary says, 'Only another writer understands what the rest of the world does not.'"

*   *   *

PULLMAN, Philip (N.) 1946-

PERSONAL: Born October 19, 1946, in Norwich, England; son of Alfred Outram (an airman) and Audrey (a housewife; maiden name, Merrifield) Pullman; married Judith Speller (a therapist), August 15, 1970; children: James, Thomas. *Education:* Oxford University, B.A., 1968. *Politics:* Socialist. *Religion:* None. *Hobbies and other interests:* Drawing, music.

ADDRESSES: Home and office—24 Templar Rd., Oxford OX2 8LT, England. *Agent*—Ellen Levine, 432 Park Ave. S., Suite 1205, New York, NY 10016; A. P. Watt, 20 John St., London WC1N 2DL, England.

CAREER: Teacher at Ivanhoe, Bishop Kirk, and Marston middle schools, Oxford, England, 1973-86; writer, 1986—. Lecturer at Westminster College, North Hinksey, Oxford.

AWARDS, HONORS: The Ruby in the Smoke received a Lancashire County Libraries/National and Provincial Children's Book Award and a Best Books for Young Adults listing from *School Library Journal,* both 1987, a Children's Book Award from the International Reading Association and a Best Books for Young Adults listing from the American Library Association, both 1988, and a Preis der Lescratten from ZDF Television (Germany); *Shadow in the North* received a Best Books for Young Adults listing from the American Library Association, 1988, and was nominated for an Edgar Allan Poe Award by the Mystery Writers of America, Inc., 1989.

WRITINGS:

Ancient Civilizations (juvenile), illustrated by G. Long, Wheaton, 1978.

Galatea (novel), Gollancz, 1978, Dutton, 1979.

Count Karlstein (juvenile), Chatto & Windus, 1982, edition with pictures by Patrice Aggs, Doubleday (England), 1991.

The Ruby in the Smoke (young adult; first novel in trilogy), Oxford University Press, 1985, Knopf, 1987.

How to Be Cool (juvenile), Heinemann, 1987, adaptation for television first broadcast by Granada, 1988.

PHILIP PULLMAN

The Shadow in the Plate (young adult; second novel in trilogy), Oxford University Press, 1987, published as *The Shadow in the North,* Knopf, 1988.
Penny Dreadful (picture book), Corgi, 1989.
Spring-Heeled Jack, pictures by David Mostyn, Doubleday (England), 1989.
Frankenstein (play; adapted from Mary Shelley's novel of the same title), Oxford University Press, 1990.
The Tiger in the Well (young adult; third novel in trilogy), Knopf, 1990.
The Broken Bridge (young adult), Macmillan (England), 1990, Knopf, 1991.

Also author of additional plays, including *The Adventure of the Sumatian Devil* and an adaptation of Alexandre Dumas's *The Three Musketeers.*

WORK IN PROGRESS: A fourth and final novel for young adults to follow the trilogy begun with *The Ruby in the Smoke; The White Mercedes,* a novel for young adults; *Torn Jasmine,* an adventure story for adults.

SIDELIGHTS: Philip Pullman told *SATA:* "I am first and foremost a storyteller. In whatever form I write—whether it's the novel, or the screenplay, or the stage play, or even if I tell stories (as I sometimes do)—I am always the servant of the story that has chosen me to tell it and I have to discover the best way of doing that. I believe there's a pure line that goes through every story and the more closely the telling approaches that pure line, the better the story will be.

"I have other values as well as those of a storyteller. I believe passionately in social justice and in the right of every citizen to live a decent life, to be well educated, to be part of a society that does not regard money as the most important thing in life. I believe in a society that has a proper human regard for the well-being of all its members, not just the strongest. I find that as I grow older I get more angry, not less, and no doubt this is reflected in the things I'm writing about; my stories are becoming less fantastic and more realistic. Real things spark stories: an incident in a shopping mall, a friend's difficulty in getting hospital treatment, or a vagrant in a local park. And although I've been writing historical fiction, which might seem faraway from the present day, I've begun to see similarities between such things as the condition of the poor in the East End of London in the 1880s and the growing contrast between rich and poor today.

"But I don't write stories to a plan or to make a political point. I've tried, and it doesn't work. The story must tell me. If a story isn't there, no amount of research, study, or passion will make it come. If, when it does come, it's quite different from the story I thought I ought to tell, so be it. I rely on my wife to be my best critic.

"In recent years I've been very pleased to see comics becoming accepted by critics as an art form in their own right. All my life I've loved comics: Batman and Superman were two of my earliest heroes. I notice when I go into schools and talk to pupils that they are often very knowledgeable about how comics work—about how to tell a story and read the pictures—things which adults who only read books, and look down on comics, don't even notice. For some time I've been secretly wanting to write and draw a comic myself. I go to life drawing classes; I'm getting better at drawing people . . . Maybe one day soon I'll begin."

Dustjacket from Philip Pullman's Victorian thriller, the second book of a projected four-volume series.

FOR MORE INFORMATION SEE:

PERIODICALS

Bulletin of the Center for Children's Books, May, 1987.
Times Literary Supplement, December 1, 1978.

*   *   *

ROOSE-EVANS, James 1927-

PERSONAL: Born November 11, 1927, in England; son of Jack and Catherine Owen (Morgan) Roose-Evans. *Education:* Oxford University, B.A., 1952, M.A., 1957. *Politics:* None. *Religion:* Christian. *Hobbies and other interests:* Bee-keeping.

ADDRESSES: Home—Wales and London. *Agent*—David Higham Associates Ltd., 5-8 Lower John St., Golden Square, London W1R 4HA, England.

CAREER: Director and writer. Maddermarket Theatre, Norwich, England, artistic director, 1954-55; Julliard School of Music, New York City, member of faculty, 1955-56; Royal Academy of Dramatic Art, London, England, staff member and judge, 1957-62; Hampstead Theatre Club, London, founder and artistic director, 1959-71; ordained a worker priest of the Anglican Church, 1981. Pitlochry Festival Theatre, artistic director, 1960; Belgrade Theatre, resident director, 1960; director of Stage Two, a theater workshop and research center. Director of West End dramatic productions, including *Under Milk Wood, Cider with Rosie, Private Lives, Spitting Image, The Happy Apple, An Ideal Husband, 84 Charing Cross Road,* 1981-82, *The Best of Friends,* 1988; also directed French production of *The Best of Friends,* 1989;

directed *Oedipus* at Greek Contemporary Theatre, Athens, and Vaclav Havel's *Temptation.* Director of radio documentaries *The Female Messiah,* 1975, *The Third Adam,* 1976, *Topsy and Fred, Acrobats of God, A Well-Conducted Theatre,* and *Lady Managers,* all for British Broadcasting Corp. (BBC). Lecturer; adjudicator for National Union of Students Drama Festival, 1970, and National Drama Festival of Zambia, 1973. Member of drama committee and dance committee of Welsh Arts Council; member of combined arts panel of Southeast Wales Art Association; council member of Welsh Dance Theatre. Founder and chairman of Bleddfa Trust-Centre for Caring and the Arts, Wales. Has preached in Westminster Abbey and other cathedrals in England; heads workshop on ritual. *Military service:* Royal Army Educational Corps, 1947-49.

MEMBER: Garrick Club, Dramatists Club.

AWARDS, HONORS: Arts Council Bursary to Finland, 1968; *The Female Messiah* was chosen by the BBC as its entry for the 1975 Italia Prize; Society of West End Theatre Managers nominated Roose-Evans best director for *84 Charing Cross Road,* 1982; nominated for British Drama Association awards.

WRITINGS:

JUVENILE; "ODD AND ELSEWHERE" SERIES;
ILLUSTRATED BY BRIAN ROBB

The Adventures of Odd and Elsewhere, Deutsch, 1971.
The Secret of the Seven Bright Shiners, Deutsch, 1972.
Odd and the Great Bear, Deutsch, 1973.
Elsewhere and the Gathering of the Clowns, Deutsch, 1974.
The Return of the Great Bear, Deutsch, 1975.
The Secret of Tippity-Witchit, Deutsch, 1976.
The Lost Treasure of Wales, Deutsch, 1977.

JAMES ROOSE-EVANS

OTHER

(Adapter) *The Little Clay Cart,* Elek Books, 1965.
Directing a Play: James Roose-Evans on the Art of Directing and Acting, foreword by Vanessa Redgrave, Theatre Arts Inc., 1968.
Experimental Theatre from Stanislavsky to Today, Universe, 1970, third edition published as *Experimental Theatre from Stanislavsky to Peter Brook,* 1984, fourth revised edition, Routledge, 1989.
London Theatre: From the Globe to the National, Phaidon, 1977.
(Adapter and director) *84 Charing Cross Road* (stage play; based on a book by Helene Hanff; produced on the West End, 1981, produced on Broadway, 1982), S. French, 1983.
Newness of Life, Routledge & Kegan Paul, 1984.
Inner Journey, Outer Journey, Rider, 1987, reprinted as *The Inner Stage: Finding a Center in Prayer and Ritual,* Cowley, 1990.
(Editor and author of introduction) Joyce Grenfell, *The Time of My Life,* (diaries and correspondence), Hodder & Stoughton, 1989.
(Editor and author of introduction) Joyce Grenfell, *Darling Ma: Letters to Her Mother, 1932-1944* (correspondence), Hodder & Stoughton, 1990.

Contributor to *Actor Training Two,* edited by Richard Brown, Drama Book Specialists, 1976. Author of introduction for Andrew Sinclair's *Adventures in the Skin Trade,* New Directions, 1968. Author of weekly column for *Woman* magazine, 1986-88. Contributor to periodicals, including *Financial Times* and *Drama.*

WORK IN PROGRESS: The Journey into Ritual, a sequel to *Inner Journey, Outer Journey.*

SIDELIGHTS: Primarily a theater director, James Roose-Evans is the author of a well-received series of children's books. "Odd" and "Elsewhere," the featured characters, are based on toys belonging to the author. "Odd" is a teddy bear similar to one he parted with when he moved from his childhood home; "Elsewhere" was inspired by a Russian clown doll that Roose-Evans bought in New York. Another character of the series, Mrs. Fenton, is an affectionate representation of the author's late friend, children's writer Eleanor Farjeon. Roose-Evans takes "Odd" and "Elsewhere" on many visits to schools and libraries, and even helps the toys to write their own signatures in books.

Roose-Evans told *SATA:* "My life is so full—what with writing, directing, teaching, leading workshops, being a priest, running the Bleddfa Trust Centre for Caring and the Arts, and traveling, living sometimes in Wales and sometimes in London (which is in England, as opposed to Wales, which is not!). I am delighted that the seven books of 'Odd and Elsewhere' are at last appearing in America. I am still amazed that I wrote them. In fact, they really seemed to write themselves, and I wonder if I ever shall write any more children's books! I have planned a special eighth book about Odd, and I hope one day to write a book about a unique dollhouse—now owned by a doll museum. There really isn't another like it!

"I enjoy writing, but books take a long time to mature. I keep files, and some books grow slowly; the files get larger and larger, with more and more research material, and odd chapters get written, until one day I sit down and start to

THE ADVENTURES OF ODD AND ELSEWHERE

James Roose-Evans

A CHILDREN'S CLASSIC

Cover for the 1971 debut book in James Roose-Evans's well-received "Odd and Elsewhere" series about the exploits of a teddy bear and a clown doll.

write the book. People are sometimes surprised to learn how much research has gone into the books of 'Odd and Elsewhere' series—research on clowns, bees, butterflies and moths, and Welsh folklore. (There really is an Odd's Own Honey. It comes in half pound jars, especially for children, with a label designed by Brian Robb.)

"I use charts. Once I know the main outline I divide a large sheet of paper into squares, and these are the requisite number of chapters. I write into the squares the substance of each chapter as I discover it. Many remain blanks and I meditate on the chart, trying to imagine how the blank spaces, the unknown chapters, will link up with the known chapters. I also do drawings of the characters, maps of the terrain, trying to visualize the scene. All this stems from my background as a theatre director, where one works on a ground plan with a model of the set and cut-outs for the characters of the play, thinking how to move characters from point A to point Z.

"I owe everything to Pam Royds, my editor at Andre Deutsch, who taught me about the craft of writing for children. She has been, and remains, my most challenging critic. That is important—to be challenged. I suppose if I did not have such a variety of creative outlets I would write more children's books. I don't think it matters what one 'achieves.' One simply expresses oneself in different ways. The only sad

thing would be if one couldn't express oneself at all. Creation is a process of growing, so one doesn't have to keep churning out work to justify oneself. 'Give me a piece of earth' says the small girl in Frances H. Burnett's *The Secret Garden*. 'What for?' asks her guardian. 'To grow things in,' is the reply. We are all growing things."

FOR MORE INFORMATION SEE:

Camden Journal, February-March, 1968.
Drama, winter, 1968.
Junior Bookshelf, April, 1977.
New York Times, June 3, 1970.
Times Literary Supplement, March 25, 1977.

*   *   *

ROSS, Tony 1938-

PERSONAL: Born August 10, 1938, in London, England; son of Eric Turle Lee (a magician) and Effie Ross; married Carole Jean D'Arcy (divorced); married second wife, Joan (divorced); married third wife, Zoe, 1979; children: (first marriage) Philippa (adopted); (second marriage) George (stepson), Alexandra; (third marriage) Katherine. *Education:* Liverpool College of Art, diplomas, 1960, 1961. *Politics:* None. *Religion:* Methodist. *Hobbies and other interests:* Sailing small boats, cats, the monarchy, collecting toy soldiers, lamb cutlets.

ADDRESSES: Home—Whisket Cottage, 5 Pexhill Rd., Broken Cross, Macclesfield, Cheshire, England.

CAREER: Smith Kline & French Laboratories, graphic designer, 1962-64; Brunnings Advertising, art director, 1964-

TONY ROSS

65; Manchester Polytechnic, Manchester, England, lecturer, 1965-72, senior lecturer in illustration, 1972-85; full-time writer and illustrator, 1985—. Consultant in graphic design.

MEMBER: Society of Industrial Artists and Designers.

AWARDS, HONORS: I'm Coming to Get You! was named a Children's Choice by the International Reading Association/CBC, and a Best Children's Picture Book of the Year by *Redbook,* both 1985; Greenaway commended book, 1986, for *I Want My Potty.*

WRITINGS:

JUVENILES; SELF-ILLUSTRATED

Tales from Mr. Toffy's Circus, six volumes, W. J. Thurman, 1973.
(Reteller) *Goldilocks and the Three Bears,* Andersen, 1976.
Hugo and the Wicked Winter, Sidgwick & Jackson, 1977.
Hugo and the Man Who Stole Colors, Follett, 1977.
(Reteller) *The Pied Piper of Hamelin,* Andersen, 1977.
Norman and Flop Meet the Toy Bandit, W. J. Thurman, 1977.
(Reteller) *Little Red Riding Hood,* Andersen, 1978.
Hugo and Oddsock, Andersen, 1978.
(Reteller) *The True Story of Mother Goose and Her Son Jack,* Andersen, 1979.
The Greedy Little Cobbler, Andersen, 1979.
Hugo and the Ministry of Holidays, Andersen, 1980, David & Charles, 1987.
Jack and the Beanstalk, Andersen, 1980, Delacorte, 1981.
Puss in Boots: The Story of a Sneaky Cat, Delacorte, 1981.
Naughty Nigel, Andersen, 1982.
(Reteller) *The Enchanted Pig: An Old Rumanian Tale,* Andersen, 1982.
The Three Pigs, Pantheon, 1983.
(Reteller) *Jack the Giantkiller,* Andersen, 1983, Dial Books for the Young, 1987.
I'm Coming to Get You!, Dial Books for the Young, 1984.
Towser and Sadie's Birthday, Pantheon, 1984.
Towser and the Terrible Thing, Pantheon, 1984.
Towser and the Water Rats, Pantheon, 1984.
Towser and the Haunted House, Andersen, 1985, David & Charles, 1987.
The Boy Who Cried Wolf, Dial Books for the Young, 1985.
Lazy Jack, Andersen, 1985, Dial Books for the Young, 1986.
(Reteller) *Foxy Fables,* Dial Books for the Young, 1986.
I Want My Potty, Kane/Miller, 1986.
Towser and the Funny Face, David & Charles, 1987.
Towser and the Magic Apple, David & Charles, 1987.
(Reteller) *Stone Soup,* Dial Books for the Young, 1987.
Oscar Got the Blame, Andersen, 1987, Dial Books for the Young, 1988.
Super Dooper Jezebel, Farrar, Straus, 1988.
I Want a Cat, Farrar, Straus, 1989.
Treasure of Cozy Cove, Andersen, 1989, Farrar, Straus, 1990.
Mrs. Goat and Her Seven Little Kids, Atheneum, 1990.
Hansel and Gretel, David & Charles, 1990.
This Old Man, Aladdin Books, 1990.

ILLUSTRATOR

Iris Grender, *Did I Ever Tell You ... ?,* Hutchinson, 1977.
Grender, *The Second Did I Ever Tell You ... ? Book,* Hutchinson, 1978.
Patricia Gray and David Mackay, *Two Monkey Tales,* Longman, 1979.
Bernard Stone, *The Charge of the Mouse Brigade,* Andersen, 1979.

Ross spent a happy childhood with a vivacious mother and a father who moonlighted as a magician.

Jean Russell, editor, *The Magnet Book of Strange Tales,* Methuen Children's, 1980.
Philip Curtis, *Mr. Browser Meets the Burrowers,* Andersen, 1980.
Curtis, *Invasion from below the Earth,* Knopf, 1981.
Curtis, *Mr. Browser and the Comet Crisis,* Andersen, 1981.
Stone, *The Tale of Admiral Mouse,* Andersen, 1981.
Grender, *Did I Ever Tell You about My Irish Great Grandmother?,* Hutchinson, 1981.
Naomi Lewis, *Hare and Badger Go to Town,* Andersen, 1981.
Grender, *But That's Another Story,* Knight, 1982.
Eric Morecambe, *The Reluctant Vampire,* Methuen Children's, 1982.
Curtis, *The Revenge of the Brain Sharpeners,* Andersen, 1982.
J. K. Hooper, *Kaspar and the Iron Poodle,* Andersen, 1982.
Russell, editor, *The Magnet Book of Sinister Stories,* Methuen Children's, 1982.
Curtis, *Mr. Browser and the Mini-Meteorites,* Andersen, 1983.
Curtis, *Invasion of the Comet People,* Knopf, 1983.
Curtis, *Mr. Browser and the Brain Sharpeners,* Andersen, 1983.
Grender, *Did I Ever Tell You about My Birthday Party?,* Andersen, 1983.
Hazel Townson, *The Shrieking Face,* Andersen, 1984.
Alan Sillitoe, *Marmalade Jim and the Fox,* Robson, 1984.
Roger Collinson, *Paper Flags and Penny Ices,* Andersen, 1984.
W. J. Corbett, *The End of the Tale,* Methuen, 1985.
Curtis, *Mr. Browser in the Space Museum,* Andersen, 1985.
Curtis, *The Quest of the Quidnuncs,* Andersen, 1986.
Hiawyn Oram, *Jenna and the Troublemaker,* Holt, 1986.
Townson, *Terrible Tuesday,* Morrow, 1986.
Grender, *The Third Did I Ever Tell You ... ?,* David & Charles, 1987.

Grender, *Did I Ever Tell You . . . What the Children Told Me?*,
    David & Charles, 1987.
Pat Thomson, *The Treasure Sock*, Delacorte, 1987.
Trinka H. Noble, *Meanwhile Back at the Ranch*, Dial Books
    for the Young, 1987.
Heather Eyles, *Well I Never!*, Stoddart, 1988.
Jeanne Willis, *Earthlets, As Explained by Professor Xargle*,
    Dutton, 1989.
Oram, *Anyone Seen Harry Lately?*, David & Charles, 1989.
Barbara S. Hazen, *The Knight Who Was Afraid of the Dark*,
    Dial Books for the Young, 1989.
The Pop-up Book of Nonsense Verse, Random House, 1989.

OTHER

Author of several animated television films. Contributor of
cartoons to magazines, including *Punch* and *Town*.

ADAPTATIONS: I'm Coming to Get You! has been made
into a filmstrip; some of Ross's books have been adapted for
television.

WORK IN PROGRESS: Writing and illustrating *Dear
Mole*, and other children's books; illustrating Jon Talbot's
The Most Unusual Computer, to be published by Kaye &
Ward.

SIDELIGHTS: "My training as an etcher, and my liking of
graphic, rather than fine, artists, gave me a love of black line
on white paper," Tony Ross once told *Something about the
Author (SATA)*. "My colours tend to be transparent inks and
watercolours, laid lightly, not obscuring the line. To me, a
children's illustrator is a creator of worlds for kids, and so I
prefer to write my own texts. I like telling stories, I like to see
children laugh, I like to draw." In books such as *I'm Coming
to Get You!*, *Lazy Jack*, and *Super Dooper Jezebel*, Ross
brings a humorous writing and drawing style to both original
and traditional stories. This unique approach has quickly
boosted Ross's reputation as a author and illustrator of
books for children.

Ross was born just before the onset of World War II in 1938
in Streatham, a suburb of London. His father worked as a
magician, and many of his relatives worked in films as extras.
During the day Ross's father worked for a wine firm, and at
night he did stage work.

Ross said his mother "was very vivacious," as he related in a
special interview with *SATA*. "I don't think she had jobs of
any sort. I never recall her working until I was a teenager and
then she joined up in business with her sister and they had a
baby linen shop together. But prior to that I don't remember
her working; she looked after me all the time."

"I adored my parents," Ross continued. "They were very
easy going and they enjoyed fun and they had parties. I was
the little boy looking through the bannisters or peeping out of
my bedroom window down at the wonderful evenings my
parents seemed to have. I remember things like my father
wearing a lampshade and dressed in a rug dancing round the
floor. I was very young when I was in London. When I was
about three we moved away up to the north of England to get
away from the bombs." The family moved to Runcorn, a
small town on the Mersey River near Liverpool.

The war caused shortages of food and other products, and of
toys as well. "It was during the war so most toys were either
wooden or pre-war Japanese ones, or German ones," the
author said. "It was high priority to have anything metal with
a clockwork motor that still worked. A lot of the second-
hand toys were brought out at Christmases because there
were no toys being made. All the metal was on the western
desert. So the toys were either clumsy wooden ones, which
weren't very satisfying, or these second-hand, slightly black
markety things that my father used to bring in his coat pocket
which were terribly exciting. I remember a Japanese motorcycle and a marvelous Mecanno aeroplane with nuts and bolts
and the propeller went round. Wonderful metal things, they
were wonderful because no one else had them. All kids had
little secrets."

Ross didn't keep many memories of the war, for the family
was away from the bombing that destroyed many other
English towns. "The one thing I do remember was I couldn't
understand how the Germans were our enemies," he explained to *SATA*. "We had some German prisoners of war
who were building something or other quite close to me and I
used to go and sit in their hut. They gave me sweets and made
little toys for me and then I'd go home and find the Germans
were our enemies. Then the next day I'd go out to the
Germans who were my friends. I really got quite mixed up.
My parents didn't seem to mind me going. When at school we
played games, the English versus the Germans, I didn't mind
being picked as a German because the Germans I knew were
quite nice. I've often thought about that afterwards, how
paradoxical it was, how strange to have an experience like
that.

"It didn't seem like war," Ross added. "The Germans didn't
seem like enemies and no bombs were falling where I lived,
the nearest bombs were in Liverpool. We heard stories of the
war but they were, to me, very unreal, they didn't touch me at
all, my life went along much the same. When it ended things
didn't seem any different except there were a few more sweets
in the shops."

Reading also played a part in Ross's childhood. "I can
remember clearly a picture of my father sitting on my bed and
my mother sitting on my bed at different times, reading out of
a big book of fairy stories with a spine hanging off, so it must
have been an old book, I don't know where it came from. And
me wanting every night another story. What the stories were,
I can't remember."

One book that did impress the young artist was an edition of
Cervantes's *Don Quixote*, illustrated by Paul Gustav Dore. "I
was ill in bed one time, mumps or maybe it was one of the
excuses for not going to school. The room was a bit dark. My
grandfather collected books and the earliest illustrated book
I can remember was *Don Quixote* by Dore. A book four
inches thick, a heavy book. I stared and stared and stared at
the picture of the windmill lifting Don Quixote off his horse."
The book, Ross added, had "creepy pictures for a small child.
I did spend a lot of time with it because it was so fascinating, it
was so different."

While Ross was a young boy he also watched his father work
as a magician. "I used to go to lots of his shows. With it being
wartime he used to do a lot of bases, forces bases, American
air force bases as well as small theatres here and there and
everywhere. I used to go around with him to the extent of
learning some of the tricks myself so when I was eleven or
twelve I had my own small act. . . . He gave me some tricks he
didn't use any more and I put them in a bag and off I went. I
performed at small town cinemas and places like that." But
Ross's short magic career didn't overshadow his childhood.
"It was only a part of my life," he continued. "I didn't do it to

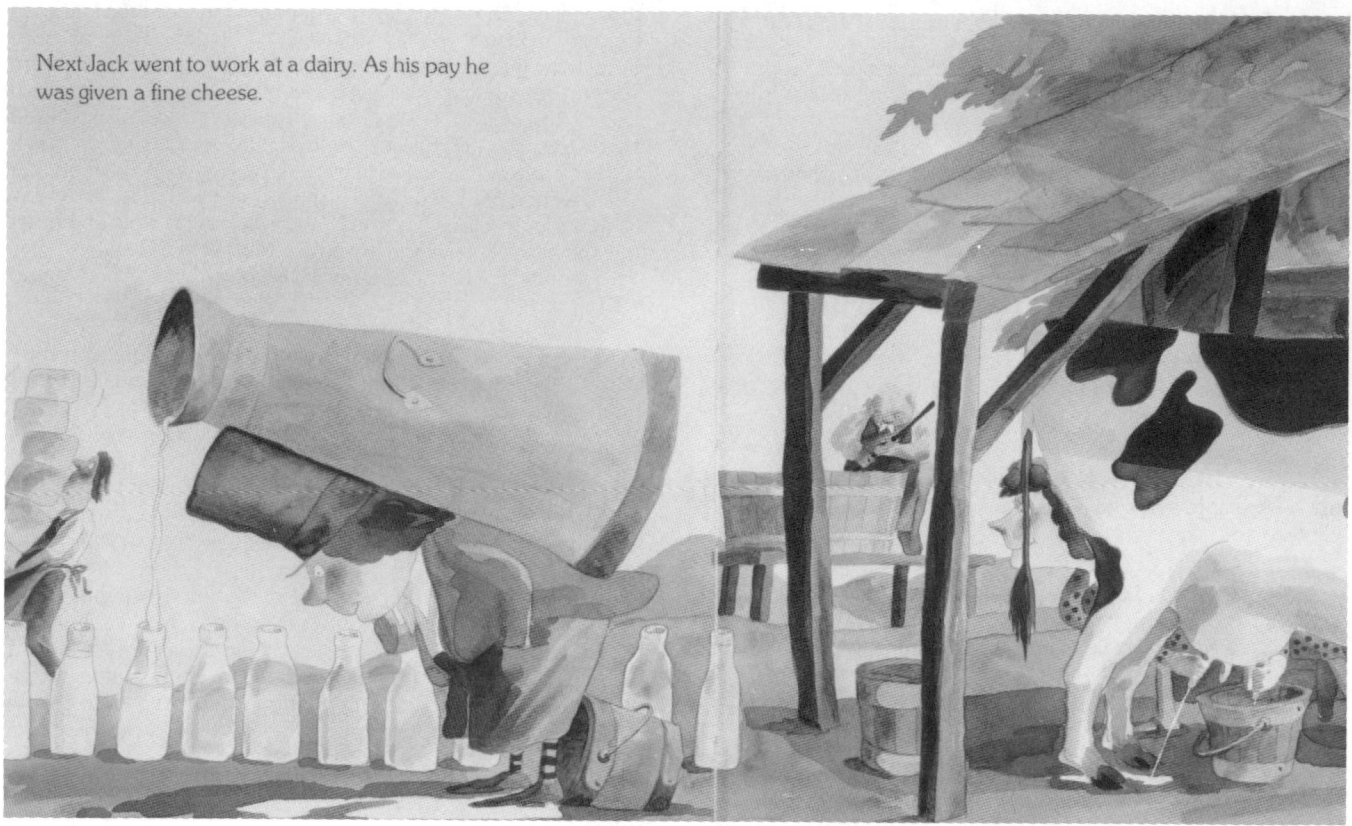

Next Jack went to work at a dairy. As his pay he was given a fine cheese.

(From *Lazy Jack,* written and illustrated by Tony Ross.)

any great extent. I can't have done more than a dozen performances ever. My normal childhood far eclipsed that."

Ross enjoyed his years as a schoolboy. "I was quite good at sports, and I think at school, if you're good at sports, you can survive school. I was at one primary school and then one grammar school." In addition, he said, "It was good because, being an only child, it was a source of friends. I would go to school and that's where all my friends were."

Ross had fun during his school years, but he didn't really excel at his studies. "I wasn't a good student," he remarked. "I was bad at nearly everything. I could draw quite well and I was all right once I got out into the playground or into the sports hall but everything else I was pretty resistant to." Although Ross did well in art class, he didn't see it as a way to improve his skills. "In those days I had no ideas of career or anything so I didn't look towards the teachers for any sort of guidance. School to me was just one of those things that you had to do like clean your teeth. I thought no more about it than that. I didn't regard it as the start of anything."

When Ross was a boy in school, it was during a time when children were less assertive than today. "You got through school by keeping your nose down and being diplomatic. Which is what I did. School was a thing to be survived." As a teenager, however, Ross saw his first James Dean movie and his whole attitude changed.

James Dean's films of teenage rebellion presented new ideas to the young Ross. "It's difficult to say when it happens to yourself but when you've gone through a childhood of doing what you're told, as you were at school and that was the way I reacted to my parents—you didn't think twice about it you just did as you were told. If any adult told me to do

something, I'd do it because that was the way I was brought up. Then you see 'Rebel without a Cause' and he *didn't* do it! He hit his Dad! You think, 'Ah, kids can do that, can they?' So it was really quite radical."

Unlike James Dean in the movies, Ross didn't rebel against his parents. "There were the odd screaming matches, but I never was in a situation of thinking my values were better than theirs because their values were quite liberal and I admired a lot of what they stood for." In particular, Ross respected his parents for "their humanity, their tolerance. They could see the point of view of nearly everybody who bothered to explain it to them. They were very tolerant people."

Meanwhile, Ross kept up an interest in art outside of school. "I'd been drawing since I was a child but I never went to galleries. We had some nice things around the house, reasonably good pictures; some old family portraits in pastels and oils, a plaque of my father's grandfather in plaster, he was a composer of very pompous church and institutional music." The young Ross also noticed national events in art. "I was aware of a new typeface, Profil—that's pretty good for someone of thirteen, to be aware of Profil typeface which was designed for the Festival of Britain, I think."

At age eighteen, Ross found himself in art school. "My parents didn't really have any ambitions for me and I had none for myself and it was really a case of the only thing I could do." Ross had considered joining the Air Force, he added. "I liked the idea of flying aeroplanes and shooting people down because I suppose I was brought up on Spitfires and that sort of thing." But the modern air force needed outstanding students for their new, complicated jets and

Remembering his mother's advice, Jack heaved the donkey onto his back. (From *Lazy Jack,* written and illustrated by Tony Ross.)

Ross's mathematics weren't good enough. "I was offered other careers but I wanted to be a pilot."

So Ross began studying art in Liverpool, where he became involved in the social scene. "It was great, the late fifties, early sixties, and the whole Liverpool beat thing was on," Ross said. "It was the tail end of being a teddy boy, with your hair slicked back and leather jackets and very very tight jeans and winklepicker shoes. Everybody tried to look like that. There was the general hard look." Ross also assumed a tough attitude like other students, because "it was the way you had to be. There was a lot of pretence."

While Ross was at school, he spent a lot of time playing music, and he met John Lennon, a man who would become famous as one of the Beatles. His art studies took a back seat to experiencing Liverpool's exciting social scene. "I was more intent on having a good time. I wasn't terribly interested in the course. My course threw me in the path of artists, I came across the whole string of artists that every art student knows, Renoir, Bonnard, Magritte, people like that. And also a great mate of mine in those days was Mickey Isaacson, who for years drew the cartoons on the back of the *New Statesman*. I was a cartoonist then, I drew some drawings for *Punch* and things like that. We used to talk about our heroes, who were Saul Steinberg and Andre Francois, the graphic artists rather than painters. So I was always interested in people who worked in black line." Ross added, "I think the main influences I had all started when I was in this silly period at art school, when I was just starting cartooning."

Ross graduated, and soon married Carol D'Arcy, whom he'd met at school. Starting out was hard for the young couple. "We lived with her parents. I was an impoverished artist, I couldn't afford anything, so we lived with her parents who didn't approve of me at all." Ross began teaching high school during the day and at an art school at night. Neither job was very satisfying. But Ross and his wife eventually moved into their own apartment, and Ross found a job he enjoyed more than teaching. "I was only teaching school children for one term. I left that and became a typographer and worked in advertising and publicity." Eventually Ross became art director for an advertising agency.

Although Ross had found a better job, there was trouble in his marriage. The couple's first child died before birth. "That was traumatic. In many ways it clouded that first marriage." The couple later adopted a daughter, Phillipa, but divorced soon after. Ross married again, this time to a woman he'd met in the village where he was living. Ross's second wife, Joan, "had a small child of Phillipa's age. The child and the cat, the whole lot, came with the mother. We went as far away from that village as we could find because by then there was a lot of gossip and jokes and it was quite impossible to do the shopping there and keep a straight face. . . . We moved to a little cottage right in the Pennines, away from anybody because we found we needed to be out of the glare. We picked an isolated cottage and moved into it."

By then, in the late sixties, Ross was making his living teaching at Manchester Polytechnic, a small college. At first, he taught advertising there. In addition, he "was doing design, designing letterheads and posters and pamphlets for other people."

At the same time, Ross began developing an interest in illustration. "When I was in advertising and I was drawing cartoons in magazines," Ross said, "I was trained as an illustrator. I just wanted to do it, nobody ever asked me to illustrate a book because I was working in advertising. I sat down and wrote some stories one day and illustrated them. The first one was called *Hugo and the Wicked Winter*, which was a ridiculous book. It was far too long, too many words, not enough illustrations. . . . But that was just a whimsical thing."

Later that year, however, Ross's job took a turn that led him further into the field. "I became part of Manchester Polytechnic, teaching advertising and in a time of crisis the Poly decided that there was nobody to look after the illustration group, there were illustration students and no member of staff. So they said, 'Well, you've drawn cartoons, you do it.' I said, 'I can't. I'm a designer, not an illustrator.' They said, 'You're the only one who's drawn things, so you'd better look after them.' So I took over the illustration group and thought 'Well, if I'm doing illustration I'd better do some. I'd better find out what all this nonsense is about.' So I illustrated some books that I wrote, called *Tales from Mr. Toffy's Circus,* simply because I felt I'd better become an illustrator."

Ross took his books to Jack Fermin, who was with the Fabbri publishing company. "He said, 'I like the stories, but the drawings are a bit labored, aren't they?'" Ross related. "He said, 'Why don't you draw like you draw your cartoons?' So I said, 'Well, can I do that?'

"I'd done [cartoons] steadily. I said, 'Those are cartoons for grown ups, these are children's books.' He said, 'No, there's no difference. Just draw like you draw in the cartoons.' So I took away my stories and re-drew them in a funnier—in my cartoon way. I was trying to draw like a children's book illustrator before," Ross continued.

Ross had pictured in his mind many different children's books, "a sort of composite image of what a children's book should be like." His attempt to follow that image wasn't very serious, he said. "It was just memories of what I'd seen. I didn't make any effort. It was just a light-hearted thing, really. So I thought, 'Well, if that's what he wants, I'll give it a whirl.' So I went off and drew in my own way and he published six of them." Since then, Jack Fermin's advice to "Just enjoy yourself with the drawings" has always remained with Ross.

Ross developed a distinctive drawing style that involves the black lines and bold colors of the graphic artists he admires. In *I'm Coming to Get You!,* for instance, "the illustrations are in colors as loud as a yell, rendered in a scratchy fashion that intensifies the speedy effects," a *Publishers Weekly* reviewer comments. "There is a dynamic quality to Tony Ross's illustrations, a quality created with raw hues of blue, green, and red and with strong contrasts between light and dark areas," a *Wilson Library Bulletin* critic similarly observes of *Hugo and Oddsock.* "But more important are the slashing, diagonal shapes and lines." The result of these "strong contrasts of light and dark and big and little," according to Donnarae MacCann and Olga Richard of *Wilson Library Bulletin,* is a sly, lively humor.

With the publication of the six *Mr. Toffy's* books, Ross's career "took off from there," the author said in his *SATA* interview. "Jack died and I wasn't very happy with what happened to the company after that. That was in the early seventies." Ross knew someone who worked in publishing, and through her found a publisher for *Hugo and the Wicked Winter.* "They weren't very happy with that one. They stopped doing children's books. It didn't sell. So I hit the road again." Through the same acquaintance Ross next met Klaus Flugge, who wanted to publish Ross's work with his own company. *Goldilocks and the Three Bears* became Andersen Press's first publication, and since then Ross has stayed with Andersen. "I've got a terrific publisher," Ross said. "Everybody admires him, the way be works, he's a good publisher in as much as he respects what artists want. . . . I think if Klaus gave up publishing, I'd give up drawing."

But as Ross's career as an author was expanding, his marriage was failing. Ross and his wife Jane had had a daughter together, Alexandra. The strain of parenting both a natural child and stepchild created a strain in the marriage, and the couple divorced about four years later.

By this time, Ross had already met the woman who would become his third wife, Zoe. "She was a student at the Polytechnic, not one of my students," Ross stated. "An art student. She was an advertising person and a copywriter. She left art school with a degree and became a copywriter and then we got married." In 1980, Ross and his wife Zoe had a daughter, Katherine.

Ross was busy helping raise his daughter, and at the same time he was beginning to make a full-time career out of writing. "It just got going. All the time I was teaching and loving life. I actually knew I could tell the students something real because I was beginning to know what I was doing. Quite

The fox could only get his snout into the very top of the glass, but the stork could sink his long beak right down to the bottom (From *Foxy Fables,* retold and illustrated by Tony Ross.)

rare in a Polytechnic lecturer. So I was enjoying my life then. It got to a state that five years or so ago I couldn't keep the two things going. I was so busy with my own work I just had not the time to teach any more—for the kind of money they were offering me. I was getting far more from publishing. I couldn't devote four days a week to the Polytechnic for the money they were offering. I needed to devote more time to my own work. So I had to leave, reluctantly." Still, Ross added, "I don't miss it at all. No gap was left in my life. As soon as I left the gap closed because other things had to be done."

Ross keeps very busy with his books, generally creating the illustrations and the words at the same time. "With a lot of people one comes before the other. But with me . . . the first thing, obviously, that comes is a vague idea. Like my recent book about nose picking started when the curtain went up at my kid's play and all three of the angels—my daughter was one of the angels—had their fingers up their noses . . . at primary school. I thought it was hilariously funny so something went on as a story there. So it starts like that.

"So that's the first thing that happens," Ross continued. "Something in real life happens and starts you thinking; it's an imaginary friend or it's a problem on a potty or it's something that starts the process. And once it's started, of course, it won't go away. Once the idea is there it won't go away. It may be years before it comes into a book but in all that time it just will not go away. It gnaws and gnaws and gnaws and while it's gnawing it's forming and evolving. Then it gets to a stage where you can actually see a book in it, so you start work properly. At that stage it's got a beginning, a middle and an end. I'm not happy with any idea until it has an end. Ends are really important, I think. So once I think of a satisfying end, I'm ready to start: not a word has been written and at that point the drawings start and then the phrases come. I write a phrase, do a bit of drawing, sometimes wake up in the night and scribble a phrase down because I've thought of something really nice. If I can read my writing in the morning it's possibly in. So they do run pretty parallel from there on."

Ross added, "Sometimes it takes a bit of conscious work to beat it out. But no hard and fast rule. Sometimes they come nearly perfect, other times they come as just a ghost and need fleshing out and fleshing out and working and working and fleshing out and rewriting. Both things happen."

Super Dooper Jezebel, the story of a smug little girl who meets an untimely end, took many years to develop in Ross's mind. "The little paragon girl is based on a girl I knew at primary school called Nancy Peacock, who was superb at everything. As I say, these things fester. That must have festered about forty years. I always hoped something horrible would happen. . . . I've always felt this about really superb people at school, because I was never very good at school myself. I'd be delighted if they came to sticky ends. I've always had this idea of somebody being absolutely perfect and then their own perfection being their downfall."

Super Dooper Jezebel "is typical Ross from the zany cartoon-style watercolors to the ironic biting humor," Heide Pilcher says in *School Library Journal.* Jezebel is perfect in every way: she is tidy, polite, clever in school, and does what she's told. But she is only too ready to tell other people how to behave properly, and so she is not very likable. When she is too busy instructing others to avoid being eaten by a crocodile, Ross makes us "cheer the crocodile for ridding the world of that prim, supercilious, rigid, prudish, gloating Jezebel," MacCann and Richard note in *Wilson Library Bulletin.* Ross

manages this feeling with his superb drawings of Jezebel, the critics add.

Ross also gets inspirations from the traditional stories that he retells. "They're largely sentimental," he said in his *SATA* interview. Ross thinks of certain tales "as being part of childhood and as I'm fond of childhood and as these things always change. . . . I was castigated for changing, it may have been *Red Riding Hood,* by a silly woman who accused me of changing the story from the traditional story. What she meant was I was changing it from the Victorian version she heard. She seemed unaware that the story goes back nine hundred years or more and has changed a thousand times since then and is in existence in every country in the world in a different form. That story simply stems out of a time when children lived in a tight community, probably with a palisade all round them and the mother or grandmother would tell the child—usually a girl child—a story to frighten her and prevent her straying away, just to keep her at home."

Ross tends to avoid such scary parts in his stories. "I don't see it as my role to set out and scare the hell out of children so all my monsters are a bit unfrightening and all the events I show are a bit unfrightening. If I deal with a monster I'm always setting out to show how un-monstrous they really are." Besides, Ross added, "my drawing is too funny, I just can't resist taking the piss out of absolutely everything. I just can't help it, it's something that's ingrained in me."

Ross brings this unusual, humorous perspective to his retellings of traditional tales. *Foxy Fables,* for example, a reworking of Aesop's fables, is "an exceptional renovation of a tried-and-true text," remark MacCann and Richard of *Wilson Library Bulletin.* "While the situations may be familiar, the settings, tone, and style are definitely changed" from old-fashioned to modern, a *Horn Book* reviewer notes. And in *Jack and the Beanstalk* "almost every page reveals an offbeat item amidst the 18th-century details," Patricia Dooley observes in *School Library Journal.*

Ross doesn't have a system for selecting an old story to rework. "It's just as it grabs me," he said in his *SATA* interview. "It depends what comes along at the time. When I did *Lazy Jack* I just stumbled across that particular story, which I thought was very funny, and it reminded me [of something] I read somewhere." If an old story catches Ross's attention, he is likely to write about it. "A lot of them are so boring, very often nothing jumps out at all. *Lazy Jack* did, popped out of an old *Mother Goose,* I think."

Lazy Jack, like many of Ross's other books, adds amusing details to the old story of a lazy fellow who wins a sad princess by making her laugh. "Ross' spacious watercolors add narrative twists of their own to this traditional tale," a critic for the *Bulletin of the Center for Children's Books* says. *Lazy Jack* "is tongue-in-cheek, the art absurd, the overall effect a super-silly read aloud," the critic adds. Christina L. Olson also enjoys what she calls "some very Monty Pythonish touches," and adds in her *School Library Journal* review that Ross's "strong color sense creates enormously light-spirited fun."

Ross's books are also inspired by things his children have done. "A lot of my books are about my children," he added in his *SATA* interview. "Very often the heroes of my books are little girls just because my own natural children have been girls." But Ross's characters are only *based* on his kids. He said, "I don't often put real people in." But Ross considers the characters in his books realistic, if not real. "Someone the other day called my work whimsical and I said it isn't whimsical, everything I do is real. Absolutely everything is drawn from life. I went through book after book after book saying, 'that's real.' "

The mothers in his books, for example, are "based very loosely on the women I see hanging around the school gates waiting to pick up their children," Ross explained. "I just drew a grandmother in my latest book and she's wearing a headband and a jogging suit. She's just come in from jogging. The friend who was calling me whimsical said, 'Look at her.' I said, 'Open your eyes. That's what grannies are like now. Do you think grannies have grey hair and hold knitting with their feet in slippers? They don't, they jog, they do aerobics.' That's the sort of grandmother I think a little child now would associate with, not this thing with grey hair like Little Red Riding Hood has. Grandmothers are something entirely different now. Maybe I've changed my attitude on grandmothers since becoming a grandfather!"

Ross also gets visual details from real life. "Certain things are from my house. In *I'm Coming to Get You,* the bedroom is my daughter's bedroom and lots of my daughter's toys are in there. Sometimes my house has been in books and some details of it have. Often they're masked by things that are not accurate, not taken from anywhere. They're all an amalgam."

Ross experiments with the shape and structure of his books, something that results from what he said is his "interest in the book form. You assume that a book starts at the beginning and ends at the end, but it's only an assumption," he continued in his interview. "You can actually play with the form and get a great deal of fun out of the plastic form of a book. Like *I'm Coming to Get You!* has the front cover and the back cover has the monster going through the book from the back and out at the front. [In] *Lazy Jack,* I decided to have a picture in front of the title page. So there was a picture, the story starts, and then there's the title page and then the story. I did that because it was convenient to me. There's this little princess, sad little princess, and I wanted to establish who she was before the book started so that when the story got to her the reader already knew who she was. I didn't want to get to her and then to stop the story and start explaining who she was. I thought the form of the book, of covers, title page, text is accepted but it's not necessarily the only the way that those pages can be opened."

Ross's willingness to go beyond what's accepted gives his work a uniquely funny viewpoint. But it is the combination of pictures and words that makes his books so enjoyable, says the *Horn Book* reviewer. The artist's illustrations "add much to the humor, interacting with the text in a lively interchange that enriches and extends both." Ross's work is distinguished by his "comic imagination and a superb sense of theater," MacCann and Richard likewise state. As a result, they conclude, "it is hard to think of many cartoonists in recent years who have developed as rapidly as Ross with both a comic touch and a serious design interest."

WORKS CITED:

"Children's Books," *Publishers Weekly,* October 26, 1984, p. 104.

Dooley, Patricia, review of *Jack and the Beanstalk, School Library Journal,* April, 1981, p. 117.

Review of *Foxy Fables, Horn Book,* September/October, 1986, p. 604.

Review of *Hugo and Oddsock, Wilson Library Bulletin,* January, 1979, p. 378.

Review of *Lazy Jack, Bulletin of the Center for Children's Books,* July-August, 1986, p. 217.

MacCann, Donnarae and Olga Richard, "Picture Books for Children," *Wilson Library Bulletin,* March, 1985, pp. 482-3.

MacCann, Donnarae and Olga Richard, "Picture Books for Children," *Wilson Library Bulletin,* November, 1986, pp. 47-8.

MacCann, Donnarae and Olga Richard, "Picture Books for Children," *Wilson Library Bulletin,* June, 1989, pp. 96-7.

Olson, Christina L., review of *Lazy Jack, School Library Journal,* September, 1986, p. 127.

Pilcher, Heide, review of *Super Dooper Jezebel, School Library Journal,* December, 1988, p. 92.

Ross, Tony, interview with Cathy Courtney for *Something about the Author.*

Something about the Author, Volume 17, Gale, 1979, pp. 203-4.

FOR MORE INFORMATION SEE:

PERIODICALS

New York Times Book Review, November 13, 1983.
School Library Journal, July, 1989.

*   *   *

RYDER, Joanne (Rose) 1946-

PERSONAL: Born September 16, 1946, in Lake Hiawatha, NJ; daughter of Raymond and Dorothy (McGaffney) Ryder; married Lawrence Yep (an author). *Education:* Re-

JOANNE RYDER

ceived degree in journalism from Marquette University, 1968; graduate study at University of Chicago, 1968-69. *Hobbies and other interests:* "Traveling whenever I can, spending time walking or hiking outdoors to enjoy nature, gardening and flower arranging, reading and listening to poetry, working and playing with puppets, sharing my interest in animals with children."

ADDRESSES: Home—San Francisco, CA.

CAREER: Harper & Row Publishers, Inc., New York City, editor of children's books, 1970-80; full-time writer, 1980—. Docent (tour guide) at the San Francisco Zoo; lecturer at schools and conferences.

MEMBER: Society of Children's Book Writers, California Academy of Sciences, San Francisco Zoological Society.

AWARDS, HONORS: Simon Underground was selected for the Children's Book Showcase, 1977; New Jersey Author's Award from the New Jersey Institute of Technology, for *Fireflies,* 1978, *Fog in the Meadow,* 1980, and *Snail in the Woods,* 1980; *Fog in the Meadow* was named Outstanding Science Trade Book of the Year for Children by the National Science Teachers Association, 1979, and a Children's Choice Book by the Children's Book Council and the International Reading Association, 1980; *The Snail's Spell* was named a Parents Choice Book by *Parents Magazine* and received the New York Academy of Sciences Children's Science Book Award, younger category, 1982; *Inside Turtle's Shell, and Other Poems of the Field* was named Outstanding Book of the Year for Children by the National Council of Teachers of English, 1985, Outstanding Science Trade Book of the Year for Children by the National Science Teachers Association, 1985, and was included on the Bluebonnet Award list and the Bank Street Outstanding Book of the Year list; *Step into the Night* was named Outstanding Science Trade Book of the Year for Children by the National Science Teachers Association and received the Commonwealth Club of Northern California Children's Book Medal, 1988; *Where Butterflies Grow* was named Outstanding Science Trade Book of the Year for Children by the National Science Teachers Association, 1989.

WRITINGS:

FOR CHILDREN

Simon Underground, illustrated by John Schoenherr, Harper, 1976.
A Wet and Sandy Day, illustrated by Donald Carrick, Harper, 1977.
Fireflies, illustrated by Don Bolognese, Harper, 1977.
Fog in the Meadow, illustrated by Gail Owens, Harper, 1979.
(With Harold S. Feinberg) *Snail in the Woods,* illustrated by Jo Polseno, Harper, 1979.
The Spiders Dance, illustrated by Robert Blake, Harper, 1981.
Beach Party, illustrated by Diane Stanley, F. Warne, 1982.
The Snail's Spell, illustrated by Lynne Cherry, F. Warne, 1982.
The Incredible Space Machines, illustrated by Gerry Daly, Random House, 1982.
C-3PO's Book about Robots, illustrated by John Gampert, Random House, 1983.
Inside Turtle's Shell, and Other Poems of the Field, illustrated by Susan Bonners, Macmillan, 1985.

The Night Flight, illustrated by Amy Schwartz, Four Winds Press, 1985.
The Evening Walk, illustrated by Julie Durrell, Western Publishing, 1985.
Old Friends, New Friends, illustrated by Jane Chambless-Rigie, Western Publishing, 1986.
Chipmunk Song, illustrated by Cherry, Lodestar, 1987.
Animals in the Woods, illustrated by Lisa Bonforte, Western Publishing, 1987, published as *Animals in the Wild,* 1989.
Step into the Night, illustrated by Dennis Nolan, Four Winds Press, 1988.
My Little Golden Book about Cats, illustrated by Dora Leder, Western Publishing, 1988.
Puppies Are Special Friends, illustrated by James Spence, Western Publishing, 1988.
(Adapter) *Hardie Gramatky's Little Toot,* illustrated by Larry Ross, Platt, 1988.
(Adapter) Charles Dickens, *A Christmas Carol,* illustrated by John O'Brien, Platt, 1989.
White Bear, Ice Bear (A "Just for a Day" Book), illustrated by Michael Rothman, Morrow, 1989.
Catching the Wind (A "Just for a Day" Book), illustrated by Rothman, Morrow, 1989.
Mockingbird Morning, illustrated by Nolan, Four Winds Press, 1989.
Where Butterflies Grow, illustrated by Cherry, Lodestar, 1989.
Under the Moon, illustrated by Cheryl Harness, Random House, 1989.
Lizard in the Sun (A "Just for a Day" Book), illustrated by Rothman, Morrow, 1990.
Under Your Feet, illustrated by Nolan, Four Winds Press, 1990.
When the Woods Hum, illustrated by Catherine Stock, Morrow, 1991.
Hello, Tree!, illustrated by Michael Hays, Lodestar, 1991.
The Bear on the Moon, illustrated by Carol Lacey, Morrow, 1991.
Winter Whale, illustrated by Rothman, Morrow, 1991.

Contributor to periodicals.

WORK IN PROGRESS: Several books, including *Dancers in the Garden,* Sierra Club Books, 1993; *Without Words,* Sierra Club Books, 1993; *My Father's Hands,* Morrow, 1994; *Turtle Time,* Knopf, 1994; *The Waterfall's Gift,* Sierra Club Books, 1994; and *The Goodbye Walk,* Lodestar, 1994, all with tentative publication dates.

SIDELIGHTS: Joanne Ryder is an award-winning children's writer who specializes in books about nature. Her works are a unique blend of scientific fact and fantasy. Through simple, poetic prose, Ryder provides her readers with knowledge of the different life forms that exist all around us. Her books describe the growth and life cycles of small creatures, like fireflies, snails, and spiders. Ryder's works also expand young readers' imaginations by challenging them to view the world as an insect or an animal would. In books like *Lizard in the Sun, Catching the Wind,* or *White Bear, Ice Bear,* for instance, Ryder takes children on dreamlike, imaginary travels that change them into lizards, geese, or bears. With more than thirty popular books to her credit, Ryder ranks among the leading writers of children's nature books.

In an interview with *Something about the Author,* Ryder described her life and work: "I was born in Lake Hiawatha, New Jersey, which was then a small, rural town. My parents moved there from New York City during World War II when my father, a rubber chemist, found a job nearby. For my parents, Lake Hiawatha was the 'country'—very different from the crowded city they knew. For me, it was a wonderful place to explore, full of treasures to discover. There were just a few houses on our street, but there were woods all around. There was a waterfall tucked in the woods to visit and a man-made lake (that gave the town its name) where my father and I could sail in our big yellow rubber raft.

"I loved living there and playing outdoors. There were always animals around to observe and encounter. We had moles who would burrow under our lawn at night and leave their mounds for me to find in the morning. Chipmunks and lizards darted this way and that across our backyard. Striped garter snakes made their home in the stone wall around ours. I'd see them on sunny days warming themselves on top of the rocky wall. One of my earliest memories is trying to follow a butterfly darting across the road and being scolded by a neighbor for running into the street.

"My parents, probably because they had spent all of their lives in the city, were also fascinated with the country. They both shared with me their different loves. My mother taught me to watch sunsets and to take time to stop and enjoy special moments in nature. I remember her stopping her chores—which she didn't often do—to sit for hours just so she could enjoy observing a hundred tiny birds, migrating spring warblers, who had paused to rest in our tree. 'When Mother Nature puts on a show,' she would say, 'I don't want to miss it. My work can wait till tomorrow.'

"My mother loved nature's grand displays—sunsets, ocean walks, spring trees all in bloom. But my father liked to pick things up and examine them. He was the one who introduced me to nature up close and made the discoveries we shared very personal ones.

"He loved to work in his garden. Whenever he would find something interesting, he would call me to come and see. If he could catch it, he would cup the tiny creature in his hands and wait until I ran to him. Then he would open his fingers and show me whatever it was he had found—a beetle, a snail, a fuzzy caterpillar. Then gently he would let me hold it, and I could feel it move, wiggle, or crawl—even breathe—as I held it in my hand.

"I discovered that beetles had feet that tickle and that snails feel cool like creeping Jello. My father's excitement was easy to catch. As he pointed out amazing features of each animal, I could see that, even though it had a few more legs or less legs than I was used too, it was rather marvelous.

"So tiny, hidden animals became very much a part of my world, as real to me as the people I knew. When my father and I took walks together into the woods or to the waterfall, it was natural for me to feel comfortable and part of the world around me.

"We lived in the country until I was almost five years old. Then we moved to Brooklyn, a part of New York City. We lived in the same apartment building where my mother had grown up. It was a bit of a shock for me to live where there were so many people all around. But the city seemed also a magical land, full of special places for me. I loved going to the park and to the museums where there were gigantic dinosaur bones and mysterious mummies and sparkling gems. There were wonders in my own neighborhood too. Every day on my way to school, I passed an old stone lion. I believed he could

understand my thoughts, and I would tell him secrets. He was one of my first friends in the city. I also began to have lovely dreams at night in which I could fly over the tall trees outside my home.

"I tell children if they would like to imagine what I was like when I was six, they might read my book, *The Night Flight.* I was very much like Anna, the girl in my story. She also gets to do some extraordinary things I wished I could—talk to the fish in the park and have her stone lion become real to take her for a ride through the jungle. But the dream she has of flying easily over the city was very much like my favorite dream. Every now and then, I still dream I can fly, and I always wake up feeling delighted.

"When I was almost seven, my family moved to a house on Long Island. I grew up in the town of New Hyde Park, and my parents still live there. I began writing poems when I was about eight. Though I've always had trouble spelling words correctly, my parents and teachers encouraged me to keep on writing even when I made mistakes. I liked playing with words and making them up. I wrote about animals and everyday things—and also about imaginary people and creatures. I liked to read fantasy stories and to pretend that I was in another world sharing in the exciting adventures. Every week I rode my bike to the town hall to borrow six new books from the public library that was tucked in the basement. Reading so much made it easier for me to write. Since I enjoyed imagining other author's worlds, it seemed natural for me to create stories and worlds of my own. I started writing my first book when I was eleven. But I have never finished it. It was a fantasy called *The Marvelous Adventures of Georgus Amaryllis the Third.* Maybe someday, I'll go back to it and see how it might end.

"Actually I must admit, there are quite a few stories I've started that I didn't finish. Sometimes when I'm writing I hit what I call a black hole. I will have no idea what will happen next. I may have to put a story away and wait until I know how to fix it. That may take a few days, months, or even years. I may know how the story begins and ends but not what happens in between. I seem to enjoy writing beginnings and endings more than writing middles! All writers have different problems, and we all have difficulties sometimes. Creating a world from scratch, which is what a story is, takes time, and often there are different choices you can make. Taking one choice will make the story short and funny, another may make the story long and sad. Sometimes I need to try different ways to find the best one for me.

"By the time I was ten, I suspected I might want to be a writer. I also thought I might like to be a ballet dancer or a veterinarian, too. But I kept on writing, and the writing won out. I went to high school, edited the school newspaper, then studied journalism in college and edited the college literary magazine. Then I studied library science and worked for a number of years as an editor of children's books in New York City. During the day I worked on other people's books. Then at night I worked on my own stories. After writing several books this way, I decided I wanted to take a leap. I quit my editing job to become a full-time writer. It was the right choice for me, and I have been writing ever since.

"My first book published was *Simon Underground.* It's about a mole, like the ones I remembered in Lake Hiawatha, who spends the winter burrowing deep below the frost line. When I was living in New York, I liked to visit the American Museum of Natural History. One of the exhibits was a cutaway of a field showing the animals in winter and

On the top of your head
you have two long feelers.
You can stretch and stretch
these feelers
till they look like
long, long horns.

In her award-winning 1982 book, *The Snail's Spell,* **Joanne Ryder uses a characteristic blend of scientific fact and fantasy.** (Illustrated by Lynne Cherry.)

spring—some were sleeping, some were active. A tiny mole dug deep tunnels all winter long and then dug up near the surface in springtime. The exhibit inspired me to write about a mole's life and also about my own feelings of life in winter and in spring.

"My books are fairly short in length, yet it can take me a long time to write one. I have written a book in as short as an evening and as long as five years. My poetry collection *Inside Turtle's Shell, and Other Poems of the Field* took much longer than I ever imagined it would. I began writing the poems on a vacation in Cape Cod. They came quickly, and I thought I would have thirty poems done in a month. Five years later, I finished the collection. I had written a lot more than thirty poems, but it took me a while to realize that the focus of the poems was on two turtles in a field on a single day. Actually it is a birthday book of sorts. On this day in mid-September, one turtle turns one-hundred-years-old and the other is born. The reader begins to realize what is happening, just as I did, slowly and gradually as the poems unfold. (It tickled me to learn a box turtle's birthday is mid-September. That's my birthday too.) I had to take out all the poems about animals in the summer or winter and about animals who wouldn't live in the field or pond nearby. Coming up with just the right poems to make the day unfold from morning to night took me years to do.

"If you read my books, you will probably discover the things that are special to me, things I like very much. You can tell because I write about them again and again. I love night—walking at dusk, looking at the sky and stars. I enjoy imagining what hidden animals are doing in the ground under my feet. There are a lot of moles and chipmunks and even worms in my stories. I like watching dragonflies and butterflies on a sunny day and fireflies flickering at night. In my books there are many creatures who fly, just as I wish I could. I may not be able to fly myself, but I can write about being someone who can. I love all kinds of bears, and I always love seeing the moon—thin or chunky or round and full. I love sitting under trees and looking at water—at the ripples in the pond or at the waves tumbling on a sandy beach.

"My husband and I live now in California. He is a native of San Francisco, and I've enjoyed exploring a new city and a new coast, even a new ocean. Living near water seems important to me, perhaps even a part of me. I like going down to the beach and walking in the sand. I find that looking at the ocean gives me the kind of quiet I need to sort out my thoughts and to imagine new things. Then I can dream and pretend, and that's what I enjoy most of all. I like using my imagination to see the world in new ways.

"Many of my books ask you to imagine with me what it would be like to live a very different life as another creature. I ask you to be a shapechanger—to imagine shrinking small or growing large, to imagine being covered in fur or being a tiny creeper clinging to a leaf. To write these stories, I have to learn about an animal and imagine what it would feel like to live as an animal in its world. This is like a puzzle and a game for me, and I enjoy thinking it out.

"Often I need to observe an animal carefully before I write about it. I've had a great many pets—including rabbits, salamanders, ducks, pigeons, canaries, hamsters, fish, and snails—and some of them have found their way into my books. Before writing *Lizard in the Sun,* I watched anoles or American chameleons near my aunt's house in Florida. I also kept one in a tank at home. Having a pet lizard can be complicated. They need to eat live food. So I had to keep a tank of crickets in my study. I liked to hear them sing but didn't like to feed them to the lizard. I also fed it meal worms I kept in a container in our fridge. I labeled the dish 'LIZARD FOOD. DO NOT OPEN!' so my husband who hates being surprised by small creeping creatures would not open it by mistake. When my book was finished, I found a better home for my lizard, but I kept the crickets. They were nice to watch and listen to!

"When I was six, I got a delightful birthday present, a big box turtle who I named Myrtle. She was my inspiration for the old turtle in *Inside Turtle's Shell, and Other Poems of the Field.* When we moved to Long Island, she kept wandering out of our yard and surprising our neighbors. Finally my parents set her free in a nearby park. Since turtles can live a long time, I like to think she still may be creeping here and there in the park even today—like the one-hundred-year-old turtle in my book.

"I do not have any children of my own, but I enjoy being with children whenever I can. I often visit schools and do presentations with puppets and slides about animals and writing. And I have been a volunteer at the San Francisco Zoo as a docent or guide for classes touring the zoo. The children and I share our love of animals, and that's fun for me. I like ending my tours at the polar bears' den. Seeing the young male and female polar bears play one day made me wonder what it would be like to be a polar bear. I tried to imagine how I would feel if I could wake up one snowy morning in my bed and suddenly be a bear—big and furry. What would it be like to spend a day at the top of the world doing polar bear things? What would my world look like? What would I do? I wrote *White Bear, Ice Bear* to share my imagined experience with others.

"Children sometimes ask me if I could be any animal which one I would be. That's a tough question, but I think it would be fun to be an otter-either a river otter or a sea otter. They are curious and playful, and they seem to have fun. I also would like to be an animal that flies. It must be exciting to be able to fly, to soar high, and to go wherever you wish.

"Story ideas come to me from many places. Poems, and even books, may begin with some wonderful fact I find in an article or scientific report. Once I read that moles may purr when they eat. It tickled me to imagine moles purring softly inside their tunnels as they eat their food, and I had to write about them in *Under Your Feet*. Sometimes I can be working on one book and read something that starts me thinking about another. I was doing research for my book on fireflies when I read a passage about snails that intrigued me. When they are young, fireflies are glowworms who eat snails. The description I read of the glowworm's attack was so vivid, I felt sorry for the snail and began to wonder about its life. I wanted to find a book on snails and learn more. I became fascinated with these cool, tiny creatures who have eyes that can slide into their heads. How marvelous they seemed! So I read more about them, kept snails in my apartment to watch them, and finally wrote *The Snail's Spell* imagining what it would be like if I could shrink and be just two inches long, creeping around a huge garden world.

"My books sometimes are built on memories of my childhood. As long as I can remember, my father has been planting parsley in our garden—more than our family could ever eat. We discovered that if we planted lots and lots of parsley, swallowtail butterflies would lay their eggs on our plants. The eggs hatched into caterpillars who ate the parsley and then changed into butterflies. It was always a magic moment to watch a chrysalis break open and a wet butterfly emerge. I wrote *Where Butterflies Grow* from my own memories of watching creepers turn into sleepers and then into flyers in our yard and home.

"*When the Woods Hum* is a very personal story, because it's about a father who shares a special event in nature with his daughter, Jenny. Of course, it's really about my father and me. I wanted to write about a family, like my own, in which sharing cycles in nature is important. I was also fascinated by the story of periodical cicadas who live underground for thirteen or seventeen years. It seemed so incredible to me to imagine tiny creatures living under tree roots for years and years. No one realizes these harmless insects are there until

they emerge in the millions to fill the woods with their songs. Theirs was a story I just had to write!

"The world I see each day and night seems full of things to wonder and write about. Whenever I look at the full moon, I see the profile of a white bear on it. Each month I watch for its return. I began to wonder about this bear. What would a bear be doing in the sky? My story *The Bear on the Moon* was my way of answering my own question. I enjoyed writing a tale that bears might tell each other about a very curious polar bear who, a little like me, wonders about things.

"Sometimes I write about my family. Often I write about myself, my dreams and wishes. But you may not always recognize me. I am quite like the two little sheep in *Beach Party,* Rose and Kate. I am also like the small mouse in *Under the Moon* who looks for the moon over her home. And like the chipmunk in *Chipmunk Song*. I enjoy eating in bed whenever I can!

"I like to ride on trains and planes, and often in the quiet movement as I am suspended in space from one town to the next, lines of poetry will come to me. I grab whatever piece of paper I have and write the lines down. Later on when I clean out my purse, I find these notes. I record my notes in my computer. Some of my books have begun just this way. Ideas are like butterflies; you have to catch them quickly and carefully or they will escape and you may lose them forever. They dart off when the phone rings or someone calls you. Sometimes I lose my ideas, but I have learned to try to catch them and put them down right away so I can remember them.

"I usually work on several books at a time. When I am stumped on one, I go and work on another. I am never quite sure which one I will finish first. I enjoy writing poetry, and often my books are like short or long poems. I like to paint pictures with words so that you can see and feel what I saw or imagined. I expect that someday I will write longer stories, perhaps novels about children who discover amazing things and have funny and fantastic adventures. But I will probably keep on writing poems too, poems that become picture books for young readers.

"I may enjoy painting pictures with words, but I cannot paint with paint! I wish I could draw well. But I have been very fortunate because very talented artists have illustrated my poems and stories. I do not work with an artist while I am writing my book. I write my story and submit it to an editor at a publishing company. If the story is accepted, the editor and art director decide who they think would be the right illustrator for my words. If the illustrator likes my story, he or she begins thinking of pictures and drawing sketches. Making a picture book is a team effort, and the editor is the captain who works with the artist, the publishing staff, and me so we can make the best book possible. I may or may not meet my illustrators, but often I share my research material with them so they can draw the nature scenes accurately.

"Sometimes children ask me if I like writing. I tell them I am very glad and feel fortunate to be a writer. It makes me happy to play with words and create an experience to share with readers. Writing is not always easy, and sometimes I get stuck or disappointed with what I've done. The hardest thing for me to do is to keep revising a story to make it better. It isn't easy for me to change a story once it's written. But if something isn't clear or smooth, it bothers me until I can fix it. My favorite part of the writing process is the beginning—when a story is just starting to emerge in my mind, when it has a million possibilities, and when I can go anywhere with it.

That's really exciting for me. It's a great deal of fun for me to play with those ideas and to discover where they take me. I love doing that!

"For a person who enjoys thinking in images and writing poems, writing picture books is a good life and a joyful way to make a living. It's a life I like *very* much. I do believe that the books you read when you are young leave a lasting impression. I am surprised when I reread books I loved as a child to discover the ways they have changed me and become part of me. They are my treasures. When I read them again, they make me smile fondly as if I were meeting old friends. It's nice for me to think that children might have fun reading my books and using their own imaginations to enjoy the natural world. I would wish that my books would turn into old and good friends for them too."

WORKS CITED:

Ryder, Joanne, interview with Chris Hunter for *Something about the Author,* conducted in Golden Gate Park, San Francisco, CA, August, 1990.

FOR MORE INFORMATION SEE:

PERIODICALS

Appraisal, spring, 1980; fall, 1981.
Bulletin of the Center of Children's Books, September, 1976; November, 1982; June, 1985; November, 1985.
Language Arts, December, 1987.
New York Times, June 13, 1982; November 14, 1982.
New York Times Book Review, November 17, 1985.
Publishers Weekly, July 30, 1982; January 20, 1989; February 24, 1989.
Santa Rosa Kidnews, June, 1990.
School Library Journal, April, 1981; April, 1985; November, 1985; June/July, 1987.

*   *   *

SAKHARNOV, S.
See SAKHARNOV, Svyatoslav

*   *   *

SAKHARNOV, Svyatoslav (Vladimirovich) 1923-
(S. Sakharnov)

PERSONAL: Born March 12, 1923, in Artemovsk, Ukrainian S.S.R.; son of Vladimir (a metallurgist) and Maria (a homemaker) Sakharnov; married first wife, Aleksandra, 1947 (marriage ended, 1978); married second wife, Larisa (a physics professor), 1978; children: Igor, Vladimir, Olga. *Education:* Attended naval academy in Leningrad, 1940-44.

ADDRESSES: Home—22-1-18 Novorossiyskaya Str., Leningrad 194018, U.S.S.R.

CAREER: Red Navy, 1944-60, retiring as commodore; captain of petty torpedo boat, 1944-45; staff officer, 1945-60; writer, 1960—. Editor in chief of children's magazine *Kostyor* (title means "Campfire"), 1973-88.

SVYATOSLAV SAKHARNOV

WRITINGS:

IN ENGLISH TRANSLATION

(Under name S. Sakharnov) *Wondrous Ships,* translation from the original Russian manuscript, Progress, 1975.
(Under name S. Sakharnov) *Who Lives in the Warm Sea?,* translation from the original Russian by Eve Manning, illustrations by N. Ustinov, Progress, 1975.
Lions and Sailing Ships (fiction for children), translation from the original Russian manuscript, *L'vy i parusniki,* by Glenys Ann Kozlov, illustrations by Mikhail Belomlinsky, Raduga Publishers, 1982.

IN RUSSIAN

Morskie skazki (fairy tales), [Leningrad], 1958.
Gak i Burtik v Strane bezdel'nikov (stories), [Leningrad], 1959.
Solnechnyi mal'chik (stories), [Leningrad], 1961.
(Under name S. Sakharnov) *Puteshestvie na "Trigle"* (stories), Detskaya Literatura (Leningrad), 1963.
(Under name S. Sakharnov) *Odinadtsat' vos'minogikh* (fiction), Detskaya Literatura (Moscow), 1965.
Kak ya spas Magellana (stories), [Moscow], 1965.
Beznogie golovonogie (stories), [Moscow], 1968.
(Under name S. Sakharnov) *Trepangolovy* (sequel to *Puteshestvie na "Trigle"*), Sovetskaya Rossiya (Moscow), 1968.
Ram i Rum, Detskaya Literatura, 1969.
Del'finii ostrov (stories), [Moscow], 1969.
Tsunami (stories), [Moscow], 1971.
Ostrov vodolazov (stories), [Leningrad], 1972.

(Under name S. Sakharnov) *Podvodnye priklyucheniya* (stories), Detskaya Literatura, 1972.

(Under name S. Sakharnov) *Po moryam vokrug Zemli* (for children), Detskaya Literatura, 1972.

Raznotsvetnoe more (stories and fairy tales), [Moscow], 1974.

V gostyakh u krokodilov (for children), Detskaya Literatura, 1974.

Os'minogi za steklom (stories), [Moscow], 1975.

Skazki o l'vakh i parusnikakh (fairy tales), [Moscow], 1975.

Devochka i del'fin (stories), [Moscow], 1977.

(Under name S. Sakharnov) *Belye kity: Puteshestviya i priklyucheniya* (stories for children), Lenizdat (Leningrad), 1978.

Skazki iz dorozhnogo chemodana (fairy tales), [Moscow], 1979.

Slony na asfal'te (stories), [Moscow], 1979.

Chto ya videl v Tanzanii (stories), [Moscow], 1981.

(Under name S. Sakharnov) *Bukhta komandora* (stories), Molodaya Gvardia (Moscow), 1983.

Skazanie o Rama, Site i letayushchei obez'yane Khanumane, [Moscow], 1986.

Pochemu u kita bol'shoi rot (stories and fairy tales), [Leningrad], 1987.

V mire del'fina i os'minoga (stories), [Moscow], 1987.

Izbrannoe, Volume I: *Rasskazy i skazki,* Volume II: *Povesti i rasskazy,* [Moscow], 1987.

OTHER

Translator of books from English, German, and Polish.

WORK IN PROGRESS: Tales from My Suitcase, a collection of world folk tales; *Leopard and Turtle,* a volume of fairy tales; *Stories about the Ships,* a history of ships.

Dustjacket from the Russian edition of Sakharnov's 1987 collection of stories and fairy tales.

SIDELIGHTS: Svyatoslav Sakharnov told *SATA:* "My books contain much of my biography. I was a diver; I took part in the war against Nazi Germany and Japan; I traveled a great deal in Africa, Cuba, India, and the Arctic; I have lived in national parks; I have spent much time in underwater laboratories and swum among coral reefs."

*   *   *

SAVAGE, Blake
See GOODWIN, Harold L(eland)

*   *   *

SCHAEFER, Jack (Warner) 1907-1991

OBITUARY NOTICE—See index for *SATA* sketch: Born November 19, 1907, in Cleveland, OH; died of congestive heart failure, January 24, 1991, in Santa Fe, NM. Editor, journalist, and author. With his very first novel, Schaefer made a lasting mark on the genre of western fiction: *Shane* has been hailed by many as one of the best novels of the Old West ever written. The story, a boy's observations of a former gunfighter who comes to work on his family's farm and becomes involved in the struggle between farmers and cattlemen, was also made into a well-received film. Schaefer began his career in journalism, working variously for the United Press wire service and newspapers such as the New Haven *Journal-Courier* and Baltimore *Sun* between 1930 and 1949. He had not been west of Ohio when he wrote *Shane;* he based the book on his study of American history, drawing on diaries and old newspapers. His later writings included a number of other novels about the West, such as *Old Ramon, Monte Walsh,* and *The Canyon,* and the nonfiction works *Heroes without Glory: Some Goodmen of the Old West* and *An American Bestiary.* Schaefer also edited the anthology *Out West.*

OBITUARIES AND OTHER SOURCES:

PERIODICALS

Chicago Tribune, January 27, 1991.
Los Angeles Times, January 27, 1991.
New York Times, January 27, 1991.
Washington Post, January 27, 1991.

*   *   *

SHORT, Michael 1937-

PERSONAL: Born February 27, 1937, in Paget, Bermuda; son of Reginald and Bella (McLean) Short; married Elaine Braithwaite (a weaver). *Education:* University of Bristol, B.Sc., 1958; attended Morley College and University of London. *Hobbies and other interests:* Windmills.

ADDRESSES: Home—73 Trowbridge Rd., Bradford-on-Avon, Wiltshire BA15 1EG, England. *Agent*—Mark Paterson, 10 Brook St., Wivenhoe, Essex CO7 9DS, England.

CAREER: Musical composer. Bath College of Higher Education, Bath, England, principal lecturer in music, 1981-87. Worked as a music librarian during 1960s; has taught music for Open University and at Cambridge University; composer in residence at Dolmetsch Summer School of Music.

MEMBER: Composers Guild of Great Britain, Scottish Society of Composers.

AWARDS, HONORS: Mendelssohn Scholarship recipient, 1966.

WRITINGS:

Windmills in Lambeth: An Historical Survey, London Borough of Lambeth, Director of Library and Amenity Services, 1971.
(Editor) Gustav Holst, *Letters to W. G. Whittaker,* University of Glasgow Press, 1974.
Gustav Holst: A Centenary Documentation, White Lion, 1974.
Your Book of Music (for children), Faber, 1982.
Gustav Holst: The Man and His Music, Oxford University Press, 1990.

Also composer of musical pieces commissioned for and performed by professional musical ensembles, including the London Sinfonietta, the Scottish Baroque Ensemble, the Alberni String Quartet, the Philip Jones Brass Ensemble, and the British Broadcasting Corporation Singers. Compiler of booklets on music. Contributor to music journals.

SIDELIGHTS: Michael Short commented: "My main creative activity is composing music; writing books is a secondary occupation. During the 1960s I worked as a music librarian, and I compiled and published some library booklets listing the available literature, music scores, and recordings of various composers and types of music. Looking ahead, I saw that the centenary of the birth of the British composer Gustav Holst was approaching in 1974, and that I would have to do a lot of work to compile a complete list of his compositions. I immediately contacted his daughter, Imogen Holst, and thus began a working relationship which lasted until her death in 1984. We compared notes, exchanged information, and were each able to compile a separate list of works: her *Thematic Catalogue* and my *Centenary Documentation.* I also edited a selection of Holst's letters for publication by the University of Glasgow Press.

"In 1974 I organized and compiled the Holst Centenary Exhibition, which was shown at the Royal Festival Hall in London. This brought together a large amount of biographical and musical material, and gave me the idea of writing another book, *Gustav Holst: The Man and His Music,* an enormous task which occupied me until 1987.

"Apart from that book, most of my work on the composer consists of specialized information useful to librarians, students, scholars, and musicians, but probably of little interest to young people. However, in 1979 Imogen Holst asked me to collaborate with her on producing a new edition of *Your Book of Music,* a children's book originally published in the 1950s. At first, my role was just to add some extra chapters on jazz, sound recording, and electronic music, but Miss Holst found that she did not have time to revise the main text, and I was asked to rewrite the entire book and provide a new set of illustrations. Rather than tinker with her original work, I started again from scratch, writing the text as if it were a completely new book. This task gave me much pleasure, as I had to solve the problem of how to cover the entire range of music in a few pages, yet make it understandable and interesting to young people.

"The aim of the book is to provide an introduction to the subject for children and teenagers (and even adult beginners), and to lead them on to an active interest in playing, singing, and listening to music. In addition to the originally requested chapters, topics include 'How Music Began,' 'How Musical Sounds Are Made,' 'The Instruments of Music,' 'How to Read Music,' 'How Music Is Composed,' 'Instrumental Music,' 'Orchestral Music,' 'Vocal Music,' and 'Folk Music.' There are also advisory appendices on 'Learning an Instrument,' 'Music as a Career,' 'Musical Terms,' and 'Suggestions for Further Reading'—all this in the space of eighty pages. The extent of my success can be judged by the fact that one reviewer described the book as 'a masterpiece of compression without falsification.'

"My own compositions range widely in scope and include orchestral, choral, instrumental, vocal, and chamber music. They vary from works for professional ensembles to advertising jingles and jazz arrangements. As composer in residence at the annual Dolmetsch Summer School of Music, I have written a number of compositions for the recorder, both solo and ensemble, that are suitable for performance by amateur musicians.

"Apart from music, I have a secret vice—I am a windmill enthusiast! I have amassed a large amount of literature on the subject, and in 1971 my own contribution was published: *Windmills in Lambeth: An Historical Survey.* This is a specialized study of the mills that once stood in an area of London, but I think it contains some useful general information, particularly the brief summary of the history and development of the windmill in Europe."

*   *   *

SHURA, Mary Francis
See CRAIG, Mary (Francis) Shura

*   *   *

SILLY, E. S.
See KRAUS, (Herman) Robert

*   *   *

SMITH, Dodie
See SMITH, Dorothy Gladys

*   *   *

SMITH, Dorothy Gladys 1896-1990
(Dodie Smith; C. L. Anthony, Charles Henry Percy, pseudonyms)

OBITUARY NOTICE—See index for *SATA* sketch: Born May 3, 1896, in Whitefield, Lancashire, England; died November 24, 1990. Actress, furnishings buyer, playwright, screenwriter, and author. Widely known for her children's book *The Hundred and One Dalmatians,* adapted as the classic animated Walt Disney film *One Hundred and One Dalmatians,* Smith began her career in British theatre. She was an amateur actress as a child and wrote her first screenplay, *Schoolgirl Rebels,* under the pseudonym Charles Henry Percy while a student at the Royal Academy of Dramatic Art. The film was bought and produced by a small film company. From 1915 to 1922 she acted on the British stage, then worked briefly as a buyer for a furnishing company. Her first play, *British Talent,* was produced in London in 1924.

Smith's theatrical works, often about daily life, include *Autumn Crocus* and *Call It a Day,* which was also filmed. Using the name C. L. Anthony until 1935, Smith wrote novels after World War II under her own name, achieving particular success with *I Capture the Castle.* She also penned autobiographical volumes such as *Look Back with Love.*

OBITUARIES AND OTHER SOURCES:

BOOKS

Smith, Dodie, *Look Back with Love,* Heinemann, 1974.
Smith, *Look Back with Mixed Feelings,* W. H. Allen, 1978.
Smith, *Look Back with Astonishment,* W. H. Allen, 1979.
Smith, *Look Back with Gratitude,* Muller, 1985.
Who's Who, 143rd edition, St. Martin's, 1991.
The Writers Directory: 1988-1990, St. James Press, 1988.

PERIODICALS

Times (London), November 27, 1990.

*   *   *

SMITH, Wanda VanHoy 1926-

PERSONAL: Born February 5, 1926, in Portland, OR; daughter of Eugene Virgil (a farmer) and Violet Jane (a school assistant; maiden name, Freer) VanHoy; married Bill G. Smith (a boat manufacturer), 1946; children: Wynn Trent, Christy Smith McCartney. *Education:* Attended Oregon State College, 1944, University of California at Los Angeles, 1960, and El Camino College, 1960-64.

ADDRESSES: Home—144 Monterey Blvd., Hermosa Beach, CA 90254.

CAREER: Writer. Associated Press, Portland, OR, teletype attendant, 1944; California State Office of Vital Statistics, Sacramento, computer operator, 1946; Redondo Beach Sailing Academy, Redondo Beach, CA, sailing coordinator, 1968-75; Capital Yachts (advertising agency), Harbor City, CA, copywriter, 1970-88.

MEMBER: Society of Children's Book Writers, Surfwriters (program chairman, 1986), Southwest Manuscripters (president), Southern California Council on Literature for Children and Young People.

WRITINGS:

Ash Brooks, Super Ranger (for children), illustrations by Gail Owens, Scribners, 1984.
Love Knots (for young adults), Willowisp Press, 1987.

Also author of *A Pearl for Francie,* Dutton. Short story, "Amy's Birthday Surprise," appeared in *Highlights for Children.*

WORK IN PROGRESS: David and the Giant Tree, a biography of David Douglas; *Tazzy and the Appaloosa; Chief Joseph and the Nez Perce Indians; Save the Spotted Horse.*

SIDELIGHTS: Wanda VanHoy Smith told *SATA:* "I won an essay contest while in high school. This achievement encouraged me to be a writer. I was editor of the school paper and on the staff of the yearbook. I entered a journalism course at Oregon State expecting to set the world on fire and

WANDA VANHOY SMITH

was too easily discouraged when a professor advised me to 'write about what you know.' Being young and foolish, I didn't think I knew about anything, so I set out to see the world.

"I went to work as a teletype attendant for the Associated Press in Portland, Oregon. Working in the newspaper office where Ernest Hemingway was everyone's hero was exciting. One Sunday afternoon when I was alone in the Oregonian office, a 'flash' came through on the teletype. This meant I was to call in all the editors . . . what excitement getting out an EXTRA. A mob had murdered and hung Benito Mussolini in the streets in Italy.

"I moved to Sacramento, California, with a friend who went there to marry an air force cadet. Sacramento was exciting in the war years, with flyers in air force uniforms dancing to big-name bands with the girls who worked at the capital.

"Still wanting to see more of the world so that I would have something to write about, I moved on to Los Angeles, California. Hollywood in the 1940s was clean and glamorous. Harry James and Benny Goodman bands were playing at the United Service Organizations and the Hollywood Palladium.

"I didn't get back into writing until after I married Bill Smith (a musician), and had a son and daughter. I regret those wasted years. I should have gone on writing no matter how busy a life I led. So I returned to writing and completed my education. My college major was recreation administration. Engineer students liked to refer to it as basket weaving under water, but recreation is an ideal course for a writer, since it includes journalism, literature, theater arts, and creative writing.

"When my husband went into sailboat manufacturing, I became involved in a sailing school. This experience was the basis for my book for young adults, *Love Knots. Ash Brooks, Super Ranger* came about from watching my son, my nephew, and their friends.

"We have a horse, and I just completed a book called *Tazzy and the Appaloosa.* So I have learned the lesson that authors should write about what they know. But it sometimes is difficult to recognize what we know. Now I intend to do a novel located in the beautiful Columbia River region where I lived as a child. I am doing research on the Nez Perce tribe.

"There is a sign on my desk saying The Quitter Never Wins, The Winner Never Quits."

FOR MORE INFORMATION SEE:

PERIODICALS

School Library Journal, March, 1985.

EDWARD SOREL

SOREL, Edward 1929-

PERSONAL: Surname originally Schwartz, legally changed to Sorel; born March 26, 1929, in Bronx, NY; son of Morris (a salesman) and Rebecca (a factory worker; maiden name, Kleinberg) Schwartz; married Elaine Rothenberg, July 1, 1956 (divorced, 1965); married Nancy Caldwell (a writer), May 29, 1965; children: (first marriage) Madeline, Leo; (second marriage) Jenny, Katherine. *Education:* Cooper Union College, diploma, 1951.

CAREER: Esquire, New York City, assistant art director, 1951-53; Push Pin Studios (commercial and graphic arts studio), New York City, co-founder, 1953, staff artist, 1953-56; Columbia Broadcasting System (CBS-TV), New York City, art director in promotion department, 1956-57; free-lance artist, political satirist, cartoonist, and illustrator of children's books, 1958—.

Exhibitions include the Push Pin Studio retrospective at the Louvre, 1970, and other Europe galleries, 1970-71; one-man shows at Graham Galleries, New York City, 1973 and 1978, New School for Social Research, New York City, 1974, and Galerie Bartsch & Charian, Munich, 1986; Retrospective Exhibition, Cooper Union, 1987.

MEMBER: American Institute of Graphic Arts, Alliance Graphique Internationale.

AWARDS, HONORS: King Carlo of Capri was named one of the fifty books of the year, 1958, by the American Institute of Graphic Arts; *Pablo Paints a Picture* was named one of the ten best illustrated books of the year, 1959, by the *New York Times;* Spring Book Festival Award, 1961, and first prize for illustration of children's books, *New York Herald Tribune,* 1962, both for *Gwendolyn, the Miracle Hen; Gwendolyn and the Weather Cock* was named one of the ten best illustrated books of the year, 1963, by the *New York Times; Magical Storybook* was among the fifty books of the year exhibition of the American Institute of Graphic Arts, 1972, and among the U.S. books in the Children's Book International Biennial of Illustrations in Bratislava, 1973; Augustus St. Gaudens Medal, Cooper Union, 1973, for professional achievement; George Polk Award, 1981, for satiric drawing; Page One Award, Newspaper Guild of New York, for best editorial cartoon (magazines), 1988; additional awards for illustration from Society of Illustrators, American Institute of Graphic Arts, and Art Directors Club of New York.

WRITINGS:

SELF-ILLUSTRATED

How to Be President: Some Hard and Fast Rules, Grove, 1960.
Moon Missing: An Illustrated Guide to the Future, Simon & Schuster, 1962.
Sorel's World's Fair, New York, 1964, McGraw, 1964.
Making the World Safe for Hypocrisy: A Collection of Satirical Drawings and Commentaries, Swallow Press, 1972.
Superpen: The Cartoons and Caricatures of Edward Sorel, edited by Lidia Ferrara, Random House, 1978.
The Zillionaire's Daughter (juvenile), Warner Books, 1990.

ILLUSTRATOR

Warren Miller, *King Carlo of Capri* (adapted from Charles Perrault's *Riquet with the Tuft of Hair*), Harcourt, 1958.
Miller, *The Goings-On at Little Wishful,* Little, Brown, 1959.

From the uppermost deck, Papa Max, Claire and Jacques waved happy good-byes to the folks on the dock. (From *The Zillionaire's Daughter*, written and illustrated by Edward Sorel.)

Miller, *Pablo Paints a Picture,* Little, Brown, 1959.

Nancy Sherman, *Gwendolyn, the Miracle Hen,* Golden Press, 1961.

Sherman, *Gwendolyn and the Weather Cock,* Golden Press, 1963.

Joy Cowley, *The Duck in the Gun* (Junior Literary Guild selection), Doubleday, 1969.

William Cole, *What's Good for a Five-Year-Old?* Holt, 1969.

Nancy Caldwell Sorel, *Word People,* American Heritage Press, 1970.

Jay Williams, *Magical Storybook,* American Heritage Press, 1972.

Ward Botsford, *The Pirates of Penzance* (adapted from the Gilbert and Sullivan operetta), Random House, 1981.

OTHER

Author of introduction to Charles Le Brun's *Resemblances, Amazing Faces,* Harlin Quist, 1980. Contributing editor of *New York, Gentlemen's Quarterly,* and *Village Voice.* Creator of syndicated feature "Sorel's News Service," for King Features, 1969-70, and of other cartoon features, including "The Spokesman" for *Esquire,* and "Unfamiliar Quotations" for the *Atlantic.* Contributor to additional periodicals, including the *Village Voice, Rolling Stone, Realist, Ramparts,* and *Time.*

SIDELIGHTS: Edward Sorel is an award-winning political satirist and illustrator of children's books. Probably best known for his political cartoons and caricatures of public figures, he uses his biting wit and artistic flair to expose abuses of power, especially among government officials. Drawn in a vigorous, free flowing, almost scratchy style, Sorel's pen and ink sketches often depict corrupt officials involved in ridiculous situations. Though his drawings have the old-fashioned look of Victorian sketches from the nineteenth century, Sorel's cartoons and caricatures are actually timely reactions to current political and social issues. Like the best political satirists always have done, Sorel calls attention to society's vices and generates considerable controversy with his artwork.

Sorel was born in 1929, the year of the legendary stock market crash that marked the beginning of the Great Depression. He grew up in a politically conservative household and pursued a career in art as an act of rebellion against his father. "I became an artist because my father was opposed to the idea," he noted in *Illustrators of Children's Books: 1957-1966.* After attending New York's High School of Music and Art, the young artist was admitted to Cooper Union, a school specializing in science and art. In an interview published in Steven Heller's *Innovators of American Illustration,* Sorel criticized the approach to art education at Cooper Union. His teachers stressed design over drawing, and he became frustrated over his failure to acquire new drawing skills. Commenting in the Heller interview on his lack of practical instruction at Cooper Union, the artist claimed that after his years of schooling, he "no longer knew how to draw."

Following his graduation in 1951, Sorel was fired from nearly a dozen graphic arts positions before landing a job as assistant art director at *Esquire* magazine. He worked there for two years before teaming up with fellow Cooper Union graduates Milton Glaser and Seymour Chwast to establish Push Pin Studios, a highly acclaimed commercial arts workshop. His assignments included the design of record covers and dust jackets for hardcover books—jobs that were very different from his earlier work and much more challenging. "The varied nature of the assignments that we received as a

studio demanded different styles and techniques, different solutions that we would not have found had we remained at our previous staff jobs," Sorel informed Frederic Whitaker in *American Artist.* "The studio proved to be a wonderful workshop for experimentation." Feeling he had contributed all he could to the success of the studio, Sorel left Push Pin in 1956 to accept a job offer in the promotions department of Columbia Broadcasting System (CBS-TV). He designed advertisements for the station for two years before embarking on a career as a free-lance artist in 1958.

As Sorel freed himself from the standards of his formal art training, he began to develop narrative skills. "I had for some time wanted to illustrate a children's book and realized that I could not tell a story, could not show those details of costume, expression, or movement which children love, unless I forgot all about style or manner and concentrated on telling a story in pictures," he said in *American Artist.* "This need to describe rather than decorate was one turning point in my development." Sorel illustrated his first children's book, the award-winning *King Carlo of Capri,* in 1958, and followed it the next year with *Pablo Paints a Picture,* another award winner.

At about the same time, Sorel began to focus his attention and creative abilities on political issues. He explained in the interview with Heller the source of his political concerns: "I grew up poor and realized that other people were rich. This made me sore as hell. . . . I think about half my political stuff is in some way or other a cry against authority."

Between 1959 and 1969, Sorel published his own periodical, *Sorel's Affiche,* which he distributed free of charge to hundreds of art directors. "The purpose of the *Affiche,*" he told Whitaker in 1960, "in addition to bringing my work before the art directors in advertising agencies and publishing houses, is to express something of what I think about certain things that are going on in the world around me, to ridicule the sacred cows of our society. . . . I am concerned only with getting my ideas across as bitingly as possible. . . . My main interest in the *Affiche* has been to show the absurdity of some of our mores and of the leaders of our political and cultural life." Throughout his career, Sorel has expressed his disenchantment with the trends of modern society while maintaining a love of an earlier, simpler time in history. He noted his fondness for the past in a *Gentleman's Quarterly* interview with Hilary Sterne, exclaiming: "I *hate* modern art. I hate modern music. I hate modern everything."

In the early 1960s, Sorel illustrated Nancy Sherman's *Gwendolyn, the Miracle Hen* and *Gwendolyn and the Weather Cock.* The first received the Spring Book Festival Award and the second was named one of the best illustrated books of the year by the *New York Times.* Sorel's first cartoon book for adults, *How to Be President: Some Hard and Fast Rules,* was published in 1960, followed by *Moon Missing: An Illustrated Guide to the Future,* which depicts world events following the disappearance of the moon. His earliest political cartoons were featured in underground periodicals, such as *The Realist,* but did not appeal to a general audience. By the mid-1960s, however, Sorel's political commentary was being published in his own monthly column—"Sorel's Bestiary"—in *Ramparts* magazine. His caricatures began to appear in established periodicals, including the *Atlantic* and *Esquire.*

From the late 1960s through the early 1970s, Sorel's satire became even more piercing. The artist explained in a *New York* article, "Vietnam changed everything. Suddenly out-

Edward Sorel's political cartoons make effective magazine covers.

rage was more than permissible— it was fashionable." At the height of the U.S. involvement in the civil war in Vietnam in the late 1960s, a cartoon feature titled "Sorel's News Service" was syndicated to about forty American newspapers. But Sorel apparently carried his satire too far: "Sorel's News Service" was canceled by almost all of the papers in response to a humorless cartoon depicting Richard M. Nixon, then president of the United States, juggling the skulls of the week's Vietnam casualties.

Cartoons from the syndicated feature were collected in Sorel's 1972 anthology *Making the World Safe for Hypocrisy.* In an article for *Graphis,* Steven Heller declared that the publication of the collection "helped change the course of modern graphic commentary in a more personally oriented direction." In the same article, Sorel offered his own thoughts on the significance of his profession: "A political cartoonist is important because he is working out his own frustrations publicly. Most of us are not in control of our destiny, and are powerless politically. A humorist corrects this in comic fashion while opening the door for others to express themselves. The indignance I exhibit represents the rage of many people."

In addition to commenting on the controversy generated by the Vietnam crisis, Sorel reacted to other factors that contributed to a general feeling of disillusionment among Americans in the 1960s and 1970s. Blatant abuses of civil rights, for instance, prompted a surge in the movement for equality among all races. And in 1973 a political scandal now known as "Watergate"—a conspiracy involving Republican party officials who engineered an elaborate network to spy on the activities of the Democratic National Committee—rocked

the credibility of the U.S. government. Focusing on these and other political and social issues, Sorel continued to inspire debate by calling attention to the crises that threatened the nation.

While poking fun at politicians with his comics throughout the 1960s and 1970s, Sorel continued to develop his narrative and drawing skills by illustrating children's books. Sorel admitted to Heller in the *Innovators of American Illustration* interview, "I never had the confidence that I could draw." He first realized his artistic abilities while illustrating *Word People,* a children's book written by his wife, Nancy. "The book was about people whose names became part of the language, like 'Sandwich,'" he told Heller. "Books are a marvelous chance for an artist to try out new stuff. . . . And in *Word People,* for the first time, I did drawings without any kind of tracing."

In 1978 a number of Sorel's satiric magazine covers, drawings, and cartoons were collected in *Superpen.* He received the George Polk Award for satiric drawings in 1981, and that same year he provided the color paintings for Ward Botsford's highly praised adaptation for children of Gilbert and Sullivan's operetta *The Pirates of Penzance.* In 1990 Sorel wrote and illustrated his first original children's book, *The Zillionaire's Daughter,* about the adventures of a rich little French girl who sails to New York aboard the S. S. *Gigantic* with her zillionaire father. Commenting on the book in *Publishers Weekly,* one reviewer noted, "Sorel's resplendent pen and ink, color-enhanced drawings are perfectly matched by his effortless verse." Sorel's recent work consists largely of magazine contributions and continued progress on a history of caricature.

In an article for *American Heritage,* Sorel summarized his artistic philosophy, stressing the boundlessness of human creativity: "The world no longer needs artists to record its momentous events. It has the camera. . . . But the camera has one serious limitation; it can only record what appears before its lens. The creative artist, on the other hand, can reproduce anything he can imagine. His mind's eye can see through brick walls and closed doors, and can even travel back through time." Modest, however, about his own artistic talent, he offered the following critique of his work in the interview with Heller: "I am seldom able to draw entirely from my imagination. I always need some kind of reference material as a starting point. This is my great lack of as an illustrator. I think it stems from not having enough life drawing at a crucial time in my development." In spite of this shortcoming, critics rank Sorel among the most influential and important caricaturists and illustrators of the twentieth century.

WORKS CITED:

Heller, Steven, *Graphis,* "Edward Sorel," July/August, 1983, p. 66.
Heller, Steven, editor, *Innovators of American Illustration,* Reinhold, 1986, pp. 61-69.
Kinsman, Lee, editor, *Illustrators of Children's Books: 1957-1966,* Hornbooks, 1968, p. 179.
Publishers Weekly, review of *The Zillionaire's Daughter,* February 9, 1990, p. 60.
Sorel, Edward, "Character Assassination Doesn't Pay Too Well But the Work Is Steady," *New York,* May 8, 1978, p. 38.
Sorel, Edward, "Footnotes to History," *American Heritage,* February, 1990, p. 55.
Sterne, Hilary, "Edward Sorel: The Artist's Studio," *Gentleman's Quarterly,* June, 1988, p. 231.
Whitaker, Frederic, "Edward Sorel," *American Artist,* May, 1960, pp. 40-58.

FOR MORE INFORMATION SEE:

BOOKS

Contemporary Graphic Artists, Volume 1, Gale, 1985.
Illustrators of Books for Young People, 2nd edition, Scarecrow, 1975.
World Encyclopedia of Cartoons, Chelsea House, 1980.

PERIODICALS

American Artist, August, 1989.
American Heritage, August/September, 1982.
Atlantic, May, 1968; June, 1968; February, 1971.
Esquire, November, 1983.
Forbes 400, October 24, 1988.
Graphis, Number 62, 1955; January, 1963; Number 154, 1971-1972.
Horizon, September, 1961.
Library Journal, May 15, 1978.
Nation, April 30, 1988.
New York, May 25, 1960.
New York Times Book Review, May 14, 1978.
Ramparts, January, 1969; April, 1973; May, 1973.
Time, October 18, 1968.

SPERLING, Dan(iel Lee) 1949-

PERSONAL: Born December 22, 1949, in New York, NY; son of Allen Aaron (an attorney) and Helen (a systems analyst; maiden name, Cohen) Sperling. *Education:* Duke University, B.A., 1971.

ADDRESSES: Home—Washington, DC.

CAREER: Chesapeake and Potomac (C & P) Telephone Co., Wheaton, MD, marketing representative, 1973-75; operator of a marketing business in Silver Spring, MD, 1975-76; free-lance writer, 1977—; reporter for *USA Today,* 1983-90.

WRITINGS:

A Spectator's Guide to Baseball, Avon, 1983.
A Spectator's Guide to Football, Avon, 1983.
A Spectator's Guide to Basketball, Avon, 1983.

Contributor of articles and reviews to magazines and newspapers, including *Eastern Review, Rolling Stone, Geo, Us, Washington Post,* and *Success.*

SIDELIGHTS: Dan Sperling told *SATA:* "Getting mediocre grades on school essays, compositions, and papers doesn't necessarily mean a student lacks writing ability; it may simply mean he or she has little interest in the arid subject matter."

HOBBIES AND OTHER INTERESTS: Bees, edible and useful wild plants, traditional psychology, decorative knots.

*   *   *

SPRINGER, Nancy 1948-

PERSONAL: Born July 5, 1948, in Montclair, NJ; daughter of Harry E. (in business) and Helen (an artist; maiden name, Wheeler) Connor; married Joel Springer (a Lutheran minister), September 13, 1969; children: Jonathan, Nora. *Education:* Gettysburg College, B.A. (cum laude), 1970. *Hobbies and other interests:* Horseback riding.

ADDRESSES: Home and office—360 West Main St., Dallastown, PA 17313. *Agent*—Jean Naggar, 216 East 75th St. #1E, New York, NY 10021.

CAREER: Writer, 1971—. Delone Catholic High School, McSherrystown, PA, teacher, 1970-71; University of Pittsburgh at Johnstown, personal development plan instructor, 1983-85; York College of Pennsylvania, special programs instructor, 1985—. Guitarist for amateur musical productions.

MEMBER: Science Fiction Writers of America, Society of Children's Book Writers, Children's Literature Council of Pennsylvania, Phi Beta Kappa.

AWARDS, HONORS: Distinguished Alumni Award, Gettysburg College, 1987; nominations for Nebula Award, Hugo Award, and World Fantasy Award, all 1987, all for short story, "The Boy Who Plaited Manes"; International Reading Association/Children's Book Council Children's

Dustjacket for Nancy Springer's 1988 mythic-fantasy novel, which combines a coming-of-age theme with a love of horses.

Choice award, 1988, for *A Horse to Love;* Nebula Award nomination, 1989, for *Apocalypse.*

WRITINGS:

FOR CHILDREN

A Horse to Love, Harper, 1987.
Not on a White Horse, Atheneum, 1988.
They're All Named Wildfire, Atheneum, 1989.
Red Wizard, Atheneum, 1990.

FANTASY NOVELS

The Book of Suns (also see below), Pocket Books, 1977.
The White Hart, Pocket Books, 1979.
The Silver Sun (based on *The Book of Suns*), Pocket Books, 1980.
The Sable Moon, Pocket Books, 1981.
The Black Beast (also see below), Pocket Books, 1982.
The Golden Swan (also see below), Pocket Books, 1983.
The Book of Vale (contains *The Black Beast* and *The Golden Swan*), Doubleday, 1983.
Wings of Flame, Tor Books, 1985.
Chains of Gold, Tor Books, 1986.
Madbond (first novel in "The Sea King Trilogy"), Tor Books, 1987.
Mindbond (second novel in "The Sea King Trilogy"), Tor Books, 1987.
Chance—And Other Gestures of the Hand of Fate, Baen Books, 1987.
Godbond (third novel in "The Sea King Trilogy"), Tor Books, 1988.

The Hex Witch of Seldom, Baen Books, 1988.
Apocalypse, Baen Books/Underwood-Miller, 1989.

OTHER

Contributor of stories to *The Magazine of Fantasy and Science Fiction.*

WORK IN PROGRESS: Volos the Unholy, a fantasy novel; *Colt,* a novel for children; *The Friendship Song,* a fantasy for children.

SIDELIGHTS: Nancy Springer told *SATA:* "I think much of my writing has been an attempt to revise my childhood, which was unsatisfactory. Not that I had any terrible troubles. Mine was just the usual sort of unhappiness: I was miserably shy, and very small and skinny, and of course I was picked on (all that has changed now). Without quite knowing why, when I was in my teens I started to daydream a lot about heroes facing an evil, hostile world, and when I was in my early twenties I started to write the daydreams down in the form of fantasy novels. Eventually these books earned me enough money to let me fulfill a childhood dream: at the age of thirty-three I bought myself a horse. I enjoyed this somewhat unruly animal very much, learned from it, gained confidence on it, and found myself writing books specifically for children and young adults. The horse, for me, was like a key that let me back into my own childhood in a more complete and realistic way than my fantasy heroes had. And once I started writing books for children, I finally started growing up.

Dustjacket from Springer's 1989 novel, depicting youthful idealism and love of horses in the everyday setting of a small Pennsylvania town.

"It occurs to me that writing books may just be a job to some people, but it obviously is not to me. My writing is part of my life, a way to manage my life. It took me a while to find this way, though. As a child and a teenager, I did not write much except for school. Instead, I lived to read. I kept notebooks in which I listed books read and vocabulary words learned. In college I studied English literature. Not until after college did I begin my own first fumbling attempts at fiction, and they were shallow and set in places far from where I lived. It took me awhile to dare to really write.

"It took me awhile also to realize how much my writing reflected my own identity. I wrote books about courageous people who were steadfast friends, yet I did not perceive myself as particularly brave or loyal. Now, years later, I understand that yes, I am brave in my way, and loyal to my ideals. Ideals I discovered through writing."

FOR MORE INFORMATION SEE:

PERIODICALS

Apprise, November, 1987.
Patriot-News, September 14, 1989.
York Sunday News, March 4, 1990.

* * *

STECKLER, Arthur 1921-1985

PERSONAL: Born January 23, 1921, in White Plains, NY; died November 1, 1985; son of Samuel (a merchant) and Sadie (Hollander) Steckler; married Marjorie Schneider, December 20, 1964; children: Lisa, Erika. *Education:* Attended high school in White Plains, NY.

ADDRESSES: Residence—New London, CT. *Agent*—Franklin Heller, 1364 Rockrimmon Rd., Stamford, CT 06903.

CAREER: Free-lance production manager for films, 1947-81; writer, 1981-85. Photographer and public relations representative for a Bermuda hotel chain. *Military service:* U.S. Marine Corps, 1940-47; served as cinematographer; became staff sergeant.

MEMBER: Screen Directors International Guild, Directors Guild of America, Motion Picture Assistant Directors/Production Managers Guild.

WRITINGS:

One Hundred and One Words and How They Began, illustrated by James Flora, Doubleday, 1979.
One Hundred One More Words and How They Began, illustrated by Flora, Doubleday, 1981.

Contributor of articles to *Action.*

* * *

STERLING, Helen
See HOKE, Helen (L.)

STEVENS, Bryna 1924-
(Bryna Donaldson)

PERSONAL: Born October 22, 1924, in New Rochelle, NY; daughter of Alexander (a pharmacist) and Amy (a business manager; maiden name, Rosenfield) Stevens; divorced; children: Joseph Meyer, Janice Puls, Mark Donaldson. *Education:* Attended New York University, Drury College, and Wayne State University; University of Wisconsin—Madison, B.Mus., 1967. *Politics:* Democrat. *Religion:* Jewish.

ADDRESSES: Home—491 31st Ave., No. 304, San Francisco, CA 94121.

CAREER: Private piano teacher, 1942-62 and 1965—; writer, 1954—. Part-time or substitute teacher of vocal music and stringed instruments in various locations in Wisconsin, including Monona, Middleton, Madison, and Dane County; choir director. Conducted writing workshops in juvenile writing, self-publishing, and critiquing at West Virginia Writers Workshop, 1982.

MEMBER: San Francisco Writers Workshop.

AWARDS, HONORS: Madison Area Writers Contest awards include honorable mention, 1968, for poetry, and 1971, 1972, and 1973, for articles; *Deborah Sampson Goes to War* was chosen as an honor book by the Virginia Library Association, 1985.

BRYNA STEVENS

WRITINGS:

(Editor) *Borrowed Feathers and Other Fables,* Random House, 1977.
The Harbor Book (juvenile), Random House, 1977.
Ben Franklin's Glass Armonica (juvenile), illustrated by Priscilla Kiedrowski, Carolrhoda, 1983.
Deborah Sampson Goes to War (juvenile), illustrated by Florence Hill, Carolrhoda, 1984.
How to Succeed in Popular Music, J. Weston Walch, 1987.
Witches: Opposing Viewpoints (juvenile), Greenhaven, 1987.
Handel and the Famous Sword Swallower of Halle, Philomel Books, 1990.

Author and publisher of keyboard books *Musical Miniatures,* 1975, and *One One One Have Some Fun,* 1976. Contributor to *Disney's Book of Tall Tales,* Random House, 1976, *Charlie Brown's Third Super Book of Questions and Answers,* Random House, 1978, and *Charlie Brown's Fourth Super Book of Questions and Answers,* Random House, 1978. Contributor, under name Bryna Donaldson, to periodicals.

WORK IN PROGRESS: Civil War female spy stories.

SIDELIGHTS: Bryna Stevens told *SATA:* "As soon as I attended school and learned to read and write, I began writing poetry. Perhaps I was inspired by Robert Louis Stevenson's *A Child's Garden of Verses,* given to me by my first-grade teacher. My early poetry attempts were published in the school paper, and perhaps it was then that I got printer's ink in my veins. At about the same time, I began taking piano lessons. Music and writing still exist as my main interests in life. As I write, I'm constantly aware of the sound of words and hear them in my mind.

"I have always had a strong interest in history, in learning how other people of long ago lived. I love doing research, searching for fascinating tidbits of the past. My aim has been to present historical events in an interesting and lively manner, so people, particularly children, will view history as a living, vibrant subject and not as something that is dead with no meaning for them.

"Once my own children were grown, I believe it's been my piano students who have kept me in touch with today's children. A writer, even a history writer, needs to stay in tune with the contemporary world."

HOBBIES AND OTHER INTERESTS: "I spend a lot of time knitting, crocheting, often designing the things I make. Also, I was bitten by the computer bug and use my computers for writing, music, and graphics. I'm strongly interested in photography; when I wrote newspaper articles, I often used my own pictures."

*　　*　　*

STOCK, Catherine 1952-

PERSONAL: Born November 26, 1952, in Stockholm, Sweden; daughter of Vere Guildford (a career diplomat) and Frances B. C. (an artist; maiden name, Coetzee) Stock. *Education:* University of Cape Town, B.F.A., 1974; University of London, postgraduate certificate in education, 1976; Pratt Institute, M.A., 1978. *Hobbies and other interests:* Hiking, swimming, reading, tennis, opera, ballet, chess, skiing, wildlife conservation, crossword puzzles, jazz, chamber music, cooking.

ADDRESSES: Home and office—20 East 88th St., New York, NY 10128.

CAREER: Hewat Teacher's Training College, Cape Town, South Africa, lecturer in drawing and art history, 1975; Putnam Publishing Group, New York City, art director, 1978-81; University of Cape Town, lecturer in children's book writing, illustration, and design, 1982-83; Macmillan Publishing Co., Inc., New York City, designer, 1984-85; Houghton Mifflin Co., New York City, art director of Clarion Books, 1985-86; author and illustrator.

AWARDS, HONORS: Award from the American Institute of Graphic Arts, 1981, for design of *A Little Interlude,* written by Robert Maiorano and illustrated by Rachel Isadora; Christopher Award, 1983, for *Posy; Justin and the Best Biscuits in the World* was selected one of Child Study Association of America's Children's Books of the Year, 1987.

WRITINGS:

JUVENILE; SELF-ILLUSTRATED

A Christmas Angel Collection, Scribner, 1978.
Emma's Dragon Hunt ("Reading Rainbow" selection), Lothrop, 1984.
Sampson, the Christmas Cat, Putnam, 1984.
Sophie's Bucket, Lothrop, 1985.
Sophie's Knapsack, Lothrop, 1988.
Alexander's Midnight Snack: A Little Elephant's ABC, Clarion, 1988.
Armien's Fishing Trip, Morrow, 1990.
Halloween Monster, Bradbury, 1990.
Thanksgiving Treat, Bradbury, 1990.
Christmas Time, Bradbury, 1990.
Secret Valentine, Bradbury, 1991.
Easter Surprise, Bradbury, 1991.
Birthday Present, Bradbury, 1991.

ILLUSTRATOR

Vernon Pizer, *Shortchanged by History,* Putnam, 1979.
Betty Baker, *All-by-Herself,* Greenwillow, 1980.
Maggie Duff, *The Princess and the Pumpkin,* Macmillan, 1980.
Helen Reader Cross, *Isabella Mine,* Lothrop, 1980.
Sally Major, *Eating Out: A Guide to European Dishes,* Grastorf & Lang, 1981.
Lucia Moira Thatcher, *Mr. Tiki Wok,* Tafelberg, 1981.
Marietta Moskin, *A Royal Gift,* Coward, 1981.
Corlia Fourie, *Marianne and the Lion in the Dollhouse,* Human & Rousseau, 1982.
Heinz Winckler, *Tina,* Tafelberg, 1983.
Martin Versfeld, *Food for Thought,* Tafelberg, 1983.
Charlotte Pomerantz, *Posy,* Greenwillow, 1983.
May Joyce Jones, *The Choice of the Herd,* Human & Rousseau, 1984.
De Waal Venter, *Loutjie Helps Find,* Human & Rousseau, 1984.
Liza Fosburgh, *Bella Arabella,* Macmillan, 1985.
Ann Whitford Paul, *Owl at Night,* Putnam, 1985.
Mildred Pitts Walter, *Justin and the Best Biscuits in the World,* Lothrop, 1986.
Alane Ferguson, *That New Pet!,* Lothrop, 1986.
Pomerantz, *Timothy Tall Feather,* Greenwillow, 1986.
Ann Turner, *Street Talk* (poems), Houghton, 1986.
Carol Ra, editor, *Trot, Trot to Boston: Play Rhymes for Baby,* Lothrop, 1987.
Caroline Bauer, *Midnight Snowman,* Atheneum, 1987.
Claudia Mills, *Melanie Magpie,* Bantam, 1987.

Catherine Stock's 1984 picture book, *Emma's Dragon Hunt,* **reflects the period of her life spent in Hong Kong.** (Illustrated by the author.)

Kathryn Lasky, *Sea Swan,* Macmillan, 1988.

Carol Beach York, *Miss Know-It-All and the Three Ring Circus,* Bantam, 1988.

Charlotte Zolotow, *Something Is Going to Happen,* Harper, 1988.

Barbara Joosse, *Better with Two,* Harper, 1988.

Zolotow, *A Tiger Called Thomas,* Lothrop, 1988.

Molly D'Arcy Thompson, *Willie Stories,* Human & Rousseau, 1988.

Kathleen Hersom and Donald Hersom, *The Copycat,* Atheneum, 1989.

York, *Miss Know-It-All and the Magic House,* Bantam, 1989.

Grace Chetwin, *Mr. Meredith and the Truly Remarkable Stone,* Bradbury, 1989.

Karen Williams, *Galimoto,* Lothrop, 1990.

Joanne Ryder, *When the Woods Hum,* Morrow, 1991.

C. B. Christiansen, *Mara in the Morning,* Atheneum, 1991.

Contributor of illustrations to magazines and newspapers, including *New Yorker* and *New York Times.*

WORK IN PROGRESS: Illustrating *The Willow Umbrella,* a book by Christine Widman set in Zimbabwe.

SIDELIGHTS: Catherine Stock told *SATA:* "Children's literature seems to be the field in which I can contribute something to the world. I'm a rather quiet and shy person, and I've always loved books. I also grew up continually painting pictures—my mother was a painter. Perhaps because we were always moving, our family was very close. Thus, childhood memories are very special to me and a constant source of inspiration. My own stories reflect periods of my life spent in France, England, South Africa, the United States, and Hong Kong. Eventually I hope to buy an old house in the French or Italian countryside with artist friends and to divide my time between Europe and New York."

*   *   *

STONE, Peter 1930-

PERSONAL: Born February 27, 1930, in Los Angeles, CA; son of John (a motion picture producer) and Hilda (a film writer; maiden name, Hess) Stone; married Mary O'Hanley, February 17, 1961. *Education:* Bard College, B.A., 1951; Yale University, M.F.A., 1953.

ADDRESSES: Home—Stony Hill Rd., Amagansett, NY 11930. *Office*— 160 East 71st St., New York, NY 10021. *Agent*—Sam Cohn, I.C.M., 40 West 57th St., New York, NY 10019.

CAREER: Playwright and film and television scenarist.

MEMBER: Dramatists Guild (member of executive council; president, beginning in 1981), Authors League of America, Writers Guild of America.

AWARDS, HONORS: National Academy of Television Arts and Sciences Emmy Award, 1962, for *The Defenders;* Writers Guild of America award nomination for television play, 1962, for *The Benefactors;* Writers Guild of America award for best comedy film, 1963, for *Charade,* 1964, for *Father Goose,* 1974, for *The Taking of Pelham 1-2-3,* and 1978, for *Who's Killing the Great Chefs of Europe?;* Mystery Writers of America award for best mystery film, 1963, for *Charade;* Academy Award for best original story and screenplay, 1964, for *Father Goose;* Tony Award for best musical, 1969, Drama Desk Award for best book of a musical, 1969, and New York Drama Critics Circle Award and *Plays and Players* award for best new musical, both 1970, all for *1776;* D.Litt., Bard College, 1971; Christopher Award, 1973, for film *1776;* Tony Award for best book of a musical, 1981, for *Woman of the Year.*

WRITINGS:

PLAYS

Friend of the Family, produced in St. Louis, MO, at Crystal Palace, December 9, 1958.
(Adaptor) Erich Maria Remarque, *Full Circle* (produced on Broadway at ANTA Theatre, November 7, 1973), Harcourt, 1974.

BOOKS FOR MUSICALS

Kean, music and lyrics by Robert Wright and George Forrest, produced on Broadway at Broadway Theatre, November 2, 1961.
Skyscraper, music by James Van Heusen, lyrics by Sammy Cahn, produced on Broadway at Lunt-Fontanne Theatre, November 13, 1965.
1776 (also see below; music and lyrics by Sherman Edwards, produced in New Haven at Shubert Theatre, February 10, 1969, produced on Broadway at Forty-Sixth Street Theatre, March 16, 1969), Viking, 1970.
Two by Two (based on play *The Flowering Peach* by Clifford Odets), music by Richard Rodgers, lyrics by Martin Charnin, produced on Broadway at Imperial Theatre, November 19, 1970.
Georgy, produced on Broadway at Winter Garden Theatre, February 26, 1970.

Sugar (based on film *Some Like It Hot*), music by Jule Styne, produced on Broadway at Majestic Theatre, April 9, 1972.
Goodtime Charley, produced on Broadway at Palace Theatre, March 3, 1975.
Woman of the Year (based on film of the same title; music by John Kander, lyrics by Fred Ebb, produced in Boston at Colonial Theatre, February, 1981, produced on Broadway at Palace Theatre, March 29, 1981), Samuel French, 1984.
(With Timothy S. Mayer) *My One and Only,* music by George and Ira Gershwin, produced on Broadway at St. James Theatre, May 1, 1983.
Grand Hotel, produced on Broadway at Martin Beck Theatre, November 12, 1989.

SCREENPLAYS

Charade, Universal, 1963, novelization by Stone published under same title, Gold Medal books, 1963, reprinted, Avon, 1980.
Father Goose, Universal, 1964.
Mirage (based on novel *Fallen Angel* by Howard Fast), Universal, 1965.
Arabesque, Universal, 1966.
(With Frank Tarloff) *The Secret War of Harry Frigg,* Universal, 1968.
Sweet Charity (based on play of same title by Neil Simon), Universal, 1969.
Skin Game, Warner Bros., 1971.
1776 (based on Stone's play of same title), Jack Warner and Columbia, 1972.
The Taking of Pelham 1-2-3, United Artist, 1974.
The Silver Bears, Columbia, 1978.
Who's Killing the Great Chefs of Europe?, Lorimar-Warner Bros., 1978.
Why Would I Lie?, Metro-Goldwyn-Mayer, 1980.

OTHER

Also author of television scripts for *Studio One,* Columbia Broadcasting System, Inc. (CBS), 1956; *Brenner,* CBS, 1959; *Witness,* CBS, 1961; *Asphalt Jungle,* American Broadcasting Companies, Inc. (ABC), 1961; *The Defenders,* CBS, 1961-62; and *Espionage,* National Broadcasting Co., Inc. (NBC), 1963. Author of script for musical special *Androcles and the Lion,* music and lyrics by Richard Rodgers, NBC, 1968. Creator of and writer for television series *Adam's Rib,* ABC, 1973-74, and *Ivan the Terrible,* CBS, 1976.

WORK IN PROGRESS: A Broadway musical, *Will Rogers at the Ziegfeld Follies,* scheduled for the 1990-91 season.

SIDELIGHTS: Recipient of numerous prestigious awards, Peter Stone writes for television, film, and stage. His most popular work, the play titled *1776,* is a historical comedy-drama that focuses on various events that surrounded the drafting of the Declaration of Independence. Written in 1969, the work has been adapted as a novel and a film. Stone explained in a March 18, 1969, *New York Times* article why he decided to write *1776:* "I was fascinated with the idea. . . . But more than that, I was astonished at what I didn't know about American history, especially that period. I spent seven years in college. I didn't shirk history. But as [I was told] about what went on I found myself appalled at my ignorance. Of the 56 men involved in the momentous decision I knew four of five and they were only cardboard figures. I didn't know the dates, the compromises, the sellouts. This is a national legend and it's not really taught in the schools."

WORKS CITED:

Funke, Lewis, "'1776' Reaps Fruit of Long Research," *New York Times,* March 18, 1969, p. 38.

* * *

SWEENEY, Joyce (Kay) 1955-

PERSONAL: Born November 9, 1955, in Dayton, OH; daughter of Paul (an engineer) and Catherine (an accounting clerk; maiden name, Spoon) Hegenbarth; married Jay S. Sweeney (a hospital public relations director) September 20, 1979. *Education:* Wright State University, B.A. (summa cum laude), 1977; graduate work in creative writing, Ohio University, 1977-78.

ADDRESSES: Home—Atlanta, GA. *Agent*—Marcia Amsterdam, 41 West 82nd St., New York, NY 10024.

CAREER: Philip Office Associates, Dayton, OH, ad copywriter, 1978; Rike's Department Store, Dayton, ad copywriter, 1979-81, legal secretary, 1980-81; free-lance ad copywriter in Dayton, 1981-82; writer, 1982—. Book critic for *Atlanta Constitution,* 1986—, and *Fort Lauderdale Sun/Sentinel,* 1989—. Conductor of creative writing workshops in Ormond Beach, FL, 1985, and Pompano Beach, FL, 1988-89.

MEMBER: Book Group of South Florida (secretary), Broward County Humane Society.

AWARDS, HONORS: Delacorte Press Prize for Outstanding First Young Adult Novel, 1983, and Best Young Adult Books citation, American Library Association, 1984, both for *Center Line;* Best Books for Reluctant Readers citation, American Library Association, 1989, for *The Dream Collector.*

WRITINGS:

Center Line, Delacorte, 1984.
Right behind the Rain, Delacorte, 1987.
The Dream Collector, Delacorte, 1989.
Face the Dragon, Delacorte, 1990.

Contributor of short stories and articles to periodicals, including *New Writers, Playgirl, CO-ED, Green's Magazine,* and *Writer.*

SIDELIGHTS: "All I ever wanted was to be a novelist," Joyce Sweeney wrote in a *Writer* article. When she started writing in grade school, however, she wrote poetry because she could finish poems quickly. In high school, she wrote fiction, gradually lengthening her attention span by making her new stories a few pages longer than the last ones. The day when she finally wrote a story long enough to submit to a magazine was a landmark for Sweeney, who remembers it fondly.

Stories she published during her college days were just practice for the day when she would start writing a novel, she said. This was her goal because, as she explained in *Writer,* "for one thing, I could think of very few famous writers who only did short stories. Novels clearly got all the attention. Also, I was tired of mailing out endless submissions to magazines, to see a story in print only every two years or so."

She continued, "More important, I wanted to do something deep, something complex, something *long.* I wanted to let characters develop slowly. I wanted time to coax emotions from my readers. I wanted to write something that would resonate for a few minutes after the last page was turned."

Again, she warmed-up for this larger project by first writing a novella, or short novel. Then she added a day of full-time writing into her weekly schedule and hired an agent. There was still a struggle ahead, as the story she was working on seemed uninteresting and unbelievable. A new idea about a group of runaway boys and their leader worked out much better for Sweeney, who says she wrote their story in "perfect bliss."

Sweeney had yet to experience the anxiety of submitting the novel to publishers. Some were careless with the manuscript; others weren't sure if it was for young readers or adults. But when the manuscript won a young adult fiction contest sponsored by Delacorte, Sweeney knew she had reached her goal. "None of this means, of course, that I will live happily ever after," she wrote in *Writer.* "Now I have a whole new set of problems. . . . But when somebody asks me what I do for a living, I can answer without any qualifications, 'I'm a novelist.'"

Sweeney also told *Something about the Author* that she is quite comfortable writing for young adults. "I seem to identify very strongly with teenagers and their problems, and, as a writer, I find them to be a very receptive and enthusiastic audience. While I hope to write adult mainstream novels someday, I also plan to do several more books for young adults—just for the sheer love of it."

WORKS CITED:

Sweeney, Joyce, "Author of *Center Line,*" *Writer,* October, 1984.

FOR MORE INFORMATION SEE:

PERIODICALS

Daytona Beach Sunday News-Journal, December 18, 1983.
Dayton Daily News Magazine, February 20, 1983.
Dayton Journal Herald, June 9, 1984.
Orlando Sentinel, April 15, 1984.
Ormond Beach News and Observer, September 27, 1984.
Times Literary Supplement, August 24, 1984.

* * *

THEMERSON, Stefan 1910-1988

PERSONAL: Born January 25, 1910, in Plock, Poland; son of a physician; naturalized British citizen, 1954; died September 6, 1988, in London, England; married Franciszka Weinles (an artist), 1931. *Education:* Attended the University and Ecole Polytechnique in Warsaw, Poland.

CAREER: Typographer, literary critic, philosopher, photographer, filmmaker, and writer. Founder of filmmakers' cooperative S.A.F. (Spoldzielnia Autorow Filmowych), 1935; cofounder and director of Gaberbocchus Press, 1948-

79. Works have been exhibited at galleries in Europe. *Military service:* Polish Army, 1940-44; served in France and England.

AWARDS, HONORS: Polish Order of Merit, 1976.

WRITINGS:

Dno Nieba (poems; title means "On the Bottom of the Sky"), [London], 1943.
Croquis dans les tenebres (poems; title means "Sketches in Darkness"), Hachette, 1944.
The Lay Scripture (prose poem), Froshaug, 1947.
Jankel Adler; or, An Artist Seen from One of Many Possible Angles (essay), Gaberbocchus, 1948.
Bayamus (novel), Editions Poetry London, 1949, revised edition, Gaberbocchus, 1965.
Mr. Rouse Builds His House (for children), Gaberbocchus, 1951, new edition, 1955.
Adventures of Peddy Bottom (for children), Editions Poetry London, 1951, revised edition, Gaberbocchus, 1954.
Wooff Wooff; or, Who Killed Richard Wagner? (fiction), Gaberbocchus, 1951, revised edition, 1967.
Professor Mmaa's Lecture (novel), Gaberbocchus, 1953, re-printed, Overlook Press, 1976.
"Factor T" and "Semantic Sonata" (essays), Gaberbocchus, 1956, revised edition, 1972.
Kurt Schwitters in England: 1940-1948 (essays), Gaberbocchus, 1958.
Cardinal Polatuo (novel), Gaberbocchus, 1961, new edition, 1965.
(With wife, Franciszka) *Semantic Divertissements* (humor), Gaberbocchus, 1962.
Tom Harris (novel), Gaberbocchus, 1967, Knopf, 1968.
Appolinaire's Lyrical Ideograms, Gaberbocchus, 1968.
St. Francis and the Wolf of Gubbio (opera), Gaberbocchus, 1972.
Special Branch (novel), Gaberbocchus, 1972.
Logic, Labels, and Flesh (philosophical essays), Gaberbocchus, 1974.
On Semantic Poetry, Gaberbocchus, 1975.
General Piesc; or, The Case of the Forgotten Mission (novel), Gaberbocchus, 1976.
The Chair of Decency (the 1981 Johan Huizinga Lecture), Atheaneum (Amsterdam), 1982.
The Urge to Create Visions (avant-garde film and photography), De Harmonie-Gaberbocchus, 1983.
The Mystery of the Sardine (novel), Faber (London), 1986, Farrar, Straus (New York), 1986.
Hobson's Island (novel), Faber, 1988.

Author of children's books in Polish, 1930-37. Wrote stories and verse for Polish school books, 1937. Contributor to *The Scientist Speculates*, edited by I. J. Good, Heinemann, 1962, and *Explorations in the Field of Nonsense*, edited by Wim Tigges, DQR Studies in Literature 3, Rodopi (Amsterdam), 1987. Also contributor to weekly periodical *Nova Polska*, 1943-46; contributor of poetry, essays on aesthetics, semantics, philosophy, art, and science to journals, including *Il Caffe, New Departures, Other Voices, Pagina, Poetry Review, The Painter and Sculptor,* and *Typographica*, during the 1950s, 1960s, and 1970s.

Creator with wife, Franciszka, of avant-garde films *Apteka*, 1931, *Europa,* 1932, *Drobiazg Melodyjny* (title means "Moment Musical"), 1933, *Zwarcie* (title means "Short Circuit"), 1935, *Przygoda Czlowieka Poczciwego* (title means "The

Adventures of a Good Citizen," 1937, *Calling Mr. Smith,* 1943, and *The Eye and the Ear,* 1944.

Editor of avant-garde cinema review *Film Artistique,* 1937; editor of children's magazine *Moja Gazetka,* 1937.

SIDELIGHTS: Stefan Themerson was a noted avant-garde filmmaker and novelist who wrote a number of children's books in Polish. Born the son of a doctor in Plock, Poland, Themerson lived in Russia from 1914 to 1918 while his father served as a captain in the Russian army. Returning to Poland, he later studied physics and architecture in Warsaw. In 1931 Themerson married the painter Franciszka Weinles, and he went on to pursue a variety of career interests. During the 1930s he wrote ten books for children, which were illustrated by his wife and published in Poland. He also collaborated with Franciszka on filmmaking endeavors, creating such experimental movies as *Apteka, Europa,* and *Przygoda Czlowieka Poczciwego* ("The Adventures of a Good Citizen").

In 1937 Themerson moved to Paris where he wrote stories and verse for Polish school books. He also edited a magazine for children, titled *Moja Gazetka.* During World War II Themerson served in the Polish Army, after which time he and his wife moved to England. Creating two more films in the 1940s, the couple also founded the Gaberbocchus Press, which published more than sixty titles over the next three decades. In addition, Themerson wrote poems, novels, essays, and the children's works *Mr. Rouse Builds His House* and *Adventures of Peddy Bottom.* Among his acclaimed novels for adults is *The Mystery of the Sardine,* which combines philosophical thought with humor. Themerson's works have been published in Polish, Italian, French, German, Swedish, and Dutch.

FOR MORE INFORMATION SEE:

OBITUARIES

Daily Telegraph (London), September 8, 1988.
Guardian (London), September 8, 1988.
Times (London), September 8, 1988.

*   *   *

THORNDYKE, Helen Louise
See BENSON, Mildred (Augustine Wirt)

*   *   *

TIBURZI, Bonnie 1948-

PERSONAL: Born August 31, 1948, in Danbury, CT; daughter of August Robert (a pilot) and Gunvor (an artist; maiden name, Dahlberg) Tiburzi; married Bruce Caputo (a lawyer), April 1, 1983; children: A. Anthony Caputo, B. Britt Caputo. *Education:* Attended Santa Fe College and University of Paris. *Politics:* Republican. *Religion:* Presbyterian.

ADDRESSES: Home—New York City. *Office*—1170 Fifth Ave., New York, NY 10029. *Agent*—Eleanor Friede Books Inc., 45 W. Twelfth St., New York, NY 10011.

CAREER: American Airlines Inc., New York City, 1973—, began as flight engineer, became captain on B-727 airplane at John F. Kennedy Airport; writer.

AWARDS, HONORS: Takeoff!! was named Best Book for Young Adults by American Library Association, 1984.

WRITINGS:

Takeoff!! The Story of America's First Woman Pilot for a Major Airline, Crown, 1984.

SIDELIGHTS: Bonnie Tiburzi told *SATA:* "I was the first female flight engineer in the United States and the first female pilot hired by a major U.S. airline."

*   *   *

TUBBY, I. M.
See KRAUS, (Herman) Robert

*   *   *

TYLER, Linda
See TYLER, Linda W(agner)

*   *   *

TYLER, Linda W(agner) 1952-
(Linda Tyler)

PERSONAL: Born February 15, 1952, in Milwaukee, WI; daughter of Anthony John (an application engineer) and Claire (a secretary; maiden name, Landry) Wagner; married Patrick Edward Tyler (a foreign correspondent), September 1, 1973; children: Silas, Landry. *Education:* University of South Carolina, degree in child development, 1974. *Religion:* Catholic.

ADDRESSES: Home and office—1750 Lamont St. NW, Washington, DC 20010.

CAREER: Kiddie Korner Day Schools, Charlotte, NC, teacher, 1975; teacher at Mt. Pleasant Montessori Day Care, 1980-81; teacher and board member at Mt. Pleasant Montessori School, 1982-86; All Saints Cathedral Preschool, Cairo, Egypt, teacher, 1987; British International School, Cairo, Egypt, board member, 1987-89; writer.

MEMBER: Society of Children's Book Writers.

AWARDS, HONORS: Children's Choice Award from International Reading Association and Children's Book Council, 1988, for *The Sick-in-Bed Birthday Book.*

WRITINGS:

JUVENILE; ILLUSTRATED BY SUSAN DAVIS

When Daddy Comes Home, Viking, 1986.
Waiting for Mom, Viking, 1987.
(Under name Linda Tyler) *The Sick-in-Bed Birthday Book,* Viking, 1988.
My Brother Oscar Thinks He Knows It All, Viking, 1989.
After Christmas Tree, Viking, 1990.

LINDA W. TYLER

WORK IN PROGRESS: A manuscript about a great-grandmother, publication expected in 1991; manuscripts for the Smithsonian Institute's children's books series.

SIDELIGHTS: Linda W. Tyler told *SATA:* "I grew up as an only child for eight years and always enjoyed inventing imaginary playmates and characters. I knew from the beginning of my college education that I wanted to teach young children or contribute to their lives. It was only when I started a day care program in my home in 1983 that I had the privilege of becoming emotionally involved with a select group of children who were in my care for eight or more hours a day, and I recognized then that it was my opportunity to influence them and shape their lives in any way I saw fit. I was also starting a family of my own and spending many hours reading to them and the day care children. I was checking out as many as fifty books a week from the local library in Washington, D.C., and thus living inside of their literature every day. I started a diary of daily problems and circumstances. I started to record them and write down those ideas that I thought could be developed into picture books.

"I met my illustrator, Susan Davis, at a Washington dinner party, where we just happened to be seated at the same table. It was a marriage made in Heaven. She is a well-known artist in Washington for her soft water color paintings of the city. At the time she was just beginning her career as a cover artist for the *New Yorker* magazine.

"We put together a mock up of our first book and went to New York City for one day trying to sell it. We left photo copies at six publishers, and Viking was the only one that allowed us through the door far enough to meet an editor. We have remained with that editor since then and have enjoyed a partnership through five books.

"I moved to Cairo, Egypt, in November of 1986, when my husband accepted the challenge of being a foreign correspondent in the Middle East. We have traveled extensively for the past three years throughout the Middle East and Europe. It has been a marvelous adventure and challenge to live in the Third World.

"I have enjoyed listening to children and writing about the subjects that most concern their daily lives. I will continue to do this and begin works on the unusual historical events that have shaped Washington in a language for young people. The Smithsonian Institution is just beginning a line of children's books and they are anxious to negotiate on several of our ideas. Perhaps at sometime in the near future I will write about our life in Cairo and what it was like for my children. I am still enchanted by that four to six age group and will continue to focus on it.

"I think there is a great need for books that children can use to see themselves and that will help them to understand that the trials of growing happen to all of them. I thoroughly enjoy practicing my sensitivity to their level.

"I hope to spend a great deal of time volunteering my time in the private and public schools in my area, reading to classes and conducting story hours in the branches of our public libraries to keep in touch with what the children are thinking. Susan Davis and I are great lovers of animals and we think that children relate well to the characters that we have developed."

* * *

USTON, Ken(neth Senzo) 1935-1987

PERSONAL: Surname originally Usui; born January 12, 1935, in New York, NY; died from a heart ailment, September 19, 1987, in Paris, France; son of Senzo (a professor) and Elsie (Lubitz) Usui; children: Beth Anne, Katie, John. *Education:* Yale University, B.A., 1955; Harvard University, M.B.A., 1959.

CAREER: Affiliated with Southern New England Telephone Co., Connecticut; served as financial consultant to Stanford University, Stanford, CA, and to various companies, including Douglas Aircraft and American Cement; Pacific Stock Exchange, San Francisco, CA, began as vice-president for finance, personnel, and planning, became senior vice-president; also served as president of Pacific Clearing Corp.; gambler and writer, 1975-87. Guest on television programs, including *Sixty Minutes. Military service:* U.S. Army, 1956; became second lieutenant.

MEMBER: Phi Beta Kappa.

WRITINGS:

(With Roger Rappaport) *The Big Player: How a Team of Blackjack Players Made a Million Dollars,* Holt, 1977.
One-Third of a Shoe, Uston Institute of Blackjack, 1979.
Million Dollar Blackjack, Gambling Times, 1981.

Mastering PAC-MAN, New American Library, 1982.
SCORE: Beating the Top Sixteen Video Games, New American Library, 1982.
Ken Uston's Guide to Buying and Beating the Home Video Games, New American Library, 1982.
Ken Uston's Guide to Home Computers, New American Library, 1982.

Contributor to periodicals, including *Gambling Times, Boardwalker, Electronic Games,* and *New Jersey Monthly.* Contributing editor to *Electronic Games.*

FOR MORE INFORMATION SEE:

PERIODICALS

Chicago Tribune Book World, February 21, 1982.
New York Times, June 27, 1976; May 20, 1977.

OBITUARIES

New York Times, October 8, 1987.
Times (London), October 7, 1987.

* * *

VEDRAL, Joyce L(auretta) 1943-

PERSONAL: Born July 23, 1943, in Bronx, NY; daughter of David (a boxer, wrestler, and mathematician) and Martha (a communications technician; maiden name, Dash) Yellin; married Charles J. Vedral (divorced April 11, 1976); children: Marthe Simone. *Education:* City College of the City University of New York, B.S., 1966, M.A., 1970; New York University, Ph.D., 1980. *Politics:* Republican. *Religion:* Protestant. *Hobbies and other interests:* Mountain climbing (including the Grand Tetons and Mount Kenya), martial arts (holds belts in Judo, Jui-Jitsu, and Go-Ju Karate), bodybuilding.

ADDRESSES: Home—P.O. Box A433, Wantagh, NY 11793-0433. *Office*— Department of English, Pace Univer-

Joyce L. Vedral and her daughter

sity—New York, Pace Plaza, New York, NY 10038. *Agent*—Pam Burnstein, William Morris Agency, 1350 Avenue of the Americas, New York, NY 10019.

CAREER: Julia Richman High School, New York City, teacher of English, 1974—; Pace University—New York, New York City, member of faculty, 1980—.

MEMBER: National Council of Teachers of English, New York City Council of Teachers of English.

AWARDS, HONORS: I Dare You, I Can't Take It Any More, and *My Parents Are Driving Me Crazy* were listed among the Best Three Hundred Books for Teens by the American Library Association; prizes for bodybuilding.

WRITINGS:

A Literary Survey of the Bible (textbook), Logos International, 1972.
I Dare You! How to Use Psychology to Get What You Want Out of Life, Holt, 1983.
Now or Never, Warner Books, 1985.
(With Bill Reynolds, Jr.) *Supercut: Nutrition for the Ultimate Physique,* Contemporary Books, 1985.
(With Gladys Portugues) *Hard Bodies,* Dell, 1986.
My Parents Are Driving Me Crazy, Ballantine, 1986.
I Can't Take It Any More, Ballantine, 1987.
(With Rachel McLish) *Perfect Parts,* Warner Books, 1987.
(With Portugues) *The Hard Bodies Express Workout,* Dell, 1988.
The Opposite Sex Is Driving Me Crazy. Ballantine, 1988.
My Teenager Is Driving Me Crazy, Ballantine, 1989.
(With Cameo Kneuer) *Cameo Fitness,* Warner, 1990.
Boyfriends: Getting Them, Keeping Them, Living without Them, Ballantine, 1990.
The Fat-Burning Workout, Warner Books, 1991.
Teachers: How to Get the Best Mark—No Matter What, Ballantine, 1991.

Contributor to periodicals, including *Female Bodybuilding, Muscle and Fitness, Parents', Seventeen, Shape, Sports Fitness,* and *Your Health.*

WORK IN PROGRESS: The Shape Workout, with Betty Weider.

SIDELIGHTS: Joyce L. Vedral told *SATA:* "I have been teaching English to teenagers in the high school for the past twenty-five years, and to college freshmen for the past ten years. However, I have been teaching a lot more than English!! Why is this so?

"After I started teaching, I quickly discovered that there were some basic needs that had to be addressed before I could hope to interest my students in what for many of them, considering the pressing problems on their minds, boiled down to educational luxuries (vocabulary, grammar, wonderful literature, and so on). I realized that if I could not reach down into the very core of their beings, and tap something that would motivate them to fight their way through the many obstacles in their lives, I would have a slim chance of getting these students to take an interest in education.

"It wasn't too difficult for me to find the answer, because growing up, I had to fight through some obstacles of my own.

It's quite a story, but suffice it to say, 'Bronx ghetto,' welfare family, low self-esteem. The answer for me then, as for today's youth who are searching for their place in this increasingly confusing world, is to spark something deep within that will motivate them to fulfill their potential, in spite of, indeed perhaps even because of the fact that it is a challenge.

"It has always been my belief that every human being is born with the potential to contribute something wonderful and positive to the world. However, since none of us were able to choose the circumstances of our birth, we have to take the 'given' and make the best of it. As card-players might say, every one of us was dealt a hand at birth. It's up to each one of us to take that hand and play it out to the best of our ability.

"My mission is to help each and every teenager who crosses my path to become inspired, even driven, to find his or her potential or talent and to use it to the fullest extent—and, in effect, to become 'self-actualized.' But how was I to do this? I started out by having my students read various adult self-help books. While the teenagers related enthusiastically to the ideas in these books, they were unable to fully comprehend their message because these books largely overlooked teen issues. My work was cut out for me. I wrote my first self-help book for teens, *I Dare You.* It became an immediate success in hardcover, and was put out in paperback so that more teenagers could have access to it. Since that date, I have insisted that each of my teen books skip the hardcover step and go straight to the paperback. There is simply no time to waste. Teens need help now.

"What do my books say? Why do I write them? My first book, *I Dare You,* inspires teens to overcome obstacles and achieve goals. It motivates them to use their potential to the fullest. It also teaches them to use basic psychology in dealing with people so that instead of getting into trouble with words, they can make things go smoothly (something we adults wish we had learned as teens). But what's most important, this book is written with virtually no difficult vocabulary. A teen with a fifth-grade reading level can handle it, yet it doesn't talk down to the teen. I have gotten thousands of letters from teenagers from all over the United States, telling me that this book has turned their lives around.

"From the many letters I received from teens, I soon discovered that one of the biggest problems faced by teens is getting along with parents. If a parent-teen relationship is troubled, that teen is in danger of depression, drug abuse, and worse. So I wrote *My Parents Are Driving Me Crazy,* a book that helps teens to cope with all kinds of parents— normal, frustrated parents who are trying to survive raising teens, as well as neurotic, disturbed parents who make teenagers' lives miserable. Teens tell me that after reading this book, they no longer have major fights with their parents. Parents loved the book so much (it helped teens to understand and have compassion for their parents and to get along with them) that they asked me to write one for them, so I did: *My Teenager Is Driving Me Crazy.* This book helps parents to cope with all sorts of maddening teen behavior, and to realize that they're not in it alone.

"My next book was born out of sadness. The teen suicide rate was on the rise. I was getting letters from hundreds of teens who were depressed about situations ranging from break-ups with sweethearts to self-disgust because of failure in school or depression due to drug or alcohol abuse. So I wrote the uplifting book that teaches teens how to sublimate anger and frustration from failure and rejection, and to turn it into positive energy and to use that energy to accomplish goals. Some have called this book a suicide prevention guide. Many have told me that it has saved their lives. It is called: _I Can't Take It Any More._

"There was yet another problem on teenagers' minds—the opposite sex. Teenagers spend at least half of their time worrying about male-female relationships. I became a spy for each of the sexes in order to show them what each other feels. I interviewed hundreds of teenage girls and guys and asked them what they wanted to know about the opposite sex. I then asked the opposite sex to answer these questions—which covered everything from sex, jealousy, and cheating to spending time and money. I also offered my advice on these issues. Teens have written to me expressing that now, at least they know that they are not 'weird,' or rejects, and that they now know how to cope with even the most cruel behavior of the opposite sex. That's how _The Opposite Sex Is Driving Me Crazy_ was born. This book has become a big seller, and because of it, I've been asked to write a book especially for girls—_Boyfriends: Getting Them, Keeping Them, Living without Them._

"In addition to all of this work with teenagers, I have pursued a hobby which turned into a writing career too! At the age of thirty-five, my body began to go 'over the hill.' Instead of allowing this to happen, I began working with champion bodybuilders. After learning their secrets and discovering that there were no realistic modified programs for the average person, I began putting the secrets into writing. The results: a series of bestselling fitness books.

"I have been touring the country for the past five years appearing on local and national radio and television shows and lecturing to parent-teen groups as well as fitness-oriented groups. My life is exciting and fulfilling because I maintain a healthy balance: mind and body. I use my mind to the best of my ability to help young adults, and I engage in appropriate physical activities to keep my body in its best possible form. This combination keeps me from going off either the intellectual or the physical 'deep end.' I do believe balance is the key to a happy life."

*   *   *

VERRAL, Charles Spain 1904-1990
(George L. Eaton, a joint pseudonym)

OBITUARY NOTICE—See index for _SATA_ sketch: Born November 7, 1904, in Highfield, Ontario, Canada; died of complications from lung cancer, April 1, 1990, in New York, NY. Artist, editor, and writer. Verral was known for his numerous books of action and adventure for young people. He began his career writing pulp fiction, and from 1934 to 1943 he wrote numerous stories for the "Bill Barnes" adventure series under the joint pseudonym George L. Eaton. Also writing radio scripts and comic strips, Verral later penned adventure books for children, nonfiction works about space, and biographies of sports figures. His titles include _Mighty Men of Baseball, Lassie and the Daring Rescue, Zorro and the Secret Plan, The Flying Car, Babe Ruth: Sultan of Swat,_ and _Popeye Goes Fishing._ Verral also had worked in New York City as a commercial artist, free-lance writer, and editor and writer for the Reader's Digest Association.

OBITUARIES AND OTHER SOURCES:

BOOKS
Who's Who in the East, 22nd edition, Marquis, 1988.

PERIODICALS
New York Times, April 3, 1990.

*   *   *

VISCOTT, David S(teven) 1938-

PERSONAL: Born May 24, 1938, in Boston, MA; son of Hiram (a pharmacist) and Shirley (Levy) Viscott; married Judith Ann Finn (a figure skater), July 12, 1959 (divorced); married Katherine Random (a designer); children: (first marriage) Elizabeth, Penelope, Jonathan. _Education:_ Dartmouth College, A.B., 1959; Tufts University, M.D., 1963. _Hobbies and other interests:_ Writing music and lyrics, skiing, playing the piano.

ADDRESSES: Office—c/o Pocket Books, 1230 Avenue of the Americas, New York, NY 10020.

CAREER: Barnes Hospital, St. Louis, MO, intern, 1963-64; University Hospital, Boston, MA, resident in psychiatry, 1964-67; Boston University, School of Medicine, instructor in psychiatry, beginning 1967. President of Sensitivity Games, Boston, 1970—; radio host, ABC Talkradio network.

MEMBER: American Psychiatric Association, Authors Guild, Authors League of America, Royal Society for Health, New York Academy of Science (fellow), Massachusetts Medical Society, Phi Sigma Delta.

AWARDS, HONORS: Mosby Book Award, 1963, for research as a medical student; Law Medicine Institute fellow, 1967-68.

WRITINGS:

Labyrinth of Silence (novel), Norton, 1970.
Feel Free, Peter Wyden, 1971.
Winning, Peter Wyden, 1972, reprinted, Pocket Books, 1987.
The Making of a Psychiatrist (autobiography), Arbor House, 1973.
Dorchester Boy: Portrait of a Psychiatrist as a Very Young Man (autobiography), Arbor House, 1973.
How to Live with Another Person (also see below), Arbor House, 1974.
The Language of Feelings (also see below), Arbor House, 1976.
(With Jonah Kalb) _What Every Kid Should Know_ (also see below), Houghton, 1976.
Risking: How to Take Chances and Win (also see below), Simon & Schuster, 1977.
The Viscott Method, Houghton, 1984.
Taking Care of Business: A Psychiatrist's Guide to Success, Morrow, 1985.
I Love You, Let's Work It Out, Simon & Schuster, 1987.

Also author of motivational audio cassettes, _How to Make Winning Your Lifestyle, Taking Risks for Personal Growth, Fifty-Two Minutes to Turn Your Life Around_ and _Building a Magic Relationship._ Writings adapted to audio cassette, _How_

DAVID S. VISCOTT

to Live with Another Person, The Language of Feelings, Risking, and *What Every Kid Should Know.* Contributor of articles to *Psychiatry, Archives of General Psychiatry, Bulletin of Tufts New England Medical Center, Cosmopolitan, Marketing Age, New Woman,* and *Today's Health.*

Viscott's book *The Language of Feelings* has been translated into Spanish.

WORK IN PROGRESS: The Making of a Psychiatrist II: Natural Therapy; a collection of essays; an art book on Oriental rugs, filmscripts, poetry, and a novel.

SIDELIGHTS: David S. Viscott commented: "I first began writing when I was about eight. . . . Throughout grade and secondary school I experimented with different forms, always attracted to dialogue, the drama, musical settings for spoken voice and the short story. My artistic interest was mainly music and perhaps the greatest influence on my writing is still music. I am most concerned with the sound of the spoken word. I read aloud everything I write to myself and always have. At Dartmouth I was in English Honors and edited the literary magazine. Honors English was closely copied from the Cambridge Don system and for two years I studied the English language from Beowulf to Virginia Woolf and became steeped in the English tradition. With this background I entered Tufts medical school and of course quickly published, wrote scientific papers on my own cancer research and eventually drifted into psychiatry. . . .

"I write sporadically, but I am always gathering material. I have day books in which I keep a running account of ideas. When I am working on a book the day book will contain first draft material. Often it contains lists of errands. When I write I can sit at the typewriter 6 to 10 hours a day, the highest

output I have is around 20,000 words per day. There are months when I don't write at all."

FOR MORE INFORMATION SEE:

PERIODICALS

Detroit News, January 23, 1975.
Fort Worth Star-Telegram, December 17, 1974.
People, August 18, 1986.

AUDIO RECORDINGS

Your Mental Health (interview), The Christophers, 1979.

* * *

WATTS, Helen L. Hoke
  See HOKE, Helen (L.)

* * *

WEAVER, Harriett E. 1908-

PERSONAL: Born June 18, 1908, in Burlington, IA; daughter of James R. and Agnes (Cox) Weaver. *Education:* University of California, Los Angeles, A.B., 1930. *Politics:* Democrat. *Religion:* Protestant. *Hobbies and other interests:* Wildlife photography, exploration, reading, painting.

CAREER: Teacher in Pico, CA, 1932-33, Santa Paula, CA, 1933-38, and Camarillo, CA, 1939-41; American Red Cross and U.S. Government, Ventura County, CA, first aid instructor, 1941-44; 9th Service Command Special Training Center, Camp McQuaide, Watsonville, CA, academic instructor, 1944-45; Fillmore Junior High School, Fillmore, CA, science teacher, 1947-68; Sunset Books/Lane Publishing Co., Menlo Park, CA, company representative and editorial consultant, 1960—. Summer employee as recreation leader, ranger, naturalist, California State Parks, 1929-50. Member of Ventura County Grand Jury, 1970-71, and Fillmore City Planning Commission, 1971-77. American Red Cross, board member of Santa Paula Chapter, 1938-44. Area commander of Women's Ambulance Corps, 1942-44; board member, Humboldt County Humane Society, 1979-84.

MEMBER: Wilderness Society, Audubon Society, Save-the-Redlands League, Westerners, Farmland Trust, Nature Conservancy, California Retired Teachers Association, Southern California Historical Society, Des Moines County (Iowa) Historical Society.

AWARDS, HONORS: First place, professional color block prints, Southern California Festival of Allied Arts, 1938; named honorary lifetime ranger; California State Park Ranger Association, 1970.

WRITINGS:

Cartooning Plus Drawing, Davis, 1938.
Cartooning Sports, Davis, 1949.
There Stand the Giants, Lane, 1960, revised edition, 1966.
California's Giant Trees: The Coast Redwoods and the Sequoias of the Sierra, Lane, 1969.
Redwoods: A Teaching Unit, California Redwood Association, 1973.
Frosty: A Raccoon to Remember, illustrations by Jennifer Owings Dewey, Chronicle Books, 1973.

Cover from the 1973 paperback edition of Harriett E. Weaver's true story about an orphaned raccoon that she raised. (Illustration by Jennifer Owings Dewey.)

Beloved Was Bahamas: A Steer to Remember, Vanguard, 1974.

Adventures in the Redwoods, Chronicle Books, 1975, revised edition published as *Redwood Country: A Pictorial Guide through California's Magnificent Redwood Forests,* photographs by David Swanlund, 1983.

Indomitable: The Only Salmon Who Could—and Did, Friends of the Redwood Library, 1984.

Also author of three booklets on California redwood trees. Contributor to books, including *Illustrated Library of Natural History,* American Museum of Natural History, 1958, and Sterling North's *Raccoons Are the Brightest People,* Dutton, 1966. Books have been included in readers for youths, including *Treasure Gold,* D.C. Heath, 1964; *Keystone,* Houghton, 1976; *Banners,* Houghton, 1981; and a Japanese textbook, *Mighty English I.*

Contributor to periodicals, including *Westways, School Arts, Ford Times, Natural History,* and *Pacific Pathways.*

Weaver and friend

WORK IN PROGRESS: "A full-length autobiographical book on my twenty years as California's first woman state park ranger."

SIDELIGHTS: Harriett E. Weaver told *SATA:* "For me, life has been wonderful all the way. From my very first years in Burlington, Iowa, my big delights have been to write and paint; my burning ambitions to live in the wilds and to enjoy animals, any animals—all animals.

"My first 'book'—complete with illustrations and four complete sentences about the amazing adventures of a rabbit that bounded through our back yard one day—made its debut when I was in the third grade. Now if I could just spark all that excitement in any four of my sentences these days!

"Throughout junior high in Denver, Colorado, and then high school and college in southern California, words and drawings rushed onward. That was nothing short of a miracle, too, for during my seventh and eighth grade English classes the teachers put me over in one corner of the room to work on my novel of a lifetime, *Jaco, Jacob, and Chatter*—the story of a circus clown, a lion, and a squirrel. How wild imagination can get! The rest of the class—poor things—labored on through nouns and verbs, capitalization and punctuation and 'all of that junk.' My teachers meant well: they simply wanted to help me create fabulous new literature for the amazement of the world. It was new all right. The only trouble was that afterwards I really had to sweat to learn those basic tools of my ambition the hard way—alone. One simply can't write what one wants to tell without knowing how to manage the nuts and bolts that structure the factual account or the plot or the creation of a scene or a mood or action—or anything at all. Over the years I gathered plain old English books and triple-checked every manuscript I wrote for all the details I should have learned in elementary school. *Jaco, Jacob, and Chatter* never made it into *Ladies' Home Journal* or *Saturday Evening Post,* although their patient (and probably amused) editors wrote me sympathetic rejections.

"Anyway, by my sophomore year in high school I had absorbed enough of how to express myself that my writings began to appear in the *Los Angeles Times* junior section, in the *Long Beach Telegram,* and finally once or twice in *St. Nicholas Magazine*—a favorite juvenile magazine of that time.

"More English rules and uses I absorbed as my sophomore and junior years moved on and I was taken on as a columnist and front page news reporter for the *Lomita Progress,* the town weekly. My English teacher there got me started keeping little pocket notebooks in which I recorded at least five new words and their meanings every day and saw to it that I used them when appropriate from then on, in both writing and speaking. Bless her forever. Thanks to her I discovered the fascination of our language and how to work with it so I could express accurately, humorously, colorfully, and powerfully whatever I wanted to say.

"The world opened up. I could now earn my own way with words and the surprising variety of sentences possible. What I could do was read books I liked and admired, analyze whatever expressions had caught my eye, then go over them carefully to see what in them had stirred me, how they were put together, the smooth flow of thought, and the movement of one event to the next. No more of this 'I see the cat. The cat sees me' stuff. I have to hope that the hundreds of eighth graders I taught later on reaped from all I continued to learn from both reading and writing.

"Twenty summers as California's first woman park ranger led me to another big love—the outdoors and its natural inhabitants. During that time I conducted nature walks through the forests and gave talks at the evening campfires in Big Basin Redwoods State Park, Richardson Grove on the Redwood Highway, and at Big Sur on the Monterey-Carmel coastline. I found plenty to write about. So much that I haven't yet been able to stop.

"A number of books emerged from those wonderful days in the state parks with tourists, vacationers, and campers from everywhere, all enjoying the giant trees and the delightful animal characters that lived among them—some of whom became sociable indeed.

"Frosty was one of them. He was a sweet little masked character who as the result of an accident I took to raise until time for him to . . . well, best to read and find out. And I must add that as it turned out, he raised me.

"Later on, after I retired from the state parks and still lived in southern California, I happened upon a many-page special edition of the *Del Norte Triplicate.* It was full of photos and accounts of the great flood of 1964 in northwestern California. In it was a picture and brief report of a black Angus steer that had, during the disaster, somehow survived a terrible ordeal and was still alive. Boom! Animal high drama for sure! I hurried up-coast as fast as I could and for two weeks petted the big black flood victim, stared at massive destruction everywhere, and talked with all who had seen it happen and had been a part of it.

" 'Truth is stranger than fiction?' You bet it is. I couldn't wait to start melding my notes into the most exciting story I would ever write—*Beloved Was Bahamas: A Steer to Remember.* What a tingle ran up my spine the moment I knew that the account of Bahamas was too terrific to ever let slip into oblivion; that it contained achievements and values both human and animal that should be recognized, remembered, and honored.

"Another instance of the same kind of thing came to me some years after that, when I inquired why a twenty-one foot long, five-ton salmon, carved from a redwood log, was mounted high above the entrance to Prairie Creek Fish Hatchery near where Redwood Creek empties into the Pacific ocean. The plaque beneath it read like a memorial. A memorial? To a silver salmon named Indomitable?

"Yes, and for good reason. Again—a real life happening, *incredible!* Not too incredible for words, though, and so I committed myself to writing that story. For the next year I submerged myself in it. In the writing I found that I literally had to remain under water, rarely coming up for air. For me, a brand new experience. But that's often how it is with recording fact. Yet I had learned that this was definitely my best way. I kept asking myself who in the world wants to create a story out of pure imagination when there were events like these to tell about that had actually happened! That belongs to someone else's talents, not mine.

"I spent time doing my homework on the story, making inquiries, interviewing, reading, and walking over the entire scene where the drama took place. And so that special salmon is celebrated again, in *Indomitable: The Only Salmon Who Could—and Did.* Long may his memory reign where the rivers sometimes become mighty and where true stories can match the grandeur of the redwood giants hovering all around.

"The world is so full of real live stories; fact-based autobiographies, like *Frosty;* others that can be written as fiction, like *Bahamas* and *Indomitable.* In my time I have learned of or witnessed many. So will today's young folks—from childhood to their later years. We just need to be alert to them, then zero in on the research and deskwork that makes them authentic and readable—and enjoyable.

"Finally comes this: apply the seat of the pants to the seat of the chair and hurl yourself into the excitement and delight and enrichment of creating a good story. You can't beat it!"

*   *   *

WEISS, Jaqueline Shachter 1926-

PERSONAL: Born May 28, 1926, in San Antonio, TX; daughter of Albert O. (a businessman) and Yetta (a registered nurse and businesswoman; maiden name, Zalinsky) Nelson; married Samuel O. Shachter, June 29, 1950 (divorced, 1979); married George Henry Weiss (a physician), March 28, 1982; children: Sherry Shachter Kandell, Ross

David Shachter, Scott Jay Shachter, Steven Bertram Weiss. *Education:* University of Texas at Austin, B.A., 1946; University of Pennsylvania, M.S., 1963, Ed.D., 1969; attended National University of Mexico, summers, 1943 and 1966. *Politics:* Democrat. *Religion:* Jewish. *Hobbies and other interests:* Sports, nature, reading, and the arts.

ADDRESSES: Home—3023 DeKalb Blvd., Norristown, PA 19401.

CAREER: Food, Tobacco, and Agricultural Workers Union, business agent in Houston, TX, 1946-47, international representative in Philadelphia, PA, 1948-50; peace activist, 1951-62; Oak Lane Day School, Blue Bell, PA, elementary teacher, 1963-68; Temple University, Philadelphia, assistant professor, 1968-72, associate professor, 1973-83, senior associate professor of education, 1983-90, associate professor emerita, 1990—; Philadelphia School District, Philadelphia, reading teacher, 1984—. Junior high school Spanish teacher in Haverford, PA, fall, 1983. Member of Jane Addams Children's Book Award selection committee, c. 1976-88, and International Board on Books for Young People.

MEMBER: Philadelphia Children's Round Table (member of executive board), Phi Beta Kappa.

AWARDS, HONORS: Nominee for Temple University Creativity Award, 1981; *Young Brer Rabbit and Other Trickster Tales from the Americas* was named a Notable Children's Trade Book in the Field of Social Studies by National

JAQUELINE SHACHTER WEISS

Council for the Social Studies and Children's Book Council, 1985; Drexel Citation, Drexel University and The Free Library of Philadelphia, 1988, for contributions to children's literature; Helen Keating Ott Award, Church and Synagogue Library Association, 1988, for children's literature contributions.

WRITINGS:

Mexico: Spanish Selections Freely Translated and Augmented, University of Pennsylvania Press, 1967.
(With Max Rosenfeld) *Old Testament Tales as Literature in Grades Three through Eight,* Sholom Aleichem Publications, 1976.
Prizewinning Books for Children: Themes and Stereotypes in U.S. Prizewinning Prose Fiction for Children, Lexington Books, 1983.
Young Brer Rabbit and Other Trickster Tales from the Americas (juvenile), illustrated by Clinton Arrowood, Stemmer House, 1985.
(With Carolyn W. Field) *Values in Selected Children's Books of Fiction and Fantasy,* Shoe String Press, 1987.

Contributor of more than twenty-five articles to education and library journals, including *The Reading Teacher, School Library Journal, English Journal, Elementary School Journal, Social Education,* and *The Gifted Child Quarterly.*

ADAPTATIONS: A cassette recording of *Young Brer Rabbit and Other Trickster Tales from the Americas,* narrated by Eartha Kitt, was released by Stemmer House in 1987.

WORK IN PROGRESS: Articles on international interviews with children's authors, published in periodicals including *Bookbird, Judaica Librarianship,* and *Newsletter* of the U.S. Board on Books for Young People; additions to the "Profiles in Literature" series of video cassettes; "a self-illustrated storybook on our family's playful black toy poodle, Shlomo."

SIDELIGHTS: Jaqueline Shachter Weiss told *SATA:* "It was in the public library of Corpus Christi, Texas, where I first became acquainted with children's literature. My mother, who had come to this country alone from Poland at the age of thirteen, did not have an English literary background. Widowed young, she had high expectations for her three children. She applauded when the whispering public librarian guided me first to all the Louisa May Alcott books, and, when I entered high school, to debating materials for statewide contests.

"After graduating as a scholarship student from the University of Texas in Austin, I was filled with student idealism. I joined a campaign to interest Houston cotton compress, rice mill, and cannery workers in the Food, Tobacco, and Agricultural Worker's Union. At first I awakened at 4 a.m. to work in a cannery where my Spanish knowledge helped me as an organizer. I was one of three who protested segregation at a Houston hotel in 1947 before I came to Philadelphia as a union representative.

"Twenty years later I completed a new cycle of my life, having had three children to whom I read the bedtime stories I had never known. After I began to teach at Oak Lane Day School, its sister school in Mexico City welcomed my children as exchange students one summer while I attended the National University of Mexico. By then I had my master's degree in reading from the University of Pennsylvania and was completing my doctorate at the same institution.

"In 1968 I was hired by Temple University's Early Childhood and Elementary Education Department. During my fourteen years there I led two Latin American children's literature study tours. While I was teaching 'kiddy lit,' I began to interview important local children's authors and illustrators on videotape so other classes could see replays. It was Carolyn W. Field, then Coordinator of the Office of Work with Children of The Free Library of Philadelphia, who became co-interviewer.

"Formalizing the separate thirty-minute videotapes into the 'Profiles in Literature' series, I copyrighted each program and reached out nationally for guests. James Michener is the sole 'Profiles' celebrity who writes exclusively for adults. The other interviewees, some sixty-five to date, include Maurice Sendak, authors of twenty-two Newbery Medal winners, and recipients of other major prizes. These book creators, 'the cream of the crop,' have enriched me enormously! I have also learned television techniques and on some programs have presented dramatized vignettes from a guest's book or a dance rendering of a book's theme.

"I have acquired other knowledge as the producer and distributor of the 'Profiles' series. I publicized programs by getting more than twenty-five articles published in leading professional journals and announcements in others. I won a grant from The Public Committee for the Humanities in Pennsylvania, which recognized the archival importance of videotaping children's literary celebrities in their prime. Now-deceased 'Profiles' guests include Pura Belpre, Arna Bontemps, John Ciardi, Marguerite de Angeli, Ezra Jack Keats, Joseph Krumgold, Arnold Lobel, and Evaline Ness; their programs have become priceless. Moreover, they are forever vibrant on videocassette, and they continue to be publicized, for well over 100,000 people have seen the 'Profiles' interviews in the United States, Canada, Australia, and even in distant Singapore.

"Fortunately, I can now boast that 'Profiles' is prizewinning. It influenced my winning the 1988 Drexel Citation from Drexel University and The Free Library of Philadelphia.

"On the topic of prize winners, in 1983 I wrote *Prizewinning Books for Children: Themes and Stereotypes in U.S. Prizewinning Prose Fiction for Children,* published by D.C. Heath's Lexington division. This book— written for librarians, teachers, parents, and college or secondary students—focuses on the primary theme of 717 awarded books. It also discusses methods of helping children discern themes.

"The groups reading *Prizewinning Books* are also the target for *Values in Selected Children's Books of Fiction and Fantasy,* a 1987 Shoe String Press release that I wrote with Carolyn W. Field. This work, useful in low-key child guidance, categorizes 713 children's books by one of ten positive values, like self-respect or cooperation. It was mainly due to *Values* that Carolyn and I won the 1988 Helen Keating Ott Award of the Church and Synagogue Library Association. After two years of intense labor on this project, my co-author and I have increased feelings of respect for each other, a genuine happy ending.

"My only children's book to date is *Young Brer Rabbit and Other Trickster Tales from the Americas,* published by Stemmer House with cassette recording by Eartha Kitt. My humorous African-South American tales were honored as a

Dustjacket from Jaqueline Shachter Weiss's 1985 collection that features a character from the well-known Uncle Remus folk tales. (Illustration by Clinton Arrowood.)

1985 Notable Children's Trade Book in the Field of Social Studies by a joint committee from the National Council for the Social Studies and the Children's Book Council. Clinton Arrowood's full-color illustrations merited the Parents' Choice Award. The book's foreword is by Anne Pellowski, former Director-Librarian of the Information Center on Children's Cultures, a service of the United States Committee for UNICEF.

"I collected the Brer Rabbit stories over a five-year period. When I led two children's literature study tours to Latin America in 1974 and 1977, I hunted my elusive cottontail. In Venezuela I realized he is still a folk hero because I saw his costumes for puppet theater presentations of 'Brer Rabbit Astronaut.' I could translate from Spanish and French before I began this study, but I enrolled in a college Portuguese class in order to translate the marvelous stories I received in Brazil. I also collected in the Caribbean area, making special trips to Puerto Rico and Cuba. It was important for me not to have an Uncle Remus presenter of stories. Joel Chandler Harris in *Nights with Uncle Remus* depicted an aged former slave narrating to 'Massa's' son, and I felt this subservient intermediary detracted from the stories themselves. I eliminated dialect for ease in reading and deliberately kept the language simple enough for those at a third-grade level and above to enjoy the content.

"My search for Brer Rabbit was just the beginning of my travels. I enjoy going abroad to interview children's authors in other countries. I am accompanied by my husband,

George Weiss, a physician who translates from German for me. Thus far our interviews have taken place in Jerusalem, Tel Aviv, Madrid, Montreal, Moscow, Munich, Vienna, London, and Paris. The resultant articles have been printed in *Bookbird, Judaica Librarianship,* and the *Newsletter* of the U.S. Board on Books for Young People.

"In 1984 I was forced to retire early from Temple University due to declining enrollment in my Early Childhood and Elementary Education Department. Since then I have been a public school teacher, one semester instructing Spanish in a junior high and thereafter teaching elementary reading classes. From 1988 to the present I have been the reading teacher in several large urban schools. Currently I even teach parents and staff in a special composition/literature class and am in charge of a school anthology. In Moscow the twelve children's authors I interviewed respected my teaching inner-city pupils more than work at a prestigious university, where egotism may exceed humility.

"My husband and I find relief from work-related pettiness in sports, nature, reading, and the arts. We enjoy year-round tennis and have made winter more exciting by skiing in Pennsylvania's Pocono Mountains or Canada's Laurentian Mountains. Our parakeet, Amadeus, sings when water runs from the faucet near his cage. It must seem like Niagara Falls to him! One day I may be an author/illustrator of a child's book about our black toy poodle, Shlomo, a constant clown. It should tickle our granddaughters, Sophia, Naomi, and Yani, as well as other young readers."

* * *

WEST, Dorothy
See BENSON, Mildred (Augustine Wirt)

* * *

WIRT, Ann
See BENSON, Mildred (Augustine Wirt)

* * *

WIRT, Mildred A.
See BENSON, Mildred (Augustine Wirt)

* * *

ZIMELMAN, Nathan 1921-

PERSONAL: Born May 8, 1921, in San Francisco, CA; son of Jacob Zimelman (a general store owner) and Sarah Sugarman (a shopkeeper). *Education:* Sacramento Junior College (now City College), A.B., 1939; University of California, Berkeley, B.A. with teaching certificate, 1942.

ADDRESSES: Home—2025 28th St. Apt. 206, Sacramento, CA 95818.

CAREER: Alaska Bargain Store (family-owned general store), Sacramento, CA, worked for his father, 1943-50, co-manager of the store with his mother after his father's death, 1950-62; free-lance author, 1964—.

AWARDS, HONORS: I Will Tell You of Peach Stone was chosen as a Children's Book of the Year by the Child Study Association of America, 1976; *Positively No Pets Allowed*

was chosen for the 1981 Children's Book Council notable book list; *Mean Chickens and Wild Cucumbers* was chosen as a notable children's trade book in the field of social studies by the National Council of Social Studies/Children's Book Council Joint Committee, 1983.

WRITINGS:

FOR CHILDREN

A Secret for Christmas, illustrated by Chester Sullivan, Augsburg, 1964.

Beneath the Oak Tree, illustrated by Carol Rogers, Steck-Vaughn, 1966.

Once When I Was Five, illustrated by Rogers, Steck-Vaughn, 1967.

Pepito, illustrated by Ann Grifalconi, Reilly & Lee, 1967.

To Sing a Song as Big as Ireland, illustrated by Joseph Low, Follett, 1967.

A Good Morning's Work (Junior Literary Guild selection), illustrated by Rogers, Steck-Vaughn, 1968.

The First Elephant Comes to Ireland, illustrated by Quentin Blake, Follett, 1969.

What Shall We Have for Breakfast?, illustrated by John Paul Richards, Steck-Vaughn, 1969.

So You Shouldn't Waste a Rhinoceros (Junior Literary Guild selection), illustrated by Dennis Lyall, Steck-Vaughn, 1970.

The Cats of Kilkenny, illustrated by Nancy Inderieden, Carolrhoda, 1972.

Michael Allen Found a Dime, illustrated by Inderieden, Carolrhoda, 1972.

Look, Hiroshi!, illustrated by Dan Quest, Aurora, 1973.

I Will Tell You of Peach Stone (Junior Literary Guild selection), illustrated by Haru Wells, Lothrop, 1974.

The Lives of My Cat Alfred (Junior Literary Guild selection), illustrated by Evaline Ness, Dutton, 1976.

Walls Are to Be Walked (Junior Literary Guild selection), illustrated by Donald Carrick, Dutton, 1977.

Positively No Pets Allowed, illustrated by Pamela Johnson, Dutton, 1980.

If I Were Strong Enough . . . , illustrated by Diane Paterson, Abingdon, 1982.

Mean Chickens and Wild Cucumbers, illustrated by David Small, Macmillan, 1983.

How to Fly Like a Bird, Even If You're Only a Boy, illustrated by Pam Summertree, Green Tiger, 1983.

Mean Murgatroyd and the Ten Cats (Junior Literary Guild selection), Dutton, 1984.

Shaughnessy (bound with *Humanization of Freddie Mouse* by Richard Blake), Davenport, 1984.

Why Do We Not See Little People, Miss Wintergreen? (bound with *The Magga Birds of Ranatan* by Herbert L. McClelland and *Spots and Splashes and a Million Butterflies* by Joyce Deedy), Davenport, 1984.

Please Excuse Jasper, illustrated by Ray Cruz, Abingdon, 1987.

The Star of Melvin, illustrated by Olivier Dunrea, Macmillan, 1987.

Treed by a Pride of Irate Lions, illustrated by Toni Goffe, Little, Brown, 1990.

The Crime of Hubie Hemplewhite, illustrated by Stephanie Newman, Harbinger, 1990.

Lovely, Lovely Mehitchabel, illustrated by Newman, Harbinger, 1990.

WORK IN PROGRESS: A Sitting of Cats.

SIDELIGHTS: Nathan Zimelman once said in the *Junior Literary Guild* that to him "a great part of writing is remembering." He has drawn on his own memories of childhood and his family to write a number of his books. Born in San Francisco, CA, in 1921, Zimelman is the son of a general store owner and his mother was a Jewish immigrant from Poland. "My father was in Sacramento and then he met my mother in San Francisco," the author said in a *Something about the Author* interview. His mother's "first eighteen years were spent in Poland, which was very fortunate for me. I've gotten a great many stories from them."

Zimelman also spoke about his mother later in the interview: "My mother told quite a few stories about her time in Poland. Her father used to peddle from village to village. She used to go with him when she was a little kid. There was a time when her father was sick and she and her sister had to go out and peddle around. That was a time a dog bit her so she was afraid to get off the wagon. That was a hell of a life, but very interesting. I've got all the stories there. I think I've milked about everything there is. That one with the dog biting her, I haven't used that one yet. But someday I may." After leaving Poland, his mother lived in New York City before moving to California. "She remembered those eight years in New York as paradise. She was fascinating," Zimelman said. "She did everything. Couldn't paint—she admitted that. I've got a series of stories about a Jewish family in New York around World War I. I hope someday to publish them."

From 1938 to 1939, Zimelman attended Sacramento Junior College. He finished his college education in 1942 at the University of California, Berkeley. "I got a B.A. and then I got a teacher's credential, which I never used. By popular demand, I think." After his graduation, Zimelman fell ill due to jaundice. "I was sick for about a year. My mother was a good nurse. It gives you a lot of time to read." He commented that he had learned more reading on his own than while studying at the University of California. "In school, you generally chew over one book over and over. There are other authors besides Shakespeare, God knows. You never read Fielding and Dickens. You never even hear about Trollope. I didn't like Cal. I liked the Sacramento Junior College. Frankly, that was a good place."

Instead of finding a job as a teacher, Zimelman went to work at his father's general store, the Alaska Bargain Store, in Sacramento. When his father died in 1950, Zimelman ran the business with his mother. However, as the city's population began to grow there was little room for a small rural business. "I think we got out of the business by 1962," the author remembered at one point in the interview. "That's when we were freewayed out. By then, of course, we were ready to move. They paid a disgusting price. They destroyed the business by then. We had a lot of business with farmers and they just pushed the farmers out. Well, you've seen what they've done with Sacramento. When they used to break the sound barrier, we had a flat roof. Never be under a flat roof when they break the sound barrier. Oh, God. A little time passes and you've got a lovely set of cracks.

"I wrote my best poetry in the store. I also did my best reading in the store. In those days, you could go into the Sacramento State Library and take a book out. Now I think you need a gun, practically, to take a book out." He told *SATA* early in the interview: "I was always writing. Then for a while I was writing poetry. Have you ever tried to publish poetry if you're not an educator? Did you ever notice when they have the biography, it's always they're a teacher in some university?

And it's pretty lousy poetry. Did you ever notice that in poetry now they just make statements? It's not poetry; they just make statements.

"About 1950, I started writing really good poetry. My favorite rejection slip, if you can have such a thing, said, 'This is too good for you. You'll never publish it.' And, God, was that prophetic.

"Contemporary poetry is garbage. They just make straight statements. There's no imagination. Poetry should really concentrate. Well, it's helped me a lot in writing the children's books." Zimelman's love for good poetry has influenced his writing for children: "I have a certain rhythm in my writing. How it happens, I don't know. It just happens. I'm not going to fight it. It has a nice run to it."

Although Zimelman has written several books featuring cats and dogs, he said, "I'm not a dog lover and I'm not a cat lover. We had a collie. I use the word loosely. He ran the place." Later, he added, "Our neighbors had a couple of black and white cats who were by us more than they were by them. You treat a dog or a cat like part of the family. Of course, the collie would have objected otherwise. Frankly, he is my base for anything I've involved with dogs. He was a creative artist. He was unbelievable. My sister was a librarian in Auburn and he was just hanging around the field, sort of the dog-of-the-field. And one day he got his foot hurt so my sister took him to the doctor and the next thing she knows there's a scratching or rapping on the door. She opens up; he walks in. After that, he moved in with her. Then for some reason, they started writing letters objecting about him, so she moved him by us. Frankly, I think he wrote the letters because I think he was planning on moving in with us. My mother was a great cook and he was a gourmet. So he lived with us for the last seven years of his infinite life. I wrote about thirty poems on him. We referred to him as George Shep."

The writer has also set several of his books in foreign countries like Japan and Ireland, although he has never traveled very far in his life. "I've only been from Sacramento to Berkeley and back to Sacramento," he said later. "I've never been out of that particular area. Well, a friend of mine took me for a drive once and we got as far as Lake Tahoe once. You don't have to travel. I mean F. Scott Fitzgerald may have had to live that peculiar life to be F. Scott Fitzgerald. On the other hand, Emily Dickinson did pretty well not traveling at all."

"We never owned a car," Zimelman also related. "My sister learned to drive, but I never learned to drive. I never missed it. I haven't been on public transportation since the last strike they pulled in Sacramento and I said 'to hell with you' and started walking. I found out you can see more things walking than any other way. My mother used to walk around when she was well into her seventies." However, the author did reveal one reason why he writes about people in foreign lands. "I love dialects," he explained at one time. "I do great dialects. I don't explore differences in ethnic culture, I just write. I think if you write, you're a minority in a sense. I think everyone thinks you're a little peculiar. I enjoy writing."

When asked why he wrote books for children, Zimelman noted, "I'm not a novelist. The way I regard novelists nowadays—it doesn't apply to the Victorians—it seems to be saying nothing at great length. When you write poetry you have a tendency to say a lot within a confined space. Now if I could write novels, I'd do it. I'd kind of been poking around children's stories for quite a while. Then all of a sudden, I started writing them on and off fairly well. It was Augsburg that brought out *A Secret for Christmas.* Now they didn't change a word. Didn't pay much, but they didn't change a word. I really don't expect to get rich from this business."

Publishing his first book, *A Secret for Christmas,* was a matter of determination for Zimelman. "Well, I just looked up addresses and started sending" the manuscripts, the writer explained. "Of course, you had to start learning about" the publishers first. "You dig out addresses anyway you can. At least that's the way I do. I think I got the Augsburg one in the *Writer's Digest.* Fortunately I discovered Steck-Vaughn and Follett, both of whom are no longer in the children's book business. Practically everyone's out of the children's book business now. So many of them have been swallowed by a few publishers. Seems to me there are some places—doesn't matter how well you write and the garbage they publish, it doesn't matter—you haven't got a chance in the world. And some people work out. I don't know how it works out. Sometimes you're doing all right and there's a change of editor and you're out again."

The illustrations for Zimelman's books are also the decision of the author's editors, he told *SATA.* "The publishers just do my books with pictures. You just get what they give you. The first three books by Steck-Vaughn, a woman named Carol Rogers did it. She had imagination. She was really wonderful. I don't know what happened, because on the fourth one, they got somebody else. I have nothing to say about anything. I'm just happy they take me. I also work on the principle that if they stick with mine the pictures are in the books anyway. I always figure out there's got to be some action. I have the dialogue describing the action. I mean that's how Shakespeare worked it, for God's sake. It doesn't have to be a narrative."

He also made additional comments about his writing later in the interview: "If you've got the imagination—if you were lucky enough to get one—use it. I don't know how it happens, now or ever, but I'm writing better than I ever did. I threw away an awful lot of stuff. But of late, the last few years, it's been coming pretty steadily. How it happens, I don't know. You always figure that it's not going to last, this is the last one, it just can't last. As long as it goes, I'll keep at it. I hate trying to dig up an idea. I don't like to polish. I write fast, but I polish and polish and polish and polish. Once in a while, you don't have to polish too much. It seems ridiculous to try to work Flaubert and then have an editor come along and work Jack the Ripper. But it's your own satisfaction. You're going to do it as well as you can. If they want to take it and ruin it, all right. They take it and ruin it. You remember the only game in town joke? That's about what it is."

Zimelman, who has never married and has no children, does not regret his decision to remain single. His fond memories of his own childhood, however, have made his writing enjoyable to him; he does not have any particular ambition to teach children through his writing. "If they learn something, they learn," the author said during part of the interview. "I just write, that's all. I remember when I was a kid. Childhood is a great thing. It's nice to remember." But Zimelman also added at one point that he does not write for young audiences alone: "I like stuff that appeals to a grown-up, too. After all, they're going to do a good deal of the reading. You should have something that should appeal to the grown-up, too."

He concluded a little later, "I don't assume I'm just writing for children. I write it as it comes. I have one rejection slip that

says 'the children wouldn't understand this.' So? I mean, one of these days you're going to understand and be happy you read the thing."

WORKS CITED:

Junior Literary Guild, March, 1976, p. 15.
Zimelman, Nathan, interview conducted by Chris Hunter for *Something about the Author,* June 27, 1990.

FOR MORE INFORMATION SEE:

BOOKS

Ward, Martha E., and Dorothy A. Marquardt, *Authors of Books for Young People,* 2nd edition, Scarecrow, 1971.

PERIODICALS

Bulletin of the Center of Children's Books, June, 1976; May, 1978; October, 1983.
Horn Book, August, 1976.
Junior Literary Guild, September, 1976.
Library Journal, September, 1968; July, 1969; September 15, 1969; December 15, 1971; September 15, 1974.
New York Times Book Review, October 23, 1977.
Publishers Weekly, April 26, 1976; May 6, 1983.
School Library Journal, September, 1976; October, 1976; February, 1978; February, 1981; December, 1982; October, 1984.

*   *   *

ZIMMER, Dirk 1943-

PERSONAL: Born October 2, 1943, in Germany. *Education:* Attended a fine arts academy in Hamburg, Germany. *Religion:* "None (of the known kinds)."

German-born Dirk Zimmer once rejected the dominance of language, but went on to write and illustrate children's books.

ADDRESSES: Home—86 Spring St., Kingston, NY 12401. *Agent*— Edite Kroll, 31 E. Thirty-first St., No. 2E, New York, NY 10016.

CAREER: Writer and illustrator.

AWARDS, HONORS: Irma Simonton Black Award from Bank Street College of Education, 1978, for *Felix in the Attic* (with Larry Bograd); the American Library Association named *Esteban and the Ghost* and *Bony-Legs* two of its notable books of 1983; Garden State Children's Book Award, Easy to Read category, from New Jersey Library Association, 1986, for *In a Dark, Dark Room and other Scary Stories* (with Alvin Schwartz).

WRITINGS:

(And illustrator) *The Trick-or-Treat Trap,* Harper, 1982.

ILLUSTRATOR

Larry Bograd, *Felix in the Attic,* Harvey House, 1978.
Dieter Kuehn, *Die Geisterhand,* Insel Verlag, 1979.
Larry Bograd, *Egon,* Macmillan, 1980.
William H. Hooks, *Mean Jake and the Devils,* Dial, 1981.
Joseph Slate, *The Star Rocker,* Harper, 1981.
Lee B. Hopkins, editor, *The Sky Is Full of Song,* Harper, 1983.
Sibyl Hancock, *Esteban and the Ghost,* Dial, 1983.
Joanna Cole, *Bony-Legs,* Four Winds, 1983.
Alvin Schwartz, *In a Dark, Dark Room and Other Scary Stories,* Harper, 1984.
Fran Manushkin, *Buster Loves Buttons!,* Harper, 1985.
Shirley Climo, *Someone Saw a Spider,* Crowell, 1985.
Larry Bograd, *Poor Gertie,* Delacorte, 1986.
Ross M. Madsen, *Perrywinkle and the Book of Magic Spells,* Dial, 1986.
Laurence Yep, *The Curse of the Squirrel,* Random House, 1987.

Zimmer created a ghoulish collection of creatures for Alvin Schwartz's 1984 edition of frightening tales.

John Bierhorst, editor, *The Naked Bear: Folktales of the Iroquois,* Morrow, 1987.
Ted Hughes, *The Iron Giant: A Story in Five Nights,* Harper, 1988.
Caroline Feller Bauer, editor, *Windy Day: Stories and Poems,* Lippincott Junior Books, 1988.
Edward Day, *John Tabor's Ride,* Knopf, 1989.
Ann Martin, *Ma and Pa Dracula,* Holiday House, 1989.
Margery Cuyler, *Weird Wolf,* Henry Holt, 1989.
Ellen Weiss and Mel Friedman, *Ratman,* Random House, 1990.
Mary Blount Christian, *Goody Sherman's Pig,* Macmillan, 1991.
Laura Geringer, *The Cow Is Mooing Anyhow,* Harper, 1991.
Patrick Lewis, *The Moonbows of Mr. Bones,* Knopf, 1991.
Valerio Scho Carey, *Tsugele's Broom,* Harper, 1992.
Percival Everett, *The One That Got Away,* Clarion, 1992.

"Do ghosts give good treats?" Peggy Pig wanted to know. The ghost gave a fierce laugh and disappeared. (From *The Trick-or-Treat Trap,* written and illustrated by Dirk Zimmer.)

SIDELIGHTS: Dirk Zimmer told *SATA:* "I grew up in Hamburg, Germany's largest port and ship-building city, which bears the proud and—for me as a child—mystifying surname 'Tor zur Welt' ('Gateway to the World'). From my early childhood on, my family, although they were straight, down-to-earth Hamburgers, encouraged my 'artistic vein,' since it had been my father's wish to go into business as a graphic designer as soon as World War II ended. But he died instead, and I had to carry on the torch—which I did with zeal. I produced endless picture stories, and my older sister had to help me with the words, since I was too young to write them myself.

"Some years later I discovered that visual art didn't need the assistance of language to make its point. On the contrary, it presented an alternative to the dominance of language, to the way letters and words dictated to the human mind how to behave and were thought of as the naturally grown, god-given basis of all consciousness. I became quite convinced that I had to join some kind of 'anti-establishment (anti-language) conspiracy' and that some artists were actually high priests of this noble cult! The tyrant *Logos* and His machinations had to be dealt with! Along these lines I interpreted the art scene in post-war Germany, discovering 'entartete Kunst,' dadaism and surrealism, and spirits like Wassily Kandinsky, Paul Klee, Max Ernst, and George Grosz practically on my own as a school kid. In other words, I wanted to become a FINE artist—not, as my family had expected, a commercial creep and compromiser. This was the tough but necessary decision a budding *artiste* had to make during one's blood-curdling, soul-searching vision quest back in the 1950s.

"But my initiation into the secrets of the art conspiracy wasn't all that easy. Since I had left school early without a high-school diploma, I was supposed to go through a three-year apprenticeship in an art-related trade. But I was not able or willing to do that and ended up as an unskilled worker on the docks, loading and unloading ocean-liners with other rough and tough guys. But I did make it into the Academy of Fine Arts in Hamburg in spite of my unqualified status (I'd known I would), and I studied mainly with Hans Thiemann, who had been a student of Klee and Kandinsky in the legendary Bauhaus in Weimar, Germany, in the 1930s. When I finished in 1969, I had my 'first and last' one-person show in a gallery in Munich; the next radical artistic step at that particular art-historical moment was to skip producing altogether and abandon the establishment—the gallery owners and their bourgeois customers and all that. And to declare an end to painting, period.

"According to Andy Warhol and some in-crowd friends, the next thing to do was film. Well, I got involved in several film projects, lived in a 'film-commune' for awhile, etc. But that wasn't really my own thing. Yet 'one's own thing' had a flair of bourgeois individualism about it, and that was a no-no in

our heroic effort to do things right—or rather *left*—with revolutionary righteousness. And one day, in the year 1977, in America, I walked away into the sunset.

"Ironically, in order to get back in touch with the 'magic' of art (i.e. my idealistic 'understanding' of it), I had to 'prostitute' myself and work as a commercial artist. Which was okay in this country, in the Big Apple, the High Castle of Capitalism, where I lived in the Wall Street district, next to the World Trade Center, in an old, half-abandoned office building, for about seven years. Actually, I had not planned to stay, but I'd needed money to go back to Berlin, so I had started to do drawings for some magazines and newspapers. Someone saw a silly little drawing of dancing sausages and running cheese I had done for the *New York Times* and got my address from them. He offered me a job: to illustrate a children's book called *Serendipity.* I accepted and was thrilled; I thought: 'Yeah, here I am in the good old surreal synchronicity groove again.' But then, when I sobered up a bit and read the text again and again, I found it corny. It didn't inspire the awe and sense of wonder I felt could be experienced when serendipity happens. So I braced myself for exclusion from further grace and told the publisher that I couldn't do it. 'That's all right,' he said. 'We have another story here, written especially for you.' That seemed like too much, but it was true. The book was *Felix in the Attic,* by Larry Bograd, and it won a little award, given by the Bank Street College of Education with the claim that this was the only award given by children, not by publishers or educators or other grown-ups. I took that as a good omen of course, and I've been busy (in my own meandering way) doing kids' books ever since.

"Now I'm an 'old fart,' a commercial creep, a compromiser, no longer an illegal alien, a grown-up (of sorts) who gets junk mail and bills all the time and whose hippie-teeth are falling out by the dozen. As I write these WORDS, wiggling like a worm, I'm about to finish my twenty-fifth job, *The Moonbows of Mr. Bones.* After that I have two more commissions to get out of my way. After that . . . thank god (so to say) I have *no idea*—well, I have a couple of ideas, I guess. I'll deal with that if the time comes (gee, how *ambitious* a nonchalant attitude sounds as soon as one writes it down)."

Cumulative Indexes

Illustrations Index

(In the following index, the number of the volume in which an illustrator's work appears is given *before* the colon, and the page number on which it appears is given *after* the colon. For example, a drawing by Adams, Adrienne appears in Volume 2 on page 6, another drawing by her appears in Volume 3 on page 80, another drawing in Volume 8 on page 1, and another drawing in Volume 15 on page 107.)

YABC

Index citations including this abbreviation refer to listings appearing in *Yesterday's Authors of Books for Children,* also published by Gale Research Inc., which covers authors who died prior to 1960.

Author Index

The following index gives the number of the volume in which an author's biographical sketch, Brief Entry, or Obituary appears.

This index includes references to all entries in the following series, which are also published by Gale Research Inc.

YABC—*Yesterday's Authors of Books for Children: Facts and Pictures about Authors and Illustrators of Books for Young People from Early Times to 1960*, Volumes 1-2

CLR—*Children's Literature Review: Excerpts from Reviews, Criticism, and Commentary on Books for Children*, Volumes 1-22

SAAS—*Something about the Author Autobiography Series*, Volumes 1-12

Holt, Rackham
  See Holt, Margaret Van Vechten (Saunders)
Holt, Rochelle Lynn 1946- 41
Holt, Stephen
  See Thompson, Harlan H.
Holt, Victoria
  See Hibbert, Eleanor
Holton, Leonard
  See Wibberley, Leonard (Patrick O'Connor)
Holtze, Sally Holmes 1952- 64
Holtzman, Jerome 1926- 57
Holyer, Erna Maria 1925- 22
Holyer, Ernie
  See Holyer, Erna Maria
Holz, Loretta (Marie) 1943- 17
Homze, Alma C. 1932- 17
Honig, Donald 1931- 18
Honness, Elizabeth H. 1904- 2
Hoobler, Dorothy 28
Hoobler, Thomas 28
Hood, Joseph F. 1925- 4
Hood, Robert E. 1926- 21
Hook, Frances 1912- 27
Hook, Martha 1936- 27
Hooker, Ruth 1920- 21
Hooks, William H(arris) 1921- 16
Hooper, Byrd
  See St. Clair, Byrd Hooper
Hooper, Meredith (Jean) 1939- 28
Hoopes, Lyn L(ittlefield) 1953- 49
  Brief Entry 44
Hoopes, Ned E(dward) 1932- 21
Hoopes, Roy 1922- 11
Hoople, Cheryl G.
  Brief Entry 32
Hoover, Helen (Drusilla Blackburn)
  1910-1984 12
  Obituary 39
Hoover, H(elen) M(ary) 1935- 44
  Brief Entry 33
  See also SAAS 8
Hope, Christopher (David Tully) 1944- 62
Hope, Laura Lee [Collective pseudonym] 1
  See also Adams, Harriet S(tratemeyer)
Hope Simpson, Jacynth 1930- 12
Hopf, Alice
  See Hopf, Alice (Martha) L(ightner)
Hopf, Alice L(ightner) 1904- 5
Hopf, Alice (Martha) L(ightner)
  Obituary 55
Hopkins, A. T.
  See Turngren, Annette
Hopkins, Clark 1895-1976
  Obituary 34
Hopkins, Joseph G(erard) E(dward)
  1909- 11
Hopkins, (Hector) Kenneth 1914-1988
  Obituary 58
Hopkins, Lee Bennett 1938- 3
  See also SAAS 4
Hopkins, Lyman
  See Folsom, Franklin
Hopkins, Marjorie 1911- 9
Hoppe, Joanne 1932- 42
Hopper, Nancy J. 1937- 38
  Brief Entry 35
Horgan, Paul 1903- 13
Hornblow, Arthur (Jr.) 1893-1976 15
Hornblow, Leonora (Schinasi) 1920- 18
Horne, Richard Henry 1803-1884 29
Horner, Althea (Jane) 1926- 36
Horner, Dave 1934- 12
Hornos, Axel 1907- 20
Hornstein, Reuben Aaron 1912- 64
Horvath, Betty 1927- 4
Horwich, Frances R(appaport) 1908- 11
Horwitz, Elinor Lander 45
  Brief Entry 33
Hosford, Dorothy (Grant) 1900-1952 22
Hosford, Jessie 1892- 5
Hoskyns-Abrahall, Clare 13
Houck, Carter 1924- 22
Hough, (Helen) Charlotte 1924- 9
Hough, Judy Taylor 1932- 63
  Brief Entry 51
  Earlier sketch in SATA 56
Hough, Richard (Alexander) 1922- 17

Houghton, Eric 1930- 7
Houlehan, Robert J. 1918- 18
Household, Geoffrey (Edward West)
  1900-1988 14
  Obituary 59
Houselander, (Frances) Caryll 1900-1954
  Brief Entry 31
Housman, Laurence 1865-1959 25
Houston, James A(rchibald) 1921- 13
  See also CLR 3
Houton, Kathleen
  See Kilgore, Kathleen
Howard, Alan 1922- 45
Howard, Alyssa
  See Buckholtz, Eileen (Garber)
Howard, Elizabeth
  See Mizner, Elizabeth Howard
Howard, John
  See Stidworthy, John
Howard, Prosper
  See Hamilton, Charles H. St. John
Howard, Robert West 1908- 5
Howard, Vernon (Linwood) 1918- 40
Howarth, David 1912- 6
Howat, Jean
  See Herbert, Helen (Jean)
Howe, Deborah 1946-1978 29
Howe, Fanny 1940-
  Brief Entry 52
Howe, James 1946- 29
  See also CLR 9
Howell, Pat 1947- 15
Howell, S.
  See Styles, Frank Showell
Howell, Virginia Tier
  See Ellison, Virginia Howell
Howes, Barbara 1914- 5
Howker, Janni
  Brief Entry 46
  See also CLR 14
Hoy, Linda 1946- 65
Hoy, Nina
  See Roth, Arthur J(oseph)
Hoyle, Geoffrey 1942- 18
Hoyt, Edwin P(almer), Jr. 1923- 28
Hoyt, Erich 1950- 65
Hoyt, Olga (Gruhzit) 1922- 16
Hubbell, Patricia 1928- 8
Hubley, Faith (Elliot) 1924- 48
Hubley, John 1914-1977 48
  Obituary 24
Hudson, Jeffrey
  See Crichton, (J.) Michael
Hudson, (Margaret) Kirsty 1947- 32
Hudson, W(illiam) H(enry) 1841-1922 35
Huff, Vivian 1948- 59
Huffaker, Sandy 1943- 10
Huffman, Tom 24
Huggins, Nathan I(rvin) 1927- 63
Hughes, Dean 1943- 33
Hughes, (James) Langston 1902-1967 33
  Earlier sketch in SATA 4
  See also CLR 17
Hughes, Matilda
  See MacLeod, Charlotte (Matilda Hughes)
Hughes, Monica (Ince) 1925- 15
  See also CLR 9
  See also SAAS 11
Hughes, Richard (Arthur Warren)
  1900-1976 8
  Obituary 25
Hughes, Sara
  See Saunders, Susan
Hughes, Shirley 1929- 16
  See also CLR 15
Hughes, Ted 1930- 49
  Brief Entry 27
  See also CLR 3
Hughes, Thomas 1822-1896 31
Hughes, Walter (Llewellyn) 1910- 26
Hughey, Roberta 1942- 61
Hugo, Victor (Marie) 1802-1885 47
Huline-Dickens, Frank William 1931- 34
Hull, Eleanor (Means) 1913- 21
Hull, Eric Traviss
  See Harnan, Terry

Hull, H. Braxton
  See Jacobs, Helen Hull
Hull, Jesse Redding
  See Hull, Jessie Redding
Hull, Jessie Redding 1932- 51
Hull, Katharine 1921-1977 23
Hülsmann, Eva 1928- 16
Hults, Dorothy Niebrugge 1898- 6
Humble, Richard 1945- 60
Hume, Lotta Carswell 7
Hume, Ruth (Fox) 1922-1980 26
  Obituary 22
Hummel, Berta 1909-1946 43
Hummel, Sister Maria Innocentia
  See Hummel, Berta
Humphrey, Henry (III) 1930- 16
Humphreys, Graham 1945-
  Brief Entry 32
Hungerford, Pixie
  See Brinsmead, H(esba) F(ay)
Hunkin, Tim(othy Mark Trelawney)
  1950- 53
Hunt, Francis
  See Stratemeyer, Edward L.
Hunt, Irene 1907- 2
  See also CLR 1
Hunt, Joyce 1927- 31
Hunt, Linda Lawrence 1940- 39
Hunt, Mabel Leigh 1892-1971 1
  Obituary 26
Hunt, Morton 1920- 22
Hunt, Nigel
  See Greenbank, Anthony Hunt
Hunter, Bernice Thurman 1922-
  Brief Entry 45
Hunter, Clingham, M.D.
  See Adams, William Taylor
Hunter, Dawe
  See Downie, Mary Alice
Hunter, Edith Fisher 1919- 31
Hunter, Evan 1926- 25
Hunter, Hilda 1921- 7
Hunter, Jim 1939- 65
Hunter, Kristin (Eggleston) 1931- 12
  See also CLR 3
  See also SAAS 10
Hunter, Leigh
  See Etchison, Birdie L(ee)
Hunter, Mel 1927- 39
Hunter, Mollie 1922- 54
  See also SAAS 7
Hunter, Norman (George Lorimer) 1899- 26
Hunter Blair, Pauline 1921- 3
Huntington, Harriet E(lizabeth) 1909- 1
Huntsberry, William E(mery) 1916- 5
Hurd, Clement (G.) 1908-1988 64
  Obituary 54
  Earlier sketch in SATA 2
Hurd, Edith Thacher 1910- 64
  Earlier sketch in SATA 2
Hurd, Thacher 1949- 46
  Brief Entry 45
Hürlimann, Bettina 1909-1983 39
  Obituary 34
Hürlimann, Ruth 1939- 32
  Brief Entry 31
Hurwitz, Johanna 1937- 20
Hurwood, Bernhardt J. 1926-1987 12
  Obituary 50
Hutchens, Paul 1902-1977 31
Hutchins, Carleen Maley 1911- 9
Hutchins, Hazel J. 1952-
  Brief Entry 51
Hutchins, Pat 1942- 15
  See also CLR 20
Hutchins, Ross E(lliott) 1906- 4
Hutchmacher, J. Joseph 1929- 5
Hutto, Nelson (Allen) 1904- 20
Hutton, Warwick 1939- 20
Huxley, Aldous (Leonard) 1894-1963 63
Huxley, Elspeth (Josceline Grant) 1907- 62
Hyde, Dayton O(gden) 9
Hyde, Hawk
  See Hyde, Dayton O(gden)
Hyde, Margaret Oldroyd 1917- 42
  Earlier sketch in SATA 1
  See also SAAS 8

L